Revision Checklist*

WORTHWHILE CONTENT

The essay's main point is clear and sharply focused.

- ☐ Does the title attract attention and give a forecast? (49)
- ☐ Is the topic limited enough? (22)
- ☐ Do you get to your main point quickly? (50)
- ☐ Is the thesis definite, informative, and easy to find? (23)

The discussion delivers on the promise mode in the thesis.

- ☐ Will readers learn something new and useful? (86)
- ☐ Do you support every assertion with enough details? (84)
- ☐ Does everything belong, or can anything be cut? (90)
- ☐ Have you used only your best material? (33)

SENSIBLE ORGANIZATION

The essay has a definite introduction, body, and conclusion.

- ☐ Will your introduction make readers want to read on? (49)
- ☐ Does each body paragraph develop one supporting point? (54)
- ☐ Does the order of body paragraphs reveal a clear line of thought and emphasize what is most important? (9)
- ☐ Does the conclusion give a real sense of an ending? (55)
- ☐ Is everything connected? (14)
- ☐ If you varied this organization, was it for good reason? (162)

Except for paragraphs of transition or special emphasis, each body (or support) paragraph usually is a mini-essay.

- ☐ Does the paragraph have a topic (or orienting) statement? (99)
- ☐ Does the topic statement come at the beginning or end, depending on your emphasis? (99)
- ☐ Does everything stick to the point (unity), and stick together (coherence)? (102, 103)
- ☐ Is the paragraph developed enough to support the point? (89)

READABLE STYLE

Sentences are clear, concise, and fluent.

- ☐ Can each sentence be understood the first time it is read? (118)
- ☐ Is the information expressed in the fewest words possible? (124)
- ☐ Are sentences put together with enough variety? (131)

Each word does its job.

- ☐ Is a real person speaking, and is the voice likable? (138)
- ☐ Is everything in plain English? (147)
- ☐ Is your meaning precise, concrete, and specific? (139)
- ☐ Is your tone appropriate for this situation and audience? (145)

*Numbers in parentheses refer to the first page of major discussion in the text.

EIGHTH EDITION

THE WRITING PROCESS

A CONCISE RHETORIC, READER, and HANDBOOK

John M. Lannon
University of Massachusetts–Dartmouth

PEARSON

Longman

New York   Boston   San Francisco
London   Toronto   Sydney   Tokyo   Singapore   Madrid
Mexico City   Munich   Paris   Cape Town   Hong Kong   Montreal

Senior Vice President and Editor in Chief: Joseph Opiela
Senior Acquisitions Editor: Lynn M. Huddon
Executive Marketing Manager: Ann Stypuloski
Senior Supplements Editor: Donna Campion
Media Supplements Editor: Nancy Garcia
Production Manager: Ellen MacElree
Project Coordination, Text Design, and Electronic Page Makeup: Nesbitt Graphics, Inc.
Cover Design Manager: Wendy Ann Fredericks
Cover Designer: Kay Petronio
Cover Photos: Top: © StockByte/Picture Quest; Bottom: © PhotoDisc
Manufacturing Buyer: Roy Pickering
Printer and Binder: R. R. Donnelley & Sons
Cover Printer: Phoenix Color Corps.

For permission to use copyrighted material, grateful acknowledgment is made to the copyright holders on pp. 543–45, which are hereby made part of this copyright page.

Library of Congress Cataloging-in-Publication Data

Lannon, John M.
    The writing process : a concise rhetoric, reader, and handbook /
    John M. Lannon. — 8th ed.
        p. cm.
Includes bibliographical references and index.
    ISBN 0-321-13375-7
    1. English language—Rhetoric. 2. English language—Grammar—Handbooks,
manuals, etc. 3. College readers. 4. Report writing. I. Title
PE1408.L3188 2004
808'.042—dc21   2003013173

Copyright © 2004 by Pearson Education, Inc.

Please visit our Web site at http://www.ablongman.com/lannon

ISBN 0-321-13375-7

1 2 3 4 5 6 7 8 9 10—DOH—06 05 04 03

BRIEF CONTENTS

DETAILED CONTENTS   *IX*

THEMATIC CONTENTS   *XXIII*

PREFACE   *XXVII*

SECTION ONE

The Process—Decisions in Planning,
Drafting, and Revising   1

Chapter 1   Decisions in the Writing Process   8

Chapter 2   Decisions in Planning   21

Chapter 3   Decisions in Drafting   48

Chapter 4   Decisions in Revising   61

SECTION TWO

Specific Revision Strategies   79

Chapter 5   Revising the Content: Writing Something
Worthwhile   83

Chapter 6   Revising the Paragraphs: Shaping for Readers'
Access   96

Chapter 7   Revising the Sentences: Writing with Style   117

Chapter 8   Revising the Words and Phrases: Fine-Tuning   137

SECTION THREE

Essays for Various Goals   160

Chapter 9   Decisions about Reading for Writing   164

Chapter 10   Helping Others See and Share an Experience: Description and Narration   178

Chapter 11   Providing Examples: Illustration   197

Chapter 12   Explaining Parts and Categories: Division and Classification   208

Chapter 13   Explaining Steps and Stages: Process Analysis   220

Chapter 14   Explaining Why It Happened or What Will Happen: Cause-and-Effect Analysis   234

Chapter 15   Explaining Similarities or Differences: Comparison and Contrast   251

Chapter 16   Explaining the Exact Meaning: Definition   265

Chapter 17   Using Multiple Strategies in a Persuasive Argument   281

Chapter 18   Special Issues in Persuasion   310

SECTION FOUR

The Research Process   331

Chapter 19   Asking Questions and Finding Answers   342

Chapter 20   Recording, Evaluating, and Interpreting Your Findings   368

Chapter 21   Documenting Your Sources   392

Chapter 22   Composing the Research Report   417

Chapter 23   Case Study: A Sample Research Project   435

SECTION FIVE

Additional Readings and Models for Writing

Description and Narration   472

Illustration   475

Division and Classification   478

Process Analysis   482

Cause-and-Effect Analysis   486

Comparison and Contrast   490

Definition   495

Argument   498

Appendix A   Editing for Grammar, Punctuation, and Mechanics   505

Appendix B   Format Guidelines for Submitting Your Manuscript   536

Appendix C   Useful Web Sites and Electronic Library Resources   539

CREDITS   *543*

INDEX   *547*

DETAILED CONTENTS

THEMATIC CONTENTS   *XXIII*

PREFACE   *XXVII*

SECTION ONE

THE PROCESS—DECISIONS IN PLANNING, DRAFTING, AND REVISING   1

INTRODUCTION   2

Writing as Decision Making   2
How Writing Looks   3
How Writing Makes a Difference   3
Decisions in Collaborative Writing   5
Decisions about Writing with Computers   5
Applications   6

CHAPTER   1

DECISIONS IN THE WRITING PROCESS   8

Decision Making and the Writing Process   9
Case Study One Writer's Decision-Making Process   10
"Life in Full Color" *Shirley Haley* (Student)   12
The Looping Structure of the Writing Process   14
"Confessions of a Food Addict" *Wendy Gianacoples* (Student)   16
Options for Essay Writing   19
Applications   15, 18

CHAPTER   2

DECISIONS IN PLANNING   21

Deciding on a Topic, Purpose, Thesis, and Audience   22
Decide on Your Topic   22

Decide on Your Purpose   22
Decide on Your Thesis   23

Guidelines for Developing a Thesis   **27**

Decide on Your Audience   28

Case Study Analyzing Your Writing Situation   **29**

Discovering, Selecting, and Organizing Your Material   30
Discover Useful Material   31

Guidelines for Brainstorming   **32**

Select Your Best Material   33
Organize for Readers   33

Case Study Exploring and Arranging Assets   **33**

Finding Your Voice   36
Find a Voice that Connects with Readers   37
Avoid an Overly Informal Tone   37
The Writer's Planning Guide   38
Planning for Group Work   40

Guidelines for Writing Collaboratively   **40**

Applications   43

CHAPTER **3**

DECISIONS IN DRAFTING   48

Drafting the Title and Introduction   49
The Introductory Paragraph   50
Placing the Thesis   51
Selecting an Opening Strategy   51
Drafting the Body Section   54
Drafting the Conclusion   55
Selecting a Closing Strategy   55

Case Study Drafting the Essay   **56**

"Cars R Us" *Maureen Malloy* (Student)   56
Drafting on the Computer   58

Guidelines for Drafting on the Computer   **58**

Applications   59

CHAPTER **4**

DECISIONS IN REVISING   61

The Meaning of Revision   62
Revision Checklist   63
Using the Checklist   64

Case Study Revising the Draft 64
Guidelines for Reviewing and Editing the Writing of Peers 66
Revising with Peers 67
Proofreading Your Final Draft 76
Guidelines for Proofreading 76
Applications 77

SECTION TWO

SPECIFIC REVISION STRATEGIES 79

INTRODUCTION 80

How Good Is "Good Enough"? 80
Revising from the Top Down 80
Beefing Up the Content 81
Harnessing Paragraph Power 81
Honing the Sentences 81
Finding the Perfect Wording 82

CHAPTER **5**

REVISING THE CONTENT: WRITING SOMETHING
WORTHWHILE 83

Make It Credible 84
Make It Informative 86
"Walk But Don't Run" *Jeff Leonard* (Student) 87
Make It Complete 89
Credit Your Information Sources 90
Applications 91

CHAPTER **6**

REVISING THE PARAGRAPHS: SHAPING FOR
READERS' ACCESS 96

Support Paragraphs as Mini-Essays 97
Paragraph Function 98
Paragraph Length 98
The Topic Statement 99
   The Topic Statement as Readers' Framework 99
   The Topic Statement as Writers' Framework 99
   How Audience and Purpose Determine a Topic Statement's Focus 100
Structural Variations in Support Paragraphs 101

Paragraph Unity   102
Paragraph Coherence   103
   Ordering Ideas for Coherence   104
   Parallelism   108
   Repetition, Restatement, and Variation   109
   Pronouns for Coherence   110
   Consistency for Coherence   110
   Transitions   110
Applications   112

CHAPTER 7

REVISING THE SENTENCES: WRITING WITH STYLE   117

Aim for Clarity   118
   Keep Your Pronoun References Clear   118
   Avoid Ambiguous Modifiers   118
   Avoid Cramming   119
   Keep Equal Items Parallel   120
   Arrange Word Order for Coherence and Emphasis   120
   Use Active Voice Often   121
   Use Passive Voice Selectively   122
Trim the Fat   124
   Avoid Wordy Phrases   124
   Eliminate Redundancy   124
   Avoid Needless Repetition   125
   Avoid *There* and *It* Sentence Openers   125
   Avoid Needless Phrases   125
   Avoid Weak Verbs   126
   Avoid Excessive Prepositions   126
   Avoid Nominalizations   126
   Make Negatives Positive   127
   Clear Out Clutter Words   128
   Delete Needless Prefaces   128
   Delete Needless Qualifiers   129
Help Sentences Flow   131
   Combine Related Ideas   131
   Vary Sentence Construction and Length   132
   Use Short Sentences for Special Emphasis   133
Applications   123, 129, 133

CHAPTER 8

REVISING THE WORDS AND PHRASES: FINE-TUNING   137

Say Something Genuine   138
   Avoid Triteness   138

Avoid Overstatement   138
Avoid Misleading Euphemisms   138
Aim for Precision   139
Sharpen the Visual Details   143
Add Some Personality   145
Establish an Appropriate Distance   146

Guidelines for Deciding about Tone   147

Guidelines for Achieving a Conversational Tone   147

Express a Clear and Appropriate Attitude   150
Avoid Personal Bias   150
Invite Everyone In   151
Avoid Sexist Language   151

Guidelines for Nonsexist Usage   152

Avoid Offensive Usage of All Types   152
Consider the Cultural Context   153

Guidelines for Inoffensive Usage   154

Legal and Ethical Implications of Word Choice   156
Using Automated Tools Effectively   157
Applications   139, 143, 145, 155

SECTION THREE

ESSAYS FOR VARIOUS GOALS   160

INTRODUCTION   160

Three Major Goals of Writing   160
Major Development Strategies   162
Using This Section   162
A Word about Structural Variations   162

CHAPTER **9**

DECISIONS ABOUT READING FOR WRITING   164

Different Levels of Reading   165
Different Readers, Different Meanings   166
Reading Strategies for Writers   166

Case Study One Writer's Response to Reading   167

"Why I Want a Wife" *Judy Brady*   167

"A Long Way to Go" *Jacqueline LeBlanc* (Student)   171

Case Study A Second Writer's Response to Reading   172

"Seeing" *Annie Dillard*   172

"Sailboats" *Shirley Haley* (Student)   174

Suggestions for Reading and Writing   175

Guidelines for Reading to Respond   175

Applications   176

CHAPTER **10**

HELPING OTHERS SEE AND SHARE AN EXPERIENCE:
DESCRIPTION AND NARRATION   178

Using Objective Description to Inform   179

Using Subjective Description to Make a Point   180

"Off-Season" *Pam Herbert* (Student)   180

Using Objective Narration to Explain   182

Guidelines for Description   183

Using Subjective Narration to Make a Point   184

Guidelines for Narration   084

"Black Men and Public Space" *Brent Staples*   186

"Back at the Ranch" *Jay Allison*   190

Case Study Responding to Reading   193

"The Old Guy" *Al Andrade* (Student)   193

Options For Essay Writing   196

Applications   189, 195

CHAPTER **11**

PROVIDING EXAMPLES: ILLUSTRATION   197

Using Examples to Explain   198

Using Examples to Make a Point   199

Guidelines for Illustrating with Examples   201

"A Case of 'Severe Bias'" *Patricia Raybon*   202

Case Study Responding to Reading   204

"My Time Capsule" *Gina Ciolfi* (Student)   204

Options For Essay Writing   206

Applications   200, 206

CHAPTER **12**

EXPLAINING PARTS AND CATEGORIES: DIVISION
AND CLASSIFICATION   208

Using Division to Explain   210

Using Division to Make a Point   210

Using Classification to Explain   211

Guidelines for Division   212

Using Classification to Make a Point   212

Guidelines for Classification   213

"Doubts about Doublespeak" *William Lutz*   215

Case Study Responding to Reading   217

"We Like It Here" *Patrick LaChane* (Student)   218

Options For Essay Writing   219

Applications   213

CHAPTER **13**

EXPLAINING STEPS AND STAGES: PROCESS ANALYSIS   220

Using Process Analysis to Explain   221

Explaining How to Do Something   221

Guidelines for Giving Instructions   222

Explaining How Something Happens   223

Using Process Analysis to Make a Point   223

"How to Deal with Snakebites" *Frank White*   224

Case Study Responding to Reading   227

"A First-Week Survival Guide for Commuters" *Catherine Nichols* (Student)   227

"How Acid Rain Develops, Spreads, and Destroys" *Bill Kelly* (Student)   229

"Dumpster Diving" *Lars Eighner*   231

Applications   223, 229, 231

CHAPTER **14**

EXPLAINING WHY IT HAPPENED OR WHAT WILL HAPPEN: CAUSE-AND-EFFECT ANALYSIS   234

Using Causal Analysis to Explain: Definite Causes   236

Using Causal Analysis to Make a Point: Possible or Probable Causes   237

Reasoning from Effect to Cause   238

Guidelines for Effect-to-Cause Analysis   238

Reasoning from Cause to Effect   239

Guidelines for Cause-to-Effect Analysis   239

"I Don't Like What You're Wearing" *David Updike*   241

"Should Schools Try to Boost Self-Esteem?—Beware the Dark Side" *Roy F. Baumeister*   244

Case Study Responding to Reading   247

"School Uniforms: A Recipe for School Reform" *John Saurette*
(Student)   248
Options for Essay Writing   250
Applications   240

CHAPTER **15**

EXPLAINING SIMILARITIES OR DIFFERENCES: COMPARISON
AND CONTRAST   251

Developing a Comparison   252
Developing a Contrast   252
Developing a Combined Comparison and Contrast   253
Using Comparison and Contrast to Explain   254
Using Comparison and Contrast to Make a Point   254
A Special Kind of Comparison: Analogy   255
Guidelines for Comparison and Contrast   **257**
"Abortion Is Too Complex to Feel All One Way About" *Anna Quindlen*   259
Case Study Responding to Reading   **262**
"Is Online Education Taking Us Anywhere?" *John Manning* (Student)   262
Options for Essay Writing   264
Applications   255, 258

CHAPTER **16**

EXPLAINING THE EXACT MEANING: DEFINITION   265

Using Denotative Definitions to Explain   266
Using Connotative Definitions to Make a Point   267
Choosing the Level of Detail in a Definition   268
Guidelines for Definition   **270**
"Gossip" *Francine Prose*   275
Case Study Responding to Reading   **277**
"Community Service Serves Everyone" *Kerry Donahue* (Student)   278
Options for Essay Writing   279
Applications   272

CHAPTER **17**

USING MULTIPLE STRATEGIES IN A PERSUASIVE
ARGUMENT   281

Anticipating Audience Resistance   282
Having a Debatable Point   283

Supporting Your Claim   284
   Offer Convincing Reasons   284
   Provide Objective Evidence   285
   Appeal to Shared Goals and Values   286
Shaping a Clear Line of Thought   287
Connecting with Your Audience   288

Guidelines for Persuasion   **288**

Considering the Ethical Dimension   289
Various Arguments For Various Goals   290
   Arguing to Influence Readers' Opinions   291
   Arguing to Enlist Readers' Support   291
   Making a Proposal   291
   Arguing to Change Readers' Behavior   291
"On Reading Trash" *Bob Swift*   292

Case Studies Responding to Reading   **294**

"Credit Cards: Leave Home Without Them" *Julia Schoonover* (Student)   294
"Standards You Meet and Don't Duck" *William Raspberry*   297
"Save Liberal Arts" *Suzanne Gilbertson* (Student)   299
"A Proposal for Better Use of the Television Set in the Campus Center"
   Patricia Haith (Student)   302
"Letter to the Boss" *Marcia White* (Student)   304
Options for Essay Writing   296, 301, 304, 306
Applications   292, 297, 302, 304, 306

C H A P T E R   **1 8**

SPECIAL ISSUES IN PERSUASION   310

Appealing to Reason   310
   Using Induction   312
   Using Deduction   314
Recognizing Invalid or Deceptive Reasoning   317
   Fallacies That Break the Chain of Logic   317
   Fallacies That Evade the Issue   320
Appealing to Emotion   321

Guidelines for Making Emotional Appeals   **322**

   Showing Empathy   322
   Acknowledging Opposing Views   323
   Maintaining a Moderate Tone   323
   Using Satire in Appropriate Circumstances   325
   "Bonfire" *Adam Symkowicz* (Student)   325
   Adding Humor Where Appropriate   326
Applications   326

SECTION FOUR

THE RESEARCH PROCESS   331

INTRODUCTION—THINKING CRITICALLY ABOUT
THE RESEARCH PROCESS   332

   Asking the Right Questions   334
   Exploring a Balance of Views   334
   Achieving Adequate Depth in Your Search   336
   Evaluating Your Findings   337
   Guidelines for Evaluating Expert Information   **338**
   Interpreting Your Findings   338

CHAPTER 19

ASKING QUESTIONS AND FINDING ANSWERS   342

   Deciding on a Research Topic   343
   Guidelines for Choosing a Research Topic   **343**
   Primary versus Secondary Sources   344
   Hard Copy versus Electronic Sources   344
   Exploring Internet Sources   345
      Usenet   345
      Listservs   346
      Library Chatrooms   347
      Electronic Magazines (Zines)   347
      Email Inquiries   347
      World Wide Web   347
   Guidelines for Researching on the Internet   **348**
   Exploring Other Electronic Sources   350
      Compact Disks   350
      Online Retrieval Services   350
      Electronic Reference Books, Indexes, and Journals   351
   Key Word Searches Using Boolean Operators   351
   Using Electronic Mail   352
   Guidelines for Using Email   **353**
   Exploring Hard Copy Sources   354
      Reference Works   354
      Card Catalog   355
      Guides to Literature   356
      Indexes   356
      Abstracts   357
      Access Tools for U.S. Government Publications   357
      Microforms   358

Informative Interviews   359

Surveys and Questionnaires   359

Inquiry Letters, Phone Calls, and Email Inquiries   359

Public Records and Organizational Publications   359

Guidelines for Informative Interviews   **360**

Personal Observation   362

Guidelines for Developing a Questionnaire   **364**

Applications   362

CHAPTER **20**

RECORDING, EVALUATING, AND INTERPRETING
YOUR FINDINGS   368

Taking Notes   369

Guidelines for Recording Research Findings   **369**

Quoting the Work of Others   370
Paraphrasing the Work of Others   372

Guidelines for Quoting the Work of Others   **373**

Preparing Summaries and Abstracts   373

Guidelines for Paraphrasing the Work of Others   **373**

What Readers Expect from a Summary or Abstract   374

Guidelines for Summarizing Information and Preparing an Abstract   **374**

Ethical Considerations in Summarizing Information   375
Evaluating the Sources   376

Guidelines for Evaluating Sources on the Web   **378**

Evaluating the Evidence   379
Interpreting Your Findings   380
Identify Your Level of Certainty   380
Be Alert for Personal Bias   381
Examine the Underlying Assumptions   382
Avoiding Statistical Fallacies   382
Common Statistical Fallacies   383

Guidelines for Critically Analyzing Information   **386**

Assessing Your Inquiry   387
Applications   388

CHAPTER **21**

DOCUMENTING YOUR SOURCES   392

Why You Should Document   392
What You Should Document   393

How You Should Document   393
MLA Documentation Style   394
   MLA Parenthetical References   394
   MLA Works-Cited Entries   395
   MLA Sample List of Works Cited   406
APA Documentation Style   406
   APA Parenthetical References   406
   APA Reference-List Entries   407
   APA Sample List of References   416
Application   416

C H A P T E R   **2 2**

COMPOSING THE RESEARCH REPORT   417

Developing a Working Thesis and Outline   417
Drafting Your Report   418
Revising Your Report   419
A Sample Report in APA Style   420
"Campus Crime: A Hidden Issue" *Julia Schoonover* (Student)   421

C H A P T E R   **2 3**

CASE STUDY: A SAMPLE RESEARCH PROJECT   438

Discovering a Worthwhile Topic   438
Focusing the Inquiry   439
Searching the Literature   440
Recording and Reviewing Findings   440
Settling on a Thesis   441
Writing and Documenting the Report in MLA Style   442
"Students Under Stress: College Can Make You Sick" *Shirley Haley*
   (Student)   443

SECTION FIVE

ADDITIONAL READINGS AND MODELS FOR WRITING   471

Description and Narration   472
"On the Ball" *Roger Angell*   472
"Grandmother's Sunday Dinner" *Patricia Hampl*   473

Illustration   475
"No Zeal for New Zealand" *Jaclyn Thomas*   475
"All You Can Eat" *Michelle Stacey*   477

Division and Classification 478
"All Junk, All the Time" *Richard Brookhiser* 478
"The Dog Ate My Disk, and Other Tales of Woe" *Carolyn Foster Segal* 480

Process Analysis 482
"How to Write a Personal Letter" *Garrison Keillor* 482
"How Boys Become Men" *Jon Katz* 484

Cause-and-Effect Analysis 486
"Why We Crave Horror Movies" *Stephen King* 486
"I Just Wanna Be Average" *Mike Rose* 488

Comparison and Contrast 490
"Parallel Worlds: The Surprising Similarities (and Differences) of
    Country-and-Western and Rap" *Denise Noe* 490
"Neat People vs. Sloppy People" *Suzanne Britt* 493

Definition 495
"The Company Man" *Ellen Goodman* 495
"What's a Hillbilly?" *Rebecca Thomas Kirkendall* 496

Argument 498
"Let Teenagers Try Adulthood" *Leon Botstein* 498
"In Defense of Elitism" *William A. Henry III* 500

APPENDIX A

EDITING FOR GRAMMAR, PUNCTUATION, AND MECHANICS 505

Common Sentence Errors 505
  Sentence Fragment 505
  Acceptable Fragment 507
  Faulty Coordination 508
  Faulty Subordination 509
  Comma Splice 510
  Run-On Sentence 512
  Faulty Agreement—Subject and Verb 513
  Faulty Agreement—Pronoun and Referent 514
  Faulty Modification 514
  Faulty Pronoun Case 516
  Sentence Shifts 518
Effective Punctuation 519
  End Punctuation 520
  Semicolon 521
  Colon 522
  Comma 523
  Apostrophe 527
  Quotation Marks 529

Ellipses 530
Italics 530
Parentheses 531
Brackets 531
Dashes 532
Effective Mechanics 532
Abbreviations 532
Hyphen 533
Capitalization 534
Use of Numbers 534
Spelling 535
Applications 508, 510, 512, 516, 518, 522, 526, 530, 532, 535

A P P E N D I X B

FORMAT GUIDELINES FOR SUBMITTING YOUR MANUSCRIPT 536

Format Guidelines for Submitting Your Manuscript 537
Format Checklist 538

A P P E N D I X C

USEFUL WEB SITES AND ELECTRONIC LIBRARY RESOURCES 539

Useful Web Sites 539
Search Engines 539
Subject Directories (or Catalogs) 540
Almanacs 540
Associations and Organizations 540
Business Directories 541
Dictionaries 541
Encyclopedias 541
Journal Articles 541
News Organizations 541
U.S. Government Information 542
Writing and Research Guides 542
Electronic Library Resources 542

Credits *543*

Index *547*

THEMATIC CONTENTS

BIOGRAPHY AND AUTOBIOGRAPHY

"Life in Full Color" *Shirley Haley*   12
"Confessions of a Food Addict" *Wendy Gianacoples*   16
"Black Men and Public Space" *Brent Staples*   186
"Back at the Ranch" *Jay Allison*   190
"The Old Guy" *Al Andrade*   193
"Dumpster Diving" *Lars Eighner*   231
"Grandmother's Sunday Dinner" *Patricia Hampl*   423
"No Zeal for New Zealand" *Jaclyn Thomas*   475
"I Just Wanna Be Average" *Mike Rose*   488

EDUCATION

"A First-Week Survival Guide for Commuters" *Catherine Nichols*   227
"Should Schools Try to Boost Self-Esteem?" *Roy Baumeister*   244
"School Uniforms: A Recipe for School Reform" *John Saurette*   248
"Is Online Education Taking Us Anywhere?" *John Manning*   262
"Community Service Serves Everyone" *Kerry Donahue*   278
"Credit Cards: Leave Home without Them" *Julia Schoonover*   294
"Standards You Meet and Don't Duck" *William Raspberry*   297
"Save Liberal Arts" *Suzanne Gilbertson*   299
"A Proposal for Better Use of the TV Set in the Campus Center" *Patricia Haith*   302
"Campus Crime: A Hidden Issue" *Julia Schoonover*   421
"Students Under Stress: College Can Make You Sick" *Shirley Haley*   443
"The Dog Ate My Disk, and Other Tales of Woe" *Carolyn Foster Segal*   480
"I Just Wanna Be Average" *Mike Rose*   488
"Let Teenagers Try Adulthood" *Leon Botstein*   498
"In Defense of Elitism" *William A. Henry III*   500

FAMILY

"Life in Full Color" *Shirley Haley*   12
"Why I Want a Wife" *Judy Brady*   167

"A Long Way to Go" *Jacqueline LeBlanc*   171
"The Old Guy" *Al Andrade*   193
"I Don't Like What You're Wearing" *David Updike*   241
"Grandmother's Sunday Dinner" *Patricia Hampl*   473

HUMAN BEHAVIOR

"Confessions of a Food Addict" *Wendy Gianacoples*   16
"Cars R Us" *Maureen Malloy*   56
"Black Men and Public Space" *Brent Staples*   186
"Back at the Ranch" *Jay Allison*   190
"A Case of Severe Bias" *Patricia Raybon*   202
"My Time Capsule" *Gina Ciolfi*   204
"I Don't Like What You're Wearing" *David Updike*   241
"Should Schools Try to Boost Self-Esteem?" *Roy Baumeister*   244
"Gossip" *Francine Prose*   275
"All You Can Eat" *Michelle Stacey*   477
"How Boys Become Men" *Jon Katz*   484
"Neat People vs. Sloppy People" *Suzanne Britt*   493

HUMOR

"Cars R Us" *Maureen Malloy*   56
"My Time Capsule" *Gina Ciolfi*   204
"Bonfire" *Adam Symkowicz*   325
"The Dog Ate My Disk, and Other Tales of Woe" *Carolyn Foster Segal*   480
"Neat People vs. Sloppy People" *Suzanne Britt*   493

MEDIA, ENTERTAINMENT, COMPUTERS

"A Case of Severe Bias" *Patricia Raybon*   202
"Is Online Education Taking Us Anywhere?" *John Manning*   262
"All Junk, All the Time" *Richard Brookhiser*   478
"Why We Crave Horror Movies" *Stephen King*   486
"Parallel Worlds: The Surprising Similarities (and Differences) of Country-and-Western and Rap" *Denise Noe*   490

NATURE

"Seeing" *Annie Dillard*   172
"Off-Season" *Pam Herbert*   180
"How Acid Rain Develops, Spreads, and Destroys" *Bill Kelly*   229

PLACES

"Sailboats" *Shirley Haley*   174
"Off-Season" *Pam Herbert*   180
"Back at the Ranch" *Jay Allison*   190
"We Like It Here" *Patrick LaChane*   218
"No Zeal for New Zealand" *Jaclyn Thomas*   475

RACE, CLASS, AND CULTURE

"In Defense of Elitism" *William A. Henry III*   50
"Black Men and Public Space" *Brent Staples*   186
"Back at the Ranch" *Jay Allison*   190
"A Case of Severe Bias" *Patricia Raybon*   202
"Dumpster Diving" *Lars Eighner*   231
"No Zeal for New Zealand" *Jaclyn Thomas*   475
"I Just Wanna Be Average" *Mike Rose*   488
"Parallel Worlds: The Surprising Similarities (and Differences) of Country-
  and-Western and Rap" *Denise Noe*   490
"What's a Hillbilly?" *Rebecca Thomas Kirkendall*   496

SOCIAL AND ETHICAL ISSUES

"Black Men and Public Space" *Brent Staples*   186
"A Case of Severe Bias" *Patricia Raybon*   202
"Dumpster Diving" *Lars Eighner*   231
"Abortion Is Too Complex to Feel All One Way About" *Anna
  Quindlen*   259
"Community Service Serves Everyone" *Kerry Donahue*   278
"Campus Crime: A Hidden Issue" *Julia Schoonover*   421

HEALTH, MEDICINE, SPORTS, AND FITNESS

"Walk but Don't Run" *Jeff Leonard*   87
"How to Deal with Snakebites" *Frank White*   224
"On the Ball" *Roger Angell*   472
"Students Under Stress: College Can Make You Sick" *Shirley
  Haley*   443
"All You Can Eat" *Michelle Stacey*   477

THE WORKPLACE

"How Acid Rain Develops, Spreads, and Destroys" *Bill Kelly*   229
"Letter to the Boss" *Marcia White*   304
"The Company Man" *Ellen Goodman*   495

WOMEN AND MEN

"Why I Want a Wife" *Judy Brady*   167
"A Long Way to Go" *Jacqueline LeBlanc*   171
"Black Men and Public Space" *Brent Staples*   186
"How Boys Become Men" *Jon Katz*   484

LANGUAGE, READING, AND WRITING

"Doubts about Doublespeak" *William Lutz*   215
"On Reading Trash" *Bob Swift*   292
"How to Write a Personal Letter" *Garrison Keillor*   482

This text promotes rhetorical awareness by treating the writing process as a set of deliberate and recursive decisions. It promotes rhetorical effectiveness by helping develop the problem-solving skills essential to reader-centered writing. Practical guidelines, accessible models, and case studies enable students to produce writing that works.

ORGANIZATION OF *THE WRITING PROCESS*, EIGHTH EDITION

Section One, THE PROCESS, covers planning, drafting, and revising. Students learn to invent, select, organize, and express their material recursively. They see how initial decisions about purpose and audience influence later decisions about what will be said and how it will be said. They see that writing is essentially a "thinking" process; they also learn to work collaboratively.

Section Two, SPECIFIC REVISION STRATEGIES, focuses on top-down revision: content, organization, and style. Students learn to support their assertions; to organize for the reader; and to achieve prose maturity, precise diction, and appropriate zone.

Section Three, ESSAYS FOR VARIOUS GOALS, shows how the *strategies* (or modes) of discourse serve the particular *goals* of a discourse; that is, how description, narration, exposition, and argument are variously employed for expressive, referential, or persuasive ends. The opening chapter explains how reading and writing are linked and offers strategies for reading and responding to essays by others. Subsequent chapters cover each rhetorical mode, using a balance of student and professional writing samples to touch on current and lasting issues. Beyond studying the samples and case studies as models, students are asked to respond to the issues presented; that is, to write in response to a specific rhetorical situation.

Section Four, THE RESEARCH PROCESS, approaches research as a process of deliberate inquiry. Students learn to formulate significant research questions; to explore a selective range of primary and secondary sources; to record, summarize, and document their findings; and, most important, to evaluate sources and evidence and interpret findings accurately.

Section Five, ADDITIONAL READINGS AND MODELS FOR WRITING, serves as a concise reader, offering a collection of short essays employing various rhetorical strategies and exploring a wide range of themes.

Finally, for easy reference, Appendix A is a concise handbook, with exercises. Appendix B—an additional, brief appendix—offers advice on formatting a manuscript. Appendix C lists useful Web sites and electronic information resources for writing students.

THE FOUNDATIONS OF *THE WRITING PROCESS*

- Writers with no rhetorical awareness overlook the decisions that are crucial for effective writing. Only by defining their rhetorical problem and asking the important questions can writers formulate an effective response to the problem.

- Although it follows no single, predictable sequence, the writing process is not a collection of random activities; rather it is a set of deliberate decisions in problem solving. Beyond emulating this or that model essay, students need to understand that effective writing requires critical thinking.

- Students write for audiences other than teachers and for purposes other than completing an assignment. To view the act of writing as a mere display of knowledge or fluency, an exercise in which writer and reader (i.e., "the teacher") have no higher stake or interest, is to ignore the unique challenges and constraints posed by each writing situation. In every forum beyond the classroom, we write to forge a specific connection with a specific audience.

- Students at any level of ability can develop audience awareness and learn to incorporate within their writing the essential rhetorical features: worthwhile content, sensible organization, and readable style.

- In addition to being a fluent *communicator,* today's educated person needs to be a discriminating *consumer* of information, skilled in the methods of inquiry, retrieval, evaluation, and interpretation that constitute the research process.

- As an alternative to reiterating the textbook material, classroom workshops apply textbook principles by focusing on the students' writing. These workshops call for an accessible, readable, and engaging book to serve as a comprehensive resource. (Suggestions for workshop design are in *The Instructor's Manual.*)

- Finally, writing classes typically contain students with all types of strengths and weaknesses. *The Writing Process* offers explanations that are thorough, examples and models that are broadly intelligible, and goals that are rigorous yet realistic. The textbook is flexible enough to allow for various course plans and customized assignments.

The Writing Process proceeds from writer-centered to reader-centered discourse. Beginning with personal topics and a basic essay structure, the focus shifts to increasingly complex rhetorical tasks, culminating in argument. Within this cumulative structure, each chapter is self-contained for flexible course planning. The sample essays represent a balance of student and professional authorship. Exercises (or Applications) in each chapter offer various levels of challenge. (All material has been class-tested.)

HALLMARKS OF THIS EDITION

- **More essays by professionals.** Section Five offers sixteen additional sample essays.
- **More student-written model essays.** Although professional examples enhance skills in reading and responding, reviewers agree that students are more comfortable emulating essays written by other students.
- **Case studies throughout.** Concise case studies show student writers at work as they read, plan, draft, and revise.
- **Expanded guidelines for writing and research.** Boxed "Guidelines" help students synthesize and apply the information in each chapter.
- **Increased coverage of collaboration.** To reflect the increasing importance of collaborative activities, this edition features collaborative projects throughout the text, including guidelines for computer-mediated collaboration.
- **Increased coverage of computers and the Internet.** Fully integrated computing advice is supplemented by end-of-chapter Web-based projects and Appendix C, listing useful Web sites and electronic resources for student writers and researchers.
- **Increased emphasis on information literacy.** *Information-literate people* are those who "know how knowledge is organized, how to find information, and how to use information in a way that others can learn from them." Critical thinking—the basis of information literacy—is covered extensively in Section Four.*

NEW TO THIS EDITION: A CHAPTER-BY-CHAPTER GUIDE

- Chapter 1, overview of the writing process: discussion of the looping structure of the writing process.
- Chapter 2, planning the essay: new examples throughout, guidelines for developing a thesis, and additional thesis exercises.
- Chapter 3, drafting the essay: advice on overcoming writer's block.
- Chapter 4, revising: step-by-step guidelines for proofreading the final draft.
- Chapter 5, content revision: a section on crediting information sources.

*American Library Association Presidential Committee on Information Literacy: Final Report, Chicago: ALA, 1989.

- Chapter 6, paragraph revision: advice on focusing a topic statement on the basis of audience and purpose.
- Chapter 7, sentence-level revision: an expanded definition of "style."
- Chapter 8, word- and phrase-level revision: a table of commonly confused words, discussion of legal and ethical implications of word choice.
- Chapter 9, reading for writing: two new essays for reading and responding.
- Chapter 10, description and narration: expanded guidelines.
- Chapter 11, illustration: new writing samples and expanded guidelines.
- Chapter 12, division and classification: new model essay.
- Chapter 13, process analysis: expanded guidelines for giving instructions.
- Chapter 14, causal analysis: expanded guidelines and a new case study.
- Chapter 15, comparison/contrast: expanded guidelines.
- Chapter 16, definition: expanded guidelines and a new case study.
- Chapter 17, argument: expanded guidelines.
- Chapter 18, special issues in persuasion: more detailed treatment of logical fallacies.
- Chapter 19, the inquiry process: up-to-date coverage of electronic and Web-based sources, expanded guidelines for using email.
- Chapter 20, recording, evaluating, and interpreting information: discussion of ethical considerations in summarizing information, expanded guidelines for evaluating sources on the Web and for critically analyzing information.
- Chapter 21, documenting sources: the latest MLA and APA guidelines.
- Chapter 22, composing the research report: fully updated sample report.
- Chapter 23, a sample research project: fully updated case study.
- An expanded Appendix C offers an annotated listing of useful Web sites and electronic library resources.
- Web-based projects added throughout.

The Instructor's Manual contains general suggestions and ideas for teaching composition, sample syllabi, chapter overviews, suggested responses to exercises and additional sample essays, collaborative projects, and options for writing.

The Companion Website to accompany *The Writing Process, 8/e* <http://www.ablongman.com/lannon> offers a wealth of resources for both students and instructors. Students can access detailed chapter overviews, writing exercises, Web resources, and criteria and checklists to help them in their own writing process. In addition, instructors will find Web resources, and *The Instructor's Manual* available for download.

ACKNOWLEDGMENTS

Much of the improvement in this edition was inspired by helpful reviews from Mary A. Gervin, Albany State University; Samuel B. Olorounto, New River Community College; Edward A. Preston, Howard University; Francie

Quaas-Berryman, Cerritos College; Angela M. Rhoe, Prince George's Community College: Kathleen Sole, University of Phoenix; Ester A. Stinnett, Montana State University, Great Falls; and Patricia Vazquez, Community College of Southern Nevada. I am also grateful to the reviewers of the last edition: Jan Coulson, Okmulgee State University; Marie Garrett, Patrick Henry Community College; Frederic Giacobazzi, Kirtland Community College; Jeanne Ann Graham, Ivy Tech State College; Lee Ann Hodges, Tri-County Community College; Kathleen Kelly, Northeastern University; Catherine Rahmes, Cincinnati State Technical and Community College; Denise M. Rogers, University of Southwestern Louisiana; Kathleen M. Sole, University of Phoenix; Esther A, Stinnett, Montana State University, Great Falls; Todd Travaille, Buena Vista University; John Wolff, West Shore Community College.

For examples, advice, and support, I thank colleagues and friends at the University of Massachusetts, Dartmouth, especially Tish Dace, Barbara Jacobskind, Louise Habicht, and Richard Larschan. As always, Raymond Dumont helped in countless ways.

A special thanks to my students who allowed me to reproduce versions of their work: Chris Adley for selections on privacy in America, Al Andrade for "The Old Guy," Joe Bolton on toys of violence, Julia Schoonover for her research essay and other excellent work, Mike Creeden on physical fitness, Wendy Gianacoples for "Confessions of a Food Addict," Liz Gonsalves on rap music, Shirley Haley for her research essay and other excellent work, Cheryl Hebert on single-sex schools and standardized testing, Pam Herbert on summer beaches, Jeff Leonard for "Walk but Don't Run," John Manning on the American Dream and "Is Online Education Taking Us Anywhere?" Maureen Malloy for "Cars R Us," Cathie Nichols for "A First-Week Survival Guide for Commuters," Adam Szymkowicz for "Bonfire," and the many other student writers named in the text.

From my publisher I received excellent editorial support, especially from Lynn Huddon. Thanks to Michael Greer for his help with the Web-based projects and to Janet Nuciforo for managing production with her usual expertise and grace.

For Chega, Daniel, Sarah, and Patrick—without whom not.

JOHN M. LANNON

SECTION ONE

The Process—Decisions in Planning, Drafting, and Revising

Introduction 2

CHAPTER 1
Decisions in the Writing Process 8

CHAPTER 2
Decisions in Planning 21

CHAPTER 3
Decisions in Drafting 48

CHAPTER 4
Decisions in Revising 61

Introduction

Writing as Decision Making   **2**

How Writing Looks   **3**

How Writing Makes a Difference   **3**

Decisions in Collaborative Writing   **5**

Decisions about Writing with Computers   **5**

Applications   **6**

WRITING AS DECISION MAKING

Writing has no recipes

People who succeed usually are those who make the right decisions—about a career, an investment, a relationship, or anything else. Like any decision making, good writing requires hard work. If we had one recipe for all writing, our labors would be small. We could learn the recipe ("Do this; then do that"), then apply it to every writing task—from love letters to lab reports. But we write about various subjects for various audiences for various purposes—at home, at school, on the job. For every writing task, we make our own decisions.

Most writers face problems like these

Still, most of us face identical problems: in deciding on who our audience is and how to connect with it; in deciding on what goal we want to achieve and on how to make the writing achieve that goal. This book introduces strategies that help us succeed as writers.

Writing can be hard work for anyone

Most writing is a conscious, deliberate *process*—not the result of divine intervention, magic, miracles, or last-minute inspiration. Nothing ever leaps from the mind to the page in one neat and painless motion—not even for creative geniuses. Instead, we plan, draft, and revise. Sometimes we know right away what we want to say; sometimes we discover our purpose and meaning only as we write. But our finished product takes shape through our decisions at different stages in the writing process.

Note

This book shows you how to plan, draft, and revise in a suggested sequence of activities. But just as no two people use an identical sequence of activities to drive, ski, or play tennis, no two people write in the same way. How you decide to use this book depends on your writing task and on what works for you.

HOW WRITING LOOKS

Writing appears in many shapes

The neat and ordered writing samples throughout this book show the *products* of writing—not the *process*. Every finished writing task begins with messy scribbling, things crossed out, lists, arrows, and fragments of ideas, as in the section from my first draft of this introduction shown in Figure I.1.

Just as the writing process has no one recipe, the finished products have no one shape. In fact, very little writing published in books, magazines, and newspapers looks exactly like the basic college essay discussed in this book's early chapters (an introductory paragraph beginning or ending with a thesis statement; three or more support paragraphs, each beginning with a topic sentence; and a concluding paragraph). But all effective writers use identical skills: they know how to discover something worthwhile to write about, how to organize their material sensibly, and how to express their ideas clearly and gracefully.

Why college essays are important

College essays offer a good model for developing these skills because they provide you with a basic structure for shaping your thinking. They also supply an immediate, helpful audience—your instructor and classmates. Unlike many audiences who read only your final draft and from whom you could not reasonably expect helpful and sympathetic advice, your teacher and classmates can give you valuable feedback as you continue to shape and rework drafts of your writing.

What any reader expects

Like any audience, your classroom readers will expect you finally to give them something worthwhile—some useful information, a new insight on some topic, an unusual perspective or an entertaining story—in a form easy to follow and pleasing to read.

HOW WRITING MAKES A DIFFERENCE

Surface reasons for writing

Deeper reasons for writing

All through school, we write too often for surface reasons: to show we can grind out a few hundred words on some topic, cook up a thesis, and organize paragraphs; to show we can punctuate, spell, and use grammar; or to pass the course. These surface reasons mask the deeper reasons we write: to explore something important to us, to connect with our readers, to make a difference—as students, as employees, as citizens, or as friends.

Differences writing can make

What kind of difference can any writing make? It might move readers to act or reconsider their biases; it might increase their knowledge or win their support; it might broaden their understanding. Whether you're giving instructions for running an electric toothbrush or pouring out your feelings to a friend, effective writing brings writer and reader together.

As you read the essays in this book, you will see how student and professional writers in all kinds of situations manage to make a difference with their readers. These models, along with the advice and assignments, should help your writing make a difference of its own.

FIGURE I.1
Part of a typical first draft

Messiness is a natural and
often essential part of
writing in its early stages

*Wouldn't it be nice if there were a formula for writing:
*"this is the way you do it"?   *Any kind of decision-
⟨USE⟩ + ⟨DEVELOP⟩ making is hard

Introduction
-buy a car
-a house
-getting married
-having children   ⟨CHANGE THESE⟩

⟨In writing, as in the rest of life,
decisions are important⟩

Later you will write all kinds of documents for all
kinds of purposes: -letters to the school board

all goals
that need
a plan
All these
are designed
to get the
reader to do
something
or at least
to like
you

-job application letters
-love letters
-requests for pay raises
-apologize for mistakes
-memos or reports for clients and colleagues
-poetry, fiction,?
-computer documentation   ⟨NO⟩
? ⟨Transitional writing⟩ ?

Those who
succeed generally
are those who
make good
decisions

Instead of
just letting
things happen

⟨?⟩ So, what ~~does writing~~ do college essays have to do with
these varied tasks? "Why am I doing this?" is a
⟨MAYBE⟩ question asked by ~~many~~ people who find themselves in
a composition class. ~~And this question deserves an answer.~~
⟨If there were I could write this section in a couple of hours,⟩
There is no one way of "doing it right." ⟨instead of a week⟩
But all writers in all situations face certain ~~comm~~
⟨USE⟩ common problems: they need to ~~figure out~~ decide what to say;
they need to ~~figure out~~ decide why they're saying it; they
need to organize to make their thinking clear; they
need to express themselves line of

DECISIONS IN COLLABORATIVE WRITING

Many of the Applications in this book ask you to collaborate with peers. Especially now that the Internet simplifies collaborative work, countless documents in the workplace are produced collaboratively; effective collaboration enables a group to synthesize the *best* from each member. Collaboration allows us to:

Benefits of collaboration

- Share in new perspectives
- Test and sharpen ideas
- Recognize our biases and assumptions
- Get feedback from group members
- Enjoy group support instead of working alone

But like all writing, collaborative work demands decisions. Group members have to find ways of expressing their views persuasively, of accepting constructive criticism, of getting along and reaching agreement with others who hold different views. Collaborators may face these potential problems:

Things that go wrong in collaborative work

- Differences in personality, working style, commitment, standards, or ability to take criticism
- Disagreements about exactly what or how much the group should accomplish, who should do what, or who should make the final decisions
- Feelings of intimidation or reluctance to speak out

Guidelines in the following chapters will help make collaborative projects useful for you

DECISIONS ABOUT WRITING WITH COMPUTERS

Like collaborative writing, computers can provide tremendous advantages if you understand their limitations. Here are some of the decisions you will be making about computers as you progress through this book:

1. *How should I use computers to write my papers?* Working directly on the computer screen reduces the drudgery of writing and revising. You can brainstorm, develop different outlines, and design countless versions of a document without retyping the entire piece. You can also insert, delete, or move blocks of text; search the document to change a word or phrase; or have your document examined automatically for correct spelling, accurate word choice, and readable style. You then can file your finished document electronically, for easy retrieval.
2. *How should I use computers to enhance my research?* Instead of thumbing through newspapers, journals, reference books, or printed card catalogs,

you can do much of your research at the computer terminal. See Chapter 19 for detailed descriptions of computerized research and reference tools (card catalogs, online databases, Internet resources, and so on).

3. *How should I use computers for collaborative projects?* Computers facilitate collaborate writing. For instance, group members might review, edit, or proofread your writing directly from a disk you have provided. The latest software even enables readers to comment on your writing without altering the text itself. Finally, using electronic mail, you can transmit copies of your writing to classmates, and they can respond.

But your decisions about these issues should take the following cautions into account:

Limitations of writing with a computer

- Messages still need to be *written*. The task of sorting, organizing, and interpreting information still belongs to the writer.
- No computerized device can convert bad writing to good. Moreover, the ease of "fixing" our writing on a computer might encourage minimal revision. (Sometimes the very act of rewriting an entire page in longhand or type causes us to rethink that whole page or discover something new.)
- A computer is not a substitute brain. Shabby thinking produces shabby writing.

The following chapters will help you make thoughtful decisions about the part computers can play in your work.

Application **A**

Identify a situation in which your writing (or someone else's) has made a difference. Be prepared to describe the situation in class.

Application **B**

Locate a piece of nonfiction writing that you think "makes a difference." Bring a copy to class and be prepared to explain why this particular piece qualifies.

Application **C**

COLLABORATIVE PROJECT

INTRODUCING A CLASSMATE

Class members will work together often this semester. So that everyone can become acquainted, your task is to introduce to the class the person seated next to you. (That person, in turn, will introduce you.) To prepare your introduction, follow this procedure—either face to face or via email:

a. Exchange with your neighbor whatever personal information you think the class needs: background, major, computer experience (email, Internet, other), career plans, communication needs of your intended profession, and so on. Each person gets five minutes (or, via email, a few hundred words) to tell her or his story.

b. If working face to face, take careful notes; ask questions if you need to.

c. Take your notes home (or review the email message) and select only what you think will be useful to the class.

d. Prepare a one-page description for your classmates about who this person is. Ask your neighbor to review your description for accuracy; revise as needed.

e. Read your description to the class and submit a copy to your instructor.

Application **D**

Web-based Project: A friend in your major believes that computers have made college writing courses and the skills they teach irrelevant. Information, after all, is readily available on the Web, and grammar and spelling checkers eliminate the need for editing and revising skills. Basically, your friend argues, anyone with decent computer skills "already knows how to write."

Write a letter summarizing the points you would make in response to your friend's assertions. Visit the Purdue University Online Writing Lab and read the discussion of key questions ("higher order concerns") to ask during the writing process:

<http://owl.english.purdue.edu/handouts/general/gl_hocloc.html>

How many of these questions can be addressed by a computer? How many require a creative human mind? Use a paraphrase of the Purdue OWL questions to help structure the main points in the letter to your friend.

Page 374 offers guidelines for summarizing information. You may also want to review "Decisions about Writing with Computers," above. See pages 402, 414 for citation formats for electronic sources.

CHAPTER 1

Decisions in the Writing Process

Decision Making and the Writing Process   **9**

CASE STUDY: One Writer's Decision-Making Process   **10**

The Looping Structure of the Writing Process   **14**

Options for Essay Writing   **19**

Readings   **12, 16**

Applications   **15**

During the writing process, you transform the material you discover—by inspiration, research, accident, or other means—into a message that makes a difference for readers. In short, writing is a process of making deliberate decisions.

For example, consider a Dear John or Jane letter, an essay exam, a job application, a letter to a newspaper, a note to a sick friend, or your written testimony as a witness to a crime. In each of these situations, you write because you have a definite *viewpoint*—a definite position on the topic—and you want to respond or speak out. By asserting your viewpoint, you let readers know exactly where you stand; you announce your position.

Here are just a few examples of the viewpoints any writer might assert:

Examples of viewpoints

> College is not for everyone.
>
> I deserve a raise.
>
> Food can be just as addictive as a drug.
>
> I want my life to be better than that of my parents.
>
> It's time to bring back school uniforms.

Later, you will see how ideas like these serve as thesis statements for essays.

But merely expressing a viewpoint doesn't tell readers very much. To understand and appreciate your ideas, readers need clear explanations. Any useful writing—whether in the form of a book, a news article, a memo, a report, or an essay—displays a sensible line of thinking, often in a shape like this:

Much of your writing will have this basic shape

INTRODUCTION

The introduction attracts attention, announces the topic and viewpoint, and previews what will follow. All good introductions invite readers in.

BODY

The body explains and supports the viewpoint, achieving *unity* by remaining focused on the viewpoint. It achieves *coherence* by carrying a line of thinking from sentence to sentence in logical order. Body sections come in all different sizes, depending on how much readers need and expect.

CONCLUSION

The conclusion sums up the meaning of the piece or points toward other meanings to be explored. Good conclusions give readers a clear perspective on what they have just read.

Writers also make decisions about who they're writing to (their *audience*) and how they want to sound: whether they want to sound formal, friendly, angry, or amused.

DECISION MAKING AND THE WRITING PROCESS

Composing words on paper or your computer screen is only one small part of the writing process. Your real challenge lies in making decisions like those in Figure 1.1:

FIGURE 1.1
Typical decisions during
the writing process

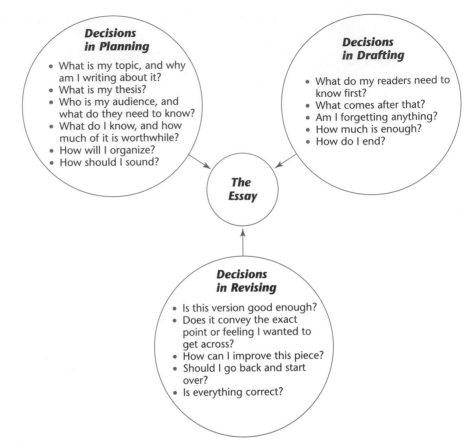

**Decisions
in Planning**

- What is my topic, and why
  am I writing about it?
- What is my thesis?
- Who is my audience, and
  what do they need to know?
- What do I know, and how
  much of it is worthwhile?
- How will I organize?
- How should I sound?

**Decisions
in Drafting**

- What do my readers need to
  know first?
- What comes after that?
- Am I forgetting anything?
- How much is enough?
- How do I end?

**The
Essay**

**Decisions
in Revising**

- Is this version good enough?
- Does it convey the exact
  point or feeling I wanted to
  get across?
- How can I improve this piece?
- Should I go back and start
  over?
- Is everything correct?

CASE STUDY

ONE WRITER'S DECISION-MAKING PROCESS

To appreciate writing as a deliberate process, let's follow one student
through two approaches to the same writing situation. We'll see how decisions about planning, drafting, and revising like those shown in Figure 1.1
distinguish this writer's quickest effort from her best effort.

Shirley Haley has been assigned an essay on this topic: How do you
want your life to be different from (or similar to) that of your parents?
Haley's twofold goal is to explore her feelings about this topic and to share
that exploration with us. Her first response, a random piece of freewriting,
took about 30 minutes:

Haley's freewriting

When my mother was my age, life was simple. Women really didn't have
to study in college. They came primarily to find a husband, and they majored

in liberal arts or teaching. They knew they were going to be wives and mothers. My mother says she got an education so she would have "something to fall back on" in case something ever happened to my father—which was a good thing, I suppose. Maybe it was her attitude about "family first, me second" that made our home life so stable.

I appreciate the fact that my parents have given me a stable home life, and I want parts of my life to turn out like theirs. But my parents are slaves to their house; they never go anywhere or do anything with their spare time. They just work on the house and yard. They never seem to do anything they want to do—only what other people expect of them.

I wish my parents would allow themselves to enjoy life, have more adventure. They go to the same place every year for their vacation. They've never even seen a country outside the United States.

I'll have a family some day, and I'll have responsibilities, but I never want to have a boring life. When I'm on my own, I want my life to be full of surprises. And even though I want to provide a stable home life for my children and husband someday, I hope I never forget my responsibility to myself as well.

Discussion of Haley's freewriting

Freewriting is a valuable invention tool—but only a first step. Haley's draft has potential, but she hints at lots of things in general and points at nothing in particular. Without a thesis to assert a controlling viewpoint, neither writer nor reader ever finds an orientation. Lacking a definite thesis, Haley never decided which material didn't belong, which was the most important, and which deserved careful development.

At first, the essay seems to be about a change in women's roles, but the end of the first paragraph and the beginning of the second suggest that Haley's topic has shifted to ways in which she wants her life to resemble her parents'. But the second, third, and fourth paragraphs discuss what Haley dislikes about her parents' lives. The final sentence adds confusion by looking back to a now-defunct topic in the first paragraph: stable family life.

The lack of an introduction and conclusion deprives us of a way of narrowing the possible meanings of the piece and of finding a clear perspective on what we have just read. The paragraphs also either lack development or fail to focus on one specific point. And some sentences (like the last two in paragraph 1) lack logical connections.

Finally, we get almost no sense of a real person speaking to real people. Haley has written only for herself—as if she were writing a journal or diary.

A quick effort (as in a journal or diary) offers a good way to get started. But when writers go no further, they bypass the essential stages of *planning* and *revising*. In fact, putting something on the page or screen is relatively easy. But in order to get the piece to *succeed*, to make a difference for readers, tougher decisions need to be made.

Now let's follow Haley's thinking as she struggles through her planning decisions.

What exactly is my topic, and why am I writing about it? *My intended topic was "How I Want My Life to Be Different from That of My Parents," but my first draft got off track. I need to focus on the specific differences!*

I'm writing this essay to discover my own feelings and to help readers understand these feelings by showing them specific parts of my parents' lifestyle that I hope will be different for me.

What is my thesis? *After countless tries, I think I've finally settled on my thesis: "As I look at my parents' life, I hope my own will be less ordinary, less duty-bound, and less predictable."*

Who is my audience, and what do they need to know? *My audience consists of my teacher and classmates. (This essay will be discussed in class.) Each reader already is familiar with this topic; everyone, after all, is someone's son or daughter! But I want my audience to understand specifically the differences I envision.*

What do I know about this topic? *A better question might be, What don't I know? I've spent my life with this topic, so I certainly don't have to do any research.*

Of all the material I've discovered on this topic, how much of it is worthwhile (considering my purpose and audience)? *Because I could write volumes here, I'll have to resist getting carried away. I've already decided to focus on the feeling that my parents' lives are too ordinary, duty-bound, and predictable. One paragraph explaining each of these supporting points (and illustrating them with well-chosen examples) should do. How will I organize? I guess I've already made this decision by settling on my thesis: moving from "ordinary" to "duty-bound" to "predictable." Predictability is what I want to emphasize, so I will save it for last.*

How do I want my writing to sound? *I'm sharing something intimate with my classmates, so my tone should be relaxed and personal, as when people talk to people they trust.*

In completing her essay, Haley went on to make similar decisions for drafting and revising. Here is her final draft.

LIFE IN FULL COLOR

I'm probably the only person I know who still has the same two parents she was born with. We have a traditional American family: We go to church and football games; we watch the Olympics on television and argue about politics; and we have Thanksgiving dinner at my grandmother Clancy's and Christmas dinner with my father's sister Jess, who used to let us kids put pitted olives on our fingertips when we were little. Most of my friends are struggling with the problems of broken homes; I'll always be grateful to my

Thesis statement

Topic sentence and first support paragraph

Topic sentence and second support paragraph

Topic statement and third support paragraph

Concluding paragraph

parents for giving me a loving and stable background. *But sometimes I look at my parents' life and hope my life will be less ordinary, less duty-bound, and less predictable.*

I want my life to be imaginative, not ordinary. Instead of honeymooning at Niagara Falls, I want to go to Paris. In my parents' neighborhood, all the houses were built alike about twenty years ago. Different owners have added on or shingled or painted, but the houses basically all look the same. The first thing we did when we moved into our house was plant trees; everyone did. Now the neighborhood is full of family homes on tree-lined streets, which is nice; but I'd prefer a condo in a renovated brick building in Boston. I'd have dozens of plants, and I'd buy great furniture one piece at a time at auctions and dusty shops and not by the roomful from the local furniture store. Instead of spending my time trying to be similar to everyone else, I'd like to explore ways of being different.

My parents have so many obligations, they barely have time for themselves; I don't want to live like that. I'm never quite sure whether they own the house or the house owns them. They worry constantly about taxes, or the old furnace, or the new deck, or mowing the lawn, or weeding the garden. After spending every weekend slaving over their beautiful yard, they have no time left to enjoy it. And when they're not buried in household chores, other people are making endless demands on their time. My mother will stay up past midnight because she promised some telephone voice 3 cakes for the church bazaar, or 5 dozen cookies for the Girl Scout meeting, or 76 little sandwiches for the women's club Christmas party. My father coaches Little League, wears a clown suit for the Lions' flea markets, and both he and my mother are volunteer firefighters. In fact, both my parents get talked into volunteering for everything. I hate to sound selfish, but my first duty is to myself. I'd rather live in a tent than be owned by my house. And I don't want my life to end up being measured out in endless chores.

Although it's nice to take things such as regular meals and paychecks for granted, many other events in my parents' life are too predictable for me. Every Sunday at two o'clock we dine on overdone roast beef, mashed potatoes and gravy, a faded green vegetable, and sometimes that mushy orange squash that comes frozen in bricks. It's not that either of my parents is a bad cook, but Sunday dinner isn't food anymore; it's a habit. Mom and Dad have become so predictable that they can order each other's food in restaurants. Just once I'd like to see them pack up and go away for a weekend, without telling anybody; they couldn't do it. They can't even go crazy and try a new place for their summer vacation. They've been spending the first two weeks in August on Cape Cod since I was two years old. I want variety in my life. I want to travel, see this country and see Europe, do things spontaneously. No one will ever be able to predict my order in a restaurant.

Before long, Christmas will be here, and we'll be going to Aunt Jess's. Mom will bake a walnut pie, and Grandpa Frank will say, "Michelle, you sure know how to spoil an old man." It's nice to know that some things never change. In fact, some of the ordinary, obligatory, predictable things in life are the most comfortable. But too much of any routine can make life seem dull and gray. I hope my choices lead to a life in full color.

—*Shirley Haley*

Discussion of Haley's final draft

Here are some of Haley's major improvements:

- The distinct shape (introduction, body, conclusion) enables us to organize our understanding and follow the writer's thinking.
- The essay no longer confuses us. We know where Haley stands because she tells us, with a definite thesis; and we know why because she shows us, with plenty of examples.
- She wastes nothing; everything seems to belong, and everything fits together.
- Now each paragraph has its own design, and each paragraph enhances the whole.
- We now see real variety in the ways in which sentences begin and words are put together. We hear a genuine voice.

All good writing has these qualities

Because she made careful decisions, Haley produced a final draft that displays the qualities of all good writing: *content* that makes it worth reading; *organization* that reveals the line of thinking and emphasizes what is most important; and *style* that is economical and convincingly human.

THE LOOPING STRUCTURE OF THE WRITING PROCESS

Writers rarely struggle with these decisions about planning, drafting, and revising in a predictable sequence. Instead, writers choose sequences that work best for them. Figure 1.2 diagrams this looping ("recursive") structure of the writing process.

In some ways, the writing process is always different; in some ways, it's always the same. For example, we tackle a research paper differently from questions on an essay exam. Memos, letters, reports, emails, or other workplace documents call for their own, specific approaches. In some of these cases (say, an essay exam), immediate time pressures might force you to find shortcuts. When you're writing about a topic you already know well, you might spend less time planning what to say. When you're writing a document that will be posted online (say, a Web page) the updating and revising might be endless. But even though any writing situation poses its own particular challenges, the basic loop of planning, drafting, and revising remains pretty much constant.

Note

Rarely is any piece of writing ever strictly "finished." Even famous writers have returned to a successful published work years later to revise it once again.

FIGURE 1.2
The looping structure of
the writing process

Decisions in the writing
process are recursive; no
one stage is complete until
all stages are complete.

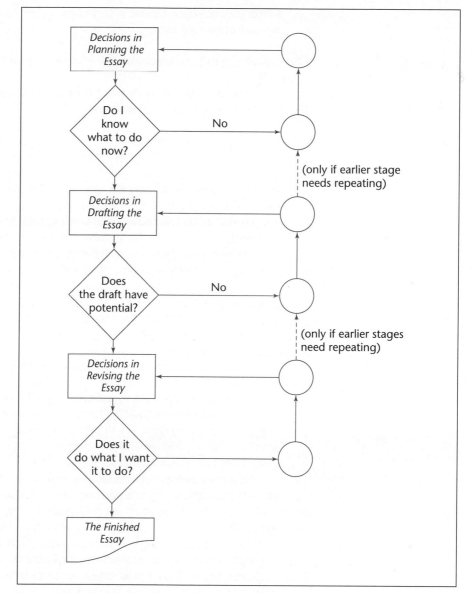

A writer might even revisit
the "finished" essay for
additional revision.

Application **1-1**

The essay that follows (a third draft) was written in response to this assignment:

> Identify a personal trait that is so strong you cannot control it (a quick temper,
> the need for acceptance, a fear of failure, shyness, a bad habit, a phobia, an
> obsession, or the like). In a serious or humorous essay, show how this trait

affects your behavior. Provide enough details for readers to understand clearly this part of your personality.

Our writer, Wendy Gianacoples, decided to explore a personal obsession: food.

Read Wendy's essay once or twice. Then read it again, using the questions that follow the essay for your analysis.

Essay for analysis

CONFESSIONS OF A FOOD ADDICT

Like many compulsive eaters, I eat to fill a void—an emptiness within. I feed my feelings. Food can be my best friend, always there when I need it. This friend, however, actually is a tyrant that dominates my life through endless cycles of need, indulgence, and guilt.

Thanks to my food obsession, I seem to have two personalities: the respected, self-controlled Wendy who eats properly all day, and the fat Wendy who emerges after dark to gobble everything in sight. Lying in bed, I wait for the house to be silent. Feeling excited and giddy, I sneak to the kitchen and head straight for the freezer to begin my search. My initial prize is an unopened pint of Ben & Jerry's chocolate chip ice cream. I break the container's seal, dig in with my spoon, and shovel down massive gobs. (I have a love/hate relationship with food: I want all or nothing.) Next thing I know the container is empty.

Stashing the empty container deeply in the trash, I continue my rampage. From the cookie drawer, I snatch a nearly full package of Fig Newtons. As I tiptoe toward the milk, I ask myself what the folks at Weight Watchers would say if they could see me standing half-awake in my ice cream splattered Lanz nightgown, popping down Fig Newtons and swigging milk from the carton. After pushing the few remaining cookies to the front of the package so it looks fuller, I rummage around for my next "fix."

Beneath a bag of frozen Bird's Eye vegetables, I find a frozen pizza—the ultimate midnight snack. The oven will take too long but the microwave is too noisy—all that beeping could get me busted. Feeling daring, I turn on the kitchen faucet to drown out the beeps, place the pizza in the microwave, set the timer, grab the last handful of Fig Newtons, and wait.

By the time I polish off the pizza, it's 1:00 a.m. and I crave Kraft Macaroni & Cheese. Standing on a chair I reach for a box from the overhead cabinet. Trying to be quiet, I dig out a spaghetti pot from a pile of pots and pans. Grabbing the handle, I hold my breath as I pull the pan from the clutter. While the water boils and the macaroni cooks, I fix a bowl of Rice Krispies. Just as I finish chowing down "Snap, Crackle, and Pop," the macaroni is ready. After eating the whole package, I bury the box in the trash.

After a binge, I panic: "What have I done?" Setting a hand on my bulging stomach, I think of the weight I'll gain this week. Climbing the stairs to my bed, I feel drained, like a person on drugs who is now "coming down." In my bedroom, I study myself in the full-length mirror, looking for visible signs of my sins. Lying in bed, I feel fat and uncomfortable. Although I usually sleep on my stomach, on "binge" nights, I assume the fetal position, cradling my full belly, feeling ashamed and alone, as if I were the only person who overeats and uses food as a crutch. When the sugar I've consumed keeps me awake, I plead with God to help me overcome this weakness.

The next morning I kick myself and feel guilty. I want to block out last night's memories, but my tight clothes offer a painful reminder. My stomach is sick all day and I have heartburn. During the following week, I'll eat next to nothing and exercise constantly, hoping to break even on the scale at Weight Watchers.

Most people don't consider compulsive eating an addiction. Substance abusers can be easy to spot, but food addicts are less obvious. Unlike drugs, one can't live without food. People would never encourage a drug addict or alcoholic to "have another hit" or "fall off the wagon." However, people constantly push food on overeaters: "Come on, one brownie won't hurt. I made them especially for you," says a friend. When I decline, she scowls and turns away. Little does she know, while she was in the bathroom, I had four.

—*Wendy Gianacoples*

Questions about the reading

Does the Content of the Essay Make It Worth Reading?

- Can you find a definite thesis that announces the writer's viewpoint? Where?
- Do you have enough information to understand the viewpoint?
- Do you learn something new and useful? Explain briefly.
- Does everything belong, or should any material be cut? Where?

Does the Organization Reveal the Writer's Line of Thinking?

- Is there an introduction to set the scene, a middle to walk us through, and a conclusion to sum up the meaning?
- Does each support paragraph present a distinct unit of meaning?
- Does each paragraph stick to the point and stick together?

Is the Style Economical and Convincing?

- Can you understand each sentence the first time you read it? If not, which?
- Should any words be cut? If so, where?
- Are sentences varied in the way they're put together? Examples?
- Is the writer's meaning always clear? If not, where?
- Can you hear a real person speaking? Describe the person you hear.
- Do you like the person you hear? Why or why not?

Write out your answers to these questions and be prepared to discuss them in class.

Application **1-2**

Collaborative Project: In class, write your "quickest effort" essay about a personal trait, or about this subject: "Important Differences or Similarities Between My Life and That of My Parents." Exchange papers with a classmate, and evaluate your classmate's paper, using the questions from Application 1-1. In one or two paragraphs, give your classmate advice for revising. Don't be afraid to mark up (with your own questions, comments, and suggestions) this paper you're evaluating. Discuss with your classmate your evaluation of his/her work. At home, read the evaluation of your paper carefully, and write your "best" version of your original essay. List the improvements you made in moving from your quickest effort to your best effort. Be prepared to discuss your improvements in class.

Also, in two or three paragraphs, trace your own writing process for this essay by describing the decisions you made. Be prepared to discuss your decisions in class.

Note: Don't expect miracles at this stage, but do expect some degree of frustration and confusion. Things will improve quickly, though.

Application **1-3**

Collaborative Project: Out of class (drawing on your personal experience with group work if possible), write down one thing you look forward to in working with peers and one potential problem you find especially important. In class, share your expectations and concerns with a small group. Do group members raise similar issues, or does everyone have different concerns? As a group, craft these issues and concerns into a list of group goals: benefits you hope to achieve and pitfalls you hope to avoid.

Application **1-4**

Web-based Project: Visit the Colorado State University Web pages on "Writing Guides" at

<http://writing.colostate.edu/references/>

Under the *Understanding Writing Processes* link, explore one of these sections:

> *Writing Academic Evaluations*
> *Scientific Writing*
> *Answering Exam Questions*

In 200 to 300 words, describe how the process for one of these three types of writing projects follows the recursive, looping process shown in Figure 1.2.

What are the key stages in the process? How do you know when to move forward and when to back up and repeat a stage?

Attach a copy of the relevant Web page(s) to your explanation.

Note | *Instead of quoting your source(s) directly, paraphrase (page 372). Be sure to credit each source of information (page 392).*

OPTIONS FOR ESSAY WRITING

The following topics offer ideas for essays to get you started. People write best about things they know, so we begin with personal forms of writing. You might want to return to this list for topic ideas when essays are assigned throughout the early chapters of this book.

1. What major effects has television had on your life (your ambitions, hopes, fears, values, consumer habits, awareness of the world, beliefs, outlook, faith in people, and so on)? Overall, has television been a positive or negative influence? Have you learned anything from TV that you couldn't have learned elsewhere? Support your thesis with specific details.

2. How do advertising and commercials shape our values (notions about looking young, being athletic, being thin, smoking, beer drinking, and so on)? Does advertising present an unrealistic view of life? In what ways? What kinds of human weaknesses and aspirations do commercials exploit? Support your viewpoint with examples your readers will recognize.

3. If you could repeat your high school years, what three or four things would you do differently? Write for a younger brother or sister entering high school, and provide enough detail to get your viewpoint across.

4. Do some music videos communicate distorted and dangerous messages? If so, what should be done? Discuss specific examples and their effect on viewers.

5. Americans often are criticized for their emphasis on competing and succeeding (academically, financially, physically, socially, and so on). Is this criticism valid? Has emphasis on competition and success been mostly helpful or harmful for you? Why?

6. Our public schools have been accused of failing to educate America's students. Does your high school typify the so-called failure of American education? Why or why not? How well did your school prepare you for college—and for life?

7. College students commonly are stereotyped as party animals. Explain to a skeptical nonstudent audience that college life is harder than people imagine—but don't sermonize or complain. For instance, if you attend a public university, you might write for state legislators who want to cut the school budget.

8. Write about a job you've had and explain what you liked and disliked about the job. Show readers exactly what the job was like. Would you recommend this job to a friend? Why or why not?

9. Describe the good and bad points of being a "nontraditional" student (returning to school after military service, employment, raising a family, or the like). Write for readers in a similar situation who are thinking about returning to school. What are the most important things they should know?

10. Explain to a skeptical audience the benefits of an alternative lifestyle choice you or someone you know has made (vegetarianism, co-housing, nontraditional family, male homemaker, back-to-nature, or the like). Dispel the negative stereotypes.

11. As a part-time student who balances work and school, give advice to a friend in your situation who wants to follow your example but feels fearful or discouraged. Explain how you manage to cope.

CHAPTER 2

Decisions in Planning

Deciding on a Topic, Purpose, Thesis, and Audience **22**

.**Guidelines** for Developing a Thesis **27**

CASE STUDY: Analyzing Your Writing Situation **29**

Discovering, Selecting, and Organizing Your Material **30**

Guidelines for Brainstorming **32**

CASE STUDY: Exploring and Arranging Assets **33**

Finding Your Voice **36**

The Writer's Planning Guide **38**

Planning for Group Work **40**

Guidelines for Writing Collaboratively **40**

Applications **43**

Why writers need to plan

Writing is a battle with impatience, a fight against the natural urge to "be done with it." Effective writers win this battle by *planning*: analyzing their writing situation, exploring their assets, and finding a voice. Of course, planning continues throughout the writing process, but an initial plan gives you a place to start and a direction for your decisions.

DECIDING ON A TOPIC, PURPOSE, THESIS, AND AUDIENCE

Your earliest planning decisions will require that you analyze your writing situation:

Questions for Analyzing a Writing Situation

- *What, exactly, is my topic?*
- *Why am I writing about it?*

- *What is my viewpoint?*
- *Who is my audience?*

Of course, you won't always follow a single order in making these decisions; in Chapter 1, Shirley Haley discovers her thesis before brainstorming for material. The key is to make all the decisions—in whichever order works best for you.

As with any stage in the writing process, you might have to return again and again to your plan.

Decide on Your Topic

In most out-of-school writing ("Why I deserve a promotion"; "Why you should marry me"; "How we repaired the computer"), topics are decided for you by the situation. But when you are asked to choose your own topic, remember one word: *focus.*

"What, exactly, is my topic?"

Sometimes, afraid we'll have too little to say, we mistakenly choose the broadest topic. But a focused topic actually provides more to write about by allowing for the nitty-gritty details that show readers what we mean.

For instance, if you wanted to know the "personality" of a particular town, walking around and talking with the people would show a lot more than flying over the place at 10,000 feet. A *focused topic,* then, is something you know and really can talk about, something that has real meaning for you.

Decide on Your Purpose

"Why am I writing?"

Finding a *purpose* means asking yourself, "Why am I writing this piece?" Each writing situation has a specific goal. Perhaps you want audience members to see what you saw, to feel what you felt, or to think differently. To achieve your goal, you will need a definite *strategy.*

Goal plus strategy equals purpose. Consider one writer's inadequate answers to the familiar question, Why am I writing this paper?

Inadequate statements of purpose

(a) I'm writing this essay to pass the course.

(b) My goal is to write an essay about college life.

(c) My goal is to describe to classmates the experience of being a nontraditional student.

Responses **a** and **b** above tell nothing about the specific goal. Response **c** defines the goal but offers no strategy. Here, finally, is our writer's purpose statement (goal plus strategy):

A useful statement of purpose

My purpose is to describe to classmates the experience of being a nontraditional student. I'll focus on the special anxieties, difficulties, and rewards.

Sometimes you will be unable to define your purpose immediately. You might need to jot down as many purposes as possible until one pops up. Or you might need to write a rough draft first or make an outline. In any case, the purpose statement should provide the raw material for your thesis.

Note   *While the purpose statement is part of the discovery process, the thesis is part of the finished essay. (See pages 56–58.)*

Decide on Your Thesis.

What a thesis is

Your purpose statement identifies exactly what you want to *do*. Your thesis announces exactly what you want to *say*—the "big picture" boiled down to one or two (or sometimes three) sentences. Usually appearing early in your essay, the thesis conveys two kinds of information: It names the topic, and it states your viewpoint about the topic:

Topic plus viewpoint

| TOPIC | VIEWPOINT |
| [Chemical pesticides and herbicides] | [are not only hazardous but also ineffective]. |

The essay can then be built around this central idea.

What a thesis does

By telling readers exactly what to expect, your thesis makes a definite commitment. Besides serving as the reader's road map, the thesis serves as your planning tool—the basic thread that holds your ideas together and that makes your thinking clear in your own mind.

The thesis itself can be expressed in various ways, as in these examples:

As an opinion	Starting college after the age of 30 hasn't been easy, but the good points definitely outweigh the bad.
As an evaluation	I want my life to be better than that of my parents.
As a suggestion	Computers should be provided for all students.

As a question	Should college be for everyone?
As a debatable claim	College is not for everyone.

Each of these thesis statements creates a clear expectation. They don't keep readers guessing. They make their points quickly.

Note | *Think of your thesis as "the one sentence you would keep if you could keep only one"* (U.S. Air Force Academy 11).

Thesis as Framework.   Consciously or unconsciously, readers look for a thesis, usually in the essay's early paragraphs. Even a single paragraph is hard to understand if the main point is missing. Read this paragraph once, only— then try answering the questions that follow.

A paragraph with its main point omitted

> His [or her] job is not to punish, but to heal. Most students are bad writers, but the more serious the injuries, the more confusing the symptoms, the greater the need for effective diagnostic work. When an accident victim is carried into the hospital emergency ward, the doctor does not start treating the patient at the top and slowly work down without a sense of priority, spending a great deal of time on the black eye before [getting] to the punctured lung. Yet that is exactly what the English teacher too often does. The doctor looks for the most vital problem; he [or she] wants to keep the patient alive, and . . . goes to work on the critical injury.
>
> *—Donald Murray*

Can you identify the paragraph's main idea? Probably not. Without the topic sentence, you have no framework for understanding this information in its larger meaning.

Now, insert the following sentence at the beginning and reread the paragraph.

The missing main idea | The writing teacher must not be a judge, but a physician.

This orientation makes the message's exact meaning obvious.

In the basic essay framework, each body paragraph supports its own *topic statement,* which focuses on one aspect of the thesis. The thesis is the controlling idea; each topic statement treats one part of the controlling idea, as diagrammed here:

Introductory paragraph

Support paragraphs

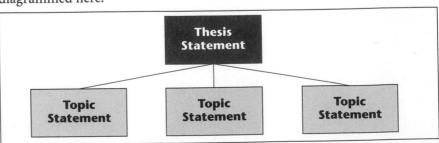

Some writers include in the thesis an explicit preview of supporting points; some don't. For instance, an essay titled "Beef Cost and the Cattle Rancher" might have this thesis statement:

A thesis that includes a preview

> Because of rising costs, unpredictable weather, and long hours, many cattle ranchers have trouble staying in business.

An alternative is to omit such a preview:

> Cattle ranchers' biggest challenge is survival for their businesses.

Including a preview in their thesis helps some writers stay on track as they develop each support paragraph. With or without the preview, be sure that supporting points appear as topic statements in subsequent paragraphs, as in this next example:

Introductory paragraph

Thesis

> _____
> _____
> _____ Starting college after age 30 hasn't been easy, but the good points definitely outweigh the bad.

Although the above thesis does not preview the main supporting points, each point is spelled out in respective topic statements:

First support paragraph

> My major obstacles were lack of self-confidence and fear of failure. [_topic statement_] _____
> _____
> _____

Second support paragraph

> While struggling to overcome my panic, I worked at developing good study habits and sharpening my basic skills. [_topic statement_] _____
> _____
> _____

Third support paragraph

> After realizing I could do the work, I began to relax and savor the "joy of learning." [_topic statement_] _____
> _____
> _____

Evaluating Your Thesis. The first thing readers want to know is this:

What readers ask about your thesis

> What, exactly, is your point, and why is it worth reading about?

Always check to see that your thesis provides a sharp focus and a definite and significant viewpoint.

A. *Is the Topic Sharply Focused?* In a short essay, avoid broad topics:

> **Too broad**   Some experiences can be unforgettable.

B. *Is a Definite Viewpoint Expressed?* Convey your exact position. These next thesis statements are not clear:

> **No clear viewpoint**   I started college at age 35 *[Merely states a fact.]*
>
> College can be a complex experience.

C. *Is the Viewpoint Worthwhile?* Whether your thesis is expressed as an opinion, evaluation, suggestion, question, or debatable claim, it should trigger some fresh insight or have some value or importance for readers. A thesis that contributes nothing new is worthless:

> **Insignificant viewpoints**   The college years can be traumatic. *[Everyone would agree, so why discuss it?]*
>
> Every nontraditional student has a unique college experience. *[No big surprise here!]*

D. *Is the Point Supportable?* Avoid any claim that you can't back up with credible evidence (page 84):

> **Unsupportable claim**   Older students are more serious about schoolwork than their younger counterparts.

E. *Does the Thesis Offer a Preview?* Provide a concise but clear picture of where your essay is headed. This next sentence offers no such preview:

> **No preview**   My experience as a nontraditional student has been interesting, to say the least.

In this next sentence, the preview is adequate but the preface is needless:

> **Needless preface**   In this essay, I will discuss how the good points of starting college after the age of 30 definitely outweigh the bad.

How thesis form and location can vary

Variations in Your Thesis.   The thesis statement can take different forms:

- The thesis need not be limited to one sentence.
- The main supporting points are not always explicitly previewed.
- A thesis does not automatically call for only three supporting points. Three is a good minimum, but some topics call for more, others for less.

How you phrase the thesis and how you support it depends on your purpose and audience.

When to Compose Your Thesis. In an ideal world, writers would be able to (1) settle on a topic, (2) compose a purpose statement, and (3) compose a thesis. But these steps rarely occur in such neat order. If you have trouble coming up with a thesis right away, go on to some other activity: list some ideas, work on an outline, do some freewriting, or take a walk. Writing, after all, is a way of discovering what you want to say.

Even if you do begin with a workable thesis, it might not be the one you end up with. As you work and discover new meanings, you might need to revise or start again.

GUIDELINES FOR DEVELOPING A THESIS

1. *Allow plenty of time for getting your thinking straight.* Writing expert Peter Elbow defines *writing* as "a way to end up thinking something [we] couldn't have started out thinking" (15). And we usually end up a long way from where we started. So don't expect your thesis to pop into your head automatically. For any writer, deciding on a solid thesis is often half the battle.

2. *Use whatever works to get yourself started.* Try writing a *working thesis,* summarizing in one or two sentences the main point you want your essay to convey. If you get stuck, try freewriting, brainstorming, or other discovery strategies from pages 30–33. Keep at it until a working thesis emerges.

3. *Settle on a specific topic.* Never tackle something too broad. Instead of writing, say, about *school reform* (a huge topic), focus on *school uniforms or dress codes.*

4. *Stick to one clear and definite main point.* Spell out your viewpoint on the topic: for example, "School uniforms offer one promising way of improving the learning environment." Take a position that leads somewhere; don't merely state a *fact,* as in "Nearly three-fourths of New York City schools now have dress codes." Facts serve as evidence to *support* a thesis, but once a

fact has been verified (page 84), there is little else to say about it. However, your viewpoint about what a fact "means" could serve as a thesis, as in "The growing popularity of dress codes is one more sign that school reform is headed 'back to the basics.'"

Once you have settled on a position, don't be vague about it: Instead of "School dress codes have benefits and drawbacks," write "The benefits of school dress codes outweigh the drawbacks."

5. *Make a worthwhile point.* Be sure your point is worth discussing or arguing—that it offers something new or significant (page 86). Don't merely restate the obvious, as in "School uniforms are a controversial issue." Instead, share a useful insight, offer a different perspective, make a debatable claim, answer a question you've researched—in short, help readers see the topic in a new way.

6. *Make your point supportable.* Readers always want to know this: "Says who?" Don't make an overstated claim, as in "Uniforms and dress codes are the best way to improve our schools." Don't make a highly opinionated claim that can't be backed up, as in "Uniforms make students look and feel more attractive." Instead, rely on the

GUIDELINES FOR DEVELOPING A THESIS (continued)

evidence: "As many schools are discovering, uniforms and dress codes can enhance the learning environment." Be sure you can support your point within the length of your essay. Also be sure that you have enough to say to justify an entire essay.

7. *Get your facts straight.* Some claims will require research; some will not. For example, research would be needed to support this thesis: "Evidence increasingly suggests that dress codes promote a more disciplined learning environment." But your personal experience should be adequate to support this thesis: "Coping with the illness of a loved one can be a valuable learning experience." (Of course, this essay might provide the basis for a subsequent research paper about strategies for coping with personal tragedy.)

8. *Offer a preview of the whole essay.* Key words or phrases in your thesis tell readers what to expect in terms of the essay's purpose, scope, and direction. Replace abstract and general words ("good," "poor," "interesting," "significant," "complex") with concrete and specific ones ("evidence suggests," "disciplined learning environment"). Avoid needless and self-evident prefaces, as in "The purpose of this essay is to . . ." or "In this paper, I will show. . ."; instead, let your key words provide the forecast.

For a more explicit preview, list your supporting points in your thesis, which might require two or more sentences, as in this example: "School uniforms and dress codes are on the rise and for good reason: They work. School districts across the country are finding that uniforms promote discipline, safety, and learning, along with a sense of equality among differing social groups." Each of these four supporting points then will appear in its own topic sentence.

9. *Use the thesis to check on your paper.* As you work on your paper, keep checking back to make sure you haven't wandered—but if you happen to discover some new, promising direction, you might rethink your thesis and adjust it as needed.

10. *Always leave room for revision.* Plan on writing numerous versions before you get it right, and be prepared to revise the thesis while you are writing your essay, all the way to the end. And don't be surprised if the thesis you end up with looks nothing like the working thesis you began with!

11. *Decide where to place your thesis.* In a college essay, the thesis usually appears as the final sentence(s) of the essay's introduction. But in some writing situations, it can appear elsewhere, as shown on page 51.

Decide on Your Audience

"Who is my audience and what do they expect?"

Audiences you might encounter

Except for a diary or a journal, everything you write is for readers who will react to your information. You might write to a prospective employer who wants to know why you quit a recent job; to a committee who wants to know why you deserve a scholarship; to a classmate who wants to know you better; or to a professor who wants to know whether you understand the material. For any audience, your task is to deliver a message that makes a difference with readers, that helps them see things your way.

What audiences expect

Out of school, you will write for diverse audiences (customers, employers, politicians, and so on). But in school, you can envision a definite audience besides your instructor: your classmates. Like any audience, they expect your writing to be clear, informative, and persuasive. Whoever your readers are, they need enough material to understand your position and to react appropriately. Readers don't need repetition of material they already know. To put readers in your place, first put yourself in theirs. Anticipate their most probable questions.

Anticipating your readers' questions gives you a better chance of discovering and selecting material that really makes a difference—that offers readers what they need and expect.

CASE STUDY

ANALYZING YOUR WRITING SITUATION

Assume you are writing in response to this assignment:

> Illustrate some feature of our societal values or behavior that you find humorous, depressing, contemptible, or admirable. Possible topics: our consumer or dress habits, the cars we drive, our ideas of entertainment, and so on.

First, focus your topic:

Focusing your topic

societal values or behavior
↓
the cars we drive
↓
our love affair with cars
↓
why we love our cars

This last topic seems focused enough for a short essay. But what in this topic do you wish to explore? What do you want readers to see and understand?

Your focused topic

How cars appeal to our sense of individuality

Now that you have a suitable topic, you're on your way. You might get stuck later and have to discard the whole thing, but for now you can decide on your purpose.

Because the essay examines "How," you organize a rough outline to lay out a sequence of examples:

Your rough outline

(a) The car as an individual statement

(b)   The car as a political statement

(c)   The car as a personal sanctuary

Now you can compose your statement of purpose:

Your purpose statement

My purpose is to poke fun at our obsession with cars by explaining to classmates how cars appeal to our sense of individuality. I'll discuss uses of the car as lifestyle statement, personal billboard, and private sanctuary.

This is your map for reaching your goal. (Keep in mind that the purpose statement is part of the discovery process, but the thesis is part of the finished essay.)

Based on the above purpose statement, assume you derive the following thesis:

Your thesis

Today's self-centered consumers demand cars that satisfy our craving for individuality.

As you consider your audience here (teacher and classmates), you anticipate the following general questions about your thesis:

General questions you can anticipate

- *Exactly what do you mean by "individuality"?*
- *What is the connection between cars and individuality?*
- *Can you give examples?*
- *Who cares?*

As this case continues, after the following section, you will identify more specific audience questions you need to answer.

DISCOVERING, SELECTING, AND ORGANIZING YOUR MATERIAL

Once you have analyzed your writing situation, you set out to answer these questions:

Questions for Exploring Your Assets

- *What do I know about the topic?*
- *How much of my material is useful in this situation?*

- *How will readers want this organized?*

Discover Useful Material

"What do I know about the topic?"

Discovering useful material is called *invention*. When you begin working with an idea or exploring a topic, you search for useful material, for content—insight, facts, statistics, opinions, examples, images—that might help answer the question, *How can I find something worthwhile to say—something that will advance my meaning?*

Some people use invention as an early writing step, a way of getting started. Others save the invention stage until they've made other decisions. Regardless of the sequence, all writers use invention throughout the writing process.

The goal of invention is to get as much material as possible on paper, through the use of strategies like the following.

Keeping a Journal. A *journal* is an excellent way to build a personal inventory of ideas and topics. Here you can write for yourself only.

How to make a journal

To start, buy a hardcover notebook with a sewn binding (so that whatever you write becomes a permanent part of your journal). Record your reactions to something you've read or seen; ask questions or describe people, places, things, feelings; explore fantasies, daydreams, nightmares, fears, hopes; write conversations or letters that never will be heard or read; examine the things you hate or love. Write several times a day, once a week, or whenever you get the urge—or put aside some regular time to write. Every so often, go back and look over your entries—you might be surprised by the things you find.

Note *You can also keep an online journal as a storehouse for ideas.*

Freewriting. *Freewriting* is a version of the "quickest-effort" approach discussed in Chapter 1. Shirley Haley's first attempt (page 10) is the product of freewriting. As the term suggests, when freewriting, you simply write whatever comes to mind, hoping that the very act of recording your thinking will generate some useful content.

How to freewrite

Try freewriting by exploring what makes you angry or happy or frightened or worried. Write about what surprises you or what you think is unfair or what you would like to see happen. Don't stop writing until you've filled a whole page or two, and don't worry about organization or correctness—just get it down. Although it will never produce a finished essay, freewriting can give you a good start by uncovering all kinds of buried ideas. It can be especially useful for curing "writer's block."

Using Journalists' Questions. To probe the many angles and dimensions of a topic, journalists ask these questions:

Questions Journalists Ask

- *Who was involved?*
- *What happened?*
- *When did it happen?*

- *Where did it happen?*
- *How did it happen?*
- *Why did it happen?*

Unlike freewriting, the journalists' questions offer a built-in organizing strategy—an array of different "perspectives" on your topic.

Asking Yourself Questions.   If you can't seem to settle on a definite viewpoint, try answering any of these questions that apply to your topic.

Discovery Questions You Can Ask

- *What is my opinion of X?*
- *Am I for it or against it?*
- *Does it make me happy or sad?*
- *Is it good or bad?*
- *Will it work or fail?*
- *Does it make sense?*
- *What have I observed about X?*

- *What have I seen happen?*
- *What is special or unique about it?*
- *What strikes me about it?*
- *What can I suggest about X?*
- *What would I like to see happen?*
- *What should or should not be done?*

From your answers, you can zero in on the viewpoint that will provide the organizing insight for your essay.

Brainstorming.   You can also try brainstorming—a sure bet for coming up with useful material. Its aim is to produce as many ideas as possible. Here is how brainstorming works:

GUIDELINES FOR BRAINSTORMING

1. Find a quiet spot, and bring an alarm clock, a pencil, and plenty of paper.
2. Set the alarm to ring in 30 minutes.
3. Try to protect yourself from interruptions: phones, music, or the like. Sit with eyes closed for two minutes, thinking about absolutely nothing.
4. Now, concentrate on your writing situation. If you've already spelled out your purpose and your audience's questions, focus on these. Otherwise, repeat this question: *What can I say about my topic, at all?*
5. As ideas begin to flow, record every one. Don't stop to judge relevance or worth, and don't worry about complete sentences (or even correct spelling). Simply get everything on paper. Even the wildest idea might lead to some valuable insight.

6. Keep pushing and sweating until the alarm rings.
7. If the ideas are still flowing, reset the alarm and go on.
8. At the end of this session, you should have a chaotic mixture of junk, irrelevancies, and useful material.
9. Take a break.
10. Now confront your list. Strike out what is useless, and sort the remainder into categories. Include any other ideas that crop up. Your finished list should provide plenty of raw material.

Note   *Try brainstorming at the computer. Try freewriting with the monitor turned off or covered, then, after 15 minutes, look at the screen and review your list.*

Reading and Researching. Some of our best ideas, insights, and questions often come from our reading (as discussed in Chapter 9). Or we might want to consider what others have said or discovered about our topic (as discussed in Chapter 19) before we reach our own conclusions. Reading and research are indispensable tools for any serious writer.

Select Your Best Material

"How much of my material is useful in this situation?"

Invention invariably produces more material than a writer needs. Select only the material that best advances your meaning (see Chapter 5, "Revising the Content").

If you do find yourself trying to include everything you've discovered, you probably need to refocus on your purpose and audience.

Organize for Readers

"How will readers want this organized?"

When material is left in its original, unstructured form, readers waste time trying to understand it. With an outline, you move from a random listing of items as they occurred to you to a deliberate map that will guide readers from point to point.

All readers expect a definite beginning, middle, and ending that provide orientation, discussion, and review. But specific readers want these sections tailored to their expectations. Identify your readers' expectations by (1) anticipating their probable questions about your thesis and (2) visualizing the sequence in which readers would want these questions answered.

Some writers can organize merely by working from a good thesis statement. Others prefer to begin with some type of outline. And some writers like to write a draft and then an outline to check their line of thinking. You might outline early or later. But you need to move from a random collection of ideas to an organized list that helps readers to follow your material.

Note *No single form of outline should be followed slavishly by any writer. The organization of any writing ultimately is determined by its audience's needs and expectations.*

CASE STUDY

EXPLORING AND ARRANGING ASSETS

For your essay on our obsession with cars, assume you've developed the brainstorming list that follows.

Your brainstorming list

1. to get us from point A to point B, junkers would suffice
2. we demand variety in our lives
3. we want cars that make us look cool
4. people seem to love their bumper stickers

5. with bumper stickers we exercise our right to free speech

6. nobody likes driving an old bomber

7. no matter what the sticker price we don't care

8. off-road vehicles are everywhere, but most of them never leave the pavement

9. "creativity is more important than knowledge"—what kind of bumper-sticker logic is that?

10. Henry Ford's Model Ts all looked exactly alike—they were basic transportation, not fashion statements!

11. today's cars are fiberglass and metal gods

12. today's automakers cater to our self-centered fantasies

13. we can run much of our lives without leaving the comfy car

14. the car is the ultimate personal space

15. a great way to escape the daily hassles

16. cars give us the freedom to go where we want when we want

17. we love to do our own thing—what America's all about

18. the car's popularity has led to the phenomenon of drive-up windows

19. people in other countries don't mind public transportation, but we seem to hate it

20. what about the bumper stickers that announce "I'm a tough guy" or "I'm an intellectual"?

21. we can even sing aloud in the car without seeming weird

With your raw material collected, you can now move into the selection phase—leaving open the possibility that new material may surface.

As you review your brainstorming list, you decide to cut items 11, 16, and 19.

Your selection of material to omit

- *Item 11 doesn't relate to the theme of individualism*
- *Item 16 is a cliché and too general to have real meaning in this essay*
- *Item 19 makes an unsupportable generalization*

(If you end up trying to include *all* your raw material, you probably need to refocus on your purpose and audience. Chapter 6 offers advice for selecting fresh and worthwhile material.)

Next you try to anticipate specific readers' questions about your essay, and you come up with this list of possibilities:

Specific reader questions you anticipate

- *Can you set the scene for us and give us a context for your thesis?*
- *Why do we identify so strongly with our cars?*
- *Where do bumper stickers fit in?*

- *Why do we often hang out in the car?*
- *What does all this say about us as a culture?*

Your readers' expectations give you a basis for organizing your brainstorming material into categories:

Your general outline

    I. How Our Relationship to Cars Has Evolved

    II. How Cars Help Us Project an Ideal Self

    III. Why We Decorate Our Cars with Stickers

    IV. How Cars Provide a Private Space

    V. How Cars Serve as the Ultimate Mechanism for Achieving Individuality

Within each category, you arrange your brainstorming items, along with any other worthwhile material that occurs to you. Your final outline might resemble this one:

Your final outline

I. Why do we love our cars so much?

    A. Cars originally were merely basic transportation.

    B. All Model Ts looked alike.

    C. Today's automakers cater to our urge to do our own thing.

    D. Consumers love this kind of attention.

    E. Thesis: Today's self-centered consumers demand cars that satisfy our craving for individuality.

II. We want cars that make a unique lifestyle statement.

    A. If basic transportation was the issue, an old junker would do.

    B. But we want to project that special image.

    C. Roughly 50 percent of consumers buy some type of off-road vehicle.

    D. Most of these jeeps and SUVs never leave the pavement.

    E. Driving a sports car really makes us feel special.

III. Stickers serve as our own personal billboard.

    A. They allow us to exercise our right to free speech.

    B. They announce exactly where we stand.

    C. They tell the world that we're animal lovers, intellectuals, tough guys, or whatever.

    D. Volvos often display political or intellectual statements.

    E. NRA stickers, especially on trucks, intimidate wimps like me.

    F. I hurry to get out of the way.

IV. Public transportation is torture for individuals like us.

    A. America's cars are personal hideaways, places to escape other humans.

B. Drive-up windows are one popular form of escape.

C. We can transact business, order meals, and dine without ever leaving the car.

D. We can sing along with the radio as we eat our Big Fat.

E. If you try singing on a bus or subway, people look at you funny.

V. Cars entice us because they provide the ultimate mechanism for achieving individuality.

A. The cars we drive and the stickers we sport proclaim our prepackaged uniqueness.

B. We can do what we want without seeming weird.

C. We can avoid direct human contact.

D. Our car is who we are.

This outline takes the form of short, kernel sentences that include key ideas for later expansion. Some writers use a less formal outline—a simple list of phrases without numerals or letters. (Use the form that works best for you.)

Later, during various drafts, you will discover more material and probably will delete some original material (as in the final draft, pages 56–58).

FINDING YOUR VOICE

Your planning inventory is nearly complete: you have a topic and a thesis, a clear sense of purpose and audience, a stock of material, and some sort of outline. In fact, if you were writing merely to get your message across, you could begin drafting the essay immediately. Except for diaries or some technical reports, however, we write not only to transmit information, but also to connect with readers.

Why voice matters

Whether your writing connects with readers depends on how it "sounds." The way your writing sounds depends on its *tone*, your personal mark—the voice readers hear between the lines. Readers who like the tone like the writer; they allow contact.

Consciously or unconsciously, readers ask three big questions about the writer:

Readers' questions in sizing up a writer

■ *What type of person is this (somebody businesslike, serious, silly, sincere, phony, boring, bored, intense, stuck-up, meek, confident, friendly, hostile)?*

■ *How is this person treating me (as a friend, acquaintance, stranger, enemy, nobody, superior, subordinate, bozo, somebody with a brain and feelings)?*

■ *What does this person really think about the topic (really involved or merely "going through the motions")?*

Why fancy words don't always work

How readers answer these questions will depend on your voice.

Some inexperienced writers mistakenly think that fancy words make them sound more intelligent and important. And sometimes, of course, only the complex word will convey your exact meaning. Instead of saying "Sexist language contributes to the ongoing existence of stereotypes," you could say more accurately and concisely, "Sexist language perpetuates stereotypes." (One "fancy" word effectively replaces six "simpler" words.) But when you use fancy words only to impress, your writing sounds stuffy and pretentious.

Find a Voice that Connects with Readers

Personal essays ordinarily employ a conversational tone: You write to your audience as though you were speaking to them. Look again at Shirley Haley's opening lines from page 12:

Conversational tone

> I'm probably the only person I know who still has the same two parents she was born with. We have a traditional American family: We go to church and football games; we watch the Olympics on television and argue about politics; and we have Thanksgiving dinner at my grandmother Clancy's and Christmas dinner with my father's sister Jess, who used to let us kids put pitted olives on our fingertips when we were little.

Haley's tone is friendly and relaxed—the voice of a writer who seems at home with herself, her subject, and her readers. We are treated to comfortable images of family things. But the long list of "traditional" family activities also hints at the writer's restlessness and lets us share her mixed feelings of attraction and repulsion.

Suppose Haley had decided to sound more "academic":

Academic tone

> Among my friends and acquaintances, I am apparently the only individual with the good fortune to have parents who remain married. Our family activities are grounded in American tradition: We attend church services and football games; we watch televised sporting events and engage in political debates; at Thanksgiving, we dine at Grandmother's, and at Christmas, with an aunt who has always been quite tolerant of children's behavior.

Which is better? To see for yourself which version is more inviting, test each against the three big questions for readers on page 36.

Avoid an Overly Informal Tone

How tone can be too informal

We generally do not write in the same way we would speak to friends at the local burger joint or street corner. Achieving a conversational tone does not mean lapsing into substandard usage, slang, profanity, or excessive colloquialisms. *Substandard usage* ("He ain't got none"; "I seen it today"; "She brang the book") ignores standards of educated expression. *Slang* ("hurling," "phat," "newbie") usually has specific meaning only for members of a particular in-group. *Profanity* ("pissed off"; "This idea sucks"; "What the hell") not only displays contempt for the audience but often triggers contempt for the person using it. *Colloquialisms* ("okay," "a lot," "snooze," "in the bag") are understood more widely than slang but tend to appear more in speaking than in writing.

How tone can offend

Tone is considered offensive when it violates the reader's expectations: when it seems disrespectful or tasteless, distant and aloof, or too "chummy," casual, or otherwise inappropriate for the topic, the reader, and the situation.

When to use an academic tone

A formal or academic tone, in fact, is perfectly appropriate in countless writing situations: a research paper, a job application, a report for the company president, and so on. In a history essay, for example, we would not refer to George Washington and Abraham Lincoln as "those dudes, George and Abe." Whenever we begin with freewriting or brainstorming, our tone might be overly informal and is likely to require some adjustment during subsequent drafts.

Although slang is usually inappropriate in school or workplace writing, some situations call for a measure of informality. The occasional colloquial expression helps soften the tone of any writing.

THE WRITER'S PLANNING GUIDE

Decisions and strategies covered in this chapter apply to almost any writing situation. You can make sure your own planning decisions are complete by following the Planning Guide whenever you write. Items in the Planning Guide are reminders of things to be done.

PLANNING GUIDE

Broad subject:

Limited topic:

Purpose statement:

Thesis statement:

Audience:

Probable audience questions:

Brainstorming list (with irrelevant items deleted):

Outline:

Appropriate tone for audience and purpose:

Your instructor might ask you to use the Planning Guide for early assignments and to submit your responses along with your essay. Remember that your decisions for completing the Planning Guide need not follow the strict order of the items listed—so long as you make all the necessary decisions.

This next Planning Guide has been completed to show a typical set of decisions for "Cars R Us."

THE COMPLETED PLANNING GUIDE

Broad topic: Societal values or behavior

Limited topic: How cars appeal to our sense of individuality

Purpose statement (what you want to do): My purpose is to poke fun at our obsession with cars by explaining to my classmates how cars appeal to our sense of individuality. I'll discuss uses of the car as a lifestyle statement, personal billboard, and private sanctuary.

Thesis statement (what you want to say): Today's self-centered consumers demand cars that satisfy our craving for individuality.

Audience: Classmates

Probable audience questions:
> *Can you set the scene for us and give us a context for your thesis?*
> *Why do we identify so strongly with our cars?*
> *Where do bumper stickers fit in?*
> *Why do we often hang out in the car?*
> *What does all this say about us as a culture?*

Brainstorming list:
> 1. to get us from point A to point B, junkers would suffice
> 2. we demand variety in our lives
> 3. we want cars that make us look cool . . . and so on

Outline:
> I. Why do we love our cars with such passion?
>   A. Cars originally were merely basic transportation.
>   B. Every Model T looked alike.
>   C. Today's automakers cater to our urge to do our own thing . . . and so on.

Appropriate tone for audience and purpose: relaxed and humorous

---

Remember that your decisions for completing the Planning Guide need not follow the strict order of the items listed—so long as you make all the necessary decisions.

PLANNING FOR GROUP WORK

In the Introduction to Section One, you practiced thinking ahead to the kinds of decisions groups must make if they are to benefit from all members' contributions. The following guidelines will enable your group to prepare for collaborative work.

GUIDELINES FOR WRITING COLLABORATIVELY*

1. *Appoint a group manager.* The manager assigns tasks, enforces deadlines, conducts meetings and keeps them on track, consults with the instructor, and generally "runs the show."
2. *Compose a purpose statement* (pages 23, 30). Spell out the project's goal and the group's plan for achieving the goal.
3. *Decide how the group will be organized.* Some possibilities:
   a. The group researches and plans together, but each person writes a different part of the document.
   b. Some members plan and research; one person writes a complete draft; others review, edit, revise, and produce the final version.

   | Note | *The final revision should display one consistent style throughout—as though written by one person only.* |

4. *Divide the task.* Who will be responsible for which parts of the essay or report, or which phases of the project? Who is best at doing what (writing, editing, using a word processor, giving an oral presentation to the class)?

   | Note | *Spell out—in writing—specific expectations for each team member.* |

5. *Establish specific completion dates for each phase.* This will keep everyone focused on what is due and when.
6. *Decide on a meeting schedule and format.* How often will the group meet, where, and for how long? In or out of class? Who will take notes? Set a strict time limit for each discussion topic. Distribute copies of the meeting agenda and timetable beforehand, and stick to this plan. Meetings work best when each member prepares a specific contribution beforehand.
7. *Establish a procedure for responding to the work of other members.* Will reviewing and editing (pages 66, 67) be done in writing, face to face, as a group, one on one, or online? Will this process be supervised by the project manager?
8. *Develop a file-naming system for various drafts.* When working with multiple drafts, it's too easy to save over a previous version and lose something important.
9. *Establish procedures for dealing with group problems.* How will gripes and disagreements be aired and resolved? How will irrelevant discussion be curtailed? Can inevitable conflict be used positively?
10. *Select a group decision-making style beforehand.* Will decisions be made alone by the group manager or be based on group input or majority vote?

*Adapted from Debs 38–41; Hill-Duin 45–50; Hulbert 53–54; Matson 30–31; McGuire 467–68; Morgan 540–41.

11. *Appoint a different "observer" for each meeting.* This group member will make a list of what worked or didn't work during the meeting.

12. *Decide how to evaluate each member's contribution.* Will members evaluate each other? Criteria for evaluation might include dependability, cooperation, effort, quality of work, and the ability to meet deadlines. Figure 2.1 shows one possible form for a manager to evaluate members. Equivalent criteria for evaluating the manager include open-mindedness, fairness in assigning tasks, ability to organize the team, ability to resolve conflicts, and so on. (Members might keep a journal of personal observations for overall evaluation of the project.)

Note | *Any evaluation of strengths and weaknesses should be backed up by comments that explain the ratings (as in Figure 2.1). A group needs to decide beforehand what constitutes "effort," "cooperation," and so on.*

13. *Prepare a project management plan.* Figure 2.2 shows a sample plan sheet. Distribute completed copies to members and the instructor.

FIGURE 2.1

Sample form for evaluating team members

> **Performance Appraisal for** ___J. Fishkill___
> (Rate each element as *[superior]*, *[acceptable]*, or *[unacceptable]*, and use the "Comment" section to explain each rating briefly)
>
> - *Cooperation:* [_superior_]
>   Comment: *works extremely well with others; always willing to help out; responds positively to constructive criticism*
>
> - *Dependability:* [_acceptable_]
>   Comment: *arrives on time for meetings; completes all assigned work*
>
> - *Effort:* [_acceptable_]
>   Comment: *does fair share of work; needs no prodding*
>
> - *Quality of work produced:* [_superior_]
>   Comment: *produces work that is carefully researched, well documented and clearly written*
>
> - *Ability to meet deadlines:* [_superior_]
>   Comment: *delivers all assigned work on or before the deadline; helps other team members with last-minute tasks*
>
>   R. P. Ketchum
>   Project manager's signature

Management Plan Sheet

Project title:
Audience:
Project manager:
Team members:
Purpose of the project

Specific Assigments   **Due Dates**

  Research: Research due:
  Planning: Planning due:
  Drafting: First draft due:
  Revising: Reviews due:
  Preparing final document: Revisions due:
  Presenting oral briefing: Final document due:
                                                     Progress report(s) due:

Specific Assigments

Group meetings:	Date	Place	Time	Note taker
#1				
#2				
#3				
etc.				
Mtgs. w/instructor				
#1				
#2				
etc.				

Miscellaneous

  How will disputes and grievances be resolved?
  How will performances be evaluated?
  Other matters (Internet searches, email routing, computer conferences, etc.)?

FIGURE 2.2
Sample plan sheet for managing a collaborative project

Application **2-1**

Narrow two or three of the broad topics in this list to a topic suitable for a short essay. (Review pages 22, 26, 29.)

EXAMPLE

> social rituals
> ↓
> high school proms
> ↓
> how the romantic image of prom night has become a myth
> ↓
> how today's typical prom night is based on competition and appearances, and polluted by drugs, alcohol, and sex

TOPICS TO BE NARROWED

entertainment	careers	war	family
life	sports	crime	sex
social rituals	automobiles	fashion	music
marriage	alcohol	studying	drugs

Application **2-2**

Compose statements of purpose for essays on three or more of the topics in Application 2-1. (Review pages 23, 30.)

EXAMPLE

Topic   The problems with prom night

Purpose statement   My purpose is to persuade past and present high school students that high school proms have become a waste of time. I will discuss four major problems with prom night: drugs and alcohol, sexual promiscuity, competition, and danger.

Application **2-3**

Convert your statements of purpose from Application 2-2 into thesis statements. (Review pages 23–28.)

EXAMPLE

Purpose statement	My purpose is to persuade past and present high school students that proms have become a waste of time. I will discuss four major problems with prom night: drugs and alcohol, sexual promiscuity, competition, and danger.
Thesis statement	High school proms have lost their value as social events and have become expensive and exaggerated rituals that entrap students in situations they often despise.

Application **2-4**

For each thesis statement in Application 2-3, brainstorm and write three or four topic statements for individual supporting paragraphs. Arrange your topic statements in logical order. (Review pages 33, 34–35.)

EXAMPLE

Thesis statement	High school proms have lost their value as social events and have become expensive and exaggerated rituals that entrap students in situations they often despise.
First topic statement	Parents, teachers, coaches, and other role models seem to merely accept the fact that students are going to drink or get high on prom night.
Second topic statement	It is almost an unspoken law that a couple (no matter how unacquainted) should have sex on prom night.
Third topic statement	Competition over who has the most expensive dress, the most unusual tux, the biggest limousine, or the cutest date also detracts from the evening.
Fourth topic statement	Not only do many feel obliged to attend the prom in order to fit in, but they also feel obliged to participate in often dangerous after-prom events.

Application **2-5**

From Application 2-4, select the most promising set of materials, and write your best essay. Use selected items from your brainstorming list to develop each support paragraph. Outline as necessary. Provide an engaging introduction and a definite conclusion. Use the questions on page 17 as guidelines for revising your essay.

Application **2-6**

Revise those thesis statements below that do not already (a) focus on a limited topic, (b) establish a definite viewpoint, (c) offer a worthwhile viewpoint, (d) make a supportable claim, or (e) preview, in order, the supporting ideas.* Mark an X next to those that are adequate. (Review pages 25–26.)*

EXAMPLE

Faulty thesis Grades are a way of life in college. *[establishes no definite or worthwhile viewpoint, and fails to preview the supporting ideas]*

Revised thesis Grades are an aid to education because they motivate students, provide an objective measure of performance, and prepare people to compete successfully in their careers.

1. My academic adviser is a new professor.
2. Less than one semester in college has changed my outlook.
3. My last blind date was childish, repulsive, and boring.
4. I would love to spend a year in (name a country).
5. Nuclear power is a controversial issue.
6. I have three great fears.
7. This essay concerns my attitude toward online education.
8. Elvis Presley had an amazing career.
9. The Batmobile is a good car for students because it's inexpensive, fuel-efficient, and dependable.
10. My significant other is the kindest person in town.

Application **2-7**

Collaborative Project: Organize into small groups. Choose a subject from the list at the end of this exercise. Then decide on a thesis statement and (not necessarily in this order) brainstorm. Identify a specific audience. Group similar items under the same major categories, and develop an outline. When each group completes this procedure, one representative can write the outline on the board for class suggestions about revision. (Review pages 33–36.)

a description of the ideal classroom

instructions for surviving the first semester of college

---

*For practice, this exercise asks that each thesis statement include an explicit preview. Any of your own thesis statements that do not include such an explicit preview should nonetheless provide a clear hint of the essay's direction.

> instructions for surviving a blind date
>
> suggestions for improving one's college experience
>
> causes of teenage suicide
>
> arguments for or against a formal grading system
>
> an argument for an improvement you think this college needs
>
> the qualities of a good parent
>
> what you expect the world to be like in ten years
>
> young people's needs that parents often ignore
>
> difficulties faced by nontraditional students

Application **2-8**

Collaborative Project: Exchange electronic copies of an essay you've written (or, in a lab, switch computers) and examine your partner's essay. Saving your edits in a new file, put the main topics in boldface and underline the supporting points. Assemble this material to form an outline of your partner's essay, then try out different arrangements of the headings or suggest new ones. Show your original and new outlines to your partner and discuss whether the essay achieved what she or he intended.

Application **2-9**

Web-based Project: Go to the University of Victoria's Writer's Guide at **<http://web.uvic.ca/wguide/>**. Use the Table of Contents page to locate the section on *Audience and Tone*. Locate one item of information about audience and tone (or voice) not covered in this chapter. Take careful notes for a brief discussion of this information in class. Attach a copy of the relevant Web page(s) to your written notes.

ALTERNATIVE ASSIGNMENTS:

1. Locate additional information on thesis statements from the Writing Workshop at the University of Illinois **<www.english.uiuc.edu/cws/wworkshop/index.htm>**.
   Follow the *Tips and Techniques* link to *Developing a Thesis*.
2. For advice about organizing a paper, go to the Paradigm Online Writing Assistant at
   <www.powa.org/orgnfrms.htm>.
3. For advice about discovering useful material (invention), go to the Paradigm Online Writing Assistant at
   <www.powa.org/whtfrms.htm>.

| Note |

Instead of quoting your source(s) directly, paraphrase (page 372). Be sure to credit each source of information (page 393).

Works Cited

Debs, Mary Beth. "Collaborative Writing in Industry." In *Technical Writing: Theory and Practice*. Ed. Bertie E. Fearing and W. Keats Sparrow. New York: Modern Language Assn., 1989: 33–42.

Elbow, Peter. *Writing without Teachers*. New York: Oxford, 1973.

Hill-Duin, Ann. "Terms and Tools: A Theory and Research-Based Approach to Collaborative Writing." *Bulletin of the Association for Business Communication* 53.2 (1990): 45–50.

Hulbert, Jack E. "Developing Collaborative Insights and Skills." *Bulletin of the Association for Business Communication* 57.2 (1994): 53–56.

Matson, Eric. "The Seven Sins of Deadly Meetings." *Fast Company* Oct./Nov. 1997: 27–31.

McGuire, Gene. "Shared Minds: A Model of Collaboration." *Technical Communication* 39.3 (1992): 467–68.

Morgan, Meg. "Patterns of Composing: Connections between Classroom and Workplace Collaborations." *Technical Communication* 38.4 (1991): 540–42.

U.S. Air Force Academy. *Executive Writing Course*. Washington, D.C.: GPO, 1981.

CHAPTER 3

Decisions in Drafting

Drafting the Title and Introduction   **49**

Drafting the Body Section   **54**

Drafting the Conclusion   **55**

CASE STUDY: Drafting the Essay   **56**

Drafting on the Computer   **58**

   Guidelines for Drafting on the Computer   **58**

Reading   **56**

Applications   **59**

Why drafting is hard

Ｏne of any writer's hardest moments is facing the blank page or computer screen and actually getting the "paper" started. If you've completed the Planning Guide on page 36, you should be in pretty good shape—with a thesis, an outline, a list of ideas, and so on. But you still need to shape all this material into a unified and coherent essay. Here is where you decide on answers to some tough questions:

Decisions in Drafting Your Essay

- *How do I begin the essay?*   - *How much is enough?*
- *What comes next?*   - *What can I leave out?*
- *How will I end?*   - *Am I forgetting anything?*

Different ways of drafting

There is no simple formula for drafting. Some writers work from a brainstorming list and perhaps an outline. Others hate outlining, and they start right off writing and scribbling and rewriting. Some write a quick draft before thinking through their writing situation. Some write a whole draft all in one marathon sitting. Some write in short bursts, a few minutes at a time. Introductions often are written last. To find your own best approach(es), you will need to experiment. Don't expect to draft your essay in a neat, one, two, three order. As you work toward your finished essay, plan on several drafts—and allow yourself plenty of time.

How to beat writer's block

Everybody gets stuck sometimes. If you suffer from writer's block, try writing a page or two of gibberish. Or write yourself a sob story ("Here I sit, stuck and confused. . . .") as a way to get rolling. You might start your essay in the middle, or even at the end, or with whatever ideas you feel surest about. Or do more brainstorming (page 32). Your best bet in any case is to read through all your planning material then just plunge right in and keep filling the pages. Take breaks if you need to, but try to stop someplace at which you'll have something left to say when you return to the paper. Sooner or later—after some false starts, detours, and dead ends—the right words will begin to flow, a useful first draft will begin to emerge.

Note

As you work, remember that each writing sample in this chapter and in this book is the product of multiple drafts and revisions. None of these writers expected to get it just right the first time—nor should you.

DRAFTING THE TITLE AND INTRODUCTION

Why titles are important

Titles—which are sometimes chosen after the essay is complete—should forecast an essay's subject and approach. Clear, attention-getting titles, such as "Let's Shorten the Baseball Season" or "Instead of Running, Try Walking," help readers plan how to interpret what they read.

Assume you are continuing your work from Chapter 2, where you planned your essay about America's obsession with cars. You have chosen the title, "Cars R Us."

The Introductory Paragraph

Introductions differ in shape and size and may consist of more than one paragraph; however, basic introductory paragraphs often have a funnel shape:

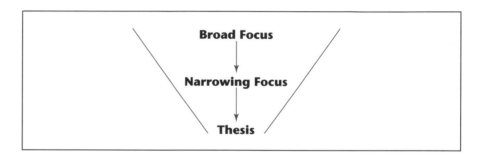

Now that you have decided on a title—"Cars R Us"—you can introduce your essay's final draft, using a funnel pattern:

Cars R Us

Broad focus (1–5)

[1]We Americans love our automobiles, no question. [2]But why is next year's new model always front-page news? [3]Cars once were merely a way to get from point A to point B faster than by foot or horse and buggy. [4]Henry Ford's Model Ts all looked identical, like boxes on wheels, all painted black. [5]People bought Model Ts for basic transportation—and not to make a fashion statement. [6]As we leave the 20th century in the dust, however, automakers cater to our desire to "do our own thing." [7]We love their attention and they know it. [8]Today's self-centered consumers demand cars that satisfy our craving for individuality.

Narrowing Focus (6–7)

Thesis (8)

Why introductions are important

Introductory paragraphs do more than just lead into the essay; they invite readers in and set a tone. The first-person plural (we, us, our) invites us to look at ourselves. Amusing images (horse and buggy, boxes on wheels) and deliberate clichés (in the dust, do our own thing) signal the writer's intention to have fun with this essay. If your only aim were to lead into the main discussion, you might have given this introduction instead:

A lifeless opening

We love our cars because they enhance our sense of individuality.

But this version lacks the inviting tone and the images that engage our attention and make us want to read on.

Placing the Thesis

In a standard essay, the thesis often appears at the end of the introductory paragraph, as a bridge to the discussion. But sometimes readers want to know where you stand immediately, especially when the topic is controversial.

A controversial thesis as opener

> *Single-sex schools offer distinct advantages over coeducational schools.* Coeducational classrooms inhibit student participation and tend to ignore gender-specific learning styles. Single-sex classrooms not only encourage participation but also allow for the kinds of gender-based teaching strategies that promote effective learning.

Sometimes, even personal writing can open directly with the thesis, especially when the viewpoint is unexpected.

A surprising thesis as opener

> *I hate summer beaches.* Ocean swimming is impossible; upon conquering a wave, I simply lose to the next, getting pushed back onto the hard-packed, abrasive sand. Booby-traps of bottles, soda cans, toys, and rocks make walking hazardous. Heavy with the stench of suntan lotion, greasy French fries, dead fish, and sweat, the thick, searing air hangs motionless about the scorching sand. Blasting radios and growling hot rods cut the slap-swoosh of the green-gray surf to a weak hiss. People devour a summer beach, gouging the sound with umbrella spikes and gripping it with oiled limbs, leaving only trampled debris at summer's end.

In some essays, the thesis appears later, even near the end (as on page 300). A delayed thesis is especially useful in a story leading to some larger meaning (*Here is what happened,* then, *Here is what it means*).

Selecting an Opening Strategy

"How do I begin?"

The specifics of your introduction are determined by what you know about your readers and your purpose.

Decisions in Analyzing Your Audience

- *Are my readers likely to be interested in this topic?*
- *How can I make them want to read on?*
- *Are they likely to react defensively?*
- *Is my purpose to describe something, to tell a story, to explain something, to change somebody's mind?*

The opening strategies that follow offer various possibilities for connecting with your audience.

Open with an Anecdote.   An anecdote is a brief, personal story that makes a point.

> Last weekend, I gave a friend's younger brother a ride from the mall. As we drove, I asked him the same old questions about high school, grades, football, and girlfriends. He answered me in one-word sentences and then pulled out a cassette tape. "Wanna hear somethin' cool?" I shrugged and popped it into the tape player. What came pouring through my car speakers made me run a stop sign. The "rap" song spelled out, in elaborate detail, 101 ways to violate a woman's body. Needless to say, it was a long ride across town.
>
> I borrowed the tape and listened to every song, horrified by their recurrent theme of sexual violence and domination. But most horrifying is that a 15-year-old kid actually considers this music "cool."

Open with a Background Story.   For example, in an essay that challenges a popular attitude, trace the development of that attitude.

> In 1945, a terrifying blast shook the New Mexico desert. Shortly afterward, the new, awesome force literally vaporized hundreds of thousands of lives, to end World War II. Thus began the atomic era. This horrid beginning, along with recent nuclear accidents and scandals, has caused increasing criticism. However, as we enter a new century the nuclear breeder reactor offers a promising energy alternative, but critics have drastically reduced its development and production. We need the breeder reactor, because it is one of our best long-range sources of energy.

This kind of opening is especially effective in persuasive writing, because it acknowledges opposing views, creating empathy (identification with the reader's attitude).

Open with a Question.   An opening question can get readers thinking right away, especially when you write instructions, give advice, or argue for action.

> What do you do when you find yourself in the produce room cooler with your manager and he nonchalantly wraps his arm around your waist? Or how about when the guys you work with come out with a distasteful remark that makes you seem like a piece of meat? These are just a couple of problems you might face as the only female in a department. There are, however, ways of dealing with this kind of harassment.

Open with a Short Quotation.   If a quotation can summarize your point, use it—and clarify its significance immediately.

> "The XL Roadster—anything else is just a car," unless the XL happens to be mine. In that case, it's just a piece of junk.

Open with a Direct Address.   The second-person *you* can involve the readers and helps them pay attention—especially when you are giving instructions or advice or writing persuasively.

> Does the thought of artificially preserved, chemically treated food make you lose your appetite? Do limp, tasteless, frozen vegetables leave you cold? Then you should try your hand at organic gardening.

Use direct address in ads, popular articles, and brochures but not in academic reports or most business and technical documents.

Open with a Brief, Vivid Description.   Instead of a thesis, some descriptive essays simply have an orienting sentence to set a scene or create a mood, to place readers at the center of things.

> The raft bobs gently as the four divers help each other with scuba gear. We joke and laugh casually as we struggle in the cramped space; but a restlessness is in the air because we want to be on our way. Finally, everyone is ready, and we split into pairs. I steal a last glance over the blue ocean. I hear the waves slap the boat, the mournful cry of a seagull, and a steady murmur from the crowded beach a mile away. With three splashes my friends jump in. I follow. There is a splash and then silence. The water presses in, and all I hear is the sound of my regulator as I take my first breath. All I see is blue water, yellow light, and endless space. While the world rushes on, we feel suspended in time. Then my buddy taps me on the shoulder, and we begin a tour of a hidden world.

Description can also be a powerful way to make a point.

> They appear each workday morning from 7:00 to 9:00, role models for millions of career-minded women. Their crisp, clear diction and articulate reporting are second only to their appearance. Slender and lovely, the female co-hosts of morning news shows radiate that businesslike "chic" that networks consider essential in their newswomen. Such perfection is precisely why the networks hire these women as anchors. Network television rarely tolerates women commentators who are other than young, stylish, and attractive.

Notice how the businesslike tone parallels the topic itself.

Open with Examples.   Examples enable readers to visualize the issue or problem.

> Privacy in America is disappearing. New technologies enable users to unearth anyone's health, credit, email, and legal records with a few keystrokes. Beyond these computerized records, our telephones, television

> sets, and even our trash can be monitored by government agencies, banks, businesses, political groups—or just plain nosy people. Current United States law does disturbingly little to protect our right to privacy.

Open with a Definition.   Clarify abstract terms for both writer and reader. This next essay, on the limits of the American Dream, begins by defining that key term.

> The American Dream has taken on different meanings for different people, but its original meaning derived from a seemingly unlimited potential for growth: in the sense of the country's great westward expansion followed by the Industrial Revolution. From this combination of geographic and economic progress emerged the correlation between the American Dream and freedom. The seemingly endless supply of land and employment let people feel there was nothing stopping them from "moving up in the world." We now recognize, however, that the Dream does have a limit.

As you draft your introduction, consider the following suggestions:

Hints for an engaging introduction

- The introduction can be the hardest part of an essay. Many writers complete it last. If you do write your introduction first, be sure to revise it later.
- In most college writing, avoid opening with personal qualifiers, such as "It is my opinion that," "I believe that," and "In this paper I will."
- Let your introduction create suspense that is resolved by your thesis statement, usually at the end of the opening paragraph(s).
- If the opening is boring, vague, long-winded, or toneless, readers may give up. Don't waste their time.

DRAFTING THE BODY SECTION

"How much is enough, and how can I shape it?"

The body section delivers on the commitment made in your thesis. Readers don't want details that just get in the way, or a jigsaw puzzle they have to unscramble for themselves. To develop the body, therefore, answer these questions:

Decisions in Developing the Body of Your Essay

- *How much is enough?*
- *How much information or detail should I provide?*

- *How can I stay on track?*
- *What shape will reveal my line of thought?*

Decide about purpose and unity. Here you discard some material you thought you might keep, and maybe discover additional material. Look hard at everything you've discovered during freewriting, brainstorming, or questioning. Stand in the reader's place. Keep whatever belongs, and discard whatever doesn't.

Decide how many support paragraphs to include. College essays typically have three or more, but use as many as you need. Decide how to develop each support paragraph and how to order them. What paragraph order will make the most sense and provide the best emphasis?

Elements affecting the shape of your writing (unity, coherence, emphasis, and transition) are discussed fully in Chapter 6, "Revising the Paragraphs." Principles of developing the individual paragraph are principles as well of creating the whole essay—or of writing at any length.

DRAFTING THE CONCLUSION

Why conclusions are important

An essay's conclusion refocuses on the thesis and leaves a final—and lasting—impression on readers. Your conclusion might evaluate the meaning or significance of the body section, restate your position, predict an outcome, offer a solution, request an action, make a recommendation, or pave the way for more exploration. Avoid conclusions that repeat, apologize, or belabor the obvious:

Don't repeat

I have just discussed my views on the role cars play in our lives.

Don't apologize

Although some readers might disagree, this is how I see it.

Don't belabor the obvious

Now that you've read my essay, you should have a clear picture of the importance we place on our cars.

Selecting a Closing Strategy

"How do I end?"

Forgettable endings drain the life from any writing. This list of strategies samples ways of closing with meaning and emphasis.

Close with a Summary.   A review of main points helps readers remember what is most important.

Close with a Question.   A closing question provides readers something to think about.

Overall, the advantages of the breeder reactor seem immeasurable. Because it can produce more fuel than it uses, it will theoretically be an infinite source of energy. And efficient use of the fuel it does burn makes it highly desirable in this energy-tight era. What other source promises so much for our long-range energy future?

Close with a Call to Action.   Tell readers exactly what you want them to do.

> Just imagine yourself eating a salad of crisp green lettuce, juicy red tomato chunks, firm white slices of cucumber, and crunchy strips of green pepper—all picked fresh from your own garden. If this picture appeals to you, begin planning your summer garden now, and by July the picture of you eating that salad will become a reality. *Bon appetit!*

Close with a Quotation.   This next writer quotes from journalist Ellen Goodman's essay, "Blame the Victim."

> I agree with Ellen Goodman's assertion that there is "something malignant about some of the extremists who make a public virtue of their health." The cancer is in the superior attitudes of the "healthy elite"—an attitude that actually discourages exercise and healthy habits by making average people feel too intimidated and inferior even to begin a fitness program.

Close with an Interpretation or Evaluation.   Help readers understand the meaning of things.

> A growing array of so-called private information about American citizens is collected daily. And few laws protect our right to be left alone. In the interest of pursuing criminals, government too often sacrifices the privacy of innocent people, and new technology is making old laws obsolete. Huge collections of data are becoming available to your insurance company, to prospective employers, to companies doing mass mailings, and even to your neighbor. The invasion continues, and no one seems to know how to stop our world from fulfilling the prophecy in George Orwell's *1984*.

Whichever strategy or combination of strategies you select, make your conclusion refocus on your main point without repeating it.

CASE STUDY

DRAFTING THE ESSAY

As an illustration of how these drafting decisions produce a completed essay, consider "Cars R Us," reproduced below. (Chapter 4 traces the steps in revision that created the final version shown here.)

Notice that the thesis and each topic sentence appear in boldface and italics.

The finished essay
Introduction

Cars R Us

We Americans love our automobiles, no question. But why is next year's new model always front-page news? Cars once were merely a way to get from point A to point B faster than by foot or horse and buggy. Henry Ford's Model Ts all looked identical, like boxes on wheels, and were all painted black. People bought Model Ts for basic transportation—and not to make a fashion statement. As we enter the 21st century, however, automakers cater to our desire to "do our own thing." We love their attention and they know it.

Thesis

Today's self-centered consumers demand cars that satisfy our craving for individuality.

First support paragraph

We want automobiles that make a unique lifestyle statement about who we think we are. If today's cars were only a means to cruise to the grocery store, we'd all be willing to drive junkers. But most people hate rusty, old bombers. We want to be able to see our ideal (or idealized) images mirrored in our car's glossy paint job or our truck's chrome hubcaps. For example, roughly fifty percent of today's rugged individuals buy 4-wheel drive, off-road vehicles that never leave the pavement. Instead we navigate our urban and suburban wilderness in Hummers, Big Wheel trucks, and SUV land barges because these vehicles symbolize toughness and an uncompromising attitude. We buy sports cars not so much to impress others, but to impress ourselves: "Hey, I'm driving this red convertible Miata and I'm special."

Second support paragraph

Cars provide each individual with a personal billboard. As a way to exercise our right to free speech, bumper stickers announce exactly where we stand. They tell the world that we're intellectuals or tough guys or sensitive types. One of mine reads, "I love my humpback whale." Another promotes my favorite radio station. For some reason Volvos often carry political statements such as "Women, unite," or "Make love, not war," or profound observations such as Einstein's "creativity is more important than knowledge"—which might be fine for an individual like Einstein, but what about the rest of us mere mortals? Some individuals like to be more rugged than others. Pick-up trucks, for instance, often sport National Rifle Association stickers, which seem to proclaim "Get out of my way!" to the rest of us wimps. I, with my stuffed Bugs Bunny doll in the back window, hurry out of the way.

Third support paragraph

Owning a car means not having to rely on—yikes—public transportation, torture for individuals like us. Americans' cars are personal sanctuaries, places to escape other humans. One popular form of escape is the drive-up window. Banks, donut shops, even dry cleaners enable us to transact business without leaving the car. Snug in our mobile dining rooms, we no longer have to budge from our orthopedically correct leather seat to order a meal. A simple adjustment of the tilt-steering allows laptop dining as we savor our grease-laden food in private, far from the noisy restaurant and screaming kids. We just stay in our cars. How convenient. We can even sing along to the stereo between bites or hum along as we chew. If you sing on a bus or subway, other commuters look at you strangely and hide their valuables.

Conclusion

Cars entice us Americans because they offer the ultimate mechanism for achieving individuality. Through the kind of car we drive and how we adorn it, we can really "be somebody" and proclaim to strangers

> our singular selves. We can dine à-la-car and sing aloud without seeming weird. Isolated in our climate controlled, stereophonic capsule, we can avoid direct human contact and concentrate full time on being individuals. At the beginning of *Mother Night,* novelist Kurt Vonnegut observes, "We are what we pretend to be"—a condition made increasingly possible by the cars we choose to drive.
>
> *—Maureen Malloy*

Discussion   This essay presents a focused picture. And the picture is unified: nothing gets in the way; everything belongs.

But content alone cannot ensure contact. Thoughts need shaping to help us organize our understanding of the writer's way of seeing. Each paragraph helps detail the prepackaged identity offered by the American automobile.

Finally, the concluding paragraph offers perspective on the whole essay, refocusing on the thesis, summing up the main points, and leaving readers with a quotation that suggests a larger meaning for the essay. Readers remember last things best, and this essay's conclusion leaves us with something worth remembering.

DRAFTING ON THE COMPUTER

Word processing is especially useful as a drafting tool, enabling you to delete, move, or design text instantly. The following guidelines will help you capitalize on all the benefits a computer can offer.

GUIDELINES FOR DRAFTING ON THE COMPUTER

1. *Decide whether to draft on the computer or by hand for later transfer to the computer.* Experiment with each approach before deciding which works best for you.

2. *Beware of computer junk.* The ease of cranking out words on a computer can produce long, windy pieces that say nothing. Cut anything that fails to advance your meaning. (See pages 124–130 for ways to achieve conciseness.)

3. *Never confuse style with substance.* Laser printers and choices of typefaces, type sizes, and other design options can produce attractive documents. But not even the most attractive format can redeem worthless or inaccessible content.

4. *Save and print your work often.* Save each paragraph as you write it; print out each page as you complete it; and keep a copy of your document on a backup disk.

5. *Consider the benefits of revising from hard copy.* Nothing beats scribbling on the printed page with pen or pencil. The hard

copy provides the whole text, right in front of you.

6. *Never depend only on automated "checkers."* Not even the most sophisticated writing aids can replace careful proofreading. A synonym found in an electronic thesaurus may distort your meaning. The spellchecker cannot differentiate among correctly spelled words, such as *their, they're,* or *there;* or *it's* versus *its.* And neither spell nor grammar checkers can evaluate *stylistic appropriateness* (the subtle choices of phrasing that determine tone and emphasis). Page 157 summarizes the limitations of computerized aids.

7. *Keep a different file for each draft.* Revision hardly ever occurs in a straight line ("good," "better," "best"). Sometimes you'll discover that parts of an earlier draft are actually better than something you've rewritten. Give each file a different name ("Draft #1," "Draft #2," and so on), in case you need to retrieve material. Make a copy of the file, and use that copy for your revision.

8. *Always print two final copies.* With all the paperwork that writing instructors (and their students) shuffle, papers sometimes get misplaced. Submit one copy and keep one for yourself—just in case!

Application **3-1**

Plan and draft an essay based on one of the writing options on pages 19–20. Decide on an audience: your classmates, readers of the campus paper, or the like. Have a thesis and deliver on it.

Also, find a voice that will appeal to your readers. Create unity so that your writing sticks to the point; create order and use transitions so that it stands together. Use the questions on page 17 for guidance in improving your essay.

Application **3-2**

Collaborative Project: Locate a good introduction or a good conclusion to a short article in a popular magazine such as *Time, Newsweek,* or *Reader's Digest.* As a group, analyze the strategies that make the writing effective. (Review pages 50–54 and 55–56.)

Application **3-3**

Computer Application: Save three copies of your essay under different file names. Revise one of the copies, keeping in mind the ideas from this chapter. Take an overnight break, then revise a second copy of the original. Print the three versions, and read them carefully. Then write a summary (pages 373–76) of your favorite version and explain why you think the changes improve the essay.

Application **3-4**

Web-based Project: Do some research on the Web about writer's block and how it can be overcome. You may want to start with the following sites:

- Purdue Online Writing Lab
  <http://owl.english.purdue.edu/handouts/general/gl_block.html>
- Capital Community College Guide to Grammar and Writing
  <http://ccc.commnet.edu/grammar/composition/brainstorm_block.htm>

Prepare a summary of different approaches and strategies your classmates might want to use to overcome writer's block. Attach copies of the relevant Web pages to your list.

Note

Instead of quoting your source(s) directly, paraphrase (page 372). Be sure to credit each source of information (page 392).

CHAPTER 4

Decisions in Revising

The Meaning of Revision   **62**

Revision Checklist   **63**

Using the Checklist   **64**

CASE STUDY: Revising the Draft   **64**

   Guidelines for Reviewing and Editing the Writing of Peers   **66**

Revising with Peers   **67**

Proofreading Your Final Draft   **76**

   Guidelines for Proofreading   **76**

Applications   **77**

Besides being a battle with impatience, writing is a battle with inertia: Once we've written a draft, we are often too easily satisfied with what we've done. Good writers win the battle by revising often. For the sake of clarity, earlier chapters have presented a single sequence of steps for composing an essay. To review:

One sequence for
composing an essay

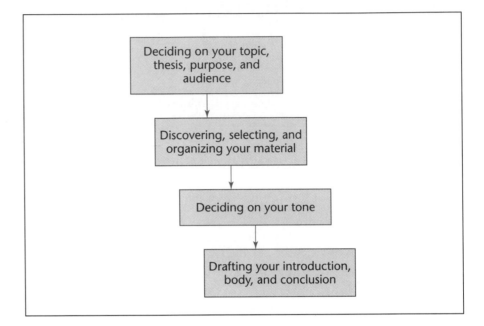

We have seen that writers rarely follow this exact sequence. But no matter what the sequence, any effective writer depends on *revision*—the one constant in the writing process. When you finish a first draft, you really have only begun.

THE MEANING OF REVISION

Revision involves more than proofreading for spelling, punctuation, or other mechanical details (discussed later in this chapter). Mechanical correctness is essential, but what matters most are the essay's *rhetorical elements: worthwhile content, sensible organization,* and *readable style.* The rhetorical elements determine whether your writing connects with readers—and makes a difference. Your instructor might write suggestions on your first draft or have you revise on your own. In any case, revision never means merely recopying; it always means *rethinking.*

Why rhetorical elements
are important

Useful revision happens only when you can evaluate accurately what you already have written. Use the Revision Checklist to pinpoint possible improvements in content, organization, and style. (Numbers in parentheses refer to the first page of discussion.)

REVISION CHECKLIST ☑

WORTHWHILE CONTENT

The essay's main point is clear and sharply focused.

- ☐ Does the title attract attention and provide a forecast? (49)
- ☐ Is the topic limited enough? (22)
- ☐ Do you get to your main point quickly? (50)
- ☐ Is the thesis definite, informative, and easy to find? (23)

The discussion delivers on the promise made in your thesis.

- ☐ Will your readers learn something new and useful? (86)
- ☐ Do you support every assertion with enough details? (84)
- ☐ Does everything belong, or can anything be cut? (90)
- ☐ Have you used only your best material? (33)

SENSIBLE ORGANIZATION

The essay has a definite introduction, body, and conclusion.

- ☐ Will your introduction make readers want to read on? (49)
- ☐ Does each body paragraph develop *one* supporting point? (54)
- ☐ Does the order of body paragraphs reveal a clear line of thought and emphasize what is most important? (9)
- ☐ Does the conclusion give a real sense of an ending? (55)
- ☐ Is everything connected? (14)

- ☐ If you varied this organization, was it for good reason? (162)

Except for paragraphs of transition or special emphasis, each body (or support) paragraph usually is a mini-essay.

- ☐ Does the paragraph have a topic (or orienting) statement? (99)
- ☐ Does the topic statement come at the beginning or end, depending on your desired emphasis? (99)
- ☐ Does everything stick to the point (unity) and stick together (coherence)? (102, 103)
- ☐ Is the paragraph developed enough to support the point? (89)

READABLE STYLE

Sentences are clear, concise, and fluent.

- ☐ Can each sentence be understood the first time it is read? (118)
- ☐ Are points made in the fewest words? (124)
- ☐ Are sentences put together with enough variety? (131)

Each word does its job.

- ☐ Is a real person speaking, and is the voice likable? (138)
- ☐ Is everything in plain English? (147)
- ☐ Is your meaning precise, concrete, and specific? (139)
- ☐ Is your tone appropriate for this situation and audience? (145)

USING THE CHECKLIST

As you use the Revision Checklist to rethink your essay, ask yourself questions such as these:

Questions for Critical Evaluation and Revision

- *Have I conveyed my exact point or feeling?*
- *Do vivid details from the event come to mind now that I've finished writing?*
- *What facts or figures or ideas do I now remember?*

- *Can I reorganize for greater emphasis or clarity?*
- *Can I find a better way of saying what I want to say?*
- *Does this draft sound as I wanted it to sound, or is it too corny or detached, or arrogant or humble?*

Eventually, you will find that you can revise almost automatically, without following the checklist item by item.

| Note |

Revising a draft doesn't always guarantee that you will improve it. Save each draft, then compare them to select the best material from each one.

CASE STUDY

REVISING THE DRAFT

Assume you've written this early draft of "Cars R Us" (whose final version appears on pages 56–58):

A draft to be revised

CAR CRAZY

We Americans love our automobiles. No question. But why do we worship them? Nearly every country has access to cars but not every country has the freedom to use them as they please. Cars were once merely a way to get from point A to point B faster than by foot or horse and buggy. Now, cars are fiberglass and metal gods. America is founded on freedom and our cars allow us to move.

In the early 1900s when Henry Ford began producing Model Ts, they all had the same body style, sort of like rectangles on wheels. Black was a buyer's only choice of paint color. People didn't purchase Model Ts because they were pretty; they were basic transportation, with no fancy options or "toys" like cars have now: tilt-steering, heated power seats, climate control, an eight-speaker stereo system with CD drive, and so on. Americans get sick of the same thing over and over. We demand variety in our lives and especially in our cars.

As we enter the 21st century automakers cater to us. We love their attention and they know it. Americans are used to instant gratification. We want and get next year's new models NOW. Because they understand our "first person on the block to have it" mentality, the car manufacturers tantalize us with concept cars—you know: those weird, space-aged looking vehicles with gull's wings and rocket packs. To please the American sense of beauty, each year the cars get more attractive. New cars are sleeker and shinier, and more pleasing to touch. With such beauty, though, comes higher sticker prices. But we don't care. We are willing to pay any price to practice the Automobile Religion.

Today, cars mean more to us than a way to cruise around town. If we saw them as only a means to get to the grocery store, then we'd all be willing to drive junkers. Instead, we see our cars as reflections of our personalities. Most people don't want to drive rusty, old bombers. We want to be able to see our ideal (or idealized) images mirrored in our car's glossy paint job. We want automobiles that make a statement about ourselves. People travel through the American wilderness in jeeps and trucks because they symbolize toughness and an uncompromising attitude. We buy sports cars not so much to impress others, but to impress ourselves: "Hey, I'm driving this red convertible Miata and I feel like the master of the highway."

That's why we love our cars and decorate them as we do, to display a little of ourselves even while we drive. With bumper stickers, we exercise our constitutional rights to free speech. One of mine reads, "I love my humpback whale." Another promotes my favorite radio station. For some reason, I often see National Rifle Association stickers on pick-up trucks. Again, the drivers are making a statement to the rest of us motorists: "I like to maim and kill! Get out of my way!" I, with my stuffed Bugs Bunny doll in the back window, get out of the way.

The word *automobile* means "self-moving." Cars give us the freedom to go where we want, when we want, across town or across the country. There is plenty of wide-open space for our cars. Even owners of land barge SUVs usually find a place to park. Let's consider the Japanese for a moment. They, too, love their cars (with good reason) yet their autos are stuck on a tiny island, and parking laws are so strict that meter-readers write in chalk on the sidewalk how long a car has been parked in a certain spot. Too long, and it's towed. In America, we can usually park our cars illegally and get away with it (for at least as long as it takes to "run" into the bank or drugstore).

When we own a car, we don't have to rely on—yikes—public transportation, something people in other countries don't mind doing. Americans' cars are personal sanctuaries, places to escape other humans. The car's popularity has led to the phenomenon of drive-up windows. Banks, donut shops, even dry cleaners allow us to transact business without leaving the comfort and safety of our autos. Try getting a bus driver to stop at Dunkin' Donuts because you have a sudden urge for a cruller. We no longer have to move from the driver's seat to order a meal. We no longer have to sit in a noisy McDonald's with screaming kids to eat our grease-laden food. We just stay in our cars. How convenient. We can even sing along to the stereo if we want. Other commuters look at you strangely and hide their valuables if you sing on a subway.

Cars entice us Americans because they allow us to do the things that appeal to us: drive where we please, when we please, dine à-la-car, sing aloud in public and not be thought insane. And through the kind of car we drive and how we adorn them, we can share with strangers our personalities. Even though we may be isolated in our automobiles, we share with other motorists the camaraderie that comes with belonging to the Car Cult.

Discussion

This draft makes a good start but it needs substantial revision. First, there seems to be too much material. This lack of a clear focus leaves lots of reader questions unanswered:

- *What and where is the thesis?*
- *Is this essay about cars and our love of freedom, of variety, of self-esteem, of free speech, of privacy, or what?*
- *What was the meaning of this whole observation for you?*

Next, the organization of this draft hints at an introduction, body, and conclusion, but some paragraphs lack definite topic sentences and clear connections between ideas. And despite the colorful images, the conversational style (like a person talking), and the use of plain English, all this could be said in fewer words and with clearer emphasis.

The following pages will show how the checklist can help you revise to achieve the finished essay on pages 56–58. For reference, the paragraphs from the draft are labeled A through H (Figure 4.1). Specific needed improvements are explained on the facing page. Notice that the original, eight-paragraph draft has been reshaped into a five-paragraph revision.

Note

This case illustrates revision for "rhetorical features" (content, organization, and style). But once the final draft is rhetorically effective, it needs to be proofread for "mechanical features" (correct grammar, punctuation, word choice, mechanics, and format)—covered in parts of Chapter 8 and in Appendixes A and B.

Revision has created an essay with worthwhile content, sensible organization, and readable style. (For detailed advice on achieving these qualities in a final draft, see Chapters 5–8.)

GUIDELINES FOR REVIEWING AND EDITING THE WRITING OF PEERS

1. *Read the entire piece at least twice before you comment.* Develop a clear sense of the assignment's purpose and its intended audience.
2. *Remember that mere correctness offers no guarantee of effectiveness.* Poor usage, punctuation, or mechanics do distract readers and harm the writer's credibility. However, a "correct" piece of writing still might contain faulty rhetorical elements (inferior content, confusing organization, or unsuitable style).

3. *Understand the acceptable limits of editing.* In the workplace, "editing" can range from fine-tuning to an in-depth rewrite. In school, however, rewriting a piece to the extent that it ceases to belong to the writer may constitute plagiarism.
4. *Be honest but diplomatic.* Most of us are sensitive to criticism—even when it is constructive—and we all respond more favorably to encouragement. Begin with something positive before moving to critique. Support rather than judge.

REVISING WITH PEERS

All writing can benefit from feedback. As part of the revision process, your writing course may include workshops for peer reviewing and editing. *Reviewing* means evaluating how well the writing connects with its intended audience and meets its intended purpose:

Questions reviewers ask

- Is the content accurate, appropriate, and useful?
- Is the material organized for the reader's understanding?
- Is the style clear, easy to read, and engaging?

In reviewing, you explain to the writer how you respond as a reader; you point out what works or doesn't work. This feedback helps a writer envision ways of revising. Criteria for reviewing an essay appear on page 63; for an argument, pages 287–88; and for a Research Report, page 420.

Editing means actually "fixing" the piece by making it more precise and readable:

Some ways in which editors "fix" writing

- rephrasing or reorganizing sentences
- clarifying a thesis or topic sentence
- choosing a better word or phrase
- correcting spelling, usage, or punctuation, and so on.

Criteria for editing appear inside the rear cover.

Note

Your task as editor is to help improve the writing—without altering the author's intended meaning.

5. *Always explain "why" something doesn't work.* Instead of "this paragraph is confusing," say, "because this paragraph lacks a clear topic sentence, I had trouble discovering the main idea" (see pages 63, 287, 420). Help the writer discover the main cause of the problem.
6. *Focus first on the big picture.* Begin with the thesis, the ideas, and the shape of the essay. (Is the thesis clear and definite? Is the supporting material relevant and convincing? Is the line of reasoning easy to follow? Does each paragraph do its job?) Then discuss specifics of style and correctness (tone, word choice, sentence structure, and so on).
7. *Make specific recommendations for improvements.* Write out suggestions in enough detail for the writer to know what to do (see pages 69, 71, 73, 75).
8. *Be aware that not all feedback has equal value.* Even professional editors can disagree. If you receive conflicting opinions from different readers, seek your instructor's advice.

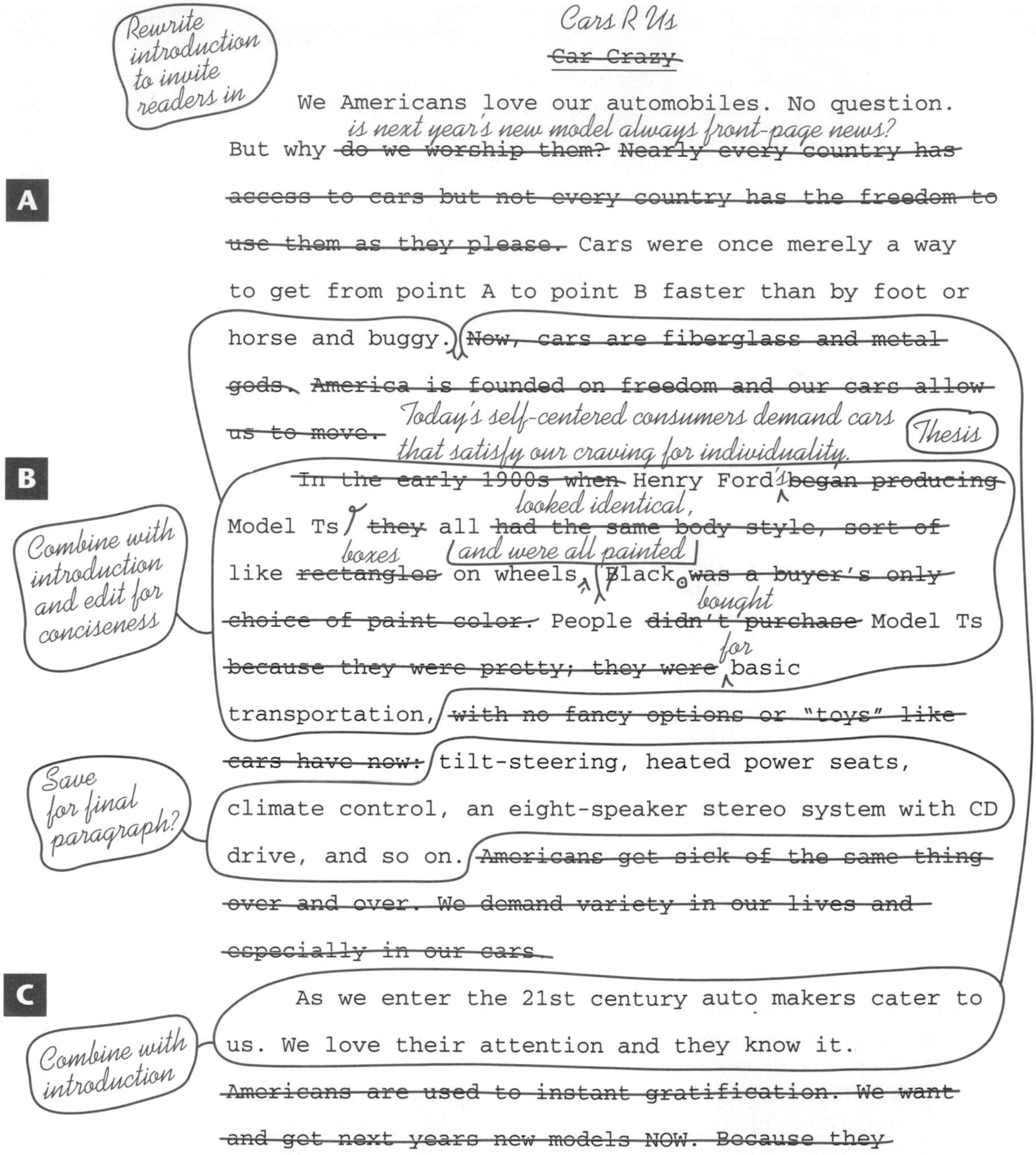

Cars R Us
~~Car Crazy~~

(Rewrite introduction to invite readers in)

We Americans love our automobiles. No question.
is next year's new model always front-page news?
But why ~~do we worship them? Nearly every country has~~

A

~~access to cars but not every country has the freedom to~~

~~use them as they please.~~ Cars were once merely a way

to get from point A to point B faster than by foot or

horse and buggy. ~~Now, cars are fiberglass and metal~~

~~gods. America is founded on freedom and our cars allow~~

~~us to move.~~ *Today's self-centered consumers demand cars*
that satisfy our craving for individuality. *(Thesis)*

B

~~In the early 1900s when~~ Henry Ford's ~~began producing~~
looked identical,
Model Ts ~~they~~ all ~~had the same body style, sort of~~
boxes *[and were all painted]*
like ~~rectangles~~ on wheels. ~~Black~~ ~~was a buyer's only~~
bought
~~choice of paint color.~~ People ~~didn't purchase~~ Model Ts
for
~~because they were pretty; they were~~ basic

(Combine with introduction and edit for conciseness)

transportation, ~~with no fancy options or "toys" like~~

~~cars have now:~~ tilt-steering, heated power seats,

climate control, an eight-speaker stereo system with CD

(Save for final paragraph?)

drive, and so on. ~~Americans get sick of the same thing~~

~~over and over. We demand variety in our lives and~~

~~especially in our cars.~~

C

As we enter the 21st century auto makers cater to

us. We love their attention and they know it.

(Combine with introduction)

~~Americans are used to instant gratification. We want~~

~~and get next years new models NOW. Because they~~

FIGURE 4.1
A draft edited for revision

Paragraph A: The essay's title could be more specific about the theme here: namely, how we identify with our cars. The paragraph itself gives readers no clear sense of what to expect. Sentences 3 and 6 refer to car worship while sentences 4 and 7 (the thesis?) are about freedom. If the final sentence is indeed the thesis, it seems to promise a discussion on the theme of worshipping our cars because they give us the freedom to move. But the final draft will explore other themes such as self-esteem, free speech, and privacy—all elements of our craving for individuality.

Paragraph B: Much of this material could be trimmed and combined with the introductory paragraph, to focus on consumer attitudes toward the Model Ts versus today's cars. The two final sentences seem awfully general; they can be cut.

Paragraph C: The two opening sentences could be combined with the introductory paragraph, to focus again on the change in consumer attitudes. The rest of the paragraph, with its wordy and irrelevant details about instant gratification, concept cars, and high sticker prices, can be cut.

None of this material relates directly to the thesis

~~understand our "first person on the block to have it" mentality, the car manufacturers tantalize us with concept cars you know: those weird, space-aged looking vehicles with gull's wings and rocket packs. To please the American sense of beauty, each year the cars get more attractive. New cars are sleeker and shinier, and more pleasing to touch. With such beauty, though, comes higher sticker prices. But we don't care. We are willing to pay any price to practice the Automobile Religion.~~

Topic sentence

We want automobiles that make a unique lifestyle statement about who we think we are.

D

Say this more concisely

Today, cars mean more to us than a way to cruise around town. If we saw them as only as a means to get to the grocery store, then we'd all be willing to drive junkers. ~~Instead, we see our cars as reflections of our personalities.~~ Most people *hate* ~~don't want to drive~~ rusty, old bombers. We want to be able to see our ideal (or idealized) images mirrored in our car's glossy paint job*, or in our truck's chrome hubcaps*. ~~We want automobiles that make a statement about ourselves.~~

Sharpen the images

People travel through the American wilderness in jeeps and trucks because they symbolize toughness and an uncompromising attitude. We buy sports cars not so much to impress others, but to impress ourselves: "Hey, I'm driving this red convertible Miata and *I'm special* (relates to theme of individuality) ~~I feel like the master of the highway.~~"

E

Topic sentence

Cars provide each individual with a personal billboard. ~~That's why we love our cars and decorate them as we do, to display a little of ourselves even while we~~

FIGURE 4.1
A draft edited for revision (continued)

Paragraph D: This paragraph provides informative details, but it lacks a topic sentence to frame readers' understanding of these details. Also, wordiness could be trimmed and images sharpened, to provide a more vivid picture. Otherwise the material here is definitely worthwhile.

Paragraph E: This paragraph, too, is generally strong, but it needs a more definite topic sentence and additional examples. Also, the tone in reference to pick-up trucks and NRA stickers lapses into name-calling.

~~drive~~. With bumper stickers, we exercise our *They tell the world that we're intellectuals or tough guys or sensitive types.* constitutional rights to free speech. One of mine

reads, "I love my humpback whale." Another promotes my

Add more examples

favorite radio station. ~~/~~~~~~~~ For some

reason, I often see National Rifle Association stickers

on pick-up trucks. Again, the drivers are making a

statement to the rest of us motorists: ~~"I like to maim~~

~~and kill!~~ Get out of my way!" to the rest of us *Too agressive*

wimps

~~motorists.~~ I, with my stuffed Bugs Bunny doll in the

back window, get out of the way. *Avoid name-calling*

F

None of this material relates to the thesis

~~The word "automobile" means self-moving. Cars give~~

~~us the freedom to go where we want, when we want,~~

~~across town or across the country. There is plenty of~~

~~wide open space for our cars. Even owners of land~~

~~barge SUVs usually find a place to park. Let's~~

~~consider the Japanese for a moment. They, too, love~~

~~their cars (with good reason) yet their autos are stuck~~

~~on a tiny island, and parking laws are so strict that~~

~~meter-readers write in chalk on the sidewalk how long a~~

~~car has been parked in a certain spot. Too long, and~~

~~it's towed. In America, we can usually park our cars~~

~~illegally and get away with it (for at least as long as~~

~~it takes to "run" into the bank or drugstore.)~~

Delete irrelevant comparison

When we own a car, we don't have to rely on--

torture for individuals like us

G yikes--public transportation, ~~something people in other~~

~~countries don't mind doing.~~ Americans' cars are

personal sanctuaries, places to escape other humans.

FIGURE 4.1
A draft edited for revision (continued)

Paragraph F: This entire paragraph strays from the essay's purpose to explore Americans' need to identify with our cars. It seems to belong to some other essay about cars and freedom, or some such.

Paragraph G: Another strong paragraph, with a basically solid topic sentence and vivid detail. The sweeping comparison with "other countries" and the "Dunkin' Donuts" reference really add nothing and can be deleted. Some sharper images would intensify the picture, and a few style changes would improve emphasis and readability.

One popular form of escape is the

~~The car's popularity has led to the phenomenon of~~

drive-up window$. Banks, donut shops, even dry

cleaners allow us to transact business without leaving

car

the ~~comfort and safety of our autos.~~ ~~Try getting a bus~~

Add more visual details like these

~~driver to stop at Dunkin' Donuts because you have a~~

Snug in our mobile dining rooms, we

~~sudden~~ urge for a cruller. (WE) no longer have to move

our orthopedically correct leather

from ~~the driver's~~ seat to order a meal. (We) no longer

Rephrase for sentence variety

have to sit in a noisy McDonald's with screaming kids

to eat our grease-laden food. (We) just stay in our

cars. How convenient. (We) can even sing along to the

between bites or hum along as we chew.

stereo ~~if we want.~~ ~~Imagine~~ Other commuters look at

Invert for emphasis

you strangely and hide their valuables *if you sing on*

a subway.

H

offer the ultimate

Cars entice us Americans because they ~~allow us to~~

mechanism for achieving individuality.

~~do the things that appeal to us: drive where we please,~~

We can   *and*   *without seeming weird.*

~~when we please,~~ dine a-la-car, sing aloud ~~in public and~~

Relate the ending directly to the thesis—without repeating it

~~not be thought insane. And~~ through the kind of car we

it   really "be somebody" and proclaim

drive and how we adorn ~~them,~~ we can ~~share with~~

singular selves

~~strangers~~ our ~~personalities.~~ Even though we may be

d

isolate~~s~~ in our automobiles, we share with other

Reverse these two sentences

motorists the camaraderie that comes with belonging to

the Car Cult.

Replace to focus on individuality

End with Kurt Vonnegut's observation that "we are what we pretend to be."

FIGURE 4.1
A draft edited for revision (continued)

Paragraph H: This conclusion needs a topic sentence that relates more explicitly to the thesis. The colorful images do a nice job of reflecting on the essay's main themes, but they should be followed by a closing statement that sums up the essay's larger meaning.

PROOFREADING YOUR FINAL DRAFT

Writers proofread as a final step, to ensure that everything is just right. No matter how engaging and informative the essay, basic errors distract the reader and make the writer look bad. Here are some types of easily correctable errors we can spot with careful proofreading:

Errors we look for during proofreading

- *Sentence errors,* such as fragments, comma splices, or run-ons (505)
- *Punctuation errors,* such as missing apostrophes or excessive commas (519)
- *Usage errors,* such as **it's** for **its, lay** for **lie,** or **their** for **there** (139)
- *Mechanical errors,* such as misspelled words, inaccurate dates, or incorrect abbreviations (532)
- *Format errors,* such as missing page numbers, inconsistent spacing, or incorrect form of documenting sources (537)
- *Typographical errors* (typos), such as repeated or missing words or letters, missing word endings (say, *-s* or *-ed* or *-ing*), or a left-out quotation mark or parenthesis

Refer to the page numbers in parentheses for advice on repairing these errors.

GUIDELINES FOR PROOFREADING

1. *Save it for the final draft.* Proofreading earlier drafts might cause writer's block and distract your focus from the rhetorical features.
2. *Take a break beforehand.* After you complete a final draft, give yourself some time before proofreading. Do something else for at least a couple of hours.
3. *Work from hard copy.* Research indicates that people read more perceptively (and with less fatigue) from a printed page than from a computer screen. Also, the page is easier to mark up, scribble on, and so on. Some people like to proofread in a comfy chair—or even lying down.
4. *Keep it slow.* Read each word—don't let yourself skim. Force yourself to slow down by sliding a ruler under each line or by moving backward throughout the essay, sentence by sentence.
5. *Be especially alert for troublesome areas in your writing.* Do you have trouble spelling? Do you get commas confused with semicolons? Do you make a lot of typographical errors (typos)? If punctuation is a problem, for example, make one final pass to check each punctuation mark.
6. *Proofread more than once.* The more you do it, the more errors you're likely to spot.
7. *Don't rely only on computerized aids.* Your spellcheckers can root out incorrectly spelled words but not incorrectly *used* words (say, "its" versus "it's") or typos that happen to spell a word (say, "cat" versus "rat"). Grammar checkers often give bizarre or inaccurate advice. In the end, nothing substitutes for your own careful reading.

Application **4-1**

Using the Revision Checklist on page 63 as a guide, return to an essay you have written earlier, and revise it.

At this early stage, you are bound to feel a little confused about the finer points of content, organization, and style. But try your best.

In later chapters, you will learn to improve your skill for diagnosing problems and prescribing cures.

Along with your revised essay, submit the original essay and an explanation of the improvements you've made.

Application **4-2**

Collaborative Project: Take an essay you have written earlier, and exchange it for a classmate's. Assume your classmate's essay has been written specifically for you as the audience. Write a detailed evaluation of your classmate's essay, making specific suggestions for revision. Using the Revision Checklist on page 63, evaluate all three rhetorical features: content, organization, and style. Use Appendix A to recommend improvements in grammar, punctuation, and mechanics. Do plenty of scribbling on the essay, and sign your evaluation.

Application **4-3**

Collaborative Project: Email a copy of your essay to a classmate and ask this reviewer to make specific comments using the Revision Checklist and then forward it to a second reviewer who repeats the exercise. Or, in a computer lab, after opening your essay file, everyone move one seat to the right and review the essay. Make comments, save the file, move again, and review the essay on the next screen.

Application **4-4**

Computer Project: Try out the spellchecker supplied by the word processing program you're using. First, learn how to add words you use often (your name, for example) to the computer's dictionary, so the program won't question you each time it encounters these words. Second, make a list of the words the computer lists as misspelled and the suggested corrections. Compare the computer's suggestions with the entries in a good dictionary. Do they match? Keep a log of the words you misspell.

Then proof your paper carefully, watching for the kinds of errors computers can't catch: *homonyms,* or words that sound alike but are spelled differently and have different meanings (*their* and *there, heel* and *heal*); and *transpositions (form for from)*. Also note that the spellchecker won't catch missing or extra words! How many of these corrections did you find?

Application **4-5**

Computer Project: Do a Web search to find dictionaries online and write a quick review of the sites you find most useful. (See also Application 16-5, page 274.)

Application **4-6**

Web-based Project: Based on information you find on the Web, develop your own list of strategies for revising and proofreading essays. Visit the following sites (you may want to search for others, as well), and compile a list of key steps and/or key questions you think would work best for revising and proofreading a paper. Be sure to include in your list at least one revision strategy and one proofreading strategy not covered in this chapter.

- Purdue Online Writing Lab
  <http://owl.english.purdue.edu/handouts/general/gl_hocloc.html>
- The Writing Center @ Rensselaer
  <http://www.rpi.edu/web/writingcenter/revise.html>
- Capital Community College Guide to Grammar and Writing
  <http://ccc.commnet.edu/grammar/composition/editing.htm>

Prepare a brief in-class presentation of this information. Attach a copy of the relevant Web page(s) to your written notes.

Note   *Instead of quoting your sources directly, paraphrase (page 372). Be sure to credit each source of information (page 392).*

Application **4-7**

Web-based Project: Web pages from The Writer's Block **<www.writersblock .ca/spring95/team.htm>** describe the relationship between writers and editors in the workplace. Prepare a one-page summary of this information, in your own words, for class discussion. (Page 373 offers guidelines for summarizing information.) Attach copies of relevant Web pages to your summary.

SECTION TWO

Specific Revision Strategies

Introduction **80**

CHAPTER 5
Revising the Content:
Writing Something Worthwhile **83**

CHAPTER 6
Revising the Paragraphs:
Shaping for Readers' Access **96**

CHAPTER 7
Revising the Sentences:
Writing with Style **117**

CHAPTER 8
Revising the Words and Phrases:
Fine-Tuning **137**

Introduction

How Good Is "Good Enough"?   **80**

Revising from the Top Down   **80**

Beefing Up the Content   **81**

Harnessing Paragraph Power   **81**

Honing the Sentences   **81**

Finding the Perfect Wording   **82**

Chapter 1 reminds us that only the rare piece of writing is ever "finished," in the strict sense. Most writing—even at later stages—is more of a work-in-progress, with considerable room for improvement. Even professional writers often revisit a "finished" work for further revision.

HOW GOOD IS "GOOD ENOUGH"?

Every writer eventually runs out of time or patience and decides that the piece is good enough. But exactly how good is "good enough"? The answer depends on your purpose and your audience's expectations. For example, a "good enough" note to a friend differs greatly from a "good enough" scholarship essay or job application. And so, to make real contact, everyone's writing at times must exceed mere adequacy and must approach excellence.

REVISING FROM THE TOP DOWN

What are some strategies for approaching excellence? One useful way to revise is to consider your essay from the top down. First, consider the actual content—your reason for writing in the first place; next, the shape and position of each paragraph; then, the flow of your sentences; and finally, the quality of your phrasing and word choice. Figure II.1 shows how essay revision can move from large matters to small.

FIGURE II.1
**Top-down decisions
in revising**

> ### Revising the Content
> - Is the thesis clear, focused, and significant?
> - Is the support credible, informative, and substantial?
>
> ### Revising the Organization
> - Is the essay's structure visible at a glance?
> - Is each support paragraph basically its own mini-essay?
>
> ### Revising the Sentences
> - Is each sentence immediately understandable?
> - Is rich information expressed in the fewest words possible?
> - Are sentences constructed with enough variety?
>
> ### Revising Word Choice
> - Does each word clarify—rather than muddle—the meaning?
> - Is the tone appropriate?

BEEFING UP THE CONTENT

Readers expect content that rewards their effort. To make it convincing, informative, and thorough, we provide plenty of *details:* facts, ideas, examples, numbers, names, events, dates, or reasons that help readers visualize what we mean. But we trim away needless details because excessive information causes readers to overlook or misinterpret the important material. Early drafts almost always need trimming.

HARNESSING PARAGRAPH POWER

Readers need structure to advance logically, so they look for shapes they can recognize. Instead of forcing readers to organize unstructured material for themselves, we shape it for their understanding. Our essential organizing tool is the paragraph: forming part of the essay's larger design while telling its own, self-contained story.

HONING THE SENTENCES

Readers have no patience with writing that's hard to interpret, takes too long to make the point, or reads like a Dick-and-Jane story from primary school. And so we work to produce razor-sharp sentences that are clear and forceful, waste no words, and make for easy reading.

FINDING THE PERFECT WORDING

Readers are turned off by wording that is poorly chosen, too fancy, or that sounds stuffy and impersonal. And so we fine-tune each word to convey precisely what we are seeing, thinking, and feeling.

Note

Like other decisions about writing, the revising process is not always as systematic as outlined here. For example, you might revisit the content while working on the organization, or you might think of a better word while reshaping a paragraph. Once you learn the strategies in this section, how you decide to use them will be up to you.

CHAPTER 5

Revising the Content: Writing Something Worthwhile

Make It Credible **84**

Make It Informative **86**

Make It Complete **89**

Credit Your Information Sources **90**

Reading **87**

Applications **91**

Readers hate to waste time. They expect an insightful thesis backed by solid content and support.

The first requirement of worthwhile content is *unity:* every word, every detail belongs. Three other qualities are also essential to worthwhile content: *credibility, informative value,* and *completeness.**

---

*Adapted from James L. Kinneavy's assertion that discourse should be factual, unpredictable, and comprehensive. See James L. Kinneavy, *A Theory of Discourse* (Englewood Cliffs, NJ: Prentice, 1971).

MAKE IT CREDIBLE

Anyone can assert opinions; *supporting* your assertion is the real challenge. We all have opinions about political candidates, cars, or controversial subjects, such as abortion or nuclear energy. But many of our opinions are *uninformed;* instead of resting on facts, they lean mostly on a chaotic collection of beliefs repeated around us, notions we've inherited from advertising, things we've read but never checked, and assumptions we've never examined.

UNINFORMED OPINIONS

Christopher Columbus was a hero.

Christopher Columbus was an oppressor.

Grindo toothpaste is best for making teeth whiter.

In a democracy, religion deserves a voice in government.

Informed opinion, in contrast, rests on fact or good sense. Any fact (*My hair is brown. Americans have more televisions than bathtubs.*) can be verified by anyone. A fact can be verified by observation (*I saw Felix murder his friend.*), by research (*Wood smoke contains the deadly chemical dioxin.*), by experience (*I was hugged this morning.*), or by measurement (*Less than 60 percent of our first-year students eventually earn a degree.*). Opinions based on these facts would be informed opinions.

INFORMED OPINIONS

Felix is guilty of murder.

Homes with woodstoves need good ventilation.

This has been a good day for me.

College clearly is not for everyone.

To *support an opinion,* you often must consider a variety of facts. You might be able to support with facts the claim that Grindo toothpaste makes teeth whiter, but a related fact may be that Grindo contains tiny silicone particles—an abrasive that "whitens" by scraping enamel from teeth. The second fact could change your opinion about Grindo.

The Grindo example illustrates that no two facts about anything are likely to have equal relevance. Assume you've asserted this opinion:

This opinion needs
supporting facts

The Diablo Canyon nuclear plant is especially dangerous.

In deciding how to support this opinion, you compare the relevance of each of these facts:

Not all supporting facts
are equal

1. The road system is inadequate for rapid evacuation of local residents.
2. Nuclear plants have no suitable way to dispose of radioactive wastes.

3. The plant is only 100 miles from sizable population centers.

4. The plant is built near a major earthquake fault.

Although all these facts support the label "dangerous," the first three can apply to many nuclear plants. Only the fourth addresses the danger specific to the Diablo Canyon plant—and therefore has most relevance. Because readers can tolerate only so many details, you must decide which of your facts offer the best support.

Besides unifying your facts, arrange them for emphasis. Consider this opening passage:

PASSAGE A—AN OPINION SUPPORTED BY FACT

Child abuse has become our national disgrace. In the past decade, reported incidence has increased an average of 20 percent yearly. This year alone, more than 500,000 children (fewer than 20 percent of cases) will be the reported victims of physical, sexual, or emotional violence by one or both parents. And among the reported offenders, only 3 percent are ever convicted. Even more tragic, the pattern of violence is cyclical, with many abused children later becoming abusive parents themselves.

We move from the disquieting numbers to the tragically cyclical process.

Instead of relying on facts, certain moral or emotional opinions (prayer in public schools, the existence of God, laws against flag desecration, children's rights) often rest on common sense and insight. The following passage supports the opinion that parents should limit their role in telling their children how to live.

PASSAGE B—AN OPINION SUPPORTED BY GOOD SENSE

The idea of the child as personal property has always bothered me, for personal reasons. . . . I lack the feeling that I own my children and have always scoffed at the idea that what they are and do is a continuation or rejection of my being. I like them, I sympathize with them, I acknowledge the obligation to support them for a term of years—but I am not so fond or foolish as to regard a biological tie as a lien on their loyalty or respect, nor to imagine that I am equipped with [special] powers of guidance as to their success and happiness. Beyond inculcating some of the obvious [manners] required in civilized life, who am I to pronounce on what makes for a happy or successful life? How many of us can say that we have successfully managed our own lives? Can we do better with our children?

—*Anonymous*

The above passage offers no statistics, research data, or observable facts. However, the support is credible because of its insight into our shared reality as parents and children.

MAKE IT INFORMATIVE

Are you one of those writers who enters college as experts in the art of "stuffing"? The stuffing expert knows how to fill pages by cramming into the essay every thought that will pile up 500 words (or any required total) with minimal pain. But readers expect *something new and useful.* Writing has informative value when it does at least one of these things:

An essay with informative value does one or more of these things

- Shares something new and significant
- Reminds us about something we know but ignore
- Offers fresh insight or perspective on something we already know

In short, informative writing gives readers exactly what they need.

Readers approach most topics with some prior knowledge (or old information). They might need reminding, but they don't need a rehash of old information; they can "fill in the blanks" for themselves. On the other hand, readers don't need every bit of new information you can think of, either.

As a reader of this book, for example, you expect to learn something worthwhile about writing, and my purpose is to provide that. Which of these statements would you find useful?

> (a) Writing is hard and frustrating work.
>
> (b) Writing is a process of deliberate decisions.

Statement a offers no news to anyone who ever has picked up a pencil. But Statement b reminds you that producing good writing can be a lot more complex than we would like. Because Statement b offers new insight into a familiar process, then we can say it has informative value.

We see that Passages A and B (page 85) satisfy our criteria for informative value. Passage A offers surprising evidence about child abuse; Passage B gives fresh insight into the familiar issue of parent–child relations.

Sometimes we write for a mixed group of readers with varied needs. How, then, can our writing have informative value for each reader?

Imagine you are an ex-jogger and a convert to walking for aerobic exercise. You decide to write an essay for classmates on the advantages of walking over running. You can assume that a few classmates are runners; others swim, cycle, or do other exercise; some don't do much but are thinking of starting; and some have no interest in any exercise. Your problem is to address all these readers in one essay that each reader finds worthwhile. Specifically, you want to

- Persuade runners and other exercisers to consider walking as an alternative
- Encourage the interested nonexercisers to try walking
- Create at least a spark of interest among the diehard nonexercisers—and maybe even inspire them to rise up out of their easy chairs and hit the bricks

First, you will need to answer questions shared by all readers:

Audience questions you
can anticipate

- *Why is walking better than running?*
- *How are they similar or different?*
- *What are the benefits in walking?*
- *Can you give examples?*
- *Why should I?*

But some readers will have special questions. Nonexercisers might ask, *What exactly is aerobic exercise, anyway?* And the true couch potatoes might ask, *Who cares?* Your essay will have to answer all these questions.

Assume that many hours of planning, drafting, and revising have enabled you to produce this final draft:

AN ESSAY WITH INFORMATIVE VALUE

WALK BUT DON'T RUN

Our bodies gain aerobic benefits when we exercise at a fast enough pace for muscles to demand oxygen-rich blood from the heart and lungs. During effective aerobic exercise, the heart rate increases roughly 80 percent above normal. Besides strengthening muscle groups—especially the heart—aerobic exercise makes blood vessels stronger and larger.

Running, or jogging, has become a most popular form of aerobic exercise. But millions of Americans who began running to get in shape are now limping to their doctors for treatment of running injuries. To keep yourself in one piece as you keep yourself in shape, try walking instead of running.

All the aerobic benefits of running can be yours if you merely take brisk walks. Consider this comparison. For enough aerobic training to increase cardiovascular (heart, lungs, and blood vessels) efficiency, you need to run three times weekly for roughly 30 minutes. (Like any efficient system, an efficient cardiovascular system produces maximum work with minimum effort.) You can gain cardiovascular benefits equivalent to running, however, by taking a brisk walk three times weekly for roughly 60 minutes. Granted, walking takes up more time than running, but it carries fewer risks.

Because of its more controlled and deliberate pace, walking is safer than running. A walker stands far less chance of tripping, stepping in potholes, or slipping and falling. And the slower pace causes less physical trauma. Anyone who has ever run at all knows that a runner's foot strikes the ground with sizable impact. But the shock of this impact travels beyond the foot—to the shins, knees, hips, internal organs, and spine. Walking, of course, creates an impact of its own, but the walker's foot strikes the ground with only half as much force as the runner's foot.

Beyond its apparent physical dangers, running can provoke subtle stress for the devoted exerciser. Because running is generally seen as more competitive than just walking, we too easily can be tempted to push our bodies too far, too fast. Even though we might not compete in races or marathons, we often tend to compete against ourselves—maybe just to keep up with a jock neighbor or to break a personal record. And by ignoring the signals of overexertion and physical stress, we can easily run ourselves into an injury—if not the grave. Slowing to a walk instead is a safe way of leaving the "competition" behind.

—Jeff Leonard

Will this essay have informative value for all readers? Probably so. It seems to answer all the readers' questions we anticipated on page 87. Will all readers become converts? Probably not. But each should have something to think about. A worthwhile message makes some kind of a difference for its readers—even if it triggers only the slightest insight.

Now let's assume that you had written the walking essay by using the old high school strategy of filling up the page. Your opening paragraph might look like this:

AN OPENING WITHOUT INFORMATIVE VALUE

WALK BUT DON'T RUN

Medical science has made tremendous breakthroughs in the past few decades. Research has shown that exercise is a good way of staying healthy, beneficial for our bodies and our minds. More people of all ages are exercising today than ever before. Because of its benefits, one popular form of exercise for Americans is aerobic exercise.

Your readers (in the situation described on page 86) already know all this. Even new material lacks informative value when it is irrelevant:

MATERIAL IRRELEVANT TO THE SITUATION

To avoid the perils of running, the Chinese attend sessions of T'ai-chi, a dancelike series of stretching routines designed to increase concentration and agility. Although T'ai-chi is less dangerous than running, it fails to provide a truly aerobic workout.

The above material might serve in an essay comparing certain aerobic and non-aerobic exercises, but not in this comparison between walking and running.

Nor would highly technical details have informative value here, as in this next example:

MATERIAL TOO TECHNICAL FOR THE SITUATION

Walking and jogging result in forward motion because you continually fall forward and catch yourself. With each stride, you lift your body, accelerate, and land. You go faster when running because you fall farther, but you also strike the ground harder, and for less time. Your increase in speed and distance fallen combine with the shorter contact period to cause an impact on your body that is more than double the impact from walking.

The above material would serve for students of biophysics, exercise physiology, or sports medicine, but seems too detailed for a mixed audience.

MAKE IT COMPLETE

All writers struggle with this question: *How much is enough?* (Or, *How long should it be?*) Again, anticipate readers' questions about your thesis.

Assume, for instance, that a friend now living in another state is thinking of taking a job similar to one you held last summer. Your friend has written to ask how you liked the job; your response will influence the friend's decision. Here is a passage from a first draft that tells but doesn't show:

NOT ENOUGH DETAIL

My job last summer as a flagger for a road construction company was boring, tiresome, dirty, and painful. All I did was stand in the road and flag cars. Every day I just stood there, getting sore feet. I was always covered with dirt and breathing it in. To make matters worse, the sun, wind, and bugs ruined my skin. By the end of summer, I vowed never to do this kind of work again.

The above passage has only limited informative value because it fails to make the experience vivid for readers. The sketchy details fail to answer our obvious questions.

- *Can you show me what the job was like?*
- *What, exactly, made it boring, tiresome, dirty, and painful?*

This next passage, on the other hand, is revised to include graphic details that make readers feel a part of it all:

ENOUGH DETAIL

My job last summer as a flagger for a road construction company was boring, tiresome, dirty, and painful. All day I stood like a robot; waving a stupid red flag at oncoming traffic, my eardrums blasted by the racket of road machinery, each day dragging by more slowly than the last. My feet would swell, and my legs would ache from standing on the hard clay and gravel for up to fifteen hours a day. And the filth was disgusting. The fumes, oil, and grime from the road machinery and the exhaust from passing cars became like a second skin. Each breath sucked up more dust, clogging my sinuses, irritating my eyes. But worst of all was the weather. Blistering from sunburn, I was being sandblasted and rubbed raw by windstorms, pounded by hail, or chewed by mosquitoes and horseflies. By the end of summer, I was a freak: swollen feet and ankles, the skin of a water buffalo, and chronic sinusitis. I'd starve before taking that job again.

In the preceding situation, even more details (say, a day-by-day description of every event) probably would clutter the message. The reader here needed and *wanted* just enough information to make an informed decision.

Giving enough detail is not the same as merely adding more words. Whatever does nothing but fill the page is puffery:

HOT AIR

My job last summer as a flagger for a road construction company was boring, tiresome, dirty, and painful. ~~Day in and day out~~, I stood ~~on that road~~ for endless hours getting ~~a severe case of~~ sore feet. My face and body were ~~always completely~~ covered with ~~the~~ dust blown up from the ~~passing cars and various other~~ vehicles, and I was forced to breathe in all ~~of~~ this ~~horrible~~ junk ~~day after day.~~ ~~To add to the problems of boredom, fatigue, and dirt,~~ the weather murdered my skin. ~~Let me tell you that~~ by the time ~~the~~ summer ended, I ~~had~~ made ~~myself~~ a solemn promise never to ~~victimize myself by~~ taking this kind of awful job again.

Although the above passage is nearly twice as long as the original (page 89), it adds no meaning; hot air (shown crossed out) offers no real information.

Note

Don't worry about not having enough to say. Once you have begun the writing process (searching for details, rephrasing, making connections), you probably will find it harder to stay within the limit than to reach it. Your purpose is to make your point—not to show how smart you are. Instead of including every word, fact, and idea that crosses your mind, learn to select. Sometimes one single detail is enough: To make the point about a "boring" job, the passage on page 89 describes the writer standing like a robot, waving a red flag.

The passages above show how you can measure the completeness of your own writing, *providing details that show*, by answering questions like the following:

Details answer these
questions

- *Who, what, when, where, and why?*
- *What did you see, feel, hear, taste, smell?*
- *What would a camera record?*
- *What are the dates, numbers, percentages?*
- *Can you compare it with something more familiar?*

CREDIT YOUR INFORMATION SOURCES

Much of any writer's information comes from other sources, and the work of others must be properly documented. In both workplace and academic settings, plagiarism (representing the words, ideas, or perspectives of others as your own) is a serious breach of ethics.

Examples of plagiarism

Blatant cases of plagiarism occur when a writer consciously lifts passages from another work (print or online) and incorporates them into his or her own work without quoting or documenting the original source. As most students know, this can result in a failing grade and potential disciplinary action. More commonly, writers will simply fail to cite a source being quoted or paraphrased, often because they misplaced the original source and publication information or forgot to note it during their research (Anson and Schwegler 633–36). Whereas this more subtle, sometimes unconscious form of misrepresentation is less blatant, it still constitutes plagiarism and can undermine a writer's credibility, or worse.

Plagiarism and the Internet

The rapid development of Internet resources has spawned a wild array of misconceptions about plagiarism. Some people mistakenly assume that, because material posted on a Web site is free, it can be paraphrased or copied without citation. Despite the ease of cutting and pasting from Web sites, the fact remains: Any time you borrow someone else's words, ideas, perspectives, or images—regardless of the medium used in the original source—you need to document the original source accurately.

Whatever your career plans, learning to gather, incorporate, and document authoritative source material is an absolutely essential job skill. By properly citing a range of sources in your work, you bolster your own credibility and demonstrate your skills as a researcher and a writer. (For more on recording, incorporating, and documenting sources, see Chapters 20 and 21.)

Application **5-1**

Each sentence below states either a fact or an opinion. Rewrite all statements of opinion as statements of fact. Remember that a fact can be verified. (Review pages 84–85.)

EXAMPLE

> **Opinion**   My roommate isn't taking college work seriously.
>
> **Fact**   My roommate never studies, sleeps through most classes, and has missed every exam.

1. Professor X grades unfairly.
2. My vacation was too short.
3. The salary for this position is $15,000 yearly.
4. This bicycle is reasonably priced.
5. We walked 5 miles last Saturday.
6. He drives recklessly.
7. My motorcycle gets great gas mileage.
8. This course has been very helpful.
9. German shepherds eat more than cocker spaniels do.
10. This apartment is much too small for our family.

Application **5-2**

Return to Shirley Haley's essay on pages 13–14. Underline all statements of fact, and circle all statements of opinion. Are all the opinions supported by facts or by good sense? Now, perform the same evaluation on an essay you have written. (Review pages 84–85.)

Application **5-3**

Assume you live in the Northeast, and citizens in your state are voting on a solar energy referendum that would channel millions of tax dollars toward solar technology. The next paragraphs are designed to help you, as a voter, make an educated decision. Do both these versions of the same message have informative value? Explain. (Review pages 86–89.)

> Solar power offers a realistic solution to the Northeast's energy problems. In recent years the cost of fossil fuels (oil, coal, and natural gas) has risen rapidly while the supply has continued to decline. High prices and short supply will continue to cause a worsening energy crisis. Because solar energy comes directly from the sun, it is an inexhaustible resource. By using this energy to heat and air-condition our buildings, as well as to provide electricity, we could decrease substantially our consumption of fossil fuels. In turn, we would be less dependent on the unstable Middle East for our oil supplies. Clearly, solar power is a good alternative to conventional energy sources.

> Solar power offers a realistic solution to the Northeast's energy problems. To begin with, solar power is efficient. Solar collectors installed on fewer than 30 percent of roofs in the Northeast would provide more than 70 percent of the area's heating and air-conditioning needs. Moreover, solar heat collectors are economical, operating for up to 20 years with little or no maintenance. These savings recoup the initial cost of installment within only 10 years. Most important, solar power is safe. It can be transformed into electricity through photovoltaic cells (a type of storage battery) noiselessly and with no air pollution—unlike coal, oil, and wood combustion. In sharp contrast to its nuclear counterpart, solar power produces no toxic wastes and poses no catastrophic danger of meltdown. Thus, massive conversion to solar power would ensure abundant energy and a safe, clean environment for future generations.

Application **5-4**

Collaborative Project: Review a classmate's essay and eliminate all statements that lack informative value (those that offer commonly known, irrelevant, or insignificant material). Be careful not to cut material the audience needs in order to understand the essay, such as:

1. Details that help us see
2. Details that help us feel
3. Numerical details
4. Vivid comparisons
5. Details that a camera would record
6. Details that help us hear

Would some parts of your classmate's essay benefit from greater detail? Use the list above as a basis for making specific suggestions.

Application **5-5**

Computer Application: Make an electronic copy of a classmate's essay. Put the main topic in boldface and underline all supporting material that has informative value. Save the file. Copy it and cut anything not in bold or underlined. Working with your classmate, compare the two versions.

Application **5-6**

Return to one of your earlier essays. Study it carefully, then brainstorm again to sharpen your details. Now write a revised version. (Review pages 84–91.)

Application **5-7**

Computer Application: Working from the joint computer file for your group, complete Application 5-4.

Application **5-8**

Computer Application: Select a paragraph you have written for an earlier assignment. Using the paragraph on page 89 as a guide, create and save at least two alternative versions of this paragraph by deleting different combinations of words and phrases. Print out all three versions. Then, from among the alternatives, choose what you think is the most effective version of *each sentence.* Recombine these sentences into a fourth version of the paragraph— one that achieves completeness without clutter.

Application **5-9**

Collaborative Project: Assume that your English teacher has just won $40 million in the state lottery. As a final grand gesture before retiring to a life of sail-

ing, collecting fine wines, and breeding polo ponies, your soon-to-be ex-
teacher makes this announcement to the class:

> After years of agonizing over ways to motivate my writing audience, I've
> discovered what could be the ultimate solution. I'm going to hold a contest
> offering $1 million to the student who writes the best essay on this topic:
> How I Would Spend $1 Million. Essays will be evaluated on the basis of
> originality, credibility, richness of detail, and clarity of explanation. The whole
> class will pick the winner from among the five finalists I select.

Write your essay, revising as often as needed to make it a winner.

Application 5-10

Web-based Project: Uninformed opinions usually are based on assumptions
or beliefs we've never really examined. (See page 382 for more discussion.)
Examples of popular assumptions that are largely unexamined:

- "Bottled water is safer and better for you than tap water."
- "Forest fires should always be prevented or suppressed immediately."
- "The fewer germs in their environment, the healthier the children."
- "The more soy products we eat, the better."

Your assignment is to identify and examine one popular assumption for accuracy. For example, you might tackle the bottled water assumption by visiting the FDA Web site <**www.FDA.gov**> or the forest fire assumption by visiting the Sierra Club pages <**www.sierraclub.org**>, for starters. (Unless you
get stuck, examine an assumption not listed above.) Trace the sites and links
you followed to get your information, and write up your findings in a memo
to be shared with the class.

Application 5-11

Web-based Project: Prepare a brief presentation for your class in which you
answer these questions: *What is plagiarism? How do I avoid it?*
   Start by exploring the following sites:

- *Plagiarism: What It Is and How to Avoid It,* from the Indiana University Writing Tutorial Services
  <**http://www.indiana.edu/~wts/wts/plagiarism.html**>
- *Avoiding Plagiarism,* from the Purdue Online Writing Lab
  <**http://owl.english.purdue.edu/handouts/research/r_plagiar.html**>

Find at least one additional Web source on plagiarism (you may need to do a search).

For your class presentation, your goal is to summarize in one page or less a practical, working definition of plagiarism and a list of suggested strategies for avoiding it. (See page 373 for guidelines for summarizing information.) Attach a copy of the relevant Web page(s) to your presentation. Be sure to credit each source of information (page 392).

Work Cited

Anson, Chris M., and Robert A. Schwegler. *The Longman Handbook for Writers and Readers.* 2nd ed. New York: Longman, 2000.

CHAPTER 6

Revising the Paragraphs: Shaping for Readers' Access

Support Paragraphs as Mini-Essays   **97**

Paragraph Function   **98**

Paragraph Length   **98**

The Topic Statement   **99**

Structural Variations in Support Paragraphs   **101**

Paragraph Unity   **102**

Paragraph Coherence   **103**

Applications   **112**

Readers look for orientation, for shapes they can recognize. But an essay's larger design (introduction, body, conclusion) depends on the smaller design of each paragraph. A paragraph is a place for things that belong together.

SUPPORT PARAGRAPHS AS MINI-ESSAYS

Paragraphs in an essay have various shapes and purposes. Introductory paragraphs draw us into the writer's reality; concluding paragraphs ease us out; transitional paragraphs help hold things together. But here we cover *support paragraphs*—those middle blocks of thought, each often a mini-shape of the whole essay. Just as the thesis is backed up by its supporting points, each major supporting point is backed up by its paragraph, as shown in Figure 6.1:

FIGURE 6.1
Support paragraphs in the basic essay

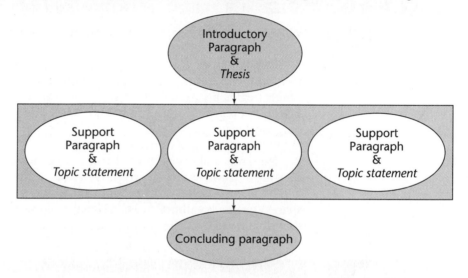

Although part of the essay's larger design, each support paragraph usually can stand alone in meaning and emphasis. Consider this paragraph by a noted psychiatrist:

A TYPICAL SUPPORT PARAGRAPH

Introduction (topic statement, 1)
Body (2–9)

[1]*Crime is everybody's temptation.* [2]It is easy to look with proud disdain upon "those people" who get caught—the stupid ones, the unlucky ones, the blatant ones. [3]But who does not get nervous when a police car follows closely? [4]We squirm over our income-tax statements and make some "adjustments." [5]We tell the customs official that we have nothing to declare—well, practically nothing. [6]Some of us who have never been convicted of any crime picked up over two billion dollars' worth of merchandise last year from the stores we patronize. [7]Over a billion dollars was embezzled by employees last year. [8]One hotel in New York lost over seventy-five thousand finger bowls, demitasse spoons, and other objects in its first ten

Conclusion (10–12)

months of operation. [9]The Claims Bureau of the American Insurance Association estimates that 75 percent of all claims are dishonest in some respect and the amount of overpayment more than $350,000,000 a year. [10]These facts disturb us or should. [11]They give us an uneasy feeling that we are all indicted. [12]"Let him who is without sin cast the first stone."

—*Karl Menninger*

Menninger's paragraph is part of a much larger design: a chapter in his book *The Crime of Punishment.* But the paragraph's shape is familiar enough: the introduction asserts a definite viewpoint; the body walks us through the writer's reasoning; the conclusion offers perspective on what we've read.

PARAGRAPH FUNCTION

Writers need definite paragraph divisions for control; readers need them for access.

Paragraphs *increase your writing control.* Each support paragraph is an idea unit, one distinct space for developing one supporting point. If Menninger begins his paragraph with the point that crime tempts everyone, he can tailor everything in the paragraph to advance that point. No matter how long your message, you can stay in control by looking for things that belong together—thinking in terms of paragraphs.

Paragraphs also *give readers orientation.* Readers need to know where they are and where they're going. By dividing a long piece of writing, paragraphs allow readers to focus on each point. The paragraph indent (five spaces) gives a breathing space, a signal that the geography is changing and that it's time to look ahead.

PARAGRAPH LENGTH

Paragraph length depends on *the writer's purpose* and the reader's capacity for understanding. Writing that carries highly technical information or complex instructions may use short paragraphs or perhaps a list. In a newspaper article, paragraphs of only one or two sentences keep the reader's attention. In writing that explains concepts, attitudes, or viewpoints (as in college essays), support paragraphs generally run from 100 to 300 words.

But word count really means very little. What matters is *how thoroughly the paragraph makes your point.* A flabby paragraph buries readers in needless words and details; but just skin and bones leaves readers looking for the meat. Each paragraph requires new decisions. Try to avoid too much of anything. A clump of short paragraphs can make some writing seem choppy and poorly organized, but a stretch of long ones is tiring. A well-placed short paragraph—sometimes just one sentence—can highlight an important idea.

More than 30 percent of our state's groundwater contains toxic wastes.

For real impact, you can even use just one word:

> Exactly.

In writing displayed on a computer screen, short paragraphs and lists are especially useful because they allow for easy scanning and navigation.

THE TOPIC STATEMENT

A college essay needs a thesis that asserts the main point, and each support paragraph needs a *topic statement* that asserts a supporting point. Sometimes the topic statement comes at the end of the paragraph; sometimes in the middle; but usually it comes first. The paragraph's first sentence should focus and forecast.

The Topic Statement as Readers' Framework

Most paragraphs in college writing begin by *telling readers what to look for.* Don't write

No focus

> Some jobs are less stressful than others.

when you mean

Better

> Mortuary management is an ideal major for anyone craving a stress-free job.

The first topic statement above doesn't give a very clear forecast; the second helps us focus.
    Don't write

No forecast

> Summers in Goonville are awful.

when you mean

Better

> I hate Goonville summers because of the chiggers, ticks, scorpions, and rattlesnakes.

The Topic Statement as Writers' Framework

Without a topic statement, writers struggle to make their paragraphs more than a collection of random thoughts. *Always take a definite stand; assert something significant.*

Imagine that you are a member of Congress, about to vote on abortion legislation. One of your constituents has responded to your request for citizens' viewpoints with a letter that begins like this:

No focus or forecast

Abortion is a very complex issue. There is a sharp division between those who are for it and those who are against it. Very few people take a neutral stand on this issue. The battle between supporters and opponents has raged for years. This is only one of the serious problems in our society. Every day, things seem to get worse.

Because this writer never identified his purpose, never discovered his own exact meaning, the above paragraph merely parrots a number of unrelated thoughts that are all common knowledge. If, instead, our writer had refined his meaning by asserting a definite viewpoint, he might have written a worthwhile paragraph. Depending on his purpose, he might have begun with, say:

Better

Abortion laws in our state discriminate against the poor.

or

Abortion is wrong because of the irresponsibility it allows.

Before you can explain yourself, you have to figure out exactly what you mean.

How Audience and Purpose Determine a Topic Statement's Focus

Your topic statement's focus governs the level of detail in the paragraph itself. Decide carefully whom you're writing for and why. Say, for example, a friend is thinking about applying to your school and has asked about life on campus. You happen to know that this person cares especially about personal identity and, thus, about attending a college that appreciates each student's unique potential. In this instance, you might come up with the following topic statement and paragraph:

A broad focus

Because you're a person who hates the idea of being lost in the crowd, I know you would enjoy Rangeley College. In a school such as this one, with limited enrollment and small classes, it's easy to make friends and get to know each professor. In no time, you'll find that all the faces look familiar, and almost everyone is on a first-name basis. Also, there will be lots of people asking you to join various organizations and activities. You can count on being welcomed here, on having a real sense of belonging, on making a difference. Why not give this place a try? You won't be sorry.

Suppose that, instead, you are working part-time in the admissions office, helping prepare a brochure that emphasizes the various activities and organizations at the college. In this case, the focus of your topic statement would be more limited than above, and the paragraph's details would be more specific:

A more limited focus

> Whether your interests are social, artistic, political, or athletic, you'll find plenty of ways to keep busy at Rangeley College. In addition to our eight sororities and seven fraternities, we have a social club that sponsors dances, parties, concerts, and whatever else might be needed to liven up even the dreariest weekend. If you like politics, run for the Student Senate or join the Visitor's Council, which brings social and political celebrities to campus. If you're musically inclined, join the marching band, chamber orchestra, or rock group. Also, the various clubs for painters, writers, actors, and dancers are always looking for new talent. To stay in shape, try out for varsity baseball, hockey, soccer, lacrosse, or track (all have both women's and men's teams), or join an intramural team. All in all, if you are looking for involvement and challenge, Rangeley College is the place for you.

Depending on your purpose and the audience's needs, a topic statement about life at Rangeley College could be narrowed even further—say, with a paragraph describing the chamber orchestra, the lacrosse team, or the activities of the Visitor's Council.

STRUCTURAL VARIATIONS IN SUPPORT PARAGRAPHS

Your main idea might have several distinct parts, which would result in an excessively long paragraph. You might then break up the paragraph, making your topic statement a brief introductory paragraph that forecasts various subparts, which are set off as independent paragraphs.

A TOPIC STATEMENT THAT SERVES SEVERAL PARAGRAPHS

> *Common types of strip-mining procedures include open-pit mining, contour mining, and auger mining. The specific type employed will depend on the type of terrain covering the coal.*
>
> Open-pit mining is employed in the relatively flat lands in western Kentucky, Oklahoma, and Kansas. Here, draglines and scoops operate directly on the coal seams. This process produces long parallel rows of packed spoil banks, 10 to 30 feet high, with steep slopes. Between the spoil banks are large pits that soon fill with water to produce pollution and flood hazards.
>
> Contour mining is most widely practiced in the mountainous terrain of the Cumberland Plateau and eastern Kentucky. Here, bulldozers and explosives cut and blast the earth and rock covering a coal seam. Wide bands are removed from the mountain's circumference to reach the embedded coal beneath. The cutting and blasting result in a shelf, along with a jagged cliff some 60 feet high at a right angle to the shelf. The blasted and churned earth is pushed over the shelf to form a massive and unstable spoil bank that creates a danger of mud slides.
>
> Auger mining is employed when the mountain has been cut so thin that it no longer can be stripped. It is also used in other difficult-access terrain. Here, large augers bore parallel rows of holes into the hidden coal seams to

extract the embedded coal. Among the three strip-mining processes, auger mining causes the least damage to the surrounding landscape.

As you can see, each paragraph begins with a clear statement of the subtopic discussed in it.

Note   *Remember that you won't always be able to think first of the right topic statement, and then of your support. Your actual framework might not appear until you've done some freewriting or brainstorming. The sequence is unimportant—as long as the finished paragraph offers a definite framework and solid support.*

PARAGRAPH UNITY

Each paragraph in an essay requires *external unity* and *internal unity*. A paragraph has external unity when (as on pages 56–58) it belongs with all the other paragraphs in an essay. But each paragraph requires internal unity as well: Every word, phrase, and sentence directly supports the topic sentence.

Imagine that you're composing a paragraph beginning with this topic statement:

Chemical pesticides and herbicides are both ineffective and hazardous.

The words that signal the meaning here are **ineffective** and **hazardous;** everything in the paragraph should advance that meaning. Here is the unified paragraph:

A UNIFIED PARAGRAPH

Chemical pesticides and herbicides are both ineffective and hazardous. Because none of these chemicals has permanent effects, pest populations invariably recover and need to be resprayed. Repeated applications cause pests to develop immunity to the chemicals. Furthermore, most pesticides and herbicides attack species other than the intended pest, killing off its natural predators, thus actually increasing the pest population. Above all, chemical residues survive in the environment (and in living tissue) for years and often are carried hundreds of miles by wind and water. This toxic legacy includes such biological effects as birth deformities, reproductive failures, brain damage, and cancer. Although intended to control pest populations, these chemicals ironically threaten to make the human population their ultimate victims.

One way to destroy unity in the paragraph above would be to veer from the focus on **ineffective** and **hazardous** to material about the cost of the chemicals, their unpleasant odor, or the number of people who oppose their use.

Every topic statement has a *signal term,* a key word or phrase that announces the viewpoint. In the paragraph below, the signal term is **intelligent,** causing readers to expect material about whale intelligence. But the shift to food problems fails to advance the meaning of intelligence, throwing the paragraph—and the reader—off track:

A DISUNIFIED PARAGRAPH

Whales are among the most intelligent of all mammals. Scientists rank whale intelligence with that of higher primates because of whales' sophisticated group behavior. These impressive mammals have been seen teaching and disciplining their young, helping their wounded comrades, engaging in elaborate courtship rituals, and playing in definite gamelike patterns. Whales continually need to search for food in order to survive. Their search for krill and other sea organisms can cause them to migrate thousands of miles yearly.

PARAGRAPH COHERENCE

In a coherent paragraph, everything not only belongs but also sticks together: Topic statement and support form *a connected line of thought,* like links in a chain.

This next paragraph (written by a track team veteran addressing new runners) is both unified and coherent: Everything relates to the topic in a continuous line of thinking.

A COHERENT PARAGRAPH

[1]*To be among the first out of the starting blocks in any race, follow these instructions.* [2]First, when the starter says "Into your blocks," make sure you are the last runner down. [3]Take your sweet time; make all the others wait for you. [4]You take your time for three good reasons: One, you get a little more stretching than your competitors do; two, they are down in the blocks getting cold and nervous while you're still warm and relaxed from stretching; and three, your deliberate manner tends to weaken other runners' confidence. [5]The second step is to lean forward over your shoulders, in the "set" position. [6]This way, you will come out of the blocks forward and low, meeting less wind resistance. [7]The third and final step is to pump your arms as fast as you can when you come off the blocks. [8]The faster your arms pump, the faster your legs will move. [9]By concentrating on each of these steps, you can expect your quickest possible start.

The material in this paragraph seems easy enough to follow:

1. The topic statement sets a clear direction.
2. The first step is introduced.
3–4. The importance of "taking your time" is emphasized and explained.
5–6. The second step is introduced and its importance explained.
7–8. The third step is introduced and its importance explained.
9. The conclusion sums up.

Because the material follows a logical order (in this case, chronological), readers know exactly where they are at any place in the paragraph. Let's now examine specific ways of achieving coherence.

Ordering Ideas for Coherence

The mind works in structured ways to arrange and make sense of its many perceptions. If you decide you like a class (a general observation), you then identify your particular reasons (friendly atmosphere, interesting subject, dynamic teacher, and so on); your thinking has followed a *general-to-specific order*. Or, if you tell a friend about your terrific weekend, you follow the order of events, how things happened over the weekend; your thinking has followed a *chronological order*. These are just two of several ordering patterns the mind uses to reveal a specific relationship. Here are the most common ordering patterns:

Common ways of arranging information

- general-to-specific order
- specific-to-general order
- emphatic order
- spatial order
- chronological order

These ordering patterns can help you answer the following questions:

- *What comes first?*
- *What comes next?*
- *Does the subject have any features that suggest an order?*

Answers will be based on your subject and purpose. In a letter describing your new car (subject) to a friend, you might decide to move from outside to inside in a spatial order, as one would when first examining the car. Or, if you decided to concentrate on the car's computerized dashboard (subject), you might move from left to right (as one would view it from the driver's seat). If, instead, you were trying to persuade someone to stay in school or to quit smoking, you probably would present your reasons in an emphatic order, from least to most important, or vice versa.

As we will see, some kinds of order call for your topic statement to come last instead of first. Even then, your opening sentence should tell readers what to expect. Before considering those variations, however, let's begin with the standard ordering pattern: general to specific.

General-to-Specific Order.   The most usual way of arranging a paragraph is from general to specific: *a general topic statement supported by specific details.* Most sample paragraphs we've seen so far follow a general-to-specific order, as this next one does:

STARTING WITH THE BIG PICTURE

General assertion (topic statement, 1)
Specific support (2–8)

Conclusion (9)

¹Americans everywhere are obsessed with speed. ²The airlines think it's so important that they've developed jets that can cross the ocean in a few hours. ³Despite energy shortages, Detroit often makes the speed of a car and the power of its engine a focal point of its advertising campaign. ⁴Ads for oil companies boast of 10-minute oil changes at their gas stations. ⁵Even pedestrians aren't spared: Some shoemakers will put soles and heels on shoes "while you wait." ⁶Fast-food restaurants prosper as increasing millions gobble increasing billions of "all-beef" hamburgers and guzzle their Cokes in seconds flat. ⁷And the Day of Rest, too, has given way to the stopwatch as more and more churches offer brief evening services or customize their offerings to suit "people on the go." ⁸Some churches even offer drive-in ceremonies—pay your money, spit out your prayer, and hit the road, streaking toward salvation with Ronald McDonald. *⁹These days, even the road to eternity has a fast lane.*

Paragraphs of general-to-specific order are the workhorses of virtually all nonfiction writing.

Specific-to-General Order. For some purposes, instead of narrowing and restricting your meaning, you will generalize and extend it. Thus, your *support will come first and your topic statement last.* A specific-to-general order is especially useful for showing how pieces of evidence add up to a convincing conclusion, as in this next paragraph.

STARTING WITH THE SUPPORTING DETAILS

Orienting statements (1–2)
Specific details (3–7)

General conclusion (topic statement, 8–9)

¹I've been thinking about seeing. ²There are lots of things to see, unwrapped gifts and free surprises. ³The world is fairly studded and strewn with pennies cast broadside from a generous hand. ⁴But—and this is the point—who gets excited by a mere penny? ⁵If you follow one arrow, if you crouch motionless on a bank to watch a tremulous ripple thrill on the water and are rewarded by the sight of a muskrat paddling from its den, will you count that sight a chip of copper only, and go your rueful way? ⁶It is dire poverty indeed when a man is so malnourished and fatigued that he won't stoop to pick up a penny. ⁷But if you cultivate a healthy poverty and simplicity, so that finding a penny will literally make your day, then, since the world is in fact planted in pennies, you have with your poverty bought a lifetime of days. *⁸It is that simple. ⁹What you see is what you get.*

—Annie Dillard

But even though the topic statement appears last, the opening statements forecast the paragraph. Whenever you decide to delay your topic sentence, be sure the paragraph's opening sentence gives readers enough orientation for them to know what's going on.

A specific-to-general order works best for supporting a position that some readers might disagree with, as in this next example:

SAVING THE BIG PICTURE FOR LAST

Specific observation in orienting statement (1)

Specific arguments (2–7)

¹Strange that so few ever come to the woods to see how the pine lives and grows and spires, lifting its evergreen arms to the light—to see its perfect success; but most are content to behold it in the shape of many broad boards brought to market, and deem *that* its true success! ²But the pine is no more lumber than [the person] is, and to be made into boards and houses is no more its true and highest use than the truest use of a [person] is to be cut down and made into manure. ³There is a higher law affecting our relations to pine as well as to [people]. ⁴A pine cut down, a dead pine, is no more a pine than a dead human carcass is a [person]. ⁵Can [one] who has discovered only some of the values of whalebone and whale oil be said to have discovered the true use of the whale? ⁶Can [one] who slays the elephant for [its] ivory be said to have "seen the elephant"? ⁷These are petty and accidental uses; just as if a stronger race were to kill us in order to make buttons and flutes of our bones; for everything may serve a lower as well as a higher use. ⁸*Every creature is better alive than dead, [people] and moose and pine trees, and [one] who understands it correctly will rather preserve its life than destroy it.*

General conclusion (topic statement, 8)

—*Henry David Thoreau*

Some readers (especially those in the paper and lumber industry, as well as hunters) would find Thoreau's main point harder to accept if it were placed at the beginning. By moving from the specific to the general, Thoreau presents his evidence before drawing his conclusion. Also, things that come last (last word in a sentence, last sentence in a paragraph, last paragraph in an essay) are the things readers remember best.

Emphatic Order. In earlier chapters, we've seen how emphasis can make important ideas stand out and become easier to remember. Writers *achieve emphasis within paragraphs by positioning material* in two common ways: (1) *from least to most important* or *serious* or *dramatic,* and (2) *vice versa.* The next paragraph is from an essay analyzing television advertisements for toys of violence. Joe Bolton places his strongest example last, for greatest emphasis.

HELPING READERS FOCUS

Topic statement (1–2)

Examples in increasing order of importance (3–5)

¹*Too many toys advertised during television programs for children are of what I call the "death and destruction" variety: toys that simulate the killing of humans by humans.* ²Such toys make children's "war games" seem far too real. ³During the pre-Christmas season, children are bombarded with ads promoting all the new weapons: guns, tanks, boats, subs, helicopters, lasers, and more. ⁴One new warplane is described as "the wickedest weapon yet," and a new mobile weapon resembles an old "Nike" missile, designed to be moved around on railroad tracks to avoid an enemy strike. ⁵One of the enemy dolls is even dubbed a "paranoid schizophrenic killer" and advertised as such on the side of the box.

Spatial Order.   Sometimes, you create a word picture by presenting the parts of your subject in the same order that readers would follow if they actually were looking at the item. In this next paragraph, the writer describes someone who is to be picked up at a busy airport.

HELPING READERS VISUALIZE

Topic statement

A gradually narrowing focus

Roger should be easy to recognize. When I last saw him, he was wearing dark blue jeans, a pair of dark brown hunting boots with red laces, and a light blue cableknit sweater with a turtleneck; he was carrying a red daypack with black trim filled with books. He stands about 6 feet 4 inches, has broad, slouching shoulders, and carries roughly 190 pounds on a medium frame. He walks in excessively long strides, like a cowboy. His hair is sunstreaked, sandy blond, cut just below his ears and feathered back on the sides. He has deep purple eyes framed by dark brown eyelashes and brows set into a clear, tanned complexion. The bridge of his nose carries a half-inch scar in the shape of an inverted crescent. His right front tooth has a small chip in the left corner.

The above sequence follows the order of features readers would recognize in approaching Roger: first, from a distance, by his clothing, size, posture, and stride; next, from a closer view—the hair, eye color, and so on; and finally, from right up close—the scar on his nose and the chip on his tooth. The earlier details, visible from a distance, would alert readers, and the later ones would confirm their impression as they moved nearer. The writer decided to take the angle of a movie camera gradually closing in.

Chronological Order.   A chronological order follows the *actual sequence of events.* Writers use chronological order to give instructions (how to be first out of the starting blocks), to explain how something works (how the heart pumps blood), or to show how something happened. This paragraph from George Orwell's essay "Shooting an Elephant" shows how something brutal happened. As with many paragraphs that tell a story, this one has no topic statement. Instead, the opening sentence places us in the middle of the action.

HELPING READERS EXPERIENCE

Orienting statement (1–2)

Sequence of events (3–16)

[1]When I pulled the trigger I did not hear the bang or feel the kick—one never does when a shot goes home—but I heard the devilish roar of glee that went up from the crowd. [2]In that instant, in too short a time, one would have thought, even for the bullet to get there, a mysterious, terrible change had come over the elephant. [3]He neither stirred nor fell, but every line on his body had altered. [4]He looked suddenly stricken, shrunken, immensely old, as though the frightful impact of the bullet had paralyzed him without knocking him down. [5]At last, after what seemed like a long time—it might have been five seconds, I dare say—he sagged flabbily to his knees. [6]His mouth slobbered. [7]An enormous senility seemed to have settled upon him. [8]One

> could have imagined him thousands of years old. [9]I fired again into the same spot. [10]At the second shot he did not collapse but climbed with desperate slowness to his feet and stood weakly upright, with legs sagging and head drooping. [11]I fired a third time. [12]That was the shot that did it for him. [13]You could see the agony of it jolt his whole body and knock the last remnant of strength from his legs. [14]But in falling he seemed for a moment to rise, for as his hind legs collapsed beneath him he seemed to tower upwards like a huge rock toppling, his trunk reaching skywards like a tree. [15]He trumpeted, for the first and only time. [16]And then down he came, his belly towards me, with a crash that seemed to shake the ground even where I lay.
>
> —*George Orwell*

The actual chronology in Orwell's paragraph is simple:

a. With the first shot, the elephant falls to its knees.
b. With the second shot, instead of collapsing, the elephant drags itself up.
c. With the third shot, the elephant falls, rises, and then falls for good.

But note that if narrating these events in order were the writer's only purpose, the paragraph might look like this:

TRACING THE EVENT

> When I pulled the trigger, a change came over the elephant. He neither stirred nor fell, but every line on his body had altered as if the impact of the bullet had paralyzed him without knocking him down. At last, he sagged to his knees. His mouth slobbered. I fired again into the same spot. At the second shot, he did not collapse but climbed slowly to his feet and stood with legs sagging and head drooping. I fired a third time. That was the shot that did it for him. But in falling he seemed for a moment to rise. And then, down he came, with his belly towards me, with a crash that shook the ground.

The above paragraph presents the kinds of details a camera might record.

Compare the first and second version of Orwell's paragraph. Which has the greatest impact? Why?

Note

This chapter asks you to practice specific strategies, but remember: When you write on your own, you won't begin by saying, "I've decided to write a spatial paragraph, and so now I need to find a subject that will fit that order." Instead, you will say, "I want to discuss X; therefore, I need to select the ordering pattern that best reveals my thinking." Much of your writing will, in fact, call for a combination of these ordering patterns.

Parallelism

Several other devices enhance coherence. The first is *parallelism*—similar grammatical structures and word order for similar items or for items of equal importance. Note how parallelism is employed in this next paragraph:

EXPRESSING EQUAL ITEMS EQUALLY

[1]*What is the shape of my life?* [2]The *shape* of my life today starts with a family. [3]I *have* a husband, five children, and a home just beyond the suburbs of New York. [4]I have also a craft, writing, and therefore work I want to pursue. [5]The *shape* of my life is, of course, determined by many other things: *my background* and childhood, *my mind and* its education, *my conscience and* its pressures, *my heart and* its desires. [6]I want *to give and take* from my children and husband, *to share* with friends and community, *to carry out* my obligations to [humanity] and *to the world, as a woman, as an artist, as a citizen.* [emphasis added]

—*Anne Morrow Lindbergh*

The above paragraph displays parallelism between as well as within sentences. Sentences 2 and 5 open with identical structures ("The shape of my life . . .") to signal that both sentences treat the same subject. Sentence 5 has four parallel phrases ("my background and . . . , my mind and . . . , my conscience and . . . , my heart and . . ."). These similar structures emphasize similarity between ideas, thereby tying the paragraph together. See page 120 for further discussion of parallelism.

Can you identify additional examples of parallelism in Morrow Lindbergh's paragraph?

Repetition, Restatement, and Variation

To help link ideas, repeat key words or phrases or rephrase them in different ways, as in this next paragraph (emphasis added):

FORWARDING THE MAIN IDEA

[1]*Whales are among the most intelligent of all mammals.* [2]Scientists rank whale *intelligence* with that of higher primates because of whales' *sophisticated* group behavior. [3]These *bright* creatures have been seen teaching and disciplining their young, helping their wounded comrades, engaging in elaborate courtship rituals, and playing in definite gamelike patterns. [4]They are able to coordinate such *complex cognitive activities* through their highly effective communication system of sonar clicks and pings. Such *remarkable social organization* apparently stems from the *humanlike* devotion that whales seem to display toward one another.

The signal word **intelligent** in the topic statement reappears as **intelligence** in sentence 2. Synonyms (different words with similar meaning) describing intelligent behavior (**sophisticated, bright, humanlike**) reinforce and advance the main idea throughout.

Note

Keep in mind that needless repetition makes writing tedious and annoying to read. For a clear distinction between effective and ineffective repetition, see page 125.

Pronouns for Coherence

Instead of repeating certain nouns, it is sometimes more natural to use pronouns that refer to an earlier key noun. Pronouns improve coherence by relating sentences, clauses, and phrases to each other. This next paragraph uses pronouns to avoid repeating **the bull fighters** (emphasis added):

USING PRONOUNS AS CONNECTORS

> The *bull fighters* march in across the sand to the president's box. *They* march with easy professional stride, swinging along, not in the least theatrical except for *their* clothes. *They* all have the easy grace and slight slouch of the professional athlete. From *their* faces *they* might be major league ball players. *They* salute the president's box then spread out along the barrera, exchanging *their* heavy brocaded capes for the fighting capes that have been laid along the red fence by the attendants.
>
> —*Ernest Hemingway*

Be sure each pronoun refers clearly to the appropriate noun. The pronouns in Hemingway's paragraph, for example, clearly refer to the **bull fighters.** See page 118 for a full discussion of pronoun-antecedent agreement.

Consistency for Coherence

Coherence always relies on consistent tense, point of view, and number. In general, do not shift from past to present tense, from third- to first-person point of view, or from singular to plural nouns or pronouns. See Appendix A for a discussion of shifts that destroy coherence.

Transitions

The above devices for achieving coherence (order, parallelism, repetition and restatement, pronouns) *suggest* specific relations between ideas. Transitional expressions, on the other hand, *announce* those relations. Words or phrases such as **for example, meanwhile, however,** and **moreover** work like bridges between thoughts. Each has a definite meaning—even without a specific context—as shown below.

TRANSITION	RELATION
X; meanwhile, Y	X and Y are occurring at the same time.
X; however, Y	Y is in contrast or exception to X.
X; moreover, Y	Y is in addition to X.
X; thus, Y	Y is a result of X.

Here is a paragraph in which these transitions are used to clarify the writer's line of thinking (emphasis added):

USING TRANSITIONS TO BRIDGE IDEAS

> Psychological and social problems of aging too often are aggravated by the final humiliation: poverty. One of every three older Americans lives near or below the poverty level. *Meanwhile,* only one of every nine younger adults lives in poverty. The American public assumes that Social Security and Medicare provide adequate support for the aged. These benefits alone, *however,* rarely are enough to raise an older person's living standards above the poverty level. *Moreover,* older people are the only group living in poverty whose population recently has increased rather than decreased. More and more of our aging citizens *thus* confront the prospect of living with less and less.

Note | *Transitional expressions should be a limited option for achieving coherence. Use them sparingly and only when a relationship is not already made clear by the devices discussed earlier.*

Whole sentences can serve as transitions between paragraphs, and a whole paragraph can serve as a transition between sections of writing. Assume, for instance, that you work as a marketing intern for a stereo manufacturer. You have just completed a section of a memo on the advantages of the new AKS amplifier and are now moving to a section on selling the idea to consumers. This next paragraph might link the two sections:

A TRANSITIONAL PARAGRAPH

> Because the AKS amplifier increases bass range by 15 percent, it should be installed as a standard item in all our stereo speakers. Tooling and installation adjustments, however, will add roughly $50 to the list price of each model. We must, therefore, explain the cartridge's long-range advantages to consumers. Let's consider ways of explaining these advantages.

Notice that this transitional paragraph *contains* transitional expressions, as well.

COMMON TRANSITIONS AND THE RELATIONS THEY INDICATE

An addition: *moreover, in addition, and, also*

> I am majoring in naval architecture; *also,* I spent three years crewing on a racing yawl.

Results: *thus, hence, therefore, accordingly, thereupon, as a result, and so, as a consequence*

> Mary enjoyed all her courses; *therefore,* she worked especially hard last semester.

An example or illustration: *for instance, to illustrate, for example, namely, specifically*

> Competition for part-time jobs is fierce; *for example,* 80 students applied for the clerk's job at Sears.

An explanation: *in other words, simply stated, in fact*

> Louise had a terrible semester; *in fact,* she flunked three courses.

COMMON TRANSITIONS AND THE RELATIONS THEY INDICATE *(Continued)*

A summary or conclusion: *in closing, to conclude, to summarize, in brief, in short, in summary, to sum up, all in all, on the whole, in retrospect, in conclusion*

> Our credit is destroyed, our bank account is overdrawn, and our debts are piling up; *in short,* we are bankrupt.

Time: *first, next, second, then, meanwhile, at length, later, now, the next day, in the meantime, in turn, subsequently*

> Mow the ball field this morning; *afterward,* clean the dugouts.

A comparison: *likewise, in the same way, in comparison, similarly*

> Our reservoir is drying up because of the drought; *similarly,* water supplies in neighboring towns are dangerously low.

A contrast or alternative: *however, nevertheless, yet, still, in contrast, otherwise, but, on the other hand, to the contrary, notwithstanding, conversely*

> Felix worked hard; *however,* his grades remained poor.

Application **6-1**

This next essay is shown without appropriate paragraph divisions. Mark the spot where each new paragraph should begin. *Hint:* Here is a rough (six-paragraph) outline: (1) introduction, (2) description of the plant, (3) a typical night shift, (4) the writer's specific job, (5) overview, (6) concluding story. Material that belongs together—and not length—should dictate specific paragraph divisions. (Review pages 98–99.)

SWING SHIFT

> Have you ever worked in a factory? Have you ever worked swing shift? Can you stand to function like a machine in 95-degree heat or more? Let alone stand it—can you work in it for eight hours of endless repetition and mindless labor? I did, for more than eight years. The Acme Tire and Rubber Company, about 5 miles east of our campus, resembles a prison. (Look for a massive and forbidding three-story building occupying two city blocks on Orchard Street.) The plant was built 50 years ago, and its windows, coated by the soot and grit of a half-century, admit no light, no hope of seeing in or out. Add to this dismal picture the drab red bricks and the stench of burned rubber. This is what I faced five nights a week at 10:00 P.M. when I reported for work. A worker's life inside the plant is arranged so as not to tax the mind. At exactly 10:00 P.M. a loud bell rings. Get to work. The bell has to be loud in order to be heard over the roar of machinery and hissing steam escaping from the

high-pressure lines. In time you don't even notice the noise. It took me about two weeks. At midnight the bell rings again: a ten-minute break. At 2:00 A.M. it rings again: lunch, 20 minutes. Two hours later, it rings for the last break of the night. At 6:00 A.M. the final bell announces that the long night is over; it's time to go home. My dreary job was stocking tires. (I say "was" because I quit the job last year.) I had to load push trucks, the kind you see in railroad depots. I picked the tires up from the curing presses. A curing press is an 8-foot-high by 6-foot-wide by 6-foot-deep pressure cooker. There are 18 curing presses all in a row, and the temperature around them is over 100 degrees. Clouds of steam hang just below the 20-foot ceiling. By the time I had worked for ten minutes, my clothes were drenched with sweat and reeked with the acrid stench of steamed rubber. Once the truck was full, I'd push it to the shipping department on the other side of the plant. It's quiet there; they ship only during the day. And it's cooler. I'd feel chilled even though the temperature was around 75 degrees. Here I would leave the full truck, look for an empty one, push it back, and start again. It was the same routine every night: endless truckloads of tires, five nights a week—every week. Nothing ever changed except the workers; they got older and worn out. I wasn't surprised to hear that a worker had hanged himself there a few weeks ago. He was a friend of mine. Another friend told me that the work went on anyway. The police said to leave the body hanging until the medical examiner could clear it—like so much meat hanging on a hook. Someone put a blanket around the hanging body. They had to move around it. The work went on.

—*Glenn Silverberg*

Application **6-2**

Identify the subject and the signal term in each of these sentences. (Review pages 102–03.)

EXAMPLE

The pressures of the sexual revolution are everywhere.

—*Joyce Maynard*

Subject   pressures of the sexual revolution
Signal term   everywhere

1. High voltage from utility transmission lines can cause bizarre human and animal behavior.
2. Nuclear power plants need stricter supervision.
3. Producers of television commercials have created a loathsome gallery of men and women patterned, presumably, on Mr. and Mrs. America.

—*Marya Mannes*

4. From the very beginning of school, we make books and reading a constant source of possible failure and possible humiliation.

—*John Holt*

5. High interest rates cripple the auto and housing industries.

Application **6-3**

Collaborative Project and Computer Application: The paragraph below is unified but not coherent, because the sentences are not in logical order. On computer disks, each member of your group should individually rearrange the sentences so that the line of thinking is clear, and then print a hard copy. As a group, compare your different versions, with each member explaining the order he or she chose. Then agree on a final version, which one group member will create by rearranging the sentences on his or her disk. Print this final version for the entire class, justifying your group's decisions.

> [1]Conditions in the state mental hospital are shameful. [2]Sedatives, soothing baths, occupational therapy, and individual counseling rarely are used because the hospital cannot afford them. [3]Hundreds of patients are left in filthy conditions, never receiving the care they desperately need. [4]When my sociology class toured the hospital, we spent the entire morning walking through the wards and talking to the attendants. [5]Because the windows are kept closed, the air is damp and musty. [6]On the whole, anyone who tours the mental hospital can't help feeling ashamed of this state. [7]Patients lie for hours staring vacantly at the dirty ceiling. [8]Some of them listen to the radio or watch television hour after hour. [9]The big brick building is two miles from the main highway, and many people do not even know there is such a place. [10]The food is cold and unappetizing. [11]The hospital has only three physicians for more than 500 patients. [12]Straitjackets, ropes, and leather straps are used to tie down violent patients.

Application **6-4**

Select one of these assignments and write a paragraph organized from the general to the specific.

- Picture the ideal summer job. Explain to an employer why you would like the job.
- Assume that it's time for end-of-semester student course evaluations. Write a one-paragraph evaluation of your favorite course to be read by your professor's department chairperson.
- Explain your views on video games. Write for your classmates.
- Describe the job outlook in your chosen field. Write for a high school senior interested in your major.

Application **6-5**

Identify a problem in a group to which you belong (such as family, club, sorority). Or select a topic from the following list or make up one of your own. After reviewing page 106, write two emphatic paragraphs, one featuring the emphatic material at the beginning and the other positioning it at the end. Be prepared to explain which version works best for you and why.

- Advice to an entering freshman about surviving in college
- Your life goal to your academic advisor, who is recommending you for a scholarship
- Your reasons for wanting to live off campus to the dean of students

Application **6-6**

Select the best paragraph or essay you have written thus far (or one that your instructor suggests). Using the strategies in this chapter, revise the paragraph or essay for improved coherence. After revising, list the specific strategies you employed (logical order, parallelism, repetition of key terms, restatement, pronouns, transitions).

Application **6-7**

Web-based Project: Even after reading this chapter, a classmate of yours admits to not having a good understanding of how and when to start a new paragraph, let alone how to use paragraphs effectively to structure and develop an argument. "I just indent and start a new paragraph when it looks right," she says. Your project is to do some research on the Web in order to develop a one-page handout for your classmate (and others who may have similar difficulties grasping the subtleties of paragraphs) that presents some practical strategies for using paragraphs more effectively.

Here are some good places to start your search:

- A basic review of paragraph elements
  <http://owl.english.purdue.edu/handouts/general/gl_pgrph2.html>
- A closer look at paragraph balance and length consistency; a visual model for evaluating paragraph development
  <http://owl.english.purdue.edu/handouts/general/gl_pgrph.html>
- Guidelines on using paragraphs to build an argument, with a sample exercise in paragraph unity
  <http://www.eslplanet.com/teachertools/argueweb/chlcare.htm>

- Good information on paragraph development and focus
  <http://ccc.commnet.edu/grammar/paragraphs.htm>
- An overview of paragraph strategies, primarily for argumentative writing
  <http://www.uottawa.ca/academic/arts/writcent/hypergrammar/paragrph.html#paragraphs>

Attach a copy of the relevant Web page(s) to your presentation. Be sure to credit each source of information (page 392).

CHAPTER 7

Revising the Sentences: Writing with Style

Aim for Clarity **118**

Trim the Fat **124**

Help Sentences Flow **131**

Applications **123, 129, 133**

A definition of style

Every bit as important as *what* you have to say is *how* you decide to say it. Your particular *writing style* is a blend of these elements:

What determines your style

- The way in which you construct each sentence
- The length of your sentences
- The way in which you connect sentences
- The words and phrases you choose
- The tone you convey

No matter how vital your content and how sensible your organization, readers' needs will not be served unless your style is *readable:* sentences easy to navigate and words precisely chosen.

Note

One requirement for readable sentences is, of course, correct grammar, punctuation, and spelling. But beyond being merely "correct," readable sentences emphasize relationships among ideas, make every word count, and flow smoothly.

117

These guidelines will help you write clear sentences that convey your meaning on the first reading.

Keep Your Pronoun References Clear

Pronouns (**she, it, his, their,** and so on) must clearly refer to the nouns they replace.

Ambiguous referent	Our patients enjoy the warm days while **they** last. [*Are the patients or the warm days on the way out?*]

Depending on whether the referent (or antecedent) for *they* is *patients* or *warm days,* the sentence can be clarified.

Clear referent	While these warm days last, our patients enjoy them.
	or
	Our terminal patients enjoy these warm days.
Ambiguous	Sally told Sarah that **she** was obsessed with **her** job.
Revised	Sally told Sarah, "I'm obsessed with my job."
	Sally told Sarah, "I'm obsessed with your job."

What other interpretations are possible for the ambiguous sentence above?
    Avoid using **this, that,** or **it**—especially to begin a sentence—unless the pronoun refers to a specific antecedent (referent).

Vague	The problem with our defective machinery is only compounded by the new operator's incompetence. **This** annoys me!
Revised	I am annoyed by the problem with our defective machinery, as well as by the new operator's incompetence.

See Appendix C for more on pronoun reference and pages 151–52 for avoiding sexist bias in pronoun usage.

Avoid Ambiguous Modifiers

A modifier is a word (usually an adjective or adverb) or a group of words (usually a phrase or a clause) that provides information about other words or groups of words. If a modifier is too far from the words it modifies, the message can be ambiguous.

Misplaced modifier	**Only** press the red button in an emergency. [*Does "only" modify "press" or "emergency"?*]
Revised	Press **only** the red button in an emergency.
	or
	Press the red button in an emergency **only.**

Another problem with ambiguity occurs when a modifying phrase has no word to modify.

Dangling modifier	**Being so well respected in the scientific field,** I would appreciate your recommendation.

The writer meant to say that the *reader* is well known, but with no word to connect to, the modifying phrase dangles. Eliminate the confusion by adding a subject:

Revised	Because **you** are so well respected in the scientific field, I would appreciate your recommendation.

See Appendix A for more on modifiers.

Avoid Cramming

A sentence crammed with ideas makes details hard to remember and relationships hard to identify.

Crammed	A smoke-filled room causes not only teary eyes and runny noses but also can alter people's hearing and vision, as well as creating dangerous levels of carbon monoxide, especially for people with heart and lung ailments, whose health is particularly threatened by "second-hand" smoke.

Clear things up by sorting out the relationships:

Revised	Besides causing teary eyes and runny noses, a smoke-filled room can alter people's hearing and vision. One of "second-hand" smoke's biggest dangers, however, is high levels of carbon monoxide, a particular health threat for people with heart and lung ailments.

Give readers no more information in one sentence than they can retain and process.

Keep Equal Items Parallel

To reflect relationships among items of equal importance, express them in identical grammatical form (see also page 108).

For example, if you begin the series with a noun, use nouns throughout the series; likewise for adjectives, adverbs, and specific types of clauses and phrases.

Faulty	The new tutor is **enthusiastic, skilled,** and **you can depend on her.**
Revised	The new tutor is **enthusiastic, skilled,** and **dependable.** [*all subjective complements*]
Faulty	In his new job, Ramon felt **lonely** and **without a friend.**
Revised	In his new job, Ramon felt **lonely** and **friendless.** [*both adjectives*]
Faulty	Lulu plans **to study** all this month and **on scoring** well in her licensing examination.
Revised	Lulu plans **to study** all this month and **to score** well in her licensing examination. [*both infinitive phrases*]

Arrange Word Order for Coherence and Emphasis

In coherent writing, everything sticks together; each sentence builds on the preceding sentence and looks ahead to the following sentence. Sentences generally work best when the beginning looks back at familiar information and the end provides the new (or unfamiliar) information.

Effective word order

FAMILIAR		UNFAMILIAR
My dog	has	fleas.
Our boss	just won	the lottery.
This company	is planning	a merger.

Besides helping a message stick together, the familiar-to-unfamiliar structure emphasizes the new information. Just as every paragraph has a key sentence, every sentence has a key word or phrase that sums up the new information. That key word or phrase usually is emphasized best when it appears at the end of the sentence.

Faulty emphasis	We expect a **refund** because of your error in our shipment.
Correct	Because of your error in our shipment, we expect a **refund.**
Faulty emphasis	After your awful behavior, an **apology** is something I expect. But I'll probably get an excuse.
Correct	After your awful behavior, I expect an **apology.** But I'll probably get an excuse.

One exception to placing key words last occurs with an imperative statement (a command, an order, an instruction) with the subject [*you*] understood. For instance, each step in a list of instructions should contain an action verb (**insert, open, close, turn, remove, press**). To give readers a forecast, place the verb in that instruction at the beginning.

Correct	**Insert** the diskette before activating the system.
	Remove the protective seal.

With the key word at the beginning of the instruction, readers know immediately the action they need to take.

av Use Active Voice Often

A verb's *voice* signals whether a sentence's subject acts or is acted upon. The active voice (**I did it**) is more direct, concise, and persuasive than the passive voice (**It was done by me**). In active voice sentences, a clear agent performs the action on a recipient:

	AGENT	ACTION	RECIPIENT
Active	Leslie	lost	your report.
	SUBJECT	VERB	OBJECT

Passive voice reverses this pattern, placing the recipient of the action in the subject slot:

	RECIPIENT	ACTION	AGENT
Passive	Your report	was lost	by Leslie.
	SUBJECT	VERB	PREPOSITIONAL PHRASE

Sometimes the passive eliminates the agent altogether:

Passive	Your report was lost. [*Who lost it?*]

Note	*Passive voice is unethical if it obscures the person or other agent who performed the action when that responsible person should be identified.*

Some writers mistakenly rely on the passive voice because they think it sounds more objective and important. But the passive voice often makes writing seem merely wordy or evasive and harder to understand:

Concise and direct (active)	**I underestimated** expenses for this semester. [*6 words*]
Wordy and indirect (passive)	Expenses for this semester **were underestimated by me.** [*8 words*]
Evasive (passive)	Expenses for this semester **were underestimated.**

In reporting errors or bad news, use the active voice for clarity and sincerity. Do not evade responsibility by hiding behind the passive voice:

Passive	A mistake was made in your shipment. [*By whom?*]
"irresponsibles"	It was decided not to hire you. [*Who decided?*]

Use the active voice when you want action. Otherwise, your statement will have no power:

Weak passive	If my claim is not settled by May 15, the Better Business Bureau will be contacted, and their advice on legal action will be taken.
Strong active	If you do not settle my claim by May 15, I will contact the Better Business Bureau for advice on legal action.

Ordinarily, use the active voice for giving instructions:

Faulty passive	The door to the cobra's cage should be locked.
	Care should be taken with the dynamite.
Correct active	Lock the door to the cobra's cage.
	Be careful with the dynamite.

pv

Use Passive Voice Selectively

Passive voice is appropriate in lab reports and other documents in which the agent's identity is immaterial to the message.

Use the passive voice if the person behind the action needs to be protected.

Correct passive	The criminal **was identified.**
	The victim **was asked** to testify.

Similarly, use the passive when the agent is unknown, unapparent, or unimportant:

Correct passive	Mr. Jones **was brought** to the emergency room.
	The bank failure **was publicized** statewide.
	All policy claims **are kept** confidential.

Prefer the passive when you want to be indirect or inoffensive:

Active but offensive	**You have not paid** your bill.
	You need to overhaul our filing system.
Inoffensive passive	This bill **has not been paid.**
	Our filing system **needs overhauling.**

Application **7-1**

These sentences are unclear because of faulty modification, unclear pronoun reference, overstuffing, faulty parallelism, or key words buried in midsentence. Revise them so that their meaning is clear. For sentences suggesting two meanings, write separate versions—one for each meaning intended. (Review pages 118–21.)

1. Bill told Fred that he was mistaken.
2. In all writing, revision is required.
3. Only use this elevator in a fire.
4. Making the shelves look neater was another of my tasks at X-Mart that is very important to a store's business because if the merchandise is not always neatly arranged, customers will not have a good impression, whereas if it is neat they probably will return.
5. Wearing high boots, the snake could not hurt me.
6. As Pierre drove away from his menial job, boring lifestyle, and damp apartment, he was happy to be leaving it behind.
7. While they snacked on dead fish, our kids enjoyed watching the alligators.
8. Education enables us to recognize excellence and to achieve it.
9. Student nurses are required to identify diseases and how to treat them.
10. My car needs an oil change, a grease job, and the carburetor should be adjusted.

Application **7-2**

Convert these passive voice sentences to concise, forceful, and direct expressions in the active voice. (Review pages 121–22.)

1. The evaluation was performed by us.
2. The essay was written by me.
3. Unless you pay me within three days, my lawyer will be contacted.
4. Hard hats should be worn at all times.
5. It was decided to decline your invitation.

Application **7-3**

The sentences below lack appropriate emphasis because of improper use of the active voice. Convert each to passive voice. (Review page 122.)

1. Joe's company fired him.
2. You are paying inadequate attention to student safety.

3. A power surge destroyed more than 2,000 lines of our new computer program.

4. You did a poor job editing this report.

5. The selection committee awarded Mary a Fulbright Scholarship.

TRIM THE FAT

Concise writing conveys the most meaning in the fewest words. But it does not omit the details necessary for clarity. Use fewer words whenever fewer will do.

Cluttered	At this point in time I must say that I need a vacation.
Concise	I need a vacation now.

First drafts rarely are concise. Trim the fat:

Avoid Wordy Phrases

Each phrase here can be reduced to one word.

Revising wordy phrases

at this point in time	=	now
has the ability to	=	can
aware of the fact that	=	know
due to the fact that	=	because
dislike very much	=	hate
the majority of	=	most
on a daily basis	=	daily
in close proximity	=	near

Eliminate Redundancy

A redundant expression says the same thing twice in different words, as in **fellow classmates.**

Spotting redundant phrases

a [dead] corpse	enter [into]
the reason [why]	[totally] monopolize
[utmost] perfection	[totally] oblivious
[mental] awareness	[very] vital
[the month of] August	[past] experience
[mutual] cooperation	[future] prospects
mix [together]	[free] gift

rep Avoid Needless Repetition

Unnecessary repetition clutters writing and dilutes meaning.

Repetitious	In trauma victims, breathing is restored by **artificial respiration.** Techniques of **artificial respiration** include mouth-to-mouth **respiration** and mouth-to-nose **respiration.**

Repetition in the above passage disappears when sentences are combined.

Concise	In trauma victims, breathing is restored by artificial respiration, either mouth-to-mouth or mouth-to-nose.

Note   *Don't hesitate to repeat, or at least rephrase, if you feel that readers need reminders. Effective repetition helps avoid cross-references like these: "See page 3" or "Review page 1."*

Th Avoid *There* and *It* Sentence Openers

Many **There is, There are,** and **It** sentence openers can be eliminated.

Faulty	There are several good reasons why Boris dropped out of school.
Concise	Boris dropped out of school for several good reasons.

Of course, in some contexts, proper emphasis would call for a **There** opener.

Correct	People often have wondered about the rationale behind Boris's sudden decision. There are several good reasons for his dropping out of school.

Most often, however, **There** openers are best dropped.

Faulty	There is a serious fire danger created by your smoking in bed.
Concise	Your smoking in bed creates danger of fire.
Wordy	It gives me great pleasure to introduce our speaker.
Concise	I am pleased to introduce our speaker.

np Avoid Needless Phrases

To be, as well as **that** and **which** phrases, often can be cut.

Wordy	She seems [to be] upset.
Wordy	I find some of my classmates [to be] brilliant.

Wordy	The Batmobile is a car [that is] worth buying.
Wordy	This [is a] math problem [that] is impossible to solve.
Wordy	The book [,which is] about Hemingway [,] is fascinating.

Avoid Weak Verbs

Prefer verbs that express a definite action: **open, close, move, continue, begin.** Avoid verbs that express no specific action: **is, was, are, has, give, make, come, take.** All forms of the verb **to be** are weak.

In some cases, such verbs are essential to your meaning: "Dr. Johnson is operating at 7 A.M." "Take me to your leader."

Substitute a strong verb for conciseness:

Weak and wordy	Please **take into consideration** my application.
Concise	Please **consider** my application.

Here are some weak verbs converted to strong:

Revising weak verbs

give a summary of	=	summarize
make an assumption	=	assume
come to the conclusion	=	conclude
take action	=	act
make a decision	=	decide
come to the realization	=	realize

Strong verbs, or action verbs, suggest an assertive, positive, and confident writer.

Avoid Excessive Prepositions

Wordy	Some **of** the members **of** the committee made these recommendations.
Concise	Some committee members made these recommendations.
Wordy	I gave the money **to** Sarah.
Concise	I gave Sarah the money.

Avoid Nominalizations

Nouns manufactured from verbs (nominalizations) often accompany weak verbs and needless prepositions.

Weak and wordy	We ask for the **cooperation** of all students.

Strong and concise	We ask that all students **cooperate.**
Weak and wordy	Give **consideration** to the possibility of a career change.
Strong and concise	**Consider** a career change.

Besides causing wordiness, nominalizations can be vague—by hiding the agent of an action.

Wordy and vague	A need for immediate action exists. [*Who should take the action? We can't tell.*]
Precise	We must act immediately.

Nominalizations drain the life from your style. For example, in cheering for your favorite team, you wouldn't say "Blocking of that kick is a necessity!" instead of "Block that kick!"

Note *Avoid excessive economy. For example, "All students must cooperate" would not be an acceptable alternative to the first example in this section. But, for the final example, "Block that kick" would be.*

Here are nominalizations restored to their verb forms:

Trading nouns for verbs

conduct an investigation of	=	investigate
provide a description of	=	describe
conduct a test of	=	test
engage in the preparation of	=	prepare
make a discovery of	=	discover

Verbs are generally easier to read because they signal action.

Make Negatives Positive

A positive expression is easier to understand than a negative one.

INDIRECT AND WORDY	Please do not be late in submitting your report.
DIRECT AND CONCISE	Please submit your report on time.

Readers work even harder to translate sentences with multiple negative expressions:

CONFUSING AND WORDY	Do **not** distribute this memo to employees who have **not** received security clearance.
CLEAR AND CONCISE	Distribute this memo only to employees who have received security clearance.

Besides the directly negative words (*no, not, never*), some indirectly negative words (*except, forget, mistake, lose, uncooperative*) also force readers to translate.

CONFUSING AND WORDY	**Do not neglect** to activate the alarm system.
	My diagnosis was **not inaccurate.**
CLEAR AND CONCISE	**Be sure** to activate the alarm system.
	My diagnosis was **accurate.**

The positive versions are more straightforward *and* persuasive.

Some negative expressions, of course, are perfectly correct, as in expressing disagreement.

CORRECT NEGATIVES	This is **not** the best plan.
	Your offer is **unacceptable.**
	This project **never** will succeed.

Prefer positives to negatives, though, whenever your meaning allows:

Trading negatives for positives

did not succeed	=	failed
does not have	=	lacks
did not prevent	=	allowed
not unless	=	only if
not until	=	only when
not absent	=	present

cl Clear Out Clutter Words

Clutter words stretch a message without adding meaning. Here are some of the commonest: **very, definitely, quite, extremely, rather, somewhat, really, actually, situation, aspect, factor.**

Cluttered	**Actually,** one **aspect** of a relationship **situation** that could **definitely** make me **very** happy would be to have a **somewhat** adventurous partner who **really** shared my **extreme** love of traveling.
Concise	I'd like to meet an adventurous person who loves traveling.

pref Delete Needless Prefaces

Instead of delaying the new information in your sentence, get right to the point.

Wordy	[I am writing this letter because] I wish to apply for the position of dorm counselor.
Wordy	[The conclusion we can draw is that] writing is hard work.

 ### Delete Needless Qualifiers

Qualifiers such as **I feel, it would seem, I believe, in my opinion,** and **I think** express uncertainty or soften the tone and impact of a statement.

Appropriate qualifiers	Despite Frank's poor academic performance last semester, he will, **I think,** do well in college.
	Your product **seems to be** what I need.

But when you are certain, eliminate the qualifier so as not to seem tentative or evasive.

Needless qualifiers	[It seems that] I've wrecked the family car.
	[It would appear that] I've lost your credit card.
	[In my opinion,] you've done a good job.

Note

In communicating across cultures, keep in mind that a direct, forceful style might be considered offensive (page 153).

Application **7-4**

Make these sentences more concise by eliminating redundancies and needless repetition. (Review pages 124–25.)

1. She is a woman who works hard.
2. I am aware of the fact that Sam is a trustworthy person.
3. Clarence completed his assignment in a short period of time.
4. Bruno has a stocky build.
5. Sally is a close friend of mine.
6. I've been able to rely on my parents in the past.

Application **7-5**

Make these sentences more concise by eliminating **There is** and **There are** sentence openers, and the needless use of **it, to be, is, of, that,** and **which.** (Review pages 125–26.)

1. I consider Martha to be a good friend.
2. Our summer house, which is located on Cape Cod, is for sale.
3. The static electricity that is generated by the human body is measurable.
4. Writing must be practiced in order for it to become effective.
5. Another reason the job is attractive is because the salary is excellent.
6. There are many activities and sports that I enjoy very much, but the one that stands out in my mind is the sport of jogging.
7. Friendship is something that people should be honest about.
8. Smoking of cigarettes is considered by many people to be the worst habit of all habits of human beings.
9. There are many students who are immature.
10. It is necessary for me to leave immediately.

Application **7-6**

Make these sentences more concise by replacing weak verbs with strong ones and nouns with verbs, by changing negatives to positives, and by clearing out clutter words, needless prefatory expressions, and needless qualifiers. (Review pages 126–29.)

1. I have a preference for Ferraris.
2. Your conclusion is in agreement with mine.
3. We request the formation of a committee of students for the review of grading discrepancies.
4. I am not unappreciative of your help.
5. Actually, I am very definitely in love with you.
6. I find Susan to be an industrious and competent employee.
7. It seems that I've made a mistake in your order.
8. Igor does not have any friends at this school.
9. In my opinion, winter is an awful season.
10. As this academic year comes upon us, I realize that I will have trouble commuting to school this semester.
11. There is an undergraduate student attrition causes study needed at our school.
12. A need for your caution exists.
13. Never fail to attend classes.
14. Our acceptance of the offer is a necessity.

HELP SENTENCES FLOW

Fluent sentences are easy to read because of clear connections, variety, and emphasis. Their varied length and word order eliminate choppiness and monotony. Fluent sentences enhance *clarity*, emphasizing the most important idea. Fluent sentences enhance *conciseness*, often replacing several short, repetitious sentences with one longer, more economical sentence. To write fluently, use the following strategies:

Combine Related Ideas

| Disconnected | Jogging can be healthful. You need the right equipment. Most necessary are well-fitting shoes. Without this equipment you take the chance of injuring your legs. Your knees are especially prone to injury. [*5 sentences*] |

| Clear, concise, and fluent | Jogging can be healthful if you have the right equipment. Shoes that fit well are most necessary because they prevent injury to your legs, especially your knees. [*2 sentences*] |

Most sets of information can be combined to form different relationships, depending on what you want to emphasize. Imagine that this set of facts describes an applicant for a ski instructor's position:

- Sarah James has been skiing since age three.
- She has no experience teaching skiing.
- She has won several slalom competitions.

Assume that you are Snow Mountain Ski Area's head instructor, conveying your impression of this candidate to the manager. To convey a negative impression, you might combine the facts in this way:

| Strongly negative emphasis | Although Sarah James has been skiing since age three and has won several slalom competitions, **she has no experience teaching skiing.** |

The *independent idea* (in boldface) receives the emphasis (also see page 509 on subordination). But if you are undecided, yet leaning in a negative direction, you might write:

| Slightly negative emphasis | Sarah James has been skiing since age 3 and has won several slalom competitions, **but** she has no experience teaching skiing. |

In this sentence, the ideas before and after **but** are both independent. Joining them with the coordinating word **but** suggests that both sides of the issue are equally important (or "coordinate"). Placing the negative idea last, however, gives it slight emphasis. (See also page 508 on coordination.)

Finally, to emphasize strong support for the candidate, you could say:

> **Positive emphasis**   Although Sarah James has no experience teaching skiing, **she has been skiing since age three and has won several slalom competitions.**

Here, the earlier idea is subordinated by **although,** leaving the two final ideas independent.

Note   *Combine sentences only to simplify the reader's task. Overstuffed sentences with too much information and two many connections can be hard for readers to sort out. Notice how many times you have to read the following overstuffed instruction in order to understand what to do:*

> **Overcombined**   In developing less than a tankful of film, be sure to put in enough empty reels to fill all the space in the tank so that the film-loaded reels won't slide around when the tank is agitated.

 ## Vary Sentence Construction and Length

Related ideas often need to be linked in one sentence so that readers can grasp the connections.

> **Disconnected**   The nuclear core reached critical temperature. The loss-of-coolant alarm was triggered. The operator shut down the reactor.
>
> **Connected**   As the nuclear core reached critical temperature, triggering the loss-of-coolant alarm, the operator shut down the reactor.

But an idea that should stand alone for emphasis needs a whole sentence of its own:

> **Correct**   Core meltdown seemed inevitable.

However, an unbroken string of long or short sentences can bore and confuse readers, as can a series with identical openings:

> **Dreary**   There are some drawbacks about diesel engines. They are difficult to start in cold weather. They cause vibration. They also give off an unpleasant odor. They cause sulfur dioxide pollution.

> **Varied** Diesel engines have some drawbacks. Most obvious are their noisiness, cold-weather starting difficulties, vibration, odor, and sulfur dioxide emission.

Similarly, when you write in the first person, overusing **I** makes you appear self-centered. Do not, however, avoid personal pronouns if they make the writing more readable (say, by eliminating passive constructions).

Use Short Sentences for Special Emphasis

All this talk about combining ideas might suggest that short sentences have no place in good writing. Wrong. Short sentences (even one-word sentences) provide vivid emphasis. They stick in a reader's mind. Consider a student pilot's description of taking off:

> Our airspeed increases. The plane vibrates. We reach the point where the battle begins.

Instead, the student might have written:

> As our airspeed increases, the plane vibrates, and we reach the point where the battle begins.

However, she wanted to emphasize three discrete phases here: (1) the acceleration, (2) the vibration, and (3) the critical point of lifting off the ground.

Application **7-7**

The sentence sets below lack fluency because they are disconnected, have no variety, or have no emphasis. Combine each set into one or two fluent sentences.

> **Choppy** The world's forests are now disappearing. The rate of disappearance is 18 to 20 million hectares a year (an area half the size of California). Most of this loss occurs in humid tropical forests. These forests are in Asia, Africa, and South America.
>
> **Revised** The world's forests are now disappearing at the rate of 18 to 20 million hectares a year (an area half the size of California). Most of this loss is occurring in the humid tropical forests of Africa, Asia, and South America.*

---

*Sample sentences are adapted from *Global Year 2000 Report to the President: Entering the 21st Century* (Washington, DC: Government Printing Office, 1980).

1. The world's population is growing.
   It has grown from 4 billion in 1975.
   It has reached 6.5 billion in 2000.
   This is an increase of more than 50 percent.

2. In sheer numbers, population is growing.
   It is growing faster than in 1975.
   It adds 100 million people each year.
   This figure compares with 75 million in 1975.

3. Energy prices are expected to rise.
   Many less-developed countries will have increasing difficulty.
   Their difficulty will be in meeting energy needs.

4. One-quarter of humanity depends primarily on wood.
   They depend on wood for fuel.
   For them, the outlook is bleak.

5. The world has finite fuel resources.
   These include coal, oil, gas, oil shale, and uranium.
   These resources, theoretically, are sufficient for centuries.
   These resources are not evenly distributed.

Application **7-8**

Combine each set of sentences below into one or two fluent sentences that provide the requested emphasis.

Sentence set	John is a loyal employee. John is a motivated employee John is short-tempered with his colleagues.
Combined for positive emphasis	Even though John is short-tempered with his colleagues, he is a loyal and motivated employee.
Sentence set	This word processor has many excellent features. It includes a spelling checker. It includes a thesaurus. It includes a grammar checker.
Combined to emphasize the thesaurus	Among its many excellent features, such as spelling and grammar checkers, this word processor includes a thesaurus.

1. The job offers an attractive salary.

   It demands long work hours.

   Promotions are rapid.

   (*Combine for negative emphasis.*)

2. The job offers an attractive salary.

   It demands long work hours.

   Promotions are rapid.

   (*Combine for positive emphasis.*)

3. Company X gave us the lowest bid.

   Company Y has an excellent reputation.

   (*Combine to emphasize Company Y.*)

4. Superinsulated homes are energy efficient.

   Superinsulated homes can promote indoor air pollution.

   The toxins include radon gas and urea formaldehyde.

   (*Combine for negative emphasis.*)

5. Computers cannot think for the writer.

   Computers eliminate many mechanical writing tasks.

   They speed the flow of information.

   (*Combine to emphasize the first assertion.*)

Application **7-9**

Collaborative Project and Computer Application: Have each group member revise this next passage to improve fluency by combining related ideas; by varying sentence structure, openings, and length; and by using short sentences for special emphasis. (*Note:* When rephrasing to achieve conciseness, be sure to preserve the meaning of the original.) Then compare your versions and collaborate on an effective revision to present to the class.

Each summer, semitropical fish appear in New England salt ponds. They are carried northward by the Gulf Stream. The Gulf Stream is a warm ocean current. It flows like a river through the cold Atlantic. It originates in the Caribbean. It winds through the Florida straits. It meanders northward along the eastern coast of the United States. Off the shore of Cape Hatteras, North Carolina, the Gulf Stream's northerly course veers. It veers slightly eastward. This veering moves the stream and its warming influence farther from the coast. Semitropical fish are swept into the Gulf Stream from their breeding ground. The breeding ground is south of Cape Hatteras. The fish are carried northward. The strong current carries them. The current is often 20 degrees warmer than adjacent waters. Some of these fish are trapped in eddies. Eddies are pools of warm water that split from the Gulf Stream. These pools drift shoreward. By midsummer the ocean water off the New England coast is warm. It is warm enough to attract some fish out of the eddies and nearer to shore. In turn, even warmer water flows from the salt ponds. It flows to the ocean. It attracts these warm-water fish. They are attracted into the ponds. Here they spend the rest of the summer. They die off in the fall. The ponds cool in the fall.

Application **7-10**

Computer Application: Try the grammar function of your word processing program. First, look for problems with clarity, conciseness, and fluency yourself. Then compare your changes with those the computer suggests. If the computer contradicts your own judgment, ask a classmate or your peer group for feedback. If the computer suggests changes that seem ungrammatical or incorrect, consult a good handbook for confirmation. Try to assess when and how the grammar function can be useful and when you can revise best on your own.

For class discussion, prepare a list of the advantages and disadvantages of your automated grammar checker: Use your grammar checker on the first two sentences from Applications 7-1 through 7-6. Are the suggested changes correct? Which of the topics covered in this chapter does the checker miss?

Application **7-11**

Web-based Project: Based on material you assemble from a Web search, develop a set of "key questions about sentence structure and style" that your classmates can use when responding to each other's drafts (or their own). For example: *Where can any words be trimmed? Where can visual details be added? Where can sentences be combined?*

Design your questions as a one-page response form that your classmates could actually use to evaluate and assess the style of a peer's draft essay.

Here are some good places to start your online research:

- *The Elements of Style,* complete text online
  <http://www.bartleby.com/141/index.html>
- *Guide to Grammar and Style,* by Jack Lynch
  <http://newark.rutgers.edu/~jlynch/Writing/>
- *Paradigm Online Writing Assistant, The Editing Process*
  <http://www.powa.org/editfrms.htm>

Attach a copy of the relevant Web page(s) to your presentation. Be sure to credit each source of information (page 392).

CHAPTER 8

Revising the Words and Phrases: Fine-Tuning

Say Something Genuine   **138**

Aim for Precision   **139**

Sharpen the Visual Details   **143**

Add Some Personality   **145**

   Guidelines for Deciding about Tone   147

   Guidelines for Achieving a Conversational Tone   147

Invite Everyone In   **151**

   Guidelines for Nonsexist Usage   152

   Guidelines for Inoffensive Usage   154

Legal and Ethical Implications of Word Choice   **156**

Using Automated Editing Tools Effectively   **157**

Applications   **139, 143, 145, 155**

The quality of our contact with an audience ultimately depends on the wording we choose and the tone we convey.

SAY SOMETHING GENUINE

Readers look between the lines for a real person; don't disappoint them.

Avoid Triteness

Writers who rely on tired old phrases (clichés) come across as too lazy or too careless to find exact, unique ways to say what they mean:

Worn-out phrases

first and foremost	tough as nails
in the final analysis	holding the bag
needless to say	up the creek
work like a dog	over the hill
last but not least	bite the bullet
dry as a bone	fly off the handle
victim of circumstance	get on the stick

If it sounds like a "catchy phrase" you've heard before, don't use it.

Avoid Overstatement

Exaggeration sounds phony. Be cautious when using words such as **best, biggest, brightest, most,** and **worst.** Recognize the differences among **always, usually, often, sometimes,** and **rarely** or among **all, most, many, some,** and **few.**

Overstated
> You never listen to my ideas.
> Everything you say is obnoxious.
> This is the worst essay I've ever read.

How would you rephrase the above examples to make them more reasonable?

Avoid Misleading Euphemisms

A form of understatement, euphemisms are expressions aimed at politeness or at making unpleasant subjects seem less offensive. Thus, we **powder our noses** or **use the boy's room** instead of **using the bathroom;** we **pass away** or **meet our Maker** instead of **dying.**

When euphemisms avoid offending or embarrassing people, they are perfectly legitimate. But they are unethical if they understate the truth when only the truth will serve:

When a euphemism is deceptive

- Instead of being **laid off** or **fired,** employees are **surplused** or **deselected,** or the company is **downsized.**
- Instead of **lying** to the public, the government engages in a **policy of disinformation.**
- Instead of **wars** and **civilian casualties,** we have **conflicts** and **collateral damage.**

Application **8-1**

Revise these sentences to eliminate triteness, overstatements, and euphemisms.

1. This course gives me a pain in the neck.
2. There is never a dull moment in my dorm.
3. Television is rotting everyone's brain.
4. I was less than candid.
5. This student is poorly motivated.
6. You are the world's most beautiful person
7. Marriage in America is a dying institution.
8. I love you more than life itself.
9. We have decided to terminate your employment.
10. People of our generation are all selfish.

AIM FOR PRECISION

ww

Even words listed as synonyms can carry different shades of meaning. Do you mean to say "I'm slender; you're slim; he's lean; and she's scrawny"? The wrong choice could be disastrous. A single, wrong word can be offensive, as in this statement by a college applicant:

Another attractive feature of the college is its **adequate** track program.

While **adequate** might convey honestly the writer's intended meaning, the word seems inappropriate in this context (an applicant expressing a judgment about a program). Although the program may not have been highly ranked, the writer could have used any of several alternatives (**solid, promising, growing**—or no modifier at all).

Be especially aware of similar words with dissimilar meanings, as in Table 8.1.

Table 8.1   COMMONLY CONFUSED WORDS

SIMILAR WORDS	USED CORRECTLY IN A SENTENCE
Affect means "to have an influence on."	Meditation positively *affects* one's concentration.
Affect can also mean "to pretend."	Boris likes to *affect* a French accent.
Effect used as a noun means "a result."	Meditation has a positive *effect* on one's concentration.
Effect used as a verb means "to make happen" or "to bring about."	Meditation can *effect* an improvement in one's concentration.
Already means "before this time."	Our new laptops are *already* sold out.
All ready means "prepared."	We are *all ready* for the summer tourist season.
Among refers to three or more.	The prize was divided *among* the four winners.
Between refers to two.	The prize was divided *between* the two winners.
Climatic (from *climate*) refers to the weather.	Recent *climatic* changes are worrisome.
Climactic (from *climax*) refers to the point of greatest intensity, as in a drama.	The hero's wedding was the *climactic* event of the play.
Continual means "repeated at intervals."	Our lower field floods *continually* during rainy season.
Continuous means "without interruption."	His headache has been *continuous* for three days.
Could of is an incorrect form of *could have*. (*Should of* and *would of* also are incorrect.)	Boris *could have* danced all night.
Criteria is the plural form of *criterion*.	Our school's *criteria* for applicants are demanding.
Criterion is the singular form.	The most important *criterion* is grade-point average.
Differ from refers to unlike things.	This plan *differs* greatly *from* our earlier one.
Differ with means "to disagree."	Mary *differs with* John about the feasibility of this project.

| **Table 8.1**   COMMONLY CONFUSED WORDS *(Continued)* | |

SIMILAR WORDS	USED CORRECTLY IN A SENTENCE
Disinterested means "unbiased" or "impartial."	Good science calls for *disinterested* analysis of research findings.
Uninterested means "not caring."	Junior high school students often are *uninterested* in science.
Eminent means "famous" or "distinguished."	Dr. Ostroff, the *eminent* physicist, is lecturing today.
Imminent means "about to happen."	A nuclear meltdown seemed *imminent*.
Farther refers to physical distance (a measurable quantity).	The school is 20 miles *farther*.
Further refers to extent (not measurable).	*Further* discussion of this issue is vital.
Fewer refers to things that can be counted.	*Fewer* than 50 students responded to our survey.
Less refers to things that can't be counted.	This survey had *less* of a response than our earlier one.
Good is always an adjective.	The food here is *good*. The young chef does a *good* job.
Well is usually an adverb.	The young chef cooks *well*.
In referring to health, *well* is an adjective.	When I feel *well*, I feel good.
Hanged refers to an execution.	The assassin was *hanged* at noon.
Hung is used for all other past-tense forms of *hang*.	The portraits of George and Martha were *hung* side by side.
Healthy means to be in good health.	To remain *healthy*, try skiing.
Healthful refers to things that promote health.	Skiing can be a *healthful* activity.
Imply means "to hint at" or "to insinuate."	This report *implies* that a crime occurred.
Infer means "to reason from evidence."	From this report, we can *infer* that a crime occurred.
Its means "belonging to."	The cost of the project has exceeded *its* budget.
It's is a contraction for "it is." (See page 528 for use of *they're, who's,* and other contractions.)	*It's* a good time for a club meeting.

Table 8.1   COMMONLY CONFUSED WORDS *(Continued)*

SIMILAR WORDS	USED CORRECTLY IN A SENTENCE
Lay means "to place or set something down." It always takes a direct object.	Please *lay* the blueprints on the desk.
Lie means "to recline." It takes no direct object.	This patient needs to *lie* on his right side all night.
(Note that the past tense of *lie* is *lay.*)	The patient *lay* on his right side all last night.
Media is the plural form of medium.	The crime received extensive *media* coverage.
Medium is the singular form.	Television is arguably our most influential *medium*.
Phenomena is the plural form of *phenomenon.*	Many scientific *phenomena* remain unexplained.
Phenomenon is the singular form.	Tiger Woods continues to be a golfing *phenomenon*.
Precede means "to come before."	Audience analysis should *precede* a written report.
Proceed means "to go forward."	If you must wake the cobra, *proceed* carefully.
Principle is always a noun that means "basic rule or standard."	Ethical *principles* should govern all our communications.
Principal, used as noun, means "the major person(s)."	All *principals* in this purchase must sign the contract.
Principal, used as adjective, means "leading."	Martha was the *principal* negotiator for this contract.
Who refers to a grammatical subject.	*Who* let the tarantulas out of their cage?
Whom refers to a grammatical object.	To *whom* was tarantula security assigned?
(See page 516 for *she/her, we/us,* and other forms of pronoun case.)	

Be on the lookout for imprecisely phrased (and therefore illogical) comparisons:

Faulty	Your bank's interest rate is higher than BusyBank. [*Can a rate be higher than a bank?*]
Revised	Your bank's interest rate is higher than BusyBank's.

Imprecision can create ambiguity. For instance, is **send us more personal information** a request for more information that is personal or for information that is more personal? Does your professor expect **fewer** or **less** technical details in your essay?

Precision ultimately enhances conciseness when one exact word replaces multiple inexact words.

Wordy and less exact	I have **put together** all the financial information.
	Keep doing this exercise for 10 seconds.
Concise and more exact	I have **assembled** all the financial information.
	Continue this exercise for 10 seconds.

Application **8-2**

Revise these sentences to make them precise.

1. Our outlet does more business than San Francisco.
2. Low-fat foods are healthy.
3. Marie's license is for driving an automatic car only.
4. This is the worse course I've taken.
5. Unlike many other children, her home life was good.
6. State law requires that restaurant personnel serve food with a sanitation certificate.

SHARPEN THE VISUAL DETAILS

spec

General terms traded for specific terms

General words name broad classes of things, such as **job, car,** or **person.** Such terms usually need to be clarified by more *specific* ones:

job = senior accountant for Rockford Press

car = red, four-door, Ford Escort station wagon

person = male Caucasian, with red hair, blue eyes (and so on)

The more specific your words, the sharper your meaning:

How the level of generality affects writing's visual quality

General 1. structure   1. animal
         2. dwelling   2. pet
         3. vacation home   3. dog
         4. log cabin   4. Doberman
         5. log cabin in Vermont 5. my Doberman, Fang
Specific 6. a three-room log cabin 6. my 90-pound, black
            on the banks of the   and tan Doberman,
            Battenkill River in Vermont   Fang

Notice how the picture becomes more vivid as we move to lower levels of generality. To visualize your way of seeing and your exact meaning, readers need specifics.

Abstract words name qualities, concepts, or feelings (**beauty, luxury, depression**) whose exact meaning has to be nailed down by *concrete* words—words that name things we can visualize:

Abstract terms traded for concrete terms

> a beautiful view = snowcapped mountains, a wilderness lake, pink granite ledge, 90-foot blue spruce trees
>
> a luxury condominium = redwood hot tub, hand-painted Mexican tile counters, floor-to-ceilng glass walls, oriental rugs
>
> a depressed person = suicidal urge, feelings of worthlessness, no hope for improvement, insomnia

Your discussion must be concrete and specific enough to provide clear and convincing support. Let's say that your topic statement is this one:

> Pedestrians crossing the street in front of my house place their lives in danger.

In supporting your main point you need to **show** with concrete and specific examples.

General For example, a person was injured there by a vehicle recently.

Specific My Uncle Albert was hit by a speeding garbage truck last Tuesday and had his leg broken.

Similarly, don't write **thing** when you mean **problem, pencil,** or **gift.** Instead of evaluating a coworker as **nice, great,** or **terrific,** use terms that are more concrete and verifiable, such as **reliable, skillful,** and **competent** or **dishonest, irritable,** and **awkward**—further clarified by examples (**never late for work**).

Note *In some instances, of course, you may wish to generalize. Instead of writing* **Bill, Mary, and Sam have been tying up the office phones with personal calls,** *you might prefer* **Some employees have been tying up. . . .** *The second version gets your message across without pointing the finger.*

Most good writing offers both general and specific information. The more general material is in the topic statement and sometimes in the conclusion because these parts, respectively, set the paragraph's direction and summarize its content. Informative writing invariably has a balance of *telling* and *showing*. Abstract and general expressions tell, and concrete and specific expressions show.

Meaningless abstraction	Professor Able's office is a sight to behold. [*What does "a sight to behold" mean?*]
Informative abstraction	Professor Able's office looks like a dump.

Now, the telling needs clarification through concrete and specific showing:

Concrete showing	The office has a floor strewn with books, a desk buried beneath a mountain of uncorrected papers, and ashtrays overflowing with ripe cigar butts.

Application **8-3**

In each set of terms, identify the most abstract or general and the most concrete or specific. Give reasons for your choices.

1. a presidential candidate, a U.S. senator, Edward Kennedy, a politician
2. a favorite spot, a beautiful place, an island in the Bahamas, a hideaway
3. woman, surgeon, person, professional individual
4. an awful person, a cruel and dishonest person, a nasty person
5. a competitor, a downhill racer, an athlete, a skier, a talented amateur
6. violence, assassination, terrorism, political action

ADD SOME PERSONALITY

tone

Your tone is your personal stamp—the personality that takes shape between the lines. The tone you create depends on (1) the distance you impose between yourself and the reader and (2) the attitude you show toward the subject.

How tone is created

Assume, for example, that a friend is going to take over a job you've held. You're writing your friend instructions for parts of the job. Here is your first sentence:

Informal

> Now that you've arrived in the glamorous world of office work, put on your track shoes; this is no ordinary clerical job.

This sentence imposes little distance between you and the reader (it uses the direct address, **you,** and the humorous suggestion to **put on your track shoes**). The ironic use of **glamorous** suggests just the opposite, that the job holds little glamour.

For a different reader (say, the recipient of a company training manual) you would have chosen some other opening:

Semiformal

> As an office assistant with Acme Explosives Corporation, you will spend little of your day seated at your desk.

The tone now is serious, no longer intimate, and you express no distinct attitude toward the job. For yet another audience (say, clients or investors who will read an annual report) you might alter the tone again:

Formal

> Office assistants at Acme Explosives are responsible for duties that extend far beyond desk work.

Here, the businesslike shift from second- to third-person address makes the tone too impersonal for any writing addressed to the assistants themselves.

Similarly, letters to your professor, your grandmother, and your friend, each about a disputed grade, would have a different tone:

Formal

> Dear Professor Snapjaws:
>   I am convinced that my failing grade in calculus did not reflect a fair evaluation of my work over the semester.

Semiformal

> Dear Granny,
>   Thanks for your letter. I'm doing well in school, except for my unfair grade in calculus.

Informal

> Dear Carol,
>   Have I been shafted or what? That old turkey, Snapjaws, gave me an F in calculus.

Establish an Appropriate Distance

We already know how tone works in speaking. When you meet someone new, for example, you respond in a tone that defines your relationship.

Tone announces
interpersonal distance

> Honored to make your acquaintance. [*formal tone—greatest distance*]
>
> How do you do? [*formal*]
>
> Nice to meet you. [*semiformal—medium distance*]

Hi. [*informal—least distance*]

What's happening? [*informal*]

Each of these responses is appropriate in some situations, inappropriate in others.

GUIDELINES FOR DECIDING ABOUT TONE

1. Use a formal or semiformal tone in writing for superiors, professionals, or academics (depending on what you think the reader expects).
2. Use a semiformal or informal tone in essays and letters (depending on how close you feel to your reader).
3. Use an informal tone when you want your writing to be conversational, or when you want it to sound like a person talking.
4. Above all, find out what tone your particular readers prefer.

Whichever tone you decide on, be consistent throughout your message:

| Inconsistent tone | My dorm room isn't fit for a pig: it is ungraciously unattractive. |
| Revised | My dilapidated dorm room is unfit to live in. |

In general, lean toward an informal tone without falling into slang. Make your writing conversational by following these suggestions:

GUIDELINES FOR ACHIEVING A CONVERSATIONAL TONE

1. Use simple and familiar words.
2. Use an occasional contraction.
3. Address readers directly when appropriate.
4. Use **I** and **We** when appropriate.
5. Prefer active to passive voice.

Use Simple and Familiar Wording. Say it in plain English. Try not to use a three-syllable word when one syllable will do. Don't write like the author of a report from the Federal Aviation Administration who suggested that manufacturers of the DC-10 be directed **to reevaluate the design of the entire**

pylon assembly to minimize design factors, which are resulting in sensitive and/or critical maintenance and inspection procedures (*25 words, 50 syllables*). Here is a plain-English translation: **Redesign the pylons so they are easier to maintain and inspect** (*11 words, 18 syllables*). Here are other instances of inflated language:

Inflated	Upgrade your present employment situation. [*5 words, 12 syllables*]
Revised	Get a better job. [*4 words, 5 syllables*]
Inflated	I am thoroughly convinced that Sam is a trustworthy individual.
Revised	I trust Sam.

Whenever possible, choose words you use and hear in everyday speaking.

Multiple syllables traded for fewer

utilize	=	use
to be cognizant	=	to know
to endeavor	=	to try
endeavor	=	effort
to secure employment	=	to find a job
concur	=	agree
effectuate	=	do
terminate	=	end
deem	=	think

Of course, now and then the complex or more elaborate word best expresses your meaning or it replaces a handful of simpler words.

Weak	Six loops around **the outside edges** of the dome tent **are needed for** the pegs **to fit into.**
Informative and precise	Six loops around the dome tent's **perimeter accommodate** the pegs.
Weak	We need a **one-to-one exchange of ideas and opinions.**
Informative and precise	We need a **dialogue.**

Use an Occasional Contraction.   Unless you have reason to be formal, use (but do not overuse) contractions. Balance an **I am** with an **I'm,** a **you are** with a **you're,** an **it is** with an **it's.** Generally, use contractions only with pronouns—not with nouns or proper nouns (names).

Awkward contractions	Barbara'll be here soon.
	Health's important.
	Love'll make you happy.
Ambiguous contractions	The dog's barking.
	The baby's crying.

These ambiguous contractions could be confused with possessive constructions.

Note *The contracted version often sounds less emphatic than the two-word version: for example, "**Don't** handle this material without protective clothing" versus "**Do not** handle this material without protective clothing." If your message requires emphasis, you should not use a contraction.*

Address Readers Directly. Use the personal pronouns **you** and **your** to connect with readers.

Impersonal tone	Students at our college will find the faculty always willing to help.
Personal tone	As a student at our college, **you** will find the faculty always willing to help.

Readers relate better to something addressed to them directly.

Note *Use **you** and **your** only to correspond directly with the reader, as in a letter, instructions, or some form of advice, encouragement, or persuasion. By using **you** and **your** in a situation that calls for first or third person, you might write something like this:*

Wordy and awkward	When **you** are in northern Ontario, **you** can see wilderness lakes everywhere around **you.**
Appropriate	Wilderness lakes are everywhere in northern Ontario.

Use "I" and "We" When Appropriate. Instead of disappearing behind your writing, use **I** or **we** when referring to yourself or your group.

Distant	This writer would like a refund.
Revised	**I** would like a refund.
Distant	The fear was awful until the police arrived.
Revised	**We** were terrified until the police arrived.

Prefer the Active Voice. Because the active voice is more direct and economical than the passive voice, it generally creates a less formal tone. Review pages 121–22 for use of active and passive voice.

Express a Clear and Appropriate Attitude

In addition to setting the distance between writer and reader, your tone implies your *attitude* toward the subject and the reader:

Tone announces attitude

> We dine at seven.
>
> Dinner is at seven.
>
> We eat at seven.
>
> We chow down at seven.
>
> We strap on the feedbag at seven.
>
> We pig out at seven.

The words you choose tell readers a great deal about where you stand.

One problem with tone occurs when your attitude is unclear. Say **I enjoyed the course** instead of **My attitude toward the course was one of high approval.** Try to convey an attitude that reflects your relationship with the reader. For instance, in an upcoming conference about a later paper, does the professor expect to **discuss the situation, talk it over, have a chat,** or **chew the fat?** Decide how casual or serous your attitude should be.

Don't be afraid to inject personal commentary when it's called for. Consider how the message below increases in force and effectiveness with the boldfaced commentary:

> In 1972, 56,000 people died on America's highways; 200,000 were injured, 15,000 children were orphaned. In that year, if you were a member of a family of five, chances are that someone related to you, by blood or law, was killed or injured by **one of the most violent forms of self-elimination ever devised by humanity**—an auto accident.

If, however, your job is to report objectively, try to suppress any bias you might have; do not volunteer your attitude.

Avoid Personal Bias

If people expect an impartial report, try to keep your own biases out of it. Imagine, for instance, that you are a campus newspaper reporter, investigating a confrontation between part-time faculty and the administration. Your initial report, written for tomorrow's edition, is intended simply to describe what happened. Here is how an unbiased description might read:

A factual account

> At 10:00 a.m. on Wednesday, October 24, 80 adjunct faculty members set up picket lines around the college's administration building, bringing business to a halt. The group issued a formal protest, claiming that their salary scale was unfair, their fringe benefits [health insurance, and so on] inadequate, and their job security nonexistent. The group insisted that the

> college's wage scales and employment policies be revised. The demonstration ended when Glenn Tarullo, vice-president in charge of personnel, promised to appoint a committee to investigate the group's claims and to correct any inequities.

Notice the absence of implied judgments. A less impartial version of the event, from a protestor's point of view, might read like this:

A biased version

> Last Wednesday, adjunct faculty struck another blow against exploitation when 80 members paralyzed the college's repressive administration for more than six hours. The timely and articulate protest was aimed against unfair salary scales, inadequate fringe benefits, and lack of job security. Stunned administrators watched helplessly as the group organized their picket lines, determined to continue their protest until their demands for fair treatment were met. An embarrassed vice-president quickly agreed to study the group's demands and to revise the college's discriminatory policies. The success of this long-overdue confrontation serves as an inspiration to oppressed adjunct faculty everywhere.

Note

Writing teacher Marshall Kremers reminds us that being unbiased, of course, doesn't mean remaining "neutral" about something you know to be wrong or dangerous.* If, for instance, you conclude that the college protest was clearly justified, say so.

INVITE EVERYONE IN

Not only do the words you choose reveal your way of seeing, but they also influence your reader's way of seeing. Insensitive language carries built-in judgments, and as the renowned linguist S. I. Hayakawa reminds us: Judgment stops thought. Writing that makes human contact is writing that excludes no one.

Avoid Sexist Language

Sexist usage refers to doctors, lawyers, and other professionals as **he** or **him** and to nurses, secretaries, and homemakers as **she** or **her.** This traditional stereotype suggests that males do the jobs that really matter and that pay higher wages, whereas females serve only as support and decoration. And when females do invade traditional "male" roles, we might express our surprise at their boldness by calling them **female executives, female sportscasters, female surgeons,** or **female hockey players.** Likewise, to demean males who have taken "female" roles, we sometimes refer to **male secretaries, male nurses, male flight attendants,** or **male models.**

---

*See *IEEE Transactions on Professional Communication* 32.2 (1989): 58–61.

GUIDELINES FOR NONSEXIST USAGE

1. Use neutral expressions:

chair, or **chairperson**	rather than	**chairman**
supervisor	rather than	**foreman**
police officer	rather than	**policeman**
letter carrier	rather than	**postman**
homemaker	rather than	**housewife**
humanity	rather than	**mankind**
actor	rather than	**actor vs. actress**

2. Rephrase to eliminate the pronoun, but only if you can do so without altering your original meaning.

Sexist	A writer will succeed if he revises.
Revised	A writer who revises succeeds.

3. Use plural forms.

Sexist	A writer will succeed if **he** revises.
Revised	Writers will succeed if **they** revise. (But *not a writer will succeed if **they** revise.*)

   When using a plural form, don't create an error in pronoun-referent agreement by having the plural pronoun **they** or **their** refer to a singular referent:

   Each writer should do **their** best.

4. When possible (as in direct address), use **you:**

Direct address	You will succeed if you revise.

   But use this form only when addressing someone directly. (See page 149.)

Avoid Offensive Usage of All Types

Enlightened communication respects all people in reference to their specific cultural, racial, ethnic, and national background; sexual and religious orientation; age or physical condition. References to individuals and groups should be as neutral as possible; no matter how inadvertent, any expression that seems condescending or judgmental or that violates the reader's sense of appropriateness is offensive. Detailed guidelines for reducing biased usage appear in these two works:

Schwartz, Marilyn et al. *Guidelines for Bias-Free Writing.* Bloomington: Indiana UP, 1995.

Publication Manual of the American Psychological Association, 5th ed. Washington, D.C.: American Psychological Association, 2001.

Page 154 offers a sampling of suggestions adapted from the works above.

5. Use occasional pairings (**him or her, she or he, his or hers, he/she**):

> **Effective pairing**   A writer will succeed if **she or he** revises.

But note that overuse of such pairings can be awkward:

> **Awkward pairing**   A writer should do **his or her** best to make sure that **he or she** connects with **his or her** readers.

6. Use feminine and masculine pronouns alternately:

> **Alternating pronouns**   An effective writer always focuses on **her** audience.
>
> The writer strives to connect with all **his** readers.

7. Drop condescending diminutive endings such as **-ess** and **-ette** used to denote females (**poetess, drum majorette, actress,** etc.)

8. Use **Ms.** instead of **Mrs.** or **Miss,** unless you know that the person prefers one of the traditional titles. Or omit titles completely: **Jane Kelly** and **Roger Smith; Kelly and Smith.**

9. In quoting sources that have ignored present standards for nonsexist usage, consider these options:

- Insert [**sic**] (for **thus** or **so**) following the first instance of sexist terminology in a particular passage.
- Use ellipses to omit sexist phrasing.
- Paraphrase instead of quoting directly.

Consider the Cultural Context

Cultures differ in their style preferences

The style guidelines throughout Chapters 7 and 8 apply specifically to standard English in North America. But practices and preferences differ widely in various cultural contexts.

Certain cultures have long preferred sentences and elaborate language to convey an idea's full complexity. Other cultures value expressions of politeness, respect, praise, and gratitude more than mere clarity or directness (Hein 125–26; Mackin 349–50).

Writing in non-English languages tends to be more formal than in English, and some relies heavily on the passive voice (Weymouth 144). French readers, for example, may prefer an elaborate style that reflects sophisticated and complex modes of thinking. In contrast, our "plain English," conversational style might connote simple-mindedness, disrespect, or incompetence (Thrush 277).

GUIDELINES FOR INOFFENSIVE USAGE

1. When referring to members of a particular culture, be as specific as possible about that culture's identity: Instead of **Latin American** or **Asian** or **Hispanic,** for instance, prefer **Cuban American** or **Korean** or **Nicaraguan.** Instead of **American students,** specify **U.S. students** when referring to the United States.

   Avoid judgmental expressions: Instead of **third-world** or **undeveloped nations** or the **Far East,** prefer **developing** or **newly industrialized nations** or **East Asia.** Instead of **nonwhites,** refer to **people of color.**

2. When referring to someone who has a disability, avoid terms that could be considered pitying or overly euphemistic, such as **victims, unfortunates, special** or **challenged** or **differently abled.** Focus on the individual instead of the disability: Instead of **blind person** or **amputee,** refer to a **person who is blind** or a **person who has lost an arm.**

   In general usage, avoid expressions that demean those who have medical conditions: **retard, mental midget, insane idea, lame excuse, the blind leading the blind, able-bodied workers,** and so on.

3. When referring to members of a particular age group, prefer **girl** or **boy** for people of age 14 or under; **young person, young adult, young man** or **young woman** for those of high school age; and **woman** or **man** for those of college age. (**Teenager** or **juvenile** carries certain negative connotations.) Instead of **the elderly,** prefer **older persons.**

In translation or in a different cultural context, certain words carry offensive or unfavorable connotations. For example, certain cultures use "male" and "female" in referring only to animals (Coe 17). Other notable disasters (Gesteland 20; Victor 44):

- The Chevrolet *Nova*—meaning "don't go" in Spanish
- The Finnish beer *Koff*—for an English-speaking market
- Colgate's *Cue* toothpaste—an obscenity in French
- A bicycle brand named *Flying Pigeon*—imported for a U.S. market

Idioms ("strike out," "over the top,") hold no logical meaning for other cultures. Slang ("bogus," "phat") and colloquialisms ("You bet," "Gotcha") can strike readers as too informal and crude.

Offensive writing can alienate audiences—toward you *and* your culture (Sturges 32).

Application **8-4**

Rewrite these statements in plain and precise English, with special attention to tone.

1. This writer desires to be considered for a position with your company.
2. My attitude toward your behavior is one of disapproval.
3. A good writer is cognizant of how to utilize grammar in correct fashion.
4. Replacement of the weak battery should be effectuated.
5. Sexist language contributes to the ongoing prevalence of gender stereo-types.
6. Make an improvement in your studying situation.
7. We should inject some rejuvenation into our lifeless and dull relationship.

Application **8-5**

Find examples of overly euphemistic language (such as "chronologically challenged") or of insensitive language—possibly on the Internet or in a newsgroup. Discuss your examples in class.

Application **8-6**

Collaborative Project and Computer Application: A version of this next letter was published in a local newspaper. Working on the computer, each group member should rewrite the letter in plain English, then email your version to group members. Discuss the changes electronically, and agree on a final version that one group member will compose. Print this final version for the whole class, justifying your group's revision.

> In the absence of definitive studies regarding the optimum length of the school day, I can only state my personal opinion based upon observations made by me and upon teacher observations that have been conveyed to me. Considering the length of the present school day, it is my opinion that the school day is excessive lengthwise for most elementary pupils, certainly for almost all of the primary children.
>
> To find the answer to the problem requires consideration of two ways in which the problem may be viewed. One way focuses upon the needs of the children, while the other focuses upon logistics, scheduling, transportation, and other limits imposed by the educational system. If it is necessary to prioritize these two ideas, it would seem most reasonable to give the first consideration to the primary and fundamental reason for the very existence of

the system itself, i.e., to meet the educational needs of the children the system is trying to serve.

Application **8-7**

Rewrite these statements to eliminate sexist and other offensive expressions—without altering the meaning.

1. An employee in our organization can be sure he will be treated fairly.
2. Almost every child dreams of being a fireman.
3. The average man is a good citizen.
4. The future of mankind is uncertain.
5. Being a stewardess is not as glamorous as it may seem.
6. Everyone has the right to his opinion.
7. Every married surgeon depends on his spouse for emotional support.
8. Dr. Marcia White is not only a female professor, but also chairman of the English department.
9. The accident left me blind as a bat for nearly an hour.
10. What a dumb idea!

LEGAL AND ETHICAL IMPLICATIONS OF WORD CHOICE

We are each accountable for the words we use—intentionally or not—in framing the audience's perception and understanding. Imprecise or inappropriate word choice in the workplace, for example, can spell big trouble, as in the following examples:

Situations in which word choice has ethical or legal consequences

- *Assessing risk.* Is the investment you are advocating "a sure thing," merely "a good bet," or even "somewhat risky?" Are you announcing a "caution," a "warning," or a "danger?" Should methane levels in mineshaft #3 "be evaluated," or be "routinely monitored," or do they "pose a definite explosion risk?" Never downplay the risks involved.
- *Offering a service or product.* Are you proposing to "study the problem," to "explore solutions to the problem," or to "eliminate the problem?" Do you "stand behind" your product or do you "guarantee" it? Never promise more than you can deliver.
- *Giving instructions.* Before inserting the widget between the grinder blades, should you "switch off the grinder," "disconnect the grinder from its power source," "trip the circuit breaker," or do all three? Always triple-check the clarity of your instructions.
- *Comparing your product with competing products.* Instead of referring to a competitor's product as "inferior," "second-rate," or "substandard," talk

about your own "first-rate product" that "exceeds (or meets) all standards." Never run down the competition.

■ *Evaluating an employee* (Clark 75–76). In a personnel evaluation, don't refer to the employee as a "troublemaker," "unprofessional," "too abrasive," "too uncooperative," "incompetent," or "too old" for the job. Focus on the specific requirements of this job, and offer factual instances in which these requirements have been violated: "Our monitoring software recorded five visits by this employee to X-rated Web sites during working hours." or "This employee arrives late for work on average twice weekly, has failed to complete assigned projects on three occasions, and has difficulty working with others." Instead of expressing personal judgments, offer the facts. Otherwise, you risk violating federal laws against discrimination and libel (damaging someone's reputation) and facing lawsuits.

USING AUTOMATED EDITING TOOLS EFFECTIVELY

The limits of automation

Many of the strategies in Chapters 7 and 8 could be executed rapidly with word-processing software. By using the global *Search-and-replace function* in some programs, you can command the computer to search for ambiguous pronoun references, overuse of passive voice, **to be** verbs, **There** and **It** sentence openers, negative constructions, clutter words, needless prefatory expressions and qualifiers, sexist language, and so on. With an online dictionary or thesaurus, you can check definitions or see a list of synonyms for a word you have used in your writing.

But these editing aids can be extremely imprecise. For example, both **its** and **it's** are spelled correctly, but only one of them means "it is." Your spellchecker is great for words that are spelled incorrectly—but not for words that are *used* incorrectly or for typos that create the wrong word but are correctly spelled words on their own, such as **howl** or **fort** instead of **how** or **for.** Likewise, grammar checkers are great for helping you spot a possible problem, but don't rely only on what the software tells you. For example, not every sentence that the grammar checker flags as "long" should be shortened. These tools simply can't eliminate the writer's burden of *choice*.

Also, none of the rules offered in this chapter applies universally. Ultimately, your own sensitivity to meaning, emphasis, and tone—the human contact—will determine the effectiveness of your writing style.

Application **8-8**

Computer Application: Explore the thesaurus function on your word-processing program. Remember that a thesaurus never can provide an exact synonym. Check the computer's suggestions against the dictionary definitions of the words. Compare the computer's suggestions with a good traditional thesaurus and with *Roget's Thesaurus* online <**http://www.thesaurus .com**>. Assess the advantages and disadvantages of each.

Application **8-9**

Web-based Project: Do a Web search to find an online style guide that expands on style advice offered in this chapter. Consider the following sites, but do not limit yourself to these:

- For decisions about word choice and tone, *Paradigm Online Writing Assistant* <**http://powa.org/revifrms.htm**>
- For avoiding biased language, the *Guide to Writing and Grammar* <**http://ccc.commnet.edu/grammar/unbiased.htm**>
- and the *Purdue Online Writing Lab* <**http://owl.english.purdue.edu/handouts/general/gl_nonsex.html**>

Prepare a one-page presentation, in your own words, with examples, for the class. Attach a copy of the relevant Web page(s) to your presentation. Be sure to credit each source of information (page 392).

Works Cited

Clark, Thomas. "Teaching Students How to Write to Avoid Legal Liability." *Business Communication Quarterly* 60.3 (1997): 71–77.

Coe, Marlana. "Writing for Other Cultures." *Intercom* Jan. 1997: 17–19.

Gesteland, Richard R. "Cross-Cultural Compromises." *Sky* May 1993: 20+.

Hein, Robert G. "Culture and Communication." *Technical Communication* 38.1 (1991): 125–26.

Mackin, John. "Surmounting the Barrier between Japanese and English Technical Documents." *Technical Communication* 36.4 (1989): 346–51.

Sturges, David L. "Internationalizing the Business Communication Curriculum." *Bulletin of the Association for Business Communication* 55.1 (1992): 30–39.

Thrush, Emily A. "Bridging the Gap: Technical Communication in an Intercultural and Multicultural Society." *Technical Communication Quarterly* 2.3 (1993): 271–83.

Victor, David A. *International Business Communication.* New York: Harper, 1992.

Weymouth, L. C. "Establishing Quality Standards and Trade Regulations for Technical Writing in World Trade." *Technical Communication* 37.2 (1990): 143–47.

SECTION THREE

Essays for Various Goals

Introduction **160**

CHAPTER 9
Decisions about Reading
for Writing **164**

CHAPTER 10
Helping Others See and Share
an Experience: Description
and Narration **178**

CHAPTER 11
Providing Examples:
Illustration **197**

CHAPTER 12
Explaining Parts and Categories:
Division and Classification **208**

CHAPTER 13
Explaining Steps and Stages:
Process Analysis **220**

CHAPTER 14
Explaining Why It Happened
or What Will Happen: Cause-and-
Effect Analysis **234**

CHAPTER 15
Explaining Similarities or
Differences: Comparison and
Contrast **251**

CHAPTER 16
Explaining the Exact Meaning:
Definition **265**

CHAPTER 17
Using Multiple Strategies in a
Persuasive Argument **281**

CHAPTER 18
Special Issues in Persuasion **310**

Introduction

Three Major Goals of Writing   **160**

Major Development Strategies   **162**

Using This Section   **162**

A Word about Structural Variations   **162**

Earlier chapters have stressed the importance of deciding on a goal and of refining the goal into a purpose (goal plus plan). This section shows you how to focus on your purpose in order to achieve a variety of writing goals.

THREE MAJOR GOALS OF WRITING

Most writing can be categorized according to three major goals: expressive, referential, and persuasive.

Expressive writing is mostly about you, the writer (your feelings, experiences, impressions, personality). This personal form of writing helps readers understand something about you or your way of seeing.

Expressive writing situations

- You write to cheer up a sick friend with a tale about your latest blind date.
- You write a Dear John (or Jane) letter.
- You write to your parents, explaining why you've been feeling down in the dumps.

Examples of expressive writing appear in the sample essays in Section One on pages 12 and 16. Many students find expressive writing easiest because it is a kind of storytelling.

Instead of focusing on the writer, *referential (or explanatory) writing* refers to some outside subject. Your goal might be (a) to inform readers about something they need to know or (b) to explain something they need to understand. Referential writing doesn't focus on your feelings and experiences but on the subject at hand.

Referential writing
situations

- You write to describe the exterior of your new dorm so that your parents can find it next weekend.
- You define *condominium* for your business law class.
- You report on the effects of budget cuts at your college for the campus newspaper.
- You write to advise a younger sibling about how to prepare for college-level work.

An example of referential writing appears on page 56.

Persuasive writing is mostly about your audience. Beyond merely imparting information or making something understandable, your goal is to win readers' support, to influence their thinking, or to motivate them in some way. Persuasive writing appeals to both the audience's reason and emotions.

Persuasive writing
situations

- You write an editorial for the campus newspaper, calling for a stricter alcohol policy in the dorms.
- You write a diplomatic note to your obnoxious neighbor, asking him to keep his dogs quiet.
- You write to ask a professor on sabbatical to reconsider the low grade you received in history.
- You write to persuade citizens in your county to vote against a proposal for a toxic-waste dump.

These three goals (expressive, referential or explanatory, and persuasive) often overlap. For example, persuading the dean to beef up campus security might mean discussing your personal fears (expressive goal) and explaining how some students have been attacked (referential goal). But most writing situations have one primary goal. Keeping that goal in focus can help you choose the best strategies for getting the job done.

Traditionally, the strategies for writing are considered to be *description, narration, exposition* (informing or explaining), and *argument*. But description, narration, and exposition can be used for expressive, referential, or persuasive goals. While Chapter 1 focuses on expressive writing, Section Three is mostly about communication between readers and writers on subjects of interest to both. Therefore, it focuses primarily on referential and persuasive uses of these strategies—that is, writing to inform, explain, or make a point. Persuasive writing, however, raises special concerns that we will cover in Chapters 17 and 18.

Note   *Keep in mind that none of these development strategies is an end in itself. In other words, we don't write merely for the sake of contrasting or discussing causes and effects, and so on. Instead, we use a particular strategy because it provides the best framework for organizing our information and clarifying our thinking on a particular topic. Each strategy is merely one way of looking at something— another option for gaining control of the countless writing situations we face throughout our lives and careers.*

MAJOR DEVELOPMENT STRATEGIES

A *development strategy* is simply a plan for coming up with the details, events, examples, explanations, and reasons that convey your exact meaning—a way of answering readers' questions. *Description* paints a word picture, while *narration* tells a story or depicts a series of related events, usually in chronological order. Narration relies on descriptive details to make the events vivid. *Exposition,* meanwhile, relies on description and narration, but it does more than paint a picture or tell a story: This strategy explains the writer's viewpoint. Strategies of exposition include *illustration, classification, process analysis, cause-effect analysis, comparison-contrast,* and *definition,* all of which are explored in the following chapters. Essays often employ some combination of these strategies but usually have one primary strategy.

Finally, *argument* strives to win readers to our point of view. Whereas the main point in exposition can usually be shown to be true or valid, the main point in an argument is debatable—capable of being argued by reasonable people on either side. The stronger argument, then, would be the one that makes the more convincing case.

| Note |

Although argument follows its own specified patterns of reasoning, it also relies on the strategies of description, narration, and exposition.

USING THIS SECTION

This section begins with a chapter on methods for reading and responding to written essays by others. The following chapters then introduce a particular strategy and show how the strategy can support referential and persuasive writing.

Next, the chapters provide guidelines for using the strategy yourself, along with a sample essay for your analysis and response. When you read these sample essays, refer to the Chapter 9 questions, as well as to the more specific questions provided in each chapter. Then examine the case study that shows one student's response to the sample essay.

For additional readings, Section Five offers professional essays that illustrate each development strategy.

A WORD ABOUT STRUCTURAL VARIATIONS

Most sample essays in earlier chapters have a basic introduction-body-conclusion structure: a one-paragraph introduction that leads into the thesis; several support paragraphs, each developed around a topic statement that treats one part of the thesis; and a one-paragraph conclusion that relates to the main point. But a quick glance at published writing shows much variation from this formula: Some topics call for several introductory paragraphs;

some supporting points require that one topic statement serve two or more body paragraphs; some paragraphs may be interrupted by digressions, such as personal remarks or flashbacks that are linked to the main point; some conclusions take up more than one paragraph. Single-sentence paragraphs will open, support, or close an essay.

Instead of the final sentence in the introduction, the thesis might be the first sentence of the essay, or it may be saved for the conclusion or not stated at all—although a definite thesis almost always is unmistakably implied.

Still other essays have neither introductory nor concluding paragraphs. Instead, the opening or closing is incorporated into the main discussion. Such *structural variations are a part of a writer's deliberate decisions*—decisions that determine the ultimate quality of an essay. Many of the essays in the following chapters embody one or more of these variations. Use them as inspiration for your own writing, but remember that *effective writing always reveals a distinct beginning, middle, and ending*—and a clear line of thought.

CHAPTER 9

Decisions about Reading for Writing

Different Levels of Reading   **165**

Different Readers, Different Meanings   **166**

Reading Strategies for Writers   **166**

CASE STUDY: One Writer's Response to Reading   **167**

CASE STUDY: A Second Writer's Response to Reading   **172**

Suggestions for Reading and Writing   **175**

   Guidelines for Reading to Respond   175

Readings   **167, 171, 172, 174**

Applications   **176**

This book asks you to read other people's writing (students and professionals) in order to consider their ideas and trace their decision making. Reading also provides raw material that helps you craft your own writing. But not all reading is equal in terms of the level of interaction it requires.

DIFFERENT LEVELS OF READING

Reading to be entertained

Reading to get information

Reading to make a critical judgment

Different reasons for reading call for different levels of interacting with a piece of writing. In reading something like a Stephen King novel, for instance, we tend to skim the surface, flipping pages to find the juicy scenes and basically enjoying the ride.

In reading a textbook in psychology or some other discipline, we work to grasp important facts and main ideas. Later, we often write to demonstrate our knowledge or understanding.

For this course, we go beyond merely retrieving and absorbing information. In *critical reading*, we dig beneath the surface and examine the writing itself—its content, organization, and style. Instead of accepting the ideas at face value, we weigh the evidence, the assumptions, and the reasoning behind them.

Questions for Critical Reading

ABOUT PURPOSE

- *What is the author asking us to think or do?*
- *In what ways does this piece succeed or fail in its purpose?*

ABOUT CONTENT

- *Is the title effective? Why?*
- *What is the thesis? Is it stated, or is it implicit? Where does it appear?*
- *Does this placement contribute to the main point?*
- *Does the piece offer something new and useful?*
- *Does the reasoning make sense?*
- *Is the essay convincing? What kinds of support does the writer offer for the main points?*
- *Are other conclusions or interpretations possible?*

ABOUT ORGANIZATION

- *Is the discussion easy to follow?*
- *How is the introduction structured? Are the writer's decisions effective? Why?*
- *Does the essay vary the standard introduction-body-conclusion format (page 162)? If so, how? Do the writer's decisions help promote the purpose?*
- *How is the conclusion structured? Is it effective? Why?*

ABOUT STYLE

- *What is the outstanding style feature of this essay? Give examples.*
- *How effective is the tone? Give examples of word choice and sentence structure that contribute to the tone.*

This critical evaluation provides essential groundwork for writing about reading. But much of the energy for *any* writing comes from our *personal* response to something we read.

Reading to discover
personal meaning

In reading for personal meaning, we join a "conversation": Reacting to something that was said, we offer something of our own. We read to explore and inspire our own thinking, to make up our minds, or to discover buried feelings or ideas. Then we reinvent that material with a force and passion that will make a difference to our own readers.

Questions for Personal Responses to Reading

- *What special meaning does this piece have for me?*
- *What grabs my attention?*
- *Does this piece make me angry, defensive, supportive, or what?*
- *Why do I feel this way?*

- *With which statements do I agree or disagree?*
- *Has the piece reminded me of something, taught me something, changed my mind, or what?*
- *How do I want to reply?*

DIFFERENT READERS, DIFFERENT MEANINGS

The connection that writing creates is both public and private. On the one hand, a piece of writing connects publicly with its entire audience; on the other hand, the writing connects privately with each of its readers. Consider, for example, "Confessions of a Food Addict" (pages 16–17): Most readers of this essay feel the writer's anxiety and sense of failure. Beyond our common reaction, however, each of us has a unique and personal reaction, as well—special feelings or memories or thoughts.

You as the reader interpret and complete the "private" meaning of anything you read. And, like you, other readers come away from the same piece with a personal meaning of their own. It is this personal meaning that ultimately inspires your own writing.

READING STRATEGIES FOR WRITERS

A worthwhile critical and personal response to writing calls for a good strategy. Instead of just a single reading, you need to really "get into" the piece. And you do this by rereading and by writing *while* you read: First you take notes, underline, scribble questions and comments in the margins, and summarize the main ideas. Then you examine the author's technique, evaluate the ideas, and discover what the piece means to you personally. Once you have a genuine grasp of the piece, you can decide exactly how you want to respond.

The following case study shows how student writer Jacqueline LeBlanc employs each of these strategies in preparing her response to a reading.

CASE STUDY

ONE WRITER'S RESPONSE TO READING

Judy Brady's "Why I Want a Wife" was published in the very first issue of *Ms.* magazine in spring 1972. Even though Brady seems to write for married readers in particular, her essay speaks to anyone familiar with married people in general.

As you read, consider this question: Based on your experience, how much have male and female roles really changed since this essay was written?

Essay for analysis and response

WHY I WANT A WIFE

I belong to that classification of people known as wives. I am A Wife. And, not altogether incidentally, I am a mother.

Not too long ago a male friend of mine appeared on the scene fresh from a recent divorce. He had one child, who is, of course, with his ex-wife. He is looking for another wife. As I thought about him while I was ironing one evening, it suddenly occurred to me that I, too, would like to have a wife. Why do I want a wife?

I would like to go back to school so that I can become economically independent, support myself, and, if need be, support those dependent upon me. I want a wife who will work and send me to school. And while I am going to school I want a wife to take care of my children. I want a wife to keep track of the children's doctor and dentist appointments. And to keep track of mine, too. I want a wife to make sure my children eat properly and are kept clean. I want a wife who will wash the children's clothes and keep them mended. I want a wife who is a good nurturant attendant to my children, who arranges for their schooling, makes sure that they have an adequate social life with their peers, takes them to the park, the zoo, etc. I want a wife who takes care of the children when they are sick, a wife who arranges to be around when the children need special care, because, of course, I cannot miss classes at school. My wife must arrange to lose time at work and not lose the job. It may mean a small cut in my wife's income from time to time, but I guess I can tolerate that. Needless to say, my wife will arrange and pay for the care of the children while my wife is working.

I want a wife who will take care of my physical needs. I want a wife who will keep my house clean. A wife who will pick up after my children, a wife who will pick up after me. I want a wife who will keep my clothes clean, ironed, mended, replaced when need be, and who will see to it that my personal things are kept in their proper place so that I can find what I need the minute I need it. I want a wife who cooks the meals, a wife who is a good cook. I want a wife who will plan the menus, do the necessary grocery shopping, prepare the meals, serve them pleasantly, and then do the cleaning up while I do my studying. I want a wife who will care for me when I am sick and sympathize with my pain and loss of time from school. I want a wife to go along when our family takes a vacation so that someone can continue to care for me and my children when I need a rest and change of scene.

I want a wife who will not bother me with rambling complaints about a wife's duties. But I want a wife who will listen to me when I feel the need to explain a rather difficult point I have come across in my course of studies. And I want a wife who will type my papers for me when I have written them.

I want a wife who will take care of the details of my social life. When my wife and I are invited out by my friends, I want a wife who will take care of the babysitting arrangements. When I meet people at school that I like and want to entertain, I want a wife who will have the house clean, will prepare a special meal, serve it to me and my friends, and not interrupt when I talk about things that interest me and my friends. I want a wife who will have arranged that the children are fed and ready for bed before my guests arrive so that the children do not bother us. I want a wife who takes care of the needs of my guests so that they feel comfortable, who makes sure that they have an ashtray, that they are passed the hors d'oeuvres, that they are offered a second helping of the food, that their wine glasses are replenished when necessary, that their coffee is served to them as they like it. And I want a wife who knows that sometimes I need a night out by myself.

I want a wife who is sensitive to my sexual needs, a wife who makes love passionately and eagerly when I feel like it, a wife who makes sure that I am satisfied. And, of course, I want a wife who will not demand sexual attention when I am not in the mood for it. I want a wife who assumes the complete responsibility for birth control, because I do not want more children. I want a wife who will remain sexually faithful to me so that I do not have to clutter up my intellectual life with jealousies. And I want a wife who understands that my sexual needs may entail more than strict adherence to monogamy. I must, after all, be able to relate to people as fully as possible.

If, by chance, I find another person more suitable as a wife than the wife I already have, I want the liberty to replace my present wife with another one. Naturally, I will expect a fresh, new life; my wife will take the children and be solely responsible for them so that I am left free. When I am through with school and have a job, I want my wife to quit working and remain at home so that my wife can more fully and completely take care of a wife's duties.

My God, who *wouldn't* want a wife?

—*Judy Brady*

Discussion

Now let's examine our critical and personal opinions of "Why I Want A Wife." Is this bleak view of the "housewife's" destiny basically accurate, in your view? What particular meaning does this essay have for you?

Maybe Brady's essay leaves you feeling irate toward (1) men, (2) the writer, (3) yourself, or (4) someone else. Or maybe you feel threatened or offended. Or maybe you feel amused or confused about your own attitudes toward gender roles. The questions on pages 165 and 166 will help you explore your reactions.

Before you decide on a response to Brady's essay, see how another student responded. Here are some of the notes Jacqueline LeBlanc wrote in her journal after first reading the essay:

One of Jackie's journal entries

This essay is annoying because it reminds me too much of some women in my own generation who seem to want nothing more than a wifely role for themselves. For all we hear about "equal rights," women still feel the pressure to conform to old-fashioned notions. I can really take this essay personally.

After rereading the essay and reviewing her journal entries, Jackie highlighted and annotated key passages. Here is what she jots on one paragraph of the Brady essay:

Jackie's highlighting and annotations of one paragraph

extremely self-centered

I want a wife who will take care of my physical needs. I want a wife who will keep my house clean. A wife who will pick up after my children, a wife who will pick up after me. I want a wife who will keep my clothes clean, ironed, mended, replaced when need be, and who will see to it that my personal things are kept in their proper place so that I can find what I need the minute I need it. I

a maid/ house- keeper

not just any old cook!

want a wife who cooks the meals, a wife who is a good cook. I want a wife who will plan the

a cook

service with a smile!

menus, do the necessary grocery shopping, prepare the meals, serve them pleasantly, and then

wants to be pampered, too!

do the cleaning up while I do my studying. I want a wife who will care for me when I am sick and sympathize with my pain and loss of time from

a nurse

How common is all this in today's marriages?

school. I want a wife to go along when our family takes a vacation so that someone can continue to care for me and my children when I need a rest and change of scene.

a nanny

What about women's view of "husbandly" duties? How are they similar or different?

To ensure her grasp of Brady's position, Jackie follows page 374 guidelines to summarize the essay in her own words:

Jackie's summary of the essay

> In "Why I Want a Wife," Judy Brady offers a graphic view of the lowly status of women in marriage. The typical wife is expected to serve as financial provider, nanny, nurse, maid, cook, secretary, and sex slave. And no matter how well she performs these and other oppressive duties, this wife is ultimately disposable in the event that the husband finds someone "more suitable" for the role.

Sometimes a direct quotation is necessary to preserve a special meaning or emphasis (page 370). Notice that Jackie is careful to place Brady's exact wording in quotation marks.

Next, Jackie uses the critical-reading questions on page 165 to evaluate Brady's case. She measures the piece's strengths and weaknesses in terms of its purpose, thesis, support, line of reasoning, accuracy, and style. Here is part of her analysis:

Jackie's partial analysis

> Brady sets out here to shock women (as well as men) out of traditional attitudes by defining her concept of "wife." Even though she offers no explicit thesis, her main point might be stated like this: *Women in the traditional "wifely" role are exploited and unappreciated.*
>
> Her many vivid examples are extremely depressing and somewhat exaggerated, but most of them should be familiar to anyone who has experienced the "traditional" family—and they really don't seem all that outdated, either.
>
> Brady's tone certainly is sarcastic, but, given the situation, her sarcasm seems justified, and it adds to the essay's shock value.

She continues her critical evaluation using the Revision Checklist facing the inside front cover.

Now that she has a solid handle on the essay, Jackie uses the personal-response questions on page 166 to explore the special meaning she finds here. Finally, she decides on the viewpoint that will guide her own response:

Jackie's own viewpoint as a basis for responding

> The stereotypical role condemned by Brady three decades ago continues to be disturbingly evident.

Jackie expresses her viewpoint in a definite thesis statement:

Jackie's thesis

> Although today's "equality-minded" generation presumably sees marriage as more than just an occupation, the wifely stereotype persists.

Here, after several revisions, is the essay that explains Jackie's viewpoint:

Jackie's final response to Brady's essay

A Long Way to Go

Judy Brady's portrait of a servile wife might appear somewhat dated—until we examine some of today's views about marriage. Brady defines a wife by the work she does for her husband: She is a secretary, housemaid, babysitter, and sex object. She is, in a word, her husband's employee. Although today's "equality-minded" generation presumably sees marriage as more than an occupation, the wifely stereotype persists.

Among a few of my women friends, I continue to encounter surprisingly traditional attitudes. Last week, for instance, I was discussing my career possibilities with my roommate, who added to the list of my choices by saying, "You can always get married." In her view, becoming a wife seems no different from becoming a teacher or journalist. She implied that marriage is merely another way of making a living. But where do I apply for the position of wife? The notion struck me as absurd. I thought to myself, "Surely, this person is an isolated case. We are, after all, in the twenty-first century. Women no longer get married as a substitute for a job—do they?"

Of course, many women do have both job and marriage, but as I look closely at others' attitudes, I find that my roommate's view is not so rare. Before the recent wedding of a female friend, my conversations with the future bride revolved around her meal plans and laundry schedule. To her vows "to love, honor, and cherish" she could have added, "to cook, serve, and clean up." She had been anticipating the first meal she would prepare for her husband. Granted, nothing is wrong with wanting to serve and provide for the one you love—but she spoke of this meal as if it were a pass-or-fail exam given by her employer on her first day on the job. Following the big day of judgment, she was elated to have passed with flying colors.

I couldn't help wondering what would have happened if her meal had been a flop. Would she have lost her marriage as an employee loses a job? As long as my friend retains such a narrow and materialistic view of wifely duties, her marriage is not likely to be anything more than a job.

Not all my friends are obsessed with wifely duties, but some do have a definite sense of husbandly duties. A potential husband must measure up to the qualifications of the position, foremost of which is wealth. One of the first questions about any male is, "What does he do?" Engineering majors or pre-med students usually get highest ranking, and humanities or music majors end up at the bottom. College women are by no means opposed to marriage based on true love, but, as we grow older, the fantasy of a Prince Charming gives way to the reality of an affluent provider. Some women look for high-paying marriages just as they look for high-paying jobs.

Some of my peers may see marriage as one of many career choices, but my parents see it as the only choice. To my parents, my not finding a husband is a much more terrifying fate than my not finding a job. In their view, being a wife is no mere occupation, but a natural vocation for all women. But not just any man will do as a husband. My parents have a built-in screening procedure for each man I date. Appearance, money, and general background are the highest qualifications. They ignore domestic traits because they assume that his parents will be screening me for such qualifications.

I have always tried to avoid considering male friends simply as prospective husbands; likewise, I never think of myself as filling the stereotypical position of wife. But sometimes I fall into my parents' way of thinking. When I invite a friend to dinner at my house, I suddenly find myself fretting about his hair, his religion, or his job. Will he pass the screening test? Is he the right man for the role of husband? In some ways, my attitudes seem no more liberated than those of my peers or parents.

Today's women have made a good deal of progress, but apparently not enough. Allowing the practical implications of marriage to overshadow its emotional implications, a surprising number of us seem to feel that we still have to fit much of the stereotype that Brady condemns.

—*Jacqueline LeBlanc*

Jackie LeBlanc reached deep into her reading and into her own insights to discover a real connection. Her writing, in turn, makes us part of that connection.

In writing about reading, each of us expresses a unique and personal response. Maybe, like Jackie LeBlanc, you will respond in a way that sticks closely to what you've read. Or maybe you will decide to use the reading as a launching toward new exploration, in the way Shirley Haley does after reading the following selection.

CASE STUDY

A SECOND WRITER'S RESPONSE TO READING

This next selection is taken from Annie Dillard's prize-winning book, *Pilgrim at Tinker Creek,* in which she examines the wonders of the natural world in the ordinary places all around her.

As you read, consider this question: Can you identify anything in your life that deserves a closer look?

Essay for analysis and response

Seeing

It is still the first week in January, and I've got great plans. I've been thinking about seeing. There are lots of things to see, unwrapped gifts and free surprises. The world is fairly studded and strewn with pennies cast broadside from a generous hand. But—and this is the point—who gets excited by a mere penny? If you follow one arrow, if you crouch motionless on a bank to watch a tremulous ripple thrill on the water and are rewarded by the sight of a muskrat kit paddling from its den, will you count that sight a chip of copper only, and go your rueful way? It is dire poverty indeed when a man is so malnourished and fatigued that he won't stoop to pick up a penny. But if you cultivate a healthy poverty and simplicity, so that finding a penny will literally make your day, then, since the world is in fact planted in pennies, you have with your poverty bought a lifetime of days. It is that simple. What you see is what you get.

I used to be able to see flying insects in the air. I'd look ahead and see, not the row of hemlocks across the road, but the air in front of it. My eyes would focus along that column of air, picking out flying insects. But I lost interest, I guess, for I dropped the habit. Now I can see birds. Probably some people can look at the grass at their feet and discover all the crawling creatures. I would like to know grasses and sedges—and care. Then my least journey into the world would be a field trip, a series of happy recognitions. Thoreau, in an expansive mood, exulted, "What a rich book might be made about buds, including, perhaps, sprouts!" It would be nice to think so. I cherish mental images I have of three perfectly happy people. One collects stones. Another—an Englishman, say—watches clouds. The third lives on a coast and collects drops of seawater which he examines microscopically and mounts. But I don't see what the specialist sees, and so I cut myself off, not only from the total picture, but from the various forms of happiness.

Unfortunately, nature is very much a now-you-see-it, now-you-don't affair: A fish flashes, then dissolves in the water before my eyes like so much salt. Deer apparently ascend bodily into heaven, the brightest oriole fades into leaves. These disappearances stun me into stillness and concentration; they say of nature that it conceals with a grand nonchalance, and they say of vision that it is a deliberate gift, the revelation of a dancer who for my eyes only flings away her seven veils. For nature does reveal as well as conceal: now-you-don't-see-it, now-you-do. For a week last September migrating red-winged blackbirds were feeding heavily down by the creek at the back of the house. One day I went out to investigate the racket; I walked up to a tree, an Osage orange, and a hundred birds flew away. They simply materialized out of the tree. I saw a tree, then a whisk of color, then a tree again. I walked closer and another hundred blackbirds took flight. Not a branch, not a twig budged: the birds were apparently weightless as well as invisible. Or, it was as if the leaves of the Osage orange had been freed from a spell in the form of red-winged blackbirds; they flew from the tree, caught my eye in the sky, and vanished. When I looked again at the tree the leaves had reassembled as if nothing had happened. Finally I walked directly to the trunk of the tree and a final hundred, the real diehards, appeared, spread, and vanished. How could so many hide in the tree without my seeing them? The Osage orange, unruffled, looked just as it had looked from the house, when three hundred red-winged blackbirds cried from its crown. I looked downstream where they flew, and they were gone. Searching, I couldn't spot one. I wandered downstream to force them to play their hand, but they'd crossed the creek and scattered. One show to a customer. These appearances catch at my throat; they are the free gifts, the bright coppers at the roots of the trees.

—Annie Dillard

In her response to Annie Dillard, Haley sets out to reinvent the meaning of "Seeing," for herself and her readers. Here, after multiple revision, is her finished essay. Even though Haley presents no explicit thesis, her writing clearly enough implies one: Things we truly see outside ourselves sometimes can help ease the pain we feel inside.

Shirley's response to Dillard's essay

SAILBOATS

On an afternoon in late June I stomped out of the house to walk off the frustration of an argument. White fists jammed into my pockets, I rehearsed what I should have said as I tromped fiercely away from the people, the village, the wharf, and the lifeguarded beaches toward the path. A fringe benefit of putting in town sewage four or five years ago, the path begins with the gravel road to the pumping station and moves on around the deepest curve of the harbor, tracing the old railroad bed. It is by no means private there, but by mutual understanding, speaking is optional, nodding preferable; the illusion of privacy is preserved. It's where I walk when I walk and fancy I'll run when I take up running, and today it was where I was stomping.

Like a child more determined to stay angry the harder you coax and tickle, I was determined to stay hurt. The walk would do no good beyond creating space between me and the house. *Pilgrim at Tinker Creek* lay on the table by my bed, and I was angry at Annie Dillard, too. She makes such work of simply being here: marveling at caterpillar foreheads and all the time refocusing to "see." When I refocus, I see places that need cleaning; better to glance and be happy in my ignorance. I cannot see the universe in a drop of water. Hers is not a gift for seeing; it's a gift for applying imagination. I walked the path that day wanting not to think, or feel or see, wishing to be transformed, melted away like the Little Mermaid into the foam at the tip of a wave.

Not far along the way, the path falls away to brackish water (neither salt nor fresh); on either side, the eel pond. It's only a baby pond on the left connected to the expanse of water on the right by a culvert, a giant corrugated tunnel for boys to hoot into and make echos. The bright sky paled against the vivid blue of the pond. The warming air had freed the scent of beach rose and marsh grass. And across the pond, across the buckskin marsh not yet turned jewel green, was the swans' nest. The swans were there like plastic swans on a wedding cake, one on the giant nest, one swimming near with wings slightly raised in a gesture of vigilance.

The growth of land separating pond and marsh from harbor and beach is called Goodspeed Island. It's not really an island, of course, but it's a good place to pretend and to camp out if you're careful about poison ivy. As the path curves from behind it, dissolving from packed dirt to sand, the harbor opens up on the left. A sandy isthmus between pond and ocean, the path continues; I digressed to my destination. The beach is cluttered with beachy clutter: seaweed, shells, waterlogged wood, and plastic rings from six-packs. Aged quarry stones strewn in odd arrangement make ideal seats for the contemplation of universes, if you're so inclined—or of hurts.

The view is of sailboats, mostly moored; the curve of the shore with houses, shops, wharves, and beaches; and, at the farthest point on the far side, the lighthouse, white. Above, the trees, which from here are a solid green rolling back from the harbor, hiding the village, reach the tips of the steeples, a Congregational Church, white, Center School, yellow, marking the block where I live.

I wonder about the boats sometimes; they never seem to go out. Dangling there at their moorings all summer, they float like vanes into the wind. And when weather comes, and it blows, one always slips its mooring and runs with the storm across the harbor to the rocks. I remember clearly going out like ghouls once in the rain to see such a one, its side torn open, and a lady in a yellow slicker picking up silverware in the dark in the surf.

I stayed a while, nursing my hurts and contemplating boats. Dog walkers passed behind me. A resolute lady strode briskly by in warm-up suit zipped to the chin, and the tide began to change. I headed home by the populated route. Still hurt but no longer angry, I walked quietly, carrying beach roses for the dining-room table. At the wharf a 40-foot wooden sailboat, a mahogany beauty, slid into the water and then motored to the dock to have her mast and rigging fitted. At home I took care in arranging my flowers and felt better.

—Shirley Haley

We have seen how two student writers reached deep into their reading and into themselves to make something happen, to discover a real connection. Their writing, in turn, makes us part of that connection.

SUGGESTIONS FOR READING AND WRITING

Some of the readings in later chapters are professionally written, others student written. Besides triggering your own writing, each reading provides a model of worthwhile content, sensible organization, and readable style.

Here are suggestions for reading to respond to the selections assigned throughout the semester:

GUIDELINES FOR READING TO RESPOND

1. Read the piece at least three times: first, to get a sense of the geography; next, to explore your reactions; finally, to see what you find most striking or important or outrageous.

2. Record initial impressions, ideas, or other reactions to the piece, using a journal (page 31).

3. Highlight and annotate passages, underlining the statements that strike you or set

GUIDELINES FOR READING TO RESPOND (continued)

you off, and jot questions and comments in the margins.

4. Summarize the entire piece, to be sure you understand the author's purpose, meaning, and main ideas. (See the guidelines on page 374.)

5. Using the critical questions on page 165, evaluate the content, organization, and style to see exactly how well the author connects with readers.

6. Answer the personal questions on page 166.

7. Once you see what makes the piece tick, settle on the main thing you want to say in reply—your viewpoint.

8. Express your viewpoint in a thesis statement. (See pages 23–28.)

Application **9-1**

Respond to Brady's essay with an essay of your own. Share with us a new way of seeing. Imagine you are conversing with the writer: How would you reply if someone had just spoken what you have read? The above guidelines will help you reach deep into your reading experience. Record your responses in a hard-copy or electronic reading journal. Compose your essay based on your responses.

Application **9-2**

Collaborative Project: Share or email your essay from Application 9-1 with others in your group who have responded to the same essay. Can you pinpoint any places where your responses were very similar or where they were radically different? As a group, discuss the possible reasons for the differences. Have one group member record the reasons for discussion with the entire class.

Application **9-3**

Computer Application: Using your group's listserv or email network, conduct Application 9-2 electronically. Transmit and exchange your documents as email attachments.

Application **9-4**

Web-based Project: Locate advice that expands on this chapter. Look for key principles (say, active versus passive reading) and strategies (say, "rephrase ideas in your own words"). Begin with the following sites but do not limit yourself to these:

- York University Counselling and Development Centre Tips on Reading Skills
  <http://www.york.ca/cdc/lsp/downloads/reading_brochure.PDF>
- Colorado State University page on Reading Processes
  <http://writing.colostate.edu/references/reading.cfm>

Prepare a one-page presentation for classmates on some aspect of reading to write, in your own words. Attach a copy of the relevant Web page(s) to your presentation. Be sure to credit each source of information.

Application **9-5**

Web-based Project: Does Brady's essay describe an essentially timeless situation? Have gender roles changed at all since this essay was written (1972)? Do some roles never change? Are there valid male points of view on these issues, as well?

For contrasting perspectives, visit the following Web sites, but do not limit yourself to these:

- National Organization for Women (NOW)
  <www.now.org>
- Men's Issues Virtual Library
  <http://www.vix.com/men/>

Identify one issue in the ongoing gender debate (say, workplace equity, scholastic performance, or health care differences) and compare the prevailing female and male viewpoints on the issue. In your own words, summarize each contrasting viewpoint in a one-page presentation for your classmates. Attach a copy of the relevant Web pages to your presentation. Be sure to credit each source of information.

CHAPTER 10

Helping Others See and Share an Experience: Description and Narration

Using Objective Description to Inform   **179**

Using Subjective Description to Make a Point   **180**

Using Objective Narration to Explain   **182**

Guidelines for Description   183

Using Subjective Narration to Make a Point   **184**

Guidelines for Narration   188

CASE STUDY: Responding to Reading   **193**

Options for Essay Writing   **196**

Readings   **180, 186, 190, 193**

Applications   **189, 195**

escription creates a word picture, a clear mental image of how something looks. Because it helps readers *visualize*, description is a common denominator in all writing.

What readers expect to learn from a description

- *What is it?*
- *What does it look like?*
- *How could I recognize it?*
- *What is it made of?*
- *What does it do?*
- *How does it work?*
- *What is your impression of it?*
- *How does it make you feel?*

Narration also creates a word picture, telling how events occur in time. It relies on the showing power of descriptive details to make the story vivid, but its main goal is to help readers follow events.

What readers expect to learn from a narrative

- *What happened?*
- *Who was involved?*
- *When did it happen?*
- *Where did it happen?*
- *Why did it happen?*

Because any topic or event can be viewed in countless ways, your decisions about descriptive and narrative details depend on your purpose and the reader's needs. Both strategies can serve either *objective (referential) goals*—that is, they can merely report—or they can be selected and used differently by different writers. They then fill *subjective (and often persuasive) goals*—they make a point.

USING OBJECTIVE DESCRIPTION TO INFORM

Objective description filters out—as much as appropriate—personal impressions, focusing instead on observable details. It provides factual information about something for someone who will use it, buy it, or assemble it, or who needs to know more about it for some good reason. Objective description records exactly what is seen from the writer's vantage point. If your CD player has been stolen, the police need a description that includes the brand name, serial number, model, color, size, shape, and identifying marks or scratches. For this audience, a subjective description (that the item was a handsome addition to your car; that its sound quality was superb; that it made driving a pleasure) would be useless.

AN OBJECTIVE DESCRIPTION

Orienting sentence (1)

View from water (2–5)

View from shoreline (6–7)

[1]The 2-acre building lot for my proposed log cabin sits on the northern shore of Moosehead Lake, roughly 1000 feet east of the Seboomook Point camping area. [2]The site is marked by a granite ledge, 30 feet long and 15 feet high. [3]The ledge faces due south and slopes gradually east. [4]A rock shoal along the westerly frontage extends about 30 feet from the shoreline. [5]On the easterly end of the frontage is a landing area on a small gravel beach immediately to the right of the ledge. [6]Lot boundaries are marked by yellow stakes a few feet from the shoreline. [7]Lot numbers are carved on yellow-marked trees adjacent to the yellow stakes.

The above paragraph, written to help a soil engineer locate the property by boat, follows a spatial order, moving from whole to parts—the same order in which we would actually view the property. Instead of a standard topic statement, the paragraph begins with a simple description, which nonetheless gives us a definite sense of what to expect.

Because the goal above is referential, only factual information appears: a brief but specific catalog of the lot's major features. Other situations might call for more specifics. For instance, the soil engineer's evaluation of the Moosehead site, written for officials who approve building permits, might look like this:

> Hand-dug test holes revealed a well-draining, granular material, with a depth of at least 48 inches to bedrock.

The quantity of detail in a description is keyed to the writer's purpose and the audience's needs.

Note   *Pure objectivity is, of course, humanly impossible. Each writer has a unique perspective on the facts and their meaning, and chooses what to put in and what to leave out.*

USING SUBJECTIVE DESCRIPTION TO MAKE A POINT

No useful description can be strictly subjective; to get the picture, readers need some observable details. Subjective description colors objective details with personal impressions and metaphors. It usually strives to draw readers into the writer's view of the world, often by creating a mood or sharing a feeling, as shown in the italicized expressions below.

A SUBJECTIVE DESCRIPTION

OFF-SEASON

Thesis

I hate summer beaches. Ocean swimming is impossible; upon conquering a wave, I simply lose to the next, getting pushed back onto the hard-packed, abrasive sand. *Booby-traps* of bottles, soda cans, toys, and rocks make walking hazardous. *Heavy with the stench* of suntan lotion, greasy French fries, dead fish, and sweat, *the thick, searing air hangs motionless about the scorching sand.* Blasting radios and growling dune buggies cut the *slap-swoosh* of the green-gray surf to a *weak hiss. People devour a summer beach, gouging the sand with umbrella spikes and gripping it with oiled limbs, leaving only trampled debris at summer's end.*

My interest in beaches begins, then, after the summer people leave. Gone are the trash and trappings. The winter wind is bitter but clean, *fresh with the damp, earthy scent* of cold seaweed. Only broken shells litter the sand, and nearer the water, ice-gray, surf-worn rocks rise like *smooth serpents' backs.* Wave upon wave, the *bruise-colored* sea thunders in, each rolling arc pouring ahead of the next, breaking into smaller and smaller waves, crawling up the beach.

Things endure but things change. Constant waves wash the face of the shore into roundness. Dunes fuse and slide apart, transformed into new mounds by the *coarse* wind. Erosion fences *whistle and ripple and clack, protesting* the sand shifting between the slats. No longer covered by sprawling sun worshippers, the beach forms *a smooth slide of continent into ocean.*

Waves naturally push and pull and wear things down. In time, the ocean will claim as its own the snack shack and the parking lots, the sea walls and the cottages. *Walking the ocean's edge awakens a small fear that the waves might slither around my ankles and draw me into that icy foam. Paralyzed with cold, I will be worn and washed by the surf until I become just another part of the ever-shrinking beach.*

So far, at least, I've been lucky: I walk winter beaches often and see nothing more sinister than gulls cracking crabs on the rocks. But I still avoid the water's edge—*beaches ravaged in summer might harbor a winter impulse for revenge.*

—*Pam Herbert*

Pam's essay blends objective and subjective description (in italics) to help us visualize the contrast between the summer beach, with its "stench" of various offensive odors, and the "clean, fresh" winter beach. The writer's impressions give us a real feel for the place and a new way of seeing.

Beyond creating a mood or sharing a feeling, description can serve practical purposes. The following selection conveys personal impressions to make a persuasive point.

SUBJECTIVE DESCRIPTION IN PERSUASIVE WRITING

Close your eyes for a moment, and picture a professional baseball game. You probably see something like this: a hot summer afternoon, complete with sizzling bats, fans clad in the reds and yellows and pastels of summer, and short-sleeved vendors yelling "ICE CREAM HEEERE!" If you recall some recent World Series, though, you might envision a scene more like this: a c-c-cold starlit night highlighted by players in Thinsulate gloves and turtlenecks, fans in ski hats instead of baseball caps, and vendors hurriedly hawking coffee. This "football-like" image suggests that baseball season is just plain too long!

—*Mike Cabral*

Similarly, a colorful description of your messy dorm or apartment might encourage roommates to clean up their act. Or a nauseating catalog of greasy food served in the college dining hall might prompt school officials to improve the menu. Subjective writing can move readers to see things your way.

USING DESCRIPTION BEYOND THE WRITING CLASSROOM

- **In other courses:** Whether you are describing a lab experiment, a field trip, or a fire hazard in the dorm, you would focus on the observable details, not on your feelings. What specific types of objective description have you written in other courses?

- **In the workplace:** Your descriptions might inform customers about a new product or service. Banks require applicants for loans to describe the property or venture. Architects and engineers would describe their proposed building on paper before construction begins. Medical professionals write detailed records of a patient's condition and treatment. Whenever readers need to visualize the item itself, objective description is essential. What specific types of objective description do you expect to write in your career?

- **In the community:** You might describe the problems with discipline or drugs or violence or overcrowding at the local junior high in an attempt to increase community awareness.

Can you think of other situations in which objective description could make a difference?

USING OBJECTIVE NARRATION TO EXPLAIN

To see how narration, like description, can serve both referential and persuasive purposes, let's look first at narration that informs, reports, or explains. These narratives simply give a picture of what happened, without stating—or even implying—any particular viewpoint. Newspaper stories or courtroom testimonies often provide only the bare facts. This next paragraph simply describes events without inserting personal impressions.

A NARRATIVE THAT MERELY REPORTS

The climactic scene (1)

A related detail (2)

Background (3–9)

[1]Two [suspects] hobbled into Federal Court in Brooklyn on crutches yesterday, each with a leg missing and each charged with smuggling cocaine and marijuana stored in the hollowed-out parts of their confiscated artificial limbs. [2]A third suspect, a . . . woman, was also accused of taking part in the smuggling of $1 million worth of cocaine from Bogota to Kennedy International Airport. [3]Acting on confidential information, customs agents took the three into custody Monday night. [4]The agents took one of the suspects . . . to St. Vincent's Hospital in Manhattan, where physicians removed his plastic

Conclusion (10–11)

leg. [5]Inside, they said, they found one kilo (2.2 pounds) of cocaine wrapped in plastic bags. [6]The suspect told them he had lost his leg during a guerrilla uprising in Colombia two years ago. [7]Agents said they found six ounces of marijuana in the artificial right limb worn by . . . another suspect. [8]The woman . . . was allegedly found to be wearing three girdles, each concealing quantities of plastic-wrapped cocaine totaling one kilo. [9]Agents reported that each suspect had more than $400 and return tickets to Bogota. [10]United States Magistrate Vincent A. Catoggio held each in $100,000 bail. [11]Expressing concern over the missing artificial limbs, which had been described as damaged, he directed that customs agents return them in good condition. . . .

—*The New York Times*

GUIDELINES FOR DESCRIPTION

1. *Always begin with some type of orienting statement.* Objective descriptions rarely call for a standard topic or thesis statement, because their goal merely is to catalog the details that readers can visualize. Any description, however, should begin by telling readers what to look for.

2. *Choose descriptive details to suit your purpose and the reader's needs.* Brainstorming yields more details than a writer can use. Select only those details that advance your meaning. Use objective details to provide a picture of something exactly as a camera would record it. Use subjective details to convey your impressions—to give us a new way of seeing or appreciating something, as in "Off-Season."

3. *For subjective description, focus on a dominant impression.* What specific feeling or sensation about your subject do you want readers to experience? For example, "Off-Season" conveys the dominant impression of an intimidating but pristine and private place, freed from the chaos and pollution of summer crowds. Do you want your own picture to be scary, ugly, humorous, relaxed, or what? The particular impression you decide on will help you select what to include in your description and what to leave out.

4. *Select details that are concrete and specific enough to convey an unmistakable picture.* Most often description works best at the lowest levels of abstraction and generality.

VAGUE	EXACT
at high speed	80 miles an hour
a tiny office	an 8-by-12-foot office
some workers	the accounting staff

5. *Use plenty of sensory details.* Allow readers to *see* "gulls cracking crabs on the rocks," *hear* "the slap-swoosh of the . . . surf," *smell* "the stench of suntan lotion and greasy French fries," *feel* "the hard-packed, abrasive sand." Let readers touch and taste. Use vivid *comparisons* such as "surf-worn rocks rise like smooth serpents' backs" or "bruise-colored sea," to make the picture come to life. Rely on *action verbs* to convey the energy of movement, to show how the erosion fences "whistle and ripple and clack." Sensory details bring a description to life.

6. *Order details in a clear sequence.* Descriptions generally follow a spatial or general-to-specific order—whichever parallels the angle of vision readers would have if viewing the item. Or the details are arranged according to the dominant impression desired.

The paragraph on page 182 implies no main point. The writer simply reports the details of the bizarre smuggling strategy.

Note, however, that the writer juggles the sequence of events to attract our interest. The first two sentences place us at the story's climax. Then the background details follow strict chronological order so that we can keep track of events leading to the courtroom scene. Consistent use of past tense and third-person point of view helps us follow the story.

USING NARRATIVE REPORTS BEYOND THE WRITING CLASSROOM

- **In other courses:** You might report on experiments or investigations in chemistry, biology, or psychology. Or you might retrace the events leading up to the Russian Revolution or the 1929 stock market crash. What specific types of narrative reports have you written in other courses?

- **On the job:** You might report on the events that led up to an accident on the assembly line or provide daily accounts of your crew's progress on a construction project. Whenever readers need to understand *what happened,* narrative reporting is essential. What specific types of narrative reports might you write in your career?

- **In the community:** As a witness to an accident, a crime, or some other incident, you might report what took place.

In what other situations might a narrative report make a difference?

USING SUBJECTIVE NARRATION TO MAKE A POINT

Narration can be an excellent strategy for advancing some definite viewpoint or thesis because a well-told story is easy to remember. When you recount last night's date, your purpose usually is to suggest a particular viewpoint: say, that some people can be fickle, or that first dates can be disastrous. The following brief story shares a special moment in the author's favorite activity—flying a small plane.

A NARRATIVE THAT MAKES A POINT

Orienting sentence

    Rolling down Runway Alpha, I feel so intensely alone that I become part human, part machine—everything working together. My mind's eye is locked on the runway's center line while my eyes flash from windshield to instruments, reading, calculating, missing nothing. Meanwhile, feet and hands make delicate adjustments on the pedals and control yoke, gently . . . gently.

    Relaxed, yet poised, I concentrate so intensely that I and the plane are one. Our airspeed increases. The plane vibrates. We reach the point where the battle begins. Time stops as *83 Bigdog* and I wage silent war with gravity. It pulls at us, insisting that we are bound to the earth, slaves of its laws, this vibrating second seeming like an eternity. But in the end we win. The wheels leave the ground and we climb, that empty-stomach feeling one gets in an elevator intensified threefold. As the ground recedes, we glide above the stress of life down below. *This burst of sensations, these physical and emotional responses to each takeoff, draw me back to the cockpit, again and again.*

—*Phoebe Brown*

Main point

Notice how the entire event is filtered through the author's impressions. The subjective details make the author's sensations real and vivid to readers and support her point about the thrill of taking off. Telling a story can be an effective way of *showing.*

The present tense and first-person point of view give the paragraph a consistent sense of direction (the author tells of her experience). An alternative point of view for narration is the third person (telling of someone else's experience).

Like description, narratives also can move readers to change their attitudes or take action. For instance, you might tell about a boating accident to elicit voter support for tougher boating laws. You might recount the details of a conflict among employees to persuade your boss to institute a stress-management program. By telling the story, you can help readers see things your way.

SUBJECTIVE NARRATION IN PERSUASIVE WRITING

I entered community college at 17 and began taking classes with some 25- and 30-year-old students. Such an age difference made me feel much luckier than these older people. What were they doing in a freshman class, anyway? Compared to them, I had unlimited time to succeed—or so I thought. Soon after my eighteenth birthday, the horrid piece of lung tissue I coughed into the sink gave a whole new meaning to my notion of "youth." Five years of inhaling hot smoke, carbon monoxide, nicotine, and tobacco pesticides finally had produced enough coughing and sickness to terrify me. "Oh, my god, I'm going to die young; I'm going to die before all those 30-year-olds." For years, I had heard my mother tell me that I was committing suicide on the installment plan. Now I seemed to be running out of installments.

—*Chris Adey*

By letting the story make the point, Chris's narrative seems more persuasive than the usual sermons: "Smoking is bad for you," and so on.

The main point in a narrative might be expressed as a topic or thesis statement at the beginning or end of the story. Or, as in the two narratives above, the main point might not be stated at all, but only implied by the story. But even when its point is saved for last or just implied, the story often opens with some statement that orients readers to the events.

The most powerful narratives often are those that combine objective and subjective details to reveal their point. In the following essay, an African American explores how a black man can induce paranoia among people who react to a racial stereotype. As you read, think about any hasty assumptions you may have made on the basis of a person's appearance.

BLACK MEN AND PUBLIC SPACE

My first victim was a woman—white, well dressed, probably in her early twenties. I came upon her late one evening on a deserted street in Hyde Park, a relatively affluent neighborhood in an otherwise mean, impoverished section of Chicago. As I swung onto the avenue behind her, there seemed to be a discreet, uninflammatory distance between us. Not so. She cast back a worried glance. To her, the youngish black man—a broad six feet two inches with a beard and billowing hair, both hands shoved into the pockets of a bulky military jacket—seemed menacingly close. After a few more quick glimpses, she picked up her pace and was soon running in earnest. Within seconds she disappeared into a cross street.

That was more than a decade ago. I was twenty-two years old, a graduate student newly arrived at the University of Chicago. It was in the echo of that terrified woman's footfalls that I first began to know the unwieldy inheritance I'd come into—the ability to alter public space in ugly ways. It was clear that she thought herself the quarry of a mugger, a rapist, or worse. Suffering from a bout of insomnia, however, I was stalking sleep, not defenseless wayfarers. As a softy who is scarcely able to take a knife to a raw chicken—let alone hold one to a person's throat—I was surprised, embarrassed, and dismayed all at once. Her flight made me feel like an accomplice in tyranny. It also made it clear that I was indistinguishable from the muggers who occasionally seeped into the area from the surrounding ghetto. That first encounter, and those that followed, signified that a vast, unnerving gulf lay between nighttime pedestrians—particularly women—and me. And I soon gathered that being perceived as dangerous is a hazard in itself. I only needed to turn a corner into a dicey situation, or crowd some frightened, armed person in a foyer somewhere, or make an errant move after being pulled over by a policeman. Where fear and weapons meet—and they often do in urban America—there is always the possibility of death.

In that first year, my first away from my hometown, I was to become thoroughly familiar with the language of fear. At dark, shadowy intersections, I could cross in front of a car stopped at a traffic light and elicit the thunk, thunk, thunk, thunk of the driver—black, white, male, or female—hammering down the door locks. On less traveled streets after dark, I grew accustomed to but never comfortable with people crossing to the other side of the street rather than pass me. Then there were the standard unpleasantries with policemen, doormen, bouncers, cabdrivers, and others whose business it is to screen out troublesome individuals before there is any nastiness.

I moved to New York nearly two years ago and I have remained an avid night walker. In central Manhattan, the near-constant crowd cover minimizes tense one-on-one street encounters. Elsewhere—in SoHo, for example, where sidewalks are narrow and tightly spaced buildings shut out the sky—things can get very taut indeed.

After dark, on the warrenlike streets of Brooklyn where I live, I often see women who fear the worst from me. They seem to have set their faces on neutral, and with their purse straps strung across their chests bandolier-style, they forge ahead as though bracing themselves against being tackled. I understand, of course, that the danger they perceive is not a hallucination. Women are particularly vulnerable to street violence, and young black males are drastically overrepresented among the perpetrators of that violence. Yet these truths are no solace against the kind of alienation that comes of being ever the suspect, a fearsome entity with whom pedestrians avoid making eye contact.

It is not altogether clear to me how I reached the ripe old age of twenty-two without being conscious of the lethality nighttime pedestrians attributed to me. Perhaps it was because in Chester, Pennsylvania, the small, angry industrial town where I came of age in the 1960s, I was scarcely noticeable against a backdrop of gang warfare, street knifings, and murders. I grew up one of the good boys, had perhaps a half-dozen fistfights. In retrospect, my shyness of combat has clear sources.

As a boy, I saw countless tough guys locked away; I have since buried several, too. They were babies, really—a teenage cousin, a brother of twenty-two, a childhood friend in his mid-twenties—all gone down in episodes of bravado played out in the streets. I came to doubt the virtues of intimidation early on. I chose, perhaps unconsciously, to remain a shadow—timid, but a survivor.

The fearsomeness mistakenly attributed to me in public places often has a perilous flavor. The most frightening of these confusions occurred in the late 1970s and early 1980s, when I worked as a journalist in Chicago. One day, rushing into the office of a magazine I was writing for with a deadline story in hand, I was mistaken for a burglar. The office manager called security and, with an ad hoc posse, pursued me through the labyrinthine halls, nearly to my editor's door. I had no way of proving who I was. I could only move briskly toward the company of someone who knew me.

Another time I was on assignment for a local paper and killing time before an interview. I entered a jewelry store on the city's affluent Near North Side. The proprietor excused herself and returned with an enormous red Doberman pinscher straining at the end of a leash. She stood, the dog extended toward me, silent to my questions, her eyes bulging nearly out of her head. I took a cursory look around, nodded, and bade her good night.

Relatively speaking, however, I never fared as badly as another black male journalist. He went to nearby Waukegan, Illinois, a couple of summers ago to work on a story about a murderer who was born there. Mistaking the reporter for the killer, police officers hauled him from his car at gunpoint and but for his press credentials would probably have tried to book him. Such episodes are not uncommon. Black men trade tales like this all the time.

> Over the years, I learned to smother the rage I felt at so often being taken for a criminal. Not to do so would surely have led to madness. I now take precautions to make myself less threatening. I move about with care, particularly late in the evening. I give a wide berth to nervous people on subway platforms during the wee hours, particularly when I have exchanged business clothes for jeans. If I happen to be entering a building behind some

GUIDELINES FOR NARRATION

1. *Set the scene immediately.* Place readers right at the center of the action. If you open with some sort of background explanation (as in "Back at the Ranch," page 190), keep it short and sweet. Be clear about when and where the event occurred and about who was involved.

2. *Convey your main point, whether stated or implied, through the narrative details.* A narrative that simply reports, of course, has no main point. But if your narrative does make a point, consider delaying that point until the end; use an earlier orienting statement to let us know what's going on.

3. *Choose details to serve specifically your purpose and the reader's needs.* Select only those details that directly advance your meaning. Focus on the important details, but don't leave out lesser details that hold the story together. Decide when to describe events objectively and when to filter events through your own impressions.

4. *Choose details that are concrete and specific enough to show clearly what happened.* Narration is most effective at the lowest levels of abstraction and generality. Use plenty of visual details—the details of real life. Try to show people "doing," and let us hear them talking.

5. *Order details in a clear sequence.* Chronological ordering often works best in a nar-

rative, because it enables readers to follow events as they occurred. But for special emphasis, you might use a *flashback* or a *flashforward* to present certain events out of sequence.

6. *Control your tenses and transitions.* To keep readers on track, indicate a clear time frame for each event: present, past, past perfect ("had been"), or even future tense (as in paragraph 5, page 194). If you move from one time frame to another, be sure to keep the tense consistent within each frame (as in "The Old Guy," page 193). To create a sense of immediacy, use the present tense.

   Use transitions to mark time and sequence. Review pages 110–12 for use of transitions.

7. *Keep the point of view straight.* Decide whether you are describing an event from the perspective of a participant (first-person point of view) or an observer (third person). Narratives designed to make a point (as in "Back at the Ranch," page 190) often blend both perspectives. If you move from one perspective to another, be sure to maintain a consistent point of view for each perspective.

8. *Explore the larger meaning of the events.* Help readers process the story; tell us what all this means and what we should remember about it.

people who appear skittish, I may walk by, letting them clear the lobby before I return, so as not to seem to be following them. I have been calm and extremely congenial on those rare occasions when I've been pulled over by the police.

And on late-evening constitutionals I employ what has proved to be an excellent tension-reducing measure: I whistle melodies from Beethoven and Vivaldi and the more popular classical composers. Even steely New Yorkers bunching toward nighttime destinations seem to relax, and occasionally they even join in the tune. Virtually everybody seems to sense that a mugger wouldn't be warbling bright, sunny selections from Vivaldi's Four Seasons. It is my equivalent of the cowbell that hikers wear when they know they are in bear country.

—*Brent Staples*

Staples analyzes the links between events to argue that a racial stereotype has a double effect: in narrowing the perceptions of those who impose the stereotype and in narrowing the choices of those who endure the stereotype.

Can you identify five memorable objective details in Staples's narrative? Five subjective ones?

Application **10-1**

Paragraph Warm-Up: Description that Informs

Assume that a close friend has been missing for two days. The police have been called in. Because you know this person well, the police have asked you for a written description. Write an objective description that would help the police identify this person. To create a clear picture, stick to details any observer could recognize. If possible, include one or more unique identifying features (scar, mannerisms, and so on). Leave out personal comments, and give only objective details. Refer to the Guidelines for Description, page 183. Use the paragraph on page 107 as a model.

Application **10-2**

Paragraph Warm-Up: Description that Makes a Point

Assume that your college newspaper runs a weekly column titled "Memorable Characters." You have been asked to submit a brief sketch of a person you find striking in some way. Create a word portrait of this person in one paragraph. Your description should focus on a dominant impression, blending objective details and subjective commentary. Be sure to focus on personal characteristics that support your dominant impression. Develop your description according to the Guidelines for Description on page 183.

Application **10-3**

Paragraph Warm-Up: Narration that Informs

Assume that you have recently witnessed an event or accident in which someone has been accused of an offense. Because you are an objective witness, the authorities have asked you to write a short report, telling them exactly what you saw. Your report will be used as evidence. Tell what happened without injecting personal impressions or interpretations. Refer to the Guidelines for Narration on page 188.

Application **10-4**

Paragraph Warm-Up: Narration that Makes a Point

Tell about a recent experience or incident you witnessed that left a strong impression on you. Write for your classmates, and be sure to include the facts of the incident, as well as your emotional reaction to it. In other words, give your audience enough details so that they will understand and, ideally, share your reaction. Use Chris Adey's paragraph as a model, letting the details of the story imply your main point. Refer to the Guidelines for Narration on page 188.

Application **10-5**

Essay Practice

The following narrative, "Back at the Ranch," recalls how a dreadful moment during the writer's adolescence changed his own perception of "manhood."

As you read, think about an event in your own life that changed your attitude.

ESSAY FOR ANALYSIS AND RESPONSE

Back at the Ranch

A young boy molts. Tender skin falls off, or gets scraped off, and is replaced by a tougher, more permanent crust. The transition happens in moments, in events. All of a sudden, something is gone and something else is in its place. I made a change like that standing in the back of a pickup truck when I was 15.

It was 1967 and I had a summer job at a camp in Wyoming. It was beautiful there, high-pasture country with a postcard view of the Tetons. As an apprentice counselor I straddled the worlds of boys and men, breathing the high air, watching over kids, hanging out with cowboys. The cowboys wrangled the horses for the camp and were mostly an itinerant group, living in summer cabins below the barn, and they tolerated my loitering down there.

I hitched up my jeans just like them, braided my lasso like them, smoked and cursed and slouched like them.

On the day it happened, I was standing with a group of cowboys by the ranch office. We heard the sound of a big engine coming in the long driveway, and after a while a red Corvette Sting Ray convertible, of all things, motored up in front of us. Conversation stopped. In the driver's seat was a hippie. His hair fell straight down his back and a bandanna was tied around his head. His style may have been standard for somewhere, but not for Jackson, Wyo.

The guy was decked out with beads and earrings, and dressed in fantastic colors, and next to him his girlfriend, just as exotic, with perfect blond hair, looked up at us over little square glasses with a distracted, angelic expression. All in a red Corvette.

I was fascinated, mesmerized. I looked around me with a big grin and realized that I was alone in this feeling. The cowboys all had hard stares, cold eyes. I adjusted, a traitor to myself, and blanked out my expression in kind.

The hippie opened up a big smile, and said: "I went to camp here when I was a kid ... came by to say hi. Is Weenie around?"

In that moment, Weenie, the owner of the place, having heard the throb of the engine, appeared in the ranch office door and walked toward us with a bowlegged stride, his big belt buckle coming first. He walked right up to the driver and looked down on him.

"Get out." Weenie didn't say hi. "Get out of here now."

"What? Wait a minute. I came to say hi. I went to camp here. I just came to say hi."

"Get the hell off this ranch. Now." And staring at the hippie, Weenie kicked some dust up on the side of the Corvette.

"What's wrong with you, man?"

"You're what's wrong with me, son."

I noticed the cowboys were nodding. I nodded. Weenie's right. The guy should leave. He doesn't belong here.

"But you sent me a Christmas card!" By this time, the hippie had choked up a little. "I don't believe it. You sent me a goddamn Christmas card!"

The group of us closed in a little around the car. We-don't-like-that-kind-of-talk-from-a-hippie was the feeling I was getting. Thumbs came out of belt-loops. Jaws began to work.

"Looks like the little girlie's cryin'," said one of the cowboys, a tough one named Hondu. He spoke with his lips turned down on one side as if he was mouthing a cigarette. "Maybe so," said another, with mock consideration.

The notion rested in the air peacefully for a moment, then, in a sudden whipping motion, Hondu's jackknife was out, open and raised. With his other hand, he reached down and grabbed a fat bunch of the hippie's hair and pulled it toward him. Smiling grimly, he hacked it off and held it up for us to see.

During this, I looked down at the hippie's face, which was lifted up and sideways in such a way that he was looking right at me. Involuntarily, my head titled just like his and we froze like that for a second.

"There now, that's better, ain't it?" asked Hondu.

The hippie, stunned, turned to his girlfriend, whose eyes and mouth had been wide open as long as he had been sitting there. Then he turned back to us, his face contorted, helpless. And then he went wild. He threw open his door and tried to jump up from the seat, but forgot that his seat belt was fastened and it held him in place. He struggled against it, screaming, swinging his arms like a bar fighter trying to shrug off his buddies restraining him. It was funny. Like a cartoon.

I looked around. We were all laughing. Our group closed up a little more, and came toward the car. The air bristled. He was the one who started the trouble. Well, he would get what he was looking for, all right.

The hippie stopped struggling, threw the Vette into gear, and fishtailed in the dust. We all jumped out of the way, but the open door of the car bumped into Weenie's favorite dog, a Rhodesian Ridgeback, an inside-out-looking animal that gave a wild yelp and ran straight into a willow thicket. We could hear his yips over the sound of the big engine as the hippie gunned it and took off.

That settled it. The hippie hit the dog.

Without hesitation, we jumped into one of the trucks. Rifles were drawn from the rack in the cab. Other weapons were thrown up into the bed of the pickup. I was standing there and caught one.

We took off, and because the rough road slowed down the Corvette, we were gaining. I was filled with a terrible, frightening righteousness. I was holding a rifle, chasing a man and a woman with a rifle in my hand. I looked around at my partners in the truck, and the air came out of me. We meant harm. We didn't care. I wondered who I was exactly. I needed to know. And in that moment, it happened: I switched sides and never said a word about it.

We hit the asphalt road and floored it, but we couldn't catch the Corvette. No way. The smoke from its exhaust settled around us like fog in the valley.

Still, 23 years later, I can see the two of us clearly, chosen by the same moment. Memory cuts back and forth between our faces. The wind pulls tears from the hippie's eyes; his long hair waves behind him in his fiery convertible rocketing down Route 191 under the Tetons. I with my short hair stand in the back of a pickup truck watching after him, chasing after him, following, facing the same wind.

—*Jay Allison*

QUESTIONS ABOUT YOUR READING

Refer to the general questions on page 165, as well as these specific questions:

PURPOSE

- In your view, what does Allison want the audience to be thinking or feeling after reading this piece?
- Does the essay succeed in making a difference with readers? If so, how?

CONTENT

- Does this essay merely inform or does it make a point, and if so, what is the point?
- Can you identify any new insights or unusual perspectives?

ORGANIZATION

- What major devices lend coherence to this narrative? Give examples of each.

STYLE

- What about the short sentences and paragraphs? Are they effective? Explain.
- What is the writer's attitude toward his subject, toward his audience? How do we know? What are the signals?
- Which images here most help us visualize?

RESPONDING TO YOUR READING

"Back At the Ranch" proves that an essay about "What I Did Last Summer" can be much more than a tired list of worn-out images and travel clichés—that telling your own story can make a difference. Explore your personal reactions to this essay by using the personal response questions on page 166. Then respond with your own narrative about an event that has made a difference in your life. Work to recapture for us the force of the event and its impact on you. Tell us what happened, but be sure to let us know what meaning the event ultimately had for you.

CASE STUDY

RESPONDING TO READING

After reading Jay Allison's "Back at the Ranch," Al Andrade decides to write about a turning point in his own awareness of his coming of age. To analyze Allison's technique and respond to that essay, Al combines the Reading Guidelines on page 175 with the questions about the reading, pages 165, 166.

As he works through various drafts, Al relies on the Narration Guidelines on page 188 and the Revision Checklist on page 63 to produce the final draft that follows.

Alternates first- and third-person points of view throughout

Paragraph 1 sets the scene

Begins in past tense

Uses present tense to give background

THE OLD GUY

¹The workout was progressing as it usually does. My father and I took turns grunting the weights up and down off our chests. Our pectorals, shoulders, and arms were shaking. Throughout the one-hour session, we encouraged and coached one another. Fortunately, weight lifting demands short breaks after each set. Without these breaks our workouts might last only two minutes. The time spent preparing for the next set (or recovering from the last one) is important, not because I'm lazy but because it gives me a chance to catch up on things with Dad. Since we don't get to see each

Paragraph 2 leads into orienting statement

Returns to past tense for main events

Events throughout follow chronological order

Paragraphs 1–4 offer a participant's perspective

Shows someone talking

Orienting statement previews the main point

Transitions throughout mark time and sequence

Shows someone "doing"

Paragraphs 4–5 focus on the author's impressions

Paragraphs 5–6 offer an observer's perspective

Uses future tense for flashforward

Uses present tense to explore the larger meaning of these events

other very often, the latest news, gossip, and philosophies get aired in the weight room.

²While I was changing the weight on the barbell for our next set, Dad was hanging around the exercise room. We'd been talking about the possibility of building an apartment on the lot next door. This discussion led to real estate, which led to the stock market, which led to his retirement. Lately Dad has been complaining a lot about his company's lousy retirement plan. I figured he was just a practical guy planning for more comfortable retirement. Then he looked up from behind the squat rack and said, "You know, Al, if I'm lucky, I have only twenty or twenty-five years left, and I don't want to be eating dog food when I retire." I snickered at the dog food remark. He's always overstating things for emphasis. The other part of his remark—the part about having only twenty or twenty-five years left—seemed a bit melodramatic. At first, Dad's comment rolled off me like a bead of sweat, until I began doing some personal arithmetic of my own.

³Our workout moved from the bench press to the chinning bar. I went first. Then I watched while Dad strained to pull himself up for the tenth repetition. "Not bad for an old guy," he said after he jumped down off the bar. I looked at him and thought he really wasn't bad. Aside from a minor middle-aged belly, he is more powerful now than ever. He routinely dead lifts 450 pounds. And even with a bad shoulder, Dad can still bench press over 250 pounds. Not bad for an old guy is right—or a young guy, for that matter. This time, however, the reference to his age wasn't as easy for me to shrug off.

⁴No longer concentrating on the weights, I thought about aging. The thought of Dad aging didn't overly distress me. I mean, the man was healthy, strong, and sweating just a few feet away. But then I pictured myself getting old, considered what I'd be doing and saying in twenty-five years. Would I be grousing about retirement plans? Would I be working out twice as hard with the notion that I might live a little longer?

⁵Most likely I'll be doing the same things Dad is doing now. A 50-year-old family man counting the years he has left. I'll be a man too busy making a living to ever make enough money. Instead of counting up the years, I'll be counting them down: five years until my retirement, ten years until I can withdraw money from my IRA without penalty, and two years before my son's twenty-fifth birthday. The cycle will be complete. I will replace my father and a son will replace me.

⁶I understand how "life goes on" and how "we're not getting any younger." But I now worried about the inevitability of middle age. I couldn't help putting myself in the Old Guy's place—of retirement worries and declining chin-ups. Twenty-three-year-old people aren't supposed to worry about retirement, or even middle age. Brilliant careers and healthy, productive lives lie ahead for us, right? We've got everything to look forward to. We think about raising families, achieving goals, and becoming successful—not about our own mortality. But we all eventually reach a time when thoughts of our own old age and death become an everyday reality.

Paragraph 7 returns to participant's perspective and past tense *Ends with implied thesis (main point)*	⁷Dad wrapped his hands around the chinning bar for his last set. This time he struggled to get six repetitions. I jabbed him and jokingly scolded, "What's the matter with you?" He turned and grinned and shook his finger at me and said, "We'll see what you can do at fifty years old." *I told him I could wait.* <div align="right">—Al Andrade</div>

Application **10-6**

Web-based Project: Describe some special place where you've lived or visited or would like to visit. Or describe a notable person whom you consider special in some way. For either assignment, prepare two versions, one objective and one subjective, in which you convey a dominant impression of the person or place. For ideas and raw material, begin with the following sites, but do not limit yourself to these:

- *Fodor's Online,* for exotic vacation destinations
  <www.fodors.com>
- *Tourism Offices Worldwide Directory*
  <www.towd.com>
- *Biography.com,* for profiles of famous people
  <www.biography.com>
- *Historical Biographical Dictionary*
  <www.s9.com/biography/>

Be sure to credit each source of information and to attach copies of relevant Web pages to your descriptions.

Be prepared to explain the differences in your two versions to the class.

Application **10-7**

Web-based Project: To get ideas for a compelling narrative, visit the following Web sites, but do not limit yourself to these:

- University of Oregon resources on literary nonfiction
  <http://Inf.uoregon.edu>
- A brief Introduction to Narrative Nonfiction
  <http://www.edwardhumes.com/narrative.htm>
- *Storyteller.net*
  <www.storyteller.net>

In a one-page presentation for your class, describe the kinds of helpful advice about nonfiction narratives visitors can find there. Trace the links they should follow to reach advice that relates to college essays. Attach a copy of the relevant Web page(s) to your presentation.

OPTIONS FOR ESSAY WRITING

1. Explore your reactions to "Off-Season" (page 180) by using the personal response questions on page 166. Then respond with an essay of your own. If you describe a special place, give a clear picture, as well as your dominant impression of the place.

2. Explore your reactions to "Black Men and Public Space" by using the questions on pages 165, 166, and those below.

   - For whom does Staples seem to be writing?
   - What assumptions does he make about his audience's knowledge and attitudes? Are these assumptions accurate? Why or why not?
   - What are the main issues here? How has this essay affected your thinking about these issues?
   - What point is Staples making about stereotypes?
   - What is this writer's attitude toward his subject? Toward his audience? How do we know? What are the signals?
   - How would you characterize the tone of this essay? Is it appropriate for this writer's audience and purpose?

   Most of us want to be liked and accepted and respected. As you reread the essay, try to recall a situation in which you or someone close to you was the object of someone's hostility or rejection—say, because of resentment or fear or anger or scorn. (Or perhaps someone else was the object of yours!) Perhaps the reaction was based on a stereotype or misunderstanding or personal bias. Perhaps, after realizing rejection, you modified your behavior to fit in; you invented a self that seemed more acceptable. Identify your audience, and decide what you want these readers to be doing or thinking or feeling after reading your essay. Describe the events and your reactions in enough detail for readers to visualize what happened and what resulted. Without preaching or moralizing, try to explain your view of this experience's *larger meaning*.

3. Do you have a hero or know a villain? Describe this person in an essay for your classmates. Provide enough descriptive details for your audience to understand why you admire or despise this person. Supply at least three characteristics to support your dominant impression.

4. Assume that you are applying for your first professional job after college. Respond to the following request from the job application:

   Each of us has been confronted by an "impossible situation"—a job that appeared too big to complete, a situation that seemed too awkward to handle, or a problem that felt too complex to deal with. Describe such a situation and how you dealt with it. Your narrative should make a point about the situation, problem solving, or yourself.

5. Tell an audience about the event that has caused you the greatest guilt, anger, joy, or other strong emotion, and how you reacted.

CHAPTER 11

Providing Examples: Illustration

Using Examples to Explain   **198**

Using Examples to Make a Point   **199**

Guidelines for Illustrating with Examples   **201**

CASE STUDY: Responding to Reading   **204**

Options for Essay Writing   **206**

Readings   **202, 204**

Applications   **200, 206**

The backbone of explanation, *examples* are concrete and specific instances of a writer's main point.

What readers expect to learn from examples

- *What makes you think so?*
- *Can you show me?*

Examples provide the evidence that enables readers to understand your meaning and accept your viewpoint. The best way to illustrate what you mean by an "inspiring teacher" is to use one of your professors as an example. You might illustrate this professor's qualities by describing several of her teaching strategies. Or you might give an extended example (say, how she

197

helped you develop confidence). Either way, you have made the abstract notion "inspiring teacher" concrete and, thus, understandable. (Notice how this paragraph's main point is clarified by the professor example.)

USING ILLUSTRATION BEYOND THE WRITING CLASSROOM

- **In other courses:** For a psychology course, you might give examples of paranoid behavior among world leaders; for an ecology course, an example of tree species threatened by acid rain.

- **On the job:** You might give examples of how the software developed by your company can be used in medical diagnosis, or examples of how certain investments have performed in the recent decade.

- **In the community:** You might give examples of how your town can provide a favorable economic climate for new industry, or examples of how other towns have coped with cutbacks in school funding.

What other specific uses of examples can you envision in any of the above three areas?

USING EXAMPLES TO EXPLAIN

In referential writing, examples help readers grasp an abstract term or a complex principle. You could explain what grunge music is by pointing out examples of well-known bands that have incorporated its influence. Or suppose you wanted to explain how the *liberal arts* have practical value in one's career; for this purpose, the paragraph below would not be very understandable:

A PASSAGE NEEDING EXAMPLES

The irony of the emphasis being placed on careers is that nothing is more valuable for anyone who has had a professional or vocational education than to be able to deal with abstractions or complexities, or to feel comfortable with subtleties of thought or language, or to think sequentially. People who have such skills will have a major advantage in just about any career. In all these respects, the liberal arts have much to offer. Just in terms of career preparation, therefore, a student is shortchanging himself or herself by shortcutting the humanities.

Because this paragraph tells, but doesn't show, it fails to make a convincing case for a liberal arts education. Any reader will have unanswered questions:

- *What do you mean by "abstractions or complexities," "subtleties of thought or language," or "to think sequentially"?*

- *How, exactly, do students "shortchange" themselves by shortcutting the humanities?*
- *Can you show me how a liberal arts education is useful in one's career?*

Now consider the revised version of the same paragraph:

A REVISION THAT INCLUDES EXAMPLES

Main point (1)

Examples (2–5)

Summary (6)

Conclusion explains how the examples fit the main point (7)

[1]*The irony of the emphasis being placed on careers is that nothing is more valuable for anyone who has had a professional or vocational education than to be able to deal with abstractions or complexities, or to feel comfortable with subtleties of thought or language, or to think sequentially.* [2]*The doctor* who knows only disease is at a disadvantage alongside the doctor who knows at least as much about people as [he or she] does about pathological organisms. [3]*The lawyer* who argues in court from a narrow legal base is no match for the lawyer who can connect legal precedents to historical experience and who employs wide-ranging intellectual resources. [4]*The business executive* whose competence in general management is bolstered by an artistic ability to deal with people is of prime value to [her] company. [5]For *the technologist,* the engineering of consent can be just as important as the engineering of moving parts. [6]In all these respects, the liberal arts have much to offer. [7]Just in terms of career preparation, therefore, a student is short-changing himself by shortcutting the humanities. [*emphasis added*]

—*Norman Cousins*

The examples (in italics) help convince us that the author has a valid point.

USING EXAMPLES TO MAKE A POINT

Because examples so often provide the evidence to back up assertions, they have great persuasive power. For one thing, they can make writing more convincing simply by making it more interesting. This next writing sample employs vivid examples as a basis for the author's judgment about a controversial trend in American society.

EXAMPLES THAT MAKE A POINT

Main point (1)

[1]*In a society based on self-reliance and free will, the institutionalization of life scares me.* [2]Today, America has government-funded programs to treat all society's ills. [3]We have day-care centers for the young, nursing homes for the old, psychologists in schools who use mental health as an instrument of discipline, and mental hospitals for those whose behavior does not conform to the norm. [4]We have drug-abuse programs, methadone-maintenance programs, alcohol programs, vocational programs, rehabilitation programs, learning-how-to-cope-with-death-for-the-terminally-ill programs, make-friends-with-your-neighborhood-policeman programs, helping-emotionally-

Conclusion explains how
the examples fit the main
point (10–12)

disturbed-children programs, and how-to-accept-divorce programs.
[5]Unemployment benefits and welfare are programs designed to institutionalize a growing body of citizens whose purpose in life is the avoidance of work. [6]They are dependent on the state for their livelihood. [7]We can't even let people die in peace. [8]We put them in hospitals for the dying, so that they can be programmed into dying correctly. [9]They don't need to be hospitalized; they would be better off with their families, dying with dignity instead of in these macabre halfway houses. [10]All this is a displacement of confidence from the individual to the program. [11]We can't rely on people to take care of themselves anymore so we have to funnel them into programs. [12]This is a self-perpetuating thing, for the more programs we make available, the more people will become accustomed to seeking help from the government. [emphasis added]

—*Ted Morgan*

In what order (chronological, general-to-specific, and so on) are the above examples presented? Is this order effective? Explain.

In contrast to the previous writing sample, with its series of brief examples, this next persuasive paragraph presents one, single extended example:

Acid rain indirectly threatens human health. Besides containing damaging chemicals, acid rain percolates through the soil, leaching out naturally present heavy metals, such as arsenic and mercury. Surface runoff then carries these pollutants into streams, lakes, and ponds, where they accumulate permanently in the fatty tissue of fish. In turn, any organisms eating the fish—or drinking the water—build up these poisons in their own body tissue. Moreover, acidified water can release strong concentrations of lead, copper, and aluminum from metal plumbing, making ordinary tap water hazardous. Even in the tiniest amounts, the gradual ingestion of these heavy metals has been shown to cause cancer, birth defects, and a host of other ailments.

—*Bill Kelly*

To support his point about the dangers of acid rain, this author offers a vivid example of how the process occurs.

Application 11-1

PARAGRAPH WARM-UP: USING EXAMPLES TO EXPLAIN

Pierre, a French student who plans to attend an American university, has asked what the typical American college student is like. He has inquired about interests, activities, attitudes, and tastes. Selecting one or more characteristics *you* think typify American college students, write a response to Pierre.

GUIDELINES FOR ILLUSTRATING WITH EXAMPLES

1. *Fit the examples to your purpose and the readers' needs.* An effective example fits the point it is designed to illustrate. Also, the example is familiar and forceful enough for readers to recognize and remember.
2. *Use brief or extended examples.* Some examples need more explanation than others. For example, Bill Kelly (page 200) spells out the details of a single process, whereas Ted Morgan (page 199) catalogs the many threats to self-reliance that he observes.
3. *Make the example more specific and concrete than the point it illustrates.* Vivid examples usually occupy the lowest level of generality and abstraction. They enable readers to *visualize.*
4. *Arrange examples in a series in an accessible order.* If your illustration is a narrative or some historical catalog, order your examples chronologically. Otherwise, try a "least-to-most" (least-to-most-dramatic or important or useful) order. Placing the most striking example last ensures greatest effect.
5. *Know "how much is enough."* Overexplaining insults a reader's intelligence.
6. *Explain how the example fits the point.* Close by refocusing on the larger meaning of your examples.

Application **11-2**

PARAGRAPH WARM-UP: USING EXAMPLES TO MAKE A POINT

Assume your campus newspaper is inviting contributions for a new section called "Insights," a weekly collection of one-paragraph essays by students. Student contributors should focus on examples gained by close observation of campus life and American values or habits to offer some fresh insight on a problem facing our culture. Using Morgan's paragraph (page 199) as a model, write such a paragraph for the newspaper. Choose examples to convince your audience that the problem you discuss is real.

Application **11-3**

ESSAY PRACTICE

The following essay appeared in *Newsweek* magazine. Read this essay, and answer the questions that follow it, as well as those on page 165. Then select one of the essay assignments.

As you read, think about instances in which media stereotypes may have influenced your own opinions about people.

ESSAY FOR ANALYSIS AND RESPONSE

A CASE OF "SEVERE BIAS"

[1]This is who I am not. I am not a crack addict. I am not a welfare mother. I am not illiterate. I am not a prostitute. I have never been in jail. My children are not in gangs. My husband doesn't beat me. My home is not a tenement. None of these things defines who I am, nor do they describe the other black people I've known and worked with and loved and befriended over these 40 years of my life.

[2]Nor does it describe most of black America, period.

[3]Yet in the eyes of the American news media, this is what black America is: poor, criminal, addicted and dysfunctional. Indeed, media coverage of black America is so one-sided, so imbalanced that the most victimized and hurting segment of the black community—a small segment, at best—is presented not as the exception but as the norm. It is an insidious practice, all the uglier for its blatancy.

[4]In recent months, oftentimes in this very magazine, I have observed a steady offering of media reports on crack babies, gang warfare, violent youth, poverty and homelessness—and in most cases, the people featured in the photos and stories were black. At the same time, articles that discuss other aspects of American life—from home buying to medicine to technology to nutrition—rarely, if ever, show blacks playing a positive role, or for that matter, any role at all.

[5]Day after day, week after week, this message—that black America is dysfunctional and unwhole—gets transmitted across the American landscape. Sadly, as a result, America never learns the truth about what is actually a wonderful, vibrant, creative community of people.

[6]Most black Americans are not poor. Most black teenagers are not crack addicts. Most black mothers are not on welfare. Indeed, in sheer numbers, more white Americans are poor and on welfare than are black. Yet one never would deduce that by watching television or reading American newspapers and magazines.

[7]Why does the American media insist on playing this myopic, inaccurate picture game? In this game, white America is always whole and lovely and healthy while black America is usually sick and pathetic and deficient. Rarely, indeed, is black America ever depicted in the media as functional and self-sufficient. The free press, indeed, as the main interpreter of American culture and American experience, holds the mirror on American reality—so much so that what the media says is, even if it's not that way at all. The media is guilty of a severe bias and the problem screams out for correction. It is worse than simply lazy journalism, which is bad enough; it is inaccurate journalism.

[8]For black Americans like myself, this isn't just an issue of vanity—of wanting to be seen in a good light. Nor is it a matter of closing one's eyes to the very real problems of the urban underclass—which undeniably is disproportionately black. To be sure, problems besetting the black underclass deserve the utmost attention of the media, as well as the understanding and concern of the rest of American society.

⁹But if their problems consistently are presented as the only reality for blacks, any other experience known to the black community ceases to have validity, or to be real. In this scenario, millions of blacks are relegated to a sort of twilight zone, where who we are and what we are isn't based on fact but on image and perception. That's what it feels like to be a black American whose lifestyle is outside of the aberrant behavior that the media presents as the norm.

¹⁰For many of us, life is a curious series of encounters with white people who want to know why we are "different" from other blacks—when, in fact, most of us are only "different" from the now common negative images of black life. So pervasive are these images that they aren't just perceived as the norm; they're accepted as the norm.

¹¹I am reminded, for example, of the controversial Spike Lee film, "Do the Right Thing," and the criticism by some movie reviewers that the film's ghetto neighborhood isn't populated by addicts and drug pushers—and thus is not a true depiction.

¹²In fact, millions of black Americans live in neighborhoods where the most common sights are children playing and couples walking their dogs. In my own inner-city neighborhood in Denver—an area that the local press consistently describes as "gang territory"—I have yet to see a recognizable "gang" member or any "gang" activity (drug dealing or drive-by shootings), nor have I been the victim of "gang violence."

¹³Yet to students of American culture—in the case of Spike Lee's film, the movie reviewers—a black, inner-city neighborhood can only be one thing to be real: drug-infested and dysfunctioning. Is this my ego talking? In part, yes. For the millions of black people like myself—ordinary, hard-working, law-abiding, tax-paying Americans—the media's blindness to the fact that we even exist, let alone to our contributions to American society, is a bitter cup to drink. And as self-reliant as most black Americans are—because we've had to be self-reliant—even the strongest among us still crave affirmation.

¹⁴I want that. I want it for my children. I want it for all the beautiful, healthy, funny, smart black Americans I have known and loved over the years.

¹⁵And I want it for the rest of America, too.

¹⁶I want America to know us—all of us—for who we really are. To see us in all our complexity, our subtleness, our artfulness, our enterprise, our specialness, our loveliness, our American-ness. That is the real portrait of black America—that we're strong people, surviving people, capable people. That may be the best-kept secret in America. If so, it's time to let the truth be known.

—*Patricia Raybon*

QUESTIONS ABOUT THE READING

Refer to the general questions on page 165, as well as these specific questions.

PURPOSE

■ Does the essay succeed in making a difference with readers? If so, how?

CONTENT

- What are Raybon's assumptions about her audience's knowledge and attitudes? Are these assumptions accurate? Why or why not?
- Identify one paragraph developed through an extended example and one through a series of brief examples.
- Should the examples be more specific? Why or why not?

ORGANIZATION

- Is ordering of the examples effective? Explain.
- Are the two single-sentence paragraphs appropriate? Explain.

STYLE

- What is the writer's attitude toward her subject? Toward her audience? How do we know? Where are the signals?
- Is the tone appropriate for this writer's audience and purpose? Explain.

RESPONDING TO YOUR READING

Explore your personal reactions to "A Case of Severe Bias" by using the questions on page 165. Then respond with an essay of your own, using powerful examples to make your point.

Perhaps someone has misjudged or stereotyped you or a group to which you belong. If so, set the record straight in a forceful essay to a specified audience. Or perhaps you can think of other types of media messages that seem to present a distorted or inaccurate view (say, certain commercials or sports reporting or war movies, and so on). For instance, do certain movies or TV programs send the wrong message? Give your readers examples they can recognize and remember.

Or you might challenge readers' assumptions by asserting a surprising or unorthodox viewpoint: that some natural foods can be hazardous, that exercise can be bad for health, or that so-called advances in electronics or medical science leave us worse off.

Or maybe you want to talk about examples of things we take for granted or what makes a good friend. Whatever the topic, be sure your examples illustrate and explain a definite viewpoint.

CASE STUDY

RESPONDING TO READING

After reading Patricia Raybon's "A Case of Severe Bias," Gina Ciolfi settles on a more lighthearted goal for her own essay: She decides to challenge our assumptions about the value of junk-filled purses by giving us colorful examples of her own buried treasures. To analyze Raybon's techniques, Ciolfi combines the reading guidelines on page 175 with questions about the essay on page 203.

As she composes various drafts, Ciolfi relies on the Illustration Guidelines on page 201 and the Revision Checklist on page 63 to produce the final draft below.

MY TIME CAPSULE

Opening paragraph invites us in and sets the tone

I always seem to be searching for the right change at checkout counters, rummaging through junk in my little brown change purse for those few extra pennies and usually coming up red-faced and empty-handed. But despite repeated frustrations, I just can't bring myself to clean that purse. I guess I hang onto things I don't need because some of my worst junk holds vivid memories. *If someone were to find the purse, they would have a record of my recent life—a kind of time capsule.*

Thesis

One extended example Gives vivid and visual examples throughout

Whenever I dig for coins, I encounter an old car key. It belonged to my '91 Chevy, a car that rarely started on cold mornings. I still remember the hours spent huddled on that frosty front seat, flicking the ignition on and off, pumping the accelerator, and muttering various profanities every time the engine sputtered and died. Even though I junked the car last year, the key survives in my so-called change purse.

A second extended example

Also in there is a torn half-ticket to the Broadway musical, *Cats,* which I've saved for years. The show is outstanding. Unfortunately, though, I had to miss a good part of it simply because I needed to use the bathroom at the same time as half the audience. And much of what I did see was obscured by the green, porcupine hairdo of the guy in front of me. From my view behind Mr. Porcupine, the actors looked like they were in the woods. But I still keep my ticket stub—in my purse, of course.

A third extended example

Somewhere near the key and the ticket sits another artifact; the coat button that came undone earlier this year. (The same button I always initially mistake for a coin.) The button helps me remember the day I wore not only a turtleneck sweater but also two scarves for one of last winter's coldest days. Like a fool, I tried tying my coat collar around what had now become a 20-inch neck. Naturally the button popped off, and naturally, it got thrown into my purse.

Saves strongest extended example for last

For months I've been buying "micro-rays of hope" toward millionairehood in the state's lottery game. I can't resist playing my usual six numbers on Wednesdays and Saturdays—even though I always lose. *Not winning* poses no real problem for me, but kissing my obsolete ticket good-bye does. Somehow the act of throwing away even a losing ticket symbolizes admitting defeat. It means the state's racket has caught another sucker. It means my latest tangible flash of financial hope must sit among the soggy potato skins in my garbage pail. So I "temporarily" save my defunct tickets by folding them neatly away in my purse. Every time I see them, I'm reminded of the many times I COULD have become a millionaire.

Concludes with a series of brief but visual examples

The passage of time seems directly related to the bloatedness of my change purse because it's forever expanding. In fact, if I opened it right now, I'd find many more memories than the few just mentioned. I'd see the semiwrapped sourball I almost ate, until I realized it was lime green. I'd find

Avoids overexplaining

Explains how the examples illustrate the main point

Facetiously suggests other meanings to be explored

the three unmated earrings, each with its own life history. I'd rediscover the safety pin that once saved me from awful embarrassment. And my old pen cap (minus the pen), a golf tee, a matchbook, a packet of sugar, and a few expired coupons would all be in there, all with legends of their own.

Even though I'm a slow learner, I know now that metal money belongs not in a purse but in a piggy bank. I'll never have to worry about a coin in my time capsule again—unless, of course, it's my old Susan B. Anthony quarter. But that's another story.

—Gina Ciolfi

Application **11-4**

Collaborative Project and Computer Application: Use email or your listserv to brainstorm collectively for examples to support one or more claims your group has generated in response to one of the readings or essay options in this chapter.

Application **11-5**

Web-based Project: Look up the homepage for a business and, pretending you're the public-relations manager for that company, write an essay to convince a new client to use the business's services or products. Use the Web to find specific examples to support your claim.

OPTIONS FOR ESSAY WRITING

1. Write a human interest essay for your campus newspaper in which you illustrate some feature of our society that you find humorous, depressing, contemptible, or admirable. Possible subjects: our eating, consumer, or dress habits; our idea of a vacation or a good time; the cars we drive, and so on. Provide at least three well-developed examples to make your point. Ted Morgan's passage (page 199) offers one example of how you might approach this assignment.
2. What pleases, disappoints, or surprises you most about college life? Illustrate this topic for your parents (or some other specific audience) with at least three examples.
3. Assume you've been assigned a faculty adviser who likes to know as much as possible about each advisee. The adviser asks each student to write an essay on this topic:

   Is your hometown (city, neighborhood) a good or a bad place for a child to grow up?

4. Using Gina Ciolfi's essay as a model, explore or poke fun at one of your own idiosyncracies by using a series of vivid examples to illustrate your point.

Notice that you are not asked to write about yourself directly (as in a personal narrative). Support your response with specific examples that will convince the reader of your sound judgment.

CHAPTER 12

Explaining Parts and Categories: Division and Classification

Using Division to Explain **210**

Using Division to Make a Point **210**

Using Classification to Explain **211**

Guidelines for Division **212**

Using Classification to Make a Point **212**

Guidelines for Classification **213**

CASE STUDY: Responding to Reading **217**

Options for Essay Writing **219**

Readings **215, 218**

Applications **213**

Division and classification are both strategies for sorting things out, but each serves a distinct purpose. *Division* deals with *one thing only*. It separates that thing into parts, pieces, sections, or categories—for closer examination (say, an essay divided into introduction, body, and conclusion).

What readers expect to learn from a division

- ■ *What are its parts?*
- ■ *What is it made of?*

Classification deals with *an assortment of things* that share certain similarities. It groups these things systematically (say, a record collection into categories—jazz, rock, country and western, classical, and pop).

What readers expect to learn from a classification

- ■ *What relates to what?*
- ■ *In what categories do X, Y, and Z belong?*

We use division and classification in many aspects of our lives. Say you are shopping for a refrigerator. If you are mechanically inclined, you could begin by thinking about the major parts that make up a refrigerator: storage compartment, cooling element, motor, insulation, and exterior casing. You can now ask questions about these individual parts to determine the efficiency or quality of each part in different kinds of refrigerators. You have *divided* the refrigerator into its components.

After shopping, you come home with a list of 20 refrigerators that seem to be built from high-quality parts. You make sense of your list by grouping items according to selected characteristics. First, you divide your list into three *classes* according to size in cubic feet of capacity: small, middle-sized, and large refrigerators. But you want economy, too, so you group the refrigerators according to cost. Or you might *classify* them according to color, weight, or energy efficiency. Here is how division and classification are related:

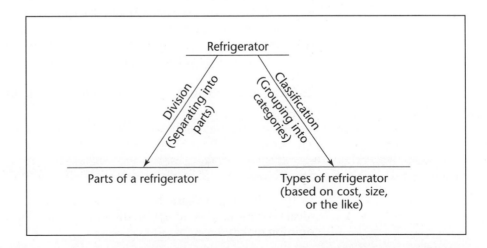

Whether you choose to apply division or classification depends on your purpose. An architect designing a library will think almost entirely of *division*. Once she has defined the large enclosed area that is needed, she must identify the parts into which that space must be divided: the reference area, reading areas, storage areas, checkout facilities, and office space. She might consider providing space for special groups of users (such as reading areas for children). In very large libraries she might need to divide further into specialized kinds of space (such as highly secure areas for rare manuscripts or special collections, or areas with special acoustic provisions for listening to recorded materials). But however simple or complex her problem, she is thinking now only about the appropriate division of space. She is not worrying about how the library will classify its books and other material.

But *classification* is one of the library staff's main problems. The purpose of a library is not only to store books and other forms of information, but above all to make the information retrievable. In order for us to find a book or item, the thousands or millions of books stored in the library must be arranged in logical categories. That arrangement becomes possible only if the books are carefully classified.

USING DIVISION TO EXPLAIN

We encounter referential uses of division every day. Division is used in manuals to help us understand, for example, how a computer or a car engine works. Division allows readers to tackle a complex task one aspect at a time, as in the following instructions for campers.

A DIVISION THAT EXPLAINS

Before pitching your tent, take the time to prepare the area that will be under the tent. Not only does this step prevent damage to the tent floor, but it also helps you get a good night's sleep. Begin by removing all stones, branches, and other debris. Use your camping shovel for anything too large or deep to remove by hand. Next, fill in any holes with dirt or leaves. Finally, make a few light sweeps with the shovel or a leafy branch to smooth the area.

To increase readability, the steps or substeps in a complex task often appear in list form.

USING DIVISION TO MAKE A POINT

In the following paragraph, Watts uses division to explain his view of the ideal education. If we accept his divisions, we are more likely to agree that his opinion makes sense.

DIVISION THAT MAKES A POINT

Lead-in to main point
(1–3)

Main point (4)

Parts of the "ideal
education" (5)

Most important part (6)

[1]It is perhaps idle to wonder what, from my present point of view, would have been an ideal education. [2]If I could provide such a curriculum for my children they, in their turn, might find it all a bore. [3]But the fantasy of what I would have liked to learn as a child may be revealing, since I feel unequipped by education for problems that lie outside the cloistered, literary domain in which I am competent and at home. [4]Looking back, then, I would have arranged for myself to be taught survival techniques for both natural and urban wildernesses. [5]I would want to have been instructed in self-hypnosis, in aikido (the esoteric and purely self-defensive style of judo), in elementary medicine, in sexual hygiene, in vegetable gardening, in astronomy, navigation, and sailing; in cookery and clothesmaking, in metalwork and carpentry, in drawing and painting, in printing and typography, in botany and biology, in optics and acoustics, in semantics and psychology, in mysticism and yoga, in electronics and mathematical fantasy, in drama and dancing, in singing and in playing an instrument by ear; in wandering, in advanced daydreaming, in prestidigitation, in techniques of escape from bondage, in disguise, in conversation with birds and beasts, in ventriloquism, in French and German conversation, in planetary history, in morphology,* and in Classical Chinese. [6]Actually, the main thing left out of my education was a proper love for my own body, because one feared to cherish anything so obviously mortal and prone to sickness.

—*Alan Watts*

The topic statement *tells;* the rest *shows* by dividing the ideal education into specific kinds of instruction. This writer knew the guidelines on page 212.

USING CLASSIFICATION TO EXPLAIN

Like division, classifying as a referential or informative strategy is a part of our lives. Your biology textbook shows you how scientists have classified life-forms into plants, animals, bacteria, and other categories; scientists examining fossils write up their discoveries by assigning them to one of these classes. A city planner might write a report classifying plans for conserving water on the basis of cost, efficiency, or some other basis. The following classification explains major career specialties in computer science on the basis of their central tasks.

CLASSIFICATION THAT EXPLAINS

Specialties in computer science can be grouped into three major categories. First, systems programmers write programs that run the computer equipment itself. Next, applications programmers develop programs that put the computer to work on specific jobs (such as keeping track of bank accounts).

---

*The structure of organisms.

Finally, systems analysts troubleshoot, debug, and update both systems and applications programs, and they develop specifications for new computer systems. All three specialties involve analyzing a problem and then reducing it to a sequence of small, deliberate steps that a computer can carry out.

GUIDELINES FOR DIVISION

1. *Apply the division to a singular item.* Only one item at a time can be divided (*ideal education*; not *ideal education* and *ideal career*).

2. *Make the division consistent with your purpose.* Watts could have divided education into primary, secondary, and higher education; into social sciences, humanities, sciences, and mathematics—and so on. But his purpose was to explain a view that goes beyond traditional categories. We are given "parts" of an education that we may not yet have considered.

3. *Make your division complete.* Only 100 percent of something can be divided, and the parts, in turn, should add up to 100 percent. If a part is omitted, the writer should say so ("some of the parts of an ideal education").

4. *Subdivide the subject as needed to make the point.* Watts's first division is into survival techniques for (a) natural and (b) urban wildernesses. He then subdivides each of these into the specific parts listed in sentences 5 and 6. If he had stopped after the first division, he would not have made his point.

5. *Follow a logical order.* In sentence 5 the parts of an ideal education range from practical to recreational to intellectual skills. In sentence 6 the most important part appears last—for emphasis.

USING CLASSIFICATION TO MAKE A POINT

Like division, classification also can be persuasive. This next paragraph uses classification to analyze the motives behind attending the high school prom.

CLASSIFICATION THAT MAKES A POINT

Why must everyone who counts be at the prom? The answer is simple: peer pressure. Prom-goers often feel compelled to attend, as the prom represents in many ways their last chance, their last hurrah. For the popular, it is their final opportunity to saunter into a room filled with people who admire them not so much for who they are or what they've achieved, but instead for the shallow ideal they represent—the football star, the homecoming queen, the rich kid. For the borderline types, the prom is their final chance to mimic the popular, to rub elbows with those who really matter. For the losers—the nerds, geeks, dweebs, wallflowers, and other loners— prom night is their last, desperate chance to try fitting in, to matter at all.

—*Julia Schoonover*

In developing her message, Schoonover observed the following guidelines.

GUIDELINES FOR CLASSIFICATION

1. *Apply the classification to a plural subject.* In Schoonover's paragraph, the subject is types who attend the prom.
2. *Make the basis of the classification consistent with your purpose.* To make her point about needs, Schoonover classifies the three groups on the basis of their respective popularity. For a different purpose, she might have classified students on prom night according to their behavior, style of dress, and so on.
3. *Make the classification complete.* All three broad stereotypes of high school culture are represented.

4. *Arrange the categories in logical order.* The categories Schoonover uses move from "winners" to "losers."
5. *Don't let categories overlap.* If she had added the category *truly needy* to the three stereotypes she identifies, Schoonover's classification would overlap, because all three categories represent some type of need.

    Or suppose a supermarket classified its meats as *pork, beef, ham,* and *lamb.* This classification would overlap because ham is a product of pork meat, rather than an exclusive category.

Application **12-1**

PARAGRAPH WARM-UP: DIVIDING TO EXPLAIN

Addressing a prospective new member, use division to explain either the organization or the function of committees in a social or service group you belong to.

Application **12-2**

PARAGRAPH WARM-UP: DIVIDING TO MAKE A POINT

Using the paragraph on page 211 as a model, write a paragraph for the college curriculum committee, explaining your idea of an ideal education.

Application **12-3**

PARAGRAPH WARM-UP: CLASSIFYING TO EXPLAIN

You are helping prepare the orientation for next year's incoming students. Your supervisor asks you to write a paragraph outlining the jobs available to graduates in your major by organizing the jobs into major categories. Your piece will be published in a career pamphlet for new students. (You may need to do some library research, say in *The Occupational Outlook Handbook.*)

Application 12-4

PARAGRAPH WARM-UP: CLASSIFYING TO MAKE A POINT

Identify a group you find in some way interesting. Sort the members of that group into at least three categories. Your basis for sorting (say, driving habits, attitudes toward marriage, hairstyles) will depend on the particular point you want to make about the group.

Application 12-5

Web-based Project: A World Wide Web homepage is an excellent example of classification and division at work. Browse your institution's homepage. Explore the arrangement of the page, deciding to what extent the divisions and classifications follow the guidelines in this chapter.

- Do all the arrangements make sense?
- How do the divisions and classifications made by the creators of the page affect the way visitors to the page see the school?
- Could the page have been arranged differently for different effects? Your instructor may ask that your analysis/critique be submitted in writing.

Application 12-6

*Web-based Project:** Harvard researcher Howard Gardner and others have classified seven different categories of "intelligence," or styles of thinking and learning. To learn more about Multiple Intelligences, visit the following Web sites and explore links that will help you answer this question: Which one or more of these basic categories seem to fit your thinking and learning style(s)?

- <http://www.d.umn.edu/student/loon/acad/strat/lrnsty.html>
- <www.geocities.com/Athens/column/7568/gardner.html>

Prepare an essay that explains the categories you have identified. Work from a clear and definite thesis. Be sure to provide convincing personal examples and to document all sources of information.

*My thanks to Georgia State University's George Pullman for inspiring this exercise.

Application **12-7**

ESSAY PRACTICE

Too often, language can camouflage rather than communicate. People see many reasons to hide behind language, as when they

Situations in which people often hide behind language

- speak for their organization or company but not for themselves
- fear the consequences of giving bad news
- are afraid to disagree with company policy
- make a recommendation some readers will resent
- worry about making a bad impression
- worry about being wrong
- pretend to know more than they do
- avoid admitting a mistake or ignorance

Inflated and unfamiliar words, euphemisms, and needlessly technical terms are some of the ways of hiding one's real meaning. Whether intentional or accidental, poor word choices produce unethical writing that resists interpretation and drives people apart instead of bringing them together.

In this next selection, English professor William Lutz categorizes four major types of deceptive language. Read the essay and answer the questions that follow it, as well as those on page 165. Then select one of the essay assignments.

Before you read, think about language you've encountered that was deceptive or downright impossible to understand.

DOUBTS ABOUT DOUBLESPEAK

[1] During the past year, we learned that we can shop at a "unique retail biosphere" instead of a farmers' market, where we can buy items made of "synthetic glass" instead of plastic, or purchase a "high-velocity, multipurpose air circulator," or electric fan. A "waste-water conveyance facility" may "exceed the odor threshold" from time to time due to the presence of "regulated human nutrients," but that is not to be confused with a sewage plant that stinks up the neighborhood with sewage sludge. Nor should we confuse a "resource development park" with a dump. Thus does doublespeak continue to spread.

[2] Doublespeak is language which pretends to communicate but doesn't. It is language which makes the bad seem good, the negative seem positive, the unpleasant seem attractive, or at least tolerable. It is language which avoids, shifts or denies responsibility; language which is at variance with its real or purported meaning. It is language which conceals or prevents thought.

[3] Doublespeak is all around us. We are asked to check our packages at the desk "for our convenience" when it's not for our convenience at all but for someone else's convenience. We see advertisements for "preowned," "experienced" or "previously distinguished" cars, not used cars and for "genuine imitation leather," "virgin vinyl" or "real counterfeit diamonds." Television offers not reruns but "encore telecasts." There are no slums or ghettos just the "inner

city" or "substandard housing" where the "disadvantaged" or "economically nonaffluent" live and where there might be a problem with "substance abuse." Nonprofit organizations don't make a profit, they have "negative deficits" or experience "revenue excesses." With doublespeak it's not dying but "terminal living" or "negative patient care outcome."

⁴There are four kinds of doublespeak. The first kind is the euphemism, a word or phrase designed to avoid a harsh or distasteful reality. Used to mislead or deceive, the euphemism becomes doublespeak. In 1984 the U.S. State Department's annual reports on the status of human rights around the world ceased using the word "killing." Instead the State Department used the phrase "unlawful or arbitrary deprivation of life," thus avoiding the embarrassing situation of government-sanctioned killing in countries supported by the United States.

⁵A second kind of doublespeak is jargon, the specialized language of a trade, profession or similar group, such as doctors, lawyers, plumbers or car mechanics. Legitimately used, jargon allows members of a group to communicate with each other clearly, efficiently and quickly. Lawyers and tax accountants speak to each other of an "involuntary conversion" of property, a legal term that means the loss or destruction of property through theft, accident or condemnation. But when lawyers or tax accountants use unfamiliar terms to speak to others, then the jargon becomes doublespeak.

⁶In 1978 a commercial 727 crashed on takeoff, killing three passengers, injuring 21 others and destroying the airplane. The insured value of the airplane was greater than its book value, so the airline made a profit of $1.7 million, creating two problems: the airline didn't want to talk about one of its airplanes crashing, yet it had to account for that $1.7 million profit in its annual report to its stockholders. The airline solved both problems by inserting a footnote in its annual report which explained that the $1.7 million was due to "the involuntary conversion of a 727."

⁷A third kind of doublespeak is gobbledygook or bureaucratese. Such doublespeak is simply a matter of overwhelming the audience with words—the more the better. Alan Greenspan, a polished practitioner of bureaucratese, once testified before a Senate committee that "it is a tricky problem to find the particular calibration in timing that would be appropriate to stem the acceleration in risk premiums created by falling incomes without prematurely aborting the decline in the inflation-generated risk premiums."

⁸The fourth kind of doublespeak is inflated language, which is designed to make the ordinary seem extraordinary, to make everyday things seem impressive, to give an air of importance to people or situations, to make the simple seem complex. Thus do car mechanics become "automotive internists," elevator operators become "members of the vertical transportation corps," grocery store checkout clerks become "career associate scanning professionals," and smelling something becomes "organoleptic analysis."

⁹Doublespeak is not the product of careless language or sloppy thinking. Quite the opposite. Doublespeak is language carefully designed and constructed to appear to communicate when in fact it doesn't. It is a language designed not to lead but mislead. Thus, it's not a tax increase but "revenue

enhancement" or "tax-base broadening." So how can you complain about higher taxes? Those aren't useless, billion-dollar pork barrel projects; they're really "congressional projects of national significance," so don't complain about wasteful government spending. That isn't the Mafia in Atlantic City; those are just "members of a career-offender cartel," so don't worry about the influence of organized crime in the city.

—*William Lutz*

QUESTIONS ABOUT YOUR READING

Refer to the general questions on page 165, as well as these specific questions.

CONTENT

- What basis can you identify in Lutz's classification? Is this basis consistent with the writer's purpose? Explain.
- Is the classification offered there complete? Explain.

ORGANIZATION

- Does the arrangement of supporting paragraphs help make the classification convincing? Explain.
- What major devices lend coherence to this essay? Give samples of each.

STYLE

- What is the writer's attitude toward his subject? Toward his audience? How do we know? Where are the signals?
- Is the tone appropriate for this writer's audience and purpose? Explain.

RESPONDING TO YOUR READING

Explore your reactions to the Lutz essay by using the questions on page 166. Then respond with an essay of your own that supports some particular point about uses of language. You might describe an experience in which you have been misled by doublespeak. Or you might discuss situations in which doublespeak can be beneficial. Whether your approach is humorous or serious, be sure your essay makes a definite point.

Or, instead of writing about language, you might write about different types of people in your life, different places you've lived or schools you've attended, different types of students you've known or friends you've had, and so on.

CASE STUDY

RESPONDING TO READING

After reading and analyzing Lutz's essay and answering the questions above, Patrick LaChane decides to diverge from the focus on language and to examine his neighborhood on the basis of those characteristics that make it such a likable place to live. To sort out the elements of this complex subject, Patrick settles on three main categories (the neighborhood's convenience, housing, and people).

In drafting and revising his essay, Patrick relies on the Division and Classification Guidelines and the Revision Checklist on pages 212–13, and 63.

| Note |

Even though classification is the dominant strategy in Patrick's essay, note how he also relies on the strategies of description, narration, and illustration to get his point across.

Title gives a clear forecast

Opening uses descriptive and narrative details to set the scene and give background

Thesis divides the neighborhood into three categories, in logical order (location—architecture—people)

First category: types of convenient facilities

Uses visual examples throughout

Second category: types of houses

Third category: types of people

WE LIKE IT HERE

Our family lives on Elgin Avenue, a busy one-way street near Rideau Park in Bitmore, Michigan, an industrial city of fifty thousand. Sixteen years ago when we first bought the house we planned to live there only a few years before we could afford to realize the all-American dream of buying property in the suburbs. But as the years have passed, we've come to love our blue-collar neighborhood and to feel that it truly is "home." *What makes this place special for us is the convenient location, the modest character of the houses, and—most of all—the special people we call neighbors.*

Within easy walking distance are all kinds of stores: barbershop, pharmacy, bakery, jeweler, hardware store, convenience store, and even a clothing store. All the shopkeepers know most of the local people by name, take an interest in them, and often go out of their way to provide great service. Because fast food has yet to invade the neighborhood, we still savor "slow" food—mashed potatoes, pork chops, and ham sandwiches on fresh-baked bread—right around the corner at Ellie's diner. Schools, churches, and all the facilities at Rideau Park are easily accessible, and the bus stops right at the corner every half hour.

Since our neighborhood was built nearly fifty years ago to house factory workers, the homes are not exactly fancy; they aren't even modern. No gambrels, split-levels, or ranches here. Instead we have a mixture of nondescript bungalows, brick row houses, two-family, three-family, and even six-family tenements, most of them no more than twenty feet apart. Many of the houses have been remodeled inside and most are well kept, both inside and out. Because of the number of multiple-family dwellings, however, parking spaces are at a premium in the evenings, when everyone is home from work. Neighborly cooperation helps alleviate the parking problem, though.

Because of the various kinds of affordable housing available in our neighborhood, we have a complex mix of generations and ethnic groups. Originally a French-Canadian area, Elgin Avenue has gradually welcomed people from various ethnic backgrounds. All of them have shared their native foods, their gardening tricks, and their child-rearing theories. But the glue that holds the neighborhood together is its children. Almost forty children under age fifteen keep our homes, yards, porches, and sidewalks very lively. They rollerskate, play street hockey and kickball, douse each other with water balloons, invite one another to share a meal, sleep out in tents, and fight and make up. They watch the little babies and run errands for the elderly. They

Conclusion reemphasizes the main point

grow up and move away, only to be replaced by a new crop of kids. The older generations get along because the children do.

We have seen and shared many sides of life during our sixteen years on this street. Having so many stores and other facilities nearby has been very convenient for our family. Seeing the homes being kept up has increased our pride in the neighborhood. Learning to love and respect our neighbors—and enjoying lifelong friendships—has been our greatest privilege.

—*Patrick LaChane*

OPTIONS FOR ESSAY WRITING

1. Television seems to invade every part of our lives. It can influence our buying habits, political views, attitudes about sex, marriage, family, and violence. Identify a group of commercials, sitcoms, talk shows, sports shows, or the like that have a bad (or good) influence on viewers. Sort the group according to a clear basis, using at least three categories, and be sure your essay supports a definite thesis.

2. Reread the passage by Alan Watts (page 211), and respond with an essay that lays out as specifically as possible the types of knowledge that you hope to acquire in college or the types you think everyone should acquire in higher education.

CHAPTER 13

Explaining Steps and Stages: Process Analysis

Using Process Analysis to Explain   **221**

Guidelines for Giving Instructions   222

Using Process Analysis to Make a Point   **223**

CASE STUDY: Responding to Reading   **227**

Readings   **224, 227, 229, 231**

Applications   **223, 229, 231**

A *process* is a sequence of actions or changes leading to a product or result (say, in producing maple syrup). A *procedure* is a way of carrying out a process (say, in swinging a golf club). A *process analysis* explains these various steps and stages to instruct or inform readers.

USING PROCESS ANALYSIS BEYOND THE WRITING CLASSROOM

- **In other courses:** You might instruct a classmate in dissecting a frog or in using the school's email network. You might answer an essay question about how economic inflation occurs or how hikers and campers can succumb to hypothermia.

- **On the job:** You might instruct a colleague or customer in accessing a database or shipping radioactive waste. You might explain to coworkers how the budget for various departments is determined or how the voice-mail system works.

- **In the community:** You might instruct a friend in casting for large-mouth bass or preparing for a job interview. You might explain to parents the selection process for new teachers followed by your local parent-teacher group.

What additional audiences and uses for process analysis can you think of?

USING PROCESS ANALYSIS TO EXPLAIN

The most common referential uses of process analysis are to give instructions and to explain how something happens.

Explaining How to Do Something

As the above examples show, anyone might need to write instructions. And everyone reads some sort of instructions. The new employee needs instructions for operating the office machines; the employee going on vacation writes instructions for the person filling in. A car owner reads the manual for service and operating instructions.

What readers want to
know about a procedure

- *How do I do it?*
- *Why do I do it?*
- *What materials or equipment will I need?*
- *Where do I begin?*
- *What do I do next?*
- *Are there any precautions?*

Instructions emphasize the reader's role, explaining each step in enough detail for the reader to complete the task safely and efficiently. This next passage is aimed at inexperienced joggers:

EXPLAINING HOW TO DO SOMETHING

Main point (1)

First step (2)

Supporting detail (3)

Second step (4)

Supporting detail (5)

Transitional sentence (6)

Third step (7–8)

[1]Instead of breaking into a jog too quickly and risking injury, take a relaxed and deliberate approach. [2]Before taking a step, spend at least ten minutes stretching and warming up, using any exercises you find comfortable. [3](After your first week, consult a jogging book for specialized exercises.) [4]When you've completed your warm-up, set a brisk pace walking. [5]Exaggerate the distance between steps, taking long strides and swinging your arms briskly and loosely. [6]After roughly 100 yards at this brisk pace, you should feel ready to jog. [7]Immediately break into a very slow trot: lean your torso forward and

let one foot fall in front of the other (one foot barely leaving the ground while the other is on the pavement). [8]Maintain the slowest pace possible, just above a walk. [9]Do not bolt like a sprinter! [10]The biggest mistake is to start fast and injure yourself. [11]While jogging, relax your body. [12]Keep your shoulders straight and your head up, and enjoy the scenery—after all, it is one of the joys of jogging. [13]Keep your arms low and slightly bent at your sides. [14]Move your legs freely from the hips in an action that is easy, not forced. [15]Make your feet perform a heel-to-toe action: land on the heel; rock forward; take off from the toe.

Precaution (9–10)
Supporting details
(11–15)

Note that these instructions do not explain terms such as *long stride*, *torso*, and *sprinter* because these should be clear to the general reader. But a *slow trot*

GUIDELINES FOR GIVING INSTRUCTIONS

1. *Know the procedure.* Unless you have performed the task, do not try to write instructions for it.
2. *Explain the purpose of the procedure.* Give users enough background to understand why they need your instructions.
3. *Make instructions complete but not excessive.* Don't assume that people know more than they really do, especially when you can perform the task almost automatically. (Think about when someone taught you to drive a car—or perhaps you have tried to teach someone else.) As in the previous jogging instructions, include enough detail for users to understand what to do, but omit general information that users probably know. Excessive details get in the way.
4. *Show users what to do.* Give them enough examples to visualize the procedure clearly.
5. *Divide the procedure into simple steps and substeps.* Allow readers to focus on one task at a time.
6. *Organize for the user's understanding.* Instructions almost always are arranged in chronological order, with notes and precautions inserted for specific steps.

7. *Make instructions immediately readable.* Instructions must be understood upon first reading, because users usually take immediate action. Because they emphasize the user's role, write instructions in the second person, as direct address.

Begin all steps and substeps with action verbs by using the *active voice* (**move your legs** versus **your legs should be moved**) and the *imperative mood* (**rock forward** versus **you should rock forward**), giving an immediate signal about the specific action to be taken.

Use shorter sentences than usual: Use one sentence for one step, so users can perform one action at a time.

Finally, use transitional expressions (**while, after, next**) to show how the steps are connected.
8. *Maintain a user-friendly tone.* Be encouraging instead of bossy.
9. *Include troubleshooting advice.* Explain what to do when things go wrong.

| Note | *If X doesn't work, first check Y and then do Z.* |

Place this advice near the end of your instructions.

is explained in detail; different readers might have differing interpretations of this term.

Explaining How Something Happens

Besides showing how to do something, you often have to explain how things occur: how sunlight helps plants make chlorophyll; how a digital computer works; how your town decided on its zoning laws. *Process explanation* emphasizes the process itself—instead of the reader's or writer's role.

What readers want to
know about a process

- *How does it happen? Or, how is it made?*
- *When and where does it happen?*
- *What happens first, next, and so on?*
- *What is the result?*

USING PROCESS ANALYSIS TO MAKE A POINT

Although many process explanations are referential, others are closely related to cause and effect (see Chapter 14). In these cases, providing complete explanations and clear connections between steps helps convince readers that the process you're describing really does happen as you say. These kinds of causal chains often support larger arguments. In the next example, Julia Schoonover uses a process analysis to support her claim that credit cards and college students create a dangerous combination.

PROCESS ANALYSIS THAT MAKES A POINT

Orienting statement (1)
Details of the process and
its results (2–8)

[1]Granted, the temptation is hard to refuse. [2]Credit card companies marketing on campus offer free cards and sign-up gifts "with no obligation." [3]The "gifts" might include candy, coffee mugs, T-shirts, sports squeeze bottles, hip bags, and other paraphernalia. [4]The process seems harmless enough: Just fill in your social security number and other personal information, take your pick from the array of gifts, and cancel the card when it arrives. [5]But these companies know exactly what they're doing. [6]They know that misusing the card is often easier than cancelling it. [7]They know that many of us work part time and are paid little. [8]They know that most of us will be unable to pay more than the minimum balance each month—meaning big-time interest for years.

Main point (9)

[9]Don't be seduced by instant credit.

—*Julia Schoonover*

Application **13-1**

PARAGRAPH WARM-UP: GIVING INSTRUCTIONS

Choose some activity you perform well. Think of a situation requiring you to write instructions for that activity. Single out a major step within the process (such as pitching a baseball or adjusting ski bindings for safe release). Provide enough details so that the reader can perform that step safely and efficiently.

Application **13-2**

PARAGRAPH WARM-UP: EXPLAINING HOW SOMETHING HAPPENS

Select some process in your university—admissions, registration, changing majors, finding a parking place. Write a process analysis that could anchor an argument for changes in the procedure.

Application **13-3**

ESSAY PRACTICE: GIVING INSTRUCTIONS

Read Frank White's essay, and answer the questions following it, along with those on page 165. Then select one of the essay assignments.

    The writer of these instructions is a counselor at the North American Survival School, which offers courses ranging from mountaineering to desert survival. Besides being a certified Emergency Medical Technician, White has extensive experience hiking and camping in snake-infested terrain. The school is preparing a survival manual for distribution to all its students. This writer's contribution is a set of instructions on dealing with snakebites. Many of the readers will have no experience with snakes (or first aid), so White decides to be brief and simple, for quick, easy reading as needed.

ESSAY FOR ANALYSIS AND RESPONSE

HOW TO DEAL WITH SNAKEBITES

    [1]Every year, thousands of Americans are injured—sometimes fatally—by poisonous snakebites. Fewer than one percent of poisonous snakebites are fatal. But many of the injuries and most fatalities can be avoided as long as you are alert and cautious and follow a few instructions.

    [2]Although most snakes bite, in the United States only rattlesnakes, copperheads, coral snakes, and water moccasins are poisonous. All these are most dangerous in early spring, when venom sacs are full from winter hibernation. Rattlers are found in most of the United States, while copperheads are only in the East. Coral snakes range throughout the South, while water moccasins live in Southern lowlands and swampy areas.

    [3]Some simple precautions can help you avoid snakebites. Since most bites occur around the ankles, wear long, thick pants and high boots of heavy rubber or leather. Also, watch where you walk, swim, or sleep. As you walk, watch where you put your feet, especially in climbing over fallen trees or stone walls. In moccasin country, swim only where the water is moving and the shoreline is free of heavy vegetation. If you cannot sleep in a closed tent with a snakeproof floor, place your sleeping bag on a high, dry, open spot, and

keep it zipped. When you do encounter a snake, freeze! Then move backwards *very* slowly, making no moves that will frighten the snake. In case these precautions fail, always carry a snakebite kit.

[4]A poisonous snakebite is easy enough to recognize. Within minutes the wound will swell and turn bright red. You will feel a throbbing pain that radiates from the bite. The swelling, redness, and pain will spread gradually and steadily. (Bites from nonvenomous snakes, in contrast, resemble mere pinpricks.) You may experience nausea and/or hot flashes. In any case, if you are not certain whether the bite is poisonous, treat it as poisonous.

[5]If you have been bitten, *do nothing to hasten the spread of the poison.* Above all, don't panic. Resist the temptation to walk, run, or move quickly. And stay away from stimulants such as coffee, tea, cola, alcohol, or aspirin. In fact, don't ingest anything. Instead, take a minute to think calmly about what you *should* do.

[6]Take the following steps immediately. Remain calm and move as little as possible. Keep the wound lower than the rest of your body so the poison remains localized. Have companions get you to a hospital as quickly as possible, without causing you needless exertion. If the hospital is more than an hour away, apply an icepack to retard the spread of the poison, or a tourniquet (snugly enough to stop venous flow but not so tight as to stop arterial flow—and loosened briefly every five minutes). If you lack a snakebite kit, you might cut a small X about 1/4-inch deep at the point of greatest swelling on the wound to suck out and spit out some poison. Perform this last procedure *only* if you have no oral cuts or injuries and there is no chance of getting medical treatment for several hours.

[7]By taking precautions and remaining alert, you should not have to fear snakebites. But if you are bitten, your best bet is to remain calm.

—Frank White

QUESTIONS ABOUT THE READING

CONTENT

- What opening strategy is used to create interest?
- Is the information adequate and appropriate for the stated audience and purpose? Explain.
- What specific readers' questions are answered here?

ORGANIZATION

- What is the order of the body paragraphs? Is this the most effective order? Explain.
- Is the conclusion adequate and appropriate? Explain.

STYLE

- Are these instructions immediately readable? Explain.
- Is the tone of these instructions too "bossy"? Explain.

RESPONDING TO YOUR READING

Assume a specific situation and audience (like those for snakebite procedures), and write instructions for a specialized procedure, or for anything that you can do well (no recipes, please). Be sure you know the process down to the smallest detail. Narrow your subject (perhaps to one complex activity within a longer procedure) so you can cover it fully. Avoid day-to-day procedures that college readers would already know (brushing teeth, washing hair, and other such elementary activities).

Application **13-4**

Web-based Project: Write instructions for conducting a Web search using one of the popular Internet search engines. Hint: Consult the site's Help, FAQ, or Search Tips page for raw material. Be sure to cite the exact source of any material you quote or paraphrase (pages 370–73).

SAMPLE SEARCH ENGINES

Alta Vista
<http://www.altavista.com>

Ask Jeeves
<http://www.aj.com>

Google
<http://www.google.com>

HotBot
<http://www.hotbot.com>

Ixquick Metasearch
<http://www.ixquick.com>

Lycos
<http://www.lycos.com>

Application **13-5**

Web-based Project: Assume that you and your classmates are preparing to spend a semester abroad in an international exchange program in one particular country. People from different cultures will need to communicate effectively and sensitively, so your group will need to develop a measurable degree of cultural awareness.

Your assignment is to select a country and to research that culture's behaviors, attitudes, values, and social system in terms of how these variables influence the culture's communication preferences and expectations. For example, some cultures are offended when confronted with argument, criticism, or expression of emotion. Some cultures observe special formalities in communicating (say, friendly inquiries and displays of concern about one's family). Some cultures observe rigidly prescribed etiquette while dining or visiting other people's homes.

What should you and your colleagues know about this culture in order to communicate effectively and diplomatically? Prepare a set of instructions for the basic "do's and don'ts."

Begin with the following sites, but do not limit yourself to these:

- *American University's Education Lab on Cross Cultural Communication*
  <http://www.nwrel.org/cnorse/booklets/ccc>
- *The Global Village*
  <http://www.bena.com/ewinters/xculture.html>

Be sure to credit each source of information and to attach copies of relevant Web pages to your instructions.

CASE STUDY

RESPONDING TO READING

After reading and analyzing Frank White's essay and answering the questions on pages 165 and 225, Cathy Nichols recalls her own experience as a new commuter student and decides to write a basic "survival guide" for commuters during their first week of school. To keep her instructions brief and straightforward, Cathy divides the procedure into four basic steps: getting essential items, checking out the library, meeting one's advisor, and establishing a support network.

In drafting and revising her essay, Cathy follows the Instruction Guidelines and Revision Checklist on pages 222 and 63.

Note

Even though process analysis is the dominant rhetorical strategy in Cathy's essay, she also relies on other strategies, such as description, illustration, division, and classification.

Title gives a forecast

*Uses encouraging tone
Establishes writer's knowledge on this topic*

Explains the procedure's purpose, in a friendly tone

First major step (classifies "essential items")

A FIRST-WEEK SURVIVAL GUIDE FOR COMMUTERS

Welcome, first-year students! You've probably read most of the "official" literature provided by this university. But as a recent first-year commuter who spent most of her first week lost, I'd like to offer some "unofficial" advice! If, like many commuters, you've managed to avoid freshman orientation, I hope you'll consider this a crash course for avoiding needless stress and dodging some common headaches.

Begin by getting the essential items: campus map, ID card, books, and a parking sticker. First, pick up a campus map at the Registrar's office. Next, find the Campus Center, and go to the Student Services office to pick up your

Transitions throughout mark time and sequence
Gives example
Uses chronological order for steps and substeps

Uses note to emphasize vital information
Second major step (divides each major step into simple substeps)

Addresses the readers directly throughout

Third major step (gives just enough detail for this audience)

Fourth major step (uses a short sentence for each substep)

Includes detail as needed

Maintains an encouraging tone throughout
Includes troubleshooting advice

student ID. Adjacent to Student Services is your next stop, the bookstore. Bring your class schedule so that you buy the right books for your class "section." If your schedule says "ENL 101–09," that means the subject is English, the class name is Reading and Writing I, and at least nine separate classes of that course exist. (Different teachers assign different texts.) Finally, head for the Campus Police office to pick up your parking sticker. Bring your student ID and car registration. *Note:* Try to do these things *before* classes begin.

As a commuter, your best bet for studying on campus is the school library, so get to know it right away. Jot down the library hours, usually posted by the entrance. (The library closes for federal holidays and has some quirky weekend hours.) Library seating is ample, but noisy groups tend to collect at the larger tables. Look for a quiet corner on one of the upper floors. English 101 classes usually take a group library tour during the semester. If your class doesn't, or if you miss it, make an appointment with one of the librarians. No one graduates without producing research papers, and acquainting yourself with the computers and research materials ahead of time will save valuable study hours.

As soon as classes begin, get to know your advisor—the person you see for choosing or adding and dropping courses, and for any kind of advice. Offices are usually on the third floor of academic buildings, organized by departments. Each department has a main office and a secretary. If you don't know who your advisor is, the secretary can tell you. The department office can also provide you with a course "checklist." This will tell you which courses you need to complete your degree. Unlike high school teachers, college professors are not required to be on campus all day. Jot down your advisor's office hours (posted outside individual offices or in the department), office phone number, and email address.

Commuters don't have the luxury of always being on campus, so establish a support network during your first week of classes. As corny as it sounds, find a buddy in each class. Or better yet, find someone who shares more than one class with you. Exchange phone numbers (and email addresses if possible). This way, if you do have to miss a class you will be able to keep up with the assignments. Also, check out the Tutoring Center (Blake Hall, second floor)—in case you ever need help. Paid for by your basic tuition, tutors are available for most subjects. They are fellow students who are not only familiar with the university but with the specific courses and professors as well. Tutoring is available on a walk-in basis or by regular appointment.

You're being asked to adjust to many different expectations, all at the same time. A little confusion and anxiety are understandable. But the entire university community is committed to helping its new students.

Note: If you have any questions about these steps—or about anything else—*ask someone!* Chances are other people have asked the same question or experienced the same problem. Best of luck.

—*Catherine Nichols*

Application **13-6**

ESSAY PRACTICE: EXPLAINING HOW SOMETHING HAPPENS

The next essay was written by Bill Kelly, a biologist, for a pamphlet on environmental pollution. It is aimed at an uninformed audience.

ESSAY FOR ANALYSIS AND RESPONSE

HOW ACID RAIN DEVELOPS, SPREADS, AND DESTROYS

[1]Acid rain is environmentally damaging rainfall that occurs after fossil fuels burn, releasing nitrogen and sulfur oxides into the atmosphere. Acid rain, simply stated, increases the acidity level of waterways, because these nitrogen and sulfur oxides combine with the air's normal moisture. The resulting rainfall is far more acidic than normal rainfall. Acid rain is a silent threat because its effects, although slow, are cumulative. This analysis explains the cause, the distribution cycle, and the effects of acid rain.

[2]Most research shows that power plants burning oil or coal are the primary cause of acid rain. Fossil fuels contain a number of elements that are released during combustion. Two of these, sulfur oxide and nitrogen oxide, combine with normal moisture to produce sulfuric acid and nitric acid. The released gases undergo a chemical change as they combine with atmospheric ozone and water vapor. The resulting rain or snowfall is more acid than normal precipitation.

[3]Acid level is measured by pH readings. The pH scale runs from 0 through 14; a pH of 7 is considered neutral. (Distilled water has a pH of 7.) Numbers above 7 indicate increasing degrees of alkalinity. (Household ammonia has a pH of 11.) Numbers below 7 indicate increasing acidity. Movement in either direction on the pH scale, however, means multiplying by 10. Lemon juice, which has a pH value of 2, is 10 times more acidic than apples, which have a pH of 3, and 1000 times more acidic than carrots, which have a pH of 5.

[4]Because of carbon dioxide (an acid substance) normally present in air, unaffected rainfall has a pH of 5.6. At this time, the pH of precipitation in the northeastern United States and Canada is between 4.5 and 4. In Massachusetts, rain and snowfall have an average pH reading of 4.1. A pH reading below 5 is considered to be abnormally acidic, and therefore a threat to aquatic populations.

[5]Although it might seem that areas containing power plants would be most severely affected, acid rain can in fact travel thousands of miles from its source. Stack gases escape and drift with the wind currents. The sulfur and nitrogen oxides thus are able to travel great distances before they return to earth as acid rain.

[6]For an average of two to five days after emission, the gases follow the prevailing winds far from the point of origin. Estimates show that about 50 percent of the acid rain that affects Canada originates in the United States; at the same time, 15 to 25 percent of the U.S. acid rain problem originates in Canada.

[7]The tendency of stack gases to drift makes acid rain a widespread menace. More than 200 lakes in the Adirondacks, hundreds of miles from any industrial center, are unable to support life because their water has become so acidic.

[8]Acid rain causes damage wherever it falls. It erodes various types of building rock, such as limestone, marble, and mortar, which are gradually eaten away by the constant bathing in acid. Damage to buildings, houses, monuments, statues, and cars is widespread. Some priceless monuments and carvings already have been destroyed, and even trees of some varieties are dying in large numbers.

[9]More important, however, is acid rain damage to waterways in the affected areas. Because of its high acidity, acid rain dramatically lowers the pH in lakes and streams. Although its effect is not immediate, acid rain eventually can make a waterway so acidic it dies. In areas with natural acid-buffering elements such as limestone, the diluted acid has less effect. The northeastern United States and Canada, however, lack this natural protection, and so are continually vulnerable.

[10]The pH level in an affected waterway drops so low that some species cease to reproduce. In fact, a pH level of 5.1 to 5.4 means that fisheries are threatened; once a waterway reaches a pH level of 4.5, no fish reproduction occurs. Because each creature is part of the overall food chain, loss of one element in the chain disrupts the whole cycle.

[11]In the northeastern United States and Canada, the acidity problem is compounded by the runoff from acid snow. During the cold winter months, acid snow sits with little melting, so that by spring thaw, the acid released is greatly concentrated. Aluminum and other heavy metals normally present in soil also are released by acid rain and runoff. These toxic substances leach into waterways in heavy concentrations, affecting fish in all stages of development.

—Bill Kelly

QUESTIONS ABOUT THE READING

Refer also to the general questions on page 165.

CONTENT

- Is the information appropriate for the intended audience (uninformed readers)? Explain.
- What specific readers' questions are answered in the body?

ORGANIZATION

- Are the body paragraphs arranged in the best order for readers to follow the process? Explain.
- Why does this essay have no specific conclusion?

STYLE

- Is the discussion easy to follow? If so, what style features help? If not, what might be changed?

■ Give one example of each of the following sentence constructions, and explain briefly how each reinforces the writer's meaning: passive construction, subordination, short sentence.

RESPONDING TO YOUR READING

Select a specialized process that you understand well (from your major or from an area of interest) and explain that process to uninformed readers. Choose a process that has several distinct steps, and write so that your composition classmates gain detailed understanding. Do not merely generalize. Get down to specifics.

Application **13-7**

ESSAY PRACTICE: USING PROCESS ANALYSIS TO MAKE A POINT

Processes occur in our personal experiences, as well—for example, our stages of maturation, of emotional growth and development, of intellectual awareness. The following essay traces a personal process some readers might consider horrifying: the stages of learning to live by scavenging through garbage. As you read, think about how the factual and "objective" style paints a gruesome portrait of survival at the margin of American affluence.

ESSAY FOR ANALYSIS AND RESPONSE

DUMPSTER DIVING

[1]I began Dumpster diving about a year before I became homeless.

[2]I prefer the term scavenging. I have heard people, evidently meaning to be polite, use the word foraging, but I prefer to reserve that word for gathering nuts and berries and such, which I also do, according to the season and opportunity.

[3]I like the frankness of the word scavenging. I live from the refuse of others. I am a scavenger. I think it a sound and honorable niche, although if I could I would naturally prefer to live the comfortable consumer life, perhaps—and only perhaps—as a slightly less wasteful consumer owing to what I have learned as a scavenger.

[4]Except for jeans, all my clothes come from Dumpsters. Boom boxes, candles, bedding, toilet paper, medicine, books, a typewriter, a virgin male love doll, coins sometimes amounting to many dollars: all came from Dumpsters. And, yes, I eat from Dumpsters, too.

[5]There is a predictable series of stages that a person goes through in learning to scavenge. At first the new scavenger is filled with disgust and self-loathing. He [or she] is ashamed of being seen.

[6]This stage passes with experience. The scavenger finds a pair of running shoes that fit and look and smell brand-new. He finds a pocket calculator in perfect working order. He finds pristine ice cream, still frozen, more than he can eat or keep. He begins to understand: people do throw away perfectly good stuff, a lot of perfectly good stuff.

[7]At this stage he may become lost and never recover. All the Dumpster divers I have known come to the point of trying to acquire everything they

touch. Why not take it, they reason; it is all free. This is, of course, hopeless, and most divers come to realize that they must restrict themselves to items of relatively immediate utility.

[8]The finding of objects is becoming something of an urban art. Even respectable, employed people will sometimes find something tempting sticking out of a Dumpster or standing beside one. Quite a number of people, not all of them of the bohemian type, are willing to brag that they found this or that piece in the trash.

[9]But eating from Dumpsters is the thing that separates the dilettanti from the professionals. Eating safely involves three principles: using the senses and common sense to evaluate the condition of the found materials; knowing the Dumpsters of a given area and checking them regularly; and seeking always to answer the question "Why was this discarded?"

[10]Yet perfectly good food can be found in Dumpsters. Canned goods, for example, turn up fairly often in the Dumpsters I frequent. I also have few qualms about dry foods such as crackers, cookies, cereal, chips, and pasta if they are free of visible contaminants and still dry and crisp. Raw fruits and vegetables with intact skins seem perfectly safe to me, excluding, of course, the obviously rotten. Many are discarded for minor imperfections that can be pared away.

[11]A typical discard is a half jar of peanut butter—though nonorganic peanut butter does not require refrigeration and is unlikely to spoil in any reasonable time. One of my favorite finds is yogurt—often discarded, still sealed, when the expiration has passed—because it will keep for several days, even in warm weather.

[12]No matter how careful I am I still get dysentery at least once a month, oftener in warm weather. I do not want to paint too romantic a picture. Dumpster diving has serious drawbacks as a way of life.

[13]I find from the experience of scavenging two rather deep lessons. The first is to take what I can use and let the rest go. I have come to think that there is no value in the abstract. A thing I cannot use or make useful, perhaps by trading, has no value, however fine or rare it may be. The second lesson is the transience of material being. I do not suppose that ideas are immortal, but certainly they are longer-lived than material objects.

[14]The things I find in Dumpsters, the love letters and rag dolls of so many lives, remind me of this lesson. Now I hardly pick up a thing without envisioning the time I will cast it away. This, I think, is a healthy state of mind. Almost everything I have now has already been cast out at least once, proving that what I own is valueless to someone.

[15]I find that my desire to grab for the gaudy bauble has been largely sated. I think this is an attitude I share with the very wealthy—we both know there is plenty more wherever we have come from. Between us are the rat-race millions who have confounded their selves with the objects they grasp and who nightly scavenge the cable channels for they know not what.

[16]I am sorry for them.

—*Lars Eighner*

QUESTIONS ABOUT THE READING

Refer also to the general questions on page 165.

CONTENT

- What are Eighner's assumptions about his audience's knowledge and attitudes? Are these assumptions accurate? Why or why not?
- Point out some of the referential details Eighner selects to make his point. How selective do you think he has been? Explain.

ORGANIZATION

- How does Eighner "frame" his process analysis through his introduction and conclusion? Do these framing elements make the depiction of the process itself more or less convincing? Explain.

STYLE

- What is the writer's attitude toward his subject? Toward his audience? How do we know? Where are the signals?
- Is the tone appropriate for this writer's audience and purpose? Explain.

RESPONDING TO YOUR READING

Explore your reactions to "Dumpster Diving" (pages 231–32) by using the questions on page 166. What is Eighner's point about values? What are the main issues? How has this essay affected your thinking about these issues? As you reread the essay, try to recall some process that has played a role for you personally or for someone close to you. Perhaps you want to focus on the process of achievement (say, preparing for academic or athletic or career competition). Perhaps you have experienced or witnessed the process of giving in to human frailty (say, addiction to drugs, tobacco, alcohol, or food). Perhaps you know something about the process of enduring and recovering from personal loss or misfortune or disappointment. Identify your audience, and decide what you want these readers to do, think, or feel after reading your essay. Should they appreciate this process, try it themselves, avoid it, or what?

Whatever you write about—college or high school or family life or city streets—make a definite point about the larger meaning beyond the details of the process, about the values involved.

CHAPTER 14

Explaining Why It Happened or What Will Happen: Cause-and-Effect Analysis

Using Causal Analysis to Explain: Definite Causes **236**

Using Causal Analysis to Make a Point:
Possible or Probable Causes **237**

Reasoning from Effect to Cause **238**

> **Guidelines** for Effect-to-Cause Analysis **238**

Reasoning from Cause to Effect **239**

> **Guidelines** for Cause-to-Effect Analysis **239**

CASE STUDY: Responding to Reading **247**

Options for Essay Writing **250**

Readings **241, 244, 248**

Applications **240**

Analysis of reasons (causes) or consequences (effects) explains why something happened or what happens as a result of some event or incident.

What readers of causal
analysis want to know

- *Why did it happen?*
- *What caused it?*
- *What are its effects?*
- *What will happen if it is done?*

For example, if you awoke this morning with a sore shoulder (effect), you might recall exerting yourself yesterday at the college Frisbee olympics (cause). You take aspirin, hoping for relief (effect). If the aspirin works, it will have *caused* you to feel better. But some causes and effects are harder to identify:

[CAUSE]   [EFFECT]

1. I tripped over a chair and broke my nose.

   [EFFECT]   [CAUSE]

2. I never studied because I slept too much.

Other causes or effects could be identified for each of the above statements.

[EFFECT]   [CAUSE]
I tripped over the chair because my apartment lights were out.

[EFFECT]   [CAUSE]
The lights were out because the power had been shut off.

[EFFECT]   [CAUSE]
The power was off because my roommate forgot to pay the electric bill.

or

[CAUSE]   [EFFECT]
Because I slept too much, my grades were awful.

[CAUSE]   [EFFECT]
Because my grades were awful, I hated college.

[CAUSE]   [EFFECT]
Because I hated college, I dropped out.

[CAUSE]   [EFFECT]
Because I dropped out of college, I lost my scholarship.

In the examples above, the causes or effects become more distant. The *immediate* cause of example 1, however—the one most closely related to the effect—is that the writer tripped over the chair. Likewise, the *immediate* effect of example 2 is that the writer did no studying. Thus, the challenge is often to distinguish between immediate causes or effects and distant ones. Otherwise, we might generate illogical statements like these:

[CAUSE]   [EFFECT]

Because my roommate forgot to pay the electric bill, I broke my nose.

[EFFECT]   [CAUSE]

I lost my scholarship because I slept too much.

USING CAUSAL ANALYSIS TO EXPLAIN: DEFINITE CAUSES

As in process analysis (Chapter 13), writing that connects definite causes to their effects clarifies the relations among events in a causal chain. A *definite cause is apparent* ("The engine's overheating is caused by a faulty radiator cap"). You write about definite causes when you explain why the combustion in a car engine causes the wheels to move, or why the moon's orbit makes the tides rise and fall.

USING CAUSAL ANALYSIS BEYOND THE WRITING CLASSROOM

- **In other courses:** A research paper might explore the causes of the Israeli-Palestinian conflict or the effects of stress on college students. A report for the Dean of Students might explain students' disinterest in campus activities or the effect of a ban on smoking in public buildings.

- **On the job:** In workplace problem solving, you might analyze the high absenteeism among company employees or the malfunction of equipment.

- **In the community:** Perhaps local citizens need to know how air quality will be affected if your power plant changes from coal to oil or how increasing enrollment has affected education quality at your local high school.

In what other situations might causal analysis make a difference?

EXPLAINING A DEFINITE CAUSE

Topic sentence (1)
Causal chain (2–3)

[1]Some of the most serious accidents involving gas water heaters occur when a flammable liquid is used in the vicinity. [2]The heavier-than-air vapors of a flammable liquid such as gasoline can flow along the floor—even the length of a basement—and be explosively ignited by the flame of the water heater's pilot light or burner. [3]Because the victim's clothing often ignites, the resulting

Effects (4)
Conclusion (5)

burn injuries are commonly serious and extremely painful. [4]They may require long hospitalization, and can result in disfigurement or death. [5]Never, under any circumstances, use a flammable liquid near a gas heater or burner.

—*Consumer Product Safety Commission*

USING CAUSAL ANALYSIS TO MAKE A POINT: POSSIBLE OR PROBABLE CAUSES

Causal writing often explores *possible or probable causes—causes that are not apparent.* In these cases, much searching, thought, and effort usually are needed to argue for a specific cause.

Suppose you ask: "Why are there no children's day-care facilities on our college campus?" Brainstorming yields these possible causes:

lack of need among students

lack of interest among students, faculty, and staff

high cost of liability insurance

lack of space and facilities on campus

lack of trained personnel

prohibition by state law

lack of legislative funding for such a project

Say you proceed with interviews, questionnaires, and research into state laws, insurance rates, and availability of personnel. You begin to rule out some items, and others appear as probable causes. Specifically, you find a need among students, high campus interest, an abundance of qualified people for staffing, and no state laws prohibiting such a project. Three probable causes remain: lack of funding, high insurance rates, and lack of space. Further inquiry shows that lack of funding and high insurance rates are issues. You think, however, that these causes could be eliminated through new sources of revenue: charging a modest fee per child, soliciting donations, diverting funds from other campus organizations, and so on. Finally, after examining available campus space and speaking with school officials, you conclude that the one definite cause is lack of space and facilities.

The persuasiveness of your causal argument will depend on the quality of research and evidence you bring to bear, as well as your ability to clearly explain the links in the chain. You must also convince audiences that you haven't overlooked important alternative causes.

Any complex effect is likely to have more than one cause; you have to make sure that the cause you have isolated is the right one.* You must also

---

*For example, one could argue that the lack of space and facilities somehow is related to funding. And the college's inability to find funds or space may be related to student need, which is not sufficiently acute or interest sufficiently high to exert real pressure. Lack of space and facilities, however, does seem to be the immediate cause.

demonstrate sound reasoning. For example, the fact that one event occurs just before another is no proof that the first caused the second. You might have walked under a ladder in the hallway an hour before flunking your chemistry exam—but you would be hard-pressed to argue convincingly that the one event had caused the other.

REASONING FROM EFFECT TO CAUSE

In reasoning from effect to cause we examine a particular result, *consequence*, or outcome, and we try to determine the circumstances that may produce such a result.

AN EFFECT-TO-CAUSE ANALYSIS

Effect (main point)(1)

Distant cause and examples (2)

Examples (3–4)

Evidence (5)

Immediate cause (6–7)

[1]In the right situation, a perfectly sane person can hallucinate. [2]It is most likely to happen when [he or she] is in a place that provides little stimulation to [the] senses, such as a barren, unbroken landscape or a quiet, dimly lit room. [3]Hallucinations are an occupational hazard of truck drivers, radar scanners, and pilots. [4]These occupations have in common long periods of monotony: lengthy stretches of straight highway, the regular rhythms of radar patterns, the droning hum of engines. [5]A. L. Mosely of the Harvard School of Public Health found that every one of 33 long-distance truck drivers he surveyed could recall having at least one hallucination. [6]Monotony means that

GUIDELINES FOR EFFECT-TO-CAUSE ANALYSIS

1. *Be sure the cause fits the effect.* Identify the immediate cause (the one most closely related to the effect), as well as the distant cause(s) (the ones that precede the immediate cause). For example, the immediate cause of a particular airplane crash might be a fuel-tank explosion, caused by a short circuit in frayed wiring, by faulty design, or by poor quality control by the manufacturer. Discussing only the immediate cause often merely scratches the surface of the problem. To clarify his point, author Daniel Goleman shows examples of "right" situations and of "sane" persons. Research from Harvard provides convincing support.

2. *Make the links between effect and cause clear.* Goleman's reasoning follows:

   [DISTANT CAUSE] [IMMEDIATE CAUSE]
   nonstimulating places ⟶ monotony

   [EFFECT]
   ⟶ hallucination

   The distant cause is discussed first so that the immediate cause will make sense.

3. *Distinguish clearly between possible, probable, and definite causes.* Unless the cause is obvious, limit your assertions by using *perhaps, probably, maybe, most likely, could, seems to, appears to,* or similar qualifiers that prevent you from making an unsupportable claim.

the brain gets fewer sensory messages from the outside. [7]As external stimulation drops off, the brain responds more to messages from inside itself.
—*Daniel Goleman*

Note

Keep in mind that faulty causal reasoning is extremely common, especially when we ignore other possible causes or we confuse mere coincidence with causation. (See page 318 for examples and discussion.)

REASONING FROM CAUSE TO EFFECT

In reasoning from cause to effect, we examine a given set of circumstances, and we try to ascertain the outcome of these circumstances.

A CAUSE-TO-EFFECT ANALYSIS

[1]What has the telephone done to us, or for us, in the hundred years of its existence? [2]A few effects suggest themselves at once. [3]It has saved lives by getting rapid word of illness, injury, or famine from remote places. [4]By joining with the elevator to make possible the multistory residence or office building,

GUIDELINES FOR CAUSE-TO-EFFECT ANALYSIS

1. *Show that the effects fit the cause.* To clarify and support his point, the author John Brooks shows the telephone's effects on familiar aspects of modern life. Because his purpose is to discuss effects in general (not only positive effects), the author balances his development with both positive and negative effects.

2. *Make links between cause and effects clear.* The reasoning goes like this:

   [CAUSE]   [IMMEDIATE EFFECT]
   telephone ➞ created rapid communication

   [ULTIMATE EFFECTS]
   ➞ saved lives, led to the modern city, and so on

   [CAUSE]   [IMMEDIATE EFFECT]
   telephone ➞ enabled people to live alone

   [ULTIMATE EFFECT]
   ➞ led to breakup of multigenerational household

   Without the link provided by the immediate effects, the ultimate effects would make no sense:

   The telephone has saved lives. [*Why?*]
   It has made possible the modern city. [*Why?*]
   It perhaps has caused wars. [*Why?*]

   For further linking, the paragraph groups definite effects (3–8), and then possible effects (9–10), with a conclusion that ties the discussion together.

3. *Consider "confounding factors" (alternate explanations for a particular effect).* For instance, studies indicating that regular exercise improves health might be overlooking the fact that healthy people tend to exercise more often than those who are unhealthy.

it has made possible—for better or worse—the modern city. ⁵By bringing about a quantum leap in the speed and ease with which information moves from place to place, it has greatly accelerated the rate of scientific and technological change and growth in industry. ⁶Beyond doubt it has crippled if not killed the ancient art of letter writing. ⁷It has made living alone possible for persons with normal social impulses; by so doing, it has played a role in one of the greatest social changes of this century, the breakup of the multigenerational household. ⁸It has made the waging of war chillingly more efficient than formerly. ⁹Perhaps (though not probably) it has prevented wars that might have arisen out of international misunderstanding caused by written communications. ¹⁰Or perhaps—again not probably—by magnifying and extending irrational personal conflicts based on voice contact, it has caused wars. ¹¹Certainly it has extended the scope of human conflicts, since it impartially disseminates the useful knowledge of scientists and the babble of bores, the affection of the affectionate and the malice of the malicious.

—*John Brooks*

Application **14-1**

PARAGRAPH WARM-UP: USING CAUSAL ANALYSIS TO EXPLAIN

Ordinary life in the 1990s depends on technology, but technology often frustrates us by letting us down when we most need it. Think of the last time you found yourself screaming at a machine. Using library research if necessary, explain the immediate and distant causes of the problem you experienced, limiting your discussion to definite causes as much as possible. Think of your paragraph as the heart of a letter to a friend explaining how to avoid the problem in the future.

Application **14-2**

PARAGRAPH WARM-UP: USING CAUSAL ANALYSIS TO MAKE A POINT

Identify a problem that affects you, your community, family, school, dorm, or other group ("The library is an awful place to study because _____"). In a paragraph, analyze the causes of this problem as a prelude to an argument for change. Choose a subject you know about or one you can research to get the facts. Identify clearly the situation, the audience, and your purpose.

Application **14-3**

Web-based Project: Assume that classmates will be serving six months as volunteers in agriculture, education, or a similar capacity in a developing country. Do the research and prepare an essay that alerts readers to the area's major health hazards and their causes: for example, contagious diseases or food, water, and insect-borne illnesses, and the like. *Hint:* Begin your research for this project by checking out the National Center for Disease Control's Web site at <**www.cdc.gov/travel/**>.

Application **14-4**

Essay Practice: Analyzing Causes

In the following essay from *Newsweek,* a father examines why he disapproves of his nine-year-old son's clothing and asks himself, "What's my problem?"

Before you read, think about disagreements you've had with adults (or children) over clothing. What were the causes of such disagreements? What were the effects?

ESSAY FOR ANALYSIS AND RESPONSE

I Don't Like What You're Wearing

[1]My son turned 9 recently, and I am surprised to find myself party to a subtle, low-grade tussle with him over his clothes. In the last few months he has taken up a style of dressing that, for reasons not entirely clear to me, I do not particularly like: large, baggy pants; big sneakers that bear the name of famous young basketball players; any shirt or sweat shirt with writing on it. Hats, too, he loves, and wears constantly—baseball hats, usually, though recently he has become enamored of a blue, camouflage number, pulled tightly onto his head, visor curled ominously around his eyes. No matter which corner of the cluttered closet I throw it into with my private hopes, it always reappears on his head.

[2]Attempts to get him to wear shirts without writing on them—nice, simple, collared shirts from the Gap, for example—are all for naught. They remain neatly folded in his top drawer. Nice, khaki pants remain untouched for weeks, then months, until, one morning after the usual struggle, he pulls them out and triumphantly announces, "Dad, they don't fit anymore. They're too tight!" (Time is on his side.)

[3]The struggle, I realize, is an ancient one, and I am surprised to find myself cast in the role of a doughty Ward Cleaver to the rebellious young Beaver. It's odd, as I've never been held up as a paragon of fashion myself. As a child I tended toward the conservative, and I remember a couple of titanic struggles with my parents over a pair of pants that seemed to me a half inch too short. And I was heartbroken to discover that the blue camping shorts and plaid shirt that I begged my mother to order out of a catalog did not turn me into the cherubic blond boy in the photograph. In college I grew my hair long and took on a look that now I recognize as a precursor to grunge—baggy polyester work pants and ill-fitting coats that I bought at the old-men's store.

[4]My wife does not fully share my anxieties about our son's clothes. It was she who caved in and bought him the Iverson sneakers ($69.99) and, in a moment of weakness and flagging judgment, succumbed to the camouflage hat. She is less bothered by the sight of him playing basketball with his hat on sideways, one pants leg halfway up his shin, Iversons barely attached to his

feet. But she was on the front lines of a struggle the other day at the mall, where the only coats for sale featured, in large, bold letters, the name of their manufacturer: ADIDAS, NIKE, or HILFIGER.

[5]Am I actually a cultural conservative dressed in liberal tweed, out of step with the times, nervous that my son is affecting the style of a hip-hop culture that makes me nervous? Is there a racial aspect to my ambivalence? Am I overly sensitive to the remarks of the playground moms who, as we watch our children play basketball, observe, "He's really changed!" followed by meaningful silence? Am I fearful of his going the way of the shy, smiling boys I knew when they were children, and have watched slowly turn into cigarette-smoking teenagers who glower at me? When I say hello, sometimes, they look up, surprised, and the shy smile of their childhood briefly returns.

[6]But what I once took as a largely urban phenomenon clearly is not: we went out to the small town where I grew up, the other day, an hour from the city, and as we played in the yard three or four boys strolled by, their enormous pants billowing like sails in the warm spring wind. I don't want to be an old stick-in-the-mud, but I draw the line at pants trying to slide down the backside. "Dad," he protests, "I have no belt!" Nor do I want my good-looking son turned into an unpaid walking billboard for Nike, or Adidas or Hilfiger. Beyond that, I've probably got some work to do myself, updating my own antiquated and overly mythologized sense of fashion and cultural iconography.

[7]The baseball hat, after all, is as American as apple pie, emblematic of virility and a peculiar brand of American male self-satisfaction. The fact that he likes to wear his sideways shouldn't send shivers of dread and alarm down my spine, should it? I was driven from the sport myself in the late 1960s by an overzealous coach who thought he was going to save America from communists by making me get my hair cut. When I did, finally, he said "shorter," and I quit instead.

[8]Baseball catchers wear their hats backward, and football players in postgame interviews, and half the male college students in America, drifting around in their smug little packs, looking for a woman or a beer. But sideways? What does it mean? Why does it bother me?

[9]"Dad!" my son asks during one of our morning skirmishes, rejected garments strewn around the floor, his hands raised and shoulders shrugged in an eternal gesture of astonishment and dismay. "What's your problem?"

—David Updike

QUESTIONS ABOUT YOUR READING

Refer to the general questions on page 165 as well as these specific questions.

PURPOSE

- In your view, what does Updike want the audience to be thinking or feeling after reading this piece?
- Does the essay succeed in making a difference with readers? If so, how?

CONTENT

- Are the causes presented here definite, probable, or possible? Explain.
- Has the author explored distant or alternative causes adequately? Explain.
- What assumptions does the author make about his audience's attitudes and awareness? Are these assumptions accurate? Explain.
- What are the main issues here? How has this essay affected your thinking about these issues?

ORGANIZATION

- What combination of opening strategies is used in the introduction?
- Are the body paragraphs arranged in an order (such as general-to-specific) that emphasizes the thesis? If so, what is that order?

STYLE

- What is the author's attitude toward his subject? Toward his audience? How do we know? What are the signals?
- Is the tone appropriate for the intended audience and purpose? Explain.

RESPONDING TO YOUR READING

Explore your reactions to Updike's essay by using the questions on page 166. Think about how this essay has made a difference for you and then respond with an essay of your own that examines the causes of one of your personal likes or dislikes.

Specifically, you might analyze the appeal of some activity or behavior (harmful or beneficial, pleasurable or painful) that takes up much of your (and other people's) time. Feel free to inject humor, as in Maureen Malloy's essay on page 56. Here are activities or behaviors whose causes you could analyze:

- Why do I (or we) spend so much time watching football games (or some other sport)?
- Why am I so obsessed with exercise, fashion, or diet?
- Why am I a soap opera fan?
- Why are we such party animals?

Be sure your analysis supports some definite thesis.

Application **14-5**

ESSAY PRACTICE: ANALYZING EFFECTS

In this next selection, a psychologist points out the dangers of inflated self-esteem.

Before you read, think about how certain school experiences affected your self-esteem. In what ways has your own sense of self-esteem differed in high school versus college? What were the causes of that change?

ESSAY FOR ANALYSIS AND RESPONSE

SHOULD SCHOOLS TRY TO BOOST SELF-ESTEEM?—BEWARE THE DARK SIDE

[1] "We must raise children's self-esteem!" How often has this sentiment been expressed in recent years in schools, homes, and meeting rooms around the United States? The sentiment reflects the widespread, well-intentioned, earnest, and yet rather pathetic hope that if we can only persuade our kids to love themselves more, they will stop dropping out, getting pregnant, carrying weapons, taking drugs, and getting into trouble, and instead will start achieving great things in school and out.

[2] Unfortunately, the large mass of knowledge that research psychologists have built up around self-esteem does not justify that hope. At best, high self-esteem is a mixed blessing whose total effects are likely to be small and minor. At worst, the pursuit of high self-esteem is a foolish, wasteful, and self-destructive enterprise that may end up doing more harm than good.

[3] Writers on controversial topics should acknowledge their biases, and so let me confess mine: I have a strong bias in favor of self-esteem. I have been excited about self-esteem ever since my student days at Princeton, when I first heard that it was a topic of study. Over the past two decades I have probably published more studies on self-esteem than anybody else in the United States (or elsewhere). It would be great for my career if self-esteem could do everything its boosters hope: I'd be dining frequently at the White House and advising policymakers on how to fix the country's problems.

[4] It is therefore with considerable personal disappointment that I must report that the enthusiastic claims of the self-esteem movement mostly range from fantasy to hogwash. The effects of self-esteem are small, limited, and not all good. Yes, a few people here and there end up worse off because their self-esteem was too low. Then again, other people end up worse off because their self-esteem was too high. And most of the time self-esteem makes surprisingly little difference.

[5] Self-esteem is, literally, how favorably a person regards himself or herself. It is perception (and evaluation), not reality. For example, I think the world would be a better place if we could all manage to be a little nicer to each other. But that's hard: We'd all have to discipline ourselves to change. The self-esteem approach, in contrast, is to skip over the hard work of changing our actions and instead just let us all *think* we're nicer. That won't make the world any better. People with high self-esteem are not in fact any nicer than people with low self-esteem—in fact, the opposite is closer to the truth.

[6] High self-esteem means thinking well of oneself, regardless of whether that perception is based on substantive achievement or mere wishful thinking and self-deception. High self-esteem can mean *confident* and *secure*—but it can also mean *conceited, arrogant, narcissistic,* and *egotistical.*

[7] A recent, widely publicized study dramatized the fact that self-esteem consists of perception and is not necessarily based on reality. In an international scholastic competition, American students achieved the lowest average scores among all participating nationalities. But the American kids rated themselves and their performance the highest. This is precisely what

comes of focusing on self-esteem: poor performance accompanied by plenty of empty self-congratulation. Put another way, we get high self-esteem as inflated perceptions covering over a rather dismal reality.

[8]Looking ahead, it is alarming to think what will happen when this generation of schoolchildren grows up into adults who may continue thinking they are smarter than the rest of the world—while actually being dumber. America will be a land of conceited fools.

[9]All of this might fairly be discounted if America were really suffering from an epidemic of low self-esteem, such as if most American schoolchildren generally had such negative views of themselves that they were unable to tackle their homework. But that's not the case. On the contrary, as I'll explain shortly, self-esteem is already inflated throughout the United States. The average American already regards himself or herself as above average. At this point, any further boosting of self-esteem is likely to approach the level of grandiose, egotistical delusions.

Boosting Self-Esteem: The Problem of Inflation

[10]Most (though not all) of the problems linked to high self-esteem involve inflated self-esteem, in the sense of overestimating oneself. Based on the research findings produced in laboratories all over North America, I have no objection to people forming a sober, accurate recognition of their actual talents and accomplishments. The violence, the self-defeating behaviors, and the other problems tend to be most acute under conditions of threatened egotism, and inflated self-esteem increases that risk. After all, if you really are smart, your experiences will tend to confirm that fact, and so there's not much danger in high self-esteem that is based on accurate recognition of your intelligence. On the other hand, if you overestimate your abilities, reality will be constantly showing you up and bursting your bubble, and so your (inflated) self-opinion will be bumping up against threats—and those encounters lead to destructive responses.

[11]Unfortunately, a school system that seeks to boost self-esteem in general is likely to produce the more dangerous (inflated) form of self-esteem. It would be fine, for example, to give a hard test and then announce the top few scores for general applause. Such a system recognizes the successful ones, and it shows the rest what the important criteria are (and how much they may need to improve). What is dangerous and worrisome is any procedure that would allow the other students to think that they are just as accomplished as the top scorers even though they did not perform as well. Unfortunately, the self-esteem movement often works in precisely this wrong-headed fashion.

[12]Some students will inevitably be smarter, work harder, learn more, and perform better than others. There is no harm (and in fact probably some positive value) in helping these individuals recognize their superior accomplishments and talents. Such self-esteem is linked to reality and hence less prone to causing dangers and problems.

[13]On the other hand, there is considerable danger and harm in falsely boosting the self-esteem of the other students. It is fine to encourage them to

work harder and try to gain an accurate appraisal of their strengths and weaknesses, and it is also fine to recognize their talents and accomplishments in other (including nonacademic) spheres, but don't give them positive feedback that they have not earned. (Also, don't downplay the importance of academic achievement as the central goal of school, such as by suggesting that success at sports or crafts is just as good.) To encourage the lower-performing students to regard their performance just as favorably as the top learners—a strategy all too popular with the self-esteem movement—is a tragic mistake. If successful, it results only in inflated self-esteem, which is the recipe for a host of problems and destructive patterns.

[14]The logical implications of this argument show exactly when self-esteem should be boosted. When people seriously underestimate their abilities and accomplishments, they need boosting. For example, a student who falsely believes she can't succeed at math may end up short-changing herself and failing to fulfill her potential unless she can be helped to realize that yes, she does have the ability to master math.

[15]In contrast, self-esteem should not be boosted when it is already in the accurate range (or higher). A student who correctly believes that math is not his strong point should not be given exaggerated notions of what he can accomplish. Otherwise, the eventual result will be failure and heartbreak. Along the way he's likely to be angry, troublesome, and prone to blame everybody else when something goes wrong.

[16]In my years as an educator I have seen both patterns. But which is more common? Whether boosting self-esteem in general will be helpful or harmful depends on the answer. And the answer is overwhelmingly clear. Far, far more Americans of all ages have accurate or inflated views of themselves than underestimate themselves. They don't need boosting.

[17]Dozens of studies have documented how inflated self-esteem is. Research interest was sparked some years ago by a survey in which 90 percent of adults rated themselves as "above average" in driving ability. After all, only half can really be above average. Similar patterns are found with almost all good qualities. A survey about leadership ability found that only 2 percent of high school students rated themselves as below average. Meanwhile, a whopping 25 percent claimed to be in the top 1 percent! Similarly, when asked about ability to get along with others, no students at all said they were below average.

[18]Responses to scales designed to measure self-esteem show the same pattern. There are always plenty of scores at the high end and plenty in the middle, but only a few struggle down toward the low end. This seems to be true no matter which of the many self-esteem scales is used. Moreover, the few individuals who do show the truly low self-esteem scores probably suffer from multiple problems that need professional therapy. Self-esteem boosting from schools would not cure them.

[19]Obviously there's precious little evidence of low self-esteem in such numbers. By definition, plenty of people are in reality below average, but most of them refuse to acknowledge it. Meanwhile large numbers of people clearly

overestimate themselves. The top 1 percent can really only contain 1 percent, not the 25 percent who claim to belong there. Meanwhile, the problem that would justify programs aimed at boosting self-esteem—people who significantly underestimate themselves—is extremely rare.

—*Roy F. Baumeister*

QUESTIONS ABOUT THE READING

Refer to the general questions on pages 165 and 166, as well as these specific questions.

CONTENT

- What assumptions does the author seem to make about his audience's attitudes and awareness? Are these assumptions accurate? Explain.
- What are the main issues here? How has this essay affected your thinking about these issues? Explain.
- Is Baumeister's essay credible? Are you convinced this writer knows what he is talking about? Explain.
- Is the writer arguing for definite, probable, or possible effects? Support your answer with specific examples.
- Does the essay have informative value? Explain.

ORGANIZATION

- Trace the line of reasoning from paragraph to paragraph. Is this arrangement effective in supporting Baumeister's causal claims? Explain.
- Identify four devices that increase coherence in this essay, and give examples of each.

STYLE

- What attitude does Baumeister display toward his subject? Toward his audience? How do we know? What are the signals?
- Is the tone appropriate for the audience and purpose? Explain.

RESPONDING TO YOUR READING

Explore your reactions to "Should Schools Try to Boost Self-Esteem?" by using the questions on page 166. Then respond with an essay about your own views on a related issue.

CASE STUDY

RESPONDING TO READING

After reading Updike's essay, John Saurette, an education major and parent of school-age children, decides to explore this question facing his family directly: How effective are school uniforms? John knows that this complex topic will require research on his part.

In drafting and revising his essay, John relies on the Guidelines for Cause-to-Effect Analysis and the Revision Checklist (pages 239 and 63).

| Note |

Even though causal analysis is the dominant rhetorical strategy in John's essay, he also relies on other strategies, such as vivid narration and description, colorful illustration, and process analysis.

Title announces the topic Opens with strategies being proposed Describes the overall desired effects

SCHOOL UNIFORMS: A RECIPE FOR SCHOOL REFORM

Standardized testing, teacher certification, school vouchers, metal detectors—needless to say, education reform is a top priority, from the White House to teachers' lounges, to our own kitchen tables. Political candidates, parents, and school officials across the country are looking at ways to improve our schools. Various groups argue for what they believe are the correct ways to improve education, be it testing or police in the schools. However, one controversial measure is gaining popularity from New York to Long Beach. This measure is also one of the simplest: school uniforms.

Focuses on one beneficial strategy Thesis statement is set off in its own paragraph, for emphasis Thesis includes a forecast of supporting points

Cites research findings here and throughout Gives one example of beneficial effects

School uniforms and dress codes are on the rise and for good reason: They work. School districts across the country are finding that uniforms promote order, discipline, safety, and learning, along with a sense of equality among differing social groups.

Distractions in schools over clothing seem to be an ongoing problem. For example, in a 1992 survey, 77 percent of parents in the Chicago public school system reported that their children experienced peer pressure at school over clothing (Spring 101). In hopes of improving the learning environment, New York City, the nation's largest school district, implemented standardized dress codes in nearly three-quarters of its elementary and middle schools in 1997. After two years, 95 percent of these schools reported improved discipline and a more orderly learning environment (Coles 6).

How researchers view the effects

Experts suggest that dress codes keep the school environment more orderly by reducing incidents of theft and violence over designer clothes and sneakers, and provide some protection against gang activity by prohibiting the wearing of gang colors and badges. Uniforms also enable school officials to identify intruders among the student body (Spring 103–05). In 1994, students in Long Beach, California began wearing uniforms. The effects seem impressive: Within three years, the system reported a 36 percent reduction in overall crime, 51 percent reduction in fights, 34 percent reduction in assault and battery, and 18 percent reduction in vandalism. School officials admit that uniforms were implemented as part of a larger, overall reform plan, but in the words of one principal, "though we can't attribute the improvement exclusively to uniforms [. . .] we think that it is more than coincidental" (U.S. Department of Education 1).

Gives another example

Shows people talking

How educators view the effects

Evidence suggests that dress codes also help promote discipline, and reduce distractions within the classroom itself. In the more businesslike environment created by uniforms, teachers find it easier to keep students on task. At the same time, uniforms seem to "promote a sense of pride and a sense of calmness" (U.S. Department of Education 1). Says one Seattle middle school principal, "[before we had uniforms] there were many more distractions [and] my kids were really into what others were wearing" (Coles 6).

How parents view the
effects

From a parent's point of view, uniforms also make sense, especially in terms of convenience and economics. Uniforms free parents from the chore of deciding what their children will wear each day. This can be especially trying as students reach middle- and high-school age. Economically, just a few uniforms and a child is set for the year. As children outgrow them, uniforms can be passed on to younger children or donated to the school for someone else's use. Even though the children will still want to buy new clothes to wear after school, the savings are real, compared to buying the latest styles in order to be part of the "in" crowd.

How opponents and
courts view the effects

Dress code opponents argue that uniforms violate a student's freedom of expression. However, federal courts so far have ruled that the benefits outweigh the drawbacks. Says one federal judge, "when we weigh all the evidence involved, [uniforms] seem to have had a real positive effect" (U.S. Department of Education 1).

Still, the latest court rulings do lean toward having an "opt-out" clause for parents who strongly oppose the dress code.

How negative effects of
uniforms can be avoided

In response to legal questions surrounding uniform requirements, federal officials have created a handbook for school districts that are considering dress codes. The *Manual on School Uniforms* provides guidelines for parent involvement, financial aid, protection of student rights, and use of uniforms as part of an overall safety plan.

How students view the
effects

Perhaps the greatest motivation for uniforms comes from students themselves. Researcher Richard Murray found that students in a middle school that required uniforms viewed their school much more positively than those in a school without such a requirement (cited in Isaacson 2). My own brief interviews of 16 eighth graders (8 males and 8 females) seem to support this observation.

Author describes own
research findings

All the participants in my survey presently wore uniforms. Ten had been wearing uniforms since kindergarten, and six were transfers from schools without dress codes. Two of the six had transferred within the past year. Complaints about the dress code were mainly aesthetic, ranging from "uncomfortable" to "ugly." This seems to indicate a greater need for flexibility in style selection. But, overwhelmingly, the students expressed satisfaction. When asked about suppression of individuality, the students cited ample opportunity for self-expression, including "dress-down days, hair styles, backpacks, and school accessories."

Surprisingly, those who had transferred most recently were also the most vocal in favor of uniforms. One female student accurately summed up the overall attitude of the participants:

Offers a representative
quotation

In my old school, it wasn't cool to talk to kids who wore the wrong clothes. There was always one or two kids whose parents were older and didn't dress their kids in style. They weren't bad kids but they always got made fun of because of their clothes. It's much easier to come to school here, where having the latest or most expensive clothes is not needed to be cool. We get to know other kids for who they are, not what they wear.

Admits the limitations of this solution

Conclusion reemphasizes the main point

Granted, dress codes alone are no panacea for all of education's ills. However, at a time in which calls for school reform are loud and clear, we must take advantage of all good opportunities. Uniforms offer one of these opportunities. The evidence indicates that dress codes cut down on classroom distractions and school violence, improve discipline, promote positive attitudes, and help in student socialization—all of which are needed if our schools are to recover. Simply stated, uniforms just may be an important first step on America's road to educational excellence.

—*John Saurette*

Works Cited

Albright Middle School Students. Personal Interviews. 1 Oct. 2000.

Coles, Adrienne D. "NYC Joins Growing List of Districts Dressing the Same." Education Week 24 Nov. 1994: 6. 3 Oct. 2001 <**www.edweek.org**>.

Isaacson, Lynne. "Student Dress Policies. ERIC Digest. Number 117." ERIC Digests (Jan. 1998): 1–4. ERIC. Online. 3 Oct. 2001 <**www.ed.gov/databases/ ERICDigests/ed415570.html**>.

Murray, Richard, J. "The Impact of School Uniforms on School Climate." NASSP BULLETIN 81 (December 1997): 106–112.

Spring, Joel H. *American Education:* An Introduction to Social and Political Aspects. 6th ed. New York: Longman, 1994.

U.S. Department of Education. Manual on School Uniforms. Washington, DC: GPO, 1996.

OPTIONS FOR ESSAY WRITING

As an alternative project, analyze the effects of a place, an event, or a relationship. You might trace the effects in your life from having a specific friend or belonging to a specific family or group. Or you might explain the effects on your family, school, or community of a tragic event (such as a suicide) or a fortunate one (say, a financial windfall). Or you might want to show how the socioeconomic atmosphere of your hometown, neighborhood, or family has affected the person you have become. Or you might explain how the weather, landscape, or geography of your area affects people's values, behavior, and lifestyle. Or you might speculate about the effects that today's racial or gender socioeconomic divisions will have on the next generation.

Whatever the topic, be sure your discussion supports a definite viewpoint about the effects of something.

CHAPTER 15

Explaining Similarities or Differences: Comparison and Contrast

Developing a Comparison **252**

Developing a Contrast **252**

Developing a Combined Comparison and Contrast **253**

Using Comparison and Contrast to Explain **254**

Using Comparison and Contrast to Make a Point **254**

A Special Kind of Comparison: Analogy **255**

Guidelines for Comparison and Contrast **257**

CASE STUDY: Responding to Reading **262**

Options for Essay Writing **264**

Readings **259, 262**

Applications **255, 258**

Comparison examines similarities; contrast examines differences. Comparison and contrast (sometimes just called *comparison*) help us evaluate things or shed light on their relationship; they help us to visualize the Big Picture.

What readers of comparison and contrast want to know

- *In what significant ways are X and Y similar or alike?*
- *In what significant ways are X and Y different?*
- *Can something about X help us understand Y?*
- *In what significant ways is one preferable to the other?*

DEVELOPING A COMPARISON

Comparison offers perspective on one thing by pointing out its similarities with something else. The two items compared are of the same class: two cars, two countries, two professors. The next paragraph compares drug habits among people of all times and places to those among people of modern times:

A COMPARISON

Main point (1)

Historical similarity to modern habits (2–3)

Religious similarity to modern habits (4–5)

Modern continuation of habit (6–7)

Concluding point (8)

[1]All the natural narcotics, stimulants, relaxants, and hallucinants known to the modern botanist and pharmacologist were discovered by primitive [people] and have been in use from time immemorial. [2]One of the first things that *Homo sapiens* did with his newly developed rationality and self-consciousness was to set them to work finding out ways to bypass analytical thinking and to transcend or, in extreme cases, temporarily obliterate the isolating awareness of the self. [3]Trying all things that grew in the field or forest, they held fast to that which, in this context, seemed good—everything, that is to say, that would change the quality of consciousness, would make it different, no matter how, from everyday feeling, perceiving, and thinking. [4]Among the Hindus, rhythmic breathing and mental concentration have, to some extent, taken the place of mind-transforming drugs used elsewhere. [5]But even in the land of yoga, even among the religious and even for specifically religious purposes, *Cannabis indica* (marijuana) has been freely used to supplement the effects of spiritual exercises. [6]The habit of taking vacations from the more-or-less purgatorial world, which we have created for ourselves, is universal. [7]Moralists may denounce it; but, in the teeth of disapproving talk and repressive legislation, the habit persists, and mind-transforming drugs are everywhere available. [8]The Marxian formula, "Religion is the opium of the people," is reversible, and one can say, with even more truth, that "Opium is the religion of the people."

—*Aldous Huxley*

DEVELOPING A CONTRAST

A contrast is designed to point out differences between one thing and another. This next paragraph contrasts the beliefs of Satanism with those of Christianity:

A CONTRAST

Main point (1)
First difference (2–3)

Second difference (4)
Third difference (5–8)

Final—and major—
difference (9–10)

¹The Satanic belief system, not surprisingly, is the antithesis of Christianity. ²Their theory of the universe, their cosmology, is based upon the notion that the desired end state is a return to a pagan awareness of their humanity. ³This is in sharp contrast to the transcendental goals of traditional Christianity. ⁴The power associated with the pantheon of gods is also reversed: Satan's power is waxing (increasing); God's, if he still lives, waning. ⁵The myths of the Satanic church purport to tell the true story of the rise of Christianity and the fall of paganism, and there is a reversal here too. ⁶Christ is depicted as an early "con man" who tricked an anxious and powerless group of individuals into believing a lie. ⁷He is typified as "pallid incompetence hanging on a tree." ⁸Satanic novices are taught that early church fathers deliberately picked on those aspects of human desire that were most natural and made them sins, in order to use the inevitable transgressions as a means of controlling the populace, promising them salvation in return for obedience. ⁹And finally, their substantive belief, the very delimitation of what is sacred and what is profane, is the antithesis of Christian belief. ¹⁰The Satanist is taught to "be natural; to revel in pleasure and in self-gratification; to emphasize indulgence and power in this life."

—Edward J. Moody

DEVELOPING A COMBINED COMPARISON AND CONTRAST

A combined comparison and contrast examines similarities and differences displayed by two or more things. This next paragraph first contrasts education with training and, second, compares how each serves important needs of society:

A COMBINED COMPARISON/CONTRAST

Main point (1)

Difference of purpose (2)
How "trained" people
serve society (3–5)

Similarity of effects (6)

How "educated" people
serve society (7–11)

¹To understand the nature of the liberal arts college and its function in our society, it is important to understand the difference between education and training. ²Training is intended primarily for the service of society; education is primarily for the individual. ³Society needs doctors, lawyers, engineers, and teachers to perform specific tasks necessary to its operation, just as it needs carpenters and plumbers and stenographers. ⁴Training supplies the immediate and specific needs of society so that the work of the world may continue. ⁵And these needs, our training centers—the professional and trade schools—fill. ⁶But although education is for the improvement of the individual, it also serves society by providing a leavening of men and women of understanding, of perception and wisdom. ⁷They are our intellectual leaders, the critics of our culture, the defenders of our free traditions, the instigators of our progress. ⁸They serve society by examining its function, appraising its needs, and criticizing its direction. ⁹They may be earning their livings by practicing one of the professions, or in pursuing a trade, or by engaging in business enterprise. ¹⁰They may be rich or poor. ¹¹They may

Conclusion (12)

occupy positions of power and prestige, or they may be engaged in some humble employment. [12]Without them, however, society either disintegrates or else becomes an anthill.

—*Harry Kemelman*

USING COMPARISON/CONTRAST BEYOND THE WRITING CLASSROOM

- **In other courses:** In sociology, you might assess the economic progress made by minority groups by comparing income figures from earlier decades with today's figures.
- **On the job:** You might compare the qualifications of various job applicants or the performance of various stock and bond portfolios.
- **In the community:** You might compare the voting records of two politicians or the SAT scores of local students compared to the national average.

In what other situations might comparison and contrast make a difference?

USING COMPARISON AND CONTRAST TO EXPLAIN

Referential comparison usually helps readers understand one thing in terms of another. For example, we could explain the effects of high-fat diets on heart disease and cancer by comparing disease rates in Japan (with its low-fat diet) with those in North America. To explain how new knowledge of earthquakes has affected the way engineers design buildings, we can contrast modern buildings with buildings constructed years ago.

Referential comparison also often permits us to explain a complex or abstract idea in terms of another. For example, it's easier to understand how earlier civilizations understand a term like "honor" if we contrast their concept with our own today.

USING COMPARISON AND CONTRAST TO MAKE A POINT

Like other development strategies, comparison and contrast can also support persuasion. For example, it is often used in evaluation, in which we judge the merits of something by measuring it in relationship to something else.

We might compare two (or more) cars, computers, political candidates, college courses, or careers to argue that one is better. In Chapter 1 (pages 12–14), Shirley Haley contrasts her parents' lifestyle with the one she prefers for herself.

Comparisons can support other kinds of arguments, as well. Huxley's comparison of past and present drug habits, for example (page 252), supports the thesis that any habit so long entrenched will be hard to eliminate. Kemelman's analysis of the differences and similarities between training and education (page 253) supports his claim that the liberal arts college has an important function in our society.

Do you think that Moody's contrast of Christians and Satanists (page 253) also supports an implied argument, or is it mainly referential? Explain.

As always, the evidence with which you support your content, your organizational skills, and your command of style are what make your argumentative comparisons persuasive.

A SPECIAL KIND OF COMPARISON: ANALOGY

Ordinary comparison shows similarities between two things of the same class (two teachers, two styles of dress, two political philosophies). *Analogy,* on the other hand, shows similarities between two things of *different classes* (writing and skiing, freshman registration and a merry-go-round, a dorm room and a junkyard). Analogy answers the reader's question:

Can you explain X by comparing it to something I already know?

Analogies are useful in explaining something abstract, complex, or unfamiliar, as long as the easier subject is broadly familiar to readers. This next analogy helps clarify an unfamiliar technical concept (dangerous levels of a toxic chemical) by comparing it to something more familiar (a human hair).

ANALOGY

A dioxin concentration of 500 parts per trillion is lethal to guinea pigs. One part per trillion is roughly equal to the thickness of a human hair compared to the distance across the United States.

—*Congressional Research Report*

By comparing new information to information your audience already understands, analogy helps build a bridge between their current knowledge and the new ideas. (For another example, read Annie Dillard's opening paragraph from "Seeing," page 172.)

Application 15-1

PARAGRAPH WARM-UP: COMPARISON/CONTRAST

Using comparison or contrast (or both), write a paragraph discussing the likenesses or differences between two people, animals, attitudes, activities, places, or things. Identify clearly the situation, the audience, and your purpose. Then classify your paragraph: Does it primarily inform, or does it make a point? Some possible subjects:

two places I know well

two memorable teaching styles (good or bad)

two similar consumer items

two pets I've had

the benefits of two kinds of exercise

Application **15-2**

PARAGRAPH WARM-UP: ANALOGY

Develop a paragraph explaining something abstract, complex, or unfamiliar by comparing it to something concrete, simple, or familiar. ("Writing is like . . .";
"Love is like . . ."; "Osmosis works like . . ."). Identify a specific purpose or audience. Do you have an informative or a persuasive goal?

Application **15-3**

Web-based Project: Many schools now have writing centers online. These centers often have exercises or tip sheets you can browse or download. Some even have opportunities for collaboration and consultation via email or "chat rooms." Do a Web search and compare and contrast two online writing centers, assessing the quality of the services and the information provided.

Application **15-4**

Web-based Project: Compare three popular Internet search engines on the basis of specific criteria, such as the following:

- search page (interface) is easy to use
- searches rapidly
- categories are well organized and easy to browse
- offers customizable features for finding of information
- offers good navigational aids
- offers good Help, FAQ, and Search Tips pages
- lists a large index of sites
- ratings system identifies quality sites
- site listings are up to date
- searches are easy to limit by topic or user

GUIDELINES FOR COMPARISON AND CONTRAST

1. *Compare or contrast items in the same class.* Compare dogs and cats, but not dogs and trees; men and women, but not women and bicycles. Otherwise you have no logical basis for comparison. If one item is less familiar than the other, define it immediately, as Moody does with Satanism.

2. *Rest the comparison on clear and definite criteria: costs, uses, benefits/drawbacks, appearance, results.* Huxley compares people of all times for their drug habits; Moody compares Satanism and Christianity for their primary beliefs; Kemelman compares education and training by their function in our society. In evaluating the merits of competing items, identify your specific criteria and rank them in order of importance. For example, Kemelman asserts that training supplies society's "immediate needs," but education supplies "the instigators of our progress" and the leadership required for cultural survival.

3. *Establish your credibility for evaluating items.* Instead of merely pointing out similarities and differences (as in Moody), comparisons often evaluate competing items. (See page 262.) Answer readers' implied question "How do you know *X* is better than *Y*?" by briefly describing your experience with (or research on) this issue.

4. *Give both items balanced treatment.* Discuss points for each item in identical order. Both Moody and Kemelman give roughly equal space to each item. In Huxley's paragraph, the other item in the comparison, modern drug use habits, is only briefly mentioned, but readers can infer its place in the discussion from their own general knowledge. Huxley, then, offers an implied comparison.

5. *Support and clarify the comparison or contrast through credible examples.* Use research if necessary, for examples that readers can visualize.

6. *Follow either a block pattern or a point-by-point pattern.* In the block pattern, first one item is discussed fully, then the next, as in Kemelman: "trained" people in the first block; "educated" people in the second. Choose a block pattern when the overall picture is more important than the individual points.

   In the point-by-point pattern, one point about both items is discussed, then the next point, and so on, as in Moody: The first difference between Satanism and Christianity is in their respective cosmologies; the second is in their view of God's power; the third is in their myths about the rise of Christianity, and so on. Choose a point-by-point pattern when specific points might be hard to remember unless placed side by side.

Block pattern	Point-by-point pattern
Item A	first point of A/first point of B, etc.
first point	
second point	
third point, etc.	
Item B	second point of A/
first point	second point of B, etc.
second point	
third point, etc.	

7. *Order your points for greatest emphasis.* Try ordering your points from least to most important, dramatic, useful, or reasonable. Placing the most striking point last emphasizes it best.

8. *In an evaluative comparison ("X is better than Y"), offer your final judgment.* Base your judgment squarely on the criteria presented.

- images are easy to download and waste no screen space
- supports advanced searches using Boolean operators (see page 351)

Be sure to specify the criteria you have chosen.

SAMPLE SEARCH ENGINES

- *Alta Vista*
  <http://www.altavista.com>
- *The Argus Clearinghouse*
  <http://www.clearinghouse.net>
- *Ask Jeeves*
  <http://www.askjeeves.com>
- *Excite*
  <http://www.excite.com>
- *HotBot*
  <http://www.hotbot.com>
- *Lycos*
  <http://www.lycos.com>
- *Savvy Search*
  <http://www.savvysearch.com>

Application **15-5**

GENDER DIFFERENCES

Collaborative Project: Recent research on ways men and women communicate in meetings indicates a definite gender gap. Communication specialist Kathleen Kelley-Reardon offers this assessment of gender differences in group communication:

> Women and men operate according to communication rules for their gender, what experts call 'gender codes.' They learn, for example, to show gratitude, ask for help, take control, and express emotion, deference, and commitment in different ways. (88–89)

Professor Kelley-Reardon describes specific elements of a female gender code: Women are more likely than men to take as much time as needed to explore an issue, build consensus and relationship among members, use tact in expressing views, use care in choosing their words, consider the listener's feelings, speak softly, allow interruptions, make requests instead of giving commands ("Could I have the report by Friday?" versus "Have this ready by Friday"), preface assertions in ways that avoid offending ("I don't want to seem disagreeable here, but . . .").

Divide into small groups of mixed genders and complete the following tasks to test the hypothesis that women and men communicate differently.

Each group member prepares the following brief messages—without consulting with other members.

- A thank-you note to a friend who has done you a favor.
- A note asking a friend for help with a problem or project.
- A note asking a collaborative peer to be more cooperative or to stop interrupting or complaining.
- A note expressing impatience, frustration, confusion, or satisfaction to members of your group.
- A note offering support to a good friend who is depressed.
- A note to a new student, welcoming this person to the dorm.
- A request for a higher grade, based on your hard work.
- The collaborative meeting is out of hand, so you decide to take control. Write out what you would say.
- Some members of your group are dragging their feet on a project. Write out what you would say.

As a group, compare messages, draw conclusions, and appoint one member to present the findings to the class.

Application **15-6**

ESSAY PRACTICE

The writer in this next selection reflects on her search for a rational conclusion about a volatile issue: She measures her personal reasons for supporting abortion rights against her reasons for opposing them.

Before you read, think about several topics over which people strongly disagree (gay marriage, euthanasia, Affirmative Action, and so on). Consider this question: Is it ever possible to "feel all one way" about any controversial topic?

ESSAY FOR ANALYSIS AND RESPONSE

ABORTION IS TOO COMPLEX TO FEEL ALL ONE WAY ABOUT

It was always the look on their faces that told me first. I was the freshman dormitory counselor and they were the freshmen at a women's college where everyone was smart. One of them could come into my room, a golden girl, a valedictorian, an 800 verbal score on the SATs, and her eyes would be empty, seeing only a busted future, the devastation of her life as she knew it. She had failed biology, messed up the math; she was pregnant.

That was when I became pro-choice.

It was the look in his eyes that I will always remember, too. They were as black as the bottom of a well, and in them for a few minutes I thought I saw myself the way I had always wished to be—clear, simple, elemental, at peace. My child looked at me and I looked back at him in the delivery room, and I realized that out of a sea of infinite possibilities it had come down to this: a specific person born on the hottest day of the year, conceived on a Christmas Eve, made by his father and me miraculously from scratch.

Once I believed that there was a little blob of formless protoplasm in there and a gynecologist went after it with a surgical instrument, and that was that. Then I got pregnant myself—eagerly, intentionally, by the right man, at the right time—and I began to doubt. My abdomen still flat, my stomach roiling with morning sickness, I felt not that I had protoplasm inside but instead a complete human being in miniature to whom I could talk, sing, make promises. Neither of these views was accurate; instead, I think, the reality is something in the middle. And there is where I find myself now, in the middle, hating the idea of abortions, hating the idea of having them outlawed.

For I know it is the right thing in some times and places. I remember sitting in a shabby clinic far uptown with one of those freshman, only three months after the Supreme Court had made what we were doing possible, and watching with wonder as the lovely first love she had had with a nice boy unraveled over the space of an hour as they waited for her to be called, degenerated into sniping and silences. I remember a year or two later seeing them pass on campus and not even acknowledge one another because their conjoining had caused them so much pain, and I shuddered to think of them as married, with a small psyche in their unready and unwilling hands.

I've met fourteen-year-olds who were pregnant and said they could not have abortions because of their religion, and I see in their eyes the shadows of twenty-two-year-olds I've talked to who lost their kids to foster care because they hit them or used drugs or simply had no money for food and shelter. I read not long ago about a teenager who said she meant to have an abortion but she spent the money on clothes instead; now she has a baby who turns out to be a lot more trouble than a toy. The people who hand out those execrable little pictures of dismembered fetuses at abortion clinics seem to forget the extraordinary pain children may endure after they are born when they are unwanted, even hated or simply tolerated.

I believe that in a contest between the living and the almost living, the latter must, if necessary, give way to the will of the former. That is what the fetus is to me, the almost living. Yet these questions began to plague me— and, I've discovered, a good many other women—after I became pregnant. But they became even more acute after I had my second child, mainly because he is so different from his brother. On two random nights eighteen months apart the same two people managed to conceive, and on one occasion the tumult within turned itself into a curly-haired brunet with merry black eyes who walked and talked late and loved the whole world, and on another it became a blond with hazel Asian eyes and a pug nose who tried to conquer the world almost as soon as he entered it.

If we were to have an abortion next time for some reason or another, which infinite possibility becomes, not a reality, but a nullity? The girl with the blue eyes? The improbable redhead? The natural athlete? The thinker? My husband, ever at the heart of the matter, put it another way. Knowing that he is finding two children somewhat more overwhelming than he expected, I asked if he would want me to have an abortion if I accidentally became pregnant again right away. "And waste a perfectly good human being?" he said.

Coming to this quandary has been difficult for me. In fact, I believe the issue of abortion is difficult for all thoughtful people. I don't know anyone who has had an abortion who has not been haunted by it. If there is one thing I find intolerable about most of the so-called right-to-lifers, it is that they try to portray abortion rights as something that feminists thought up on a slow Saturday over a light lunch. That is nonsense. I also know that some people who support abortion rights are most comfortable with a monolithic position because it seems the strongest front against the smug and sometimes violent opposition.

But I don't feel all one way about abortion anymore, and I don't think it serves a just cause to pretend that many of us do. For years I believed that a woman's right to choose was absolute, but now I wonder. Do I, with a stable home and marriage and sufficient stamina and money, have the right to choose abortion because a pregnancy is inconvenient right now? Legally I do have the right; legally I want always to have that right. It is the morality of exercising it under those circumstances that makes me wonder.

Technology has foiled us. The second trimester has become a time of resurrection: a fetus at six months can be one woman's late abortion, another's premature, viable child. Photographers now have film of embryos the size of a grape, oddly human, flexing their fingers, sucking their thumbs. Women have amniocentesis to find out whether they are carrying a child with birth defects that they may choose to abort. Before the procedure, they must have a sonogram, one of those fuzzy black-and-white photos like a love song heard through static on the radio, which shows someone is in there.

I have taped on my VCR a public-television program in which somehow, inexplicably, a film is shown of a fetus in utero scratching its face, seemingly putting up a tiny hand to shield itself from the camera's eye. It would make a potent weapon in the arsenal of the antiabortionists. I grow sentimental about it as it floats in the salt water, part fish, part human being. It is almost living, but not quite. It has almost turned my heart around, but not quite turned my head.

—*Anna Quindlen*

QUESTIONS ABOUT YOUR READING

Refer also to the general questions on page 165.

PURPOSE

- In addition to comparison/contrast, what other development strategies support the purpose of this essay?
- Does the essay succeed in making a difference with readers? If so, how?

CONTENT

- In your own words, restate the point of the comparison in a complete sentence.
- Does Quindlen establish credibility for making her evaluations? If so, how?

ORGANIZATION

- Does this comparison follow a block pattern, a point-by-point pattern, or a combination? Comment on the effectiveness of the pattern.
- Do both sides of the issue receive balanced treatment? Explain.
- Does Quindlen order her points for greatest emphasis? Explain.
- Does she offer a final judgment? If so, is it based convincingly on the evidence she presents?

STYLE

- Is the tone appropriate for the audience and purpose? Explain.

RESPONDING TO YOUR READING

Explore your reactions to Anna Quindlen's essay by using the questions on page 166. Then respond with an essay, *based on your own experience or observations,* that evaluates competing positions on some controversial issue. Try to arrive at a reasonable conclusion about which position seems preferable. Be sure your essay supports a clear and definite thesis. If you select some highly emotional issue, such as euthanasia, school prayer, or nationwide standards for high school graduation, be sure to avoid preaching. Let your examples convey your point instead, as does Quindlen.

CASE STUDY

RESPONDING TO READING

After reading and analyzing Quindlen's essay, John Manning decides to evaluate both sides of an issue very familiar to him: the pros and cons of online education.

John presents an implied comparison here, focusing on the benefits and drawbacks of an online "classroom," which is the less familiar item in this comparison. He can reasonably expect readers to visualize for themselves the familiar, traditional classroom.

Note   *Even though comparison/contrast is the dominant rhetorical strategy in John's essay, other strategies, such as narration, illustration, and causal analysis, play supporting roles.*

Title gives an immediate forecast

Defines the unfamiliar item in the comparison

Writer establishes his credibility on this topic

Thesis announces the basis for comparison: benefits and drawbacks

IS ONLINE EDUCATION TAKING US ANYWHERE?

As a growing alternative to the traditional classroom, we hear more and more about Internet-based learning, variously known as "cybereducation," "online education," and "virtual education." In this model, each student's computer is "wired" to an instructor's Web site at which course material and assignments are transmitted, posted, and discussed electronically. "Virtual universities" even offer entire degrees online. After taking two of these courses, I asked myself this question: Compared with a physical classroom setting, what is gained and lost in a "virtual" classroom? *While the actual benefits are undeniable, the drawbacks or potential consequences also are worth considering.*

Point-by-point comparison of benefits and drawbacks

First benefit (or criterion): access and convenience

Next benefit: economy and efficiency

Major benefit: student interest
Uses causal analysis

Gives vivid examples throughout

First drawback: lack of interpersonal relations
Gives equal attention to "benefits" and "drawbacks"—with criteria for each ranked in order of increasing importance

Writer uses narrative examples throughout to reinforce his credibility
Next drawback: practical problems

Major drawback: social costs

In terms of access and convenience, online education definitely holds the winning edge. This is especially true in Canada and Australia or parts of the American West in which relatively small populations are scattered thinly over a vast land mass. Students working online from any location now benefit from an endless variety of courses that require no travel whatsoever. Even though I live in a suburb, I personally enjoyed the luxury of commuting by computer.

Online education also is more economical and efficient than traditional schooling. The "school" itself has no need to maintain a physical structure with classrooms, faculty offices, and other expensive facilities. In the face of rising tuitions and room and board costs, the potential savings passed along to students are tremendous. Also students can participate and do most of their work at their convenience—without the time constraints of regularly scheduled classes. With work and family commitments in addition to my student responsibilities, I found this aspect especially appealing.

In terms of student interest, online courses stimulate concentration and interactivity on the student's part. Motivated students can focus their energies on the computer screen, in the relative peace and quiet of their own room, without the usual distractions in an actual classroom. Shy students might feel more comfortable about interacting in a chatroom atmosphere. Also, the Web's graphics capabilities are more dynamic than the static pages of a textbook—in a medium that today's college-age students have grown up with (video games, email, net surfing, and so on). I found the graphics especially useful in my online course, Introduction to Statistics.

Despite all these benefits, does the online learning experience itself carry interpersonal drawbacks? I personally missed the "human element" of getting to know my teachers, and having an advisor to turn to whenever some problem arises. I also missed face-to-face discussions. It seems easier to absorb what others are saying from hearing their actual voice and seeing their faces rather than reading their words from a computer screen. (Think of a poetry reading, for example.) For me, an inspiring lecture or a heated class discussion can only happen "in person."

I also worry about some practical drawbacks. For instance, online courses demand a strong desire to learn and the self-discipline and skills—and confidence—to manage one's education on one's own. I wonder how many students are ready to do this. (It was extremely hard for me.) Also, some people could abuse the system. For example, how can anyone know for sure whether other people are doing a student's work or whether unqualified students are walking away with degrees based on work others have done for them? And what about studying a language online—how does one learn pronunciation without live conversation.

My biggest concern is with the potential social costs of online education. While online dollar costs for access are low, those for training and equipment are high—in terms of fairly high-level computer skills and expensive hardware. For example, it takes nearly a top-of-the-line computer to run Web-browsing software—a computer that soon becomes obsolete. This investment in skills

Conclusion refocuses on the main question
Sums up the comparison

and equipment automatically rules out those people who can't afford it. Once again, it seems that the affluent will get another leg up based on this technology while the have-nots stay down in the dark.

All in all, do the benefits of online courses outweigh the drawbacks? On the plus side, the convenience, price, and dynamics of online education can't be beat. On the minus side, for people who come to school looking for human contact, transacting exclusively online seems awfully impersonal. Also, it's hard keeping up the motivation and self-discipline needed to do all one's work online. Finally, we have to consider the potential for creating an educated elite and even greater social division between the haves and have-nots. And so, while online education seems a powerful *supplement* to live classrooms, it's scary to think of it as a complete *substitute*.

Closes with a judgment based on the evidence

—*John Manning*

OPTIONS FOR ESSAY WRITING

1. If you had your high school years to relive, what would you do differently?
2. During your years in school you've had much experience with both good teaching and bad. Based on your experiences, what special qualities are necessary for good teaching? Use a series of contrasts to make your point.

Work Cited

Kelley-Reardon, Kathleen. *They Don't Get It, Do They?: Communication in the Workplace—Closing the Gap Between Women and Men.* Boston: Little, 1995.

CHAPTER 16

Explaining the Exact Meaning: Definition

Using Denotative Definitions to Explain **266**

Using Connotative Definitions to Make a Point **267**

Choosing the Level of Detail in a Definition **268**

Guidelines for Definition 270

CASE STUDY: Responding to Reading **277**

Options for Essay Writing **279**

Readings **275, 278**

Applications **272, 273**

All successful writing shares one feature—clarity. Clear writing begins with clear thinking; clear thinking begins with an understanding of what all the terms mean. Therefore, clear writing depends on definitions that both reader and writer agree on.

Definitions answer the question, *What, exactly, are we talking about?* by spelling out the precise meaning of a term that can be interpreted in different ways; for example, a person buying a new computer needs to understand exactly what "manufacturer's guarantee" or "expandable memory" means in the context of that purchase.

Definitions also can answer the question, *What, exactly, is it?* by explaining what makes an item, concept, or process unique; for example, an engineering student needs to understand the distinction between "elasticity" and "ductility." Inside or outside any field, people have to grasp precisely what "makes a thing what it is and distinguishes that thing from all other things" (Corbett 38).

What readers of definition want to know

- *What, exactly, are we talking about?*
- *What, exactly is it?*
- *What is its accepted meaning?*
- *What personal meaning(s) does it suggest?*

Words can signify two kinds of meaning: *denotative* and *connotative*. Denotations—the meanings in a dictionary—usually appear in referential writing. A word's denotation means the same thing to everyone. *Apple* denotes the firm, rounded, edible fruit of the apple tree.

But words have connotations as well, overtones or suggestions beyond their dictionary meanings. A word can have different connotations for different people. Thus, *apple* might connote Adam and Eve, apple pie, Johnny Appleseed, apple polisher, or good health. These meanings play an important part in persuasive writing, as writers use the possible meanings audiences find in words to elicit their emotions or to share a viewpoint.

USING DENOTATIVE DEFINITIONS TO EXPLAIN

Denotative definitions either explain a term that is specialized or unfamiliar to your readers or convey your exact definition of a word that has more than one meaning.

Most fields have specialized terms. Engineers talk about *pre-stressed concrete, tolerances,* or *trusses;* psychologists refer to *sociopathic behavior* or *paranoia;* attorneys discuss *liens, easements,* and *escrow accounts.* For readers outside the field, these terms must be defined.

Sometimes a term will be unfamiliar to some readers because it is new or no longer in use (*future shock, meltdown,* and *uptalk*) or a slang word (*bad, diss, freak*).

Some readers, though, are unaware that more familiar terms, such as *guarantee, disability, lease* or *consent,* take on very specialized meanings in some contexts. What *consent* means in one situation is not necessarily what it means in another. Denotative definition then becomes crucial if all parties are to understand.

This next definition explains the meaning of a slang term no longer in use.

A DENOTATIVE DEFINITION

Main point (1)

Contrast and division (2)

[1]During my teen years I never left the house on my Saturday night dates without my mother slipping me a few extra dollars—Mad Money, it was called. [2]I'll explain what it was for the benefit of the new generation in which

Division (3)

people just sleep with each other: the fellow was supposed to bring me home, lead me safely through the asphalt jungle, protect me from slithering snakes, rapists, and the like. [3]But my mother and I knew that young men were apt to drink too much, to slosh down so many rye-and-gingers that some hero might well lead me in front of an oncoming bus, smash his daddy's car into Tiffany's window, or, less gallantly, throw up on my dress. [4]Mad Money was for getting home on your own, no matter what form of insanity your date happened to evidence. [5]Mad Money was also a wallflower's rope ladder; if a guy you came with suddenly fancied someone else, you didn't have to stay there and suffer; you could go home.

Cause-effect (sentence definition) (4)
Cause-effect as analogy (5)

—*Anne Roiphe*

USING CONNOTATIVE DEFINITIONS TO MAKE A POINT

A denotative definition cannot communicate the personal or special meaning a writer may intend. But connotative definitions explain terms that hold personal meanings for the writer.

In the next paragraph, the denotative definition of *house* (a structure serving as a dwelling) is replaced by a more personal, artistic, and spiritual definition:

A CONNOTATIVE DEFINITION

Main Point (1)
Analogies (2–4)

[1]What is a house? [2]A house is a human circumstance in Nature, like a tree or the rocks of the hills; a good house is a technical performance where form and function are made one; a house is integral to its site, a grace, not a disgrace, to its environment, suited to elevate the life of its individual inhabitants; a house is therefore integral with the nature of the methods and materials used to build it. [3]A house to be a good home has throughout what is most needed in American life today—integrity. [4]Integrity, once there, enables those who live in that house to take spiritual root and grow.

—*Frank Lloyd Wright*

Connotative definition is especially useful when we want people to accept a particular definition of a term that carries multiple, conflicting meanings (*freedom, love, patriotism,* or the like) and especially when the meaning we advocate is unconventional or controversial.

Unless you are sure that readers know the exact or special meaning you intend, always define a term the first time you use it.

USING DEFINITION BEYOND THE WRITING CLASSROOM

■ **In other courses:** Whatever your major, much of your education focuses on definition of a virtually endless array of terms, such as *capitalism, sonnet, osmosis, existentialism,* and so on.

- **On the job:** Contracts are detailed (and legally binding) definitions of the specific terms of a business agreement. If you lease a car for company travel, for example, the printed contract will define both the *lessee's* and the *lessor's* specific responsibilities. An employment contract will spell out responsibilities for both employer and employee. Many other documents, such as employee handbooks, are considered implied contracts ("Handbooks" 5). In preparing an employee handbook for your company, you would need to define such terms as *acceptable job performance* on the basis of clear objectives that each employee can understand, such as "submitting weekly progress reports, arriving on time for meetings," and so on ("Performance Appraisal" 5–6). Because you are legally responsible for any document you prepare, clear and precise definitions are essential.

- **In the community:** Clear and accurate definitions help the general public understand and evaluate complex technical and social issues. For example, we hear and read plenty about the debates over genetic engineering. But as a first step in understanding this debate, we would need at least this basic definition:

A general but informative definition

> Genetic engineering refers to [an experimental] technique through which genes can be isolated in a laboratory, manipulated, and then inserted stably into another organism. Gene insertion can be accomplished mechanically, chemically, or by using biological vectors such as viruses. (Office of Technology Assessment 20)

Of course, as we began to follow the debate, we would need increasingly more detailed information (about specific procedures, risks, benefits, and so on). But the above definition gets us started by enabling us to *visualize* the basic concept.

CHOOSING THE LEVEL OF DETAIL IN A DEFINITION

How much detail will readers need to understand a term or a concept? Can you use a synonym (a term with a similar meaning)? Will you provide a sentence, a paragraph—or an essay?

Parenthetical Definition

Often, you can clarify the meaning of an unfamiliar word by using a more familiar synonym or a clarifying phrase:

Parenthetical definitions

> To **waffle** means to be evasive and misleading.
>
> The **leaching field** (sieve-like drainage area) requires 15 inches of crushed stone.

Note

Be sure that the synonym clarifies your meaning instead of obscuring it.

Don't say:

| A tumor is a neoplasm.

Do say:

| A tumor is a growth of cells that occurs independently of surrounding tissue and serves no useful function.

Sentence Definition

More complex terms may require a sentence definition (which may be stated in more than one sentence). These definitions follow a fixed pattern: (1) the name of the item to be defined, (2) the class to which the item belongs, and (3) the features that differentiate the item from all others in its class.

Elements of sentence definitions

Term	Class	Distinguishing features
carburetor	a mixing device	in gasoline engines that blends air and fuel into a vapor for combustion with the cylinders
diabetes	a metabolic disease	caused by a disorder of the pituitary or pancreas and characterized by excessive urination, persistent thirst, and inability to metabolize sugar
brief	a legal document	containing all the facts and points of law pertinent to a case and filed by an attorney before the case is argued in court
stress	an applied force	that strains or deforms a body

These elements are combined into one or more complete sentences:

A complete sentence definition

| Diabetes is a metabolic disease caused by a disorder of the pituitary or pancreas and characterized by excessive urination, persistent thirst, and inability to metabolize sugar.

Sentence definition is especially useful if you need to stipulate your precise definition for a term that has several possible meanings. For example, *qualified buyer* can have different meanings for different readers in construction, banking, or real estate.

Expanded Definition

The sentence definition of *carburetor* (above) is adequate for a general reader who simply needs to know what a carburetor is. An instruction manual for mechanics, however, would define *carburetor* in much greater detail; these readers need to know how a carburetor works, how it is made, what conditions cause it to operate correctly, and so on.

Your choice of parenthetical, sentence, or expanded definition depends on the amount of information your readers need. Consider the two examples that follow.

A SENTENCE DEFINITION

It [paranoia] refers to a psychosis based on a delusionary premise of self-referred persecution or grandeur (e.g., "The Knights of Columbus control the world and are out to get me"), and supported by a complex, rigorously logical system that interprets all or nearly all sense impressions as evidence for that premise.

This definition is part of an article published in *Harper's*, a magazine whose general readership will require a more detailed definition of this specialized term. The expanded version below uses several explanatory strategies.

EXPANDED DEFINITION OF A SPECIALIZED TERM

Main point (1)
Sentence definition (2)

[1]Paranoia is a word on everyone's lips, but only among mental-health professionals has it acquired a tolerably specific meaning. [2]It refers to a

GUIDELINES FOR DEFINITION

1. *Decide on the level of detail.* Definitions vary greatly in length and detail, from a few words in parentheses to a complete essay. How much does this audience need in order to follow your explanation or grasp your point?

2. *Classify the term precisely.* The narrower your class, the clearer your meaning. *Stress* is classified as an applied force; to say that stress "is what . . ." or "takes place when . . ." fails to reflect a specific classification. Diabetes is precisely classified as a *metabolic disease,* not as a *medical term.*

3. *Differentiate the term accurately.* If the distinguishing features are too broad, they will apply to more than this one item. A definition of *brief* as a "legal document

used in court" fails to differentiate *brief* from all other legal documents (*wills, affidavits,* and the like).

4. *Avoid circular definitions.* Do not repeat, as part of the distinguishing feature, the word you are defining. "Stress is an applied force that places stress on a body" is a circular definition.

5. *Expand your definition selectively.* Begin with a sentence definition and select from a combination of the following development strategies: description/narration; illustration; division/classification; process analysis; cause/effect analysis; and comparison/contrast.

6. *Know "how much is enough."* Don't insult people's intelligence by giving needless details or spelling out the obvious.

	psychosis based on a delusionary premise of self-referred persecution or grandeur (e.g., "The Knights of Columbus control the world and are out to get me"), and supported by a complex, rigorously logical system that interprets all or nearly all sense impressions as evidence for that premise. [3]The traditional psychiatric view is that paranoia is an extreme measure for the defense of the integrity of the personality against annihilating guilt. [4]The paranoid (so goes the theory) thrusts his guilt outside himself by denying his hostile or erotic impulses and projecting them onto other people or onto the whole universe. [5]Disintegration is avoided, but at high cost; the paranoid view of reality can make everyday life terrifying and social intercourse problematical. [6]And paranoia is tiring. [7]It requires exhausting mental effort to construct trains of thought demonstrating that random events or details "prove" a wholly unconnected premise. [8]Some paranoids hallucinate, but hallucination is by no means obligatory; paranoia is an interpretive, not a perceptual, dysfunction.

Effect-cause analysis (3)

Process analysis (4)

Cause-effect analysis (5–7)

Contrast (8)

—*Hendrik Hertzberg and David C. K. McClelland*

General readers are much more likely to understand this expanded definition than the sentence definition alone.

As we have seen in earlier chapters, synonyms and sentence definitions are part of most writing. But notice in turn how various development strategies from earlier chapters are employed in an expanded definition.

7. *Use negation to show what a term does not mean.* For example: Raw data is not "information"; data becomes information only after it has been evaluated, interpreted, and applied.

8. *Explain the term's etymology (its origin).* For example: Biological control of insects is derived from the Greek *bio,* meaning "*life or living organism,*" and the Latin *contra,* meaning "*against or opposite.*" Biological control, then, is the use of living organisms against insects. Check your college dictionary or, preferably, *The Oxford English Dictionary* (or its Web site).

9. *Consider the legal implications of your definition.* What does an "unsatisfactory job performance" mean in an evaluation of a company employee: that the employee could be fired, required to attend a training program, given one or more chances to improve, or what? ("Performance Appraisal" 3–4) Failure to spell out your meaning invites a lawsuit.

10. *Consider the ethical implications of your definition.* Be sure your definition of a fuzzy or ambiguous term, such as *safe levels of exposure, conservative investment,* or *acceptable risk,* is based on technical fact and not on social pressure. Consider, for example, a recent U.S. cigarette company's claim that cigarette smoking in the Czech Republic promoted "fiscal benefits," defined, in this case, by the fact that smokers die young, thus eliminating pension and health care costs for the elderly!

The following expanded definition, from an auto insurance policy, defines damages for *bodily injury to others,* a phrase that could have many possible meanings.

EXPANDED DEFINITION OF A FAMILIAR TERM WITH A SPECIAL MEANING

Main point (1)
Sentence definition (2)

Cause-effect (3–6)

Negation (7)

[1]Under this coverage, we will pay damages to people injured or killed by your auto in Massachusetts accidents. [2]Damages are the amount an injured person is legally entitled to collect through a court judgment or settlement. [3]We will pay only if you or someone else using your auto with your consent is legally responsible for the accident. [4]The most we will pay for injuries to any one person as a result of any one accident is $5,000. [5]The most we will pay for injuries to two or more people as a result of any one accident is a total of $10,000. [6]This is the most we will pay as the result of a single accident no matter how many autos or premiums are shown on the Coverage Selections page.[7]We will not pay: for injuries to guest occupants of your auto; for accidents outside of Massachusetts or in places in Massachusetts where the public has no right of access; for injuries to any employees of the legally responsible person if they are entitled to Massachusetts workers' compensation benefits.

This definition is designed to answer two basic questions:

- *Under what conditions will the insurer pay damages?*
- *Under what conditions will the insurer not pay?*

Thus, the development strategy of cause-effect, aided by *negation* (showing what something isn't), most logically serves the purpose of this definition.

Note

Because they are designed to draw readers into the writer's complex, private associations, connotative definitions almost always call for expanded treatment.

Note

*An increasingly familiar (and user-friendly) format for expanded definition, especially for Web users, is a listing of Frequently Asked Questions (FAQs), which organizes chunks of information as responses to questions users are likely to ask. This question-and-answer format creates a conversational style and conveys to users the sense that their particular concerns are being addressed. Consider using an FAQ list whenever you want to increase user interest and decrease resistance. For a Web-based example, go to <**www.3.ibm.com/ibm/easy/eou/**> and click on User Centered Design.*

Application **16-1**

Sentence definitions require precise classification and detailed differentiation. Is each of these definitions adequate for a general reader? Rewrite those that seem inadequate. If necessary, consult dictionaries and specialized encyclopedias.

1. A bicycle is a vehicle with two wheels.
2. A transistor is a device used in transistorized electronic equipment.
3. Surfing is when one rides a wave to shore while standing on a board specifically designed for buoyancy and balance.
4. Mace is a chemical aerosol spray used by the police.
5. A Geiger counter measures radioactivity.
6. A cactus is a succulent.
7. In law, an indictment is a criminal charge against a defendant.
8. Friction is a force between two bodies.
9. Hypoglycemia is a medical term.
10. A computer is a machine that handles information with amazing speed.

Application **16-2**

PARAGRAPH WARM-UP: DENOTATIVE DEFINITION THAT EXPLAINS

Using denotative definition, write a paragraph explaining the meaning of a term that is specialized, new, or otherwise unfamiliar to your reader. List in the margin the strategies for expansion you've used. Begin with a formal sentence definition (term—class—differentiation). Select a term from one of the lists below, from your major (defined for a nonmajor), or from your daily conversation with peers (defined for an elderly person). Identify clearly the situation, the audience, and your purpose.

Specialized terms	Slang terms
summons	jock
generator	Yuppie
dew point	nerd
capitalism	turkey
economic recession	sweet
microprocessor	to break
T-square	awesome

Application **16-3**

PARAGRAPH WARM-UP: CONNOTATIVE DEFINITION THAT MAKES A POINT

Using connotative definition, write a paragraph explaining the special meaning or associations that a term holds for you. Select a term from the list below, or provide your own. List in the margin the expansion strategies you've used. Identify clearly the situation, the audience, and your purpose.

patriotism	education	freedom
trust	marriage	courage
friendship	God	peace

progress	guilt	morality
beauty	the perfect date	happiness
adult	sex appeal	fear

Application **16-4**

Computer Application: Consult either a computer manual, a computer publication, or a newsgroup for computer enthusiasts. Find at least five technical terms that you—and probably most of your classmates—aren't familiar with or don't fully understand. Research these terms; then, for your classmates, write both sentence and expanded definitions for two of them. Some possibilities: FTP, MOO, MUD, IRC, HTML, memory bus, firewall, RISC, LAN, CGI, Javascript.

Application **16-5**

Web-based Project: Compare two Internet dictionaries on the basis of specific criteria, such as the following:

- search page (interface) is easy to use
- searches rapidly
- offers links to other dictionaries and language resources
- provides good navigational aids
- offers good Help, FAQ, and Search Tips pages
- entries are easy to browse

Be sure to specify the criteria you have chosen.

SAMPLE DICTIONARIES

- Dictionary.com
  <http://www.dictionary.com>
- WWWebster Dictionary
  <http://www.m-w.com/netdict.htm>
- Encyberpedia Dictionary and Glossary
  <http://www.encyberpedia.com/glossary.htm>
- Wordsmyth English Dictionary-Thesaurus
  <http://www.wordsmyth.net>

Application **16-6**

ESSAY PRACTICE

In this next selection from the *New York Times,* an essayist and novelist offers a connotative definition to shed positive light on an activity generally considered unfavorable. As you read, identify the various development strategies used to expand this definition.

ESSAY FOR ANALYSIS AND RESPONSE

GOSSIP

[1]Once I met a woman who grew up in the small North Carolina town to which Chang and Eng, the original Siamese twins, retired after their circus careers. When I asked her how the town reacted to the twins marrying local girls and setting up adjacent households, she laughed and said: "Honey, that was *nothing* compared to what happened *before* the twins got there. Get the good gossip on any little mountain town; scratch the surface and you'll find a snake pit!"

[2]Surely she was exaggerating; one assumes the domestic arrangements of a pair of Siamese twins and their families would cause a few ripples anywhere. And yet the truth of what she said seemed less important than the glee with which she said it, her pride in the snake pit she'd come from, in its history, its scandals, its legacy of "good gossip." Gossip, the juicier the better, was her heritage, her birthright; that town, with its social life freakish enough to make Chang and Eng's seem mundane, was part of who she was.

[3]Gossip must be nearly as old as language itself. It was, I imagine, the earliest recreational use of the spoken word. First the cave man learned to describe the location of the plumpest bison, then he began to report and speculate on the doings of his neighbors in the cave next door. And yet, for all its antiquity, gossip has rarely received its due; its very name connotes idleness, time-wasting, frivolity and worse. Gossip is the unacknowledged poor relative of civilized conversation: Almost everyone does it but hardly anyone will admit to or defend it; and of these only the smallest and most shameless fraction will own up to enjoying it.

[4]My mother and her friends are eloquent on the subject and on the distinction between gossiping and exchanging information: "John got a new job," is, they say, information. "Hey, did you hear John got fired?" is gossip; which is, they agree, predominantly scurrilous, mean-spirited. That's the conventional wisdom on gossip and why it's so tempting to disown. Not long ago I heard myself describe a friend, half-jokingly, as "a much better person than I am, that is, she doesn't gossip so much." I heard my voice distorted by that same false note that sometimes creeps into it when social strain and some misguided notion of amiability make me assent to opinions I don't really share. What in the world was I talking about?

[5]I don't, of course, mean rumor-mongering, outright slander, willful fabrication meant to damage and undermine. But rather, ordinary gossip, incidents from and analyses of the lives of our heroes and heroines, our relatives, acquaintances and friends. The fact is, I love gossip, and beyond that, I believe in it—in its purposes, its human uses.

[6]I'm even fond of the word, its etymology, its origins in the Anglo-Saxon term "godsibbe" for god-parent, relative, its meaning widening by the Renaissance to include friends, cronies and later what one *does* with one's cronies. One gossips. Paring away its less flattering modern connotations, we

discover a kind of synonym for connection, for community, and this, it seems to me, is the primary function of gossip. It maps our ties, reminds us of what sort of people we know and what manner of lives they lead, confirms our sense of who we are, how we live and where we have come from. The roots of the grapevine are inextricably entwined with our own. Who knows how much of our sense of the world has reached us on its branches, how often, as babies, we dropped off to sleep to the rhythms of family gossip? I've often thought that gossip's bad name might be cleared by calling it "oral tradition"; for what, after all, is an oral tradition but the stories of other lives, other eras, legends from a time when human traffic with spirits and gods was considered fit material for gossipy speculation?

[7]Older children gossip; adolescents certainly do. Except in the case of those rare toddler-fabulists, enchanting parents and siblings with fairy tales made up on the spot, gossip may be the way that most of us learn to tell stories. And though, as Gertrude Stein is supposed to have told Hemingway, gossip is not literature, some similar criteria may apply to both. Pacing, tone, clarity and authenticity are as essential for the reportage of neighborhood news as they are for well-made fiction.

[8]Perhaps more important is gossip's analytical component. Most people—I'm leaving out writers, psychologists and probably some large proportion of the academic and service professions—are, at least in theory, free to go about their lives without feeling the compulsion to endlessly dissect the minutiae of human motivation. They can indulge in this at their leisure, for pleasure, in their gossip. And while there are those who clearly believe that the sole aim of gossip is to criticize, to condemn (or, frequently, to titillate, to bask in the aura of scandal as if it were one's own), I prefer to see gossip as a tool of understanding. It only takes a moment to tell what someone did. Far more mileage—and more enjoyment—can be extracted from debating why he did it. Such questions, impossible to discuss without touching on matters of choice and consequence, responsibility and will, are, one might argue, the beginnings of moral inquiry, first steps toward a moral education. It has always seemed peculiar that a pastime so conducive to the moral life should be considered faintly immoral.

[9]I don't mean to deny the role of plain nosiness in all this, of unadorned curiosity about our neighbors' secrets. And curiosity (where would we be without it?) has, like gossip, come in for some negative press. Still, it's understandable, everyone wants to gossip, hardly anyone wants to be gossiped about. What rankles is the fear that our secrets will be revealed, some essential privacy stripped away and, of course, the lack of control over what others say. Still, such talk is unavoidable; it's part of human nature, of the human community. When one asks, "What's the gossip?" it's that community that is being affirmed.

[10]So I continue to ask, mostly without apology and especially when I'm talking to friends who still live in places I've moved away from. And when they answer—recalling the personalities, telling the stories, the news—I feel as close as I ever will to the lives we shared, to what we know and remember in common, to those much-missed, familiar and essentially beneficent snake pits I've lived in and left behind.

—Francine Prose

QUESTIONS ABOUT YOUR READING

Refer to the general questions on page 165 and the specific ones here.

PURPOSE

- Does the author succeed in making her point? If so, how?

CONTENT

- What is the primary expansion (or development) strategy in this definition? Which additional strategies can you identify?
- The author offers various connotations of gossip. Which ones seem most credible? Explain.

ORGANIZATION

- Trace the line of thought in this essay. Is this the most effective order? Explain.
- Does the organization make the expansion strategies easier to follow? Explain.

QUESTIONS ABOUT STYLE

- Identify the major devices that increase coherence.
- What attitude does the author express toward her subject? How do we know? Where are the signals?

RESPONDING TO YOUR READING

Explore your reactions to "Gossip" by using the questions on page 166. Then respond with your own essay that examines the connotations of a familiar term that evokes positive or negative feelings. For instance, you might define a term of recent vintage, such as *rap, grunge,* or *skater,* or you might examine the connotations of *fraternity, sorority, commuter, jock, remedial course,* or some other campus-related term. Or perhaps you belong to an in-group that uses words in ironic or special ways to connote meanings that could be appreciated only by members of that particular group.

Your essay should make a clear and definite point about the larger meaning behind the examples you provide.

CASE STUDY

RESPONDING TO READING

After reading "Gossip," Kerry Donahue settles on a practical goal for her own essay: As a columnist of her campus newspaper, she decides to prepare the following editorial in hopes of promoting campus-wide support for a community-service requirement for all students. Kerry knows that, to succeed, she will have to present community service in its most positive connotations—in a new light.

During her planning, drafting, and revising, Kerry relies on the Definition Guidelines and the Revision Checklist on pages 270 and 63 in producing the final draft.

Note

As Kerry's essay illustrates, expanded definition relies on a rich combination of development strategies, such as comparison/contrast and cause-effect.

Title announces the topic
Opens with vivid examples of need

COMMUNITY SERVICE SERVES EVERYONE

On Horseneck Beach in Westport, a seagull lies tangled in a web of old fishing nets that washed ashore after the last high tide. It probably will die in those nets because no one is on the beach to clean up the nets or to notice the bird trapped inside. Across town in a nursing home, an elderly man struggles to read his favorite book. He has trouble making out the words. No one is around to read to him, and so he merely sits silently on the edge of his bed, anxiously awaiting a visitor—any visitor. Scenarios like these are all too common, which is why I propose that all students at our University do roughly ten hours of community service each semester as a graduation requirement. Community service should be required for two excellent reasons: *First, countless people and animals in need of help every day could use our assistance; second, we students would enjoy future benefits in more ways than one.*

Lead-in to the thesis

Thesis

Compares different connotations of community service
Gives examples of voluntary service opportunities
Discusses beneficial effects for the community

For some people, *community service* connotes a form of punishment for breaking the law. Although certain lawbreakers are routinely assigned community service, plenty of law-abiding citizens volunteer their time, as well. Examples include working in soup kitchens, organizing food drives for the homeless, helping with after-school youth programs, visiting the elderly, cleaning up the environment, and walking/campaigning for afflictions such as AIDS, cancer, and drug addiction. These and countless other activities could benefit from the help of energetic, idealistic college students. Despite our busy schedules of going to class, working, studying, sleeping, and partying, it's hard to imagine that most of us couldn't spend an extra hour here and there to make a difference in the community.

Anticipates objections

Refutes objections by pointing out harmful effects of doing nothing

Some people may object to the idea of forced service in order to graduate. They may think it unfair to ask students to devote time and energy to something that has nothing to do with their lives. But that is where they are wrong. The events in our surrounding communities do affect our lives in some way or other. If nets and dead sea animals pollute the beaches, we will not be able to use them when school gets out for the summer. Homelessness, hunger, and drug addiction drive people to crime. Misguided and mistreated children often disrupt learning in lower grades. Ultimately, no one is immune from what goes on in our community. It is true that many students have after-school jobs. Some of us take five or six classes per semester and have tons of homework. Athletes have to juggle class, practice, and games as it is. But early in the semester, when the work load is light and sports are just getting started, asking students to spend an hour or so here and there to help those in need seems hardly a lot. (Of course, those students with genuine hardships

Acknowledges further objections

Offers a reasonable limitation

Gives a persuasive comparison

Discusses beneficial effects for students

Illustrates how a model program works

Conclusion reemphasizes main idea

Focuses on the larger meaning

of their own would be exempted.) I realize that winning games and getting good grades fills students with pride and satisfaction. However, helping the less fortunate can be just as rewarding.

Academically, community service can help students prepare for life beyond the walls of our campus. Working with others and interacting on a personal level can help us all "broaden our horizons" and can open our eyes to what the real world is really like. For students of all majors, this is a chance to develop career credentials in public leadership and public relations—as well as to prepare ourselves for helping improve the communities in which we eventually settle.

For a model community-service program, we only need to look down the road: At Polk University's Stanton Center, students can work as service coordinators or they can get advice on how to get involved in the community. The Stanton Center has various programs, including Music in Hospitals, Project HIV/AIDS, after-school programs for helping children with literacy and self-confidence, help with domestic abuse for both students as well as nonstudents, among others. The Center itself is funded by federal and state grants. Our school could explore similar sources of funding.

Some students may gripe at the notion of community service as a graduation requirement. But I firmly believe that the benefits far outweigh the costs. A little time each semester helping others could prepare each of us for the future while making life more pleasant for those in need. Teaching a child to read, saving animals, feeding those who are hungry, and walking to raise money for people with diseases—these are the biggest reasons why each of us at this university should do community service. We will be benefiting not only ourselves but the broader world as well.

—*Kerry Donahue*

OPTIONS FOR ESSAY WRITING

Along with changing times come changes in our way of seeing. Some terms that held meanings for us two or three years ago may have acquired radically different meanings by now. If we once defined *success* narrowly as social status and income bracket, we might now define it in broader words: leading the kind of life that puts us in close touch with ourselves and the world around us. Similarly, the meanings of many other terms (*education, friendship, freedom, maturity, self-fulfillment, pain, love, home, family, career, patriotism*) may have changed. Although some terms take on more positive meanings, others acquire more negative ones. Your connotations of *marriage* may depend on whether you have witnessed (or experienced) marriages that have been happy and constructive or bitter and destructive. And quite often an entire society's definition of something changes over time, *marriage* being a good example.

Identify something that has changed in meaning, either for you individually or for our society as a whole—such as "The American Dream." Discuss both the traditional and the new meanings (choose a serious, ironic, or humorous point of view) in such a way that your definition makes a specific point or commentary, either stated or implied, about society's values or your own.

Works Cited

Corbett, Edward P.J. *Classical Rhetoric for the Modern Student.* 3rd. ed. New York: Oxford, 1990.

"Handbooks." *The Employee Problem Solver.* Ramsey, NJ: Alexander Hamilton Institute: 2000.

Office of Technology Assessment. *Harmful Non-Indigenous Species in the United States.* Washington, DC: GPO, 1993.

"Performance Appraisal—Discrimination." *The Employee Problem Solver.* Ramsey, NJ: Alexander Hamilton Institute: 2000.

CHAPTER 17

Using Multiple Strategies in a Persuasive Argument

Anticipating Audience Resistance **282**

Having a Debatable Point **283**

Supporting Your Claim **284**

Shaping a Clear Line of Thought **287**

Connecting with Your Audience **288**

   Guidelines for Persuasion **288**

Considering the Ethical Dimension **289**

Various Arguments for Various Goals **290**

CASE STUDIES: Responding to Reading **294, 299**

Options for Essay Writing **296, 301, 304, 306**

Readings **292, 294, 297, 299, 302, 304**

Applications **292, 297, 302, 304, 306**

As we have seen, the strategies in Chapters 10–16 can be used to draw readers into the writer's special way of seeing. This purpose can be called "persuasive," because it asks readers to agree with particular viewpoints such as these:

- media reports on African Americans often are biased (page 202)
- the "wifely" stereotype persists in today's generation (page 171)
- most people have too much self-esteem, rather than too little (page 244)
- gossiping can be a worthwhile activity (page 275)

Writing for the *primary* goal of persuasion, however, often takes a stand on even more controversial topics—issues on which people always disagree. Examples: Do the risks of nuclear power outweigh its advantages? Should your school require athletes to maintain good grades? Should your dorm be coed? We write about these issues in hopes of winning readers over to our side—or at least inducing them to appreciate our position. Although these arguments employ various development strategies (description, comparison/contrast, and so on), their underlying goal is to persuade readers to see things the writer's way.

In a free society, you can expect some readers to disagree with your stand on a controversy, no matter how long and how brilliantly you argue. But even though you won't change *everyone's* mind, a strong persuasive argument can make a difference to *some people.*

| Note |

"Argument," in this context, means "a process of careful reasoning in support of a claim"—and not "a quarrel or dispute." People who "argue skillfully" connect with others in a rational, sensible way, without animosity. But people who are only "argumentative," on the other hand, merely make others defensive.

ANTICIPATING AUDIENCE RESISTANCE

Argument focuses on its audience; it addresses issues in which people are directly involved. But people rarely change their minds about such issues without good reason. Expect resistance from your readers and defensive questions such as these:

What readers of argument want to know

- *Why should I even read this?*
- *Why should I change my mind?*
- *Can you prove it?*
- *How do you know?*
- *Says who?*

Getting readers to admit *you* might be right means getting them to admit *they* might be wrong. The more strongly they identify with their position, the more resistance you can expect. To overcome this resistance, you have to put yourself in your audience's position and see things their way before you argue for your way. The persuasiveness of any argument ultimately depends on how convincing it is to its *audience*.

Making a good argument requires that you bring together all the strategies you've learned so far, along with features specific to any type of argumentative writing:

1. a main point or claim that the audience finds debatable
2. convincing support for the claim
3. a clear and unmistakable line of thought
4. a good relationship with the audience
5. attention to the ethics of argument

HAVING A DEBATABLE POINT

The main point in an argument must be debatable (something open to dispute, something that can be viewed from more than one angle). Statements of fact are not debatable:

A fact is something whose certainty is established

> Several near-disastrous accidents have occurred recently in nuclear power plants.
>
> Women outlive men.
>
> Economic policies of this presidential administration have led to decreases in student loan programs.
>
> More than 50 percent of traffic deaths are alcohol related.

Because these statements can be verified (shown to be true or accurate—at least with enough certainty so that reasonable people would agree), they cannot be debated. Questions of taste or personal opinion never can be debated, because they rest on no objective reasons:

Personal taste or opinion is based on preference, belief, or feeling—instead of fact.

> I love oatmeal.
>
> Catholics are holier than Baptists.
>
> Professor Dreary's lectures put me to sleep.
>
> I hate the taste of garlic.

Even many assertions that call for expository support are not debatable for most audiences:

Once reasonable people know the facts, they would have to agree with these claims

> During the last decade, the Religious Right has gained political influence.
>
> Competition for good jobs is now fiercer than ever.
>
> Police roadblocks help deter drunk driving.
>
> Lowering the drinking age increases alcohol-related traffic fatalities.

Writing that demonstrates the truth of these assertions is primarily referential. Once the facts are established, the audience almost certainly will agree, "Yes, it's true."

What, then, is a *debatable point?* It is *one that cannot be proved true, but only more or less probable.* For example, few readers would debate the notion that electronic games have altered the play habits of millions of American children. But some would disagree that electronic games are dominating children's lives.

No amount of evidence can prove or disprove these claims

> The political activities of the Religious Right violate the constitutional separation of church and state.
>
> Schools should place more emphasis on competition.
>
> Police roadblocks are a justifiable deterrent against drunk driving.
>
> All states should maintain the drinking age at twenty-one.

Even though the rightness or wrongness of these controversial issues can never be proved, writers may argue (more or less persuasively) for one side or the other. And—unlike an assertion of personal opinion or taste—an arguable assertion can be judged by the quality of support the writer presents. How does the assertion hold up against *opposing* assertions?

Always state your arguable point directly and clearly as a thesis. While other development strategies (especially description and narration) may allow the thesis merely to be implied, argumentative writing almost never does. Let readers know exactly where you stand.

SUPPORTING YOUR CLAIM

Chapter 5 shows how any credible assertion rests on opinions derived from facts. But facts out of context can be interpreted in various ways. Legitimate argument offers convincing reasons, reliable sources, careful interpretation, and valid conclusions.

Offer Convincing Reasons

Any argument is only as convincing as the reasons that support it. Before readers will change their minds, they need to know why. They expect you to complete a version of this statement, in which your reasons follow the "because":

My position is _____ because _____.

Arguing effectively means using *only* those reasons likely to move your specific audience. Assume, for instance, that all students living on your campus have a meal plan with a 15-meal requirement (for weekdays), costing $1,800 yearly. You belong to a group trying to reduce the required meals to 10 weekly. Before seeking students' support and lobbying the administration, your group constructs a list of reasons for its position. A quick brainstorming session produces this list:

Subjective support offers reasons that matter to the writer—but not always to the reader.

> The number of required weekly meals should be reduced to 10 per week because:
>
> 1. Many students dislike the food.
> 2. Some students with only afternoon classes like to sleep late and should not have to rush to beat the 9:00 a.m. breakfast deadline.
> 3. The cafeteria atmosphere is too noisy, impersonal, and dreary.
> 4. The food selection is too limited.
> 5. The price of a yearly meal ticket has risen unfairly and is now more than 5 percent higher than last year's price.

You quickly spot a flaw in this list: All these reasons rest almost entirely on *subjective* grounds, on personal taste or opinion. For every reader who dislikes the food or sleeps late, another may like the food or rise early—and so on. Your intended audience (students, administrators) probably won't think these reasons very convincing. Your reasons should be based on *objective* evidence and on goals and values you and your readers share.

Provide Objective Evidence

Evidence (factual support from an outside source) is objective when it can be verified (shown to be accurate) by everyone involved. Common types of objective evidence include factual statements, statistics, examples, and expert testimony.

A *fact* is something that can be demonstrated by observation, experience, research, or measurement—and that your audience is willing to recognize:

Offer the facts

> Each dorm suite has its own kitchen.

Be selective. Decide which facts best support your case (page 84).

Numbers can be highly convincing. Many readers are interested in the "bottom line" (percentages, costs, savings, profits):

Cite the numbers

> Roughly 30 percent of the 500 students we surveyed in the cafeteria eat only two meals per day.

But numbers can mislead. Your statistics must be accurate, trustworthy, and easy to understand and verify (see pages 383–87). Always cite your source.

Examples help people visualize and remember the point. For instance, the best way to explain what you mean by "wasteful" is to show "waste" occurring:

Show what you mean

> From 20 to 25 percent of the food prepared is never eaten.

Use examples that your audience can identify with and that fit the point they are designed to illustrate.

Expert testimony—if it is unbiased and the expert is recognized—lends authority and credibility to any claim:

Cite the experts

> Food service directors from three local colleges point out that their schools' flexible meal plans have been highly successful.

See page 338 for the limits of expert testimony.

Appeal to Shared Goals and Values

Evidence alone isn't always enough to change a reader's mind. Identify at least one goal you and your audience have in common. In the meal plan issue, for example, we can assume that everyone wants to eliminate wasteful practices. A persuasive argument will, therefore, take this goal into account:

Appeal to shared goals

> These changes in the meal plan would eliminate waste of food, labor, and money.

People's goals are shaped by their values (qualities they believe in, ideals they stand for): friendship, loyalty, honesty, equality, fairness, and so on (Rokeach 57–58). Look for a common, central goal. In the meal plan case, *fairness* might be an important value:

Appeal to shared values

> No one should have to pay for meals she or he doesn't eat.

Here is how your group's final list of reasons might read:

Persuasive claims are backed up by reasons that matter to the reader

> The number of required weekday meals should be reduced to ten per week because:
>
> 1. No one should have to pay for meals she or he doesn't eat.
> 2. Roughly 30 percent of the 500 students we surveyed in the cafeteria eat only two meals per day.
> 3. From 20 to 25 percent of the food prepared is never eaten—a waste of food, labor, and money.
> 4. Each dorm suite has its own kitchen, but these are seldom used.
> 5. Between kitchen suites and local restaurants, students on only the Monday-through-Friday plan do survive on weekends. Why couldn't they survive just as well during the week?
> 6. Food service directors from three local colleges point out that their schools' flexible meal plans have been highly successful.

Reasonable audiences should find the above argument compelling because each reason is based on a verifiable fact or (as in item 1) good sense. Even audience members not moved to support your cause will understand why you've taken your stand.

Give your audience reasons that have meaning for *them* personally. For example, in a recent study of teenage attitudes about smoking, respondents listed these reasons for not smoking: bad breath, difficulty concentrating, loss of friends, and trouble with adults. No respondents listed dying of cancer—presumably because this last reason carries little meaning for young people personally (Bauman et al. 510–30).

Finding objective evidence to support a claim often requires that we go beyond our own experience by doing some type of research (see Section Four).

SHAPING A CLEAR LINE OF THOUGHT

Like all writing, persuasive writing has an introduction, a body, and a conclusion. But within this familiar shape, your argument should do some special things, as well. Readers need to follow your reasoning; they expect to see how you've arrived at your conclusions. The following model lays out a standard shape for arguments, but remember that virtually no argument rigidly follows the order of elements shown in the model. Select whatever shape you find most useful—as long as it reveals a clear line of thought.

STANDARD SHAPE FOR AN ARGUMENT

Introduction: *Attract and Invite Your Audience, and Provide a Forecast*

- Identify the issue clearly and immediately. Show that your argument deserves attention.

- Be clear about the points over which you and opponents disagree.

- Acknowledge the opposing viewpoint accurately and concede its merit.

- Offer at least one point of your own that your audience will agree with.

- Give enough background for people to understand your position accurately.

- State a clear, concrete, and definite claim (or thesis). Never delay your claim without good reason: If the thesis is highly controversial, you might want to delay it until you've offered some convincing evidence.

- Keep the introduction short—no more than a few brief paragraphs.

Body: *Offer the Support and Refutation*

- Focus on reasons that *your audience* will consider important (impersonal grounds of support).

- Organize your supporting points for best emphasis. If you think the audience has little interest, begin with the strongest material. Sometimes you can sandwich weaker points between stronger ones. But if all your points are equally strong, begin with the most familiar and acceptable to your audience to elicit early agreement. In general, try to save the strongest points for last.

- Reinforce each supporting point with concrete, specific details (facts, examples, narratives, quotations, or other verifiable evidence).

- String your supporting points and evidence together to show a definite line of reasoning.
- In at least one separate paragraph, refute opposing arguments (including any anticipated objections to your points).

Conclusion: *Sum Up Your Case and Make a Direct Appeal*

- Summarize your main points and refutation, emphasizing your strongest material. Offer a view of the Big Picture.
- Appeal directly to readers for definite action (where appropriate).
- Let people know what they should do, think, or feel.

CONNECTING WITH YOUR AUDIENCE

In any persuasive writing, the audience is the main focus. Whenever you set out to influence someone's thinking, remember the principle on page 289.

GUIDELINES FOR PERSUASION

1. *Be clear about what you want.* Diplomacy is important, but don't leave people guessing about your purpose. Develop the clearest possible view of exactly what it is you want to see happen.
2. *Think your idea through.* Are there any holes in this argument? How will it stand up under scrutiny?
3. *Never make a claim or ask for something you know people will reject outright.* Can people live with whatever you're requesting or proposing? Get a realistic sense about what is achievable in this particular situation by asking what people are thinking. Invite them to share in decision making. Offer real choices.
4. *Do your homework.* Be sure your facts are straight and your figures are accurate.
5. *Anticipate your audience's reaction.* Few of us are anxious to admit publicly that our

way of seeing something could be the wrong one. No one likes losing face. Will people be defensive, shocked, annoyed, angry? Try to neutralize big objections beforehand. Express your judgments on the issue ("We could do better") without blaming people ("It's all your fault").

6. *Project a likable and reasonable persona.* Persona is the image or impression you project in your tone and diction. Audiences have these questions about the writer: "What do I think about the person making the argument? " "Do I like and trust this person?" "Does this person seem to know what he/she is talking about?" "Is this person trying to make me look stupid?"

Audiences tune out aggressive people—no matter how sensible the argu-

> **No matter how brilliant, any argument rejected by its audience is a failed argument.**

If readers dislike what you have to say or decide that what you have to say has no meaning for them personally, they reject your argument. Connecting with an audience means being able to see things from their perspective. The Guidelines for Persuasion on page 288 can help you make that connection.

CONSIDERING THE ETHICAL DIMENSION

Arguments can "win" without being ethical if they "win" at any cost. For instance, advertisers effectively win customers with an implied argument that "our product is just what you need!" Some of their more specific claims can be: "Our artificial sweetener is made of proteins that occur naturally in the human body [amino acids]" or "Our potato chips contain no cholesterol."

ment. Resist the urge to preach, to "sound off," or to be sarcastic. Admit the imperfections or uncertainty in your case. Invite people to respond. A little humility never hurts.

7. *Find points of agreement with your audience.* What does everyone involved want? To reduce conflict, focus early on a shared value, goal, or experience. Emphasize your similarities.

8. *Never distort the opposing position.* A sure way to alienate people is to cast the opponent in a more negative light than the facts warrant.

9. *Concede* something *to the opposing position.* Reasonable people respect an argument that is fair and balanced. Admit the merits of the opposing case before arguing for your own. Show empathy and willing-

ness to compromise. Encourage people to air their own views.

10. *Don't merely criticize.* If you're arguing that something is wrong, be sure you can offer realistic suggestions for making it right.

11. *Stick to claims or assertions you can support.* Show people what's in it for them—but never distort the facts just to please the audience.

12. *Stick to your best material.* Not all points are equal. Decide which material—from your audience's view—best advances your case.

13. *Use your skills responsibly.* The obvious power of persuasive skills creates tremendous potential for abuse. People who feel they have been bullied or "conned" will likely become your enemies.

Such claims are technically accurate but misleading: Amino acids in artificial sweeteners can alter body chemistry to cause headaches, seizures, and possibly brain tumors; potato chips often contain saturated fat—from which the liver produces cholesterol.

We often are tempted to emphasize anything that advances our case and to ignore anything that impedes it. But a message is unethical if it prevents readers from making their best decision. To ensure that your writing is ethical, answer the following questions.

REVISION CHECKLIST ✔*

ETHICS CHECKLIST FOR PERSUASIVE WRITING

☐ Do I avoid exaggeration, understatement, sugarcoating, or any distortion or omission that leaves readers at a disadvantage?

☐ Do I make a clear distinction between "certainty" and "probability"?

☐ Have I explored all sides of the issue and all possible alternatives?

☐ Are my information sources valid, reliable, and relatively unbiased?

☐ Am I being honest and fair with everyone involved?

☐ Am I reasonably sure that what I'm saying will harm no innocent persons or damage their reputation?

☐ Am I respecting all legitimate rights to privacy and confidentiality?

☐ Do I provide enough information and interpretation for readers to understand the facts as I know them?

☐ Do I state the case clearly, instead of hiding behind fallacies or generalities?

☐ Do I inform readers of the consequences or risks (as I am able to predict) of what I am advocating?

☐ Do I credit all contributors and sources of ideas and information?

VARIOUS ARGUMENTS FOR VARIOUS GOALS

"What do I want people do be thinking or doing?"

Arguments can differ considerably in what they ask readers to do. The goal of an argument might be to influence readers' opinions, seek readers' support, propose some action, or change readers' behavior. Let's look at arguments that seek different levels of involvement from readers.

---

*Adapted from Brownell and Fitzgerald 18; Bryan 87; Johannesen 21–22; Larson 39; Unger 39–46; Yoos 50–55.

Arguing to Influence Readers' Opinions

Asking only for a change in thinking

An argument intended to change an opinion asks for minimal involvement from its readers. Maybe you want readers to agree that specific books and films should be censored, that women should be subject to military draft, or that grades are a detriment to education. The specific goal behind any such argument is merely to get readers to change their thinking, to say "I agree."

Arguing to Enlist Readers' Support

Asking for active support

In seeking readers' support for our argument, we ask readers not only to agree with a position but also to take a stand. Maybe you want readers to vote for a candidate, lobby for additional computer equipment at your school, or help enforce dorm or library "quiet" rules. The goal in this kind of argument is to get people actively involved, to get them to ask, "How can I help?"

Making a Proposal

Asking for direct action

The world is full of problems to solve. And proposals are designed precisely to solve problems. The type of proposal we examine here typically asks readers to take some form of direct action (to improve dorm security, fund a new campus organization, or improve working conditions). But before you can induce people to act, you must fulfill these preliminary persuasive tasks:

A proposal involves these persuasive tasks

1. spell out the problem (and its causes) in enough detail to convince readers of its importance
2. point out the benefits of solving the problem
3. offer a realistic solution
4. address objections to your solution
5. give reasons why your readers should be the ones to act

Your goal in presenting a proposal is getting people to say, "Okay, let's do this project."

Arguing to Change Readers' Behavior

Asking for different behavior

Persuading readers to change their behavior is perhaps the biggest challenge in argument. Maybe you want your boss to treat employees more fairly, or a friend to be less competitive, or a teacher to be more supportive in the classroom. Whatever your goal, readers are bound to take your argument personally. And the more personal the issue, the greater resistance you can expect. You're trying to get readers to say, "I was wrong. From now on, I'll do it differently."

The four writing samples shown in Applications 17–1 through 17–4 are addressed to readers who have an increasing stake or involvement in the issue. Comparing these essays will show how writers in various situations can convey their way of seeing.

Application **17-1**

ESSAY PRACTICE: ARGUING TO INFLUENCE READERS' OPINIONS

The following essay from the *Miami Herald* argues that "trash" fiction (about Tarzan, Nancy Drew, Conan the Barbarian, and so on) offers children a good preparation for reading great literature. Read the essay, and answer the questions that follow. Then (as your instructor requests) select one of the essay assignments.

Before you read, think about the kinds of books, magazines, and newspapers you enjoy the most. Could some of these be considered "trash"? If so, what arguments could you make for the benefits of this type of reading?

ESSAY FOR ANALYSIS AND RESPONSE

ON READING TRASH

[1] If you want kids to become omnivorous readers, let them read trash. That's my philosophy, and I speak from experience.

[2] I don't disagree with The National Endowment for the Humanities, which says every high school graduate should have read 30 great works of literature, including the Bible, Plato, Shakespeare, Hawthorne, the "Declaration of Independence," "Catcher in the Rye," "Crime and Punishment" and "Moby Dick."

[3] It's a fine list. Kids should read them all, and more. But they'll be better readers if they start off on trash. Trash? What I mean is what some might call "popular" fiction. My theory is, if you get kids interested in reading books— no matter what sort—they will eventually go on to the grander literature all by themselves.

[4] In the third grade I read my first novel, a mystic adventure set in India. I still recall the sheer excitement at discovering how much fun reading could be.

[5] When we moved within walking distance of the public library a whole new world opened. In the library I found that wonder of wonders, the series. What a thrill, to find a favorite author had written a dozen or more other titles.

[6] I read a series about frontiersmen, learning about Indian tribes, beef jerky and tepees. A Civil War series alternated young heroes from the Blue and the Gray, and I learned about Grant and Lee and the Rock of Chickamauga.

[7] One summer, in Grandpa Barrow's attic, I discovered the Mother Lode, scores of dusty books detailing the adventures of Tom Swift, The Rover Boys, The Submarine Boys, The Motorcycle Boys and Bomba the Jungle Boy. It didn't matter that some were written in 1919; any book you haven't read is brand new.

[8]Another summer I discovered Edgar Rice Burroughs. I swung through jungles with Tarzan, fought green Martians with John Carter, explored Pellucidar at the Earth's core, flew through the steamy air of Venus with Carson Napier. Then I came across Sax Rohmer and, for book after book, prowled opium dens with Nayland Smith, in pursuit of the insidious Fu Manchu.

[9]In the seventh grade, I ran across Booth Tarkington's hilarious Penrod books and read them over and over.

[10]My cousin went off to war in 1942 and gave me his pulp magazines. I became hooked on Doc Savage, The Shadow, G8 and His Battle Aces, The Spider, Amazing Stories. My folks wisely did not object to them as trash. I began to look in second-hand book shops for past issues, and found a Blue Book Magazine, with an adventure story by Talbot Mundy. It led me back to the library, for more of Mundy's Far East thrillers. From Mundy, my path led to A. Conan Doyle's "The Lost World," Rudyard Kipling's "Kim," Jules Verne, H. G. Wells and Jack London.

[11]Before long I was whaling with Herman Melville, affixing scarlet letters with Hawthorne and descending into the maelstrom with Poe. In due course came Hemingway, Dos Passos, "Hamlet," "The Odyssey," "The Iliad," "Crime and Punishment." I had discovered "real" literature by following the trail of popular fiction.

[12]When our kids were small, we read aloud to them from Doctor Dolittle and Winnie the Pooh. Soon they learned to read, and favored the "Frog and Toad" and "Freddie the Pig" series.

[13]When the old Doc Savage and Conan the Barbarian pulps were reissued as paperbacks, I brought them home. The kids devoured them, sometimes hiding them behind textbooks at school, just as I had. They read my old Tarzan and Penrod books along with Nancy Drew and The Black Stallion.

[14]Now they're big kids. Each kid's room is lined with bookshelves, on which are stacked, in an eclectic mix, Doc Savage, Plato, Louis L'Amour westerns, Thomas Mann, Gothic romances, Agatha Christie, Sartre, Edgar Allan Poe, science-fiction, Saul Bellow, Shakespeare, Pogo, Greek tragedies, Hemingway, Kipling, Tarzan, "Zen and the Art of Motorcycle Maintenance," F. Scott Fitzgerald, "Bomba the Jungle Boy," Nietzsche, "The Iliad," "Dr. Dolittle," Joseph Conrad, Fu Manchu, Hawthorne, Penrod, Dostoevsky, Ray Bradbury, Herman Melville, "Conan the Barbarian" . . . more. Some great literature, some trash, but all good reading.

—Bob Swift

QUESTIONS ABOUT YOUR READING

Refer also to the general questions on page 165.

PURPOSE

- Who is Swift's intended audience here? How do we know?
- Does Swift succeed in connecting with his audience? If so, how?

CONTENT

- What is the primary development strategy used here? Which other strategies can you identify?
- Does the writer acknowledge the opposing viewpoint? If so, where?
- Does the thesis grow out of sufficient background details? Explain.

ORGANIZATION

- Is the material arranged in the best order? Explain.
- Are most paragraphs too short? Explain.

STYLE

- How would you characterize the tone? Is it appropriate for the audience and purpose?
- Does the writer appear likable? Is he ever too extreme? Explain.

RESPONDING TO YOUR READING

Explore your reactions to "On Reading Trash" by using the questions on page 166. You might wish to challenge the author's view by arguing your own ideas about what constitutes worthwhile reading. You might support his view by citing evidence from your own experience. Or you might set out to influence reader opinion on some other topic of interest. Decide carefully on your audience and on what you want these readers to do, think, or feel after reading your essay. Be sure your essay supports a clear and definite point.

Be sure your essay has a clear thesis and addresses a specific audience affected by the issue in some way. Although this essay will make an emotional appeal, your argument should not rest solely on subjective grounds (how you feel about it), but also on factual details.

CASE STUDY

RESPONDING TO READING

After reading and analyzing Swift's essay, Julia Schoonover decides to persuade fellow students that credit cards can be far more dangerous than they appear.

While planning, drafting, and revising, Julia refers to the Persuasion Guidelines, the Model Outline for Argument, and the Revision Checklist on pages 288, 287, and 63.

Note | *Like most arguments, Julia's piece relies on multiple development strategies, especially causal analysis, process analysis, and illustration.*

Title announces the essay's purpose
Opens directly with the thesis

CREDIT CARDS: LEAVE HOME WITHOUT THEM

Credit cards are college students' best friends and potentially their worst enemy. Credit cards provide a convenient means of purchasing much-needed textbooks, food, and dorm room essentials. Credit cards enable students to

Acknowledges opposing view

Vivid examples help establish agreement and neutralize objections

Transition to upcoming refutation

Cause/effect analysis

Process analysis

Uses examples as objective evidence

Process analysis

Gives striking statistics

Gives additional examples readers can identify with

Gives striking quotation

Gives striking statistic

Projects a reasonable, empathetic persona throughout

Cause/effect analysis

Cites an expert

Process analysis

purchase plane tickets to fly home or to Bermuda for spring break. Credit cards even make money available for those "little" extras that mom and dad would never buy—like a state-of-the-art stereo system or a new wardrobe. Long distance calls and Christmas shopping are also made a lot easier by credit cards.

Although credit cards can be very helpful to the struggling student, they also can spell big trouble. The most obvious danger comes from their misuse: that is, the temptation to go on a spending spree. It is very easy for students to run up huge debt because credit card companies don't require cardholders—indeed, they don't *want* cardholders—to pay off their debts when the bill comes in at the end of each month. Although these cards are promoted with a teaser "low interest rate," that rate soon triples. As a result, many students end up owing more than they originally borrowed, even with regular minimum monthly payments.

Three coworkers of mine who are also students know what it's like to be in debt to credit card companies. Ron, a Fallow State College junior, owes more than $5,200 to credit card companies. Ron claims that when he first got a card he "went crazy" with it. He bought exercise equipment, a couch, a CD player, and clothes for himself and his girlfriend. Ron now makes about $120 weekly at his part-time job, goes to school full-time, and knows that because the interest rate for each of his three cards is around 17 percent and he pays only the $98 monthly minimum, it will take him about ten years to repay his debt. By then, Ron will have paid the credit card companies more than double the amount he charged.

Another coworker, Jane, a sophomore at Walloon College, says she owes $1,300 on one card and $1,100 on another. Jane says most of the money she owes is from last Christmas. She tries to pay the minimum combined charge of $40 monthly but even $40 takes a big chunk out of her $64 weekly salary after she pays for meals, movies, gas, and a steep phone bill (her boyfriend goes to the University of Florida). Dave, a senior at the University of Massachusetts, worries how he will ever pay his $3,500 credit card debt on his $70 weekly paycheck. Dave can't even remember what he spent this money on. "You spend it here and there and it adds up fast." Meanwhile, Dave's debt is increasing at the rate of 18.9 percent yearly.

Because of the immediate money problems that credit cards seem to solve, it's easy to ignore the long-term effects of a bad credit history. According to accountant John Farnes, former mortgage officer at Town Savings Bank, when people apply for any type of loan, the bank immediately obtains a credit report, which lists the applicant's number of credit cards, total debt, and the amount that person is eligible to borrow. The report also shows whether the applicant has ever "maxed out" all credit cards or missed any minimum monthly payments. Applicants who have missed payments—or have been late with a payment—usually are rejected. Even people who make all minimum payments but still have outstanding or excessive credit card debt are turned down for loans. Farnes cautions that students who "run up credit card bills" can dig a big hole for themselves—a hole from which they might never climb out.

Acknowledges opposing view

Relies on visual details throughout

Conclusion refutes opposing view and reemphasizes the main point

Appeals directly to readers

Granted, the temptation is hard to refuse. Credit card companies marketing on campus offer free cards and sign-up gifts "with no obligation." The "gifts" might include candy, coffee mugs, T-shirts, sports squeeze bottles, hip bags, and other paraphernalia. The process seems so easy and harmless: Just fill in your social security number and other personal information, take your pick from the array of gifts, and cancel the card when it arrives.

But these companies know exactly what they're doing. They know that misusing the card is often easier than canceling it. They know that many of us work part time and are paid little. They know that most of us will be unable to pay more than the minimum balance each month—meaning big-time interest for years. Don't be seduced by instant credit.

—*Julia Schoonover*

OPTIONS FOR ESSAY WRITING

1. Argue for or against this assertion: Parents have the right to make major decisions in the lives of their teenagers.
2. Are grades an aid to education?
3. Sally and Sam have two children, ages two and five. Sally, an attorney, is currently not working but has been offered an attractive full-time job. Sam believes Sally should not work until both children are in school. Should Sally take the job?
4. Recently, voters in several communities defeated or repealed ordinances protecting homosexuals from discrimination in housing and employment. Defend or attack these public decisions.
5. Should college scholarships be awarded for academic achievement or promise, rather than for financial need?
6. During your more than twelve years in school, you've undoubtedly developed legitimate gripes about the quality of American education. Based on your experiences, perceptions, and research, think about one specific problem in American education and argue for its solution. Remember, you are writing an argument, not an attack; your goal is not to offend but to persuade readers—to move them to your way of seeing.

After making sure you have enough inductive evidence to support your main generalization, write an editorial essay for your campus newspaper: Identify the problem; analyze its cause(s); and propose a solution. Possible topics:

- too little (or too much) attention given to remedial students
- too little (or too much) emphasis on practical education (career training)
- too little (or too much) emphasis on competition

- teachers' attitudes
- parents' attitudes
- students' attitudes

Application **17-2**

ESSAY PRACTICE: ARGUING TO ENLIST READERS' SUPPORT

Read the essay, and answer the questions that follow. Then (as your instructor requests) select one of the essay assignments.

Before you read, think about the academic standards at your old high school. Did your school have minimum grade standards for participation in extracurricular activities? Were these standards fair, in your view? Should they be more strict, more lenient? If so, why?

ESSAY FOR ANALYSIS AND RESPONSE

STANDARDS YOU MEET AND DON'T DUCK

[1]I'm telling you about my son Mark, not because I want to embarrass him, but because I find it useful in discussing public-policy questions to ask what I would advocate if the people affected by my policy proposals were members of my own family.

[2]Mark, who is not quite twelve, is a good kid: friendly, bright, a good athlete and (potentially) a very good student. But he has a tendency to be lazy about his studies.

[3]So at the beginning of the year, I issued an edict: He would perform acceptably well in school or he wouldn't be allowed to play organized sports outside school.

[4]He talked me into a modification: Rather than penalize him for last year's grades, earned before the new rule was announced, let him sign up for the Boys Club league now, and take him off the team if his mid-terms weren't up to par.

[5]Well, the mid-terms came out, and the basketball team is struggling along without the assistance of my son the shooting guard.

[6]All of which is a roundabout and perhaps too personal a way of saying my sentiments are with the Prince George's County (Maryland) school officials. My suburban Washington neighbors, confronted with angry parents, disappointed students, and decimated athletic teams, are under pressure to modify their new at-least-C-average-or-no-extracurriculars policy.

[7]I hope they will resist it. The new policy may not be perfect, but it reflects a proper sense of priorities, which is one of the things our children ought to be learning. It may turn out to be a very good thing for all concerned—including the 39 percent of the county's students who are temporarily ineligible for such outside activities as athletics, cheerleading, dramatics, and band.

[8]I've heard the arguments on the other side, and while I don't dismiss them out of hand, they fall short of persuading me that the new standards are

too tough or their application too rigid. I know that for some students, the extracurriculars are the only thing that keep school from being a complete downer. I know that some youngsters will be tempted to pass up Algebra II, chemistry, and other tough courses in order to keep their extracurricular eligibility (weighted grade points could solve that problem). And I know that for students whose strengths are other than academic, success in music or drama or sports can be an important source of self-esteem.

[9]Still I support the C-average rule—partly because of my assumption that it isn't all that tough a standard. We're not talking here about bell-shaped curves that automatically place some students above the median and some below it. I suspect that we're talking less about acceptable academic achievement than about acceptable levels of exertion. I find it hard to believe that Prince George's teachers will flunk kids who really do try: who pay attention in class, turn in all their work, seek special assistance when they need it, and also bring athletic glory to their schools. (If it turns out that some youngsters are being penalized for inadequate gifts rather than insufficient effort, I'd support some modification of the rule.)

[10]The principal value of the new standard is that it helps the students, including those in the lower grades, to get their own priorities right: to understand that while outside activities can be an ego-boosting adjunct to classroom work, they cannot be a substitute for it. Even the truly gifted, whose nonacademic talents might earn them college scholarships or even professional careers, need as solid an academic footing as they can get.

[11]Pity, which is what we often feel for other people's children, says give the poor kids a break. Love, which is what we feel for our own, says let's help them get ready for real life—not by lowering the standards but by providing the resources to help them meet the standards. One principal who saw 38 percent of his students fall below the eligibility cutoff agrees. Said Thomas Kirby: "I don't see any point in having a kid who can bounce a basketball graduate from high school and not be able to read."

—*William Raspberry*

QUESTIONS ABOUT YOUR READING

Refer also to the general questions on page 165.

PURPOSE

■ Does Raspberry succeed in making his point? If so, how?

CONTENT

■ Does the writer acknowledge the opposing viewpoint, and does he address opponents' biggest objections to his position?
■ Where is the thesis? Is it easily found?
■ Does the writer offer sound reasons for his case? Explain.
■ Does the writer offer impersonal (as well as personal) support? Explain.

ORGANIZATION

■ Is the introduction effective? Which of the tasks on page 287 does it perform? Explain.

- Is the strongest material near the beginning or the end of the essay? Is this placement effective?
- How does the writer achieve coherence and smooth transitions between paragraphs?

STYLE

- Does the writer avoid an extreme persona here (say, sounding like a righteous parent)? Explain.

RESPONDING TO YOUR READING

Explore your reactions to "Standards You Meet and Don't Duck" by using the questions on page 166. Then respond with your own essay supporting or opposing the author's view. Your goal is to get readers involved. Perhaps you will want to argue from the viewpoint of athletes who are affected by grade standards.

Or you might argue for some other school requirement, as in urging your old high school (or your college) to require an exit essay of its graduating seniors to ensure an acceptable level of literacy.

Or maybe you feel that some school requirements are unfair. Whatever your position, be sure that your essay has a clear thesis and that you address a specific audience whose support you seek. In order to be persuasive, base your support not only on personal grounds (how you feel about it), but on impersonal grounds (verifiable evidence), as well.

CASE STUDY

RESPONDING TO READING

After reading and analyzing Raspberry's essay, Suzanne Gilbertson thinks about a current controversy at her own university: In an age when jobs require increasing specialization, the importance of the liberal arts are under question. Some people argue that students in career-oriented majors, such as computer science and engineering, actually are hurt by the university's humanities, social science, and language requirements, because these students are prevented from taking enough courses in their specialties. Beyond advocating that such requirements be dropped, some people argue that certain majors (such as fine arts and philosophy) and upper-level courses should be eliminated, thereby freeing more resources for career programs.

Suzanne decides to refute the assertion that the liberal arts have become an unaffordable luxury at her school. Her essay will be published in the campus newspaper as an open letter to faculty, administrators, trustees, and students.

Note

In shaping her argument, Suzanne combines a rich array of development strategies.

Title announces the argument's purpose
Opens with a familiar question

SAVE LIBERAL ARTS

You may be one of them. As a child you never could give a confident answer to the question "What do you want to be when you grow up?" In high school, while your friends fingered through various issues of *National*

*Gives visual examples
readers can identify with*

*Projects a reasonable
persona throughout*

*Acknowledges opposing
view without distorting it*

Refutes opposing view

Offers clear definitions

Defines by negation

Thesis

Offers a contrast

*Gives objective evidence
to support the contrast*

*Offers points of
agreement*

*Expands on above points
Cause/effect analysis*

Geographic during study hall in the library, you hovered near the Fiction section or lost yourself in *The Last Days of Pompeii*. Once in college, you couldn't bring yourself to declare a major; instead picking and choosing courses from an array of disciplines, you resembled a diner filling his or her plate at a breakfast buffet. Recognize the type? If you found yourself enjoying freshman English, if you register for beginning Spanish one semester and elementary Russian the next, or combine obscure philosophy courses with biology and write a poem on the similarities of the two, you might just be a "closet" liberal arts major.

Many folks tend to believe that education should provide the student with concrete skills that later can be applied to specific tasks. Historically, young children were apprenticed to a craftsperson to learn a skill by constant observation and imitation. Today, most people still prefer to specialize in a single field. They feel comfortable on a "career track." In our high-tech age, the liberal arts major seems to have lost its appeal. Some even label a liberal arts degree self-indulgent and impractical, and encourage students to take courses that will "guarantee" them employment after graduation.

But some students find it harder to narrow their interests and sharpen their talents to fit a practical field. Are liberal arts majors simply choosing an easy or irrelevant way to a college diploma?

Maybe we need first to examine the meaning of "education" as opposed to "schooling." The "Renaissance person" is so named after the philosophers, poets, and artists who illuminated three centuries of Western civilization through a rebirth of classical learning. Such a person is characterized by an intense love of learning, a search for excellence. Far from being self-indulgent or withdrawn from worldly and practical affairs, the Renaissance person is committed to serving the needs of society by studying humanity and the life of citizens in society.

Beyond merely imparting information or training, education in the Renaissance prepared students to be concerned citizens *in the world.* Career training alone was considered far inferior to a liberal education. *Likewise today, a liberal education teaches us to observe the human condition, synthesize what we know of that condition from our study of history and philosophy, and verbalize and communicate our perception of the needs of others besides ourselves.*

The twentieth century has produced for us complex problems beyond the comprehension of Renaissance thinkers, such as da Vinci, Galileo, or Thomas More. Our world seems smaller and more crowded. We are threatened by poisons in our air and water. Many nations are hungry and oppressed. We live under the constant fear of the ultimate weapons of destruction we have created to protect our freedoms. We continue to need skilled doctors to cure our ills, dedicated farmers to feed us, and politicians and managers to lead us. And the advanced technology at the disposal of our specialists may well be the key to our survival.

Yet, in order to understand and cope with the challenges of the twenty-first century, we must first be able to see where we have come from. Even our

Offers vivid examples throughout

Appeals to shared goals and values

Reemphasizes the main idea

present technological breakthroughs are made possible because of the questions first asked by the scholars of the Renaissance: Are there any limits to what humanity can accomplish? What are the possibilities for human achievement? How can we best take advantage of our human and natural resources?

In the Renaissance tradition, the liberal arts graduate is well equipped to meet the broadest challenges of our technological society. Now, more than ever, we need people who can step back and monitor our "progress." We need minds that can synthesize our many achievements and our aspirations, to guide us toward a safe and improved existence. In the end, what will bind us together will be our ability to formulate and question our goals and to communicate our global needs. Questioning, synthesizing, and communicating—these are the broad skills liberal arts graduates bring to the enrichment of their world.

—*Suzanne Gilbertson*

OPTIONS FOR ESSAY WRITING

1. Respond to the assertion that the liberal arts have become an unaffordable luxury. Be sure to consider the arguments for and against specialized vocational education versus a broadly humanistic—but less "practical"—education.
2. Your college is thinking of abolishing core requirements. Write a letter to the dean in which you argue for or against this change.
3. Should first-year composition be required at your school? Argue your position to the faculty senate.
4. Should your school (or institute) drop students' evaluations of teachers? Write to the student and faculty senates.
5. Perhaps you belong to a fraternity, a sorority, or some other organized group. Identify an important decision your group faces. In a letter, present your position on the issue to the group.
6. The Cultural Affairs Committee at your school has decided to sponsor a concert next fall, featuring some popular singer or musical group. Although the committee (mostly faculty) is aware that today's music reflects great diversity in personal taste and musical style, the committee members are uncertain about which performer or group would be a good choice for the event. In fact, most committee members admit to being ignorant of the characteristics that distinguish one performance or recording from another. To help in the decision, the committee has invited the student body to submit essays (not letters) arguing for a performer or group. Free tickets will be awarded to the writer of the best essay. Compose your response.
7. Should your school have an attendance policy?

8. In a letter to the college newspaper, challenge an attitude or viewpoint that is widely held on your campus. Maybe you want to persuade your classmates that the time required to earn a Bachelor's degree should be extended to five years. Or maybe you want to claim that the campus police should (or should not) wear guns. Or maybe you want to ask students to support a 10 percent tuition increase in order to make more computers and software available.

What kind of resistance can you anticipate? How can you avoid outright rejection of your claim? What reasons will have meaning for your audience? What tone should you adopt?

Application **17-3**

ESSAY PRACTICE: MAKING A PROPOSAL

This proposal addresses a fairly common problem: A large television set in the campus center is causing congestion and wasting students' time. One student confronts the problem by writing a proposal to the director of the campus center.

Read the proposal carefully, and answer the questions that follow. Select one of the essay assignments if your instructor requests you to do so.

Before you read, think about some improvement you would like to see in your school or community. How might that change be brought about?

ESSAY FOR ANALYSIS

A PROPOSAL FOR BETTER USE OF THE TELEVISION SET IN THE CAMPUS CENTER

[1]Leaving the campus center yesterday for class, I found myself stuck in the daily pedestrian jam on the second-floor landing. People by the dozens had gathered on the stairway for their daily dose of *General Hospital.* Fighting my way through the mesmerized bodies, I wondered about the appropriateness of the television set's location, and of the value of the shows aired on this set.

[2]Along with the recent upsurge of improvements at our school (in curriculum and standards), we should be considering ways to better use the campus center television. The tube plays relentlessly, offering soap operas and game shows to the addicts who block the stairway and main landing. Granted, television for students to enjoy between classes is a fine idea, but no student needs to attend college to watch soap operas. By moving the set and improving the programs, we could eliminate the congestion and enrich the learning experience.

[3]The television needs a better location: out of the way of people who don't care to watch it, and into a larger, more comfortable setting for those who do. Background noise in the present location makes the set barely audible; and the raised seating in front of the set places the viewers on exhibit to all who walk by. A far better location would be the back wall of the North

Lounge, outside the Sunset Room—a large, quiet, and comfortable space. Various meetings sometimes held in this room could be moved instead to the browsing area of the library.

[4]More important than the set's location is the quality of its programs. Videotaped movies might be a good alternative to the shows now aired. Our audiovisual department has a rich collection of excellent movies and educational programs on tape. People could request the shows they would like to see, and a student committee could be responsible for printing showtime information.

[5]The set might also serve as a primary learning tool by allowing communications students to create their own shows. Our school has the videotaping and sound equipment and would need only a faculty adviser to supervise the project. Students from scriptwriting, drama, political science, and journalism classes (to name a few) could combine their talents, providing shows of interest to their peers. We now have a student news program that is aired evenings on a local channel, but many who live some distance off campus cannot receive this channel on their sets at home. Why not make the program accessible to students during the day, here on campus?

[6]With resources already in our possession, we can make a few changes that will benefit almost everyone. Beyond providing more efficient use of campus center space, these changes could really stimulate people's minds. I urge you to allow students and faculty to vote on the questions of moving the television set and improving its programs.

—*Patricia Haith*

QUESTIONS ABOUT YOUR READING

Refer also to the general questions on page 165.

CONTENT

- Does the proposal fulfill the tasks outlined on page 291? Explain.
- Does the writer offer the best reasons for her primary audience? Explain.
- For a different audience (say, students who avidly follow the soap operas), would the writer have to change her material? Explain.
- Is this argument primarily inductive or deductive? (See page 310).
- Does the writer establish agreement with the reader? If so, where?

ORGANIZATION

- Which expository strategy is mainly used in this essay?
- Is the narrative introduction effective? Explain.
- Does the conclusion perform all the tasks on page 288?

STYLE

- How do the outstanding style features of this essay contribute to its tone?
- Should the tone of this essay be more or less formal for this audience and purpose? Or is it appropriate? Explain.
- Is the writer's voice likable? Explain.

OPTIONS FOR ESSAY WRITING

Identify a problem in your school, community, family, or job. Develop a proposal for solving the problem. Stipulate a definite audience for your proposal. Here are some possible subjects:

- improving living conditions in your dorm
- improving security in your dorm
- creating a day-care center on campus
- saving labor, materials, or money at your job
- improving working conditions
- improving the services of your college library
- improving the food service on campus
- establishing more equitable use of computer terminals on campus

Be sure to spell out the problem, explain the benefits of change, offer a realistic plan, and urge your readers to definite action. Decide exactly what you want your readers to do.

Application 17-4

ESSAY PRACTICE: CHANGING THE READER'S BEHAVIOR

This essay, a complaint letter from an employee to her boss, illustrates the challenge of trying to influence another person's behavior. Read it carefully, and answer the questions that follow. Then select one of the essay assignments.

Before you read, think about a situation in which you've wanted to confront someone about a problem in their behavior. If you did, what was the result? If you didn't, what was the result? What would you do differently now?

ESSAY FOR ANALYSIS

LETTER TO THE BOSS

[1]For several months I have been hesitant to approach you about a problem that has caused me great uneasiness at work. More recently, however, I've found that several other employees are equally upset, and I feel, as one of your close friends, that I should explain what's wrong. With you as our boss, we all have an exceptional employer-employee relationship, and I'd hate to see one small problem upset it.

[2]John, when you have criticism about any one of us at work, you never seem to deal directly with that specific person. When the chefs were coming in late, you didn't confront them directly to express your displeasure; instead, you discussed it with the other employees. When you suspected Alan's honesty and integrity as a bartender, you came to me rather than to Alan. I learned yesterday from the coat-checker that you are unhappy with the

waitpersons for laughing and joking too much. And these are just a few of many such incidents.

[3]I understand how difficult it is to approach a person with constructive criticism—in fact, it's taken me several months to mention this problem to you! Having been on the receiving end of grapevine gossip, though, I would accept the complaint much more gracefully if it came directly from you. Many of the employees are needlessly upset, and our increasing dissatisfaction harms the quality of our work.

[4]Because I've never been a supervisor, I can only imagine your difficulty. I'm sure your task is magnified because when you bought this restaurant last spring, we employees all knew one another, but you knew none of us. You've told me many times how important it is for you to be a friend to all of us, but sometimes friendship can stand in the way of communication.

[5]Our old boss used to deal with the problem of making constructive suggestions in this way: Every other Saturday evening we would have a meeting at which he would voice his suggestions and we would voice ours. This arrangement worked out well, because none of us felt singled out for criticism, and we all had the chance to discuss problems openly.

[6]I value your friendship, and I hope you will accept this letter in the sincere spirit in which it's offered. I'm sure that with a couple of good conversations we can work things out.

—*Marcia White*

QUESTIONS ABOUT YOUR READING

Refer also to the general questions on page 165.

CONTENT

- Bracket all facts in this letter, and underline all statements of opinion (see Chapter 5). Are all opinions supported by facts? Explain.
- Does the writer acknowledge the opposing viewpoint? Explain.
- Does the writer admit the imperfections in her case? Explain.

ORGANIZATION

- In the introductory paragraph, is the writer guilty of "beating around the bush"? Explain.
- Which body paragraphs spell out the problem?
- Is the final body paragraph too indirect? Explain.
- Which is the most concrete paragraph? Explain its function.

STYLE

- In the second and third body paragraphs, identify one example of coordination. How does this structure reinforce the writer's meaning?
- Is the tone appropriate for the situation, audience, and purpose? Identify three sentences that contribute to this tone.
- Identify three sentences in which the writer expresses empathy with her reader.

OPTIONS FOR ESSAY WRITING

1. Everyone has habits that annoy others or are harmful in some way. Identify the bad habit of a friend, relative, coworker, or someone you spend a lot of time with, and write a letter trying to persuade the person to break that habit. Suggest specific actions your reader might take to overcome it. (Stay away from the classic cigarette smoking.) Keep in mind you're writing to someone close to you; you want to sound like an honest friend, not a judge. Your reader will be defensive; how can you defuse that defensiveness while getting your message across?

2. Think of a situation in which you recently encountered problems—in a job, in a school, or as a consumer. Choose something about which you have a major complaint. Write a letter to the person who is in charge or is otherwise responsible, laying out the issues and suggesting appropriate changes.

Application **17-5**

Computer Application: The standard shape for an argument on pages 287–88 suggests an effective arrangement for your thesis, your response to opposing views, your support paragraphs, and your conclusion. But throughout this book, we have seen that the standard shape can be varied in many productive ways. Try out different placements for the various elements of one of your argumentative essays by cutting and pasting. (Be sure to change the file name for each version!) What happens if you position the thesis after the response to opposing arguments instead of before it? What if you place the response to your opposition after the support? Get feedback from classmates about the various options. In particular, notice how different arrangements call for different transitions (pages 110–12) between paragraphs and sections. Be sure to refine these transitions in the final version of this essay you select.

Application **17-6**

Collaborative/Computer Project: Select one of the types of essays presented in this chapter. Using your listserv or email, collaborate with a group of classmates on a joint paper addressed to an appropriate audience. Use the Guidelines for Writing Collaboratively on page 40 (Section One) to brainstorm electronically for a topic, thesis, and support. Then distribute writing tasks, exchange and peer review your work, and construct a draft using transitions to knit the sections together. Submit edited versions to the list and confer electronically about final decisions. As you work, take notes for a future paper about how the electronic process makes working together easier, more complex, or both.

Application **17-7**

Which of these statements are debatable, and why? (Review pages 283–84.)

1. Grades are an aid to education.
2. Forty percent of incoming first-year students at our school never graduate.
3. Physically and psychically, women are superior to men.
4. Pets should not be allowed on our campus.
5. Computer courses are boring.
6. Every student should be required to become computer literate.
7. The computer revolution is transforming American business.
8. French wines are better than domestic wines.
9. French wines generally are more subtle and complex than domestic wines.
10. The price of French wines has risen 20 percent in the past two years.

Application **17-8**

Using your own subjects or those following, develop five arguable assertions. (Review pages 283–84.)

EXAMPLES

[sex] The sexual revolution has created more problems than it has solved.

[education] The heavy remedial emphasis at our school causes many introductory courses to be substandard.

education	law	pollution
sex	music	jobs
drugs	war	dorm life

Application **17-9**

Web-based Project: Locate one item of information about writing argumentative essays that expands on or is not covered in this chapter. Take careful notes for class discussion or (at your instructor's request) prepare a one-page summary of this information. Attach a copy of the relevant Web page(s) to your written notes or summary (guidelines on page 374). Begin with the following sites, but do not limit yourself to these:

- Paradigm Online Writing Assistant
  <**www.powa.org/argufrms.htm**>
- The ESL Planet
  <**www.eslplanet.com/teachertools/argueweb/frntpage.htm**>
- Roane State Community College Online Writing Lab
  <**www.rscc.tn.us/owl&writingcenter/OWL/Argument.html**>

| Note | *Instead of quoting your sources directly, paraphrase. Be sure to credit each source of information (pages 392–406).* |

Application **17-10**

Web-based Project: Examine Web sites that make competing claims about a controversial topic, such as bioengineered foods and crops, nuclear power, and herbal medications or other forms of alternative medicine. For example, compare claims about biotech foods from the Council for Biotechnology Information

<**www.why.biotech.com.**>

with those from the Sierra Club

<**www.sierraclub.org**>

and from the Food and Drug Administration

<**www.fda.gov**>

Or compare claims about nuclear energy from the Nuclear Energy Institute

<**www.nei.org**>

with those from the Sierra Club

<**www.sierraclub.org**>

the American Council on Science

<**www.acsh.org**>

and from the Nuclear Regulatory Commission

<**www.nrc.gov**>

Do you find possible examples of unethical communication, such as conflicts of interest or exaggerated claims?

Refer to the Checklist for Ethical Communication (page 290) as a basis for evaluating the various claims. Also, visit the following sites for information to supplement your analysis:

- Ethics on the World Wide Web
  <**www.commfaculty.fullerton.edu/lester/ethics/ethics_list.html**>
- Institute for Globalethics
  <**www.globalethics.org/**>
- International Society for Environmental Ethics
  <**www.cep.unt.edu/ISEE.html**>

Report your findings in an essay to your instructor and classmates. Attach copies of the relevant Web page(s) to your report. Be sure to credit each source of information (pages 392–406).

Works Cited

Bauman, K. E., et al. "Three Mass Media Campaigns to Prevent Adolescent Cigarette Smoking." *Preventive Medicine* 17 (1988): 510–30.

Brownell, Judi, and Michael Fitzgerald. "Teaching Ethics in Business Communication: The Effective/Ethical Balancing Scale." *Bulletin of the Association for Business Communication* 55.3 (1992): 15–18.

Bryan, John. "Down the Slippery Slope: Ethics and the Technical Writer as Marketer." *Technical Communication Quarterly* 1.1 (1992): 73–88.

Johannesen, Richard L. *Ethics in Human Communication.* 2nd ed. Prospect Heights, IL: Waveland, 1983.

Larson, Charles U. *Persuasion: Perception and Responsibility.* 7th ed. Belmont, CA: Wadsworth, 1995.

Rokeach, Milton. *The Nature of Human Values.* New York: Free Press, 1973.

Unger, Stephen H. *Controlling Technology: Ethics and the Responsible Engineer.* New York: Holt, 1982.

Yoos, George. "A Revision of the Concept of Ethical Appeal." *Philosophy and Rhetoric* 12.4 (1979): 41–58.

CHAPTER 18

Special Issues in Persuasion

Appealing to Reason **310**

Recognizing Invalid or Deceptive Reasoning **317**

Appealing to Emotion **321**

Guidelines for Making Emotional Appeals **322**

Reading **325**

Applications **326**

A persuasive argument connects with readers by appealing to their reason and, often, to their emotions as well.

APPEALING TO REASON

Although argument relies on some combination of description, narration, and exposition, many persuasive arguments are built around one or both of these specific reasoning patterns: *induction* (reasoning from specific evidence to a general conclusion) and *deduction* (applying a proven generalization to a specific case).

Just about any daily decision (including the ones you're asked to make in this book) is the product of inductive or deductive reasoning, or both. Consider this example: You suffer from a bad case of math anxiety. On registration day, you're trying to decide on a course to fulfill your math requirement. After speaking with friends and reviewing your available evidence, you immediately decide to register for Math 101 with Professor Digit. Let's trace the reasoning that led to your decision.

First, you reasoned inductively, from this specific evidence to a generalization:

Inductive evidence

- *Fact:* Your older brother, a poor mathematician but a hard worker, took Professor Digit's course two years ago, mastered his own anxiety, and earned a B-minus.
- *Fact:* Although his course is demanding, Professor Digit is known for being friendly, encouraging, and for always being willing to help his students.
- *Fact:* The students you've talked to all praise Professor's Digit's ability to make math "fun and understandable."
- *Fact:* Many of Professor Digit's students go on to take his upper-level math courses as electives.

Based on the above evidence, you reached this generalization about Professor Digit's teaching skills:

A generalization based on inductive evidence

Professor Digit seems to be an excellent math teacher.

The evidence led you to an informed opinion (a probability, not a fact). You reached this opinion through inductive reasoning. You then used deductive reasoning to move from this generalization to a conclusion:

Generalization

Students willing to work hard succeed in Professor Digit's Math 101 course.

Specific instance

I am a hard worker.

Conclusion

I am likely to succeed in Professor Digit's course.

This conclusion led you to register for his section.

We use induction and deduction repeatedly, often unconsciously. Specific facts, statistics, observations, and experiences lead us inductively to generalizations such as these:

Other inductively based generalizations

Pre-med majors must compete for the highest grades.

Politicians can't always be trusted.

Big cities can be dangerous.

A college degree alone does not ensure career success.

On the other hand, deductive reasoning leads us from generalizations to specific instances to conclusions.

Generalization	Big cities can be dangerous.
Specific instance	New York is a big city.
Conclusion	New York can be dangerous.
Generalization	Pre-med majors must compete for the highest grades.
Specific instance	Brigitte will be a pre-med major next year.
Conclusion	Brigitte will have to compete for the highest grades.

When we write to persuade others, we need to use these processes deliberately and consciously.

Using Induction

We use induction in two situations: (1) to move from specific evidence to a related generalization or (2) to establish the cause or causes of something. Assume you've been dating a Significant Other for a while, but recently you've made these observations:

Reviewing the evidence	My Significant Other (SO) hasn't returned my phone calls in a week.
	My SO always wants to go home early.
	My SO yawns a lot when we're together.
	My SO talks to everyone but me at parties.

This evidence leads to an inductive generalization:

Generalizing from the evidence	My SO is losing interest in me.

The same kind of reasoning establishes the possible or probable causes of your SO's aloofness. As you reflect on the relationship, you recall a number of inconsiderate things you've done recently:

Establishing the cause	I've been awfully short-tempered lately.
	I forgot all about my SO's birthday last week.
	I'm usually late for our dates.
	A few times, I've made wisecracks about my SO's creepy friends.

And so you conclude that your own inconsiderate behavior probably damaged the relationship.

Although generalizations aren't proof of anything, the better your evidence, the more likely it is that your generalizations are accurate. Avoid generalizing from too little evidence. That your Significant Other yawns a lot would not be a sufficient basis to conclude that she or he is losing interest. (Maybe he or she's ill or tired!) Or if your SO had yawned during only one evening, that fact alone would not support the hasty generalization that your relationship is on the rocks. Provide enough facts, examples, statistics, and informed opinions to make your assertions believable.

Consider the inductive reasoning in this passage from a 1963 letter by Martin Luther King, Jr. to white clergy after he had been jailed for organizing a civil-rights demonstration in Birmingham, Alabama.

AN INDUCTIVE ARGUMENT

A key statistic (1)
Informed opinion (2)

Acknowledgment of opposing views (3)
Examples (4)

[1]We have waited for more than 340 years for our constitutional and God-given rights. [2]The nations of Asia and Africa are moving with jetlike speed toward gaining political independence, but we still creep at horse-and-buggy pace toward gaining a cup of coffee at a lunch counter. [3]Perhaps it is easy for those who have never felt the stinging darts of segregation to say, "Wait." [4]But when you have seen vicious mobs lynch your mothers and fathers at will and drown your sisters and brothers at whim; when you have seen hate-filled policemen curse, kick, and even kill your black brothers and sisters; when you have seen the vast majority of your twenty million Negro brothers smothering in an airtight cage of poverty in the midst of an affluent society; when you suddenly find your tongue twisted and your speech stammering as you seek to explain to your six-year-old daughter why she can't go to the public amusement park that has just been advertised on television, and see tears welling up in her eyes when she is told that Funtown is closed to colored children, and see ominous clouds of inferiority beginning to form in her little mental sky, and see her beginning to distort her personality by developing an unconscious bitterness toward white people; when you have to concoct an answer for a five-year-old son who is asking, "Daddy, why do white people treat colored people so mean?"; when you take a cross-country drive and find it necessary to sleep night after night in the uncomfortable corners of your automobile because no motel will accept you; when you are humiliated day in and day out by nagging signs reading "white" and "colored"; when your first name becomes "nigger," your middle name becomes "boy" (however old you are) and your last name becomes "john," and your wife and mother are never given the respected title "Mrs."; when you are harried by day and haunted by night by the fact that you are a Negro, living constantly at tiptoe stance, never quite knowing what to expect next, and are plagued with inner fears and outer resentments; when you are forever fighting a degenerating sense of "nobodiness"—then you will understand why we find it difficult to wait. [5]There comes a time when the cup of endurance runs over, and [people] are no longer willing to be plunged into the abyss of despair. [6]I hope, sirs, you can understand our legitimate and unavoidable impatience.

A generalization from specifics (5)
Main point as a direct appeal (6)

—*Martin Luther King, Jr.*

Notice how the inductive argument is organized: Sentence 4 carries the burden of support for Dr. King's stand. And the support itself is organized for greatest effect, with examples that progress from the injustice he has witnessed to the injustice he and his family have suffered to the humiliation he feels. Not only does he provide ample evidence to support his closing generalization (African Americans have reason to be impatient), but his evidence also adds up logically—and leads dramatically—to his conclusion.

Using Deduction

You reason deductively when you use generalizations to arrive at specific conclusions. Once the generalization "African Americans have legitimate cause for impatience" is established *inductively* (and accepted), one can argue deductively by applying the generalization to a specific instance:

Generalization	African Americans have legitimate cause for impatience
	↓
Specific instance	Ms. Gomes is African American.
	↓
Conclusion	Ms. Gomes has legitimate cause for impatience.

The conclusion is valid because (a) the generalization is accepted and (b) the specific instance is a fact. Both these conditions must exist in order for the conclusion to be sound.

Here is how you might use deductive reasoning daily:

Examples of deductive reasoning

- If you know that Professor Jones gives no make-up exams, and you sleep through her final, then you can expect to flunk her course.
- If you know that Batmobiles need frequent repairs, and you buy a Batmobile, then you can expect many repairs.

The soundness of deductive reasoning can be measured by sketching an argument in the form of a *syllogism,* the basic pattern of deductive arguments. Any syllogism has three parts: a major premise, a minor premise, and a conclusion:

A valid syllogism

All humans are mortal. [*Major premise*]

↓

Feliciana is human. [*Minor premise*]

↓

Feliciana is mortal. [*Conclusion*]

If readers accept both premises, they also must accept your conclusion. For the conclusion to be valid, the major premise must state an accepted generalization, and the minor premise must state a factual instance of that generalization. Moreover, the conclusion must express the same degree of certainty as the premises (that is, if a "usually" appears in a premise, it must appear in the conclusion, as well). Finally, the syllogism must be stated correctly, the minor premise linking its subject with the subject of the major premise; otherwise, the syllogism is faulty:

A faulty syllogism

All humans are mortal.
↓
John is mortal. [*Minor premise is stated incorrectly; all creatures are mortal, but not all are human.*]
↓
John is human.

Each premise in a syllogism actually is derived from inductive reasoning. Because every human being we've known so far has been mortal, we can reasonably conclude that all human beings are mortal. And once we have examined John thoroughly and classified him as human, we can connect the two premises to arrive at the conclusion that John is mortal.

Illogical deductive arguments may result from a faulty major premise (or generalization). We usually can verify a minor premise (as in the previous example, merely by observing John, to determine whether he is human). But the major premise is a generalization; unless we have enough inductive evidence, the generalization can be faulty. How much evidence is enough? Let your good judgment tell you. Base your premise on *reasonable* evidence, so that your generalization reflects reality as discerning people would recognize it. Avoid unreasonable premises such as these:

Faulty generalizations

All men are male chauvinists.
School is boring.
Long-haired men are drug addicts.
People can't be trusted.
Frailty, thy name is woman.

Notice the problem when one such generalization serves as the major premise in an argument:

What happens when the major premise is faulty

People can't be trusted. [*Major premise*]
↓
My grandparents are people. [*Minor premise*]
↓
My grandparents can't be trusted. [*Conclusion*]

In ordinary conversation, deductive arguments often are expressed as *enthymemes,* implicit syllogisms in which the generalizations are not stated explicitly; instead they are implied, or understood:

Enthymemes are implicit syllogisms

Joe is ruining his health with cigarettes. [*Implied generalization: Cigarette smoking ruins health.*]

Sally's low verbal scores on her college entrance exam suggest that she will need remedial help in composition. [*Implied generalization: Students with low verbal scores need extra help in composition.*]

Here's what happens to the conclusion when the unstated generalization is faulty:

Faulty enthymemes

> Martha is a feminist, and so she obviously hates men. [*All feminists hate men.*]
>
> He's a member of the clergy, and so what he says must be true. [*Clergy members never are mistaken or dishonest.*]

Another danger in deductive arguments is the overstated generalization, that is, making a limited generalization apply to all cases. Be sure to modify your assertions with qualifying words, such as **usually, often, sometimes,** and **some,** instead of absolute words, such as **always, all, never,** and **nobody:**

Overstated generalizations

> All Dobermans are vicious. [*Revised: "Some can be. . . "*]
>
> Politicians never keep their promises. [*Revised: "Some politicians seldom . . ."*]

In such cases, remember that the conclusion that follows must also be qualified.

A DEDUCTIVE ARGUMENT

> By focusing more on bits of knowledge rather than on critical thinking skills, standardized tests tend to hinder, rather than encourage, student achievement. Critics claim that standardized tests place excessive emphasis on recall and rote learning at the expense of analysis, judgment, inspiration, and reflection. Such tests encourage students to be passive learners who need only to recognize—not to construct—answers and solutions. They also promote the misleading impression that every problem or question has one, single, right answer. Finally, they trivialize knowledge and skill development by reducing whatever is taught to a fill-in-the-best-choice format. Aware of these objections, progressive learning communities nationwide are working to develop testing tools that stimulate the student's analytical and imaginative powers.
>
> —*Cheryl Hebert*

The deductive argument in the above paragraph runs like this:

Implied generalization

> Tests that focus on bits of knowledge rather than on critical thinking seem to do more harm than good.

Specific instance

> Standardized tests often focus on bits of knowledge.

Conclusion

> Therefore, standardized tests do more harm than good.

The argument is valid because it meets these criteria:

- The major premise is acceptable.
- The minor premise is verifiable.

- The argument is not overstated. Notice the limiting words.
  "tend to" [not *do*]
  "critics claim" [not *critics have proven*]
- The author limits her argument to *one* problem: How such tests may be defeating the aims of education (not how they might provide inaccurate assessment, or favor certain groups, or the like).

RECOGNIZING INVALID OR DECEPTIVE REASONING

Errors in inductive or deductive reasoning are called *fallacies*. Fallacies weaken an argument by (1) breaking the chain of logic or (2) evading the issue.

Fallacies That Break the Chain of Logic

In any valid reasoning pattern, one element logically follows from another (say, when a generalization is derived from credible evidence). But that logical chain can be broken by reasoning errors such as the following.

Faulty Generalizations.   We engage in faulty generalization when we jump from a limited observation to a sweeping conclusion. Even "proven" facts can invite mistaken conclusions.

Factual observations

> 1. "For the period 1992–2005, two-thirds of the fastest-growing occupations will call for no more than a high-school degree" (Harrison 62).
> 2. "Adult female brains are significantly smaller than male brains—about 8% smaller, on average" (Seligman 74).

How much can we generalize from these findings?

Invalid generalizations

> 1. Higher education . . . Who needs it?!
> 2. Women are the less intelligent gender.

When we accept findings uncritically and jump to conclusions about their meaning (as in 1, above) we commit the error of *hasty generalization*. When we overestimate the extent to which the findings reveal some larger truth (as in 2, above) we commit the error of *overstated generalization*.

The following generalizations are often repeated—but how true are they?

Faulty generalizations

> Teachers are mostly to blame for low test scores and poor discipline in public schools.
>
> Television is worthless.
>
> Humanities majors rarely get good jobs.

A common version of faulty generalization is *stereotyping*, the simplistic and trite assignment of characteristics to groups.

Stereotypes

> All politicians are crooks.
>
> Southern cops are brutal.
>
> The Irish are big drinkers.

Note

We often need to generalize, and we should. For example, countless studies support the generalization that fruits and vegetables help lower cancer risk. But we ordinarily limit general claims by inserting qualifiers such as "usually," "often," "sometimes," "probably," "possibly," or "some."

Faulty Causal Reasoning. Causal reasoning tries to explain *why* something happened or *what* will happen, often very complex questions. Anything but the simplest effect is likely to have multiple causes. Faulty causal reasoning oversimplifies or distorts the cause-effect relationship through errors like these:

Ignoring other causes

> Investment builds wealth. [*Ignores the role of knowledge, wisdom, timing, and luck in successful investing.*]

Ignoring other effects

> Running improves health. [*Ignores the fact that many runners get injured, and that some even drop dead while running.*]

Inventing a causal sequence

> Right after buying a rabbit's foot, Felix won the state lottery. [*Posits an unwarranted causal relationship merely because one event follows another—the* post hoc *fallacy.*]

Confusing correlation with causation

> Poverty causes disease. [*Ignores the fact that disease, while highly associated with poverty, has many causes unrelated to poverty.*]

Rationalizing

> My grades were poor because my exams were unfair. [*Denies the real causes of one's failures.*]

Media Researcher Robert Griffin identifies three criteria for demonstrating a causal relationship:

> Along with showing correlation [say, a measurable association between smoking and cancer], evidence of causality requires that the alleged causal agent occurs prior to the condition it causes (e.g., that smoking precedes the development of cancers) and—the most difficult task—that other explanations are discounted or accounted for. (240)

For example, studies found this correlation: People who eat lots of broccoli, cauliflower, and other "cruciferous" vegetables have lower rates of some cancers. But other explanations (say, that big veggie eaters might have many other healthful habits, as well) could not be ruled out until lab studies showed how a special protein in these vegetables actually protects human cells. (Wang 182)

Slippery-Slope. We ski the slippery slope when we make some overstated prediction that one action will initiate other actions or events that produce dire consequences.

Slippery-slope assertions

> Distributing condoms to high school students will lead to rampant promiscuity.
>
> Unless we stop Communist aggression in Viet Nam, all of Southeast Asia will fall to Communism.

Faulty Analogy. Our analogies are faulty when they overstate the similarities between the two items being compared.

Faulty analogies

> All my friends' parents are allowing them to hitchhike across the country. Why can't I?
>
> In many instances, cancer cells can be eliminated by the appropriate treatment. Since violent criminals are a societal cancer, they should be eliminated by capital punishment.

Question Begging. You beg the question when you base your argument on a claim that remains to be proven. In other words, you commit the fault of circular reasoning by "begging" readers to automatically accept an unproven premise:

Assertions that beg the question

> Useless subjects like composition should not be required.
>
> Voters should reject Candidate X's unfair accusation.
>
> Books like X and Y, which destroy the morals of our children, should be banned from school libraries.

If a subject is useless, obviously it should not be required. But a subject's uselessness is precisely what has to be established. Likewise, Candidate X's accusation has to be proven unfair, and books such as X and Y have to be proven corrupting.

Either/Or Thinking. You commit the either/or fallacy when you reduce an array of choices to a dilemma: only two extreme positions or sides—black or white—even though other choices exist.

False dilemmas

> Students deserve the opportunity to do their best work. But deadlines force students to hand in something not carefully done, just to make sure it's on time. [*Ignores the possibility of doing it on time* and *doing it well.*]
>
> We have the choice between polluting our atmosphere or living without energy. [*Leaves out the possibility of generating clean energy.*]
>
> Marry me or I'll join the monastery.

Arguing from Ignorance. We argue from ignorance when we contend that an assertion is true because it has not been proven false—or that the assertion is false because it has not been proven true.

Arguments from ignorance

> Drunk-driving laws are absurd: I know loads of people who drink and drive and who have never had an accident.
>
> Since the defendant can't offer evidence to prove her innocence, she must be guilty.

Fallacies That Evade the Issue

A deceptive argument clouds the main issue with fallacies such as the following.

Red Herring. Named after the practice of dragging a dead herring across a game trail to distract hunting dogs from their prey, this strategy aims at deflecting attention from the main issue. The distraction commonly involves an attempt to rationalize one's bad action by making it seem insignificant or by pointing to similar actions by others.

Trivializing one's bad action

Asserting that two wrongs make a right

> Except for my drunk-driving arrest, I've always been a law-abiding citizen.
>
> Sure, I bought my term paper from the CollegeSucks Web site, but so do lots of other students.

Bandwagon Appeal. The bandwagon approach urges readers to climb aboard by claiming that everyone else is doing it.

Bandwagon appeals

> This book is a best-seller. How could you ignore it?
>
> More Cadillac owners are switching to Continental than ever before. [*Of course, if the numbers provided real evidence, the assertion would be legitimate.*]

Irrational Appeals to Emotion. As we will see in the next section, some appeals to emotions (pity, fear, and the like) are perfectly legitimate. But you avoid the question when you distract readers from the real issue with material that is irrelevant or that obscures the issue by making an irrational appeal to emotions.

An appeal to pity

> He should not be punished for his assault conviction because as a child he was beaten severely by his parents. [*Has no legal bearing on the real issue: his crime.*]

An appeal to fear

> If we outlaw guns, only outlaws will have guns. [*Ignores the deaths and injuries caused by "legally owned" guns.*]

An appeal to normalcy

> She is the best person for the teaching job because she is happily married and has two lovely children. [*Has nothing to do with the real issue: her qualifications as a teacher.*]

An appeal to flattery	A person with your sophistication surely will agree that marriage is outmoded. [*Has nothing to do with the conclusion that remains to be verified.*]
An appeal to authority or patriotism	Uncle Sam stands behind savings bonds. [*Ignores the question of whether savings bonds are a good investment: Although they are safe, they pay lower interest than many other investments.*]

The snob appeal to emotion persuades readers to accept your assertion because they want to be identified with respected or notable people.

Snob appeal	"I want to be like Mike." [*Has nothing to do with the quality of the sneakers or hamburgers or other items being marketed.*]
	No All-American sports hero could be guilty of such a horrible crime. [*Ignores the evidence.*]

Attacking Your Opponent.   Another way to ignore the real question is by attacking your opponent through name-calling or derogatory statements about this person on the basis of age, gender, political or sexual orientation, or the like (ad hominem argument):

Ad hominem attacks	The effete intellectual snobs in academia have no right to criticize our increase in military spending. [*Calling people names does not discredit their argument.*]
	How could any man be expected to understand a woman's emotional needs?
	College students are too immature to know what they want, so why should they have a say in the college curriculum?

Instead of attacking the person, focus on refuting the argument.

Attacking a Strawperson.   You commit a Strawperson fallacy when you distort your opponent's position on the issue, and use that distortion as a basis for attack.

Strawperson fallacy	Feminists won't be satisfied until males are powerless.
	People oppose Affirmative Action because they refuse to give up their own, long-standing privilege.

When you set out to refute an argument, be sure to represent the opposing position accurately.

APPEALING TO EMOTION

Emotion is no substitute for reason, but some audiences are not persuaded by reason alone. In fact, the audience's attitude toward the writer is often the biggest factor in persuasion—no matter how solid the argument. Audiences are more receptive to people they like, trust, and respect.

Appeals to honesty, fairness, humor, and common sense are legitimate ways of enhancing a supportable argument. On the other hand, appeals to closed-mindedness, prejudice, paranoia, and ignorance (as in the logical fallacies covered earlier) merely hide the fact that an argument offers no authentic support.

Emotional transactions between writer and reader are complex, but the following strategies offer some guidance.

GUIDELINES FOR MAKING EMOTIONAL APPEALS

1. *Try to identify—empathize—with the reader's feelings.*
2. *Show respect for the reader's views.*
3. *Try to appear reasonable.*
4. *Know when and how to be forceful or satirical.*
5. *Know when to be humorous.*

Showing Empathy

To show empathy is to identify with the reader's feelings and to express genuine concern for the reader's welfare. Consider the lack of empathy in this next paragraph.

A MESSAGE THAT LACKS EMPATHY

Dear Buck,
After a good deal of thought I've decided to write to you about your weight problem. Let's face it: You're much too fat. Last week's shopping trip convinced me of that. Remember the bathing suit you liked, the one that came only in smaller sizes? If you lost weight, you might be able to fit into those kinds of suits. In addition to helping you look attractive, the loss of 30 or 40 pounds of ugly fat would improve your health. All you have to do is exercise more and eat less. I know it will work. Give me a call if you need any more help or suggestions.

This writer's superior tone can't help but alienate the reader. In this next version, he makes a distinct effort to empathize.

A MORE EMPATHETIC VERSION

Dear Buck,
Remember that great bathing suit we saw in Stuart's the other day, the one you thought would be perfect for the beach party but that didn't come in your size? Because the party is still three weeks away, why not begin dieting

and exercising so you can buy the suit? I know that losing weight is awfully hard, because I've had to struggle with that problem myself. Buck, you're one of my best friends, and you can count on me for support. A little effort on your part could make a big difference in your life.

Empathy is especially important in arguments that try getting the reader to *do* something.

Acknowledging Opposing Views

Before making your case, acknowledge the opposing case. This next writer takes a controversial position on a turning point in the high school experience. But by showing respect for the traditional view, she decreases readers' resistance to her own position.

AN ACKNOWLEDGMENT OF OPPOSING VIEWS

Orienting statement (1)

Acknowledgment of opposing view (2–3)

Writer's argument (4)

[1]From our first steps into high school we learn to anticipate an essential rite of passage: the senior prom—one of those memories that last a lifetime. [2]Traditionally, prom night suggests a magical time when it's fun to get dressed up, have pictures taken with your date, enjoy a fancy dinner, and party with your friends; then, after a perfect evening, you kiss your date goodnight and go home. [3]This fairy tale chain of events is how our parents recount their long-ago experiences and it persists as part of the prom image. [4]But this benign image too often masks the reality of a night polluted by drugs and sex, a night based on competition and looks, a night hyped to unbelievable proportions, only to become a total letdown.

—*Julia Schoonover*

Maintaining a Moderate Tone

People are more inclined to accept the viewpoint of someone they *like*—someone who seems reasonable. Never overstate your case to make your point. Stay away from emotionally loaded words that boil up in the heat of argument. This next writer is unlikely to win converts:

VOICE OF THE HOTHEAD

Scientists are the culprits responsible for the rape of our environment. Although we never see these beady-eyed, amoral eggheads actually destroying our world, they are busy in their laboratories scheming new ways for industrialists and developers to ravage the landscape, pollute the air, and turn all our rivers, lakes, and oceans into stinking sewers. How anybody with a conscience or a sense of decency would become a scientist is beyond me.

Granted, this piece is forceful and sincere and does suggest the legitimate point that scientists share responsibility—but the writer doesn't seem very likable. The paragraph is more an attack than an argument. Besides generalizing recklessly and providing no evidence for the assertions, the writer uses emotionally loaded words (**eggheads, stinking sewers**) that overstate the position and surely will make readers skeptical.

Here is another version of this paragraph. Understating the controversial point makes the argument more convincing:

A MORE REASONABLE TONE

[1]It might seem unfair to lay the blame for impending environmental disaster at the doorstep of the scientists. [2]Granted, the rape of the environment has been carried out, not by scientists, but by profiteering industrialists and myopic developers, with the eager support of a burgeoning population greedy to consume more than nature can provide and to waste more than nature can clear away. [3]But to absolve the scientific community from complicity in the matter is quite simply to ignore that science has been the only natural philosophy the western world has known since the age of Newton. [4]It is to ignore the key question: who provided us with the image of nature that invited the rape, and with the sensibility that licensed it? [5]It is not, after all, the normal thing for people to ruin their environment. [6]It is extraordinary and requires extraordinary incitement.

—*Theodore Roszak*

Notice how the above argument begins by acknowledging the opposing view (sentences 1–2). The tone is firm yet reasonable. When the writer points the blame at scientists, in sentences 3–4, he offers evidence.

Roszak softens his tone while making his point by using a rhetorical question in sentence 4. *Rhetorical questions* are really statements in the form of questions; because the answer is obvious, readers are invited (or challenged) to provide it for themselves. A rhetorical question can be a good way of impelling readers to confront the issue (as does the question in sentence 2 of the letter to Buck, page 322) without offending them.

But use rhetorical questions with caution. They can easily alienate readers, especially if the issue is personal.

RHETORICAL QUESTIONS USED OFFENSIVELY

Your constant tardiness is an inconvenience to everyone. It's impossible to rely on a person who is never on time. Do you know how many times I've waited in crummy weather for you to pick me up? What about all the appointments I've been late for? Or how about all the other social functions we haven't "quite" made it to on time? It's annoying to everyone when you're always late.

The tone above seems far too aggressive for the situation.

Some strong issues may deserve the emotional emphasis created by rhetorical questions. This is another kind of decision you need to make continually about your audience and purpose.

Using Satire in Appropriate Circumstances

Satire can be one vehicle for expressing forceful anger, frustration, or outrage without alienating readers. No one enjoys being "told off" or ridiculed, but sometimes a jolt of lucid observation—"telling it like it is"—might help readers overcome denial in order to face an issue realistically.

Satire usually relies on irony and sarcasm. *Irony* is a form of expression that states one thing while clearly meaning another, as in proclaiming a day in which everything has gone wrong as "simply wonderful!" *Sarcasm* employs a more blatant form of irony to mock or to ridicule. For instance, in the essay that follows, an undergraduate takes a hard look at the policy of eliminating "offensive" books from high school curricula.

As you read, think about how the satirical perspective forces a reexamination of attitudes.

SATIRE AS A PERSUASIVE STRATEGY

BONFIRE

I've uncovered the root of all evil today. It lurks in our schools and in our communities. It hides in children's rooms and sits on our coffee tables. Books cause all of society's problems, from drugs to homosexuality to irreverence.

Books like *Of Mice and Men* and *The Adventures of Huckleberry Finn* teach children violence, hatred, and blasphemy. After children read words like "damn," "hell," and "nigger," they will begin to use them. If they witness violence in literature, they will hit one another. After reading about George shooting Lenny in *Of Mice and Men,* they will regard killing their friends and carrying guns as acceptable. If they view a story like *Children of the Rainbow,* which contains homosexual characters, they will look at homosexuality in a positive light. Kids wouldn't think to become gay if they didn't read about it. *Brave New World* and books of that type teach our children to have sex. Teen pregnancy and overpopulation originate from romance novels about fornication. *Go Ask Alice* introduces readers to drugs and therefore contributes to our society's drug problems. Kids won't participate in such evils if they don't know they exist.

If we shield our children from the world's harsh realities, they will grow up respectable citizens. We do this by burning books. Nothing makes me smile more than the flaming corpse of a smutty novel. While other families make hamburgers and hot dogs on their grills, I barbecue Twain. The smoke of *War and Peace* refreshes my nostrils after a long day. I bought 27 copies of *Catcher in the Rye* for a bonfire last August and this Christmas my living room will glow with the flames of that ancient pornography, the *Bible.*

No writing conveys a positive message, for even Dr. Seuss distorts reality for children. We should shut down all libraries, all bookstores, and all schools and end the use of the written word. After burning all books, we should eliminate magazines, newspapers and credits at the end of movies.

Libraries house Satan worshippers. Their message reaches our children through the schools. If you see your children with a library card, a membership

> card to Lucifer's kingdom, I urge you to destroy it and punish them. The future depends on eliminating texts which show the horrors of society. Keep the fires of hell away from your doorstep by setting aflame the contents of our libraries and the volumes in your bathrooms.
>
> —*Adam Szymkowicz*

Some readers might feel offended or defensive about Adam's harsh assessment; however, satire deliberately seeks confrontation. So be sure that you understand its potential effect on your audience before deciding on a satirical perspective in your own writing.

Adding Humor Where Appropriate

Sometimes a bit of humor can rescue an argument that might cause hard feelings. In this next paragraph, the writer wanted to call attention to the delicate issue of his roommate's sloppiness.

HUMOR AS A PERSUASIVE STRATEGY

> Jack,
>
> If you never see me alive again, my body will be at the bottom of your dirty clothes pile that rises like a great mountain in the center of our room. How did I end up there? Well, while doing my math I ran out of paper and set out for my desk to get a few pieces—despite the risk I knew I was taking. I was met by a six-foot wall of dirty laundry. You know how small our room is; I could not circumnavigate the pile. I thought I'd better write this note before going to the janitor's room for a shovel to dig my way through to my desk. The going will be tough and I doubt I'll survive. If the hard work doesn't kill me, the toxic fumes will. Three years from now, when you finally decide to do your wash, just hang my body up as a reminder to stash your dirty clothes in your closet where they will be out of sight and out of smell.
>
> —*Your dead roommate*

Again, anticipate how your audience will react; otherwise, humor can backfire.

Whichever strategies you employ, don't allow your tone to be voiceless. Readers need to sense a real person behind the words.

Application **18-1**

The statements below are followed by false or improbable conclusions. What specific supporting evidence would be needed to justify each conclusion so that it is not a specious generalization? (First, you need to infer the missing generalization or premise; then you have to decide what evidence would be needed for the premise to be acceptable.) (Review pages 311–18.)

EXAMPLE

> Only 60 percent of incoming first-year students eventually graduate from this college. Therefore, the college is not doing its job.

To consider this conclusion valid, we would have to be shown that:

(a) All first-year students want to attend college in the first place.

(b) They are all capable of college-level work.

(c) They did all assigned work promptly and responsibly.

1. Abner always speeds but never has an accident. Therefore, he must be an excellent driver.
2. Fifty percent of last year's college graduates did not find the jobs they wanted. Therefore, college is a waste of time and money.
3. Olga never sees a doctor. Therefore, she must be healthy.
4. This house is expensive. Therefore, it must be well built.
5. Felix is flunking first-year composition. Therefore, he must be stupid.

Application **18-2**

PARAGRAPH WARM-UP: INDUCTIVE REASONING

Using Dr. King's paragraph (page 313) as a model, write a paragraph in which you use inductive reasoning to support a general conclusion about one of these subjects (after you have narrowed it) or about one of your own choice.

> highway safety   minorities
> a college core requirement   the legal drinking age
> the changing role of women   credit cards

Identify your audience and purpose. Provide enough evidence so that readers can follow your line of reasoning to its conclusion.

Application **18-3**

PARAGRAPH WARM-UP: DEDUCTIVE REASONING

Select an accepted generalization from this list or choose one of your own as the topic statement in a paragraph using deductive reasoning. (Review pages 314–17.)

- "Beauty is in the eye of the beholder."
- "That person is richest whose pleasures are the cheapest."

- Some teachers can have a great influence on a student's attitude toward a subject.
- A college degree doesn't guarantee career success.

Application **18-4**

Identify the fallacy in each of these sentences and revise the assertion to eliminate the error. (Review pages 317–21.)

EXAMPLE

Faulty   Television is worthless. [*sweeping generalization*]

Revised   Commercial television offers too few programs of educational value.

1. Big Goof received this chain letter, sent out twenty copies, and three days later won the lottery. Little Goof received this chain letter, threw it away, and fell off a cliff the next day.
2. Because our product is the best, it is worth the high price.
3. America—love it or leave it.
4. Three of my friends praise their Jettas, proving that Volkswagen makes the best car.
5. My grades last semester were poor because my exams were unfair.
6. Anyone who was expelled from Harvard for cheating could not be trusted as a president.
7. Until college students contribute to our society, they have no right to criticize our government.
8. Because Angela is a devout Christian, she will make a good doctor.
9. Anyone with common sense will vote for this candidate.
10. You should take up tennis; everyone else around here plays.
11. Hubert, a typical male, seems threatened by feminists.
12. Convex running shoes caused Karl Crane to win the Boston Marathon.
13. My doctor said "Mylanta."
14. How could voters expect any tax-and-spend liberal to know or understand the concerns of working people like us?
15. Sky diving is perfectly safe. After thirty dives, it hasn't killed me yet!
16. If non-smokers think their lungs are being violated by smokers, it's a fact of life. Fumes from vehicles, woodstoves, and incinerators all damage everyone's lungs. Should we ban these things, too?
17. Vote for me, or our nation is doomed.
18. How could we trust any promise made by that radical, rightwing nut?

19. Killing a bald eagle (a sacred American symbol) is a crime; therefore, burning the Flag (another sacred American symbol) should also be a crime.

20. If the present rate of immigration continues, U.S. workers will soon have no jobs left.

21. Gay-rights activists won't be satisfied until schools promote gay lifestyles for all students.

22. If everyone else filed honest tax returns, I would too.

23. "Among 20-year-olds in 1979, those who said that they smoked marijuana 11 to 50 times in the past year had an average IQ 15 percentile points higher than those who said they'd only smoked once" (Sklaroff and Ash 85). Pot, therefore, increases brain power.

Application **18-5**

Revise this next paragraph so that its tone is more moderate and reasonable, more like an intelligent argument than an attack. Feel free to add personal insights that might help the argument.

> People who argue that marijuana should remain outlawed are crazy. Beyond that, many of them are mere hypocrites—the boozers of our world who squander their salary in bars and come home to beat the wife and kids. Any intelligent person knows that alcohol burns out the brain, ruins the body, and destroys the personality. Marijuana is definitely safer: it leaves no hangover; it causes no physical damage or violent mood changes, as alcohol does; and it is not psychologically or physically addictive. Maybe if those redneck jerks who oppose marijuana would put down the beer cans and light a joint, the world would be a more peaceful place.

Application **18-6**

After reading this paragraph, answer the questions that follow.

> [1]Responsible agronomists report that before the end of the year millions of people, if unaided, might starve to death. [2]Half a billion deaths by starvation is not an uncommon estimate. [3]Even though the United States has done more than any other nation to feed the hungry, our relative affluence makes us morally vulnerable in the eyes of other nations and in our own eyes. [4]Garret Hardin, who has argued for a "lifeboat" ethic of survival (if you take all the passengers aboard, everybody drowns), admits that the decision not to feed all the hungry requires of us "a very hard psychological adjustment." [5]Indeed it would. [6]It has been estimated that the 3.5 million tons of fertilizer spread on American golf courses and lawns could provide up to 30 million tons of food in overseas agricultural production. [7]The nightmarish thought intrudes itself. [8]If we

as a nation allow people to starve while we could, through some sacrifice, make more food available to them, what hope can any person have for the future of international relations? [9]If we cannot agree on this most basic of values—feed the hungry—what hopes for the future can we entertain? [10]Technology is imitable and nuclear weaponry certain to proliferate. [11]What appeals to trust and respect can be made if the most rudimentary of moral impulses—feed the hungry—is not strenuously incorporated into national policy?

—James R. Kelly

1. Is this argument inductive or deductive? Explain.
2. Does the author appeal to our emotions? If so, where and how?
3. In which sentences does he support his position with hard evidence?
4. Restate the main point as a declarative sentence. Is the point arguable? Explain.
5. Are the rhetorical questions effective here? Explain.

Application **18-7**

Web-based Project: "Lurk" on a newsgroup for a couple of days and find examples of faulty logic used by some of the people who post.

Hint: For this and the following application, supplement the chapter's discussion of logical fallacies by visiting Stephen's Guide to the Logical Fallacies <**www.intrepidsoftware.com/fallacy/toc.htm**>.

Application **18-8**

Web-based Project: Look at the advertisements on the Web and discuss the types of arguments (and fallacies) used.

Works Cited

Griffin, Robert J. "Using Systematic Thinking to Choose and Evaluate Evidence." *Communicating Uncertainty: Media Coverage of New and Controversial Science.* Ed. Sharon Friedman, Sharon Dunwoody, and Carol Rogers. Mahwah, NJ: Erlbaum, 1999: 225–48.

Harrison, Bennett. "Don't Blame Technology This Time." *Technology Review* July 1997: 62.

Seligman, Dan. "Gender Mender." *Forbes* 6 Apr. 1998: 72+.

Sklaroff, Sara, and Michael Ash. "American Pie Charts." *Civilization* April/May 1997: 84–85.

Wang, Linda. "Veggies Prevent Cancer Through Key Protein." *Science News* 159.12 (2001): 182.

SECTION FOUR

The Research Process

Introduction—Thinking Critically
about the Research Process **332**

CHAPTER 19
Asking Questions and
Finding Answers **342**

CHAPTER 20
Recording, Evaluating, and
Interpreting Your Findings **368**

CHAPTER 21
Documenting Your Sources **392**

CHAPTER 22
Composing the Research Report **417**

CHAPTER 23
Case Study: A Sample
Research Project **438**

Introduction—Thinking Critically about the Research Process*

Asking the Right Questions   **334**

Exploring a Balance of Views   **334**

Achieving Adequate Depth in Your Search   **336**

Evaluating Your Findings   **337**

   Guidelines for Evaluating Expert Information   **338**

Interpreting Your Findings   **338**

We do research to obtain facts or expert opinions or to understand issues. For example, we might want to inquire about the prices of building lots on Boca Grande Island, the latest findings in AIDS research, or what experts are saying about global warming. Or, suppose you learn that your well water is contaminated with benzene. Should you merely ask your neighbor's opinion about the dangers, or should you track down the answers for yourself?

In the workplace, professionals need to locate all kinds of information daily (*How do we market this product? How do we avoid accidents like this one? Are we headed for a recession?*). We all have to know where and how to look for answers and how to communicate them *in writing*. Research is the way to find your own answers; a research report records and discusses your findings.

A *research report* involves a lot more than cooking up any old thesis, settling for the first material you happen to find, then blending in a few juicy quotations and paraphrases to "prove" you've done the assigned work. Re-

---

*My thanks to University of Massachusetts Dartmouth librarian Shaleen Barnes for inspiring this introduction.

search is a deliberate form of inquiry, a process of *problem solving*. And we cannot begin to solve the problem until we have clearly defined it.

Parts of the research process follow a recognizable sequence. The following steps shown in Figure IV.1 are treated in these chapters:

FIGURE IV.1
Procedural stages in the research process

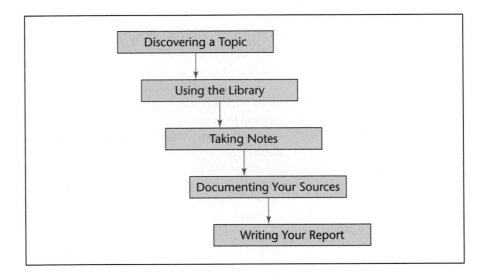

But research writing is never merely a "by-the-number" set of procedures ("First, do this; then do that"). The procedural stages depend on the many careful decisions that accompany any legitimate inquiry, depicted in Figure IV.2.

FIGURE IV.2
Inquiry stages in the research process

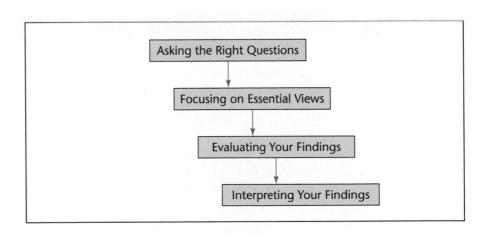

Let's consider how these inquiry stages of the research process lead to the kind of inquiry that makes a real difference.

The answers you uncover will depend on the questions you ask. Suppose, for instance, you've decided to research the following topic.

DEFINING AND REFINING A RESEARCH QUESTION

> The problem of violent crime on college campuses has received a good deal of recent publicity. So far your own school has been spared but, as a precautionary measure, campus decision makers are considering doubling the police force and allowing police to carry guns. Some groups are protesting, claiming that guns pose a needless hazard to students or that funding for additional police should be devoted to educational programs instead. On the student senate you and your colleagues have discussed the controversy, and you have been appointed to prepare a report that examines the trends regarding violent crime on campuses nationwide. Your report will form part of a document to be presented to the student and faculty senates in six weeks.

First, you need to identify the exact question or questions you want answered. Before settling on a definite question, you need to navigate a long list of possible questions, like those in the Figure IV.3 tree chart. Any *one* of the questions could serve as the topic of a worthwhile research report on such a complex topic.

Instead of settling for the most comforting or convenient answer, pursue the *best* answer. Even "expert" testimony may not be enough, because experts can disagree or be mistaken. To answer fairly and accurately, you are ethically obligated to consider a balance of perspectives from up-to-date and reputable sources (Figure IV.4).

Let's say you've chosen this question: *Violent crime on college campuses: How common is it?* Now you can consider sources to consult (journals, reports, news articles, Internet sites, database searches, and so on). Figure IV.5 lists some likely sources of information on college crime.

Note

Recognize the difference between "balance" (sampling a full range of opinions) and "accuracy" (getting at the facts). The media, for example, might present a more negative view than the facts warrant. Not every source is equal, nor should we report points of view as though they were equal (Trafford 137).

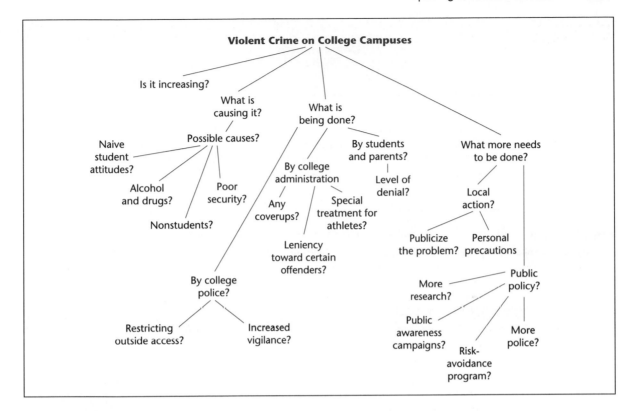

FIGURE IV.3
How the right questions help define a research problem. You cannot begin
to solve a problem until you have defined it clearly.

FIGURE IV.4
**Effective research consid-
ers multiple perspectives.**

Try to consider all the
angles.

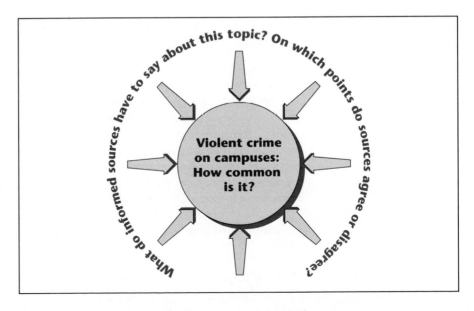

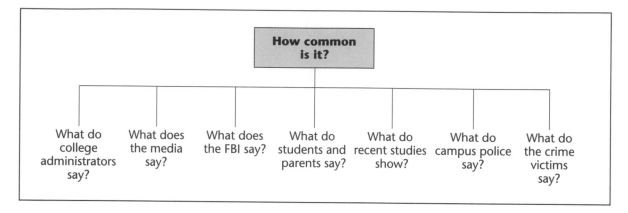

FIGURE IV.5
A range of essential viewpoints. No single source is likely to offer the "final word."

ACHIEVING ADEQUATE DEPTH IN YOUR SEARCH*

Balanced research examines a *broad range* of evidence; thorough research, however, examines that evidence in sufficient *depth*. Different sources of information have different levels of detail and dependability (Figure IV.6).

1. At the surface layer are items from the popular press (newspapers, radio, TV, magazines, certain Internet newsgroups and Web sites). Designed for general consumption, this layer of information often merely skims the surface of an issue.

2. At the next level are trade and business publications or Web sites (*Law Enforcement Digest, The Chronicle of Higher Education,* Internet listservs, and so on). Designed for readers who range from moderately informed to highly specialized, this layer of information focuses more on practice than on theory, on items considered newsworthy to group members, on issues affecting the field, and on public relations. While the information is usually accurate, viewpoints tend to reflect a field's particular biases.

3. At a deeper level is the specialized literature (journals from professional associations: academic, medical, legal, engineering, and so on). Designed for practicing professionals, this layer of information focuses on theory as well as practice: on descriptions of the latest studies (written by the researchers themselves and scrutinized by others for accuracy and objectivity), on debates among scholars and researchers, and on reviews and critiques of prior studies and publications.

---

*My thanks to University of Massachusetts Dartmouth librarian Ross LaBaugh for inspiring this section.

FIGURE IV.6
Effective research
achieves adequate depth.

The depth of a source
often determines its quality

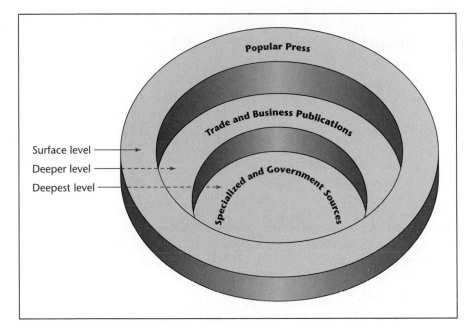

Surface level ————
Deeper level ————
Deepest level ————

Popular Press

Trade and Business Publications

Specialized and Government Sources

Also at this deeper level are government sources (studies and reports by NASA, EPA, FAA, FBI, the Congress) and corporate documents available through the Freedom of Information Act (page 358). Designed for anyone willing to investigate its complex resources, this layer of information offers hard facts and highly detailed and (in many instances) *relatively* impartial views.

Most of these sources are accessible via the Internet, through specialized search engines such as Lexis Nexis. Ask your librarian.

Note

Web pages, of course, offer links to increasingly specific levels of detail, but the actual "depth" and quality of information from a particular Web site ultimately depend on the sponsorship and reliability of that site (page 378).

How "deep" is deep enough? This depends on your topic. But the real story and the hard facts more likely reside at deeper levels. Research on college crime, for instance, would need to look beneath popular "headlines," focusing instead on studies done by experts.

EVALUATING YOUR FINDINGS

Not all findings have equal value. Some information might be distorted, incomplete, or misleading. Information might be tainted by *source bias*, in which a source might understate or overstate certain facts, depending on whose interests that source represents—say, college administrators, students, or a reporter seeking headlines.

GUIDELINES FOR EVALUATING EXPERT INFORMATION

To use expert information effectively, follow these suggestions:

1. *Look for common ground.* When opinions conflict, consult as many experts as possible and try to identify those areas in which they agree (Detjen 170)
2. *Consider all reasonable opinions.* Science writer Richard Harris notes that "Often [extreme views] are either ignored entirely or given equal weight in a story. Neither solution is satisfying. . . . Putting [the opinions] in balance means . . . telling . . . where an expert lies on the spectrum of opinion. . . . The minority opinion isn't necessarily wrong—just ask Galileo" (Harris 170).
3. *Be sure the expert's knowledge is relevant in this context.* Don't seek advice about a brain tumor from a podiatrist.
4. *Don't expect certainty.* In complex issues, experts cannot *eliminate* uncertainty; they can merely help us cope with it.
5. *Don't expect objectivity in all cases.* For example, the expert might have a financial or political stake in the issue or might hold a radical point of view.
6. *Expect special interests to produce their own experts to support their position.*
7. *Learn all you can about the issue before accepting anyone's final judgment.*

Questions for Evaluating a Particular Finding

- *Is this information accurate, reliable, and relatively unbiased?*
- *Can the claim be verified by the facts?*
- *How much of it (if any) is useful?*
- *Is this the whole or the real story?*
- *Do I need more information?*

Remember, ethical researchers don't try to prove the "rightness" of some initial assumptions; instead, they research to find the *right* answers. And only near the end of your inquiry can you settle on a *definite* thesis, based on what the facts suggest.

INTERPRETING YOUR FINDINGS

Once you have decided which of your findings seem legitimate, you must decide what they mean.

Questions for Interpreting Your Findings

- *What are my conclusions?*
- *Do any findings conflict?*
- *Are other interpretations possible?*

- *Should I reconsider the evidence?*
- *What, if anything, should be done?*

Even the best research can produce contradictory or indefinite conclusions. For example (Lederman 5): What does a reported increase in violent crime on U.S. college campuses mean—especially in light of national statistics that show violent crime decreasing?

- That college students are becoming more violent?
- That some drugs and guns in high schools end up on campuses?
- That off-campus criminals see students as easy targets?

Or could these findings mean something else entirely?

- That increased law enforcement has led to more campus arrests—and, thus, greater recognition of the problem?
- That crimes actually have not increased but fewer now go unreported?

Depending on our interpretation, we might conclude that the problem is worsening—or improving!

Note
> *Not all interpretations are equally valid. Never assume that any interpretation that is possible is also allowable—especially in terms of its ethical consequences. Certain interpretations in the college crime example, for instance, might justify an overly casual or overly vigilant response—either of which could have disastrous consequences.*

Figure IV.7 shows the critical-thinking decisions crucial to worthwhile research: asking the right questions about your topic, your sources, your findings, and your conclusions. Like the writing process (see Figure I.2), the research process is *recursive:* stages are revisited and repeated as often as necessary.

Note
> *Never force a simplistic conclusion on a complex issue. Sometimes the best you can offer is an indefinite conclusion. A wrong conclusion is far worse than no definite conclusion at all.*

Application **A**

Students in your major want a listing of one or two discipline-specific information sources from different depths of specialization.

FIGURE IV.7
Critical thinking in the
research process.

No single stage is
complete until all stages
are complete. Stages are
revisited as often as
necessary.

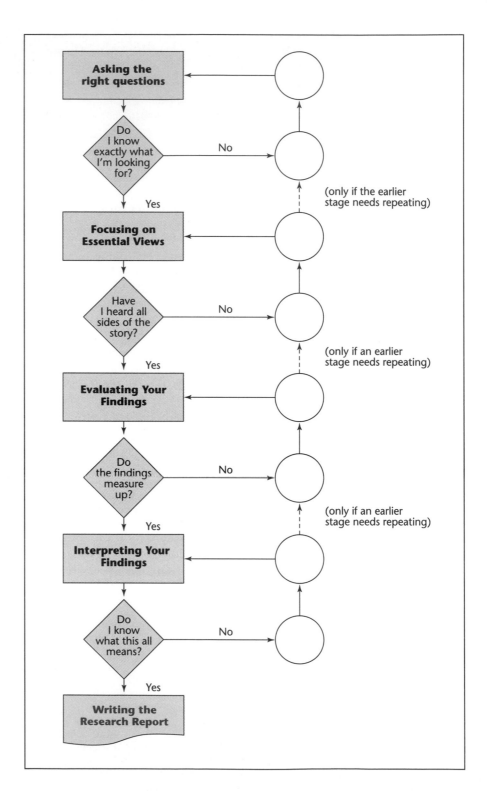

    a. the popular press (newspaper, radio, TV, magazines)

    b. trade/business publications (newsletters and trade magazines)

    c. professional literature (journals) and government sources (corporate data, technical reports, etc.)

Prepare the list (in memo form) and include a one-paragraph description of each source.

Application **B**

Web-based Project: Select a topic of interest from science or technology (benefits versus risks of genetically modified foods, feasibility of colonizing Mars, or the like). Survey expert opinions on this issue by consulting Web sources such as these:

- Ask Jeeves
  <www.askjeeves.com>
- Scientific American's "Ask the Experts" link at
  <www.sciam.com>
- Expert.com
  <www.expert.com>
- ExpertCentral.com
  <www.expertcentral.com>

Identify one example of each of the following:

- a point on which most experts agree
- a point on which many experts disagree
- an opinion that resides on a radical end of the spectrum (Cite the source clearly.)
- an opinion that seems influenced by financial or political motives (Cite the source clearly.)

Prepare a written report of your findings to be shared with the class. Attach copies of relevant Web pages to your report.

Works Cited

Detjen, Jim. "Environmental Writing." *A Field Guide for Science Writers.* Ed. Deborah Blum and Mary Knudson. New York: Oxford, 1997. 173–79.

Harris, Richard F. "Toxics and Risk Reporting." *A Field Guide for Science Writers.* Ed. Deborah Blum and Mary Knudson. New York: Oxford, 1997. 166–72.

Lederman, Douglas. "Colleges Report Rise in Violent Crime," *Chronicle of Higher Education* 3 Feb. 1995, sec. A: 5+.

Trafford, Abigail. "Critical Coverage of Public Health and Government." *A Field Guide for Science Writers.* Ed. Deborah Blum and Mary Knudson. New York: Oxford, 1997. 131–41.

CHAPTER 19

Asking Questions and Finding Answers

Deciding on a Research Topic   **343**

   Guidelines for Choosing a Research Topic   **343**

Primary versus Secondary Sources   **344**

Hard Copy versus Electronic Sources   **344**

Exploring Internet Sources   **345**

   Guidelines for Researching on the Internet   **348**

Exploring Other Electronic Sources   **350**

Keyword Searches Using Boolean Operators   **351**

Using Electronic Mail   **352**

Guidelines for Using Email   **353**

Exploring Hard Copy Sources   **354**

Informative Interviews   **359**

Surveys and Questionnaires   **359**

Inquiry Letters, Phone Calls, and Email Inquiries   **359**

Public Records and Organizational Publications   **359**

   Guidelines for Informative Interviews   **360**

Personal Observation   **362**

Applications   **362**

   Guidelines for Developing a Questionnaire   **364**

DECIDING ON A RESEARCH TOPIC

A crucial step in developing a research report is deciding on a worthwhile topic. Begin with a subject with real meaning for you, then decide on the specific question you want to ask about it. Pages 334–35 show how the subject of campus crime might be narrowed. Now let's try another subject.

Let's say you're disturbed about all the chemicals used to preserve or enhance flavor and color in foods—*food additives and preservatives.* What specific part of this subject would you like to focus on? This will be your *topic,* and it should be phrased as a question. To identify the possible questions you

GUIDELINES FOR CHOOSING A RESEARCH TOPIC

1. *Avoid topics that are too broad for a six- to twelve-page research report.* The topic "Do food additives and preservatives affect children?" would have to include children's growth and development, their intelligence, their susceptibility to diseases, and so on.

2. *Avoid topics that limit you to a fixed viewpoint before you've done your research:* "Which behavior disorders in children are caused by food additives and preservatives?" Presumably, you haven't yet established that such chemicals have any harmful effects. Your initial research is meant to find the facts, not to prove some point. Allow your thesis to grow from your collected facts, instead of manipulating the facts to fit your thesis.

3. *Avoid topics that have been exhausted:* abortion, capital punishment, gun control—unless, of course, you can approach such topics in a fresh way: "Could recent technological developments to help a fetus survive outside the womb cause the Supreme Court to reverse its 1973 ruling on abortion?"

4. *Avoid topics that can be summed up in an encyclopedia entry or in any one source:* "The Life of Thoreau," "How to Cross-Country Ski," or "The History of Microwave Technology." From a different angle, of course, any of these areas might allow you to draw your own, more interesting conclusions: "Was Thoreau Ever in Love?"; "How Do Injury Rates Compare Between Cross-Country and Downhill Skiing?"; "How Safe are Microwave Ovens?"

5. *Avoid religious, moral, or emotional topics that offer no objective basis for informed conclusions:* "Is Euthanasia Moral?"; "Will Jesus Save the World?"; "Should Prayer Be Allowed in Public Schools?" Questions debated throughout the ages by philosophers, judges, and social thinkers are unlikely to be definitively answered in your research paper.

6. *Consider narrowing your focus electronically.* For example, browse through subject and subtopic lists cataloged on *Yahoo!* <http://www.yahoo.com>. Continue exploring subtopics until you locate the right topic and the listing of related Web sites. Or explore subject categories at *WWW Virtual Library* <http://www.vlib.org>. Or scan more than 4,000 research topics listed in the *Idea Directory* at Researchpaper.com <http:www.researchpaper.com>.

might ask, develop a tree chart (as on page 335). Your interests might lead you to this question: *What effects, if any, do food additives and preservatives have on children's behavior?*

| Note |

Far more important than the topic you choose is the question you decide to ask about it. Plan to spend many hours in search of the right question.

PRIMARY VERSUS SECONDARY SOURCES

How primary and secondary sources differ

For many topics, you will want *primary* as well as *secondary* sources. Primary research is a firsthand study of the topic from observation, questionnaires, interviews, inquiry letters, works of literature, or personal documents. If your topic is the love life of Thoreau, a good primary source will be his poems, journals, and letters—or an interview with a specialist in the English department. Secondary research is based on information and conclusions that other researchers—by their primary research—have compiled in books and articles. Secondary sources are *about* primary sources. Whenever possible, combine these approaches.

HARD COPY VERSUS ELECTRONIC SOURCES

Although electronic searches for information are becoming the norm, a *thorough* search often requires careful examination of hard copy sources as well. Advantages and drawbacks of each search medium (Table 19.1) often provide good reason for exploring both.

Table 19.1   HARD COPY VERSUS ELECTRONIC SOURCES: BENEFITS AND DRAWBACKS

	BENEFITS	DRAWBACKS
Hard Copy Sources	• organized and searched by librarians • often screened by experts for accuracy • easier to preserve and keep secure	• time-consuming and inefficient to search • offer only text and images • hard to update
Electronic Sources	• more current, efficient, and accessible • searches can be narrowed or broadened • can offer material that has no hard copy equivalent	• access to recent material only • not always reliable • user might get lost

Benefits of hard copy sources

Hard copy libraries offer the judgment and expertise of librarians who organize and search for information. Compared with electronic files (on disks, tapes, hard drives), hard copy is easier to protect from tampering and to preserve from aging. (An electronic file's life span can be as brief as ten years.)

Note

For many automated searches, a manual search of hard copy is usually needed, as well. A manual search provides the whole "database" (the bound index or abstracts). As you browse, you often randomly discover something useful.

Drawbacks of hard copy sources

Manual searches (flipping pages by hand), however, are time-consuming and inefficient: Books can get lost; relevant information has to be pinpointed and retrieved or "pulled" by the user. Also, hard copy cannot be updated easily.

Benefits of electronic sources

Compared with hard copy, electronic sources are more current, efficient, and accessible. Sources are updated rapidly. Ten or fifteen years of an index can be reviewed in minutes. Searches can be customized: for example, narrowed to specific dates or topics. They also can be broadened: a keyword search (page 351) can uncover material that a hard copy search might have overlooked; Web pages can provide links to material of all sorts—much of which exists in hard copy form.

Drawbacks of electronic sources

Drawbacks of electronic sources include the fact that databases rarely contain entries published before the mid-1960s and that material, especially on the Internet, can change or disappear overnight or be highly unreliable. Also, given the potential for getting lost in cyberspace, a thorough electronic search calls for a preliminary conference with a trained librarian.

Note

One recent study found greater than 50 percent inconsistency among database indexers. Thus, even an electronic search by a trained librarian can miss improperly indexed material (Lang and Secic 174–75).

EXPLORING INTERNET SOURCES

Internet service providers (ISPs), including commercial services such as *CompuServe, America Online,* and *Microsoft Network,* provide Internet access via "gateways," along with aids for navigating its many resources (Figure 19.1). Following are common types of Internet sources.

Usenet

Usenet is a worldwide system for online discussions via newsgroups, a type of electronic bulletin board at which users post and share information and discuss topics of common interest via email.

Moderated newsgroups try to filter out unreliable material

Newsgroups are either *moderated* or *unmoderated.* In a moderated group, all contributions are evaluated by a reviewer who must approve the material before it can be posted. In an unmoderated group, any contribution at all gets posted. Most newsgroups are unmoderated and, thus, generally less reliable than moderated groups.

FIGURE 19.1
Various parts of the
Internet

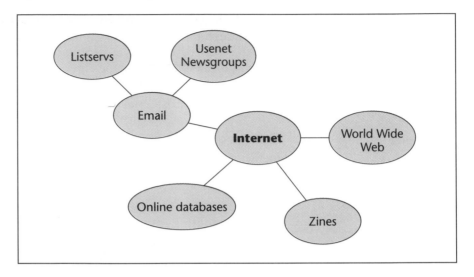

For a wealth of reliable information, consult *newsfeed* newsgroups, which post news items from wire services such as the Associated Press. Whereas newspapers can print only a fraction of the information received from wire services, newsfeed groups provide all of it online.

Newsgroups typically publish answers to frequently asked questions (FAQs) about a topic of interest (acupuncture, sexual harassment, and so on.). Although potentially informative, FAQs reflect the biases of those who contribute to and edit them (Maeglin 5). A group's particular convictions might politicize information and produce all sorts of inaccuracies (Snyder 90).

To locate newsgroups on any topic, go to <**www.lizt.com/news**>.

Listservs

Listservs usually are more specialized than newsgroups

A listserv is simply a computer-operated mailing list. Like newsgroups, listservs are special-interest groups for email discussion and information sharing. In contrast to newsgroups, listserv discussions usually focus on specialized topics, with discussions usually among experts (say, cancer researchers), often before their findings or opinions appear in published form. Many listservs include a FAQ listing.

Listserv access is available to subscribers who receive mailings automatically via email. Like a newsgroup, a listserv may be moderated or unmoderated, but subscribers/contributors are expected to observe proper Internet etiquette and to stick to discussion of the topic, without digressions, "flaming" (attacking someone), or "spamming" (posting irrelevant messages). Some lists allow anyone to subscribe, whereas others require that subscription requests be approved by the list owner. In general, only subscribers can post messages to the list.

To find listservs on your topic, go to **<www.lizt.com>** or **<http:// tile.net/lists>**.

Library Chatrooms

Major libraries are beginning to offer the research expertise of reference librarians on a round-the-clock basis via live chat. In response to a researcher query, the librarian locates the answer or guides the researcher to the appropriate sources (Kinik 38). See, for example, the Santa Monica Public Library site at **<www.smpl.org>**.

Electronic Magazines (E-zines)

E-zines offer information available only in electronic form. Despite the broad differences in quality among E-zines, this online medium offers certain benefits over hard copy magazines.

Benefits of online magazines

- links to related information
- immediate access to earlier magazine issues
- interactive forums for discussions among readers, writers, and editors
- rapid updating and error correction.

Major news publications and television and radio news programs also offer interactive editions online. Examples:

ABCNews
<www.abcnews.go.com>
National Public Radio
<www.npr.org>
PBS Online NewsHour
<www.pbs.org/newshour>

Email Inquiries

The global email network is excellent for contacting knowledgeable people in any field. Email addresses are increasingly accessible via locator programs that search various local directories listed on the Internet (Steinberg 27). But keep in mind that unsolicited and indiscriminate email inquiries might annoy the recipient.

Online reference librarians at the Library of Congress (see Appendix C for Web address) now respond directly to email queries from researchers or they forward the question to a member library (Kinik 38).

World Wide Web

The Web is a global network of databases, documents, images, and sounds. All types of information from anywhere in the Web network can be accessed and explored through navigation programs known as "browsers," such as *Netscape Navigator* or *Microsoft Internet Explorer*. Links among Web resources allow users to explore information along different paths by clicking on key words or icons.

Each Web site has its own *home page* that serves as an introduction to the site and is linked to additional "pages" that individual users can explore according to their information needs. To find various sites on the Web, we use two basic tools: *subject directories* and *search engines*.

Subject directories are maintained by humans

Subject Directories. Subject directories are compiled and maintained by editors who sift through countless Web sites and sort the most useful links into an index of subject categories. Popular subject directories include *Yahoo!* at <**www.yahoo.com**> and the *Internet Public Library* <**www.ipl.org**>; additional directories are listed in Appendix C. Supplementing these general directories are specialized directories (Quible 59) that focus on a single topic, such as software, health, or employment. See, for example, *Beaucoup* at

---

GUIDELINES FOR RESEARCHING ON THE INTERNET*

1. *Focus your search beforehand.* The more precisely you identify the information you seek, the less your chance of wandering through cyberspace.

2. *Select key words or search phrases that are varied and technical, rather than general.* Some search terms generate better hits than others. In addition to "food additives," for example, try "monosodium glutamate," "sugar and hyperactivity," or "attention deficit disorder." Specialized terms (for example, *vertigo* versus *dizziness*) offer the best access to sites that are reliable, professional, and specific. Always check your spelling.

3. *Look for Web sites that are specific.* Compile a *hotlist* of sites that are most relevant to your needs and interests. (Specialized newsletters and trade publications offer good site listings.)

4. *Set a time limit for searching.* Set a 10- to 15-minute time limit, and avoid tangents.

5. *Expect limited results from any search engine.* Each search engine (*Alta Vista, Excite, Hot Bot, Infoseek, WebCrawler*—see Appendix C) has strengths and weaknesses. Some are faster and more thorough, while others yield more targeted and updated hits. Some search titles only—instead of full text—for key words. No single search engine can index more than a fraction of rapidly increasing Web content. Broaden your coverage by using multiple engines.

6. *Use bookmarks and hotlists for quick access to favorite Web sites.* Mark a useful site with a bookmark and add it to your hotlist.

7. *Expect material on the Internet to have a brief life span.* Site addresses can change overnight; material is rapidly updated or discarded. If you find something of special value, save or print it before it changes or disappears.

<www.beaucoup.com> for a listing of hundreds of specialized directories (and search engines) organized by category.

Most search engines are maintained by computers

Search Engines. Instead of offering a directory of subject categories, search engines such as *Alta Vista* <**www.altavista.com**> scan for Web sites containing specific key words. Because most search engines are maintained exclusively by computers instead of people, none of the information gets filtered, evaluated, or organized. Even though search engines yield a lot more information than subject directories, much of it can be irrelevant or useless. Some search engines, however, are more selective than others, and some, such as *SearchIQ* <**www.searchiq.com**>, focus on specialized topics. See Appendix C for a list and description of various search engines.

Note

Assume that any material obtained from the Internet is protected by copyright. Before using this material anywhere other than in a college paper (properly documented), obtain written permission from its owner.

8. *Be selective about what you download.* Download only what you need. Unless they are crucial to your research, omit graphics, sound, and video files because these consume time and disk space. Focus on text files only.

9. *Never download copyrighted material without written authorization from the copyright holder.* It can be a federal crime to possess or give out electronic copies of copyrighted material without permission. Only material in the public domain is exempted. Such crimes are punishable by heavy fines and prison sentences.

   Before downloading *anything* from the Internet, ask yourself: "Am I violating someone's privacy (as in forwarding an email or a newsgroup entry)?" or "Am I decreasing, in any way, the value of this material for the person who owns it?" Obtain permission beforehand, and cite the source.

10. *Consider using information retrieval services.* An electronic service, such as *Inquisit* or *Dialog,* protects copyright holders by selling access to all materials in its database. For a monthly fee and or per-page fee, users can download full texts of articles. Subscribers to these Internet-accessible databases include companies and educational institutions. Check with your library.

    One drawback is that these retrieval services do not catalog material that exists only in electronic form (E-zines, newsgroup and listserv entries, and so on). Therefore, these databases exclude potentially valuable material (such as research studies not yet available in hard copy) accessible only through a general Web search.

*Guidelines adapted from Baker 57+; Branscum 78; Busiel and Maeglin 39–40, 76; Fugate 40–41; Kawasaki "Get" 156; Matson 249–52.

EXPLORING OTHER ELECTRONIC SOURCES

In addition to the Internet, other electronic technologies are used for storing and retrieving information. These technologies are accessible at libraries and, increasingly, via the Web.

Compact Discs

A single CD-ROM disc can store the equivalent of an entire encyclopedia and serves as a portable database, usually searchable via keyword. One useful CD-ROM for business information is *ProQuest*™: its ABI/INFORM database offers full text of over 600 management, marketing, and business journals published since 1989, along with indexes and abstracts of roughly 1,500 journals from the 1970s onward; its *UMI* database indexes major U.S. newspapers. A useful CD-ROM for information about psychology, nursing, education, and social policy is *SilverPlatter*™.

Note

> *In many cases, CD-ROM access via the Internet is restricted to users who have their own passwords for entering a particular library's information system.*

Online Retrieval Services

College libraries and corporations subscribe to online services that can access thousands of databases stored on centralized computers. Compared with CDs, mainframe databases are usually more specialized and more current, often updated daily (as opposed to weekly, monthly, or quarterly updating of CD databases). Online retrieval services offer three types of databases: bibliographic, full-text, and factual (Lavin 14):

Types of online databases

- *Bibliographic databases* list publications in a particular field and sometimes include abstracts of each entry.
- *Full-text databases* display the entire article or document (usually excluding graphics) directly on the computer screen, then will print the article on command.
- *Factual databases* provide facts of all kinds: global and up-to-the-minute stock quotations, weather data, lists of new patents filed, and credit ratings of major companies, to name a few.

Here are four popular database services:

- OCLC and RLIN. You easily can compile a comprehensive list of works on your subject at any library that belongs to an electronic consortium such as the Online Computer Library Center (OCLC) or the Research Libraries Information Network (RLIN). OCLC and RLIN databases are essentially giant electronic card catalogs. Using a networked terminal, you can search these databases by subject, title, or author.

- DIALOG. Many libraries subscribe to DIALOG, a network of more than 150 independent databases covering a range of subjects and searched by keywords. The system provides bibliographies and abstracts of the most recent articles on your topic. DIALOG databases include *Conference Papers Index, Electronic Yellow Pages* (for retailers, services, manufacturers), and *ENVIROLINE.*
- BRS. Bibliographic Retrieval Services (BRS), another popular database network, provides bibliographies and abstracts from life sciences, physical sciences, business, or social sciences. BRS databases include *Dissertation Abstracts International, Harvard Business Review,* and *Pollution Abstracts.*

Comprehensive databases networks, such as *DIALOG* and *BRS,* are accessible via the Internet for a fee. Specialized databases, such as MEDLINE or ENVIROLINE, offer free bibliographies and abstracts, and for a fee, copies of the full text can be ordered. Ask your librarian for help searching online databases.

Note   *Never assume that computers yield the best material. Database specialist Charles McNeil points out that "the material in the computer is what is cheapest to put there." Reference librarian Ross LaBaugh warns of a built-in bias in databases: "The company that assembles the bibliographic or full-text database often includes a disproportionate number of its own publications." Like any collection of information, a database can reflect the biases of its assemblers.*

Electronic Reference Books, Indexes, and Journals

Reference books and indexes, discussed in the section on hard copy sources, are increasingly available in electronic form. Also, hard copy journals are now increasingly available in *ejournal* format as well, with full text and editorials. Ask your librarian.

KEYWORD SEARCHES USING BOOLEAN OPERATORS

Most engines that search by keyword allow the use of Boolean* operators (commands such as AND, OR, NOT, and so on), to define relationships among various key words. Table 19.2 shows how these commands can expand a search or narrow it by generating fewer "hits."

Boolean commands also can be combined, as in

(additives *OR* preservatives) *AND* (health *OR* behavior)

The hits produced here would contain any of these combinations:

additives and health, additives and behavior, preservatives and health, preservatives and behavior

---

*British mathematician and logician George Boole (1815–1864) developed the system of symbolic logic (Boolean logic) now widely used in electronic information retrieval.

Table 19.2	USING BOOLEAN OPERATORS TO EXPAND OR LIMIT A SEARCH	
IF YOU ENTER THESE TERMS ...	**THE COMPUTER SEARCHES FOR ...**
food preservatives *AND* health	only entries that contain both terms
food preservatives *OR* health	all entries that contain either term
food preservatives *NOT* health	only entries that contain term 1 and do not contain term 2
food preserv*	all entries that contain this root within other words

Using *truncation* (cropping a word to its root and adding an asterisk), as in *preserv**, would produce a broad array of hits, including these:

> preserves, preservation, preservatives . . .

Different search engines use Boolean operators in slightly different ways; many include additional options (such as NEAR, to search for entries that contain search terms within ten or twenty words of each other). Click on the HELP option of your particular search engine to see which strategies it supports.

USING ELECTRONIC MAIL

Among the most widely used applications on or off the Internet, electronic mail connects to discussion forums on listserv, and usenets, and countless other networked locations across the globe.

Email benefits for writers and researchers

Compared to phone, fax, or conventional mail (or even face-to-face conversation, in some cases), email offers real advantages:

Email facilitates communication and collaboration

- *Email is fast, convenient, efficient, and relatively nonintrusive.* Unlike conventional mail, email travels instantly. Moreover, email makes for efficiency by eliminating "telephone tag." It is less intrusive than the telephone, offering recipients the choice of when to read a message or respond.
- *Email can foster creative thinking.* Email dialogues involve a give-and-take, much like a conversation. Writers feel encouraged to express their thoughts spontaneously as they write and respond—without worrying about page design, paragraph structure, or perfect phrasing. This relatively free exchange of views can lead to new insights or ideas (Bruhn 43).
- *Email is an excellent tool for collaborative work and research.* Collaborative teams keep in touch via email, and researchers contact people who have the answers they need. Documents or electronic files of any length can be attached and sent for downloading by the receiver.

GUIDELINES FOR USING EMAIL

Recipients who consider an email message poorly written, irrelevant, offensive, or inappropriate will only end up resenting the sender. These guidelines offer suggestions for effective email use.*

1. *Check and answer your email daily.* Like an unreturned phone call, unanswered email is annoying. If you're really busy, at least acknowledge receipt and respond later.

2. *Check your distribution list before each mailing.* Verify that your message will reach all intended recipients—but no unintended ones.

3. *Assume your email is permanent and could be read by anyone anytime.* Don't write anything you couldn't say to another person face to face. Avoid *spamming* (sending junk mail) and *flaming* (making rude remarks).

4. *Think twice before making humorous remarks.* What seems amusing to you may be offensive to others. Any email judged to be harassing or discriminatory can bring dire legal consequences.

5. *Don't use email to send confidential information.* Avoid complaining, criticizing, or evaluating people, or saying anything that should be kept private (say, a complaint against a fellow student).

6. *Before you forward an incoming message to other recipients, obtain permission from the sender.* Any email message you receive is copyrighted by the person who generated it. As the law now stands, forwarding this message to anyone for any purpose is a violation of the owner's copyright. Besides being an infringement of copyright, for-

warding a message without the original author's consent also violates that person's privacy.

7. *Limit your message to a single topic.* Remain focused and concise.

8. *Limit your message to a single screen, if possible.* Don't force recipients to scroll needlessly.

9. *Use a clear subject line to identify your topic.* ("Subject: Request for Make-up Exam in English 201.") Recipients can scan subject lines in deciding which new mail to read immediately. Messages also are easier to file and retrieve for later reference.

10. *Refer clearly to the message to which you are responding.* ("Here are the available meeting dates you requested on Oct. 10".)

11. *Keep sentences and paragraphs short, for easy reading.*

12. *Don't write in FULL CAPS—unless you want to SCREAM at the recipient!*

13. *Don't send huge attachments (or enclosures) without checking with the recipient.* Not all email browsers can handle formatted files, photos, and so on. Also, a recipient who has a slow Internet connection will take forever to download a long or complex attachment. Always ask beforehand about whether the recipient's browser can accept attachments and about which file types (*SimpleText, PDF file*, and so on) the equipment can handle.

*Adapted from Bruhn 43; "Email Etiquette 3;" Goodman 33–35, 167; Gurak and Lannon 186; Kawasaki, "The Rules" 286; Munger; Nantz, and Drexel 45–51; Peyser and Rhodes 82.

EXPLORING HARD COPY SOURCES

Where you begin your search of hard copy sources will depend on whether you are looking for background and basic facts or for the latest information. Library sources appear in Figure 19.2.

If you are an expert in the field, you might simply do a computerized database search or browse through specialized journals and listservs. If you have limited knowledge, you probably will want to begin with general reference sources.

Note

Librarian Ross LaBaugh suggests beginning with the popular, general literature, then working toward journals and other specialized sources: "The more accessible the source, the less valuable it is likely to be."

Reference Works

Reference sources provide background information

Reference works provide background that can lead to more specific information. Make sure the work is current by checking the last copyright date.

Bibliographies. These comprehensive lists of publications about a subject are generally issued yearly, or even more often. However, they quickly become dated. To locate the bibliographies published in your field, begin with the *Bibliographic Index,* a list (by subject) of bibliographies that contains at least 50 citations. To locate bibliographies on scientific and technical topics, consult *A Guide to U.S. Government Scientific and Technical Resources,* a list of everything published by the government in these broad fields. You might also look for bibliographies focused on a specific subject, such as *Health Hazards of Video Display Terminals: An Annotated Bibliography.*

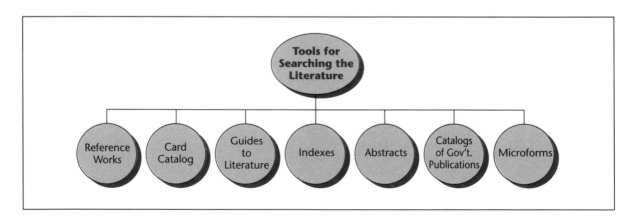

FIGURE 19.2
Ways of searching the literature. Many of these resources are now accessible via the Web.

Encyclopedias. Encyclopedias provide basic information (which might be outdated). Examples include *Encyclopedia of Building and Construction Terms, Encyclopedia of Banking and Finance, Encyclopedia of Food Technology.* The *Encyclopedia of Associations* lists over 30,000 professional organizations worldwide (American Medical Association, Institute of Electrical and Electronics Engineers, American Society of Women Accountants). Many such organizations can be accessed via their Web sites.

Dictionaries. Dictionaries may be generalized or they may focus on specific disciplines or give biographical information. Examples include the *Dictionary of Engineering and Technology, Dictionary of Telecommunications,* and *Dictionary of Scientific Biography.*

Handbooks. These research aids amass key facts (formulas, tables, advice, examples) about a field in condensed form. Examples include the *Business Writer's Handbook, Civil Engineering Handbook,* and *The McGraw-Hill Computer Handbook.*

Almanacs. Almanacs contain factual and statistical data. Examples include the *World Almanac and Book of Facts, Almanac for Computers,* and *Almanac of Business and Industrial Financial Ratios.*

Directories. Directories provide updated information about organizations, companies, people, products, services, or careers, often including addresses and phone numbers. Examples include *The Career Guide: Dun's Employment Opportunities Directory, Directory of American Firms Operating in Foreign Countries,* and *The Internet Directory.* For electronic versions of directories, ask your librarian about *Hoover's Company Capsules* (for basic information on more than 13,000 companies) and *Hoover's Company Profiles* (for detailed information on roughly 3,400 companies).

Reference works are increasingly accessible by computer. Some, such as the *Free Online Dictionary of Computing,* are wholly electronic.

Note	*Many of the reference works listed above are accessible at no charge via the Internet. Go to the Internet Public Library at <**www.ipl.org**> or consult Appendix C.*

Card Catalog

All books, reference works, indexes, periodicals, and other materials held by a library are usually listed in its card catalog under three headings: author, title, and subject. Most library card catalogs are no longer made up of actual cards; instead, they are electronic and can be accessed through the Internet or through terminals in the library. Visit the library's Web site or ask a librarian for help.

To search catalogs from many different libraries, go to the Library of Congress Gateway at <**http://lcweb.loc.gov/Z3950/gateway.html#other**> or

LibrarySpot at <**www.libraryspot.com**>, a gateway to over 5,000 libraries worldwide.

Guides to Literature

If you simply don't know which books, journals, indexes, and reference works are available for your topic, consult a guide to literature. For a general list of books in various disciplines, see Walford's *Guide to Reference Material* or Sheehy's *Guide to Reference Books.* For scientific and technical literature, consult Malinowsky and Richardson's *Science and Engineering Literature: A Guide to Reference Sources.* Ask a librarian about literature guides for your discipline.

Indexes

Indexes list current information

Indexes are lists of books, newspaper articles, journal articles, or other works on a particular subject.

Book Indexes.   A book index lists works by author, title, or subject. Sample indexes include *Scientific and Technical Books and Serials in Print* (an annual listing of literature in science and technology), *New Technical Books: A Selective List with Descriptive Annotations* (issued ten times yearly), and *Medical Books and Serials in Print* (an annual listing of works from medicine and psychology).

Note   *No book is likely to offer the very latest information because of the time required to publish a book manuscript (from several months to over a year).*

Newspaper Indexes.   These indexes list articles from major newspapers by subject. Sample titles include *The New York Times Index, Christian Science Monitor Index,* and the *Wall Street Journal Index.* Most newspapers and news magazines are searchable via their Web sites, and they usually charge a fee for searches of past issues.

Periodical Indexes.   A periodical index provides sources from magazines and journals. First, decide whether you seek general or specialized information. Two general indexes are the *Magazine Index* (a subject index on microfilm) and the *Reader's Guide to Periodical Literature* (updated every few weeks).

For specialized information, consult indexes that list journal articles by disciplines, such as *Ulrich's International Periodicals Directory, General Science Index, Applied Science and Technology Index,* or *Business Periodicals Index.* Specific disciplines have their own indexes, such as *Agricultural Index, Index to Legal Periodicals,* and the *International Nursing Index.*

Ask your librarian about the best indexes for your topic and about the many indexes searchable by computer. For example, the *Expanded Academic Index,* on CD-ROM, lists some 1,200 journals and provides full text and images from many of these works.

Citation Indexes. Citation indexes allow researchers to trace the development and refinement of a published idea. Using a citation index, you can track down the exact publications in which the original material has been cited, quoted, applied, critiqued, verified, or otherwise amplified (Garfield 200). In short, you can use them to answer this question: *Who else has said what about this idea?*

Web of Science (Science Citation Index Expanded) cross-references articles on science and technology from more than 5,700 major journals covering 164 scientific disciplines. The *Social Science Citation Index* is also searchable by computer.

Technical Report Indexes. Government and private sector reports prepared worldwide offer specialized and current information. Sample indexes include *Scientific and Technical Aerospace Reports, Government Reports Announcements and Index,* and the *Monthly Catalog of United States Government Publications.* Proprietary or security restrictions limit public access to certain corporate or government documents.

Indexes to Conference Proceedings. Many of the papers presented at the more than 10,000 yearly professional conferences are collected, then indexed in printed or computerized listings, such as *Proceedings in Print, Index to Scientific and Technical Proceedings,* and *Engineering Meetings* (an engineering index database). The very latest ideas, explorations, or advances in a field are often presented during such proceedings, before appearing as journal publications. Check your library's electronic resources to see which indexes are searchable by computer.

Abstracts

By indexing and summarizing each article, an abstract can save you from going all the way to the journal to decide whether to read the article or to skip it. Abstracts are usually titled by discipline: *Biological Abstracts, Computer Abstracts,* and so on. For some current research, consult abstracts of doctoral dissertations in *Dissertation Abstracts International.* Abstracts are increasingly searchable by computer; see, for example, *ComAbstracts* for abstracts of articles in the communications field.

Access Tools for U.S. Government Publications

The federal government publishes maps, periodicals, books, pamphlets, manuals, monographs, annual reports, research reports, and other information, often searchable by computer. A few of the countless titles include *Electromagnetic Fields in Your Environment, Major Oil and Gas Fields of the Free World,* and the *Journal of Research of the National Bureau of Standards.*

Your best bet for tapping this complex resource is to request assistance from the librarian in charge of government documents. Here are the basic access tools for documents issued or published at government expense, as well as for many privately sponsored documents.

Access tools

- *The Monthly Catalog of the United States Government,* the major pathway to government publications and reports.
- *Government Reports Announcements & Index,* a listing (with summaries) of more than a million federally sponsored research reports and patents since 1964.
- *The Statistical Abstract of the United States,* updated yearly, offers statistics on population, health, employment, and the like. It can be accessed via the World Wide Web. CD-ROM versions are available beginning with the 1997 edition.

Many unpublished documents are available under the Freedom of Information Act (FOIA). The FOIA grants public access to all federal agency records except for classified documents, trade secrets, certain law enforcement files, records protected by personal privacy law, and similar categories of exempted information.

Publicly accessible government records

Suppose you have heard that a certain toy has been recalled as a safety hazard and you want to know the details. In this case, the Consumer Product Safety Commission could help you. Perhaps you want to read the latest inspection report on conditions at a nursing home certified for Medicare. Your local Social Security office keeps such records on file. Or you might want to know if the Federal Bureau of Investigation has a file that includes you. In all these examples, you may use the FOIA to request information (U.S. General Services Administration 1).

Contact the agency that would hold the records you seek: for workplace accident reports, the Department of Labor; for industrial pollution records, the Environmental Protection Agency; and so on.

Government information is increasingly posted to the Web. For example, the Food and Drug Administration's electronic bulletin board at <**www.fda.gov**> on experimental drugs to fight AIDS, on drug recalls, and a host of related items; the Department of Energy at <**www.doe.gov**> has a Web page for information on human radiation experiments. A good starting point for government sites is the Library of Congress homepage at <**http://lcWeb.loc.gov**>. See Appendix C for other useful Web sites.

Microforms

Microform technology allows vast quantities of printed information to be stored on microfilm or microfiche. This material is read on machines that magnify the reduced image.

INFORMATIVE INTERVIEWS

An excellent source for information unavailable in any publication is the *personal interview*. Much of what an expert knows may never be published (Pugliano 6). Also, a respondent might refer you to other experts or sources of information.

Of course, an expert's opinion can be just as mistaken or biased as anyone else's (page 338). As medical patients, for example, we would seek second opinions about serious medical conditions. As researchers, we should seek a balanced range of expert opinions about a complex problem or controversial issue. For example, in assessing safety measures at a local nuclear power plant, we would question not only company spokespersons and environmentalists, but also independent and presumably more objective third parties, such as a professor or journalist who has studied the issue.

SURVEYS AND QUESTIONNAIRES

Surveys help us to develop profiles and estimates about the concerns, preferences, attitudes, beliefs, or perceptions of a large, identifiable group (a *target population*) by studying representatives of that group (a *sample group*).

- Do consumers prefer brand A or brand B?
- How many students on this campus are "nontraditional"?
- Is public confidence in technology increasing or decreasing?

The tool for conducting surveys is the questionnaire. While interviews allow for greater clarity and depth, questionnaires offer an inexpensive way to survey a large group. Respondents can answer privately and anonymously—and often more candidly than in an interview.

INQUIRY LETTERS, PHONE CALLS, AND EMAIL INQUIRIES

Letters, phone calls, or email inquiries to experts listed in Web pages are handy for obtaining specific information from government agencies, legislators, private companies, university research centers, trade associations, and research foundations such as the Brookings Institution and the Rand Corporation (Lavin 9). Keep in mind that unsolicited inquiries, especially by phone or email, can be intrusive and offensive.

PUBLIC RECORDS AND ORGANIZATIONAL PUBLICATIONS

The Freedom of Information Act and state public record laws grant access to an array of government, corporate, and organizational documents. Obtain-

GUIDELINES FOR INFORMATIVE INTERVIEWS*

Planning the Interview

1. *Focus on your purpose.* Determine exactly what you hope to learn from this interview. Write out your purpose.

Purpose statement

I will interview Carol Bono, campus police chief, to ask her about specific campus safety measures being proposed and implemented.

2. *Do your homework.* Learn all you can about the topic beforehand. If the respondent has published anything relevant, read it before the interview. Be sure the information this person might provide is unavailable in print.

3. *Request the interview at your respondent's convenience.* Give the respondent ample notice and time to prepare, and ask whether she/he objects to being quoted or taped. If possible, submit a list of questions well before the actual interview.

Preparing the Questions

1. *Make each question unambiguous and specific.* Avoid questions that can be answered with a simple "yes" or "no."

An unproductive question

In your opinion, can campus safety be improved?

Instead, phrase your question to elicit a detailed response:

A productive question

Of the various measures being proposed or considered, which do you consider most effective?

This is one instance in which your earlier homework pays off.

2. *Avoid loaded questions.* A loaded question invites or promotes a particular bias:

A loaded question

Wouldn't you agree that campus safety problems have been overstated?

An impartial question does not influence the interviewee to respond in a certain way.

An impartial question

In your opinion, have campus safety problems been accurately stated, overstated, or understated?

3. *Save the most difficult, complex, or sensitive questions for last.* Leading off with your toughest questions might annoy respondents, making them uncooperative.

4. *Write out each question on a separate notecard.* Use the notecard to summarize the responses during the interview.

Conducting the Interview

1. *Make a good start.* Arrive on time; thank your respondent; restate your purpose; explain why you believe he/she can be helpful; explain exactly how the information will be used.

2. *Ask questions clearly, in the order you prepared them.*

3. *Let the respondent do most of the talking.* Keep opinions to yourself.

4. *Be a good listener.* Don't fidget, stare out the window, or doodle.

5. *Stick to your interview plan.* If the respondent wanders, politely nudge the conversation back on track (unless the additional information is useful).

6. *Ask for clarification or explanation.* If you don't understand an answer, say so. Request an example, an analogy, or a simplified version—and keep asking until you understand.

Clarifying questions

- Could you go over that again?
- Is there a simpler explanation?

7. *Keep checking on your understanding.* Repeat major points in your own words and ask whether the details are accurate and whether your interpretation is correct.

8. *Be ready with follow-up questions.* Some answers may reveal new directions for the interview.

Follow-up questions

- Why is it like that?
- Could you say something more about that?
- What more needs to be done?
- What happened next?

9. *Keep note taking to a minimum.* Record statistics, dates, names, and other precise data, but don't record every word. Jot key terms or phrases that later can refresh your memory.

Concluding the Interview

1. *Ask for closing comments.* Perhaps the respondent can lead you to additional information.

Concluding questions

- Would you care to add anything?
- Is there anyone else I should talk to?
- Is there anyone who has a different point of view?
- Are there any other sources you are aware of that might help me better understand this issue?

2. *Request permission to follow up.* If additional questions arise, you might need to contact the respondent again, perhaps by phone, email, or fax—depending on the complexity of the questions and on the respondent's preference.

3. *Invite the respondent to review your version.* If the interview is to be published, ask the respondent to check your final draft for accuracy and to approve it before you quote him or her in print. Offer to provide copies of any document in which this information appears.

4. *Thank your respondent and leave promptly.*

5. *As soon as you leave the interview, write a complete summary* (or record one verbally). Do this while responses are fresh in your memory.

*Several guidelines are adapted from Blum 88; Dowd, 13–14; Hopkins-Tanne 23, 26; Kotulak 147; McDonald 190; Rensberger 15; Young 114, 115, 116.

ing these documents (from state or federal agencies) takes time, but in them you can find answers to questions like these (Blum 90–92):

Public records may hold answers to tough questions

- Which pharmaceutical companies are being investigated by the USDA (Dept. of Agriculture) for mistreating laboratory animals?
- Are IRS auditors required to meet quotas?
- What are the results of state and federal water-quality inspections in this region?

Most organizations publish pamphlets, brochures, annual reports, or prospectuses for consumers, employees, investors, or voters.

Note

Be alert for bias in company literature. In evaluating the safety measures at a local nuclear power plant, you would want the complete picture. Along with the company's literature, you would want studies and reports from government agencies and publications from environmental groups.

PERSONAL OBSERVATION

If possible, amplify and verify your findings with a firsthand look. Observation should be your final step, because you now know what to look for. Know how, where, and when to look, and jot down observations immediately. You might even take photos or make drawings.

Note

Even direct observation is not foolproof: For instance, you might be biased about what you see (focusing on the wrong events or ignoring something important), or, instead of behaving normally, people being observed might behave in ways they believe you expect that they should (Adams and Schvaneveldt 244).

Application 19-1

Prepare a research report by completing these steps. (Your instructor might establish a timetable for your process.)

PHASE ONE: PRELIMINARY STEPS

1. Choose a topic of *immediate practical importance,* something that affects you or your community directly. Develop a tree chart to help you ask the right questions.
2. Identify a specific audience and its intended use of your information.
3. Narrow your topic, checking with your instructor for approval and advice.
4. Identify the various viewpoints that will lead to your own balanced viewpoint.
5. Make a working bibliography to ensure sufficient primary and secondary resources. Don't delay this step!
6. List the information you already have about your topic.

7. Submit a clear statement of purpose to your instructor.
8. Make a working outline.

PHASE TWO: COLLECTING, EVALUATING AND INTERPRETING DATA

Read Chapter 20 in preparation for this phase.

1. In your research, move from the general to the specific; begin with general reference works for an overview.
2. Skim the sources, looking for high points.
3. Evaluate each finding for accuracy, reliability, fairness, and completeness.
4. Take notes *selectively.* Use notecards or electronic file software.
5. Decide what your findings mean.
6. Settle on your thesis.
7. Use the checklist on page 389 to assess your methods, interpretations, and reasoning.

PHASE THREE: ORGANIZING YOUR DATA AND WRITING THE REPORT

1. Revise your working outline, as needed.
2. Follow the introduction-body-conclusion format.
3. Fully document all sources of information.
4. Write your final draft according to the checklist on page 420.
5. Proofread carefully.

DUE DATES

- List of possible topics due: _____
- Final topic due: _____
- Working bibliography and working outline due: _____
- Notecards due: _____
- Revised outline due: _____
- First draft of report due: _____
- Final draft of report with full documentation due: _____

Application **19-2**

Collaborative Project: (For this assignment, please read Chapter 20, pages 376–87.) Divide into small groups and prepare a comparative evaluation of literature search media. Each group member will select one of the resources listed below and create an individual bibliography (listing at least twelve recent and relevant works on a specific topic of interest selected by the group):

- conventional print media
- electronic catalogs
- CD-ROM services
- a commercial database service, such as DIALOG

GUIDELINES FOR DEVELOPING A QUESTIONNAIRE

1. *Decide on the types of questions* (Adams and Schvaneveldt 202–12; Velotta 390). Questions can be *open-ended* or *closed-ended*. Open-ended questions allow respondents to express exactly what they're thinking or feeling in a word, phrase, sentence, or short essay:

Open-ended questions

- How much do you know about crime at our school?
- What do you think should be done about crime at our school?

Because one never knows what people will say, open-ended questions are a good way to uncover attitudes and obtain unexpected information. But essay-type questions are hard to answer and tabulate.

When you want to measure exactly where people stand, choose closed-ended questions:

Closed-ended questions

Are you interested in joining a group of concerned students?

| YES _____   NO _____

Rate your degree of concern about crime problems at our school.

| HIGH _____ MODERATE _____
| LOW _____ NO CONCERN _____

- Circle the number that indicates your view about the administration's proposal to allow campus police to carry handguns.

1 . . . . 2 . . . . 3 . . . . 4 . . . . 5 . . . . 6 7
STRONGLY   NO   STRONGLY
DISAPPROVE   OPINION   APPROVE

Respondents may be asked to *rate* one item on a scale (from high to low, best to worst), to *rank* two or more items (by importance, desirability), or to select items from a list. Other questions measure percentages or frequency:

How often do you . . . ?
ALWAYS _____ OFTEN _____
SOMETIMES _____ RARELY _____
NEVER _____

Although they are easy to answer, tabulate, and analyze, closed-ended questions create the potential for biased responses. Some people, for instance, automatically prefer items near the top of a list or the left side of a rating scale (Plumb and Spyridakis 633). Also, respondents are prone to agree rather than disagree with assertions in a questionnaire (Sherblom, Sullivan, and Sherblom 61).

2. *Design an engaging introduction and opening questions.* Persuade respondents that the survey relates to their concerns, that their answers matter, and that their anonymity is assured. Explain how respondents will benefit from your findings, or offer an incentive (say, a copy of your final report).

A survey introduction

Your answers will enable our Senate representative to convey your views about handguns for the campus police. Results of this survey will appear in our campus newspaper. Thank you.

Researchers often include a cover letter with the questionnaire. Begin with the easiest questions. Once respondents commit to these, they are likely to complete later, more difficult questions.

3. *Make each question unambiguous.* All respondents should be able to interpret identical questions in the same manner.

An ambiguous question

Do you favor weapons for campus police?

YES _____   NO _____

"Weapons" might mean tear gas, clubs, handguns, all three, or two out of three. Consequently, responses to the above question would produce a misleading statistic, such as "Over 95 percent of students favor handguns for campus police," when the accurate conclusion might really be "Over 95 percent of students favor some form of weapon." Moreover, the limited choice ("yes/no") reduces an array of possible opinions to an either/or response.

A clear and incisive question

Do you favor (check all that apply):

_____ Having campus police carry mace and a club?

_____ Having campus police carry nonlethal "stun guns"?

_____ Having campus police store handguns in their cruisers?

_____ Having campus police carry small-caliber handguns?

_____ Having campus police carry large-caliber handguns?

_____ Having campus police carry no weapons?

_____ Don't know

To ensure a full range of possible responses, include options such as "Other _____," "Don't know," "Not applicable," or an "Additional comments" section.

4. *Make each question unbiased.* Avoid loaded questions that invite or advocate a particular viewpoint or bias:

A loaded question

Should our campus tolerate the needless endangerment of innocent students by lethal weapons?

YES _____   NO _____

Emotionally loaded and judgmental words ("endangerment," "innocent," "tolerate," "needless," "lethal") in a survey are unethical because their built-in judgments manipulate people's responses (Hayakawa 40).

5. *Keep the questionnaire as short as possible.* Try to limit questions and their response spaces to two sides of a single page.

Respondents generally don't mind giving up some time to help, but long questionnaires usually get very few replies. And even when they do reply, people tend to give less thought and attention to their answers as a long survey progresses.

- the Internet and World Wide Web
- an electronic consortium of local libraries, if applicable

After carefully recording the findings and keeping track of the time spent in each search, compare the ease of searching and quality of results obtained from each type of search on your group's selected topic. Which medium yielded the most current sources (page 376)? Which provided abstracts and full texts, as well as bibliographic data? Which consumed the most time? Which provided the most dependable sources (page 377)? The most diverse or varied sources (page 334)? Which cost the most to use? Finally, which yielded the greatest depth of resources (page 336)? Prepare a report and present your findings to the class.

Works Cited

Adams, Gerald R., and Jay D. Schvaneveldt, *Understanding Research Methods.* New York: Longman, 1985.

Baker, Russ. "Surfer's Paradise." *Inc.* Nov. 1997: 57+.

Blum, Deborah. "Investigative Science Journalism." *Field Guide for Science Writers.* Ed. Deborah Blum and Mary Knudson. New York: Oxford, 1997. 86–93.

Branscum, Deborah. "bigbrother@the.office.com." *Newsweek* 27 Apr. 1998: 78.

Broody, Herb. "Clicking onto Webzines." *Technology Review* Aug./Sept. 1995: 24–35.

Bruhn, Mark J. "E-Mail's Conversational Value." *Business Communication Quarterly* 58.3 (1995): 43–44.

Busiel, Christopher, and Tom Maeglin. *Researching Online.* New York: Addison, 1998.

Dowd, Charles. "Conducting an Effective Journalistic Interview." *INTERCOM* May 1996: 12–14.

"Email Etiquette Revisited." *Manager's Legal Bulletin.* Ramsey, NJ: Alexander Hamilton Institute, 2000.

Fugate, Alice E. "Mastering Search Tools for the Internet." *INTERCOM* Jan. 1998: 40–41.

Garfield, Eugene. "What Scientific Journals Can Tell Us about Scientific Journals." IEEE Transactions on Professional Communication 16.4(1973): 200–02.

Goodman, Danny. *Living at Light Speed.* New York: Random, 1994.

Gurak, Laura J., and John M. Lannon. *A Concise Guide to Technical Communication.* New York: Longman, 2001.

Hayakawa, S. I. *Language in Thought and Action.* 3rd ed. New York: Harcourt, 1972.

Hopkins-Tanne, Janice. "Writing Science for Magazines." *A Field Guide for Science Writers.* Ed. Deborah Blum and Mary Knudson. New York: Oxford, 1997. 17–26.

Kawasaki, Guy. "Get Your Facts Here." *Forbes* 23 Mar. 1998: 156.

———. "The Rules of E-Mail." *MACWORLD* Oct. 1995: 286.

Kinik, Karina. "The Library that Never Closes." *Forbes ASAP* 19 Jan. 2000: 38.

Kotulak, Ronald. "Reporting on Biology of Behavior." *A Field Guide for Science Writers.* Ed. Deborah Blum and Mary Knudson. New York: Oxford, 1997. 142–51.

Lang, Thomas A., and Michelle Secic. *How to Report Statistics in Medicine.* Philadelphia: American College of Physicians, 1997.

Lavin, Michael R. *Business Information: How to Find It. How to Use It.* 2nd ed. Phoenix, AZ: Oryx, 1992.

Maeglin, Thomas. Unpublished review.

Matson, Eric. "(Search) Engines." *Fast Company* Oct./Nov. 1997: 249–52.

McDonald, Kim A. "Covering Physics." *A Field Guide for Science Writers.* Ed. Deborah Blum and Mary Knudson. New York: Oxford, 1997. 188–95.

Munger, David. Unpublished review.

Nantz, Karen S., and Cynthia L. Drexel. "Incorporating Electronic Mail with the Business Communication Course." *Business Communication Quarterly* 58.3 (1995): 45–51.

Peyser, Marc, and Steve Rhodes. "When E-Mail Is Oops-Mail." *Newsweek* 16 Oct. 1995: 82.

Plumb, Carolyn, and Jan H. Spyridakis, "Survey Research in Technical Communication: Designing and Administering Questionnaires." *Technical Communication* 39.4 (1992): 625–38.

Pugliano, Fiore. Unpublished review.

Quible, Zane K. "Guiding Students in Finding Information on the Web." *Business Communication Quarterly* 62.3 (Sept. 1999): 57–70.

Rensberger, Bayce. "Covering Science for Newspapers." *A Field Guide for Science Writers.* Ed. Deborah Blum and Mary Knudson. New York: Oxford, 1997. 7–16.

Sherblom, John C., Claire F. Sullivan, and Elizabeth C. Sherblom. "The What, the Whom, and the Hows of Survey Research." *Bulletin of the Association for Business Communication* 56:12 (1993): 58–64.

Snyder, Joel. "Finding It on Your Own." *Internet World* June 1995: 89–90.

Steinberg, Stephen. "Travels on the Net." *Technology Review* July 1994: 20–31.

U.S. General Services Administration. *Your Rights to Federal Records.* Washington: GPO, 1995.

Velotta, Christopher. "How to Design and Implement a Questionnaire." *Technical Communications* 38.3 (1991): 387–92.

Young, Patrick. "Writing about Articles for Science Journals." *A Field Guide for Science Writers.* Ed. Deborah Blum and Mary Knudson. New York: Oxford, 1997. 110–16.

CHAPTER 20

Recording, Evaluating, and Interpreting Your Findings

Taking Notes **369**

  Guidelines for Recording Research
  Findings **369**

Quoting the Work of Others **370**

  Guidelines for Quoting the Work of
  Others **370**

Paraphrasing the Work of
Others **372**

  Guidelines for Paraphrasing the Work
  of Others **373**

Preparing Summaries and
Abstracts **373**

  Guidelines for Summarizing Information
  and Preparing an Abstract **374**

Evaluating the Sources **376**

  Guidelines for Evaluating Sources on
  the Web **378**

Evaluating the Evidence **379**

Interpreting Your Findings **380**

Avoiding Statistical Fallacies **382**

  Guidelines for Critically Analyzing
  Information **386**

Assessing Your Inquiry **387**

Applications **388**

TAKING NOTES

Many researchers take notes on a laptop computer, using electronic file programs or database management software that allows notes to be filed, shuffled, and retrieved by author, title, topic, date, or key words. You can also take notes in a single word processing file, then use the "find" command to locate notes quickly. Whether you use a computer or notecards, your notes should be easy to organize and reorganize.

GUIDELINES FOR RECORDING RESEARCH FINDINGS

1. *Make a separate bibliography listing for each work you consult.* Record that work's complete entry (Figure 20.1), using the citation format that will appear in your report. (See pages 394–406) for sample entries.) Record the information accurately so that you won't have to relocate a source at the last minute. When searching online, you often can print out the full bibliographic record for each work, or save it to disk, thereby ensuring an accurate citation.

2. *Skim the entire work to locate relevant material.* Look over the table of contents and the index. Check the introduction for an overview or thesis. Look for informative headings.

3. *Go back and decide what to record.* Use a separate entry for each item.

4. *Be selective.* Don't copy or paraphrase every word. (See the Guidelines for Summarizing on page 374.)

5. *Record the item as a quotation or a paraphrase.* When quoting others directly, be sure to record words and punctuation accurately. When restating material in your own words, preserve the original meaning and emphasis.

FIGURE 20.1
Bibliography entry

Record each bibliographic citation exactly as it will appear in your final report

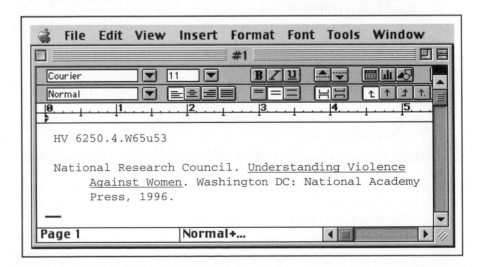

QUOTING THE WORK OF OTHERS

You must place quotation marks around all exact wording you borrow, whether the words were written or spoken (as in an interview or presentation) or whether they appeared in electronic form. Even a single borrowed sentence or phrase, or a single word used in a special way, needs quotation marks, with the exact source properly cited.

GUIDELINES FOR QUOTING THE WORK OF OTHERS

1. *Use a direct quotation only when absolutely necessary.* Sometimes a direct quotation is the only way to do justice to the author's own words—as in these instances:

Expressions that warrant direct quotation

"Writing is a way to end up thinking something you couldn't have started out thinking" (Elbow 15).

Think of the topic sentence as "the one sentence you would keep if you could keep only one" (USAF Academy 11).

Consider quoting directly for these purposes:

Reasons for quoting directly

- to preserve special meaning
- to preserve special phrasing or emphasis
- to preserve precise meaning
- to preserve an especially striking or colorful example
- to convey the authority and complexity of expert opinion
- to convey the original's voice, sincerity, or emotional intensity

2. *Ensure accuracy.* Copy the selection word for word; record the exact page numbers; and double-check that you haven't altered the original expression in any way (Figure 20.2).

3. *Keep the quotation as brief as possible.* For conciseness and emphasis, use ellipses: Use three spaced periods [. . .] to indicate each omission within a single sentence. Add a fourth period after the bracket to indicate each omission that includes the end of a sentence or sections of multiple sentences.

Ellipses within and between sentences

Use three [. . .] periods to indicate each omission within a single sentence. Add a fourth [. . .] to indicate [. . .] .

The elliptical passage must be grammatical and must not distort the original meaning. (For additional guidelines, see pages 457, 530.)

> **Note** *Use brackets for ellipses only in quoted material and not for ellipses in your own statements, as in this next example:*

I was on the verge of dropping out of school . . . but your encouragement kept me going.

Plagiarism often is unintentional

If your notes don't identify quoted material accurately, you might forget to credit the source. Even when this omission is unintentional, writers face the charge of *plagiarism* (misrepresenting as one's own the words or ideas of someone else). Possible consequences of plagiarism include expulsion from school, the loss of a job, and a lawsuit.

The perils of buying plagiarized work online

It's no secret that any cheater can purchase essays, reports, and term papers on the Web. But antiplagiarism Web sites, such as <**plagiarism.org**>

4. *Use square brackets to insert your own clarifying comments or transitions.* To distinguish your words from those of your source, place them within brackets:

Brackets setting off words within a quotation

"This occupation [campus police officer] requires excellent judgment."

Note also the bracketed insertion on page 457.

5. *Embed quoted material in your sentences clearly and grammatically.* Introduce integrated quotations with phrases such as "*Jones argues that,*" or "*Gomez concludes that.*" More importantly, use a transitional phrase to show the relationship between the quoted idea and the sentence that precedes it.

An introduction that unifies a quotation with the discussion

One investigation of sexual assault on college campuses found that "college athletes and fraternity men are a protected species." (Johnson, 1991, p. 34).

Your integrated sentence should be grammatical:

Quoted material integrated grammatically with the writer's words

"Alcohol has become the social drug of choice at American colleges," reports Mathews, "and a fuel for campus crime" (1993, p. 41).

(For additional guidelines, see pages 529–30.)

6. *Quote passages four lines or longer in block form.* Avoid relying on long quotations except in these instances:

Reasons for quoting a long passage

■ to provide an extended example, definition, or analogy

■ to analyze or discuss a particular idea or concept

Double-space a block quotation and indent the entire block ten spaces. Do not indent the first line of the passage, but do indent first lines of subsequent paragraphs three spaces. Do not use quotation marks.

7. *Introduce the quotation and discuss its significance.*

An introduction to quoted material

Here is a corporate executive's description of some audiences you can expect to address. . . .

8. *Cite the source of each quoted passage.*

now enable professors to cross-reference a suspicious paper against previously published material, flagging and identifying each plagiarized source.

Research writing is a process of independent thinking in which you work with the ideas of others in order to reach your own conclusions; unless the author's exact wording is essential, try to paraphrase, instead of quoting, borrowed material.

FIGURE 20.2

Entry for a quotation

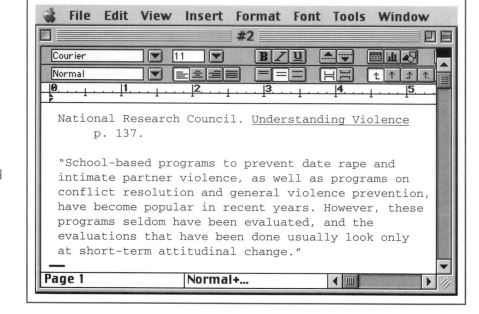

Place quotation marks around all directly quoted material

PARAPHRASING THE WORK OF OTHERS

Paraphrasing means more than changing or shuffling a few words; it means restating the original idea in your own words—sometimes in a clearer, more direct, and emphatic way—and giving full credit to the source.

Faulty paraphrasing is a form of plagiarism

To borrow or adapt someone else's ideas or reasoning without properly documenting the source is plagiarism. To offer as a paraphrase an original passage only slightly altered—even when you document the source—also is plagiarism. Equally unethical is offering a paraphrase, although documented, that distorts the original meaning.

Figure 20.3 shows an entry paraphrased from the passage in Figure 20.2. Paraphrased material is not enclosed within quotation marks, but it is documented to acknowledge your debt to the source.

FIGURE 20.3
Entry for a paraphrase

Signal the beginning of
the paraphrase by citing
the author and the end by
citing the source.

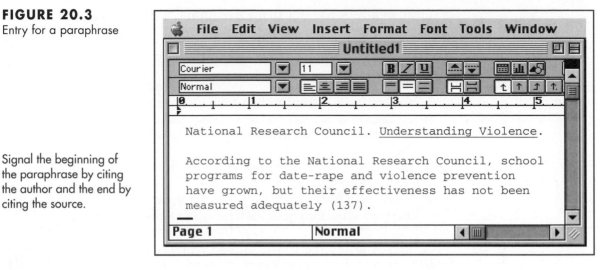

National Research Council. <u>Understanding Violence</u>.

According to the National Research Council, school programs for date-rape and violence prevention have grown, but their effectiveness has not been measured adequately (137).

GUIDELINES FOR PARAPHRASING THE WORK OF OTHERS

1. *Refer to the author early in the paraphrase to indicate the beginning of the borrowed passage.*
2. *Retain keywords from the original to preserve its meaning.*
3. *Restructure and combine original sentences for emphasis and fluency.*
4. *Delete needless words from the original for conciseness.*

5. *Use your own words and phrases to explain the author's ideas, for clarity.*
6. *Cite (in parentheses) the exact source to mark the end of the borrowed passage and to give full credit.*
7. *Be sure to preserve the author's original intent (Weinstein 3).*

PREPARING SUMMARIES AND ABSTRACTS

As we record our research findings, we summarize and paraphrase to capture the main ideas in compressed form. Also, researchers and readers who must act on information need to identify quickly what is most important in a long document. An abstract is a type of summary that does three things: (1) shows what the document is all about; (2) helps readers decide whether to read all of it, parts of it, or none of it; and (3) gives readers a framework for understanding what follows.

What Readers Expect from a Summary or Abstract

Whether you summarize your own writing (like the sample on page 422) or someone else's, readers expect these qualities:

Elements of a usable abstract

- *Accuracy:* Readers expect an abstract to sketch the content, emphasis, and line of reasoning precisely from the original.
- *Completeness:* Readers expect to consult the original document only for more detail—but not to make sense of the main ideas and their relationships.
- *Readability:* Readers expect an abstract to be clear and straightforward—easy to follow and understand.
- *Conciseness:* Readers expect an abstract to be informative yet brief, and they may stipulate a word limit (say, 200 words).

For college papers, the abstract normally appears on a separate page right before the text of the paper or report. Although the abstract is written last, it is read first; take the time to do a good job.

GUIDELINES FOR SUMMARIZING INFORMATION AND PREPARING AN ABSTRACT

1. *Be considerate of later users.* Unless you own the book, journal, or magazine, work from a photocopy.
2. *Read the entire original.* When summarizing someone else's work, grasp the total picture before picking up your pencil.
3. *Reread and underline.* Identify the issue or need that led to the article or report. Focus on the main ideas: thesis, topic sentences, findings, conclusions, and recommendations.
4. *Pare down your underlined material.* Omit lengthy background, examples, technical details, explanations, or anything not essential to the overall meaning. In abstracting the writing of others, avoid quotations; if you must quote some crucial word or phrase directly, use quotation marks.

5. *Rewrite in your own words.* Even if this first draft is too long, include everything that seems essential for this version to stand alone; you can trim later. If a direct quotation is absolutely necessary, be sure to place quotation marks around the author's own words.
6. *Edit for conciseness.* Once your draft contains everything readers need, find ways to trim the word count. (Review pages 124–29.)
   a. Cross out all needless words—but keep sentences clear and grammatical:

   Needless words omitted

   ~~As far as~~ artificial intelligence ~~is concerned,~~ ~~the~~ technology is only in its infancy.

   b. Cross out needless prefaces:

Ethical Considerations in Summarizing Information

Information in a summary format is increasingly attractive to today's readers, who often feel bombarded by more information than they can handle. Consider, for example, the popularity of the *USA Today* newspaper, with its countless news items offered in brief snippets for overtaxed readers. In contrast, The *New York Times* offers lengthy text that is information rich but more time-consuming to digest.

A summary format is especially adaptable to the hypertext-linked design of Web-based documents. Instead of long blocks of text, Web users expect pages with concise modules, or "chunks," of information that stand alone, are easy to scan, and require little or no scrolling on the reader's part. Moreover, magazine Web sites such as *Forbes* or *The Economist* offer email summaries of their hard copy editions. And while capsules or "digests" of information are an efficient way to stay abreast of new developments, the abbreviated presentation carries potential pitfalls, as media critic Alan Greenberg points out on page 376 (65).

Needless prefaces omitted

The writer argues that . . .

Also discussed is . . .

c. Combine related ideas (page 131) and rephrase to emphasize important connections:

Disconnected and rambling

A recent study emphasized job opportunities in the computer field. Fewer of tomorrow's jobs will be for programmers and other people who know how to create technology. More jobs will be for people who can use technology—as in marketing and finance (Ross, "Enjoy" 206).

Connected and concise

A recent study predicts fewer jobs for programmers and other creators of technology, and more jobs for users of technology—as in marketing and finance (Ross, "Enjoy" 206).

d. Use numerals for numbers, except to begin a sentence.

7. *Check your version against the original.* Verify this version's accuracy and completeness. Add no personal comments.

8. *Rewrite your edited version.* In this final draft, strive for readability and conciseness. Add transitional expressions (page 111) to emphasize connections. Respect any stipulated word limit.

9. *Document your source.* Cite the full source (Chapter 21) below any abstract not accompanied by its original.

Ways in which
summarized information
can be unethical

- A condensed version of a complicated issue or event may provide a useful overview, but this superficial treatment can rarely communicate the issue's full complexity—i.e., the complete story.
- Whoever summarizes a lengthy piece makes decisions about what to leave out and what to leave in, what to emphasize, and what to ignore. During the selection process, the original message could very well be distorted.
- In a summary of someone else's writing, the tone or "voice" of the original author disappears—along with that writer's way of seeing.

A summary's tip-of-the-iceberg view can alter any reader's accurate interpretation of the issue or the event, as in the following headlines that summarize the story but distort the facts:

Summaries that fail to
capture the real story

- "Cannabis makes drivers more cautious: study"—This headline from the August 21, 2000 *Ottawa Citizen* is accompanied by the following summary on page A1: "Driving while high is less dangerous than while fatigued or drunk." Unless they turn to page A2, readers never encounter the essential fact that "Experts agree that driving while high is not as safe as driving while sober."
- "Chocolate: The New Heart-Healthy Food."—Various forms of this claim have made headlines, as, for example, in the March 18, 2000 *Science News:* "Chocolate Hearts: Yummy and Good Medicine?" Although the main ingredient in chocolate (cocoa) is rich in antioxidants that prevent arterial plaque buildup, most chocolate treats also contain high concentrations of sugar, caffeine, and cholesterol-laden butterfat or tropical oils (palm or coconut)—thus offsetting any apparent health benefits.

Informed decisions about countless science and technological controversies (human cloning, bioengineered foods, global warming, estrogen therapy) require an informed public. And, although summaries do have their place in our busy world, scanning headlines or abstracts is no substitute for detailed reading and careful weighing of the facts. The more complex the topic, the more readers need the whole story.

| Note |

*For more advice about quotations, paraphrases, and summaries (including examples), go to <**www.wisc.edu/writing/Handbook/QuoSuccessfulSummary.html**>.*

EVALUATING THE SOURCES

Not all sources are equally dependable. A source might offer information that is out of date, inaccurate, incomplete, mistaken, or biased.

"Is the source up-to-date?"

- *Determine the currency of the source.* Certain types of information become outdated more quickly than others. For topics that focus on *tech-*

nology (Internet censorship, alternative cancer treatments), information more than a few months old may be outdated. But for topics that focus on *people* (student motivation, gender equality), historical perspectives often help.

Note

The most recent information is not always the most reliable—especially in scientific research, a process of ongoing inquiry in which what seems true today may be proven false tomorrow (Taubes 76). Consider, for example, the recent discoveries of fatal side effects from some of the latest "miracle" weight-loss drugs.

"Is the printed source dependable?"

■ *Assess the reputation of a printed source.* Some sources are more reputable, unbiased, and authoritative than others. For research on alternative cancer treatments, you could depend more on reports in the *New England Journal of Medicine* or *Scientific American* than on those in scandal sheets or movie magazines. Even researchers with expert credentials, however, can disagree or be mistaken.

Assess a publication's reputation by checking its copyright page. Is the work published by a university, professional society, museum, or respected news organization? Do members of the editorial and advisory board all have distinguished titles and degrees? Is the publication refereed (all submissions reviewed by experts before acceptance)? Does the bibliography or list of references indicate how thoroughly the author has researched the issue (Barnes)? Many periodicals also provide brief biographies or descriptions of authors' earlier publications and achievements.

"Is the electronic source dependable?"

■ *Assess the dependability of an Internet or database source.* The Internet offers information that never appears in other sources, for example from *listservs* and *newsgroups*. But much of this information may reflect the bias of the special-interest groups that provide it. Moreover, anyone can publish almost anything on the Internet—including a great deal of misinformation—without having it verified, edited, or reviewed for accuracy. Don't expect to find everything you need on the Internet. (Pages 378–79 offer suggestions for evaluating sources on the Web.)

Even in a commercial database such as DIALOG, decisions about what to include and what to leave out depend on the biases, priorities, or interests of those who assemble that database.

"Who sponsored the study, and why?"

■ *Consider the sponsorship and the motives for the study.* Much of today's research is paid for by private companies or special-interest groups, which have their own agendas (Crossen 14, 19). Medical research may be sponsored by drug or tobacco companies; nutritional research, by food manufacturers; environmental research, by oil or chemical companies. Instead of a neutral and balanced inquiry, this kind of "strategic research" is designed to support one special interest or another (132–34).

Furthermore, those who pay for strategic research are not likely to publicize findings that contradict their original claims or opinions or beliefs. Research consumers need to know exactly what the sponsors of a particular study stand to gain or lose from the results (234).

GUIDELINES FOR EVALUATING SOURCES ON THE WEB*

1. *Consider the site's domain type and sponsor.* In this typical address, <**http://www.umass.edu**>, the site or domain information follows the *www*. The *.edu* signifies the type of organization from which the site originates. Standard domain types in the United States:

   .com = business/commercial organization

   .edu = educational institution

   .gov = government organization

   .mil = military organization

   .net = any group or individual with simple software and Internet access

   .org = nonprofit organization

   The domain type might signal a certain bias or agenda that could distort the data. For example, at a .com site, you might find accurate information but also a sales pitch. At an .org site, you might find a political or ideological bias (say, The Heritage Foundation's conservative ideology versus the Brookings Institution's more liberal slant). A tilde (~) in the address usually signifies a personal home page. Knowing a site's sponsor can help you evaluate the credibility of its postings.

2. *Identify the purpose of the page or message.* Decide whether the message is intended simply to relay information, to sell something, or to promote a particular ideology or agenda.

3. *Look beyond the style of a site.* Fancy graphics, video, and sound do not always translate into dependable information. Sometimes the most reliable material resides in the less attractive, text-only sites.

4. *Assess the site's/material's currency.* An up-to-date site should indicate when the material was created or published and when it was posted and updated.

5. *Assess the author's credentials.* Learn all you can about the author's reputation, expertise on this topic, institutional affiliation (a university, Fortune 500 Company, reputable environmental group). Do this by following links to other sites that mention the author or by using search engines to track the author's name. Newsgroup postings often contain "a signature file that includes the author's name, location, institutional or organizational affiliation, and often a quote that suggests something of the writer's personality, political leanings, or sense of humor" (Goubril-Gambrell 229–30).

Note

Keep in mind that any research ultimately stands on its own merits. Thus, funding by a special interest should not automatically discredit an otherwise valid and reliable study.

"What are similar sources saying?"

■ *Cross-check the source against other, similar sources.* Instead of relying on a single source or study, seek a consensus among various respected sources (Cohn 106).

Note

Some issues (the need for defense spending or causes of inflation) always are controversial and will never be resolved. Although we can get verifiable data and can reason persuasively on some subjects, no close reasoning by any expert and no

| Note | *Don't confuse an author (the person who wrote the material) with a Webmaster (the person who created and maintains the Web site).* |

6. *Compare the site with other sources.* Check related sites and publications to compare the quality of information and to discover what others might have said about this site or author. Comparing many similar sites helps you create a benchmark, a standard for evaluating any particular site. Ask a librarian for help.

7. *Decide whether the assertions/claims make sense.* Decide where, on the spectrum of informed opinion and accepted theory, this author's position resides. Is each assertion supported by convincing evidence? Never accept any claim that seems extreme without verifying it through other sources, such as a professor, a librarian, or a specialist in the field.

8. *Look for other indicators of quality.*

   ■ *Worthwhile content:* The material is technically accurate. All sources of data presented as "factual" are fully documented (see Chapter 21).

■ *Sensible organization:* The material is organized for the user's understanding, with a clear line of reasoning.

■ *Readable style:* The material is well written (clear, concise, easy to understand) and free of typos, misspellings, and other mechanical errors.

■ *Objective coverage:* Debatable topics are addressed in a balanced and impartial way, with fair, accurate representation of opposing views. The tone is reasonable, with no "sounding off."

■ *Expertise:* The author refers to related theory and other work in the field and uses specialized terminology accurately and appropriately.

■ *Peer review:* The material has been evaluated and verified by related experts.

■ *Links to reputable sites:* The site offers a gateway to related sites that meet quality criteria.

■ *Follow-up option:* The material includes a signature block or a link for contacting the author or the organization.

*Guidelines adapted from Barnes; Busiel and Maeglin 39; Elliot; Facklemann 397; Grassian; Hall 60–61; Hammett; Harris; Kapoun 4; Stemmer.

supporting statistical analysis will "prove" anything about a controversial subject. Some problems simply are more resistant to solution than others, no matter how dependable the sources.

EVALUATING THE EVIDENCE

Evidence is any finding used to support or refute a particular claim. Although evidence can serve the truth, it also can create distortion, misinformation, and deception. For example:

Questions that invite
distorted evidence

- How much money, material, or energy does recycling really save?
- How well are public schools educating children?
- Which automobiles are safest?

Competing answers to such questions often rest on evidence that has been stacked to support a particular view or agenda. As consumers of research, we have to assess for ourselves the quality of evidence presented.

"Is there enough
evidence?"

- *Determine the sufficiency of the evidence.* Evidence is sufficient when nothing more is needed to reach an accurate judgment or a conclusion. Say you are researching the benefits of low-impact aerobics for reducing stress among employees at a fireworks factory. You would need to interview or survey a broad sample: people who have practiced aerobics for a long time; people of both genders, different ages, different occupations, different lifestyles before they began aerobics, and so on. Even responses from hundreds of practitioners might be insufficient unless those responses were supported by laboratory measurements of metabolic and heart rates, blood pressure, and so on.

> **Note**   *Although anecdotal evidence ("This worked great for me!") might offer a good starting point for investigation, your personal experience rarely provides enough evidence from which to generalize. No matter how long you might have practiced aerobics, for instance, you need to determine whether your experience is representative.*

"Can the evidence be
verified?"

- *Differentiate hard from soft evidence.* Hard evidence consists of factual statements, expert opinion, or statistics that can be verified. Soft evidence consists of uninformed opinion or speculation, data that were obtained or analyzed unscientifically, and findings that have not been replicated or reviewed by experts.

INTERPRETING YOUR FINDINGS

Interpreting means trying to reach an overall judgment about what the findings mean and what conclusion or action they suggest.

Unfortunately, research does not always yield answers that are clear or conclusive. Instead of settling for the most *convenient* answer, we pursue the most *reasonable* answer by examining critically a full range of possible meanings.

Identify Your Level of Certainty

Research can yield three distinct and very different levels of certainty:

1. The ultimate truth—the *conclusive answer*:

A practical definition of
"truth"

Truth is *what is so* about something, as distinguished from what people wish, believe, or assert to be so. In the words of Harvard philosopher Israel Scheffler, truth is the view "which is fated to be ultimately agreed to by all who investigate." * The word *ultimately* is important. Investigation may produce a wrong answer for years, even for centuries. For example, in the second century A.D., Ptolemy's view of the universe placed the earth at its center—and though untrue, this judgment was based on the best information available at that time. And Ptolemy's view survived for 13 centuries, even after new information had discredited this belief. When Galileo proposed a more truthful view in the fifteenth century, he was labeled a heretic.

One way to spare yourself any further confusion about truth is to reserve the word *truth* for the final answer to an issue. Get in the habit of using the words *belief, theory,* and *present understanding* more often. (Ruggiero 21–22)

2. The *probable answer:* the answer that stands the best chance of being true or accurate—given the most we can know at this particular time. Proba- ble answers are subject to revision in the light of new information.
3. The *inconclusive answer:* the realization that the truth of the matter is more elusive or ambiguous or complex than we expected.

Exactly how certain are we?

We need to decide what level of certainty our findings warrant. For ex- ample, we are *highly certain* about the perils of smoking, *reasonably certain* about the health benefits of fruits and vegetables, but *less certain* about the perils of coffee drinking or the benefits of vitamin supplements.

Can you think of additional examples of information about which we are *highly, reasonably,* or *less* certain?

Be Alert for Personal Bias

Personal bias is a fact of life

When the issue is controversial, our own bias might cause us to overestimate (or deny) the certainty of our findings.

Expect yourself to be biased, and expect your bias to affect your efforts to construct arguments. Unless you are perfectly neutral about the issue, an unlikely circumstance, at the very outset . . . you will believe one side of the issue to be right, and that belief will incline you to . . . present more and better arguments for the side of the issue you prefer. (Ruggiero 134)

Because personal bias is hard to transcend, *rationalizing* often becomes a sub- stitute for *reasoning:*

Reasoning versus rationalizing

You are reasoning if your belief follows the evidence—that is, if you examine the evidence first and then make up your mind. You are rationalizing if the evidence follows your belief—if you first decide what you'll believe and then select and interpret evidence to justify it. (Ruggiero 44)

Personal bias often is unconscious until we examine our own value systems, attitudes long held but never analyzed, notions we've inherited from our

---
*From *Reason and Teaching.* New York: Bobbs-Merrill, 1973.

backgrounds, and so on. Recognizing our own biases is a crucial first step in managing them.

Examine the Underlying Assumptions

Assumptions are notions we take for granted, things we accept without proof. The research process rests on assumptions like these: that a sample group accurately represents a larger target group, that survey respondents remember certain facts accurately, that mice and humans share enough biological similarities for meaningful research. For a particular study to be valid, the underlying assumptions have to be accurate.

Assume, for instance, you are an education consultant evaluating the accuracy of IQ testing as a predictor of academic performance. Reviewing the evidence, you perceive an association between low IQ scores and low achievers. You then check your statistics by examining a cross-section of reliable sources. Should you feel justified in concluding that IQ tests do predict performance accurately? This conclusion might be invalid unless you could verify the following assumptions:

1. That neither parents nor teachers nor the children tested had seen individual test scores and had thus been able to develop biased expectations.
2. That, regardless of their IQ scores, all children had been exposed to an identical pace, instead of being "tracked" on the basis of individual scores.

The evidence could be evaluated and interpreted only within the framework of these underlying assumptions.

| **Note** | *Assumptions are often easier to identify in someone else's thinking and writing than in our own. During collaborative discussions, ask group members to help you identify your own assumptions (Maeglin).* |

AVOIDING STATISTICAL FALLACIES

How numbers can mislead

The purpose of statistical analysis is to determine the meaning of a collected set of numbers. Surveys and questionnaires often lead to some kind of numerical interpretation. ("What percentage of respondents prefer *X*?" "How often does *Y* happen?") In our own research, we often rely on numbers collected by survey researchers.

Numbers seem more precise, more objective, more scientific, and less ambiguous than words. They are easier to summarize, measure, compare, and analyze. But numbers can be totally misleading. For example, radio or television phone-in surveys produce grossly distorted data: although 90 percent of callers might express support for a particular viewpoint, people who call tend to be those with the greatest anger or extreme feelings about the issue—representing only a fraction of overall attitudes (Fineman 24). Mail-in surveys can produce similar distortion because only people with certain attitudes might choose to respond.

Before relying on any set of numbers, we need to know exactly where they come from, how they were collected, and how they were analyzed (Lavin 275–76). Are the numbers accurate and, if so, what do they mean?

Common Statistical Fallacies

Faulty statistical reasoning produces conclusions that are unwarranted, inaccurate, or deceptive. Here are some typical fallacies:

"Exactly how well are we doing?"

- *The sanitized statistic:* Numbers are manipulated (or "cleaned up") to obscure the facts. For instance, the College Board's recent "recentering" of SAT scores has raised the "average" math score from 478 to 500 and the average verbal score from 424 to 500 (a boost of almost 5 and 18 percent, respectively), although actual student performance remains unchanged (Samuelson 44).

"How many rats was that?"

- *The meaningless statistic:* Exact numbers are used to quantify something so inexact or vaguely defined that it should only be approximated (Huff 247; Lavin 278): "Boston has 3,247,561 rats." "Zappo detergent makes laundry 10 percent brighter." An exact number looks impressive, but it can hide the fact that certain subjects (child abuse, cheating in college, virginity, drug and alcohol abuse on the job, eating habits) cannot be quantified exactly because respondents don't always tell the truth (because of denial or embarrassment or merely guessing). Or they respond in ways they think the researcher expects.

"Why is everybody griping?"

- *The undefined average:* The mean, median, and mode are confused in determining an average (Huff 244; Lavin 279). The *mean* is the result of adding up the value of each item in a set of numbers, and then dividing by the number of items. The *median* is the result of ranking all the values from high to low, then choosing the middle value (or the 50th percentile, as in calculating SAT scores). The *mode* is the value that occurs most often in a set of numbers.

Each of these three measurements represents some kind of average. But unless we know which "average" is being presented, we cannot interpret the figures accurately.

Assume, for instance, that we are computing the average salary among female vice presidents at XYZ Corporation (ranked from high to low):

Vice President	Salary
"A"	$90,000
"B"	$90,000
"C"	$80,000
"D"	$65,000
"E"	$60,000
"F"	$55,000
"G"	$50,000

In the above example, the mean salary (total salaries divided by people) equals $70,000; the median salary (middle value) equals $65,000; the mode (most frequent value) equals $90,000. Each is, legitimately, an "average," and each could be used to support or refute a particular assertion (for example, "Women receive too little" or "Women receive too much").

Research expert Michael R. Lavin sums up the potential for bias in reporting averages:

> Depending on the circumstances, any one of these measurements may describe a group of numbers better than the other two. . . . [But] people typically choose the value which best presents their case, whether or not it is the most appropriate to use. (279)

Although the mean is the most commonly computed average, this measurement is misleading when one or more values on either end of the scale deviate excessively from the normal distribution (or spread) of values. Suppose, for instance, that Vice President "A" (above) was paid $200,000: Because this figure deviates so much from the normal range of salary figures for "B" through "G," it distorts the average for the whole group—increasing the "mean salary" by more than 20 percent (Plumb and Spyridakis 636).

"Is 51 percent really a majority?"

- *The distorted percentage figure:* Percentages are reported without explanation of the original numbers used in the calculation (Adams and Schvaneveldt 359; Lavin 280): "Seventy-five percent of respondents prefer our brand over the competing brand"—without mention that only four people were surveyed.

Another fallacy in reporting percentages occurs when the *margin of error* is ignored. This is the margin within which the true figure lies, based on estimated sampling errors in a survey. For example, a claim that most people surveyed prefer Brand X might be based on the fact that 51 percent of respondents expressed this preference; but if the survey carried a 2 percent margin of error, the real figure could be as low as 49 percent or as high as 53 percent. In a survey with a high margin of error, the true figure may be so uncertain that no definite conclusion may be drawn.

"Which car should we buy?"

- *The bogus ranking:* This happens when items are compared on the basis of ill-defined criteria (Adams and Schvaneveldt 212; Lavin 284): "Last year, the Batmobile was the number-one selling car in America"—without mention that some competing car makers actually sold *more* cars to private individuals, and that the Batmobile figures were inflated by hefty sales to rental-car companies and corporate fleets. Unless we know how the ranked items were chosen and how they were compared (the criteria), a ranking can produce a scientific-seeming number based on a completely unscientific method.

"Does *X* actually cause *Y*?"

- *Confusion of correlation with causation: Correlation* is the measure of association between two variables (between smoking and increased lung cancer risk or between education and income). *Causation* is the demonstrable production of a specific effect (smoking causes lung cancer). Correlations between smoking and lung cancer or education and income signal a causal relationship that has been proven by many studies. But not every correlation implies causation. For instance, a recently discovered correlation between moderate alcohol consumption and decreased heart disease risk offers no sufficient proof that moderate drinking *causes* less heart disease.

Many highly publicized correlations are the product of "data dredging": In this process, computers randomly compare one set of variables (say, eating habits) with another set (say, a range of diseases). From these countless comparisons, certain relationships reveal themselves (say, between coffee drinking and pancreatic cancer risk). As dramatic as such isolated correlations may be, they constitute no proof of causation and often lead to hasty conclusions (Ross, "Lies" 135).

"How have assumptions influenced this computer model?"

■ *The fallible computer model:* Complex assumptions form the basis of computer models designed to predict or estimate costs, benefits, risks, or probable outcomes. But answers produced by any computer model depend on the assumptions (and data) programmed in. Assumptions might be influenced by researcher bias or the sponsors' agenda. For example, a prediction of human fatalities from a nuclear reactor meltdown might rest on assumptions about availability of safe shelter, evacuation routes, time of day, season, wind direction, and the structural integrity of the containment unit. But these assumptions could be manipulated to overstate or understate the risk (Barbour 228). For computer-modeled estimates of accident risk (oil spill, plane crash) or of the costs and benefits of a proposed project or policy (International Space Station, welfare reform), consumers rarely know the assumptions behind the numbers.

"Is this good news or bad news?"

■ *Misleading terminology:* The terms used to interpret statistics sometimes hide their real meaning. For instance, the widely publicized figure that people treated for cancer have a "50 percent survival rate" is misleading in two ways; (1) *Survival* to laypersons means "staying alive," but to medical experts, staying alive for only five years after diagnosis qualifies as survival; (2) the "50 percent" survival figure covers *all* cancers, including certain skin or thyroid cancers that have extremely high *cure rates,* as well as other cancers (such as lung or ovarian) that rarely are curable and have extremely low *survival rates* ("Are We" 6).

Even the most valid and reliable statistics require us to interpret the reality behind the numbers. For instance, the overall cancer rate today is "higher" than it was in 1910. What this may mean is that people are living longer and thus are more likely to die of cancer and that cancer today rarely is misdiagnosed—or mislabeled because of stigma ("Are We" 4). The finding that rates for certain cancers "double" after prolonged exposure to electromagnetic waves may really mean that cancer risk actually increases from 1 in 10,000 to 2 in 10,000.

GUIDELINES FOR CRITICALLY ANALYZING INFORMATION

Evaluate the Sources

1. *Check the source's date of posting or publication.* Although the latest information is not always the best, it's important to keep up with recent developments.
2. *Assess the reputation of each printed source.* Check the copyright page for background on the publisher; the bibliography for the quality and extent of research; and (if available) the author's brief biography for credentials.
3. *Assess the quality of each electronic source.* See page 378 for evaluating Internet sources. Don't expect comprehensive sources on any single database.
4. *Identify the study's sponsor.* If the study acclaims the crash-worthiness of the Batmobile but is sponsored by the Batmobile Auto Company, be skeptical.
5. *Look for corroborating sources.* Usually, no single study produces dependable findings. Learn what other sources say, why they might agree or disagree with your source, and where most experts stand on this topic.

Evaluate the Evidence

1. *Decide whether the evidence is sufficient.* Evidence should surpass mere personal experience, anecdote, or news reports. It should be substantial enough for reasonable and informed observers to agree on its value, relevance, and accuracy.
2. *Look for a reasonable and balanced presentation of evidence.* Suspect any claims about "breakthroughs" or "miracle cures," as well as loaded words that invite emotional response or anything beyond accepted views on a topic. Expect a discussion of drawbacks, as well as benefits.
3. *Do your best to verify the evidence.* Examine the facts that support the claims. Look for replication of findings. Go beyond the study to determine the direction in which the collective evidence seems to be leaning.

Interpret Your Findings

1. *Don't expect "certainty."* Most complex questions are open-ended, and a mere accumulation of "facts" doesn't "prove" anything. Even so, the weight of solid evidence usually points toward some reasonable conclusion.
2. *Examine the underlying assumptions.* As opinions taken for granted, assumptions are easily mistaken for facts.
3. *Identify your personal biases.* Examine your own assumptions. Don't ignore evidence simply because it contradicts your way of seeing, and don't focus only on evidence that supports your assumptions.

These are only a few examples of statistics and interpretations that seem highly persuasive but that in fact cannot always be trusted. Any interpretation of statistical data carries the possibility that other, more accurate interpretations have been overlooked or deliberately excluded (Barnett 45).

| Note | *For good examples of faulty (as well as correct) statistical reasoning in the news, check out Dartmouth College's Chance Project at <**www.dartmouth.edu/~chance**>.* |

4. *Consider alternate interpretations.* Consider what else this evidence might mean. Instead of settling for the most convenient conclusion, seek out the most reasonable one.

Check for Weak Spots

1. *Scrutinize all generalizations.* Decide whether the "facts" are indeed facts or merely assumptions and whether the evidence supports the generalization (page 317). Suspect any general claim not limited by some qualifier ("often," "sometimes," "rarely," or the like).

2. *Treat causal claims skeptically.* Differentiate correlation from causation, as well as possible from probable or definite causes (pages 237, 318). Consider confounding factors (other explanations for the reported outcome). For example, studies indicating that regular exercise improves health might be overlooking the fact that healthy people tend to do more exercise than those in poor health ("Walking" 3–4).

3. *Look for statistical fallacies.* Determine where the numbers come from, and how they were collected and analyzed—information that legitimate researchers routinely provide. Note the margin of error.

4. *Consider the limits of computer analysis.* Data mining (dredging) often produces intriguing but random correlations; a computer model is only as accurate as the assumptions and data programmed into it.

5. *Look for misleading terminology.* Examine terms that beg for precise definition in their specific context: "survival rate," "success rate," "customer satisfaction," "average increase," "risk factor," and so on.

6. *Interpret the reality behind the numbers.* Consider the possibility of alternative, more accurate, interpretations of these numbers. For example, "Saabs and Volvos are involved in 75 percent fewer fatal accidents than average." Is this only because of superior engineering or also because people who buy these cars tend to drive carefully ("The Safest" 72)?

7. *Consider the study's possible limitations.* Small, brief studies are less reliable than large, extended ones; epidemiologic studies are less reliable than laboratory studies (that also carry flaws); animal or human exposure studies are often not generalizable to larger human populations; "masked" (or blind) studies are not always as objective as they seem; measurements are prone to error.

8. *Look for the whole story.* Consider whether bad news may be underreported; good news, exaggerated; bad science, camouflaged and sensationalized; or research on promising but unconventional topics (say, alternative energy sources), ignored.

ASSESSING YOUR INQUIRY

The inquiry phases of the research process present a minefield of potential errors in where we search, how we interpret, and how we reason. So before preparing the actual report, examine critically your methods, interpretations, and reasoning with the checklist on page 389.

Application 20-1

Web-based/Collaborative Project: In class, form teams of students who have similar majors or interests. As a team, decide on a related topic that is currently in the news. Appoint a manager who will assign each team member a specific task. Using a combination of Web-based and hard copy versions of news coverage, compare summarized versions with more detailed coverage. For example:

- a *USA Today* hard copy version versus one from The *New York Times*
- a headline summary from The *New York Times'* "Quick News" and "Page One Plus" links
  <www.nytimes.com>
  versus the full-text hard copy version
- summarized Web versions from *Forbes*
  <www.forbes.com>
  or *The Economist*
  <www.economist.com>
  versus the whole story in hard copy
- a summarized cover story from "The Daily News Info" link on *Newsweek*'s Web site
  <www.newsweek.com>
  versus the entire story in hard copy.

(Ask your reference librarian for additional suggestions.)

Each team member should compare the benefits and drawbacks of the story's shorter and longer versions, making a copy of each. Are there instances in which a summary version simply is ethically inadequate as a sole source of information? (Consult the Checklist for Ethical Communication, page 290.) Using your sample documents, explain and illustrate.

As a full team, assemble and discuss the collected findings and appoint one member to present the findings to the class in a 15-minute oral report, showing transparencies of selected documents on the overhead projector.

Application 20-2

Web-based Project: Uninformed opinions usually are based on assumptions we've never really examined. Examples of popular assumptions that are largely unexamined:

- "Bottled water is safer and better for you than tap water."
- "Forest fires should always be prevented or suppressed immediately."
- "The fewer germs in their environment, the healthier the children."
- "The more soy we eat, the better."

REVISION CHECKLIST FOR THE RESEARCH PROCESS ☑

(Numbers in parentheses refer to the first page of discussion.)

METHODS

☐ Did I ask the right questions? (334)

☐ Are the sources appropriately up-to-date? (376)

☐ Is each source reputable, trustworthy, relatively unbiased, and borne out by other, similar sources? (377)

☐ Does the evidence clearly support the conclusions? (379)

☐ Can all the evidence be verified? (380)

☐ Is a fair balance of viewpoints presented? (334)

☐ Has my research achieved adequate depth? (336)

REASONING

☐ Am I reasonably certain about the meaning of these findings? (380)

☐ Can I rule out other possible interpretations or conclusions? (381)

☐ Am I reasoning instead of rationalizing? (381)

☐ Am I confident that my causal reasoning is correct? (384)

☐ Can all the numbers and statistics be trusted? (382)

☐ Have I resolved (or at least acknowledged) any conflicts among my findings? (339)

☐ Have I decided whether my final answer is definitive, probable, or inconclusive? (380)

☐ Is this the most reasonable conclusion (or merely the most convenient)? (339)

☐ Have I accounted for all sources of bias, including my own? (381)

☐ Should the evidence be reconsidered? (387)

Your assignment is to identify and examine one popular assumption for accuracy. For example, you might tackle the bottled water assumption by visiting the FDA Web site

   <www.FDA.gov>

and the Sierra Club site

   <www.sierraclub.org>

for starters. (Unless you get stuck, try to work with an assumption not listed above.) Trace the sites and links you followed to get your information, and write up your findings in a report to be shared with the class.

Works Cited

Adams, Gerald R., and Jay D. Schvaneveldt. *Understanding Research Methods.* New York: Longman, 1985.

"Are We in the Middle of a Cancer Epidemic?" *University of California at Berkeley Wellness Letter* 10.9 (1994): 4–5.

Barbour, Ian. *Ethics in an Age of Technology.* New York: Harper, 1993.

Barnes, Shaleen. "Evaluating Sources Checklist." Information Literacy Project. 10 June 1997. Online Posting. 23 June 1998. <http://www.2lib.umassd.edu/library2/INFOLIT/prop.html>.

Barnett, Arnold. "How Numbers Can Trick You." *Technology Review* Oct. 1994: 38–45.

Busiel, Christopher, and Tom Maeglin. *Researching Online.* New York: Addison, 1998.

Cohn, Victor. "Coping with Statistics." *A Field Guide for Science Writers.* Ed. Deborah Blum and Mary Knudson. New York: Oxford, 1997. 102–09.

Crossen, Cynthia. *Tainted Truth: The Manipulation of Fact in America.* New York: Simon, 1994.

Elbow, Peter. *Writing without Teachers.* New York: Oxford, 1973.

Elliot, Joel. "Evaluating Web Sites: Questions to Ask." 18 Feb. 1997. Online Posting. List for Multimedia and New Technologies in Humanities Teaching. 9 Mar. 1997 <http://www.learnnc.org/documents/webeval.html>.

Facklemann, Kathleen. "Science Safari in Cyberspace." *Science News* 152.50 (1997): 397–98.

Fineman, Howard. "The Power of Talk." *Newsweek* 8 Feb. 1993: 24–28.

Goubril-Gambrell, Patricia. "Designing Effective Internet Assignments in Introductory Technical Communication Courses." *IEEE Transactions on Professional Communication* 39.4 (1996): 224–31.

Grassian, Esther. "Thinking Critically About World Wide Web Resources." 1 April 1999. UCLA College Library. 12 Nov. 1999 <http://www.library.ucla.edu/libraries/college/instruct/critical.htm>.

Greenberg, Alan. "Selling News Short." *Brill's Content* Mar. 2000: 64–65.

Hall, Judith. "Medicine on the Web: Finding the Wheat, Leaving the Chaff." *Technology Review* Mar./Apr. 1998: 60–61.

Hammett, Paula. "Evaluating Web Resources." 29 Mar. 1997. Ruben Salazar Library. Sonoma State University. 26 Oct. 1997 <http://www.libweb.sonoma.edu/resources/eval.html>.

Harris, Robert. "Evaluating Internet Research Sources." 17 Nov. 1997. Online. 23 June 1998 <http://www.sccu.edu/faculty/R_Harris/evalu8it.htm>.

Huff, Darrell. *How to Lie with Statistics.* New York: Norton, 1954.

Kapoun, Jim. "Questioning Web Authority." *On Campus* Feb. 2000: 4.

Lavin, Michael R. *Business Information: How to Find It, How to Use It.* 2nd ed. Phoenix, AZ: Oryx, 1992.

Maeglin, Tom. Unpublished review.

Plumb, Carolyn, and Jan H. Spyridakis. "Survey Research in Technical Communication: Designing and Administering Questionnaires." *Technical Communication* 39.4 (1992): 625–38.

Ross, Philip E. "Enjoy It While It Lasts." *Forbes* 27 July 1998: 206.

———. "Lies, Damned Lies, and Medical Statistics." *Forbes* 14 Aug. 1995: 130–35.

Ruggiero, Vincent R. *The Art of Thinking.* 3rd ed. New York: Harper, 1991.

"The Safest Car May Be a Truck." *Fortune* 21 July 1997: 72.

Samuelson, Robert. "Merchants of Mediocrity." *Newsweek* 1 Aug. 1994: 44.

Stemmer, John. "Citing Internet Sources." 4 Mar. 1997. Online Posting. Political Science Research and Teaching List. 22 Apr. 1997 <polpsrt@h-met.msu.edu>.

Taubes, Gary. "Telling Time by the Second Hand." *Technology Review* May/June 1998: 30+.

U.S. Air Force Academy. *Executive Writing Course.* Washington: GPO, 1981.

"Walking to Health." *Harvard Men's Health Watch* 2.12 (1998): 3–4.

Weinstein, Edith K. Unpublished review.

CHAPTER 21

Documenting Your Sources

Why You Should Document   **392**

What You Should Document   **393**

How You Should Document   **393**

MLA Documentation Style   **394**

APA Documentation Style   **406**

Application   **416**

Documenting research means acknowledging one's debt to each information source. Proper documentation satisfies professional requirements for ethics, efficiency, and authority.

WHY YOU SHOULD DOCUMENT

Documentation is a matter of *ethics,* for the originator of borrowed material deserves full credit and recognition. Moreover, all published material is protected by copyright law. Failure to credit a source could make you liable to legal action, even if your omission was unintentional.

Documentation also is a matter of *efficiency.* It provides a network for organizing and locating the world's recorded knowledge. If you cite a particular source correctly, your reference will enable interested readers to locate that source themselves.

Finally, documentation is a matter of *authority*. In making any claim (say, "A Mercedes-Benz is more reliable than a Ford Taurus") you invite challenge: "Says who?" Data on road tests, frequency of repairs, resale value, workmanship, and owner comments can help validate your claim by showing its basis in *fact*. A claim's credibility increases in relation to the expert references supporting it. For a controversial topic, you may need to cite several authorities who hold various views. Readers of your research report expect the *complete picture*.

WHAT YOU SHOULD DOCUMENT

Document any insight, assertion, fact, finding, interpretation, judgment or other "appropriated material that readers might otherwise mistake for your own" (Gibaldi and Achtert 155)—whether the material appears in published form or not. Specifically, you must document these sources:

Sources that require documentation

- any source from which you use exact wording
- any source from which you adapt material in your own words
- any visual illustration: charts, graphs, drawings, or the like

How to document a confidential source

In some instances, you might have reason to preserve the anonymity of unpublished sources: say, to allow people to respond candidly without fear of reprisal (as with employee criticism of the company) or to protect their privacy (as with certain material from email inquiries or electronic newsgroups). You still must document the fact that you are not the originator of this material by providing a general acknowledgment in the text ("A number of faculty expressed frustration with …"), along with a general citation in your list of References or Works Cited ("Interviews with campus faculty, May 2003").

Common knowledge need not be documented

You don't need to document anything considered *common knowledge*: material that appears repeatedly in general sources. In medicine, for instance, it has become common knowledge that foods containing animal fat (meat, butter, cheese, whole milk) contribute to blood cholesterol levels. Thus, in a research report on fatty diets and heart disease, you probably would not need to document that well-known fact. But you would document information about how the fat-cholesterol connection was discovered, subsequent studies (say, of the role of saturated versus unsaturated fats), and any information for which some other person could claim specific credit. If the borrowed material can be found in only one specific source and not in multiple sources, document it. When in doubt, document the source.

HOW YOU SHOULD DOCUMENT

Cite borrowed material twice: at the exact place you use that material and at the end of your paper. Documentation practices vary widely, but all systems work almost identically: A brief reference in the text names the source and refers readers to the complete citation, which enables the source to be retrieved.

This chapter illustrates citations and entries for two styles widely used for documenting sources in college writing:

- Modern Language Association (MLA) style, for the humanities
- American Psychological Association (APA) style, for social sciences

Unless your audience has a particular preference, either of these styles can be adapted to most research writing. Use one style consistently throughout your paper.

MLA DOCUMENTATION STYLE

Use this alternative to footnotes and bibliographies

Traditional MLA documentation used superscripted numbers (like this:[1]) in the text, followed by complete citations at page bottom (footnotes) or at document's end (endnotes) and, finally, by a bibliography. But a more current form of documentation appears in the *MLA Handbook for Writers of Research Papers,* 6th ed., New York: Modern Language Association, 2003. Footnotes or endnotes are now used only to comment on material in the text or on sources or to suggest additional sources. (Place these notes at page bottom or in a "Notes" section at document's end.)

Cite a source briefly in your text and fully at the end

In current MLA style, in-text parenthetical references briefly identify the source(s). The complete citation then appears in a "Works-Cited" section at the paper's end.

A parenthetical reference usually includes the author's surname and the exact page number(s) of the borrowed material:

Parenthetical reference in the text

```
Recent data provided by 796 colleges indicate that violent crime

on campus is increasing (Lederman 31).
```

Readers seeking the complete citation for Lederman can refer easily to Works Cited, listed alphabetically by author:

Full citation at paper's end

```
Lederman, Douglas. "Colleges Report Rise in Violent Crime."

    Chronicle of Higher Education 3 Feb. 1995, sec. A: 31-42.
```

This complete citation includes page numbers for the entire article.

MLA Parenthetical References

How to cite briefly in your text

For clear and informative parenthetical references, observe these guidelines:

- If your discussion names the author, do not repeat the name in your parenthetical reference; simply give the page number(s):

Citing page numbers only

> Lederman points out that data provided by 796 colleges indicate that violent crime on campus is increasing (31).

- If you cite two or more works in a single parenthetical reference, separate the citations with semicolons:

Three works in a single reference

> (Jones 32; Leduc 41; Gomez 293-94)

- If you cite two or more authors with the same surname, include the first initial in your parenthetical reference to each author:

Two authors with identical surnames

> (R. Jones 32) (S. Jones 14-15)

- If you cite two or more works by the same author, include the first significant word from each work's title, or a shortened version:

Two works by one author

> (Lamont, Biophysics 100-01) (Lamont, Diagnostic Tests 81)

- If the work is by an institutional or corporate author or if it is unsigned (that is, author unknown), use only the first few words of the institutional name or the work's title in your parenthetical reference:

Institutional, corporate, or anonymous author

> (American Medical Assn. 2) ("Distribution Systems" 18)

To avoid distracting the reader, keep each parenthetical reference as brief as possible. (One method is to name the source in your discussion and to place only the page number[s] in parentheses.)

Where to place a parenthetical reference

For a paraphrase, place the parenthetical reference *before* the closing punctuation mark. For a quotation that runs into the text, place the reference *between* the final quotation mark and the closing punctuation mark. For a quotation set off (indented) from the text, place the reference two spaces *after* the closing punctuation mark.

MLA Works-Cited Entries

How to space and indent entries

The Works-Cited list includes each source that you have paraphrased or quoted. In preparing the list, type the first line of each entry flush with the left margin. Indent the second and subsequent lines one-half inch. Double-space within and between each entry. Use one character space after any period, comma, or colon.

How to cite fully at the end

Following are examples of complete citations as they would appear in the Works-Cited section of your report. Shown italicized below each citation is its corresponding parenthetical reference as it would appear in the text. Note capitalization, abbreviations, spacing, and punctuation in the sample entries.

INDEX TO SAMPLE ENTRIES FOR MLA WORKS-CITED LIST

Books

1. Book, single author
2. Book, two or three authors
3. Book, four or more authors
4. Book, anonymous author(s)
5. Multiple books, same author(s)
6. Book, one or more editors
7. Book, indirect source
8. Anthology selection or book chapter

Periodicals

9. Article, magazine
10. Article, journal with new pagination each issue
11. Article, journal with continuous pagination
12. Article, newspaper

Other Sources

13. Encyclopedia, dictionary, other alphabetical reference
14. Report
15. Conference presentation

16. Interview, personally conducted
17. Interview, published
18. Letter, unpublished
19. Questionnaire
20. Brochure or pamphlet
21. Lecture
22. Government document
23. Document with corporate authorship
24. Map or other visual aid
25. Miscellaneous (unpublished report, dissertation, and so on)

Electronic Sources

26. Online database
27. Computer software
28. CD-ROM
29. Listserv
30. Usenet
31. Email
32. Web site
33. Article in online periodical
34. Real-time communication

What to include in an
MLA citation for a book

MLA Works-Cited Entries for Books.   Any citation for a book should contain the following information (found on the book's title and copyright pages): author, title, editor or translator, edition, volume number, and facts about publication (city, publisher, date).

1. Book, Single Author—MLA

Reardon, Kathleen Kelley. They Don't Get It, Do They?:

   Communication in the Workplace—Closing the Gap Between Women

   and Men. Boston: Little, 1995.

Parenthetical reference: (Reardon 3-4)

Identify the state of publication by U.S. Postal Service abbreviations. If the city of publication is well known (Boston, Chicago, and so on), omit the state abbreviation. If several cities are listed on the title page, give only the first. For Canada, include the province abbreviation after the city. For all other countries, include an abbreviation of the country name.

2. Book, Two or Three Authors—MLA

Aronson, Linda, Roger Katz, and Candide Moustafa. <u>Toxic Waste</u>

<u>Disposal Methods</u>. New Haven: Yale UP, 2003.

Parenthetical Reference: (Aronson, Katz, and Moustafa 121-23)

Shorten publishers' names, as in "Simon" for Simon & Schuster, "GPO" for Government Printing Office, or "Yale UP" for Yale University Press. For page numbers having more than two digits, give only the final two digits for the second number if the first digit is identical.

3. Book, Four or More Authors—MLA

Santos, Ruth J., et al. <u>Environmental Crises in Developing</u>

<u>Countries</u>. New York: Harper, 2001.

Parenthetical Reference: (Santos et al. 9)

"Et al." is the abbreviated form of the Latin "et alia," meaning "and others."

4. Book, Anonymous Author(s)—MLA

<u>Structured Programming</u>. Boston: Meredith, 2002.

Parenthetical Reference: (<u>Structured</u> 67)

5. Multiple Books, Same Author(s)—MLA

Chang, John W. <u>Biophysics</u>. Boston: Little, 2002.

---. <u>Diagnostic Techniques</u>. New York: Radon, 1997.

Parenthetical Reference: (Chang, <u>Biophysics</u> 123-26) (Chang,

<u>Diagnostic</u> 87)

When citing more than one work by the same author, do not repeat the author's name; simply type three hyphens followed by a period. List the works alphabetically by title.

6. Book, One or More Editors—MLA

Morris, A. J., and Louise B. Pardin-Walker, eds. <u>Handbook of New</u>

<u>Information Technology</u>. New York: Harper, 2000.

Parenthetical Reference: (Morris and Pardin-Walker 34)

For more than three editors, name only the first, followed by "et al."

7. Book, Indirect Source—MLA

```
Kline, Thomas. Automated Systems. Boston: Rhodes, 1992.

Stubbs, John. White-Collar Productivity. Miami: Harris, 1999.
```

Parenthetical Reference: (qtd. in Stubbs 116)

When your source (as in Stubbs, above) has quoted or cited another source, list each source in its appropriate alphabetical place in the Works Cited list. Use the name of the original source (here, Kline) in your text and begin the parenthetical reference with "qtd. in," or "cited in" for a paraphrase.

8. Anthology Selection or Book Chapter—MLA

```
Bowman, Joel P. "Electronic Conferencing." Communication and
     Technology: Today and Tomorrow. Ed. Al Williams. Denton, TX:
     Assn. for Business Communication, 1994. 123-42.
```

Parenthetical Reference: (Bowman 129)

The page numbers in the complete citation are for the selection cited from the anthology.

What to include in an MLA citation for a periodical

MLA Works-Cited Entries for Periodicals. Give all available information in this order: author, article title, periodical title, volume and issue, date (day, month, year), and page numbers for the entire article—not just pages cited.

9. Article, Magazine—MLA

```
DesMarteau, Kathleen. "Study Links Sewing Machine Use to
     Alzheimer's Disease." Bobbin Oct. 1994: 36-38.
```

Parenthetical Reference: (DesMarteau 36)

No punctuation separates the magazine title and date. Nor is the abbreviation "p." or "pp." used to designate page numbers. If no author is given, list all other information:

```
"Video Games for the Next Decade." Power Technology Magazine 18
     Oct. 2002: 18+.
```

Parenthetical Reference: ("Video Games" 18)

This article began on page 18 and then continued on page 21. When an article does not appear on consecutive pages, give only the number of the first page, followed immediately by a plus sign. A three-letter abbreviation denotes any month spelled with five or more letters.

10. Article, Journal with New Pagination Each Issue—MLA

`Thackman-White, Joan R. "Computer Assisted Research." `American

`Library Journal` 51.1 (2002): 3-9.

Parenthetical Reference: (Thackman-White 4-5)

Because each issue for that year will have page numbers beginning with "1," readers need the number of this issue. The "51" denotes the volume number; the "1" denotes the issue number. Omit "The" or "A" or any other introductory article from a journal or magazine title.

11. Article, Journal with Continuous Pagination—MLA

`Barnstead, Marion H. "The Writing Crisis." `Journal of Writing

`Theory` 12 (2001): 415-33.

Parenthetical Reference: (Barnstead 418)

When page numbers continue from issue to issue for the full year, readers won't need the issue number, because no other issue in that year repeats these same page numbers. (Include the issue number if you think it will help readers retrieve the article more easily.) The "12" denotes the volume number.

12. Article, Newspaper—MLA

`Baranski, Vida H. "Errors in Medical Diagnosis." `Boston Times` 15`

`Jan. 2002, evening ed., sec. B: 3.`

Parenthetical Reference: (Baranski 3)

When a daily newspaper has more than one edition, cite the specific edition after the date. Omit any introductory article in the newspaper's name (not The Boston Times). If no author is given, list all other information. If the newspaper's name does not contain the city of publication, insert it, using brackets: "Sippican Sentinel [Marion MA]."

What to include in an MLA citation for a miscellaneous source

MLA Works-Cited Entries for Other Sources.   Miscellaneous sources range from unsigned encyclopedia entries to conference presentations to government publications. A full citation should give this information (as available): author, title, city, publisher, date, and page numbers.

13. Encyclopedia, Dictionary, Other Alphabetical Reference—MLA

`"Communication." `The Business Reference Book`. 2001 ed.`

Parenthetical Reference: ("Communication")

Begin a signed entry with the author's name. For any work arranged alphabetically, omit page numbers in the complete citation and the parenthetical reference. For a well-known reference book, include only an edition (if stated) and a date. For other reference books, give the full publication information.

14. Report—MLA

Electrical Power Research Institute (EPRI). <u>Epidemiologic Studies</u>
    <u>of Electric Utility Employees</u>. (Report No. RP2964.5). Palo
    Alto, CA: EPRI, Nov. 1994.

Parenthetical Reference: (Electrical Power Research Institute
    [EPRI] 27)

If no author is given, begin with the organization that sponsored the report.

For any report or other document with group authorship, as above, include the group's abbreviated name in your first parenthetical reference, then use only that abbreviation in any subsequent reference.

15. Conference Presentation—MLA

Smith, Abelard A. "Multicultural Stereotypes in Elizabethan Prose
    Fiction." <u>First British Symposium in Multicultural Studies.</u>
    London, 11-13 Oct. 2002. Ed. Anne Hodkins. London: Harrison,
    2002. 106-21.

Parenthetical Reference (Smith 109)

The above example shows a presentation that has been included in the published proceedings of a conference. For an unpublished presentation, include the presenter's name, the title of the presentation, and the conference title, location, and date, but do not underline or italicize the conference information.

16. Interview, Personally Conducted—MLA

Nasson, Gamela. Chief of Campus Police. Rangeley, ME. 2 Apr. 2002.

Parenthetical Reference (Nasson)

17. Interview, Published—MLA

Lescault, James. "The Future of Graphics," <u>Executive Views of</u>
    <u>Automation</u>. Ed. Karen Prell. Miami: Haber, 2002. 216-31.

Parenthetical Reference (Lescault 218)

The interviewee's name is placed in the entry's author slot.

18. Letter, Unpublished—MLA

Rogers, Leonard. Letter to the author. 15 May 2001.

Parenthetical Reference: (Rogers)

19. Questionnaire—MLA

Taynes, Lorraine. Questionnaire sent to 61 college
administrators. 14 Feb. 2002.

Parenthetical Reference: (Taynes)

20. Brochure or Pamphlet—MLA

Career Strategies for the 21st Century. San Francisco: Blount
Economics Assn., 2001.

Parenthetical Reference: (Career)

If the work is signed, begin with its author.

21. Lecture—MLA

Dumont, R. A. "Androgyny and the Rhetorical Tradition." Lecture,
University of Massachusetts at Dartmouth, 15 Jan. 2001.

Parenthetical Reference: (Dumont)

If the lecture title is not known, write Address, Lecture, or Reading but do
not use quotation marks. Include the sponsor and the location if they are
available.

22. Government Document—MLA

If the author is unknown, begin with the information in this order: name of
the government, name of the issuing agency, document title, place, publisher,
and date:

Virginia, Highway Dept. Standards for Bridge Maintenance.
Richmond: Virginia Highway Dept., 2000.

Parenthetical Reference: (Virginia Highway Dept. 49)

For any Congressional document, identify the house of Congress (Senate or
House of Representatives) before the title and the number and session of
Congress after the title:

United States Cong. House. Armed Services Committee. Funding for

the Military Academies. 103rd Cong., 2nd sess. Washington:

GPO, 2001.

Parenthetical Reference: (Armed Services Committee 41)

("GPO" is the abbreviation for the United States Government Printing Office.)

For an entry from the Congressional Record, give only date and pages:

Cong. Rec. 10 Mar. 1999: 2178-92.

Parenthetical Reference: (Cong. Rec. 2184)

23. Document with Corporate Authorship—MLA

Hermitage Foundation. Global Warming Scenarios for the Year 2030.

Washington: Natl. Res. Council, 2002.

Parenthetical Reference: (Hermitage Foun. 123)

24. Map or Other Visual Aid—MLA

Deaths Caused by Breast Cancer, by County. Map. Scientific

American Oct. 1995: 32D.

Parenthetical Reference: (Deaths Caused)

If the creator of the visual is listed, list that name first. Identify the type of visual (Map, Graph, Table, Diagram) immediately following its title.

25. Miscellaneous Items (Unpublished Report, Dissertation, and so on)—MLA

Author (if known), title (in quotes), sponsoring organization or

publisher, date, page number(s).

For any work that has group authorship (corporation, committee, task force), cite the name of the group or agency in place of the author's name.

What to include in an
MLA citation for an
electronic source

MLA Works-Cited Entires for Electronic Sources.   Citation for an electronic source with a printed equivalent should begin with that publication information (see relevant sections above). But whether or not a printed equivalent exists, any citation should enable readers to retrieve the material electronically.

The Modern Language Association recommends these general conventions:

PUBLICATION DATES   For sources taken from the Internet, include the date the source was posted to the Internet or last updated or revised; give also the date you accessed the source.

UNIFORM RESOURCE LOCATORS   Include a full and accurate URL for any source taken from the Internet (with access-mode identifier—*http, ftp, gopher,* or *telnet*). Enclose URLs in angle brackets (< >). When a URL continues from one line to the next, break it only after a slash. Do not add a hyphen.

PAGE NUMBERING   Include page or paragraph numbers when given by the source.

26. Online Database Source—MLA

```
Sahl, J. D. "Power Lines, Viruses, and Childhood Leukemia."

      Cancer Causes Control 6.1 (Jan. 1995): 83. MEDLINE. Online.

      7 Nov. 2001. Dialog.
```

```
Parenthetical reference: (Sahl 83)
```

For entries with a printed equivalent, begin with publication information, then the database title (underlined), the "Online" designation to indicate the medium, and the service provider (or URL or email address) and the date of access. The access date is important because frequent updatings of databases can produce different versions of the material.

For entries with no printed equivalent, give the title and date of the work in quotation marks, followed by the electronic source information:

```
Argent, Roger R. "An Analysis of International Exchange Rates for

      1999." Accu-Data. Online. Dow Jones News Retrieval. 10 Jan.

      2002.
```

```
Parenthetical reference: (Argent 4)
```

If the author is not known, begin with the work's title.

27. Computer Software—MLA

```
Virtual Collaboration. Diskette. New York: Harper, 1994.
```

```
Parenthetical reference: (Virtual)
```

Begin with the author's name, if known.

28. CD-ROM Source—MLA

Canalte, Henry A. "Violent-Crime Statistics: Good News and Bad

News." <u>Law Enforcement</u> Feb. 1995: 8. <u>ABI/INFORM</u>. CD-ROM.

Proquest. Sept. 2002.

Parenthetical reference: (Canalte 8)

If the material also is available in print, begin with the information about the printed source, followed by the electronic source information: name of database (underlined), "CD-ROM" designation, vendor name, and electronic publication date. If the material has no printed equivalent, list its author (if known) and its title (in quotation marks), followed by the electronic source information.

How to cite an abstract

If you are citing merely an abstract (page 422) of the complete work, insert "Abstract," followed by a period, immediately after the work's page number(s)—as in "8" in the previous entry.

For CD-ROM reference works and other material that is not routinely updated, give the work title followed by the "CD-ROM" designation, place, electronic publisher, and date:

<u>Time Almanac</u>. CD-ROM. Washington: Compact, 1997.

Parenthetical reference: (<u>Time Almanac</u> 74)

Begin with the author's name, if known.

29. Listserv—MLA

Kosten, A. "Major update of the WWWVL Migration and Ethnic

Relations." 7 April 1998. Online posting. ERCOMER News.

7 Apr. 2002 <http://www.ercomer.org/archive/

ercomer-news/002.html>.

Begin with the author's name (if known), followed by the title of the work (in quotation marks), publication date, the Online posting designation, name of discussion group, date of access, and the URL. The parenthetical reference includes no page number because none is given in an online posting.

30. Usenet—MLA

Dorsey, Michael. "Environmentalism or Racism." 25 Mar. 1998.

Online posting. 1 Apr. 2001 <news: alt.org.sierra-club>.

31. Email—MLA

```
Wallin, John Luther. "Frog Reveries." Email to the author. 12
        Oct. 2002.
```

Cite personal email as you would printed correspondence. If the document has a subject line or title, enclose it in quotation marks.

For publicly posted email (say, a newsgroup or discussion list), include the address and the date of access.

32. Web Site—MLA

```
Dumont, R. A. "An On-line Course in Composition." 10 Dec. 1999.
        UMASS Dartmouth Online. 6 Jan. 2002.
        <http://www.umassd.edu/englishdepartment.html>.
```

Parenthetical reference: (Dumont 7-9)

Begin with the author's name (if known), followed by title of the work (in quotation marks), the posting date, name of Web site, date of access, and Web address (in angle brackets). Note that a Web address that continues from one line to the next is broken only after slash(es). No hyphen is added.

33. Article in an Online Periodical—MLA

```
Jones, Francine L. "The Effects of NAFTA on Labor Union
        Membership." Cambridge Business Review 2.3 (1999): 47-64. 4
        Apr. 2002. <http://www.mun.ca/cambrbusrev/1999vol2/
        jones2.html>.
```

Parenthetical reference: (Jones 44-45)

Information about the printed version is followed by the date of access to the Web site and the electronic address.

34. Real-Time Communication—MLA

Synchronous communication occurs in a "real-time" forum and includes MUDs (multiuser dungeons), MOOs (MUD object-oriented software), IRC (Internet relay chat), and FTPs (file transfer protocols). The message typed in by the sender appears instantly on the screen of the recipient, as in a personal interview.

```
Mendez, Michael R. Online debate. "Solar Power versus Fossil Fuel
     Power." 3 Apr. 1998. CollegeTownMoo. 3 Apr. 2002.
     <telnet://next.cs.bvc.edu.777>
```

Parenthetical reference: (Mendez)

Begin with the name of the communicator(s) and indicate the type of communication (personal interview, online debate, and so on), topic title, posting date, name of forum, access date, and electronic address.

MLA Sample List of Works Cited

Place your "Works Cited" section on a separate page at document's end. (See pages 464–68.) Arrange entries alphabetically by author's surname. When the author is unknown, list the title alphabetically according to its first word (excluding introductory articles). For a title that begins with a digit ("5," "6," etc.), alphabetize the entry as if the digit were spelled out.

APA DOCUMENTATION STYLE

One popular alternative to MLA style appears in the *Publication Manual of the American Psychological Association,* 5th ed. Washington, DC: American Psychological Association, 2001. APA style is useful when writers wish to emphasize the publication dates of their references. A parenthetical reference in the text briefly identifies the source, date, and page number(s):

Reference cited in the text

```
Data provided by 796 colleges indicate that violent crime on
campus is increasing (Lederman, 1995, p. 31).
```

The full citation then appears in the alphabetical listing of "References" at the paper's end:

Full citation at paper's end

```
Lederman, D. (1995). Colleges report rise in violent crime.
     Chronicle of Higher Education, pp. 31-42.
```

Because it emphasizes the date, APA style (or any similar author-date style) is preferred in the sciences and social sciences, where information quickly becomes outdated.

APA Parenthetical References

How APA and MLA parenthetical references differ

APA's parenthetical references differ from MLA's (pages 394–95) as follows: the citation includes the publication date; a comma separates each item in the reference; and "p." or "pp." precedes the page number (which is optional in the APA system). When a subsequent reference to a work follows closely after the initial reference, the date need not be included. Here are specific guide-lines:

- If your discussion names the author, do not repeat the name in your parenthetical reference; simply give the date and page number(s):

Author named in the text

```
Lederman (1995) cites recent data provided by 796 colleges
indicating that violent crime on campus is increasing (p. 31).
```

When two authors of a work are named in your text, their names are connected by "and," but in a parenthetical reference their names are connected by an ampersand: "&."

- If you cite two or more works in a single reference, list the authors in alphabetical order and separate the citations with semicolons:

Two or more works in a single reference

```
(Jones, 2001; Gomez, 1995; Leduc, 1998)
```

- If you cite a work with three to five authors, try to name them in your text, to avoid an excessively long parenthetical reference:

A work with three to five authors

```
Franks, Oblesky, Ryan, Jablar, and Perkins (1993) studied the
role of electromagnetic fields in tumor formation.
```

In any subsequent references to this work, name only the first author, followed by "et al." (Latin abbreviation for "and others").

- If you cite two or more works by the same author published in the same year, assign a different letter to each work:

Two or more works by the same author in the same year

```
(Lamont 1999a, p. 135) (Lamont 1999b, pp. 67-68)
```

Other examples of parenthetical references appear with their corresponding entries in the following discussion of the reference-list entries.

APA Reference-List Entries

How to space and indent entries

The APA reference list includes each source you have cited in your paper. In preparing the list of references for a student paper, type the first line of each entry flush with the left margin. Indent the second and subsequent lines 5 character spaces or one-half inch. Double-space within and between each entry. Skip one character space after any period, comma, or colon.

What to include in an APA citation for a book

Following are examples of complete citations as they would appear in the "References" section of your paper. Shown immediately below each entry is its corresponding parenthetical reference as it would appear in the text. Note the capitalization, abbreviation, spacing, and punctuation in the sample entries.

INDEX TO SAMPLE ENTRIES FOR APA REFERENCES

Books
1. Book, single author
2. Book, two to five authors
3. Book, six or more authors
4. Book, anonymous author
5. Multiple books, same author(s)
6. Book, one to five editors
7. Book, indirect source
8. Anthology selection or book chapter

Periodicals
9. Article, magazine
10. Article, journal with new pagination for each issue
11. Article, journal with continuous pagination
12. Article, newspaper

Other Sources
13. Encyclopedia, dictionary, alphabetical reference

14. Report
15. Conference presentation
16. Interview, personally conducted
17. Interview, published
18. Personal correspondence
19. Brochure or pamphlet
20. Unpublished lecture
21. Government document
22. Miscellaneous items (unpublished manuscript, dissertation, and so on)

Electronic Sources
23. Online database abstract
24. Online database article
25. Computer software or software manual
26. CD-ROM abstract
27. CD-ROM reference work
28. Personal email
29. Web site
30. Newsgroup, discussion list, online forum

APA Entries for Books.   Any citation for a book should contain all applicable information in the following order: author, date, title, editor or translator, edition, volume number, and facts about publication (city and publisher).

1. Book, Single Author—APA

Reardon, K. K. (1995). *They don't get it, do they?: Communication in the workplace—closing the gap between women and men.* Boston: Little, Brown.

Parenthetical reference: (Reardon, 1995, pp. 3-4)

Use only initials for an author's first and middle name. Capitalize only the first words of a book's title and subtitle and any proper names. Identify a later edition in parentheses between the title and the period.

2. Book, Two to Five Authors—APA

Aronson, L., Katz, R., & Moustafa, C. (2002). *Toxic waste disposal methods*. New Haven: Yale University Press.

Parenthetical reference: (Aronson, Katz, & Moustafa, 2002)

Use an ampersand (&) before the name of the final author listed in an entry. As an alternative parenthetical reference, name the authors in your text and include date (and page numbers, if appropriate) in parentheses.

3. Book, Six or More Authors—APA

Fogle, S. T., et al. (1998). *Hyperspace technology*. Boston: Little, Brown.

Parenthetical reference: (Fogle, et al., 1998, p. 34)

"Et al." is the Latin abbreviation for "et alia," meaning "and others."

4. Book, Anonymous Author—APA

Structured programming. (2002). Boston: Merideth Press.

Parenthetical reference: (*Structured Programming*, 2002, p. 67)

In your list of references, place an anonymous work alphabetically by the first key word (not "The," "A," or "An") in its title. In your parenthetical reference, capitalize all key words in a book, article, or journal title.

5. Multiple Books, Same Author(s)—APA

Chang, J. W. (2002a). *Biophysics*. Boston: Little, Brown.

Chang, J. W. (2002b). *MindQuest*. Chicago: John Pressler.

Parenthetical reference: (Chang, 2002a) (Chang, 2002b)

Two or more works by the same author not published in the same year are distinguished by their respective dates alone, without the added letter.

6. Book, One to Five Editors—APA

Morris, A. J., & Pardin-Walker, L. B. (Eds.). (2000). *Handbook of new information technology*. New York: HarperCollins.

Parenthetical reference: (Morris & Pardin-Walker, 2000, p. 79)

For more than five editors, name only the first, followed by "et al."

7. Book, Indirect Source

Stubbs, J. (1999). *White-collar productivity*. Miami: Harris.

Parenthetical reference: (cited in Stubbs, 1999, p. 47)

When your source (as in Stubbs, above) has cited another source, list only this second source, but name the original source in your text: "Kline's study (cited in Stubbs, 1996, p. 47) supports this conclusion."

8. Anthology Selection or Book Chapter—APA

Bowman, J. (1994). Electronic conferencing. In A. Williams (Ed.),
   Communication and technology: Today and tomorrow. (pp.
   123-142). Denton, TX: Association for Business
   Communication.

Parenthetical reference: (Bowman, 1994, p. 126)

The page numbers in the complete reference are for the selection cited from the anthology.

What to include in an APA citation for a periodical

APA Entries for Periodicals.   A citation for an article should give this information (as available), in order: author, publication, date, article title (without quotation marks), volume or number (or both), and page numbers for the entire article—not just the page(s) cited.

9. Article, Magazine—APA

DesMarteau K. (1994, October). Study links sewing machine use to
   Alzheimer's disease. *Bobbin, 36*, 36-38.

Parenthetical reference: (DesMarteau, 1994, p. 36)

If no author is given, provide all other information. Capitalize only the first words in an article's title and subtitle. Capitalize all key words in a periodical title. Show a continuous underline for the periodical title, volume number, and comma.

10. Article, Journal with New Pagination for Each Issue—APA

Thackman-White, J. R. (2002). Computer-assisted research.
   American Library Journal, 51 (1), 3-9.

Parenthetical reference: (Thackman-White, 2002, pp. 4-5)

Because each issue for a given year has page numbers that begin at "1," readers need the issue number (in this instance, "1"). The "*51*" denotes the volume number, which is italicized.

11. Article, Journal with Continuous Pagination—APA

Barnstead, M. H. (2001). The writing crisis. *Journal of Writing Theory, 12,* 415-433.

Parenthetical reference: (Barnstead, 2001, pp. 415-416)

The "*12*" denotes the volume number. When page numbers continue from issue to issue for the full year, readers won't need the issue number, because no other issue in that year repeats these same page numbers. (You can include the issue number if you think it will help readers retrieve the article more easily.)

12. Article, Newspaper—APA

Baranski, V. H. (2002, January 15). Errors in medical diagnosis. *The Boston Times,* p. B3.

Parenthetical Reference: (Baranski, 2002, p. B3)

In addition to the year of publication, include the month and date. If the newspaper's name begins with "The," include it in your citation. Include "p." or "pp." before page numbers. For an article on nonconsecutive pages, list each page, separated by a comma.

What to include in an APA citation for a miscellaneous source

APA Entries for Other Sources. Miscellaneous sources range from unsigned encyclopedia entries to conference presentations to government documents. A full citation should give this information (as available): author, publication date, title of work, city, publisher (or volume and issue number), and page numbers (if applicable).

13. Encyclopedia, Dictionary, Alphabetical Reference—APA

Communication. (2001). In *The business reference book.*

Parenthetical reference: (Communication, 2001)

For an entry that is signed, begin with the author's name and publication date.

14. Report—APA

Electrical Power Research Institute. (1994). *Epidemiologic studies of electric utility employees.* (Report No. RP2964.5). Palo Alto, CA: Author.

Parenthetical reference: (Electrical Power Research Institute [EPRI], 1994, p. 12)

If authors are named, list them first, followed by the publication date. When citing a group author, as above, include the group's abbreviated name in your first parenthetical reference, and use only that abbreviation in any subsequent reference. When the agency (or organization) and publisher are the same, list "Author" in the publisher's slot.

15. Conference Presentation—APA

Smith, A. A. (2002). Multicultural stereotypes in Elizabethan prose fiction. In A. Hodkins (Ed.), *First British Symposium on Multicultural Studies* (pp. 106-121). London: Harrison Press, 2002.

Parenthetical reference: (Smith, 2002, p. 109)

In parentheses is the date of the presentation. The name of the symposium is a proper name, so is capitalized. Following the publisher's name is the date of publication.

For an unpublished presentation, include the presenter's name, year and month, title of the presentation (italicized), and all available information about the conference or meeting: "Symposium held at. . . ." Do not italicize this last information.

16. Interview, Personally Conducted—APA

This material is considered a "nonrecoverable" source, so it is cited in the text only, as a parenthetical reference:

Parenthetical reference: (G. Nasson, personal interview, April 2, 2002)

If you name the interviewee in your text, do not repeat the name in your citation.

17. Interview, Published—APA

Jable, C. K. (1999, June 7). The future of graphics. [Interview with James Lescault]. In K. Prell (Ed.), *Executive views of automation* (pp. 216-231). Miami: Haber Press, 2000.

Parenthetical reference: (Jable, 1999, pp. 218-223)

Begin with the name of the interviewer, followed by the interview date and title (if available), the designation (in brackets), and the publication information, including the date.

18. Personal Correspondence—APA

This material is considered nonrecoverable data, so it is cited in the text only, as a parenthetical reference:

Parenthetical reference: (L. Rogers, personal correspondence, May
15, 2001)

If you name the correspondent in your text, do not repeat the name in your citation.

19. Brochure or Pamphlet—APA

This material follows the citation format for a book entry (pages 408–410).

20. Unpublished Lecture—APA

Dumont, R. A. (2001, January 15). *Androgyny and the rhetorical
tradition.* Lecture presented at the University of
Massachusetts at Dartmouth.

Parenthetical reference: (R. A. Dumont, 2001)

If you name the lecturer in your text, do not repeat the name in your citation.

21. Government Document—APA

If the author is unknown, present the information in this order: name of the issuing agency, publication date, document title, place, and publisher.

Virginia Highway Department. (2000). *Standards for bridge
maintenance.* Richmond: Author.

Parenthetical reference: (Virginia Highway Department, 2000,
p. 49)

When the issuing agency is both author and publisher, list "Author" in the publisher's slot.

For any Congressional document, identify the house of Congress (Senate or House of Representatives) before the date.

United States Congress. House. Armed Services Committee. (2001).
Funding for the military academies. Washington, DC: U.S.
Government Printing Office.

Parenthetical reference: (Armed Services Committee, 2001, p. 41)

22. Miscellaneous Items (Unpublished manuscript, Dissertation, and so on)—APA

```
Author (if known), date of publication, title of work, sponsoring
                organization or publisher, page numbers.
```

For any work that has group authorship (corporation, committee, and so on), cite the name of the group or agency in place of the author's name.

What to include in an APA citation for an electronic source

APA Entries for Electronic Sources.   Any citation for electronic media should enable readers to identify the original source (printed or electronic) and provide an electronic path for retrieving the material.

Begin with the publication information for the printed equivalent. Then, in brackets, name the electronic source ([CD-ROM], [Computer software]), the protocol* (Bitnet, Dialog, FTP, Telnet) and any other items that define a clear path (service provider, database title, access code, retrieval number, or site address).

23. Online Database Abstract—APA

```
Sahl, J. D. (1995). Power lines, viruses, and childhood leukemia.
     Cancer Causes Control, 6 (1), 83. Abstract retrieved
        November 7, 2001, from the MEDLINE database.
```

Parenthetical reference: (Sahl, 1995)

Note that the above entry ends with a period. Only entries that close with a URL have no period at the end.

24. Online Database Article—APA

```
Alley, R. A. (1999, January). Ergonomic influences on worker
        satisfaction. Industrial Psychology, 5(11), 93-107.
           Retrieved April 8, 2002, from the PsycARTICLES database.
```

Parenthetical reference: (Alley, 1999)

25. Computer Software or Software Manual—APA

```
Virtual collaboration [Computer software]. (1994). New York:
        HarperCollins.
```

Parenthetical reference: (Virtual, 1994)

---

*A protocol is a body of standards that ensure compatibility among the different products designed to work together on a particular network.

For citing a manual, replace the "Computer software" designation in brackets with "Software manual."

26. CD-ROM Abstract—APA

Cavanaugh, H. (1995). An EMF study: Good news and bad news [CD-ROM]. *Electrical World,* 209(2), 8. Abstract retrieved April 7, 2002, from ProQuest File: ABI/INFORM.

Parenthetical reference: (Cavanaugh, 1995)

The "8" in the above entry denotes the page number of this one-page article.

27. CD-ROM Reference Work—APA

Time almanac. (1997). Washington: Compact, 1997.

Parenthetical reference: (Time almanac, 1997)

If the work on CD-ROM has a printed equivalent, APA currently prefers that it be cited in its printed form.

28. Personal Email—APA

Parenthetical reference: Fred Flynn (personal communication, May 10, 1999) provided these statistics.

Instead of being included in the list of references, personal email is cited directly in the text.

29. Web Site—APA

Dumont, R. A. (2000, July 10). An online course in composition. Retrieved May 18, 2001, from http://www.umassd.edu/englishdepartment.html

Parenthetical reference: (Dumont, 2000)

If the Web address continues from one line to the next, divide it only after the slash(es).

30. Newsgroup, Discussion List, Online Forum—APA

Labarge, V. S. (2002, October 20). A cure for computer viruses [Msg 2237]. Message posted to http://forums.ntnews.com/webin/webz198@.dsg956

Parenthetical reference: (Labarge, 2002)

APA Sample List of References

APA's "References" section (pages 434–36) is an alphabetical listing (by author) equivalent to MLA's "Works Cited" section (page 406). Like Works Cited, the References section includes only those works actually cited. (A bibliography usually would include background works or works consulted, as well.) In one notable difference from MLA style, APA style calls for only "recoverable" sources to appear in the reference list. Therefore, personal interviews, email messages, and other unpublished materials are cited in the text only.

Application **21-1**

Computer Project: Both MLA and APA have issued new guidelines (pages 402, 414) for documenting sources from the Internet or Web.

But electronic documentation presents special problems. First, authors or sponsoring organizations for material posted directly to the Internet can be hard to find. Material on the Internet may have appeared somewhere else first, and this original source is sometimes not indicated clearly. Internet addresses won't take you back to the same site if you fail to copy them exactly—even though they may be several lines long. Pages often aren't numbered. Finally, it's sometimes hard to verify the quality of Internet sources, because on the Internet, *anyone* can claim to be an expert.

As you conduct your own electronic searches, use the list of problems above as a starting point and compile your own list of documentation issues in electronic research. For your classmates, compose a set of guidelines that will help them deal with these difficulties. Then examine the MLA and APA formats for electronic documentation. Which seems most useful? Why? Can you suggest changes that will make the formats more effective for students like you as they try to document their work?

Work Cited

Gibaldi, Joseph, and Walter S. Achtert. *MLA Handbook for Writers of Research Papers.* 3rd ed. New York: Modern Language Assn., 1988.

C H A P T E R   2 2

Composing the Research Report

Developing a Working Thesis and Outline   **417**

Drafting Your Report   **418**

Revising Your Report   **419**

A Sample Report in APA Style   **420**

DEVELOPING A WORKING THESIS AND OUTLINE

Don't expect to arrive at your thesis until you have evaluated and interpreted your findings (as discussed on pages 376–87). Your thesis should emerge from the most accurate and reliable information you have been able to find.

On page 334 you phrased your topic as this question:

Research topic

| *Violent Crime on College Campuses: How Common Is It?*

Near the completion of your research, you should have at least a tentative answer to that question:

Tentative thesis

| Violent crime on college campuses is more common than many people like to believe.

As your research proceeds, you might revise this tentative thesis any number of times.

417

Now you need a road map—a working outline. Perhaps your topic itself or your reading suggested a rough, working outline:

A working outline

    I. The extent of the problem

       A. Recent examples of highly publicized campus crimes

       B. National crime statistics

       C. The 1992 Campus Awareness and Security Act

    II. Direct causes of campus crime

       A. Alcohol and drug use by students

       B. Offenders from off-campus

    III. Indirect causes of campus crime

       A. Naive assumptions by parents

       B. Carefree student attitudes

       C. Deceptive publicity by some colleges

       D. Special treatment for athletes and fraternities

       E. Denial and cover-up by administrators

    IV. Actions required

       A. Greater candor and publicity

       B. Change in student habits

       C. Prevention programs

Of course, by the time you compose your final outline the shape of your report may have changed radically (see pages 421–36).

DRAFTING YOUR REPORT

When you have collected and reviewed your material, organized your note-cards, and settled on a workable thesis, you are ready to write the first draft of your report.

Begin by revising your working outline. At this stage, try to develop a detailed formal outline, using at each level either topic phrases (page 417) or full sentences (page 444).

A formal outline needs logical notation and consistent format. *Notation* is the system of numbers and letters marking the logical divisions; *format* is the arrangement of your material on the page (indentation, spacing, and so on). Proper notation and format show the subordination of some parts of your topic to others. The general pattern of outline notation goes like this:

The logical divisions of a formal outline

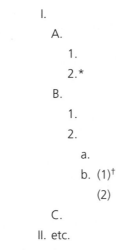

```
I.
   A.
      1.
      2.*
   B.
      1.
      2.
         a.
         b. (1)†
            (2)
   C.
II. etc.
```

(For a discussion of a sample formal outline, see page 445.) When your outline is complete, check your tentative thesis to make sure it promises *exactly* what your report will deliver.

Now you can begin to write. Students often find this the most intimidating part of research: pulling together a large body of information. Don't frantically throw everything on the page simply to get done. Concentrate on only one section at a time.

Begin by classifying your notecards or electronic notes in groups according to the section of your outline to which each note is keyed. Next, arrange the notes for your introduction in order. You are ready to write your first section. As you move from subsection to subsection, provide commentary and transitions, and document each source.

REVISING YOUR REPORT

After completing and documenting a first draft, use the Revision Checklist for essays in Chapter 4, along with the following Research Report checklist, to revise the report.

Pages 421–36 show the completed report, documented according to the APA style guidelines discussed in Chapter 21.

---

*Note each level of division yields at least two items. If you cannot divide a major item into at least two subordinate items, retain only your major heading.
†Carry further subdivisions as far as needed, but keep notation for each level individualized and consistent.

RESEARCH REPORT CHECKLIST ☑

(Numbers in parentheses refer to the first page of discussion.)

CONTENTS

☐ Does the report grow from a clear thesis? (417)

☐ Does the title offer an accurate forecast? (49)

☐ Does the evidence support the conclusion? (338)

☐ Is the report based on reliable sources and evidence? (376, 379)

☐ Is the information complete? (338)

☐ Does the report avoid reliance on a single source? (334)

☐ Is the evidence free of weak spots? (387)

☐ Are all data clearly and fully interpreted? (380)

☐ Can anything be cut? (369)

☐ Is anything missing? (380)

ORGANIZATION

☐ Does the introduction state clearly the purpose and thesis? (418)

☐ Does the report follow the outline? (418)

☐ Is each paragraph focused on one main thought? (98)

☐ Is the line of reasoning clear and easy to follow? (33)

DOCUMENTATION

☐ Is the documentation consistent, complete, and correct? (392)

☐ Is all quoted material marked clearly throughout the text? (370)

☐ Are all sources not considered common knowledge documented? (393)

☐ Are direct quotations used sparingly and appropriately? (370)

☐ Are all quotations accurate and integrated grammatically? (371)

☐ Is the report free of excessively long quotations? (370)

☐ Are all paraphrases accurate and clear? (372)

☐ Are electronic sources cited clearly and appropriately? (402, 414)

A SAMPLE REPORT IN APA STYLE

The following report was written in response to the scenario on page 334. As you read the report, evaluate its content, organization, and documentation by referring to the Checklist above.

1

Campus Crime: A Hidden Issue

Julia Schoonover

University of Massachusetts, Dartmouth
Professor J. M. Lannon

Intermediate Composition

Section 1

May 5, 2003

A research report in APA style

2

ABSTRACT

Violent crime on college campuses, usually student-on-student and triggered by alcohol and drugs, is far more common than many people like to believe. Campus crime remains a largely hidden issue because of naive assumptions by parents, carefree student attitudes, deceptive publicity by some colleges, special treatment for athletes and other privileged groups, and frequent denial and cover-up by college administrators. Recent government legislation, improved security measures, and prevention and support programs offer partial solutions. Most needed, however, is more responsible behavior from students and greater candor and publicity from college officials.

A research report in APA style (*Continued*)

DISCUSSION OF RESEARCH REPORT IN APA STYLE
APA FRONT MATTER (ITEMS THAT PRECEDE THE REPORT): 1–2

1. *Title page:* Center the title and all other lines. Do not underline the title or use all capital letters. Number the title page and all subsequent pages in the upper-right corner and include a shortened title as a running head for each page.

2. *Abstract:* Papers in APA style usually contain a one-paragraph abstract (roughly 100 words) that previews the main points and shows how they are related. Place the abstract on a separate page, following the title page. Center the heading; double-space the abstract; use no paragraph indent. (To prepare an abstract, see pages 373–76.)

3
4
5
6
7

Campus Crime: A Hidden Issue

Parents, students, and school administrators view college campuses through rose-colored glasses. We tend to think a college campus is a fairy land in which good prevails and, on rare occasions, evil briefly invades and then quickly retreats. According to journalist Anne Matthews (1993), "when aware of campus crime at all, [we] frequently attribute it to faceless hit-and-retreat raiders from the world beyond the ivy curtain" (p. 38). Like characters in a make-believe world, we enjoy feeling content and secure. The real world, however, tells a different story.

8

How Secure Is the Typical College Campus?

9
10

11

Benign images of campus life might conceal a pattern of violence. In 1986, at Lehigh University a female student was "robbed, sodomized, and murdered in her dorm bed by a fellow student she had never met" (Pfister, 1994, p. 26). In 1990, "one male and three female students at the University of Florida and another woman at Santa Fe Community College were found stabbed or bludgeoned to death. . . . Three of the victims were mutilated; one, an 18-year-old female honor student, was decapitated" (Campus ripper, 1990, p. 43). In 1991, "five University of Iowa employees—three professors, one staff member, and an associate vice president—were shot to death by a former physics graduate student irate at losing a research prize" (Matthews, 1993, p. 38). In 1992, "student Wayne Lo, 18, roamed Simon's Rock College, shooting four people and killing a professor and a fellow student" (Matthews, 1993, p. 38). Within one recent week alone, three people were shot dead at the Appalachian School of Law, and a murder-suicide killed two more at Broward Community College (Clayton, 2002).

A research report in APA style (*Continued*)

APA Body Elements: 3–11

3. Include the shortened title as a running head on each page and continue the page numbering.

4. Repeat the title exactly as it appears on the title page and center it.

5. Use one-inch margins all around. Begin the first paragraph two lines below the title and use double spacing throughout. Use a one-half inch indent for the first line of each paragraph. Do not hyphenate words at the right margin or justify the right margin (i.e., do not make it even).

6. Use the introduction to invite readers in and present your main idea. Show readers that your topic has meaning to them *personally* (as our writer here does by using "we"). For immediate credibility, try to include brief quotations from one or more authorities.

7. Introduce brief quotes by naming the author or speaker so that readers will know who said what. Combine the quoted material with your own words to make complete sentences. Use brackets to signal any alteration of the original quotation.

8. Use section headings to orient readers and show them what to expect. When you use questions as headings, phrase the questions the way readers might ask them. Phrase all section headings consistently.

9. Use vivid examples to make the problem real for readers.

10. Cite each source in parentheses, inside the period, but outside any quotation marks.

11. Use a shortened title to identify a source with no author named.

12

Countless additional crimes occur on college campuses, and their number is increasing. For example, Lederman (1995) points out that campus robberies and assaults increased by nearly 3 percent from 1992 to 1993, following a similar increase from 1991 to 1992 (p. 31). Recent evidence indicates that the violence is continuing: from 1999 to 2000, for example, the campus murder rate nearly doubled, from 11 to 20 per year (Clayton, 2002). Moreover, according to the Federal Bureau of Investigation (1999), 26 percent of all hate crimes reported in 1999 occurred on college campuses. (The Massachusetts Governor's Task Force (2001) defines *hate crime* as a crime motivated by prejudice against a victim's race, religion, ethnicity, gender, disability, or sexual orientation.)

Why Does Campus Crime Receive Scant Attention?

To find the right college for their child, parents look for many qualities in a school: a strong academic program, an accomplished faculty, an attractive campus, clean and roomy dormitories, and so on. But parents rarely consider campus crime because they assume that college campuses are safe. School officials attribute such naivete to parents' belief in the notion of *in loco parentis*— the assumption that a university stands in for the student's parents. According to a University of South Carolina law enforcement official, parents have unrealistic expectations when they send children off to college: "They expect the university to be able to control students' behavior. We can't always do that" (Dodge, 1991, p. A30). One safety official at Rutgers University agrees that too many parents "feel like they are turning their child over to the university for the university to care for in the same way that the child was cared for at home; that is just not possible" (McClarin, 1994, p. A1).

A research report in APA style (*Continued*)

APA BODY ELEMENTS (CONTINUED)

12. When you name the author in your text, include the date of the work immediately afterward, and the page numbers at citation's end. In the APA system, page numbers are optional in citing paraphrased material, but required in citing direct quotations.

Most students also feel safe in the serene and attractive setting of the typical college, failing to realize that roughly 80 percent of campus crime is student-on-student (McClarin, 1994, p. A1). In his review of recent research, Kier (1996) observes that as many as one of ten women on college campuses is sexually assaulted by an acquaintance. Pfister (1994) notes that overall estimates of campus sexual assault range from one in twenty-five to one in four (p. 26). Despite these alarming figures, student respondents to a survey at St. Augustine's College attributed the crime problem mostly to nonstudents (Ayres, 1993, p. A14).

In addition, like their parents, students assume they will be safeguarded from any danger by administrators or security personnel. They often consider themselves invincible and have the attitude "I get to do whatever I want but you have to protect me" (Matthews, 1993, p. 42). But students make themselves vulnerable to crime by drinking and partying until all hours and then just plopping down, wherever they may be, and sleeping until they sober up. Prior to the 1986 rape and murder at Lehigh University, for example, students routinely left room and dorm doors unlocked for the convenience of friends and roommates (Pfister, 1994, p. 26).

College crime statistics show that carefree attitudes about alcohol contribute to campus crime. Matthews (1993) asserts that "alcohol has become the drug of use at American Colleges, and a fuel for campus crime" (p. 41). In 1989, Towson State's Center for the Study and Prevention of Campus Violence surveyed 1,100 colleges and universities and found that "student crime victims drink and use drugs significantly more than nonvictims" (Matthews, 1993, p. 40). A 1992 survey of 17,000 students on 140 campuses found that 42 percent of college students are "binge drinkers" (five or more drinks in a row within any

A research report in APA style (*Continued*)

two weeks), and that female students on high-binge campuses reported a higher number of unwanted sexual advances (Cage, 1992, p. A30). For 1999, combined crime reports from roughly 800 campuses showed nearly 26,000 cases of illegal drinking; roughly 37,000 aggravated assaults; more than 1,800 sexual assaults; and 11 murders. Because many such crimes go unreported, experts argue, actual figures are probably much higher (Nicklin, 2001, p. A35).

Illegal drugs and alcohol abuse are common factors in about 90 percent of all campus crimes (Clery & Carter, 1997). Alcohol abuse has become such a rampant problem on campuses that a coalition of 24 Boston-area colleges recently pledged to work together to establish a discipline consistency, stronger programming, and increased alcohol awareness training (Fonseca, 1998).

The Boston coalition was formed in the wake of public outcry over a pair of recent, high-profile student deaths in the Bay State. The deaths include Massachusetts Institute of Technology freshman Scott Kreuger, who died from alcohol poisoning sustained during a freshman pledge party in Boston, and a University of Massachusetts Amherst student who died after he drank too much and collapsed through the roof of a greenhouse at the school (Fonseca, 1998).

Administrators know the exact dangers that exist on any college campus, but too often they choose to ignore the unpleasant facts—to avoid scaring off prospective students. Bright, glossy brochures promote every aspect of a particular school but rarely mention campus safety—let alone crime statistics. Transcripts of Congressional hearings (U.S. House of Representatives, 1990) reveal that, when campus crime does hit home, administrators often deny that any of their students are involved (p. 61).

A research report in APA style *(Continued)*

Administrators sometimes cover up campus crime because the offenders are prominent student athletes or drunken fraternity members. While investigating sexual assault on college campuses, Johnson (1991) found that "college athletes and fraternity men are a protected species" (p. 34). Beyond avoiding bad publicity, campus officials protect these assailants for fear of antagonizing their parents or school athletic fans and contributors (Matthews, 1993, p. 42). One prominent university recently awarded a grant to a basketball player who had pleaded guilty to sexual assault. This same school then offered his victim an academic scholarship (Blum, 1995, p. A29).

Any violent crime on a college campus causes temporary wariness among parents, students, and faculty. For a few weeks following a rape, assault, or other crime, everyone behaves more cautiously. Parents warn students to be careful. Administrators post fliers with police phone numbers in large, bold print. Students walk in groups and avoid usual shortcuts through woods or poorly lit areas. Extra police are on patrol; emergency phones are repaired; dorm security is increased. But as the immediate shock wears off, students again take their safety for granted. They begin walking alone again at night; they resume their usual shortcuts.

At our school, *only four weeks* after a female nearly was raped while awaiting a bus outside the library and a male student was assaulted by a knife-wielding attacker, most students seem to have resumed their carefree ways. On any late evening, males and females alike can be seen walking or jogging alone.

A research report in APA style (*Continued*)

Is Enough Being Done?

The rise in campus crime led to passage of the *Crime Awareness and Security Act* in 1990, requiring all schools to disclose information about security measures and crime statistics to current or prospective students and employees (Rates, 1994, p. 2). This legislation was followed in 1992 by the *Campus Sexual Assault Victim's Bill of Rights,* requiring all colleges to establish set policies for assisting victims. Also passed in 1992 was the *Buckley Amendment Clarification Act,* designating campus police records as no longer confidential (Security, 1996). Perhaps most significant, Fosley and Smith (1995) note that courts are increasingly holding schools responsible for crimes on their campuses.

But, as Clery and Carter (1997) point out in a study of security on college campuses, too many schools continue to handle serious crimes such as rape, hazing, aggravated assault, and other felonies simply as violations of student disciplinary codes. And, while the Department of Education requires that criminal incidents that are handled on campus by resident directors, administrators, or counselors must be reported in the annual crime statistics, many schools either ignore this federal law or conveniently downgrade campus crimes.

Until recently, another problem with tracking campus crime has been the lack of an official repository for campus crime statistics, similar to the FBI's Uniform Crime Reporting Program for cities (Clery & Carter, 1997). Since October 2000, however, all schools have been required to report their crime statistics online to the Department of Education (Moran, 2000). To compare schools nationwide, users can visit www.ed.edu and click on the site's on "Research and Stats" link.

A research report in APA style (*Continued*)

Additional resources are increasingly available on the Internet. For example, *Security on Campus, Inc.,* a non-profit organization for preventing campus violence, has helped victims and families take legal action against various schools for negligence and "failure to protect" (Security, 2002). *Survivors of Stalking,* an independently funded advocacy and resource center, offers help for victims (Survivors, 2002).

The Internet also makes it easier for students and their parents to find out about campus crime at particular colleges. Harvard University, for example, devotes a portion of its Web site to the university's police department. Campus crime statistics as well as safety tips and guidelines on crime reporting are available. Also, information on self-defense courses offered at the university is provided (Harvard, 2002).

Many schools routinely offer sessions on campus safety and sexual assault for incoming students, but these programs tend to be "one-shot deals." Also, safety measures such as increased lighting and police patrols, emergency phones, and escort services help prevent assault by strangers—but not by acquaintances. Clearly, more needs to be done: for example, prevention programs, periodic safety awareness sessions, self-defense classes, and mandatory crime awareness seminars in which student victims share their experiences with other students. These seminars might even be offered as one-credit classes. Current campus crime statistics could be published weekly in the campus newspaper. Measures like these would heighten safety awareness and possibly reduce campus crime.

A research report in APA style (*Continued*)

College students have every right to feel safe on campus, but they must recognize that campus crime is real. While the specter of campus crime should not taint the freedoms and joys of college life, parents must become more realistic; students, more responsible for their actions; and colleges, more candid.

Crime is a fact of life on college campuses—just as in the real world. The sooner parents, students, and administrators accept that fact, the safer college campuses might become.

A research report in APA style (*Continued*)

13

14

References

15

Ayres, B. D., Jr. (1993, September 10). College requires applicants to come clean about crime. *New York Times,* p. A14.   *[newspaper article]*

16

Blum, D. E. (1995, June 30). A controversial scholarship [CD-ROM]. *The Chronicle of Higher Education,* pp. A29, A30. Abstract retrieved from: SilverPlatter File: ERIC.   *[CD-ROM abstract]*

Cage, M. C. (1992, September 30). 42% of college students engage in "binge drinking," survey shows. *The Chronicle of Higher Education,* p. A30.

17

Campus ripper. (1990, September 14). *Time,* 43.   *[magazine article]*

Clayton, M. (2002, January 22). Latest murders highlight rise in campus crime. *The Christian Science Monitor.* Retrieved April 5, 2003, from

18

http://www.csmonitor.com/2002/0122/p03so1-ussc.html   *[online newspaper]*

Clery, B., & Carter, D. (1997). Campus crime information for college and university students. Retrieved April 4, 2003, from http://www.memexpress.com/ cc/askcc010997.html   *[Web site]*

Dodge, S. (1991, February 18). With campus crime capturing public attention, colleges re-evaluate security measures and stiffen some penalties. *The*

19

Chronicle of Higher Education, pp. A29, A31.

Federal Bureau of Investigation (1999). Hate crime statistics. *Uniform Crime Reporting Program.* Retrieved April 7, 2003, from http://www.fbi.gov/ucr/ 99hate.pdf

Fonseca, B. (1998, December 10). Colleges seek to put a cap on underage drinking. *Fall River Herald News,* p. 1.

20

Fosley R., & Smith, M. (1995, Summer). Institutional liability for campus rapes: The emerging law. [Online] *Journal of Law and Education, 24,* 377–401. Abstract retrieved April 4, 2003, from http://www.educlaw.edu/jle/cc.htm

[online abstract]

A research report in APA style (*Continued*)

APA List of References: 13–21

13. Continue the running heads and page numbers. Use one-inch margins.

14. Center the "References" title at the top of a new page. Include only recoverable data (material that readers could retrieve for themselves); cite personal interviews, unpublished lectures, email, and other personal correspondence parenthetically in the text only. (See also items 18 and 21 in this list.)

15. Double-space entries and order them alphabetically by author's last name (excluding A, An, or The). List initials only for authors' first and middle names. Write out names of all months. Capitalize only the first word in article or book titles and subtitles and any proper nouns. Capitalize all key words in magazine, journal, or newspaper titles. Do not enclose article titles in quotation marks. Italicize periodical titles.

16. In student papers, indent the second and subsequent lines of an entry one-half inch. In papers submitted for publication in an APA journal, the first line instead is indented.

17. Use the first key word in the title to alphabetize works whose author is not named.

18. List all Web sites that directly contributed to your paper, and provide the electronic address, especially for resources that readers might wish to consult. If no author is named, list the organization sponsoring the Web site (e.g., Federal Bureau of Investigation) in the author slot. Omit your punctuation from the end of an electronic address.

19. For a magazine or newspaper article on nonconsecutive pages, list each page, separated by a comma.

20. For more than one author or editor, use ampersands instead of spelling out "and." Use italics for a journal article's title, volume number, and the comma. Give the issue number in parentheses only if each issue begins on page 1. Do not include "p." or "pp." before journal page numbers (only before page numbers from a newspaper). For page numbers of three or more digits, provide all digits in the second number.

21

Harvard University Police Department. (2002). Retrieved April 1, 2003, from
   http://www.hupd.harvard.edu/

Johnson, C. (1991, October 7). When sex is the issue. *U.S. News and World Report,*
   34–35.

Kier, F. (1996, January). *Acquaintance rape on college campuses: A review of the
   literature.* Paper presented at the annual meeting of the Southwest
   Educational Research Association, New Orleans.   *[unpublished conference paper]*

Lederman, D. (1995, February 3). Colleges report rise in violent crime. *The
   Chronicle of Higher Education,* pp. A31–A42.

Massachusetts Governor's Task Force. (2001, September 18). *Advisory bulletin on
   hate crimes.* Boston: Author.

Matthews, A. (1993, March 4). The campus crime wave. *The New York Times
   Magazine,* 30–42.

McClarin, K. (1994, September 7). Fear prompts self-defense as crime comes to
   college. *New York Times,* pp. A1, A4.

Moran, K. J. (2000, September 2). Higher crime statistics at UMass due in part to
   reporting change. *Hampshire Gazette,* p. B1.

Nicklin, J. L. (2001, February 2). Drug and alcohol arrests increased in 1999. *The
   Chronicle of Higher Education,* p. A35.

Pfister, B. (1994, Spring). Swept awake! *On the Issues,* 20–26.

Rates of campus crime. (1994, March/April). *Society,* 2–3.

Security on Campus, Inc. (2002). *History, Accomplishments, and Programs.* Retrieved
   April 7, 2003, from http://www.socoline.org.htm   *[Web site]*

Survivors of Stalking. (2002). *Ending the silence that kills.* Retrieved April 3, 2003,
   from http://www.gate.net/~soshelp/one.htm

U.S. House of Representatives. (1990). *Hearing on H.R. 3344: The crime awareness
   and security act.* Washington, DC: U.S. Government Printing Office.
                                                [gov't publication—no author named]

A research report in APA style (*Continued*)

APA List of References (Continued)

21. Treat an unpublished conference presentation as a "recoverable" source, including it in your list of references instead of merely citing it parenthetically in your text.

CHAPTER 23

Case Study: A Sample Research Project

Discovering a Worthwhile Topic   **438**

Focusing the Inquiry   **439**

Searching the Literature   **440**

Recording and Reviewing Findings   **440**

Settling on a Thesis   **441**

Writing and Documenting the Report in MLA Style   **442**

This chapter will follow one student writer's problem-solving, from the day her report was assigned until she submitted her final draft.

DISCOVERING A WORTHWHILE TOPIC

As soon as Shirley Haley learned that a research report was due in six weeks, she began to search for a worthwhile topic. Although many of Haley's college friends had adjusted to the hectic pace of the first-year student, others were not doing so well: Some had developed insomnia; others had gained or lost a good deal of weight; one friend was sleeping more than 12 hours a day. Other disorders ranged from compulsive eating and indigestion to chronic headaches and skin problems—all seemingly since the beginning of the semester. Haley wondered why, beyond the obvious pressures of college life, so many of her friends had become so unhealthy.

A psychology major, Haley recently had read about *stress* in an introductory textbook. She wondered about a connection between stress and her friends' problems.

FOCUSING THE INQUIRY

But Haley knew that, to come up with the right answers, she would have to ask the right questions. Here is her tree chart:

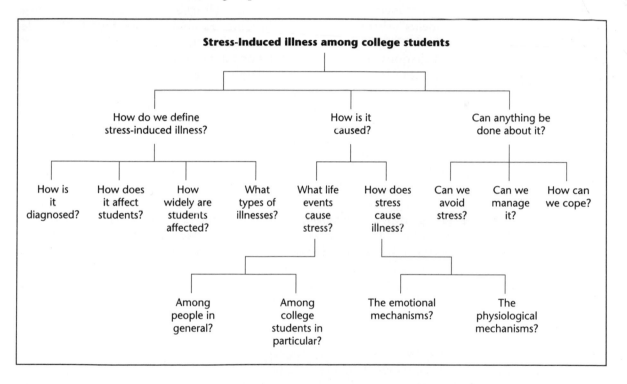

Once she knew what information she was looking for, Haley focused on the various viewpoints that would give her a balanced picture:

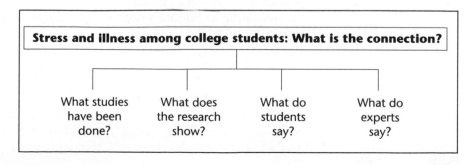

Now that she knew what questions to ask and where to get the answers, Haley was ready to research.

SEARCHING THE LITERATURE

Because Haley already had read a description of *stress* in her psychology textbook, she needed no general reference works, such as encyclopedias and specialized dictionaries. Using her library's Web page, she accessed the CD-ROM version of the *Readers' Guide to Periodical Literature,* whose recent issues listed numerous articles under "Stress." Haley also checked under "College students"; there, under the subheading "Psychology," she found other relevant titles. Also checking earlier volumes of the *Readers' Guide,* she recorded full citations of interesting articles on bibliography cards.

Next Haley searched through recent files of *Psychological Abstracts* for studies on stress and college students. Besides finding yet more titles, she looked up and read abstracts of promising articles. Under "College students" she found some key articles addressing her friends' health problems.

Now Haley checked her library's periodicals holdings to see which of these key articles the library held. Some she found collected in bound volumes; others were on microfilm and others in online databases. The librarian ordered two articles from other libraries.

Using the electronic card catalog, she did a key word search for books offering historical background on stress. At the card catalog, Haley jotted down a few book titles and call numbers. In the stacks, she browsed through the books on the shelves. She also checked the "Selected Bibliography" section of her psychology textbook, continuing to record citations.

Once she had a basic background on her topic, Haley browsed Web sites and online databases for additional sources on her topic.

RECORDING AND REVIEWING FINDINGS

Armed with a good stock of sources, Haley skimmed the most promising works, evaluating each finding for accuracy, reliability, fairness, and completeness. She recorded useful material, indicating source and page numbers and recording quotations word for word. Because she found a good body of information on stress management, she decided to structure her report in this way:

Problem ─────────→ Causes and Effects ─────────→ Solutions

SETTLING ON A THESIS

The evidence pointed toward a definite conclusion: Stress was indeed a real factor in students' poor health. Now she could formulate a tentative thesis:

| Stress is a definite cause of illness among college students.

Haley would later refine and expand her thesis, but for now, she had a good focal point for developing her report.

WRITING AND DOCUMENTING THE REPORT IN MLA STYLE

Haley continued to read, record the information, outline, and organize her notes. Finally, she decided she knew enough to write her first draft. Using the revision checklists, she reworked her first and second drafts into the final draft that appears on the following pages. (Marginal numbers refer to the writer's decisions discussed on the facing pages.)

Students Under Stress: College Can Make You Sick

by
Shirley Haley

English 101, Section 1432
Professor Lannon
May 8, 2003

A research report in MLA style

Haley   i

OUTLINE

<u>Thesis:</u> Because of disruptive changes and pressures in their personal, social, and academic lives, college students are highly vulnerable to the physical effects of stress.

2

I. <u>The Problem:</u> Stress increasingly is recognized as a definite cause of physical disorders.

   A. The mechanisms have been studied for years, but stress still is making us sick.

   B. Stress has a technical and a personal definition, and both are accurate.

   C. More and more of us suffer the physical effects of stress.

   D. College students are among the groups most affected.

II. <u>Specific Causes:</u> Stress-induced illness is caused by emotional responses that have physical consequences.

   A. Stress originates when the body works too hard to maintain equilibrium.

      1. If the alarm reaction persists, the body is forever ready for action.

      2. Psychosomatic illness is not imaginary.

   B. A major study showed a connection between the stress of common life events and illness.

   C. Even a series of ordinary events in the lives of college students can cause dangerous levels of stress.

   D. Various studies of college students confirm the stress-illness link.

III. <u>Possible Solutions:</u> Now that the problem is recognized, solutions are being found.

   A. The effect stress has on us depends on how well we cope.

      1. We need both coping strategies and help from others.

      2. Without coping mechanisms, we are almost certain to be overwhelmed.

   B. Students need to develop more realistic expectations of college life.

      1. College orientation should be more realistic.

      2. Stress-management courses should be offered by more colleges.

   C. Some type of stress-management training should be available to every college student.

A research report in MLA style (*Continued*)

1. *Title page:* Many reports for government, business, and industry are prefaced by a title page with these standard items: report title, author's name, course or department, intended reader's name, and date. Haley centers and spaces these items for visual appeal. The title page is not numbered.

2. *Outline:* The running head for all pages consists of the author's last name, followed by one space and page number (small roman numerals for outline, Arabic for paper). Haley prefaces her sentence outline with her thesis, so that readers can understand her plan at a glance. Her three major sections (*The Problem, Specific Causes,* and *Possible Solutions*) reveal a clear and sensible effect-to-cause development (see pages 238–39).

   Notice that each level of division in the outline yields at least *two* parts.

Haley   1

3

The Problem: Stress-Induced Illness

Stress can cause physical illness. The mechanisms have been studied for years, but stress still is making us sick.

4

Over 60 years ago, the search began for a link between stress and illness. Walter Cannon identified the "fight or flight" response in 1929. Showing that emotional arousal causes physical reactions such as increased respiration and pulse rate and elevated blood pressure, Cannon laid the groundwork for stress research. In the 1930s Dr. Adolf Mayer, who began charting patients' life events to aid his medical

5

diagnoses, recorded "the changes of habit, of school entrances, graduations or changes, or failures; the various jobs [. . .] and other important events" (Dohrenwend and Dohrenwend 3). And Hans Selye in 1936 described the body's

6

reaction to stress as "the syndrome of just being sick" ("Stress Concept" 72).

Stress has a technical and a personal definition. Technically, stress is a psychological and physiological response to life events that disrupt the physical being. This response evolved as a primitive and necessary defense against physical

7

danger (Adler, Kalb, and Rogers 59). But in the modern world, stress takes on a broader, more personal definition: Stress occurs, for example, when a person falls in or out of love, receives good or bad news, drives a car, receives a traffic ticket, takes final exams, or graduates. All life experiences, major or minor, entail stress and too often provoke an overreaction that Stanford stress researcher Robert Sapolsky terms "more damaging than the imaginary challenge" (qtd. in Adler, Kalb, and Rogers 60). Although some degree of anxiety is a good motivator, excessive stress endangers our health.

8

More and more of us suffer physical effects of stress: ulcers and colitis, fatigue and exhaustion, high blood pressure and headache. Stress probably makes us susceptible to infectious disease and cancer by inhibiting our "natural killer (NK) cells." These killer cells help the body fight colds, flu, pneumonia, and other

A research report in MLA style (*Continued*)

3. *Headings and page numbering:* Because she uses a title page, Haley does not repeat her title on page 1. Instead she uses section headings to keep readers on track. Each page of the paper itself (including Works Cited) has an Arabic number after the author's last name as running head.

4. *Background information:* Haley's opening grabs our attention by showing immediately that stress makes us sick. She summarizes a half-century of stress research, to show that the stress issue is no mere fad. Brief quotations from authorities lend credibility.

5. *Using quoted material:* Haley introduces brief quotes by naming the author and by combining the quotations with her own words to make complete sentences.

6. *In-text citations:* Haley cites each source in parentheses, inside the period, but outside any quotation marks. Because one of the authors cited in the first paragraph has more than one work listed in Haley's Works Cited section, Haley lists a shortened version of this work's title when she refers to that author.

7. *Defining the problem:* Haley *defines* her subject before discussing it, clarifying her definition with concrete examples. She quotes authorities to point out that *some* stress can be beneficial, but that too much is destructive.

8. *Relating the material to the audience:* Readers want to know what something means to *them* personally; Haley therefore includes a paragraph on the common effects and signs of stress.

Haley   2

infections, and they destroy malignant cells. In one study, young adults who
reported highly stressful lives showed decreased NK cell activity and a high rate of
infectious illness (Bower 141). Recent work by John Cacioppo and colleagues at
Ohio State University shows that stress definitely weakens the immune system.

In addition, two recent studies indicate a link between cortisol (an
immunosuppressant hormone produced in response to stress) and the development
of cancer and multiple sclerosis—as well as the progression of AIDS (Facklemann
350–51).

Stress has warning signs, cues to seek help before our bodies actually break
down. Among the most common signs are an overpowering urge to cry or run
away, persistent anxiety for no reason, insomnia, and a feeling of being "keyed up."
(See Appendix A for other signs.) Overeating and alcohol or drug use are often the
result of stress beyond endurance, an attempt to escape (Selye, Stress of Life 175).

Among the groups most exposed to life changes, and thus most affected by
stress, are college students. In a 1992 Irish study, Tyrell found that students' main
sources of stress were "fear of falling behind, finding the motivation to study, time
pressures, financial worries, and concern about academic ability" (185–88). Stanford
psychologist Alejandro Martinez regards stress as one of the three major problems
(along with family and relationships) faced by college students (Nikravesh).

Students' battles with stress can begin early. Even before graduating from high
school they worry about admission to the college of their choice. Or they feel
pressure to measure up to parents' achievements and expectations, or keep up with
successful older siblings. "Second-rate doesn't rate at all in a majority of the
households from which these [students] come—and they know it" (Brooks 613).
Transition to college creates more stress as students leave a friendly and familiar
environment for one that seems impersonal and demanding, academically and

A research report in MLA style (Continued)

9. *Citing an electronic source with no printed equivalent:* The page numbers for this electronic text are not available, so Haley names the author (John Cacioppo) in her discussion, to avoid the in-text parenthetical citation.

10. *Referring to appendices:* Haley refers us to an appendix at report's end for details that we might find useful but that would interrupt the flow of the report itself.

11. *Thesis paragraphs:* Now Haley can focus specifically on stress in the lives of college students. This paragraph and the next lead into her thesis (bottom of first paragraph on report page 3).

12. *Citing a source whose author is named in the text:* Because Haley has named the author (Tyrell) in her paragraph, she merely lists the page numbers in her parenthetical citation.

13. *Citing an online source:* The Nikravesh citation includes no page numbers because none are available from the online source.

Haley   3

socially (Compas et al. 243). Moreover, today's students struggle with tuition increases, reductions in financial aid, and feelings of hopelessness about finding decent jobs after graduation (Cage A2). Others worry about coping with sexual experiences or being the victims of a sexual assault (White and Humphrey). Such disruptive changes and pressures in their personal, social, and academic lives make students vulnerable to the physical effects of stress.

One example of the stress-illness cycle in students: Severed from close relationships back home, students end up feeling lonely. Rockefeller University's Dr. Bruce McEwen points out that this "lack of social support" creates a "sense of isolation" ("Demystifying Stress" 4). And feelings of isolation, as Stanford's Robert Sapolsky has shown, lead to higher levels of the stress hormone, cortisol (Leutwyler 30). This in turn suppresses the body's immunity to disease.

Specific Causes of Stress-Induced Illness

Stress originates when the body works too hard to maintain the equilibrium necessary for a healthy life. Any disruption or demand, good or bad, sets off an adjustment that allows the body to regain its equilibrium. When a stimulus sets off this adjustment, when an "alarm reaction" puts the body "on alert," adrenaline prepares the body for action: blood pressure rises to increase blood flow to muscles; digestion temporarily shuts down; blood sugar rises to increase energy; perspiration increases; and other physical changes occur, to prepare the body for "fight or flight" (Selye, "Stress Concept" 76).

If the alarm reaction persists, the body is forever ready for action. That is when stress becomes destructive. We can run away from a speeding car as we cross the street, and when the danger passes, so does the stress. But we can't run away from some inner threat, such as the pressure for good grades. And as the stress endures, our bodies become less able to maintain the equilibrium needed for health.

A research report in MLA style (*Continued*)

14. *Citing an abstract:* The White and Humphrey citation includes no page numbers because merely the abstract is being cited.

15. *Tracing the causes:* Before Haley covers the disruptive situations that cause stress, she explains how the body reacts to such situations. We need this background to understand the later connection between life events and illness.

16. *Interpreting research findings:* This paragraph shows us that Haley is interpreting her material, not merely giving us a collection of findings to sort out for ourselves.

Haley   4

Far from being imaginary, psychosomatic illness is real disease that can be diagnosed and treated. But the cause of psychosomatic illness is unmanaged stress. Until the stress is controlled, the disease can't be cured. Because of previous illness or heredity, one organ or system (heart, digestive system, skin) in a person's body tends to be most vulnerable. This part of the body is like the weak link in a chain; no matter what pulls the chain, good or bad, the chain breaks (Selye, "Stress Concept" 77).

17

A connection between the stress of common life events and illness was first demonstrated in a 1967 study. First, researchers assigned point values to 43 specific life events (divorce, illness, marriage, job loss). After collecting health histories, the researchers asked their subjects to total the points for recent events in their lives. (The scale ranged from 100 points for the death of a spouse to 11 for a traffic violation—see Appendix B for a full listing.) Comparing the health histories to point totals, the researchers discovered that any group of life events totaling 150 or more points in one year was connected to a major illness (requiring a physician's care) for 93 percent of the subjects. And the harmful effects of a high point total lasted as long as two years (Holmes and Masuda 50–56).

18

Studies of college students confirm the stress-illness link. Even a collection of ordinary events in students' lives can place them in a danger category, as shown in Table 1:

19

TABLE 1: A Life-Events Scale for College Students

Event	Points	Event	Points
Beginning or ending of school	26	Change in church activities	19
Change in living conditions	25	Change in social activities	18
Revision of personal habits	24	Loan of less than $10,000	17
Change in work hours or conditions	20	Change in sleeping habits	16
Change in residence	20	Change in eating habits	15

Source: Adapted from Holmes and Rahe, Table 3: 216.

A research report in MLA style (Continued)

17. *Establishing the link:* Haley describes the major study that demonstrated the stress-illness connection. Again, she refers us to an appendix for details.

18. *Focusing on college students:* Haley now interprets her general findings in specific relation to college students, leading into a detailed discussion of studies on college students.

19. *Using visuals:* Haley chooses a table for her numerical data. She numbers the table, introduces it, cites her source, and interprets the data for her readers. Tables longer than one text page would go in an appendix (see report pages 8–10). Other visuals (charts, graphs, diagrams, maps, photos) can provide concrete and vivid illustrations.

The life events in Table 1 alone total 200 points—disregarding any other points students collect from out-of-school experiences. For example, one study showed that, among those students who also have to work to pay for college costs, nearly two-thirds considered the job an additional source of stress (Ross, Niebling, and Heckert 315).

20

More than half of the medical students in one study "experienced major health changes" within two years after entering school. A college life-events scale was given to 54 incoming first-year medical students; those with the highest scores reported most illness before the end of the second year (Holmes and Masuda 64). The stress of starting school can strongly affect one's health.

In a related study, Holmes and Masuda found a connection between life changes and the number of injuries sustained by 100 college football players. High scores on the life-change survey equaled more injuries on the field. Of the ten players who had multiple injuries, seven were from the group with highest scores in the life-events survey (66). Furthermore, a lab study by Marucha, Kiecolt-Glaser, and Favagehi has shown that the healing of wounds is significantly impaired by the stress of college exams.

21

Pressures of college life often produce stress-induced insomnia. For instance, one survey at a Virginia university found that thirty-five percent of students sleep no more than six hours nightly—largely because of sleep disruption caused by stress (Ganeshananthan). Students who procrastinate in their college work are particularly prone to insomnia, as a recent Canadian study of 374 undergraduates has found (Glenn A1).

One major study suggests that stress-induced illness can be self-perpetuating, that symptoms initiated by stressful events can help create further stressful events: "For example, divorce of one's parents may lead to symptoms of depression [anxiety, insomnia, loss of appetite, hopelessness, etc.], which in turn may lead to

A research report in MLA style (*Continued*)

20. *Citing sources selectively:* Rather than listing all studies confirming the stress-illness link, Haley is *selective,* giving us only what we need.

21. *Citing an abstract:* No page numbers are given because the source is merely an abstract. Because there are no page numbers, Haley avoids a parenthetical citation by naming the authors in her discussion.

22 disruption of interpersonal relationships and poor performance in school" (Compas 242). Merely treating the symptoms—without confronting the causes—traps many students in this cycle of stress and illness.

23
Possible Solutions

Because stress is unlikely to disappear, our only solution is to learn to cope. "It is our ability to cope with the demands made by the events in our lives, not the quality or intensity of the events, that counts. What matters is not so much what **24** happens to us, but the way we take it" (Selye, "Stress Concept" 83). And "the way we take it" has a lot to do with heredity, with the coping strategies we've learned, and with the helping resources available to us now.

Without coping mechanisms, we are likely to be overwhelmed. Stanford **25** psychiatrist David Spiegel adds that "Living a stress-free life is not a reasonable **26** goal. The goal is to [cope][. . .] actively and effectively." (qtd. in Cowley, Underwood, and Kalb 60).

For students, coping depends on realistic expectations of college life. A 1984 counseling study at Kansas State University found that students tend to be unrealistic about their chances of succeeding in college. They suffer from what Levine calls the *Titanic Ethic:* "They see doom in the world around them but still feel they **27** [personally] will somehow survive" (qtd. in Newton 541). Students are so certain of survival, they make few plans for coping with anticipated problems; instead they rely on the hope that problems will take care of themselves (Newton 540–42).

Experts agree that "college success is largely determined by experiences during the start of freshman year" ("Coping"). To help students avoid shattered **28** expectations, counselor Fred Newton suggests that college orientation should be more realistic: it should include stress-management counseling and a no-nonsense look at all sides of college life (541).

Realistic approaches to college life also must include the effective use of leisure time. Stanford's Dr. Martinez emphasizes the importance, during stressful periods,

A research report in MLA style (*Continued*)

22. *Transition:* Haley's transitional sentence sums up the causes and leads into her final discussion of solutions.

23. *Arriving at solutions:* Haley's reasoning in this part proceeds from the importance of coping, to specific coping strategies, to students' coping needs, to programs designed to help students cope. She has *shaped* her material to clarify her thinking.

24. *Punctuating quotations.* Commas and periods following a quotation belong inside the quotation marks. Any other punctuation belongs outside the quotation marks—unless it belongs to the quoted material itself *(What did he mean when he said "I'm through"?* or *His response was "I'm through.").*

25. *Using brackets in quotations:* To clarify some quotations, Haley inserts a word or phrase in brackets. The brackets signal that the writer has altered the original quotation; the bracketed comments are Haley's, not the author's.

26. *Using ellipses in quotations:* Haley uses ellipses (. . .) to shorten otherwise long quotations. In fact, no quotation in the report is more than a few lines long. A research report does not merely catalog other people's ideas and words. Instead, writers give this material their own concise shape—without distorting the original information.

    A quotation of more than four typewritten lines would have been indented ten spaces and double-spaced, without quotation marks.

27. *Quoting an indirect source:* In her research, Haley came across a key phrase—"the Titanic Ethic"—to characterize college students. But Haley's source quoted this phrase from another source, and her source gave no page number from the original. Unable to trace the original, Haley includes the abbreviation "qtd."—for "quoted in"—in the parenthetical citation of her indirect source. As we will see, she includes the indirect source (Newton) in her Works Cited list.

28. *Paraphrased and summarized material:* To save space and improve coherence, Haley paraphrases and summarizes throughout her report. (See pages 372 and 373 for guidelines.) Here is the original passage for this paraphrase:

    > Selective blindness may be a more difficult illness to prevent when the fantasy vision may seem more pleasant than reality. As a recommendation, to shock students into an awareness of reality now may be more beneficial than the rude awakening of tomorrow. So far, the best suggestion is to conduct "future shock" and "future cope" workshops that confront students with situations and problems that will need to be resolved. Perhaps, orientation programs should strive to show more of the realities of college life rather than the present-day programs of welcoming, testing, registering, and saying "I'll see you in the fall."

of persisting with activities that do us good, such as exercise (Nikravesh). A recent study shows that students who know how to relax through recreational activities (hobbies, sports, exercise groups) report reduced feelings of stress (Mounir and McKinney 7–9). Meditation training seems particularly effective in stress reduction (Janowiak and Hackman 1008–09). And recent studies confirm the effectiveness of massage therapy, not only in reducing stress but also in bolstering the immune system ("New Study Links").

To teach students how to cope with stress and learn to relax, the University of California at Irvine offers a "stress lab." Here, students find warm surroundings, homelike furniture, literature, videotapes, interactive stress-reduction programs, and even a biofeedback machine (Murray).

These are a mere sample of the resources available to stressed-out students. A quick Internet search produces useful advice online from many colleges, such as the University of Florida Web page, "Stress and College Students," at <http://www.counsel.ufl.edu>. Online discussion groups on stress-related issues are found at <http://www.deja.com>. Also, various organizations, such as The American Institute of Stress at <http://www.stress.org>, offer Web pages with advice, newsletters, and links to additional resources.

In conclusion, although stress in college is unavoidable, it can be managed. Stress-management training should be offered to all students, to make them aware of the realities of college life and of their responsibility for their own well-being. All students should make it a point to explore the resources offered by their schools. As the research clearly shows, students who do learn to manage stress will be less likely to find that college makes them sick.

29

A research report in MLA style (*Continued*)

29. *Conclusion:* Haley's closing suggestions are keyed specifically to her thesis, summarizing and rounding out the discussion and reemphasizing the major points.

Haley   8

30

Appendix A: Warning Signals of Stress

Stress has definite warning signals, emotional and physical. Here are the commonest:

Emotional Signs of Stress

- being emotionally very "up" or very "down"
- impulsive behavior and emotional instability
- uncontrollable urge to cry or run away
- inability to concentrate
- feelings of unreality
- loss of "joy of life"
- feeling "keyed up"
- being easily startled
- nightmares; insomnia
- a general sense of anxiety or dread

Physical Signs of Stress

- pounding heart (may indicate high blood pressure)
- constantly dry throat and mouth
- weakness; dizziness
- feelings of tiredness
- trembling; nervous tics
- high-pitched, nervous laughter
- grinding of teeth
- constant aimless motion
- excessive perspiring
- diarrhea; indigestion; queasy stomach
- headaches
- pain in the neck or lower back (because of muscle tension)
- excessive or lost appetite
- proneness to accidents

Source: Adapted from Selye, The Stress of Life: 175.

A research report in MLA style (*Continued*)

30. *Appendices* (this and the next two pages): An appendix is a catchall for material that is important but difficult to integrate into the body of a report. Appendices might include:

- details of an experiment
- specific measurements
- maps
- quotations longer than one page of text
- photographs
- long lists or visuals using more than one full page
- texts of laws, regulations, literary passages, and so on

But readers should not have to turn to appendices to understand the report. Haley distills the essentials from her appendices and includes them in the main text.

Each appendix is labeled clearly, with a separate one for each major item. Appendices appear at the end of the text but before the Works Cited pages.

Appendix B: Stress Values of Common Life Events

In their 1967 study, Holmes and Rahe ranked life events in descending order according to their stress value. This table shows the rating scale.

Social Readjustment Rating Scale

Rank	Life Event	Mean Value
1	Death of spouse	100
2	Divorce	73
3	Marital separation from mate	65
4	Detention in jail or other institution	63
5	Death of a close family member	63
6	Major personal injury or illness	53
7	Marriage	50
8	Being fired at work	47
9	Marital reconciliation with mate	45
10	Retirement from work	45
11	Major change in the health or behavior of a family member	44
12	Pregnancy	40
13	Sexual difficulties	39
14	Getting a new family member (e.g., through birth, adoption, oldster moving in, etc.)	39
15	Major business readjustment (e.g., merger, reorganization, bankruptcy, etc.)	39
16	Major change in financial state (e.g., a lot worse off or a lot better off than usual)	38
17	Death of a close friend	37
18	Changing to a different line of work	36
19	Major change in the number of arguments with spouse (e.g., either a lot more or a lot less than usual regarding child rearing, personal habits, etc.)	35
20	Taking out a mortgage or loan for a major purchase (e.g., for a home, business, etc.)	31
21	Foreclosure on a mortgage or loan	30
22	Major change in responsibilities at work (e.g., promotion, demotion, lateral transfer)	29
23	Son or daughter leaving home (e.g., marriage, attending college, etc.)	29
24	Trouble with in-laws	29

A research report in MLA style (*Continued*)

Appendix B: (Continued)

Social Readjustment Rating Scale

Rank	Life Event	Mean Value
25	Outstanding personal achievement	28
26	Wife beginning or ceasing work outside the home	26
27	Beginning or ceasing formal schooling	26
28	Major change in living conditions (e.g., building a new home, remodeling, deterioration of home or neighborhood)	25
29	Revision of personal habits (dress, manners, associations, etc.)	24
30	Trouble with the boss	23
31	Major change in working hours or conditions	20
32	Change in residence	20
33	Changing to a new school	20
34	Major change in usual type and/or amount of recreation	19
35	Major change in church activities (e.g., a lot more or a lot less than usual)	19
36	Major change in social activities (e.g., clubs, dancing, movies, visiting, etc.)	18
37	Taking out a mortgage or loan for a lesser purchase (e.g., for a car, TV, freezer, etc.)	17
38	Major change in sleeping habits (a lot more or a lot less sleep, or change in part of day when asleep)	16
39	Major change in number of family get-togethers (e.g., a lot more or a lot less than usual)	15
40	Major change in eating habits (a lot more or a lot less food intake, or very different meal hours or surroundings)	15
41	Vacation	13
42	Christmas	12
43	Minor violations of the law (e.g., traffic tickets, jaywalking, disturbing the peace, etc.)	11

Source: "The Social Readjustment Scale": 216.

A research report in MLA style (*Continued*)

Haley   11

31

Works Cited

32   Adler, Jerry, Claudia Kalb, and Adam Rogers. "Stress." <u>Newsweek</u> 14 June 1999:

57+.   *[magazine article]*

Bower, Bruce. "Setting the Stage for Infection." <u>Science News</u> 26 Aug. 1989: 141.

Brooks, Andre A. "Educating the Children of Fast-Track Parents." <u>Phi Delta Kappan</u>

April 1990: 612–15.

33   Cacioppo, John T. "Stress: Interplay between Social and Biological Processes."

Homepage. 18 Dec. 1995. 8 Apr. 2003

<http://www.acs.ohio-state.edu/units/psych/s-psych/jtc.html>.   *[Web site]*

34   Cage, Mary C. "Students Face Pressures as Never Before, But Counseling Help Has

Withered." <u>Chronicle of Higher Education</u> 18 Nov. 1992, Sec A2.

[newspaper article]

Compas, Bruce E., et al. "A Prospective Study of Life Events, Social Support, and

Psychological Symptomatology During the Transition from High School to

College." <u>American Journal of Community Psychology</u> 14 (1986): 241–56.

[journal article from print source]

35   "Coping with the Stress of College Life." 25 Sept. 1998. <u>The Snapper Online</u>. 8

Apr. 2003 <http://snapper.millersv.edu/Stories/19980925/

commentary/counselor.html>.

Cowley, Geoffrey, Anne Underwood, and Claudia Kalb. "Stress Busters: What

Works." <u>Newsweek</u> 14 June 1999: 60–61.

"Demystifying Stress." <u>UC Berkeley Wellness Letter</u> June 1998: 4.

36   Dohrenwend, Barbara Snell, and Bruce Dohrenwend, eds. <u>Stressful Life Events:

Their Nature and Effects</u>. New York: Wiley, 1974.

A research report in MLA style (*Continued*)

31. *Works Cited* (including the continuation on the next page): One inch from the top of the page is the centered heading "Works Cited." Two spaces below the heading is the first entry. Each entry is double-spaced, with second and subsequent lines indented one-half inch from the left margin. Entries are in alphabetical order, with double-spacing between them. The Works Cited section follows the numbering of the text pages.

32. Article titles appear in quotation marks; book or periodical titles are underlined. All key words in the title are capitalized. Articles, prepositions, or conjunctions are capitalized only if they come first or last. Three-letter abbreviations denote months having five or more letters. Volume numbers for magazines are not cited. No punctuation separates magazine title and date.

33. A citation for a personal or professional Web site begins with the creator's name (if known), followed by the work's title (in quotation marks), the site's title (or description, such as *Homepage,* if no title is given), the posting date, and the user's access data.

34. Omit the introductory article ("The") in the newspaper's name.

35. An entry for any electronic source that is updated periodically should include your date of access (as in "8 Apr.").

36. In this collection of essays by various authors, the editors also are the authors of the introduction to the anthology.

Facklemann, Kathleen. "The Cortisol Connection: Does a Stress Hormone Play a
Role in AIDS?" <u>Science News</u> 152.22 (1998): 350–51.

Ganeshananthan, Sugi. "Nightmare on Whittier Blvd. Leaves Whitmanites
Sleepless." Nov. 1996. <u>Black and White</u>. 14 Nov. 2003
<http://www.whitman.gmu.edu/publications/bw/1996-7issue11/ind>.

Glenn, David. "Procrastination in College Students Is a Marker for Unhealthy
Behaviors, Study Indicates." <u>Chronicle of Higher Education</u> 26 Aug. 2002:
A1.

Holmes, Thomas H., and Minoru Masuda. "Life Change and Illness Susceptibility."
Dohrenwend and Dohrenwend. 45–72.

Holmes, Thomas H., and R. H. Rahe. "The Social Readjustment Scale." <u>Journal of
Psychosomatic Research</u> 11 (1967): 213–18.

Janowiak, J. J., and R. Hackman. "Meditation and College Students' Self-
Actualization and Rated Stress." <u>Psychological Reports</u> 75.2 (1994): 1007–10.

Leutwyler, Kristin. "Don't Stress." <u>Scientific American</u> Jan. 1998: 28+.

Marucha, Philip T., Janice Kiecolt-Glaser, and Mehrdad Favagehi. "Mucosal Wound
Healing Is Impaired by Examination Stress." <u>Psychosomatic Medicine</u> 60
(1998): 362–65. Abstract. 7 April 2003
<http://www.dent.ohio-state.edu/maruchalab/examinationstress.html>.

[online abstract]

Mounir, Raghet, and Jennifer McKinney. "Campus Recreation and Perceived
Academic Stress." <u>Journal of College Student Development</u> 34.1 (1993): 5–10.

Murray, Bridget. "University 'Stress Lab' Helps Students Unwind." <u>APA Monitor</u>
March 1996: n. pag. Online. 11 Apr. 2003
<http://www.apa.org/monitor/mar96/stress.html>.

37

38

A research report in MLA style (*Continued*)

37. Since this essay appears in an anthology cited elsewhere in this list (i.e., Dohrenwend and Dohrenwend), the only information needed is the editor's name and the page numbers.

38. Although this online article has a printed equivalent, "n. pag." denotes that this Web source provided no page numbers.

Haley   13

"New Study Links Massage Therapy with The Immune System." 1 Oct. 1998.

Fox Chase Cancer Center News. 13 Apr. 2002

<http://www.fccc.edu/news/Massage-Therapy-Study-10-01-1998>.

39 Newton, Fred B., et al. "The Assessment of College Student Needs: First Step in a

Prevention Response." Personnel and Guidance Journal 62 (1984): 537–43.

40 Nikravesh, Bita, "Stress in College." National Student News Service 16 Feb. 1996:

n. pag. Online. 4 Apr. 2003 <http://acs5.gac.peachnet.edu/~colonade/

1996/021396/college-stress.html>.   *[electronic publication]*

Ross, S. E., B. C. Niebling, and T. M. Heckert. "Source of Stress among College

Students." College Student Journal 33 (1999): 312–17.

41 Selye, Hans. "The Stress Concept: Past, Present, and Future." Stress Research:

Issues for the 80's. Ed. Cary L. Cooper. Chichester, England: Wiley, 1983:

69–87.   *[article, anthology]*

42 ---. The Stress of Life. Rev. ed. New York: McGraw, 1976.

43 Tyrell, Jeanne. "Sources of Stress among Psychology Undergraduates." Irish

Journal of Psychology 13.2 (1992): 184–92.

44 White, Jaquelyn W., and John A. Humphrey. "Sexual Revictimization: A

Longitudinal Perspective." Paper Presented at the 101st Annual Meeting of

the American Psychological Association, 20–24 Aug. 1993. Toronto, Ontario.

Abstract. ERIC. CD-ROM. SilverPlatter. 3 Apr. 2003. ERIC Item: ED 374 363.

[conference paper—CD-ROM abstract]

A research report in MLA style (*Continued*)

39. An entry for a work with four or more authors or editors cites only the first person's name, followed by "et al."

40. An electronic publication has no printed equivalent.

41. An entry for an article in a collection of works compiled by an editor.

42. An entry for a revised edition of a book. Books with no edition number on the title page are cited as first editions. Otherwise, the edition is identified by number, name, or year, as given on the title page. Shorten publishers' names ("McGraw" for "McGraw-Hill" or "Harper" for "HarperCollins"). Also, multiple works by the same author are listed alphabetically according to title. Three hyphens followed by a period denote a second work by the same author.

43. For page numbers with more than two digits, include only the final two digits of the second number if the first digits are identical.

44. A citation for a CD-ROM database that is updated often should include the date of electronic publication for that particular disk (as in "3 Apr. 2003"). The "Abstract" designation shows that Haley is citing merely the abstract of this conference presentation.

SECTION FIVE

Additional Readings and Models for Writing

Description and Narration **472**

Illustration **475**

Division and Classification **478**

Process Analysis **482**

Cause-and-Effect Analysis **486**

Comparison and Contrast **490**

Definition **495**

Argument **498**

T his section provides additional writing samples for you to emulate and viewpoints to consider. You can apply the skills covered in earlier chapters by developing your own questions about the reading and your own ideas for responding to the topics. Sample essays illustrate each of the eight development strategies covered in Section Three. The final two essays offer competing arguments in the ongoing controversy about improving the U.S. educational system.

| Note | *Although each essay employs a primary development strategy, it usually relies on secondary strategies as well.* |

DESCRIPTION AND NARRATION

On the Ball

Roger Angell

It weighs just over five ounces and measures between 2.86 and 2.94 inches in diameter. It is made of a composition-cork nucleus encased in two thin layers of rubber, one black and one red, surrounded by 121 yards of tightly wrapped blue-gray wool yarn, 45 yards of white wool yarn, 54 more yards of blue-gray wool yarn, 150 yards of fine cotton yarn, a coat of rubber cement, and a cowhide (formerly horsehide) exterior, which is held together with 216 slightly raised red cotton stitches. Printed certifications, endorsements, and outdoor advertising spherically attest to its authenticity. Like most institutions, it is considered inferior in its present form to its ancient archetypes, and in this case the complaint is probably justified; on occasion in recent years it has actually been known to come apart under the demands of its brief but rigorous active career. Baseballs are assembled and hand-stitched in Taiwan (before this year the work was done in Haiti, and before 1973 in Chicopee, Massachusetts), and contemporary pitchers claim that there is a tangible variation in the size and feel of the balls that now come into play in a single game; a true peewee is treasured by hurlers, and its departure from the premises, by fair means or foul, is secretly mourned. But never mind: any baseball is beautiful. No other small package comes as close to the ideal in design and utility. It is a perfect object for a man's hand. Pick it up and it instantly suggests its purpose; it is meant to be thrown a considerable distance—thrown hard and with precision. Its feel and heft are the beginning of the sport's critical dimensions; if it were a fraction of an inch larger or smaller, a few centigrams heavier or lighter, the game of baseball would be utterly different. Hold a baseball in your hand. As it happens, this one is not brand-new. Here, just to one side of the curved surgical welt of stitches, there is a pale-green grass smudge, darkening on one edge almost to black—the mark of an old infield play, a tough grounder now lost in memory. Feel the ball, turn it over in your hand; hold it across the seam or the other way, with the seam just to the side of your middle finger. Speculation stirs. You want to get outdoors and throw this spare and sensual object to somebody or, at the very least, watch somebody else throw it. The game has begun.

Grandmother's Sunday Dinner

Patricia Hampl

Food was the potent center of my grandmother's life. Maybe the immense amount of time it took to prepare meals during most of her life accounted for her passion. Or it may have been her years of work in various kitchens on the hill and later, in the house of Justice Butler: after all, she was a professional. Much later, when she was dead and I went to Prague, I came to feel the motto I knew her by best—*Come eat*— was not, after, all a personal statement, but a racial one, the *cri de coeur* of Middle Europe.[1]

Often, on Sundays, the entire family gathered for dinner at her house. Dinner was 1 P.M. My grandmother would have preferred the meal to be at the old time of noon, but her children had moved their own Sunday dinner hour to the more fashionable (it was felt) 4 o'clock, so she compromised. Sunday breakfast was something my mother liked to do in a big way, so we arrived at my grandmother's hardly out of the reverie of waffles and orange rolls, before we were propped like rag dolls in front of a pork roast and sauerkraut, dumplings, hot buttered carrots, rye bread and rollikey, pickles and olives, apple pie and ice cream. And coffee.

Coffee was a food in that house, not a drink. I always begged for some because the magical man on the Hills Brothers can with his turban and long robe scattered with stars and his gold slippers with pointed toes, looked deeply happy as he drank from his bowl. The bowl itself reminded me of soup, Campbell's chicken noodle soup, my favorite food. The distinct adultness of coffee and the robed man with his deep-drinking pleasure made it clear why the grownups lingered so long at the table. The uncles smoked cigars then, and the aunts said, "Oh, those cigars."

My grandmother, when she served dinner, was a virtuoso hanging on the edge of her own ecstatic performance. She seemed dissatisfied, almost querulous until she had corralled everybody into their chairs around the table, which she tried to do the minute they got into the house. No cocktails, no hors d'oeuvres (pronounced, by some of the family, "horse's ovaries"), just business. She was a little power crazed: she had us and, by God, we were going to eat. She went about it like a goose breeder forcing pellets down the gullets of those dumb birds.

She flew between her chair and the kitchen, always finding more this, extra that. She'd given you the *wrong* chicken breast the first time around; now she'd found the *right* one: eat it too, eat it fast, because after the chicken comes the rhubarb pie. Rhubarb pie with a thick slice of cheddar cheese that it was imperative every single person eat.

We had to eat fast because something was always out there in the kitchen panting and charging the gate, champing at the bit, some mound of rice or a Jell-O fruit salad or vegetable casserole or pie was out there, waiting to be let loose into the dining room.

She had the usual trite routines: the wheedlings, the silent pout ("What! You don't like my brussels sprouts? I thought you liked *my* brussels sprouts," versus your

---

[1]*Cri de coeur:* cry of the heart.

wife's/sister's/mother's. "I made that pie just for you," etc., etc.). But it was the way she tossed around the old cliches and the overused routines, mixing them up and dealing them out shamelessly, without irony, that made her a pro. She tended to peck at her own dinner. Her plate, piled with food, was a kind of stage prop, a mere bending to convention. She liked to eat, she was even a greedy little stuffer, but not on these occasions. She was a woman possessed by an idea, given over wholly to some phantasmagoria of food, a mirage of stuffing, a world where the endless chicken and the infinite lemon pie were united at last at the shore of the oceanic soup plate that her children and her children's children alone could drain . . . if only they would try.

She was there to bolster morale, to lead the troops, to give the sharp command should we falter on the way. The futility of saying no was supreme, and no one ever tried it. How could a son-in-law, already weakened near the point of imbecility by the once, twice, thrice charge to the barricades of pork and mashed potato, be expected to gather his feeble wit long enough to ignore the final call of his old commander when she sounded the alarm: "Pie, Fred?"

Just when it seemed as if the food-crazed world she had created was going to burst, that she had whipped and frothed us like a sack of boiled potatoes under her masher, just then she pulled it all together in one easeful stroke like the pro she was.

She stood in the kitchen doorway, her little round Napoleonic self sheathed in a cotton flowered pinafore apron, the table draped in its white lace cloth but spotted now with gravy and beet juice, the troops mumbling indistinctly as they waited at their posts for they knew not what. We looked up at her stupidly, weakly. She said nonchalantly, "Anyone want another piece of pie?" No, no more pie, somebody said. The rest of the rabble grunted along with him. She stood there with the coffeepot and laughed and said, "Good! Because there *isn't* any more pie."

No more pie. We'd eaten it all, we'd put away everything in that kitchen. We were exhausted and she, gambler hostess that she was (but it was her house she was playing), knew she could offer what didn't exist, knew us, knew what she'd wrought. There was a sense of her having won, won something. There were no divisions among us now, no adults, no children. Power left the second and third generations and returned to the source, the grandmother who reduced us to mutters by her art.

That wasn't the end of it. At 5 P.M. there was "lunch"—sandwiches and beer; the sandwiches were made from the leftovers (mysteriously renewable resources, those roasts). And at about 8 P.M. we were at the table again for coffee cake and coffee, the little man in his turban and his coffee ecstasy and his pointed shoes set on the kitchen table as my grandmother scooped out the coffee and dumped it into a big enamel pot with a crushed eggshell. By then everyone was alive and laughing again, the torpor gone. My grandfather had been inviting the men, one by one, into the kitchen during the afternoon where he silently (the austere version of memory— but he must have talked, must have said *something*) handed them jiggers of whiskey, and watched them put the shot down in one swallow. Then he handed them a beer, which they took out in the living room. I gathered that the *little* drink in the tiny glass shaped like a beer mug was some sort of antidote for the *big* drink of beer. He sat

Illustration   **475**

on the chair in the kitchen with a bottle of beer on the floor next to him and played his concertina, allowing society to form itself around him—while he lived he was the center—but not seeking it, not going into the living room. And not talking. He held to his music and the kindly, medicinal administration of whiskey.

By evening, it seemed we could eat endlessly, as if we'd had some successful inoculation at dinner and could handle anything. I stayed in the kitchen after they all reformed in the dining room at the table for coffee cake. I could hear them, but the little man in his starry yellow robe was on the table in the kitchen and I put my head down on the oil cloth very near the curled and delighted tips of his pointed shoes, and I slept. Whatever laughter there was, there was. But something sweet and starry was in the kitchen and I lay down beside it, my stomach full, warm, so safe I'll live the rest of my life off the fat of that vast family security.

ILLUSTRATION

No Zeal for New Zealand

Jaclyn Thomas

I expected New Zealand to look and feel like the miles of photographs I had studied for months before deciding to spend a semester abroad there: mountains the color of dark emeralds, sheep swirling like clouds around the ankles of happy, ruddy farmers, and electric nightlife in the cities. When our group of American college students arrived in Auckland, we were amazed at the lack of airport security; we boarded our connecting plane for Wellington as one mass of unwashed backpackers, tossing our bags on the belt without accounting for them or answering a single question about their contents. But airport protocol was forgotten when we first saw the edges of the North Island slipping into the Pacific. From the sky, New Zealand resembled everything I had imagined.

Wellington, the capital city, is clean and small, without New York's trash-mottled sidewalks or LA's dirty sky. Because of its hilly landscape and its cosmopolitan reputation, it is advertised as "the San Francisco of New Zealand." I loved the accessibility of everything. Instead of New York's West Side Highway roaring in my ears, my first walk through the city found me strolling along a road populated with university student housing and bars and delicious, overpriced cafes. New Zealand's population of around 3.3 million thinned the traffic of both wheels and feet, and I welcomed my escape from the frenzied rush of American urban life.

As for our own national identity, we American students often leapt to correct the assumption that immediately followed the sounds of our voices: "Where are you from? Canada?" To many Kiwis, as New Zealanders cheerily call themselves, there was no cultural distinction to be made between Canada and the United States; many of them announced that as soon as they began their OE ("Overseas Experience," a period of global travel for the lucky and well-funded), they were heading to Canada.

We eagerly suggested places to visit in the States, but most Kiwis I encountered seemed less than enchanted with our home country. Instead they had their hearts set somewhere between Toronto and Vancouver.

To the Kiwis, we were "Yanks"; we were worse things, muttered in guttural voices, but for the most part we were Yanks. I was prepared for Yank; I was prepared for Kiwis to ask us if we thought we "owned the place" when we stopped at a Mc-Donald's late one night. But I was not prepared to hear the word Negro twice during my first week. My cab driver in Auckland had informed me of his travels in California as we pulled away from the airport, breathlessly including a report of "Negroes with guns." I had smiled and nodded, wondering if he had not noticed my dark skin or if I was simply hearing things after fourteen hours on a plane.

A few nights later I realized that my hearing actually was okay when I saw a Kiwi boy dancing around the room at a university party and suggesting that he was being "one of those American Negroes." While several of my fellow travelers glanced at me anxiously, the Kiwi faces radiated a complete absence of concern. After one of the Americans sternly observed that, "We don't use that word in America anymore," the boy managed to shift his conversation to mock the Asian students before cursing the "bloody Maori," the native people of New Zealand. So much for our program director's earlier description of the "great respect" that the white Kiwis held for the Maori.

As soon as we began attending the university in Wellington, our instinct was to blend. Like our Kiwi classmates, we ducked out of the constant rain and drank cheap beer. Two-dollar pints were available in the bar on the ground floor of my dorm, and in the dorm across the street, and in the bars a few blocks away. Our on-campus bar served beer from noon onward—a tempting offer once I had sat through my first class: During my Reading Women Writers lecture, I was informed by a Kiwi classmate that my professor would only appreciate "like, the feminist bits" of my essay. My most discouraging university experience, however, was not the flow of beer or the apathetic classmates, but a professor's response when I told the class what American college I attended at home. She replied: "You've taken quite a step down, now, haven't you?" I guess so.

By the end of my trip to New Zealand, I had exhausted my fascination with things new and different. When I finally arrived at Los Angeles International Airport, the vendors sold cookies instead of biscuits, and responded to a higher demand for coffee than tea. For a moment I was stunned by the crowds and cacophony, strikingly dissimilar to the quiet of Wellington airport. New Zealand flights were smooth and stress-free; back at LAX I endured long lines, excessive elevator rides, announcements of delays, and general testiness. Fifteen minutes after arriving in my home country, I witnessed a battle at the baggage claim over the single remaining cart. But when I left the terminal for a moment of fresh air, the beauty of a sunny California parking lot made me forget the rush of the Wanganui River, the seals at Wellington's red rocks, and the glimpse of Mt. Cook from the North Island shore. I wanted Mexican food and television that had not been recycled from the 1980s. I went back into LAX and changed my ticket to Boston so I would have more time to revel in the joys of my arrival. In California, I could splash my feet in the side of the Pacific I preferred.

Illustration   **477**

All You Can Eat

Michelle Stacey

The capacity of the human mind for self-deception is, it appears, bottomless. I plow into the vast, raisin-dotted pillowiness of my New York-style, bakery-made morning bagel and think: Bagel and coffee for breakfast, no butter, no cream cheese, pretty virtuous, *n'est-ce pas?* But this is not a bagel as nature or the U.S. government intended, which would be a moderate two to three ounces and 150 to 250 calories; instead, this is a behemoth, puffed up to five or six ounces and probably 400 calories, accounting for almost half of the six to eleven daily bread servings recommended by the USDA's Food Guide Pyramid. If I continue my see-no-evil approach, I can easily rack up innumerable quantities of fat and calories in a day of restaurant meals: steaming heaps of pasta, usually eight ounces instead of the USDA's suggested two; gargantuan chicken breasts that look as if they were cut from a three-foot-tall hen; baked potatoes that take up half the plate. Americans are on a portion pig-out, a swing to the far side of last decade's dainty nouvelle cuisine. "I don't care," proclaims a fast-food customer in a recent TV commercial, "just SuperSize me."

The problem goes beyond a simple ratcheting-up that leaves the door open for studied ignorance ("But I only ate *one!*"). American food has strayed so far from its original standards that our eyes, and instincts, can hardly be trusted anymore. Even nutrition experts can no longer guess what's in a portion. Further complicating things are the standards put out by the government—"airline portions," according to one expert. "Portion size is reaching a crisis," says Lisa Young, nutritionist and adjunct faculty member at New York University, who is writing her doctoral dissertation on the subject. "The problem is that there's a huge discrepancy between oversize restaurant portions and tiny government portions. So while three cups of pasta, the usual restaurant size, is too much, the half cup on the USDA chart isn't a realistic serving either."

Young, who notes that "portion sizes have gotten a lot larger in the last decade, and so have people," conducted a test of 200 dietitians and nutritionists at a 1996 convention of the American Dietetic Association. She asked them to guess the fat and calorie content of various popular dishes, including Caesar salad with grilled chicken and a tuna-salad sandwich. All participants underestimated by about 20 percent. The average estimate for a hamburger and onion rings was 863 calories and 44 grams of fat; the reality was 1,550 calories and 101 grams of fat. Similarly, a study several years ago found that a group of severely overweight people trying to lose weight—people "fairly well-educated in terms of nutrition," according to the study's head researcher—were actually eating twice as many calories per day as they thought they were. Such wishful thinking may account for the fact that official dietary-intake surveys in the last few years, based on daily food diaries, showed people eating barely enough calories to maintain body weight, while actual weights have been increasing dramatically.

The inability to estimate a total calorie count may have been beside the point in the days before the car-and-computer culture, but in this stationary age, calorie-creep has put a lot of people over the edge. It's terribly tempting to let restaurant chefs or even grocery stores be one's authority on how much to eat, but mostly they're authorities on pleasing people. Listen to them for a while and your eye gets retrained; pretty soon you'll think a ten-ounce steak is average (a USDA "serving" of meat is two to three ounces, about the size of a deck of cards).

There's a route to be charted between restaurant-gargantuan and USDA-ascetic, says Young. First, fight the food-as-bargain impulse: It is not a mortal sin to leave food on your plate, even though you paid for it. Next, plan in advance: If you're going out to dinner, try to imagine what you'll want, and adjust the rest of your day accordingly. "It's absurd to go to an Italian restaurant and order the broiled filet of sole, dry," Young says. "You want pasta. So eat less bread earlier in the day and more protein. Then, for dinner, consider getting an appetizer portion of pasta—that's usually a cup and a half. By USDA standards that's three portions of bread, but I think that's a reasonable amount of food, along with a salad."

So, if you want to splurge, go ahead—just don't kid yourself that a stack of pancakes that stretches across a twelve-inch plate is magically the same as the four-inch pancakes described in the average calorie chart. The clean-plate club closed its doors a long time ago.

Michelle Stacey. "All You Can Eat" from *Elle* magazine. March 1998. Reprinted by permission.

DIVISION AND CLASSIFICATION

All Junk, All the Time

Richard Brookhiser

Like a turtle egg buried on the beach, the thought warmed, out of sight, all summer. The Olympics and the political conventions helped it grow, but the key stimulus was a passing sentence in a *New York Times Magazine* article on megachurches, which are evangelical churches that number their congregations in the thousands. The article was discussing the music used in the services, and said something to the effect that the megachurches favored rock. Just like the conventions. Just like the Olympics. Just like everyone everywhere.

Megachurches keep their eye on eternity. In the here and now, rock is triumphant and universal. Its empire will only expand, ferreting out the few nooks it does not yet command, and filling them. Francis Fukuyama alerted us (wrongly) to the End of History. But rock has ended the history of music. There are no ideological, religious, or ethnic redoubts. I once read a profile of the commander of a Salvadoran death squad. He was a Deadhead. Iranian mullahs, Chinese Communists, skinheads, rabbis expecting the return of Menachem Schneerson, Papuan savages dressed only in penis wrappers, all listen, openly or in secret, or their children will.

What is rock? A certain set of musicians—drums, guitars, a voice or two. A beat that, well, rocks. Lyrics. Pare down the music until it almost vanishes, as in rap; soften the beat until it becomes easy listening; give the songwriter the equipment and the ambitions of Brian Wilson: but the form never quite disappears. It hasn't changed for forty years, and it never will, because it is so easy to do well enough.

Consider the elements.

Music. The guitar is the ultimate E-Z-2-Play instrument. Why else was it the lyre of the American peasantry? If rock depended on some instrument—trumpet, clarinet, fiddle, piano—that required some tone of the lips or lightness of the fingers to play even barely competently, its pool of potential performers would have shrunk by 90 percent. There is only one instrument easier to fake: drums. The low standards also apply to rock vocalists. Remember Mick Jagger when he was in his prime? Heard him now, when he sounds like a voice on the subway PA system? Mr. Jagger could actually move his notes around, but they were always harsh and homely notes. That's OK—they were good enough for rock.

Words. The rock critic Elizabeth Wurtzel, reviewing an album of covers of Cole Porter songs by rock musicians, hoped the experience might inspire rock songwriters to be a little more careful of their rhyme schemes. Wrong! The whole point is not to have to worry about rhyme schemes. If you start worrying, not everyone will be able to do it. So rock will keep on rhyming "pain" and "shame," and "stop" and "stuck."

Dancing. I was in fifth and sixth grade just after kids stopped taking solemn little lessons, in gym class or after school, in the box step and the cha-cha. Those who still dance these, and all the other dances of mankind, do it, like fox hunters or Greek scholars, as a passion or a hobby. To fulfill the necessities of social intercourse, it will never be necessary to take a dance lesson again. Slow dancing to rock is what you hope to be doing horizontally with your clothes off afterward. Fast dancing is—well, look at it, at any wedding or bar mitzvah, where even the grown-ups shake their aged hams. The abolition of dance steps was a great relief to the awkward, especially the men, who once had to lead—no more visualizing the points of the compass, no more shame when you crunched the foot you were supposed to be guiding.

Entrepreneurs. There is a final way in which rock is easy, which impels the other three. It is easy to make a buck selling it. Because the product is so generic, primitive, and witless, the distributors and marketers can know nothing, ingest huge quantities of drugs, and still not be too addled to make millions. The fields I know best are journalism, publishing, and politics, and so I do know something about laziness and empty pretensions. But if there were ever a land of opportunity for the feckless, the modern music industry is it.

Rock is a form of popular culture that aims downward in terms of class and age, instead of aiming up. Rather than aspiring, it *despires*. Astronomers speak of the red shift, the change in the spectrum of the light of receding galaxies. Rock is redneck shift. The preceding phase of popular music, encompassing jazz, dance bands, and show tunes, was urban and adult. Rock is kids channeling the rhythms of bumpkins.

But the worst thing about rock is not that it fails the culture, but that it fails on its own terms. Popular music is a marker and a memory aid. Most of the important events in life—romance, courtship, celebration—are accompanied by it. We remember them because of their importance to us, no matter what was on the radio. But if the music is crude and blank, does not some of its crudity and blankness infect the experience, and the memory?

And while popular music mostly amplifies pre-existing emotions, at its best it can tug us, tease us, make us grow. Not rock. For all its supposedly revolutionary ethos, rock is a binary switch of angst and hormones—Kafka without humor, or centerfolds in notes. The emotions that unsettle, like stones under a sleeping bag—hope, regret—are beyond its ken. And they are beyond our ken, to the extent rock stuffs our ears.

It's Bottom 40, all junk, all the time. And it's here to stay.

The Dog Ate My Disk, and Other Tales of Woe

Carolyn Foster Segal

Taped to the door of my office is a cartoon that features a cat explaining to his feline teacher, "The dog ate my homework." It is intended as a gently humorous reminder to my students that I will not accept excuses for late work, and it, like the lengthy warning on my syllabus, has had absolutely no effect. With a show of energy and creativity that would be admirable if applied to the (missing) assignments in question, my students persist, week after week, semester after semester, year after year, in offering excuses about why their work is not ready. Those reasons fall into several broad categories: the family, the best friend, the evils of dorm life, the evils of technology, and the totally bizarre.

The Family. The death of the grandfather/grandmother is, of course, the grandmother of all excuses. What heartless teacher would dare to question a student's grief or veracity? What heartless student would lie, wishing death on a revered family member, just to avoid a deadline? Creative students may win extra extensions (and days off) with a little careful planning and fuller plot development, as in the sequence of "My grandfather/grandmother is sick"; "Now my grandfather/grandmother is in the hospital"; and finally, "We could all see it coming—my grandfather/grandmother is dead."

Another favorite excuse is "the family emergency," which (always) goes like this: "There was an emergency at home, and I had to help my family." It's a lovely sentiment, one that conjures up images of Louisa May Alcott's little women rushing off with baskets of food and copies of *Pilgrim's Progress,* but I do not understand why anyone would turn to my most irresponsible students in times of trouble.

The Best Friend. This heartwarming concern for others extends beyond the family to friends, as in, "My best friend was up all night and I had to (a) stay up with her in the dorm, (b) drive her to the hospital, or (c) drive to her college because (1) her boyfriend broke up with her, (2) she was throwing up blood [no one catches a cold anymore; everyone throws up blood], or (3) her grandfather/grandmother died."

At one private university where I worked as an adjunct, I heard an interesting spin that incorporated the motifs of both best friend and dead relative: "My best friend's mother killed herself." One has to admire the cleverness here: A mysterious woman in the prime of her life has allegedly committed suicide, and no professor can prove otherwise! And I admit I was moved, until finally I had to point out to my students that it was amazing how the simple act of my assigning a topic for a paper seemed to drive large numbers of otherwise happy and healthy middle-aged women to their deaths. I was careful to make that point during an off week, during which no deaths were reported.

The Evils of Dorm Life. These stories are usually fairly predictable; almost always feature the evil roommate or hallmate, with my student in the role of the innocent victim; and can be summed up as follows: My roommate, who is a horrible person, likes to party, and I, who am a good person, cannot concentrate on my work when he or she is partying. Variations include stories about the two people next door who were running around and crying loudly last night because (a) one of them had boyfriend/girlfriend problems; (b) one of them was throwing up blood; or (c) someone, somewhere, died. A friend of mine in graduate school had a student who claimed that his roommate attacked him with a hammer. That, in fact, was a true story; it came out in court when the bad roommate was tried for killing his grandfather.

The Evils of Technology. The computer age has revolutionized the student story, inspiring almost as many new excuses as it has Internet businesses. Here are just a few electronically enhanced explanations:

- The computer wouldn't let me save my work.
- The printer wouldn't print.
- The printer wouldn't print this disk.
- The printer wouldn't give me time to proofread.
- The printer made a black line run through all my words, and I know you can't read this, but do you still want it, or wait, here, take my disk. File name? I don't know what you mean.
- I swear I attached it.
- It's my roommate's computer, and she usually helps me, but she had to go to the hospital because she was throwing up blood.
- I did write to the newsgroup, but all my messages came back to me.
- I just found out that all my other newsgroup messages came up under a different name. I just want you to know that its really me who wrote all those messages, you can tel which ones our mine because I didnt use the spelcheck! But it was yours truely :) Anyway, just in case you missed those messages or dont belief its my writting, I'll repeat what I sad: I thought the last movie we watched in clas was borring.

The Totally Bizarre. I call the first story "The Pennsylvania Chain Saw Episode." A commuter student called to explain why she had missed my morning class. She had gotten up early so that she would be wide awake for class. Having a bit of extra time, she walked outside to see her neighbor, who was cutting some wood. She called out to him, and he waved back to her with the saw. Wouldn't you know it, the safety catch wasn't on or was broken, and the blade flew right out of the saw and across his lawn and over her fence and across her yard and severed a tendon in her right hand. So she was calling me from the hospital, where she was waiting for surgery.

Luckily, she reassured me, she had remembered to bring her paper and a stamped envelope (in a plastic bag, to avoid bloodstains) along with her in the ambulance, and a nurse was mailing everything to me even as we spoke.

That wasn't her first absence. In fact, this student had missed most of the class meetings, and I had already recommended that she withdraw from the course. Now I suggested again that it might be best if she dropped the class. I didn't harp on the absences (what if even some of this story were true?). I did mention that she would need time to recuperate and that making up so much missed work might be difficult. "Oh, no," she said, "I can't drop this course. I had been planning to go on to medical school and become a surgeon, but since I won't be able to operate because of my accident, I'll have to major in English, and this course is more important than ever to me." She did come to the next class, wearing—as evidence of her recent trauma—a bedraggled Ace bandage on her left hand.

You may be thinking that nothing could top that excuse, but in fact I have one more story, provided by the same student, who sent me a letter to explain why her final assignment would be late. While recuperating from her surgery, she had begun corresponding on the Internet with a man who lived in Germany. After a one-week, whirlwind Web romance, they had agreed to meet in Rome, to rendezvous (her phrase) at the papal Easter Mass. Regrettably, the time of her flight made it impossible for her to attend class, but she trusted that I—just this once—would accept late work if the pope wrote a note.

PROCESS ANALYSIS

How to Write a Personal Letter

Garrison Keillor

We shy persons need to write a letter now and then, or else we'll dry up and blow away. It's true. And I speak as one who loves to reach for the phone, dial the number, and talk. The telephone is to shyness what Hawaii is to February; it's a way out of the woods. *And yet:* a letter is better.

Such a sweet gift—a piece of handmade writing, in an envelope that is not a bill, sitting in our friend's path when she trudges home from a long day spent among wahoos and savages, a day our words will help repair. They don't need to be immortal, just sincere. She can read them twice and again tomorrow: *You're someone I care about, Corinne, and think of often, and every time I do, you make me smile.*

We need to write; otherwise nobody will know who we are. They will have only a vague impression of us as A Nice Person, because, frankly, we don't shine at conversation, we lack the confidence to thrust our faces forward and say, "Hi, I'm Heather Hooten; let me tell you about my week." Mostly we say "Uh-huh" and "Oh really." People smile and look over our shoulder, looking for someone else to meet.

So a shy person sits down and writes a letter. To be known by another person—to meet and talk freely on the page—to be close despite distance. To escape from anonymity and be our own sweet selves and express the music of our souls.

Same thing that moves a giant rock star to sing his heart out in front of 123,000 people moves us to take ballpoint in hand and write a few lines to our dear Aunt Eleanor. *We want to be known.* We want her to know that we have fallen in love, that we quit our job, that we're moving to New York, and we want to say a few things that might not get said in casual conversation: *Thank you for what you've meant to me. I am very happy right now.*

The first step in writing letters is to get over the guilt of *not* writing. You don't "owe" anybody a letter. Letters are a gift. The burning shame you feel when you see unanswered mail makes it harder to pick up a pen and makes for a cheerless letter when you finally do. *I feel bad about not writing, but I've been so busy,* etc. Skip this. Few letters are obligatory, and they are *Thanks for the wonderful gift* and *I am terribly sorry to hear about George's death* and *Yes, you're welcome to stay with us next month.* Write these promptly if you want to keep your friends. Don't worry about the others, except love letters, of course. When your true love writes *Dear Light of My Life, Joy of My Heart, O Lovely Pulsating Core of My Sensate Life,* some response is called for.

Some of the best letters are tossed off in a burst of inspiration, so keep your writing stuff in one place where you can sit down for a few minutes and—*Dear Roy, I am in the middle of an essay but thought I'd drop you a line. Hi to your sweetie too*—dash off a note to a pal. Envelopes, stamps, address book, everything in a drawer so you can write fast when the pen is hot.

A blank white 8″ × 11″ sheet can look as big as Montana if the pen's not so hot—try a smaller page and write boldly. Get a pen that makes a sensuous line, get a comfortable typewriter, a friendly word processor—whichever feels easy to the hand.

Sit for a few minutes with the blank sheet of paper in front of you, and meditate on the person you will write to, let your friend come to mind until you can almost see her or him in the room with you. Remember the last time you saw each other and how your friend looked and what you said and what perhaps was unsaid between you, and when your friend becomes real to you, start to write.

Write the salutation—*Dear* You—and take a deep breath and plunge in. A simple declarative sentence will do, followed by another and another. Tell us what you're doing and tell it like you were talking to us. Don't think about grammar, don't think about style, don't try to write dramatically, just give us your news. Where did you go, who did you see, what did they say, what do you think?

If you don't know where to begin, start with the present: *I'm sitting at the kitchen table on a rainy Saturday morning. Everyone is gone and the house is quiet.* Let your simple description of the present moment lead to something else; let the letter drift gently along.

The toughest letter to crank out is one that is meant to impress, as we all know from writing job applications; if it's hard work to slip off a letter to a friend, maybe you're trying too hard to be terrific. A letter is only a report to someone who already likes you for reasons other than your brilliance. Take it easy.

Don't worry about form. It's not a term paper. When you come to the end of one episode, just start a new paragraph. You can go from a few lines about the sad state of pro football to the fight with your mother to your fond memories of Mexico to your cat's urinary-tract infection to a few thoughts on personal indebtedness and on to the kitchen sink and what's in it. The more you write, the easier it gets, and when you have a True True Friend to write to, a *compadre,* a soul sibling, then it's like driving a car; you just press on the gas.

Don't tear up the page and start over when you write a bad line—try to write your way out of it. Make mistakes and plunge on. Let the letter cook along and let yourself be bold. Outrage, confusion, love—whatever is in your mind, let it find a way to the page. Writing is a means of discovery, always, and when you come to the end and write *Yours ever* or *Hugs and Kisses,* you'll know something you didn't when you wrote *Dear Pal.*

Probably your friend will put your letter away, and it'll be read again a few years from now—and it will improve with age. And forty years from now, your friend's grandkids will dig it out of the attic and read it, a sweet and precious relic of the ancient Eighties that gives them a sudden clear glimpse of you and her and the world we old-timers knew. You will have then created an object of art. Your simple lines about where you went, who you saw, what they said, will speak to those children, and they will feel in their hearts the humanity of our times.

You can't pick up a phone and call the future and tell them about our times. You have to pick up a piece of paper.

How Boys Become Men

Jon Katz

Two nine-year-old boys, neighbors and friends, were walking home from school. The one in the bright blue windbreaker was laughing and swinging a heavy-looking book bag toward the head of his friend, who kept ducking and stepping back. "What's the matter?" asked the kid with the bag, whooshing it over his head. "You chicken?"

His friend stopped, stood still and braced himself. The bag slammed into the side of his face, the thump audible all the way across the street where I stood watching. The impact knocked him to the ground, where he lay mildly stunned for a second. Then he struggled up, rubbing the side of his head. "See?" he said proudly. "I'm no chicken."

No. A chicken would probably have had the sense to get out of the way. This boy was already well on the road to becoming a *man,* having learned one of the central ethics of his gender: Experience pain rather than show fear.

Women tend to see men as a giant problem in need of solution. They tell us that we're remote and uncommunicative, that we need to demonstrate less machismo and more commitment, more humanity. But if you don't understand something about boys, you can't understand why men are the way we are, why we find it so difficult to make friends or to acknowledge our fears and problems.

Boys live in a world with its own Code of Conduct, a set of ruthless, unspoken, and unyielding rules:

Don't be a goody-goody.

Never rat. If your parents ask about bruises, shrug.

Never admit fear. Ride the roller coaster, join the fistfight, do what you have to do. Asking for help is for sissies.

Empathy is for nerds. You can help your best buddy, under certain circumstances. Everyone else is on his own.

Never discuss anything of substance with anybody. Grunt, shrug, dump on teachers, laugh at wimps, talk about comic books. Anything else is risky.

Boys are rewarded for throwing hard. Most other activities—reading, befriending girls, or just thinking—are considered weird. And if there's one thing boys don't want to be, it's weird.

More than anything else, boys are supposed to learn how to handle themselves. I remember the bitter fifth-grade conflict I touched off by elbowing aside a bigger boy named Barry and seizing the cafeteria's last carton of chocolate milk. Teased for getting aced out by a wimp, he had to reclaim his place in the pack. Our fistfight, at recess, ended with my knees buckling and my lip bleeding while my friends, sympathetic but out of range, watched resignedly.

When I got home, my mother took one look at my swollen face and screamed. I wouldn't tell her anything, but when my father got home I cracked and confessed, pleading with them to do nothing. Instead, they called Barry's parents, who restricted his television for a week.

The following morning, Barry and six of his pals stepped out from behind a stand of trees. "It's the rat," said Barry.

I bled a little more. *Rat* was scrawled in crayon across my desk.

They were waiting for me after school for a number of afternoons to follow. I tried varying my routes and avoiding bushes and hedges. It usually didn't work.

I was as ashamed for telling as I was frightened. "You did ask for it," said my best friend. Frontier Justice has nothing on Boy Justice.

In panic, I appealed to a cousin who was several years older. He followed me home from school, and when Barry's gang surrounded me, he came barreling toward us. "Stay away from my cousin," he shouted, "or I'll kill you."

After they were gone, however, my cousin could barely stop laughing. "You were afraid of *them?*" he howled. "They barely came up to my waist."

Men remember receiving little mercy as boys; maybe that's why it's sometimes difficult for them to show any.

"I know lots of men who had happy childhoods, but none who have happy memories of the way other boys treated them," says a friend. "It's a macho marathon from third grade up, when you start butting each other in the stomach."

"The thing is," adds another friend, "you learn early on to hide what you feel. It's never safe to say, 'I'm scared.' My girlfriend asks me why I don't talk more about what I'm feeling. I've gotten better at it, but it will *never* come naturally."

You don't need to be a shrink to see how the lessons boys learn affect their behavior as men. Men are being asked, more and more, to show sensitivity, but they dread the very word. They struggle to build their increasingly uncertain work lives but will deny they're in trouble. They want love, affection, and support but don't know how to ask for them. They hide their weaknesses and fears from all, even those they care for. They've learned to be wary of intervening when they see others in trouble. They often still balk at being stigmatized as weird.

Some men get shocked into sensitivity—when they lose their jobs, their wives, or their lovers. Others learn it through a strong marriage, or through their own children.

It may be a long while, however, before male culture evolves to the point that boys can learn more from one another than how to hit curve balls. Last month, walking my dog past the playground near my house, I saw three boys encircling a fourth, laughing and pushing him. He was skinny and rumpled, and he looked frightened. One boy knelt behind him while another pushed him from the front, a trick familiar to any former boy. He fell backward.

When the others ran off, he brushed the dirt off his elbows and walked toward the swings. His eyes were moist and he was struggling for control.

"Hi," I said through the chain-link fence. "How ya doing?"

"Fine," he said quickly, kicking his legs out and beginning his swing.

CAUSE-AND-EFFECT ANALYSIS

Why We Crave Horror Movies

Stephen King

I think that we're all mentally ill; those of us outside the asylums only hide it a little better—and maybe not all that much better, after all. We've all known people who talk to themselves, people who sometimes squinch their faces into horrible grimaces when they believe no one is watching, people who have some hysterical fear—of snakes, the dark, the tight place, the long drop . . . and, of course, those final worms and grubs that are waiting so patiently underground.

When we pay our four or five bucks and seat ourselves at tenth-row center in a theater showing a horror movie, we are daring the nightmare.

Why? Some of the reasons are simple and obvious. To show that we can, that we are not afraid, that we can ride this roller coaster. Which is not to say that a really good horror movie may not surprise a scream out of us at some point, the way we may scream when the roller coaster twists through a complete 360 or plows through a lake at the bottom of the drop. And horror movies, like roller coasters, have always been the special province of the young; by the time one turns 40 or 50, one's appetite for double twists or 360-degree loops may be considerably depleted.

We also go to re-establish our feelings of essential normality; the horror movie is innately conservative, even reactionary. Freda Jackson as the horrible melting woman in *Die, Monster, Die!* confirms for us that no matter how far we may be removed from the beauty of a Robert Redford or a Diana Ross, we are still light-years from true ugliness.

And we go to have fun.

Ah, but this is where the ground starts to slope away, isn't it? Because this is a very peculiar sort of fun, indeed. The fun comes from seeing others menaced—sometimes killed. One critic has suggested that if pro football has become the voyeur's version of combat, then the horror film has become the modern version of the public lynching.

It is true that the mythic, "fairy-tale" horror film intends to take away the shades of gray. . . . It urges us to put away our more civilized and adult penchant for analysis and to become children again, seeing things in pure blacks and whites. It may be that horror movies provide psychic relief on this level because this invitation to lapse into simplicity, irrationality, and even outright madness is extended so rarely. We are told we may allow our emotions a free rein . . . or no rein at all.

If we are all insane, then sanity becomes a matter of degree. If your insanity leads you to carve up women like Jack the Ripper or the Cleveland Torso Murderer, we clap you away in the funny farm (but neither of those two amateur-night surgeons was ever caught, heh-heh-heh); if, on the other hand, your insanity leads you only to talk to yourself when you're under stress or to pick your nose on your morning bus, then you are left alone to go about your business . . . though it is doubtful that you will ever be invited to the best parties.

The potential lyncher is in almost all of us (excluding saints, past and present; but then, most saints have been crazy in their own ways), and every now and then, he has to be let loose to scream and roll around in the grass. Our emotions and our fears form their own body, and we recognize that it demands its own exercise to maintain proper muscle tone. Certain of these emotional muscles are accepted—even exalted—in civilized society; they are, of course, the emotions that tend to maintain the status quo of civilization itself. Love, friendship, loyalty, kindness—these are all the emotions that we applaud, emotions that have been immortalized in the couplets of Hallmark cards and in the verses (I don't dare call it poetry) of Leonard Nimoy.

When we exhibit these emotions, society showers us with positive reinforcement; we learn this even before we get out of diapers. When, as children, we hug our rotten little puke of a sister and give her a kiss, all the aunts and uncles smile and twit and cry, "Isn't he the sweetest little thing?" Such coveted treats as chocolate-covered graham crackers often follow. But if we deliberately slam the rotten little puke of a sister's fingers in the door, sanctions follow—angry remonstrance from parents, aunts, and uncles; instead of a chocolate-covered graham cracker, a spanking.

But anticivilization emotions don't go away, and they demand periodic exercise. We have such "sick" jokes as, "What's the difference between a truckload of bowling balls and a truckload of dead babies?" (You can't unload a truckload of bowling balls with a pitchfork . . . a joke, by the way, that I heard originally from a ten-year-old.) Such a joke may surprise a laugh or a grin out of us even as we recoil, a possibility that confirms the thesis: If we share a brotherhood of man, then we also share an insanity of man. None of which is intended as a defense of either the sick joke or insanity but merely as an explanation of why the best horror films, like the best fairy tales, manage to be reactionary, anarchistic, and revolutionary all at the same time.

The mythic horror movie, like the sick joke, has a dirty job to do. It deliberately appeals to all that is worst in us. It is morbidity unchained, our most base instincts let free, our nastiest fantasies realized . . . and it all happens, fittingly enough, in the dark. For those reasons, good liberals often shy away from horror films. For myself, I like to see the most aggressive of them—*Dawn of the Dead,* for instance—as lifting a trap door in the civilized forebrain and throwing a basket of raw meat to the hungry alligators swimming around in that subterranean river beneath.

Why bother? Because it keeps them from getting out, man. It keeps them down there and me up here. It was Lennon and McCartney who said that all you need is love, and I would agree with that.

As long as you keep the gators fed.

I Just Wanna Be Average

Mike Rose

Students will float to the mark you set. I and the others in the vocational classes were bobbing in pretty shallow water. Vocational education has aimed at increasing the economic opportunities of students who do not do well in our schools. Some serious programs succeed in doing that, and through exceptional teachers—like Mr. Gross in *Horace's Compromise*—students learn to develop hypotheses and troubleshoot, reason through a problem, and communicate effectively—the true job skills. The vocational track, however, is most often a place for those who are just not making it, a dumping ground for the disaffected. There were a few teachers who worked hard at education; young Brother Slattery, for example, combined a stern voice with weekly quizzes to try to pass along to us a skeletal outline of world history. But mostly the teachers had no idea of how to engage the imaginations of us kids who were scuttling along at the bottom of the pond.

And the teachers would have needed some inventiveness, for none of us was groomed for the classroom. It wasn't just that I didn't know things—didn't know how to simplify algebraic fractions, couldn't identify different kinds of clauses, bungled Spanish translations—but that I had developed various faulty and inadequate ways of doing algebra and making sense of Spanish. Worse yet, the years of defensive tuning out in elementary school had given me a way to escape quickly while seeming at least half alert. During my time in Voc. Ed., I developed further into a mediocre student and a somnambulant problem solver, and that affected the subjects I did have the wherewithal to handle: I detested Shakespeare; I got bored with history. My attention flitted here and there. I fooled around in class and read my books indifferently—the intellectual equivalent of playing with your food. I did what I had to do to get by, and I did it with half a mind.

But I did learn things about people and eventually came into my own socially. I liked the guys in Voc. Ed. Growing up where I did, I understood and admired physical prowess, and there was an abundance of muscle here. There was Dave Snyder, a sprinter and halfback of true quality. Dave's ability and his quick wit gave him a natural appeal, and he was welcome in any clique, though he always kept a little independent. He enjoyed acting the fool and could care less about studies, but he possessed a certain maturity and never caused the faculty much trouble. It was a testament to his independence that he included me among his friends—I eventually went out for track, but I was no jock. Owing to the Latin alphabet and a dearth of *R*s and *S*s Snyder sat behind Rose, and we started exchanging one-liners and became friends.

There was Ted Richard, a much-touted Little League pitcher. He was chunky and had a baby face and came to Our Lady of Mercy as a seasoned street fighter. Ted was quick to laugh and he had a loud, jolly laugh, but when he got angry he'd smile a little smile, the kind that simply raises the corner of the mouth a quarter of an inch. For those who knew, it was an eerie signal. Those who didn't found themselves in big trouble, for Ted was very quick. He loved to carry on what we would come to call philosophical discussions: What is courage? Does God exist? He also loved words, enjoyed picking up big ones like *salubrious* and *equivocal* and using them in our conversations—laughing at himself as the word hit a chuckhole rolling off his tongue. Ted didn't do all that well in school—baseball and parties and testing the courage he'd speculated about took up his time. His textbooks were *Argosy* and *Field and Stream*, whatever newspapers he'd find on the bus stop—from the *Daily Worker* to pornography—conversations with uncles or hobos or businessmen he'd meet in a coffee shop, *The Old Man and the Sea*. With hindsight, I can see that Ted was developing into one of those rough-hewn intellectuals whose sources are a mix of the learned and the apocryphal, whose discussions are both assured and sad.

And then there was Ken Harvey. Ken was good-looking in a puffy way and had a full and oily ducktail and was a car enthusiast . . . a hodad. One day in religion class, he said the sentence that turned out to be one of the most memorable of the hundreds of thousands I heard in those Voc. Ed. years. We were talking about the parable of the talents, about achievement, working hard, doing the best you can do, blah-blah-blah, when the teacher called on the restive Ken Harvey for an opinion. Ken thought about it, but just for a second, and said (with studied, minimal affect), "I just wanna be average." That woke me up, Average?! Who wants to be average? Then the athletes chimed in with the clichés that make you want to laryngectomize them, and the exchange became a platitudinous melee. At the time, I thought Ken's assertion was stupid, and I wrote him off. But his sentence has stayed with me all these years, and I think I am finally coming to understand it.

Ken Harvey was gasping for air. School can be a tremendously disorienting place. No matter how bad the school, you're going to encounter notions that don't fit with the assumptions and beliefs that you grew up with—maybe you'll hear these dissonant notions from teachers, maybe from the other students, and maybe you'll read them. You'll also be thrown in with all kinds of kids from all kinds of backgrounds, and that can be unsettling—this is especially true in places of rich ethnic and linguistic mix, like the L.A. basin. You'll see a handful of students far excel you in courses that sound exotic and that are only in the curriculum of the elite: French, physics, trigonometry. And all this is happening while you're trying to shape an identity, your body is changing, and your emotions are running wild. If you're a working-class kid in the vocational track, the options you'll have to deal with this will be constrained in certain ways: You're defined by your school as "slow"; you're placed in a curriculum that isn't designed to liberate you but to occupy you, or, if you're lucky, train you, though the training is for work the society does not esteem; other students are picking up the cues from your school and your curriculum and interacting with you in particular ways. If you're a kid like Ted Richard, you turn your back on all this and let your mind roam where it may. But youngsters like Ted are rare. What Ken and so many others do is protect themselves from such suffocating madness by taking on with a vengeance the identity implied in the vocational track. Reject the confusion and frustration by openly defining yourself as the Common Joe. Champion the average. Rely on your own good sense. Fuck this bullshit. Bullshit, of course, is everything you—and the others—fear is beyond you: books, essays, tests, academic scrambling, complexity, scientific reasoning, philosophical inquiry.

The tragedy is that you have to twist the knife in your own gray matter to make this defense work. You'll have to shut down, have to reject intellectual stimuli or diffuse them with sarcasm, have to cultivate stupidity, have to convert boredom from a malady into a way of confronting the world. Keep your vocabulary simple, act stoned when you're not or act more stoned than you are, flaunt ignorance, materialize your dreams. It is a powerful and effective defense—it neutralizes the insult and the frustration of being a vocational kid and, when perfected, it drives teachers up the wall, a delightful secondary effect. But like all strong magic, it exacts a price.

COMPARISON AND CONTRAST

Parallel Worlds: The Surprising Similarities (and Differences) of Country-and-Western and Rap

Denise Noe

In all of popular music today, there are probably no two genres that are more apparently dissimilar than country-and-western and rap: the one rural, white, and southern; the other urban, black, and identified with the two coasts ("New York style" versus "L.A. style"). Yet C&W and rap are surprisingly similar in many ways. In both C&W and rap, for example, lyrics are important. Both types of music tell stories, as do folk songs, and the story is much more than frosting for the rhythm and beat.

The ideologies espoused by these types of music are remarkably similar as well. We frequently stereotype country fans as simple-minded conservatives—"redneck," moralistic super-patriots à la Archie Bunker. But country music often speaks critically of mainstream American platitudes, especially in such highly charged areas as sexual morality, crime, and the Protestant work ethic.

The sexual ethos of C&W and rap are depressingly similar: the men of both genres are champion chauvinists. Country singer Hank Williams, Jr., declares he's "Going Hunting Tonight," but he doesn't need a gun since he's hunting the "she-cats" in a singles bar. Male rappers such as Ice-T, Ice Cube, and Snoop Doggy Dogg are stridently misogynist, with "bitches" and "hos" their trademark terms for half of humanity; their enthusiastic depictions of women raped and murdered are terrifying. Indeed, the sexism of rap group NWA (Niggaz with Attitude) reached a real-life nadir when one member of the group beat up a woman he thought "dissed" them—and was praised for his brutality by the other members.

On a happier note, both rap and C&W feature strong female voices as well. Women rappers are strong, confident, and raunchy: "I want a man, not a boy / to approach me / Your lame game really insults me. . . . I've got to sit on my feet to come down to your level," taunt lady rappers Entice and Barbie at Too Short in their duet/duel, "Don't Fight the Feeling." Likewise, Loretta Lynn rose to C&W fame with defiant songs like "Don't Come Home a-Drinkin' with Lovin' on Your Mind" and "Your Squaw Is on the Warpath Tonight."

Country music can be bluntly honest about the realities of sex and money—in sharp contrast to the "family values" rhetoric of the right. "Son of Hickory Hollow's Tramp" by Johnny Darrell salutes a mother who works as a prostitute to support her children. "Fancy" by Bobbie Gentry (and, more recently, Reba McEntire) describes a poverty-stricken woman's use of sex for survival and her rise to wealth on the ancient "gold mine." Both tunes are unapologetic about the pragmatic coping strategies of their heroines.

More startling than the resemblances in their male sexism and "uppity" women are the parallels between C&W and rap in their treatment of criminality. Country-and-western music is very far from a rigid law-and-order mentality. The criminal's life is celebrated for its excitement and clear-cut rewards—a seemingly promising alternative to the dull grind of day-to-day labor.

"Ain't got no money / Ain't got no job / Let's find a place to rob," sings a jaunty Ricky Van Shelton in "Crime of Passion." In "I Never Picked Cotton," Roy Clark is more subdued but still unrepentant when he says: "I never picked cotton / like my mother did and my sister did and my brother did / And I'll never die young / working in a coal mine like my daddy did." Waylon Jennings' "Good Ole Boys" boast gleefully of having "hot-wired a city truck / turned it over in the mayor's yard."

Similarly, rap songs like "Gangsta, Gangsta" and "Dopeman" by NWA and "Drama" by Ice-T tell of the thrill and easy money offered by a life of crime. "Drama" records the dizzying high of the thief; "Gangsta, Gangsta," the rush of adrenaline experienced by a murderer making a quick getaway. Of course, both C&W and rap songs do express the idea that in the long run crime doesn't pay. The sad narrator of Merle Haggard's "Mama Tried" "turned 21 in prison / doing life without parole," while the thief of Ice-T's "Drama" is forced to realize that "I wouldn't be here if I'd fed my brain / Got knowledge from schoolbooks / 'stead of street crooks. / Now all I get is penitentiary hard looks."

Though both C&W and rap narrators are often criminals, their attitudes toward law enforcement differ radically. The Irish Rovers' "Wasn't That a Party?" ("that little drag race down on Main Street / was just to see if the cops could run") pokes lighthearted fun at the police, while the Bobby Fuller Four's "I Fought the Law and the Law Won" expresses the most common C&W attitude: an acceptance that criminals must be caught, even if you are one. Neither song displays any anger toward the police, who are, after all, just doing their job.

To rappers, on the other hand, cops are the enemy. Two of the most notorious rap songs are Ice-T's "Cop Killer" and NWA's "Fuck tha Police" (which angrily asserts, "Some police think they have the authority to kill a minority"). Despite ample evidence of police brutality in the inner city, "Fuck tha Police" was almost certainly regarded by nonblack America as a paranoid shriek—until the world witnessed the infamous videotape of several of Los Angeles' finest brutally beating Rodney King while a dozen other "peace officers" nonchalantly looked on.

Interestingly, although the C&W view of law enforcement naturally sits better with the general public (certainly with the police themselves), the fact remains that country-and-western music contains a good deal of crime, violence, and casual sex. Yet it is easily accepted by white Americans while rap arouses alarm and calls for labeling. Why?

I believe there are three major reasons. The first, and simplest, is language. Rappers say "bitch," "ho," "fuck," and "motherfucker"; C&W artists don't. Country singers may say, "I'm in the mood to speak some French tonight" (Mary Chapin-Carpenter, "How Do") or "There's two kinds of cherries / and two kinds of fairies" (Merle Haggard, "My Own Kind of Hat"), but they avoid the bluntest Anglo-Saxon terms.

A second reason is race. African Americans have a unique history of oppression in this country, and rap reflects the inner-city African American experience. Then, too, whites expect angry, frightening messages from blacks and listen for them. Many blacks, on the other hand, hope for uplifting messages—and are dismayed when black artists seem to encourage or glorify the drug abuse and violence in their beleaguered communities. Thus, the focus on violence in rap—and the dismissal of same in C&W.

While the differing attitudes toward law enforcement are real enough, much of the difference between violence in country-and-western music and in rap lies not in the songs themselves but in the way they are heard. Thus, when Ice Cube says, "Let the suburbs see a nigga invasion / Point-blank, smoke the Caucasian," many whites interpret that as an incitement to violence. But when Johnny Cash's disgruntled factory worker in "Oney" crows, "Today's the day old Oney gets his," it's merely a joke. Likewise, when Ice Cube raps, "I've got a shotgun and here's the plot / Taking niggas out with the fire of buckshot" ("Gangsta, Gangsta"), he sends shudders through many African Americans heartbroken by black-on-black violence; but when Johnny Cash sings of an equally nihilistic killing in "Folsom Prison Blues"—"Shot a man in Reno / just to watch him die"—the public taps its feet and hums along. It's just a song, after all.

There is a third—and ironic—reason why rap is so widely attacked: rap is actually closer to mainstream American economic ideology than country-and-western is. While C&W complains about the rough life of honest labor for poor and working-class people, rap ignores it almost entirely. "Work your fingers to the bone and what do you get?" asks Hoyt Axton in a satirical C&W song, then answers sardonically with its title: "Bony Fingers." Likewise, Johnny Paycheck's infamous "Take This Job and Shove It" is a blue-collar man's bitter protest against the rough and repetitive nature of his life's work. Work in C&W is hard and meaningless; it keeps one alive, but leaves the worker with little time or energy left to enjoy life.

Songs by female country singers reinforce this point in a different way; they insist that love (with sex) is more important than affluence. The heroine of Reba McEntire's "Little Rock" says she'll have to "slip [her wedding ring] off," feeling no loyalty to the workaholic husband who "sure likes his money" but neglects his wife's emotional and physical needs. Jeanne Pruett in "Back to Back" lampoons the trappings of wealth and proclaims, "I'd trade this mansion / for a run-down shack / and a man who don't believe in sleeping back to back."

Rap's protagonists, on the other hand, are shrewd, materialistic, and rabidly ambitious—although the means to their success are officially proscribed in our society. Not for them a "life that moves at a slower pace" (Alabama, "Down Home"); unlike the languorous hero of country-and-western, "catching these fish like they're going out of style" (Hank Williams, Jr., "Country State of Mind"), rap singers and rap characters alike are imbued with the great American determination to get ahead.

Rap's protagonists—drug dealers, burglars, armed robbers, and "gangstas"— live in a society where success is "a fistful of jewelry" (Eazy E, "No More ?s"), "Motorola phones, Sony color TVs" (Ice-T, "Drama"), where "without a BMW you're through" (NWA, "A Bitch Iz a Bitch"). In NWA's "Dopeman," sometimes cited as an anti-drug song, the "Dopeman" is the archetypal American entrepreneur: clever, organized, ruthless, and not ruled by impulse—"To be a dopeman you must qualify / Don't get high off your own supply."

The proximity of rap to our success ethic arouses hostility because America is torn by a deep ideological contradiction: we proudly proclaim ourselves a moral (even religious) nation and tout our capitalist economic system. But the reality of a successful capitalist system is that it undermines conventional morality. A glance at the history books shows how our supposedly moral nation heaped rewards upon the aptly named "robber barons": the Rockefellers, Vanderbilts, Carnegies, and Morgans. The crack dealer is a contemporary version of the bootlegger—at least one of whom, Joe Kennedy, Sr., founded America's most famous political dynasty. (Indeed, I would not be surprised if history repeated itself and the son—or daughter—of a drug lord becomes this country's first African American president.)

Capitalism is unparalleled in its ability to create goods and distribute services, but it is, like the hero of "Drama," "blind to what's wrong." The only real criterion of a person's worth becomes how much money she or he has—a successful crook is treated better than a poor, law-abiding failure.

In short, the laid-back anti-materialist of country-and-western can be dismissed with a shrug, but the rapper is attacked for that unforgivable sin: holding a mirror up to unpleasant truths. And one of them is that amoral ambition is as American as apple pie and the Saturday Night Special.

Neat People vs. Sloppy People

Suzanne Britt

I've finally figured out the difference between neat people and sloppy people. The distinction is, as always, moral. Neat people are lazier and meaner than sloppy people.

Sloppy people, you see, are not really sloppy. Their sloppiness is merely the unfortunate consequence of their extreme moral rectitude. Sloppy people carry in their mind's eye a heavenly vision, a precise plan, that is so stupendous, so perfect, it can't be achieved in this world or the next.

Sloppy people live in Never-Never Land. Someday is their métier. Someday they are planning to alphabetize all their books and set up home catalogs. Someday they will go through their wardrobes and mark certain items for tentative mending and certain items for passing on to relatives of similar shape and size. Someday sloppy people will make family scrapbooks into which they will put newspaper clippings, postcards, locks of hair, and the dried corsage from their senior prom. Someday they will file everything on the surface of their desks, including the cash receipts from coffee purchases at the snack shop. Someday they will sit down and read all the back issues of *The New Yorker.*

For all these noble reasons and more, sloppy people never get neat. They aim too high and wide. They save everything, planning someday to file, order, and straighten out the world. But while these ambitious plans take clearer and clearer shape in their heads, the books spill from the shelves onto the floor, the clothes pile up in the hamper and closet, the family mementos accumulate in every drawer, the surface of the desk is buried under mounds of paper and the unread magazines threaten to reach the ceiling.

Sloppy people can't bear to part with anything. They give loving attention to every detail. When sloppy people say they're going to tackle the surface of the desk, they really mean it. Not a paper will go unturned; not a rubber band will go unboxed. Four hours or two weeks into the excavation, the desk looks exactly the same, primarily because the sloppy person is meticulously creating new piles of papers with new headings and scrupulously stopping to read all of the old book catalogs before he throws them away. A neat person would just bulldoze the desk.

Neat people are bums and clods at heart. They have cavalier attitudes toward possessions, including family heirlooms. Everything is just another dust-catcher to them. If anything collects dust, it's got to go and that's that. Neat people will toy with the idea of throwing the children out of the house just to cut down on the clutter.

Neat people don't care about process. They like results. What they want to do is get the whole thing over with so they can sit down and watch the rasslin' on TV. Neat people operate on two unvarying principles: never handle any item twice, and throw everything away.

The only thing messy in a neat person's house is the trash can. The minute something comes to a neat person's hand, he will look at it, try to decide if it has immediate use and, finding none, throw it in the trash.

Neat people are especially vicious with mail. They never go through their mail unless they are standing directly over a trash can. If the trash can is beside the mailbox, even better. All ads, catalogs, pleas for charitable contributions, church bulletins and money-saving coupons go straight into the trash can without being opened. All letters from home, postcards from Europe, bills and paychecks are opened, immediately responded to, then dropped in the trash can. Neat people keep their receipts only for tax purposes. That's it. No sentimental salvaging of birthday cards or the last letter a dying relative ever wrote. Into the trash it goes.

Neat people place neatness above everything, even economics. They are incredibly wasteful. Neat people throw away several toys every time they walk through the den. I knew a neat person once who threw away a perfectly good dish drainer because it had mold on it. The drainer was too much trouble to wash. And neat people sell their furniture when they move. They will sell a La-Z-Boy recliner while you are reclining in it.

Neat people are no good to borrow from. Neat people buy everything in expensive little single portions. They get their flour and sugar in two-pound bags. They wouldn't consider clipping a coupon, saving a leftover, reusing plastic nondairy whipped cream containers or rinsing off tin foil and draping it over the unmoldy dish drainer. You can never borrow a neat person's newspaper to see what's playing at the movies. Neat people have the paper all wadded up and in the trash by 7:05 A.M.

Neat people cut a clean swath through the organic as well as the inorganic world. People, animals, and things are all one to them. They are so insensitive. After they've finished with the pantry, the medicine cabinet, and the attic, they will throw out the red geranium (too many leaves), sell the dog (too many fleas), and send the children off to boarding school (too many scuffmarks on the hardwood floors).

DEFINITION

The Company Man

Ellen Goodman

He worked himself to death, finally and precisely, at 3:00 A.M. Sunday morning.

The obituary didn't say that, of course. It said that he died of a coronary thrombosis—I think that was it—but everyone among his friends and acquaintances knew it instantly. He was a perfect Type A, a workaholic, a classic, they said to each other and shook their heads—and thought for five or ten minutes about the way they lived.

This man who worked himself to death finally and precisely at 3:00 A.M. Sunday morning—on his day off—was fifty-one years old and a vice-president. He was, however, one of six vice-presidents, and one of three who might conceivably—if the president died or retired soon enough—have moved to the top spot. Phil knew that.

He worked six days a week, five of them until eight or nine at night, during a time when his own company had begun the four-day week for everyone but the executives. He worked like the Important People. He had no outside "extracurricular interests," unless, of course, you think about a monthly golf game that way. To Phil, it was work. He always ate egg salad sandwiches at his desk. He was, of course, overweight, by 20 or 25 pounds. He thought it was okay, though, because he didn't smoke.

On Saturdays, Phil wore a sports jacket to the office instead of a suit, because it was the weekend.

He had a lot of people working for him, maybe sixty, and most of them liked him most of the time. Three of them will be seriously considered for his job. The obituary didn't mention that.

But it did list his "survivors" quite accurately. He is survived by his wife, Helen, forty-eight years old, a good woman of no particular marketable skills, who worked in an office before marrying and mothering. She had, according to her daughter, given up trying to compete with his work years ago, when the children were small. A company friend said, "I know how much you will miss him." And she answered, "I already have."

"Missing him all these years," she must have given up part of herself which had cared too much for the man. She would be "well taken care of."

His "dearly beloved" eldest of the "dearly beloved" children is a hard-working executive in a manufacturing firm down South. In the day and a half before the funeral, he went around the neighborhood researching his father, asking the neighbors what he was like. They were embarrassed.

His second child is a girl, who is twenty-four and newly married. She lives near her mother and they are close, but whenever she was alone with her father, in a car driving somewhere, they had nothing to say to each other.

The youngest is twenty, a boy, a high-school graduate who has spent the last couple of years, like a lot of his friends, doing enough odd jobs to stay in grass and food. He was the one who tried to grab at his father, and tried to mean enough to him to keep the man at home. He was his father's favorite. Over the last two years, Phil stayed up nights worrying about the boy.

The boy once said, "My father and I only board here."

At the funeral, the sixty-year-old company president told the forty-eight-year-old widow that the fifty-one-year-old deceased had meant much to the company and would be missed and would be hard to replace. The widow didn't look him in the eye. She was afraid he would read her bitterness and, after all, she would need him to straighten out the finances—the stock options and all that.

Phil was overweight and nervous and worked too hard. If he wasn't at the office, he was worried about it. Phil was a Type A, a heart-attack natural. You could have picked him out in a minute from a lineup.

So when he finally worked himself to death, at precisely 3:00 A.M. Sunday morning, no one was really surprised.

By 5:00 P.M. the afternoon of the funeral, the company president had begun, discreetly of course, with care and taste, to make inquiries about his replacement. One of three men. He asked around: "Who's been working the hardest?"

Who's a Hillbilly?

Rebecca Thomas Kirkendall

I once dated a boy who called me a hillbilly because my family has lived in the Ozarks in southern Missouri for several generations. I took offense, not realizing that as a foreigner to the United States he was unaware of the insult. He had meant it as a term of endearment. Nonetheless, it rankled. I started thinking about the implications of the term to me, my family and my community.

While growing up I was often surprised at the way television belittled "country" people. We weren't offended by the self-effacing humor of *The Andy Griffith Show* and *The Beverly Hillbillies* because, after all, Andy and Jed were the heroes of these shows, and through them we could comfortably laugh at ourselves. But as I learned about tolerance and discrimination in school, I wondered why stereotypes of our lifestyle went unexamined. Actors playing "country" people on TV were usually comic foils or objects of ridicule. Every sitcom seemed to have an episode where country cousins, wearing high-water britches and carrying patched suitcases, visited their city friends. And movies like *Deliverance* portrayed country people as backward and violent.

As a child I laughed at the exaggerated accents and dress, never imagining that viewers believed such nonsense. Li'l Abner and the folks on *Hee Haw* were amusing, but we on the farm knew that our work did not lend itself to bare feet, gingham bras and revealing cutoff jeans.

Although our nation professes a growing commitment to cultural egalitarianism, we consistently oversimplify and misunderstand our rural culture. Since the 1960s, minority groups in America have fought for acknowledgment, appreciation and, above all, respect. But in our increasingly urban society, rural Americans have been unable to escape from the hillbilly stigma, which is frequently accompanied by labels like "white trash," "redneck" and "hayseed." These negative stereotypes are as unmerciful as they are unfounded.

When I graduated from college, I traveled to a nearby city to find work. There I heard wisecracks about the uneducated rural folk who lived a few hours away. I also took some ribbing about the way I pronounced certain words, such as "tin" instead of "ten" and "agin" for "again." And my expressed desire to return to the country someday was usually met with scorn, bewilderment or genuine concern. Co-workers often asked, "But what is there to *do?*" Thoreau may have gone to Walden Pond, they argued, but he had no intention of staying there.

With the revival of country music in the early 1980s, hillbillyness was again marketable. Country is now big business. Traditional country symbols—Minnie Pearl's hat tag and Daisy Mae—have been eclipsed by the commercially successful Nashville Network, Country Music Television, and music theaters in Branson, Mo. Many "country" Americans turned the negative stereotype to their advantage and packaged the hillbilly legacy.

Yet with successful commercialization, the authentic elements of America's rural culture have been juxtaposed with the stylized. Country and Western bars are now chic. While I worked in the city, I watched with amazement as my Yuppie friends hurried from their corporate desks to catch the 6:30 line-dancing class at the edge of town. Donning Ralph Lauren jeans and ankle boots, they drove to the trendiest country bars, sat and danced together and poked fun at the local "hicks," who arrived in pickup trucks wearing Wrangler jeans and roper boots.

Every summer weekend in Missouri the freeways leading out of our cities are clogged with vacationers. Minivans and RVs edge toward a clear river with a campground and canoe rental, a quiet lake resort or craft show in a remote Ozark town. Along these popular vacation routes, the rural hosts of convenience stores, gift shops and corner cafes accept condescension along with personal checks and credit cards. On a canoeing trip not long ago, I recall sitting on the transport bus and listening, heartbroken, as a group of tourists ridiculed our bus driver. They yelled, "Hey, plow-boy, ain't ya got no terbacker fer us?" They pointed at the young man's sweat-stained overalls as he, seemingly unaffected by their insults, single-handedly carried their heavy aluminum canoes to the water's edge. That "plowboy" was one of my high-school classmates. He greeted the tourists with a smile and tolerated their derision because he knew tourism brings dollars and jobs.

America is ambivalent when it comes to claiming its rural heritage. We may fantasize about Thomas Jefferson's agrarian vision, but there is no mistaking that ours is an increasingly urban culture. Despite their disdain for farm life—with its manure-caked boots, long hours, and inherent financial difficulties—urbanites rush to imitate a sanitized version of this lifestyle. And the individuals who sell this rendition understand that the customer wants to experience hillbillyness without the embarrassment of being mistaken for one.

Through it all, we Ozarkians remind ourselves how fortunate we are to live in a region admired for its blue springs, rolling hills and geological wonders. In spite of the stereotypes, most of us are not uneducated. Nor are we stupid. We are not white supremacists, and we rarely marry our cousins. Our reasons for living in the hills are as complex and diverse as our population. We have a unique sense of community, strong family ties, a beautiful environment, and a quiet place for retirement.

We have criminals and radicals, but they are the exception. Our public-education system produces successful farmers, doctors, business professionals, and educators. Country music is our favorite, but we also like rock and roll, jazz, blues, and classical. We read Louis L'Amour, Maya Angelou, and *The Wall Street Journal*. And in exchange for living here, many of us put up with a lower standard of living and the occasional gibe from those who persist in calling us "hillbillies."

ARGUMENT

Let Teenagers Try Adulthood

Leon Botstein

The national outpouring after the Littleton shootings has forced us to confront something we have suspected for a long time: the American high school is obsolete and should be abolished. In the last month, high school students present and past have come forward with stories about cliques and the artificial intensity of a world defined by insiders and outsiders, in which the insiders hold sway because of superficial definitions of good looks and attractiveness, popularity, and sports prowess.

The team sports of high school dominate more than student culture. A community's loyalty to the high school system is often based on the extent to which varsity teams succeed. High school administrators and faculty members are often former coaches, and the coaches themselves are placed in a separate, untouchable category. The result is that the culture of the inside elite is not contested by the adults in the school. Individuality and dissent are discouraged.

But the rules of high school turn out not to be the rules of life. Often the high school outsider becomes the more successful and admired adult. The definitions of masculinity and femininity go through sufficient transformation to make the game of popularity in high school an embarrassment. No other group of adults young or old is confined to an age-segregated environment, much like a gang in which individuals of the same age group define each other's world. In no workplace, not even in colleges or universities, is there such a narrow segmentation by chronology.

Given the poor quality of recruitment and training for high school teachers, it is no wonder that the curriculum and the enterprise of learning hold so little sway over young people. When puberty meets education and learning in modern America, the victory of puberty masquerading as popular culture and the tyranny of peer groups based on ludicrous values meet little resistance.

By the time those who graduate from high school go on to college and realize what really is at stake in becoming an adult, too many opportunities have been lost and too much time has been wasted. Most thoughtful young people suffer the high school environment in silence and in their junior and senior years mark time waiting for college to begin. The Littleton killers, above and beyond the psychological demons that drove them to violence, felt trapped in the artificiality of the high school world and believed it to be real. They engineered their moment of undivided attention and importance in the absence of any confidence that life after high school could have a different meaning.

Adults should face the fact that they don't like adolescents and that they have used high school to isolate the pubescent and hormonally active adolescent away from both the picture-book idealized innocence of childhood and the more accountable world of adulthood. But the primary reason high school doesn't work anymore, if it ever did, is that young people mature substantially earlier in the late 20th century than they did when the high school was invented. For example, the age of first menstruation has dropped at least two years since the beginning of this century, and not surprisingly, the onset of sexual activity has dropped in proportion. An institution intended for children in transition now holds young adults back well beyond the developmental point for which high school was originally designed.

Furthermore, whatever constraints to the presumption of adulthood among young people may have existed decades ago have now fallen away. Information and images, as well as the real and virtual freedom of movement we associate with adulthood, are now accessible to every fifteen- and sixteen-year-old.

Secondary education must be rethought. Elementary school should begin at age four or five and end with the sixth grade. We should entirely abandon the concept of the middle school and junior high school. Beginning with the seventh grade, there should be four years of secondary education that we may call high school. Young people should graduate at sixteen rather than eighteen.

They could then enter the real world, the world of work or national service, in which they would take a place of responsibility alongside older adults in mixed company. They could stay at home and attend junior college, or they could go away to college. For all the faults of college, at least the adults who dominate the world of colleges, the faculty, were selected precisely because they were exceptional and different, not because they were popular. Despite the often cavalier attitude toward teaching in college, at least physicists know their physics, mathematicians know and love their mathematics, and music is taught by musicians, not by graduates of education schools, where the disciplines are subordinated to the study of classroom management.

For those sixteen-year-olds who do not want to do any of the above, we might construct new kinds of institutions, each dedicated to one activity, from science to dance, to which adolescents could devote their energies while working together with professionals in those fields.

At sixteen, young Americans are prepared to be taken seriously and to develop the motivations and interests that will serve them well in adult life. They need to enter a world where they are not in a lunchroom with only their peers, estranged from other age groups and cut off from the game of life as it is really played. There is nothing utopian about this idea; it is immensely practical and efficient, and its implementation is long overdue. We need to face biological and cultural facts and not prolong the life of a flawed institution that is out of date.

In Defense of Elitism

William A. Henry III

While all the major social changes in post-war America reflect egalitarianism of some sort, no social evolution has been more willfully egalitarian than opening the academy. Half a century ago, a high school diploma was a significant credential, and college was a privilege for the few. Now high school graduation is virtually automatic for adolescents outside the ghettos and barrios, and college has become a normal way station in the average person's growing up. No longer a mark of distinction or proof of achievement, a college education is these days a mere rite of passage, a capstone to adolescent party time.

Some 63% of all American high school graduates now go on to some form of further education, according to the Department of Commerce's *Statistical Abstract of the United States,* and the bulk of those continuing students attain at least an associate's degree. Nearly 30% of high school graduates ultimately receive a four-year baccalaureate degree. A quarter or so of the population may seem, to egalitarian eyes, a small and hence elitist slice. But by world standards this is inclusiveness at its most extreme—and its most peculiarly American.

For all the socialism of British or French public policy and for all the paternalism of the Japanese, those nations restrict university training to a much smaller percentage of their young, typically 10% to 15%. Moreover, they and other First World nations tend to carry the elitism over into judgments about precisely which institution one attends. They rank their universities, colleges and technical schools along a prestige hierarchy much more rigidly gradated—and judged by standards much more widely accepted—than Americans ever impose on their jumble of public and private institutions.

In the sharpest divergence from American values, these other countries tend to separate the college-bound from the quotidian masses in early adolescence, with scant hope for a second chance. For them, higher education is logically confined to those who displayed the most aptitude for lower education.

The opening of the academy's doors has imposed great economic costs on the American people while delivering dubious benefits to many of the individuals supposedly being helped. The total bill for higher education is about $150 billion per year, with almost two-thirds of that spent by public institutions run with taxpayer funds. Private colleges and universities also spend the public's money. They get grants for research and the like, and they serve as a conduit for subsidized student loans—many of which are never fully repaid. President Clinton refers to this sort of spending as an investment in human capital. If that is so, it seems reasonable to ask whether the investment pays a worthwhile rate of return. At its present size, the American style of mass higher education probably ought to be judged a mistake—and one based on a giant lie.

Why do people go to college? Mostly to make money. This reality is acknowledged in the mass media, which are forever running stories and charts showing how much a college degree contributes to lifetime income (with the more sophisticated publications very occasionally noting the counterweight costs of tuition paid and income forgone during the years of full-time study.)

But the equation between college and wealth is not so simple. College graduates unquestionably do better on average economically than those who don't go at all. At the extremes, those with five or more years of college earn about triple the income of those with eight or fewer years of total schooling. Taking more typical examples, one finds that those who stop their educations after earning a four-year degree earn about 1 1/2 times as much as those who stop at the end of high school. These outcomes, however, reflect other things besides the impact of the degree itself. College graduates are winners in part because colleges attract people who are already winners—people with enough brains and drive that they would do well in almost any generation and under almost any circumstances, with or without formal credentialing.

The harder and more meaningful question is whether the mediocrities who have also flooded into colleges in the past couple of generations do better than they otherwise would have. And if they do, is it because college actually made them better employees or because it simply gave them the requisite credential to get interviewed and hired? The U.S. Labor Department's Bureau of Labor Statistics reports that about 20% of all college graduates toil in fields not requiring a degree, and this total is projected to exceed 30% by the year 2005. For the individual, college may well be a credential without being a qualification, required without being requisite.

For American society, the big lie underlying higher education is akin to Garrison Keillor's description of the children in Lake Wobegon: they are all above average. In the unexamined American Dream rhetoric promoting mass higher education in the nation of my youth, the implicit vision was that one day everyone, or at least practically everyone, would be a manager or a professional. We would use the most elitist of all means, scholarship, toward the most egalitarian of ends. We would all become chiefs; hardly anyone would be left a mere Indian. On the surface, this New Jerusalem appears to have arrived. Where half a century ago the bulk of jobs were blue collar, now a majority are white or pink collar. They are performed in an office instead of on a factory floor. If they still tend to involve repetition and drudgery, at least they do not require heavy lifting.

But the wages for them are going down virtually as often as up. And as a great many disappointed office workers have discovered, being better educated and better dressed at the workplace does not transform one's place in the pecking order. There are still plenty more Indians than chiefs. Lately, indeed, the chiefs are becoming even fewer. The major focus of the "downsizing" of recent years has been eliminating layers of middle management—much of it drawn from the ranks of those lured to college a generation or two ago by the idea that a degree would transform them from the mediocre to magisterial.

Yet U.S. colleges blithely go on "educating" many more prospective managers and professionals than the country is likely to need. In my own field, there are typically more students majoring in journalism at any given moment than there are journalists employed at all the daily newspapers in the U.S. A few years ago, there were more students enrolled in law school than there were partners in all law firms. As trends shift, there have been periodic oversupplies of M.B.A.-wielding financial analysts, of grade school and high school teachers, of computer programmers, even of engineers. Inevitably many students of limited talent spend huge amounts of time and money pursuing some brass-ring occupation, only to see their dreams denied. As a society America considers it cruel not to give them every chance at success. It may be more cruel to let them go on fooling themselves.

Just when it should be clear that the U.S. is already probably doing too much to entice people into college, Bill Clinton is suggesting it do even more. In February 1994, for example, the President asserted that America needs a greater fusion between academic and vocational training in high school—not because too many mediocre people misplaced on the college track are failing to acquire marketable vocational skills, but because too many people on the vocational track are being denied courses that will secure them admission to college. Surely what Americans need is not a fusion of the two tracks but a sharper division between them, coupled with a forceful program for diverting intellectual also-rans out of the academic track and into the vocational one. That is where most of them are heading in life anyway. Why should they wait until they are older and must enroll in high-priced proprietary vocational programs of often dubious efficacy—frequently throwing away not only their own funds but federal loans in the process—because they emerged from high school heading nowhere and knowing nothing that is useful in the marketplace?

If the massive numbers of college students reflected a national boom in love of learning and a prevalent yen for self-improvement, America's investment in the classroom might make sense. There are introspective qualities that can enrich any society in ways beyond the material. But one need look no further than the curricular wars to understand that most students are not looking to broaden their spiritual or intellectual horizons. Consider three basic trends, all of them implicit rejections of intellectual adventure. First, students are demanding courses that reflect and affirm their own identities in the most literal way. Rather than read a Greek dramatist of 2,000 years ago and thrill to the discovery that some ideas and emotions are universal, many insist on reading writers of their own gender or ethnicity or sexual preference, ideally writers of the present or the recent past.

The second trend, implicit in the first, is that the curriculum has shifted from being what professors desire to teach to being what students desire to learn. Nowadays colleges have to hustle for students by truckling trendily. If the students want media-studies programs so they can all fantasize about becoming TV news anchors, then media studies will abound. There are in any given year some 300,000 students enrolled in undergraduate communications courses.

Of even greater significance than the solipsism of students and the pusillanimity of teachers is the third trend, the sheer decline in the amount and quality of work expected in class. In an egalitarian environment the influx of mediocrities relentlessly lowers the general standards at colleges to levels the weak ones can meet. When my mother went to Trinity College in Washington in the early 1940s, at a time when it was regarded more as a finishing school for nice Catholic girls than a temple of discipline, an English major there was expected to be versed in Latin, Anglo-Saxon and medieval French. A course in Shakespeare meant reading the plays, all 37 of them. In today's indulgent climate, a professor friend at a fancy college told me as I was writing this chapter, taking a half semester of Shakespeare compels students to read exactly four plays. "Anything more than one a week," he explained, "is considered too heavy a load."

This probably should not be thought surprising in an era when most colleges, even prestigious ones, run some sort of remedial program for freshmen to learn the reading and writing skills they ought to have developed in junior high school—not to mention an era when many students vociferously object to being marked down for spelling or grammar. Indeed, all the media attention paid to curriculum battles at Stanford, Dartmouth and the like obscures the even bleaker reality of American higher education. As Russell Jacoby points out in his book *Dogmatic Wisdom,* most students are enrolled at vastly less demanding institutions, where any substantial reading list would be an improvement.

My modest proposal is this: Let us reduce, over perhaps a five-year span, the number of high school graduates who go on to college from nearly 60% to a still generous 33%. This will mean closing a lot of institutions. Most of them, in my view, should be community colleges, current or former state teachers' colleges and the like. These schools serve the academically marginal and would be better replaced by vocational training in high school and on-the-job training at work. Two standards should apply in judging which schools to shut down. First, what is the general academic level attained by the student body? That might be assessed in a rough-and-ready way by requiring any institution wishing to survive to give a standardized test—say, the Graduate Record Examination—to all its seniors. Those schools whose students perform below the state norm would face cutbacks or closing. Second, what community is being served? A school that serves a high percentage of disadvantaged students (this ought to be measured by family finances rather than just race or ethnicity) can make a better case for receiving tax dollars than one that subsidizes the children of the prosperous, who have private alternatives. Even ardent egalitarians should recognize the injustice of taxing people who wash dishes or mop floors for a living to pay for the below-cost public higher education of the children of lawyers so that they can go on to become lawyers too.

Some readers may find it paradoxical that a book arguing for greater literacy and intellectual discipline should lead to a call for less rather than more education. Even if college students do not learn all they should, the readers' counterargument would go, surely they learn something, and that is better than learning nothing. Maybe it is. But at what price? One hundred fifty billion dollars is awfully high for deferring the day when the idle or ungifted take individual responsibility and face up to their fate. Ultimately it is the yearning to believe that anyone can be brought up to college level that has brought colleges down to everyone's level.

APPENDIX A

Editing for Grammar, Punctuation, and Mechanics

Common Sentence Errors   **505**

Effective Punctuation   **519**

Effective Mechanics   **532**

Applications   **508, 510, 512, 516, 518, 522, 526, 530, 532, 535**

The rear endsheets display editing and revision symbols and their page references. When your instructor marks a symbol on your paper, turn to the appropriate section for explanations and examples.

COMMON SENTENCE ERRORS

The following common sentence errors are easy to repair.

Sentence Fragment

A sentence expresses a logically complete idea. Any complete idea must contain a subject and a verb and must not depend on another complete idea to make sense. Your sentence might contain several complete ideas, but it must contain at least one!

	[INCOMPLETE IDEA]	[COMPLETE IDEA]	[COMPLETE IDEA]

Although Mary was injured, she grabbed the line, and she saved the boat.

Omitting some essential element (the subject, the verb, or another complete idea), leaves only a piece of a sentence—a *fragment*.

> Grabbed the line. [*a fragment because it lacks a subject*]
>
> Although Mary was injured. [*a fragment because—although it contains a subject and a verb—it needs to be joined with a complete idea to make sense*]
>
> Sam an electronics technician.

This last statement leaves the reader asking, "What about Sam the electronics technician?" The verb—the word that makes things happen—is missing. Adding a verb changes this fragment to a complete sentence.

> **Simple verb**   Sam **is** an electronics technician.
>
> **Verb plus adverb**   Sam, an electronics technician, **works hard.**
>
> **Dependent clause, verb, and subjective complement**   **Although he is well paid,** Sam, an electronics technician, **is not happy.**

Do not, however, mistake the following statement—which seems to contain a verb—for a complete sentence:

Sam being an electronics technician.

Such "-ing" forms do not function as verbs unless accompanied by such other verbs as **is, was,** and **will be.**

> **Sam,** being an electronics technician, **was responsible for checking the circuitry.**

Likewise, the "to + verb" form (infinitive) is not a verb.

> **Fragment**   To become an electronics technician.
>
> **Complete**   To become an electronics technician, **Sam had to complete a two-year apprenticeship.**

Sometimes we inadvertently create fragments by adding subordinating conjunctions (**because, since, it, although, while, unless, until, when, where,** and others) to an already complete sentence.

| **Although** Sam is an electronics technician.

Such words subordinate the words that follow them; that is, they make the statement dependent on an additional idea, which must itself have a subject and a verb and be a complete sentence. (See also "Subordination"—pages 509–10.) We can complete the subordinate statement by adding an independent clause.

> Although Sam is an electronics technician, **he hopes to become an electrical engineer.**

Note

Because the incomplete idea (dependent clause) depends on the complete idea (independent clause) for its meaning, you need only a pause *(symbolized by a comma), not a* break *(symbolized by a semicolon).*

Here are some fragments from students' writing. Each is repaired in two ways. Can you think of other ways of making these statements complete?

Fragment	She spent her first week on the job as a researcher. **Selecting and compiling technical information from digests and journals.**
Revised	She spent her first week on the job as a researcher, selecting and compiling technical information from digests and journals.
	In her first week on the job as a researcher, she selected and compiled technical information from digests and journals.
Fragment	**Because the operator was careless.** The new computer was damaged.
Revised	Because the operator was careless, the new computer was damaged.
	The operator was careless; as a result, the new computer was damaged.
Fragment	**When each spool is in place.** Advance your film.
Revised	When each spool is in place, advance your film. Be sure that each spool is in place before advancing your film.

Acceptable Fragment

A fragmented sentence is acceptable in commands or exclamations because the subject ("you") is understood.

Acceptable   Slow down.
fragments   Give me a hand.
                 Look out!

Also, questions and answers sometimes are expressed as incomplete sentences.

Acceptable   How? By investing wisely.
fragments   When? At three o'clock.
                 Who? Bill.

In general, however, avoid fragments unless you have good reason to use one for special tone or emphasis.

Application **A-1**

Correct these sentence fragments by rewriting each in two ways.

1. Fred is a terrible math student. But an excellent writer.
2. As they entered the haunted house. The floors began to groan.
3. Hoping for a A in biology. Sally studied every night.
4. Although many students flunk out of this college. Its graduates find excellent jobs.
5. Three teenagers out of every ten have some sort of addiction. Whether it is to alcohol or drugs.

Faulty Coordination

Give equal emphasis to ideas of equal importance by joining them, within simple or compound sentences, with coordinating conjunctions: **and, but, or, nor, for, so,** and **yet.**

Correct   This course is difficult, **but** it is worthwhile.
               My horse is old **and** gray.
               We must decide to support **or** reject the dean's plan.

But too much coordination can confound your meaning. Below, notice how the meaning becomes clear when the less important ideas (**nearly floating, arms and legs still moving, my mind no longer having**) are shown as dependent on, rather than equal to, the most important idea (**jogging almost by reflex**).

Excessive coordination	The climax in jogging comes after a few miles **and** I can no longer feel stride after stride **and** it seems as if I am floating **and** jogging becomes almost a reflex **and** my arms and legs continue to move **and** my mind no longer has to control their actions.
Revised	The climax in jogging comes after a few miles, when I can no longer feel stride after stride. By then I am jogging almost by reflex, nearly floating, my arms and legs still moving, my mind no longer having to control their actions.

Avoid coordinating two or more ideas that cannot be sensibly connected:

Faulty	I was late for work **and** wrecked my car.
Revised	Late for work, I backed out of the driveway too quickly, hit a truck, and wrecked my car.

sub Faulty Subordination

Proper subordination shows that a less important idea is dependent on a more important idea. A dependent (or subordinate) clause in a complex sentence is signaled by a subordinating conjunction: **because, so that, if, unless, after, until, since, while, as,** and **although.** Consider these complete ideas:

Joe studies hard. He has severe math anxiety.

Because these ideas are expressed as simple sentences, they appear coordinate (equal in importance). But if you wanted to indicate your opinion of Joe's chances of succeeding, you would need a third sentence: **His handicap probably will prevent him from succeeding** or **His willpower will help him succeed** or some such. To communicate the intended meaning concisely, combine the two ideas. Subordinate the one that deserves less emphasis and place the idea you want emphasized in the independent (main) clause.

Despite his severe math anxiety [*subordinate idea*], Joe studies hard [*independent idea*].

Below, the subordination suggests the opposite meaning:

Despite his diligent study [*subordinate idea*], Joe is unlikely to overcome his learning disability [*independent idea*].

Do not coordinate when you should subordinate:

Faulty	Television viewers can relate to a person they idolize, and they feel obliged to buy the product endorsed by their hero.

Of the two ideas in the sentence above, one is the cause, the other the effect. Emphasize this relationship through subordination.

> **Revised** Because television viewers can relate to a person they idolize, they feel obliged to buy the product endorsed by their hero.

When combining several ideas within a sentence, decide which is most important and subordinate the other ideas to it—do not merely coordinate:

> **Faulty** This employee is often late for work, and he writes illogical reports, and he is a poor manager, and he should be fired.

> **Revised** Because this employee is often late for work, writes illogical reports, and has poor management skills, **he should be fired.** (*The last clause is independent.*)

Do not overstuff sentences by excessive subordination:

> **Overstuffed** This job, which I took when I graduated from college, while I waited for a better one to come along, which is boring, where I've gained no useful experience, makes me eager to quit.

> **Revised** Upon college graduation, I took this job while waiting for a better one to come along. Because I find it boring and have gained no useful experience, I am eager to quit.

Application A-2

Use coordination or subordination to clarify relationships in these sentences. (Review pages 508–10.)

1. Martha loves John. She also loves Bruno.
2. You will succeed. Work hard.
3. I worked hard in calculus and flunked the course.
4. Now I have no privacy. My cousin moved into my room.
5. The instructor entered the classroom. Some students were asleep.

Comma Splice

In a comma splice, two complete ideas (independent clauses), which should be *separated* by a period or a semicolon, are incorrectly *joined* by a comma:

| Sarah did a great job, she was promoted.

You can choose among several possibilities for repair:

1. Substitute a period followed by a capital letter:

| Sarah did a great job. She was promoted.

2. Substitute a semicolon to signal a relationship between the two items:

| Sarah did a great job; she was promoted.

3. Use a semicolon with a connecting (conjunctive) adverb (a transitional word):

| Sarah did a great job; **consequently,** she was promoted.

4. Use a subordinating word to make the less important clause incomplete, thereby dependent on the other:

| **Because** Sarah did a great job, she was promoted.

5. Add a connecting word after the comma:

| Sarah did a great job, **and** she was promoted.

The following revisions show that your choice of construction will depend on the exact meaning or tone you wish to convey:

Comma splice	This is a fairly new product, therefore, some people don't trust it.
Revised	This is a fairly new product. Some people don't trust it.
	This is a fairly new product; therefore, some people don't trust it.
	Because this is a fairly new product, some people don't trust it.
Comma splice	Ms. Gomez was a strict supervisor, she was well liked by her employees.
Revised	Ms. Gomez was a strict supervisor. She was well liked by her employees.
	Ms. Gomez was a strict supervisor; **however,** she was well liked by her employees.
	Although Ms. Gomez was a strict supervisor, she was well liked by her employees.
	Ms. Gomez was a strict supervisor, **but** she was well liked by her employees.

Application **A-3**

Correct these comma splices by rewriting each in two ways.

1. Efforts are being made to halt water pollution, however, there is no simple solution to the problem.
2. Bill slept through his final, he had forgotten to set his alarm.
3. Ellen must be a genius, she never studies yet always gets A's.
4. We arrived at the picnic late, there were no hamburgers left.
5. My part-time job is excellent, it pays well, provides good experience, and offers a real challenge.

Run-On Sentence

The run-on sentence, a cousin to the comma splice, crams too many ideas without needed breaks or pauses.

Run-on   The hourglass is more accurate than the waterclock for the water in a waterclock must always be at the same temperature in order to flow with the same speed since water evaporates it must be replenished at regular intervals thus not being as effective in measuring time as the hourglass.

Revised   The hourglass is more accurate than the waterclock because water in a waterclock must always be at the same temperature to flow at the same speed. Also, water evaporates and must be replenished at regular intervals. These temperature and volume problems make the waterclock less effective than the hourglass in measuring time.

Application **A-4**

Revise these run-on sentences.

1. The gale blew all day by evening the sloop was taking on water.
2. Jennifer felt hopeless about passing English however the writing center helped her complete the course.
3. The professor glared at John he had been dozing in the back row.
4. Our drama club produces three plays a year I love the opening nights.
5. Pets should not be allowed on our campus they are messy and sometimes dangerous.

Faulty Agreement—Subject and Verb

The subject should agree in number with the verb. Faulty agreement seldom occurs in short sentences, where subject and verb are not far apart: "Jack eat too much" instead of "Jack eats too much." But when the subject is separated from its verb by other words, we sometimes lose track of the subject-verb relationship.

> **Faulty** The lion's **share** of diesels **are** sold in Europe.

Although **diesels** is closest to the verb, the subject is **share,** a singular subject that needs a singular verb.

> **Revised** The lion's **share** of diesels **is** sold in Europe.

Agreement errors are easy to correct once subject and verb are identified.

> **Faulty** There **is** an estimated 29,000 **women** living in our city.
>
> **Revised** There **are** an estimated 29,000 **women** living in our city.
>
> **Faulty** A **system** of lines **extend** horizontally to form a grid.
>
> **Revised** A **system** of lines **extends** horizontally to form a grid.

A second problem with subject-verb agreement occurs with indefinite subject pronouns such as **each, everyone, anybody,** and **somebody.** They usually take a singular verb.

> **Faulty** **Each** of the crew members **were** injured during the storm.
>
> **Revised** **Each** of the crew members **was** injured during the storm.
>
> **Faulty** **Everyone** in the group **have** practiced long hours.
>
> **Revised** **Everyone** in the group **has** practiced long hours.

Collective nouns such as **herd, family, union, group, army, team, committee,** and **board** can call for a singular or plural verb, depending on your intended meaning. When denoting the group as a whole, use a singular verb.

> **Correct** The **committee meets** weekly to discuss new business.
>
> The editorial **board** of this magazine **has** high standards.

To denote individual members of the group, use a plural verb.

> **Correct** The **committee disagree** on whether to hire Jim.
>
> The editorial **board are** all published authors.

When two subjects are joined by **either . . . or** or **neither . . . nor,** the verb is singular if both subjects are singular and plural if both subjects are plural. If one subject is plural and one is singular, the verb agrees with the one closer to the verb.

Correct   Neither **John** nor **Bill works** regularly.

Either **apples** or **oranges are** good vitamin sources.

Either Felix or his **friends are** crazy.

Neither the boys nor their **father likes** the home team.

If, on the other hand, two subjects (singular, plural, or mixed) are joined by **both . . . and,** the verb will be plural.

Correct   **Both** Joe and Bill **are** resigning.

A single **and** between subjects makes for a plural subject.

Faulty Agreement—Pronoun and Referent

A pronoun must refer to a specific noun (its referent or antecedent), with which it must agree in gender and number.

Correct   **Jane** lost **her** book.

The **students** complained that **they** had been treated unfairly.

When an indefinite pronoun such as **each, everyone, anybody, someone,** or **none** serves as the pronoun referent, the pronoun is singular.

Correct   **Anyone** can get **his** degree from that college.

Anyone can get **his** or **her** degree from that college.

Each candidate described **her** plans in detail.

Faulty Modification

Modifiers explain, define, or add detail to other words or ideas. Prepositional phrases, for example, usually define or limit adjacent words:

> the foundation **with the cracked wall**
> the journey **to the moon**

So do phrases with "-ing" verb forms:

> the student **painting the portrait**
> **Opening the door,** we entered quietly.

Phrases with "to + verb" limit:

| **To succeed,** one must work hard.

Some clauses also limit:

> the person **who came to dinner**
> the job **that I recently accepted**

If a modifier is too far from the words it modifies, the message can be ambiguous.

Misplaced modifier	At our campsite, **devouring the bacon,** I saw a huge bear.

Was it **I** who was devouring the bacon? Moving the modifier next to **bear** clarifies the sentence:

Revised	At our campsite, I saw a huge bear **devouring the bacon.**

The order of adjectives and adverbs also affects the meaning of sentences:

> **I often** remind myself to balance my checkbook.
> I remind myself to balance my checkbook **often.**

Position modifiers to reflect your meaning:

Misplaced modifier	Jeanette read a report on using nonchemical pesticides **in our conference room.** [*Are the pesticides to be used in the conference room?*]
Revised	In our conference room, Jeanette read a report on using nonchemical pesticides.
Dangling modifier	**Answering the telephone,** the cat ran out the door.

The cat obviously did not answer the telephone. But because the modifier **Answering the telephone** has no word to modify, the noun beginning the main clause (**cat**) seems to name the one who answered the phone. Without any word to connect to, the *modifier dangles.* Inserting a subject repairs this absurd message.

Revised	**As Mary answered the telephone,** the cat ran out the door.

A dangling modifier also can obscure your meaning.

Dangling modifier	**After completing the student financial aid application form,** the Financial Aid Office will forward it to the appropriate state agency.

Who completes the form—the student or the Financial Aid Office?
Here are other dangling modifiers:

Dangling modifier	**By planting different varieties of crops,** the pests were unable to adapt.
Revised	By planting different varieties of crops, **farmers** prevented the pests from adapting.
Dangling modifier	**As an expert in this field,** I'm sure your advice will help.
Revised	**Because of your expertise in this field,** I'm sure your advice will help.

Application **A-5**

Revise these sentences to make subjects and verbs agree in number, pronouns and referents agree in gender and number, or to clarify relations between modifiers and the words they modify.

1. Ten years ago the mineral rights to this land was sold to a mining company.
2. Each of the students in our dorm have a serious complaint about living conditions.
3. Neither the students nor the instructor like this classroom.
4. Neither Fred nor Mary expect to pass this course.
5. Anyone wanting to enhance their career should take a computer course.
6. Wearing high boots, the snake could not hurt me.
7. Having two hours left to travel, the weather kept getting worse.
8. Only use this phone during a red alert.

ca

Faulty Pronoun Case

A pronoun's case (nominative, objective, or possessive) is determined by its role in the sentence: as subject, object, or indicator of possession.

If the pronoun serves as the subject of a sentence (**I, we, you, she, he, it, they, who**), its case is *nominative*.

She completed her graduate program in record time.

Who broke the chair?

When a pronoun follows a version of the verb **to be** (a linking verb), it explains (complements) the subject, so its case is nominative.

The killer was **she.**

The professor who perfected our new distillation process is **he.**

If the pronoun serves as the object of a verb or a preposition (**me, us, you, her, him, it, them, whom**), its case is *objective.*

Object of the verb	The employees gave **her** a parting gift.
Object of the preposition	To **whom** do you wish to complain?

If a pronoun indicates possession (**my, mine, our, ours, your, yours, his, her, hers, its, their, whose**), its case is *possessive.*

The brown briefcase is **mine.**

Her offer was accepted.

Whose opinion do you value most?

Here are some frequent errors in pronoun case:

Faulty	**Whom** is responsible to **who?** [*The subject should be nominative and the object should be objective.*]
Revised	**Who** is responsible to **whom?**
Faulty	The debate was between Marsha and **I.** [*As object of the preposition, the pronoun should be objective.*]
Revised	The debate was between Marsha and **me.**
Faulty	**Us** students are accountable for our decisions. [*The pronoun accompanies the subject, "students," and thus should be nominative.*]
Revised	**We** students are accountable for our decisions.
Faulty	A group of **we** students will fly to California. [*The pronoun accompanies the object of the preposition, "students," and thus should be objective.*]
Revised	A group of **us** students will fly to California.

Deleting the accompanying noun from the two latter examples reveals the correct pronoun case ("We . . . are accountable . . ."; "A group of us . . . will fly . . .").

Application **A-6**

Select the appropriate pronoun case from each of these pairs (in parentheses).

1. By (who, whom) was the job offer made?
2. The argument was among Bill, Terry, and (I, me).
3. A committee of (we, us) concerned citizens is working to make our neigh-borhood safer.
4. (Us, we) students are being hurt by federal cuts in loan programs.
5. The liar is (he, him).

Sentence Shifts

Shifts in point of view damage coherence. If you begin a sentence or para-graph with one subject or person, do not shift to another.

Shift in person	When **one** finishes such a great book, **you** will have a sense of achievement.
Revised	When **you** finish such a great book, **you** will have a sense of achievement.
Shift in number	**One** should sift the flour before **they** make the pie.
Revised	**One** should sift the flour before **one** makes the pie. (*Or better: Sift the flour before making the pie.*)

Do not begin a sentence in the active voice, then shift to the passive voice.

Shift in voice	**He** delivered the plans for the apartment complex, and the building site **was also inspected by him.**
Revised	He **delivered** the plans for the apartment complex and also **inspected** the building site.

Do not shift tenses without good reason.

Shift in tense	She **delivered** the blueprints, **inspected** the foundation, **wrote** her report, and **takes** the afternoon off.
Revised	She **delivered** the blueprints, **inspected** the foundation, **wrote** her report, and **took** the afternoon off.

Do not shift from one verb mood to another (as from imperative to indica-tive mood in a set of instructions).

Shift in mood	**Unscrew** the valve, then steel wool **should be used** to clean the fittings.
Revised	**Unscrew** the valve, then **use** steel wool to clean the fittings.

Application **A-7**

Revise these sentences to eliminate shifts in person, mood, voice, tense, or number.

1. People should keep themselves politically informed; otherwise, you will not be living up to your democratic responsibilities.
2. Barbara made the Dean's List and the Junior Achievement award was also won by her.
3. As soon as he walked into his dorm room, George sees the mess left by his roommate.
4. When one is being stalked by a bear, you should not snack on sardines.
5. First loosen the lug nuts; then you should jack up the car.

EFFECTIVE PUNCTUATION

Punctuation marks are like road signs and traffic signals. They govern reading speed and provide clues for navigation through a network of ideas; they mark intersections, detours, and road repairs; they draw attention to points of interest along the route; and they mark geographic boundaries.

Let's review the four used most often. These marks can be ranked in order of their relative strengths.

1. *Period.* A period signals a complete stop at the end of an independent idea (independent clause). The first word in the idea following the period begins with a capital letter.

| Jack is a fat cat. His friends urge him to diet.

2. *Semicolon.* A semicolon signals a brief stop after an independent idea but does not end the sentence; instead, it announces that the forthcoming independent idea is **closely related** to the preceding idea.

| Jack is a fat cat; he eats too much.

3. *Colon.* A colon usually follows an independent idea and, like the semicolon, signals a brief stop but does not end the sentence. The colon and

semicolon, however, are never interchangeable. A colon symbolizes "explanation to follow." Information after the colon (which need not be an independent idea) explains or clarifies the idea expressed before the colon.

> Jack is a fat cat: He weighs forty pounds. [*The information after the colon answers "How fat?"*]

> *or*

> Jack is a fat cat: forty pounds worth! [*The second clause is not independent.*]

    4. *Comma.* The weakest of these four marks, a comma signals only a pause within or between ideas in the sentence. A comma often indicates that the word, phrase, or clause set off from the independent idea cannot stand alone but must rely on the independent idea for its meaning.

> Jack, a fat cat, is a jolly fellow.
> **Although he diets often,** Jack is a fat cat.

A comma is used between two independent clauses only if accompanied by a coordinating conjunction (**and, but, or, nor, yet**).

>   **Comma splice**   Jack is a party animal, he is loved everywhere.
>   **Correct**   Jack is a party animal, **and** he is loved everywhere.

End Punctuation

The three marks of end punctuation—period, question mark, and exclamation point—work like a red traffic light by signaling a complete stop.

Period.   A period ends a sentence and is the final mark in some abbreviations.

> | Ms. | Assn. | N.Y. |
> |-----|-------|------|
> | M.D. | Inc. | B.A. |

Periods serve as decimal points for numbers.

> $15.95
> 21.4%

Question Mark.   A question mark follows a direct question.

> Where is the essay that was due today?

Do not use a question mark to end an indirect question.

Faulty	Professor Grey asked whether all students had completed the essay?
Revised	Professor Grey asked whether all students had completed the essay.
	or
	Professor Grey asked, "Did all students complete the essay?"

Exclamation Point. Use an exclamation point only when expression of strong feeling is appropriate.

Appropriate	Oh, no!
	Pay up!

Semicolon

Like a blinking red traffic light at an intersection, a semicolon signals a brief but definite stop.

Semicolons Separating Independent Clauses. Semicolons separate independent clauses (logically complete ideas) whose contents are closely related and are not connected by a coordinating conjunction.

> The project was finally completed; we had done a good week's work.

The semicolon can replace the conjunction-comma combination that joins two independent ideas.

> The project was finally completed, and we were elated.
> The project was finally completed; we were elated.

The second version emphasizes the sense of elation.

Semicolons Used with Adverbs as Conjunctions and Other Transitional Expressions. Semicolons must accompany conjunctive adverbs like **besides, otherwise, still, however, furthermore, moreover, consequently, therefore, on the other hand, in contrast,** or **in fact.**

> The job is filled; however, we will keep your résumé on file.
> Your background is impressive; in fact, it is the best among our applicants.

Semicolons Separating Items in a Series.   When items in a series contain internal commas, semicolons provide clear separation between items.

> I am applying for summer jobs in Santa Fe, New Mexico; Albany, New York; Montgomery, Alabama; and Moscow, Idaho.
>
> Members of the survey crew were Juan Jimenez, a geologist; Hector Lightfoot, a surveyor; and Mary Shelley, a graduate student.

Colon

Like a flare in the road, a colon signals you to stop and then proceed, paying attention to the situation ahead. Usually, a colon follows an introductory statement that requires a follow-up explanation.

> We need this equipment immediately: a voltmeter, a portable generator, and three pairs of insulated gloves.
>
> She is an ideal colleague: honest, reliable, and competent.

Except for salutations in formal correspondence (e.g., Dear Ms. Jones:) colons follow independent (logically and grammatically complete) statements.

> **Faulty**   My plans include: finishing college, traveling for two years, and settling down in Sante Fe.

No punctuation should follow "include."
    Colons can introduce quotations.

> The supervisor's message was clear enough: "You're fired."

A colon can replace a semicolon between two related, complete statements when the second one explains or amplifies the first.

> Pam's reason for accepting the lowest-paying job offer was simple: She had always wanted to live in the Northwest.

Application **A-8**

Insert semicolons or colons as needed in these expressions.

1. June had finally arrived it was time to graduate.
2. I have two friends who are like brothers Sam and Daniel.
3. Joe did not get the job however, he was high on the list of finalists.
4. The wine was superb an 1898 Margaux.

5. Our student senators are Joan Blake, a geology major Helen Simms, a nursing major and Henry Drew, an English major.

Comma

The comma is the most frequently used—and abused—punctuation mark. It works like a blinking yellow traffic light, for which you slow down briefly without stopping. Never use a comma to signal a *break* between independent ideas.

Comma as a Pause Between Complete Ideas.   In a compound sentence in which a coordinating conjunction (**and, or, nor, for, but**) connects equal (independent) statements, a comma usually precedes the conjunction.

This is an excellent course, **but** the work is difficult.

Comma as a Pause Between an Incomplete and a Complete Idea.   A comma usually is placed between a complete and an incomplete statement in a complex sentence when the incomplete statement comes first.

Because he is a fat cat, Jack diets often.

When he eats too much, Jack gains weight.

When the order is reversed (complete idea followed by incomplete), the comma usually is omitted.

Jack diets often **because he is a fat cat.**

Jack gains weight **when he eats too much.**

Reading a sentence aloud should tell you whether or not to pause (and use a comma).

Commas Separating Items (Words, Phrases, or Clauses) in a Series.
Use commas after items in a series, including the next to last item.

Helen, Joe, Marsha, and **John** are joining us on the term project.

He works hard **at home, on the job,** and even **during his vacation.**

The new employee complained **that the hours were long, that the pay was low, that the work was boring, and that the supervisor was paranoid.**

Use no commas if **or** or **and** appears between all items in a series.

She is willing to study in San Francisco or Seattle or even in Anchorage.

Comma Setting Off Introductory Phrases.   Infinitive, prepositional, or verbal phrases introducing a sentence usually are set off by commas, as are interjections.

Infinitive phrase	**To be or not to be,** that is the question.
Prepositional phrase	**In Rome,** do as the Romans do.
Participial phrase	**Being fat,** Jack was slow at catching mice.
	Moving quickly, the army surrounded the enemy.
Interjection	**Oh, is** that the verdict?

Commas Setting Off Nonrestrictive Elements.   A *restrictive* phrase or clause modifies or defines the subject in such a way that deleting the modifier would change the meaning of the sentence.

> All students **who have work experience** will receive preference.

Without **who have work experience,** which *restricts* the subject by limiting the category **students,** the meaning would be entirely different. All students will receive preference.

Because this phrase is essential to the sentence's meaning, it is *not* set off by commas.

A *nonrestrictive* phrase or clause could be deleted without changing the sentence's meaning and *is* set off by commas.

> Our new manager, **who has only six weeks' experience,** is highly competent.

Modifier deleted	Our new manager is highly competent.

> This house, **riddled with carpenter ants,** is falling apart.

Modifier deleted	This house is falling apart.

Commas Setting Off Parenthetical Elements.   Items that interrupt the flow of a sentence (such as **of course, as a result, as I recall,** and **however**) are called parenthetical and are enclosed by commas. They may denote emphasis, afterthought, clarification, or transition.

Emphasis	This deluxe model, **of course,** is more expensive.
Afterthought	Your essay, **by the way,** was excellent.
Clarification	The loss of my job was, **in a way,** a blessing.
Transition	Our warranty, **however,** does not cover tire damage.

Direct address is parenthetical.

| Listen, **my children,** and you shall hear . . .

A parenthetical expression at the beginning or the end of a sentence is set off by a comma.

> **Naturally,** we will expect a full guarantee.
> **My friends,** I think we have a problem.
> You've done a good job, **Jim.**
> **Yes,** you may use my name in your advertisement.

Commas Setting Off Quoted Material. Quoted items within a sentence are set off by commas.

| The customer said, "I'll take it," as soon as he laid eyes on our new model.

Commas Setting Off Appositives. An appositive, a word or words explaining a noun and placed immediately after it, is set off by commas when the appositive is nonrestrictive. (See page 524.)

> Martha Jones, **our new president,** is overhauling all personnel policies.
> Alpha waves, **the most prominent of the brain waves,** typically are recorded in a waking subject whose eyes are closed.
> Please make all checks payable to Sam Sawbuck, **school treasurer.**

Commas Used in Common Practice. Commas set off the day of the month from the year, in a date.

| May 10, 1989

Commas set off numbers in three-digit intervals.

> 11,215
> 6,463,657

They also set off street, city, and state in an address.

| Mail the bill to J. B. Smith, 18 Sea Street, Albany, Iowa 01642.

When the address is written vertically, however, the omitted commas are those that would otherwise occur at the end of each address line.

> J. B. Smith
> 18 Sea Street
> Albany, Iowa 01642

Commas set off an address or date in a sentence.

> Room 3C, Margate Complex, is my summer address.
> June 15, 1987, is my graduation date.

They set off degrees and titles from proper nouns.

> Roger P. Cayer, M.D.
> Sandra Mello, Ph.D.

Commas Used Erroneously.   Avoid needless or inappropriate commas. Read a sentence aloud to identify inappropriate pauses.

Faulty   The instructor told me, that I was late. [*separates the indirect from the direct object*]

The most universal symptom of the suicide impulse, is depression. [*separates the subject from its verb*]

This has been a long, difficult, semester. [*second comma separates the final adjective from its noun*]

John, Bill, and Sally, are joining us on the trip home. [*third comma separates the final subject from its verb*]

An employee, who expects rapid promotion, must quickly prove his or her worth. [*separates a modifier that should be restrictive*]

I spoke by phone with John, and Marsha. [*separates two nouns linked by a coordinating conjunction*]

The room was, 18 feet long. [*separates the linking verb from the subjective complement*]

We painted the room, red. [*separates the object from its complement*]

Application **A-9**

Insert commas where needed in these sentences.

1. In modern society highways seem as necessary as food water or air.
2. Everyone though frustrated by pollution can play a part in improving the environment.
3. Professor Jones who has written three books is considered an authority in her field.
4. Amanda Ford of course is the best candidate for governor.

5. Terrified by the noise Sally ran never looking back.

6. One book however will not solve all your writing problems.

Application **A-10**

Eliminate needless or inappropriate commas from these sentences.

1. Students, who smoke marijuana, tend to do poorly in school.

2. As I started the car, I saw him, dash into the woods.

3. This has been a semester of happy, exciting, experiences.

4. Sarah mistakenly made dates on the same evening with Joe, and Bill, even though she had promised herself to be more careful.

5. In fact, a writer's reaction to criticism, is often defensiveness.

 ap/

Apostrophe

Apostrophes indicate the possessive, a contraction, and the plural of numbers, letters, and figures.

Apostrophe Indicating the Possessive.   At the end of a singular word or of a plural word that does not end in **s,** add an apostrophe plus **s** to indicate the possessive. Single-syllable nouns that end in **s** take the apostrophe before an added **s.**

> The **people's** candidate won.
>
> The chainsaw was **Emma's.**
>
> The **women's** locker room burned.
>
> I borrowed **Chris's** book.

Do not add **s** to words that already end in **s** *and* have more than one syllable; add an apostrophe only.

> **Aristophanes'** death

Do not use an apostrophe to indicate the possessive form of either singular or plural pronouns.

> The books was hers.
>
> Ours is the best school in the county.
>
> The fault was theirs.

At the end of a plural word that ends in **s,** add an apostrophe only.

> the **cows'** water supply
> the **Jacksons'** wine cellar

At the end of a compound noun, add an apostrophe plus **s.**

> my **father-in-law's** false teeth

At the end of the last word in nouns of joint possession, add an apostrophe plus **s** if both own one item.

> **Joe and Sam's** lakefront cottage

Add an apostrophe plus **s** to both nouns if each owns specific items.

> **Joe's** and **Sam's** passports

Apostrophe Indicating a Contraction.   An apostrophe shows that you have omitted one or more letters in a phrase that is usually a combination of a pronoun and a verb.

> I'm   they're
> he's   you'd
> you're   who's

Don't confuse **they're** with **their** or **there.**

> **Faulty**   there books
>   their now leaving
>   living their
> **Correct**   their books
>   they're now leaving
>   living there

Remember the distinction this way:

> Their friend knows they're there.

It's means "it is." **Its** is the possessive.

> It's watching its reflection in the pond.

Who's means "who is," whereas **whose** indicates the possessive.

> Who's interrupting whose work?

Other contractions are formed from the verb and the negative.

isn't	can't
don't	haven't
won't	wasn't

Apostrophe Indicating the Plural of Numbers, Letters, and Figures.

The **6's** on this new printer look like smudged **G's, 9's** are illegible, and the **%'s** are unclear.

Quotation Marks

Quotation marks set off the exact words borrowed from another speaker or writer. The period or comma at the end is placed within the quotation marks.

Periods and commas belong within quotation marks

"Hurry up," Jack whispered.

Jack told Felicia, "I'm depressed."

The colon or semicolon always is placed outside quotation marks.

Colons and semicolons belong outside quotation marks

Our student handbook clearly defines "core requirements"; however, it does not list all the courses that fulfill the requirement.

When a question mark or exclamation point is part of a quotation, it belongs within the quotation marks, replacing the comma or period.

Some punctuation belongs within quotation marks

"Help!" he screamed.

Marsha asked John, "Can't we agree about anything?"

But if the question mark or exclamation point pertains to the attitude of the person quoting instead of the person being quoted, it is placed outside the quotation mark.

Some punctuation belongs outside quotation marks

Why did Boris wink and whisper, "It's a big secret"?

Use quotation marks around titles of articles, paintings, book chapters, and poems.

Certain titles belong within quotation marks   The enclosed article, "The Job Market for College Graduates," should provide some helpful insights.

But titles of books, journals, or newspapers should be italicized.

Finally, use quotation marks (with restraint) to indicate your ironic use of a word.

Quotation marks to indicate irony   She is some "friend"!

Application A-11

Insert apostrophes and quotation marks as needed in these sentences.

1. Our countrys future, as well as the worlds, depends on everyone working for a cleaner environment.
2. Once you understand the problem, Professor Jones explained, you find its worse than you possibly could have expected.
3. Can we help? asked the captain.
4. Its a shame that my dog had its leg injured in the accident.
5. All the players bats were eaten by the cranky beaver.

Ellipses

Three dots within brackets in a row [. . .] indicate you have omitted material from a quotation. If the omitted words come at the end of the original sentence, a fourth dot, after the brackets, indicates the period. (Also see pages 370, 457.)

> "Three dots [. . .] indicate [. . .] omitted [. . .] material [. . .]. A fourth dot indicates the period."

Italics

In longhand writing, indicate italics by underlining. On a word processor, use italic print for titles of books, periodicals, films, newspapers, and plays; for the names of ships; for foreign words or scientific names; sparingly, for emphasizing a word; and for indicating the special use of a word.

The *Oxford English Dictionary* is a handy reference tool.

The *Lusitania* sank rapidly.

She reads the *Boston Globe* often.

My only advice is *caveat emptor.*

Bacillus anthracis is a highly virulent organism.

Do not inhale these fumes under any circumstances!

Our contract defines a *work-study student* as one who works a minimum of twenty hours weekly.

()/ Parentheses

Use commas normally to set off parenthetical elements, dashes to give some emphasis to the material that is set off, and parentheses to enclose material that defines or explains the statement that precedes it.

An anaerobic (**airless**) environment must be maintained for the cultivation of this organism.

The cost of running our college has increased by 15 percent in one year (**see Appendix A for full cost breakdown**).

This new calculator (**made by Ilco Corporation**) is perfect for science students.

Material between parentheses, like all other parenthetical material discussed earlier, can be deleted without harming the logical and grammatical structure of the sentence.

[]/ Brackets

Brackets in a quotation set off material that was not in the original quotation but is needed for clarification, such as an antecedent (or referent) for a pronoun. (Also see pages 371, 457.)

"She [**Amy**] was the outstanding candidate for the scholarship."

Brackets can enclose information taken from some other location within the context of the quotation.

"It was in early spring [**April 2, to be exact**] that the tornado hit."

Use **sic** ("thus," or "so") when quoting an error in a quotation.

The assistant's comment was clear: "He don't [**sic**] want any."

Dashes

Dashes can be effective—if not overused. Parentheses deemphasize the enclosed material; dashes emphasize it.

> Have a good vacation—but watch out for sandfleas.
>
> Mary—a true friend—spent hours helping me rehearse.

Application **A-12**

Insert parentheses or dashes as appropriate in these sentences.

1. Writing is a deliberate process of deliberate decisions about a writer's purpose, audience, and message.
2. Have fun but be careful.
3. She worked hard summers at three jobs actually to earn money for agricultural school.
4. To achieve peace and contentment that is the meaning of success.
5. Fido a loyal pet saved my life during the fire.

EFFECTIVE MECHANICS

Correctness in abbreviation, hyphenation, capitalization, use of numbers, and spelling demonstrates your attention to detail.

Abbreviations

Avoid abbreviations in formal writing or in situations that might confuse your reader. When in doubt, write the word out.

Abbreviate some words and titles when they precede or immediately follow a proper name, but not military, religious, or political titles.

> **Correct**   Mr. Jones
>
> Dr. Jekyll
>
> Raymond Dumont Jr.
>
> Reverend Ormsby
>
> President Clinton

Abbreviate time designations only when they are used with actual times.

> **Correct**   400 B.C.
>
> 5:15 a.m.

| **Faulty** | Plato lived sometime in the B.C. period. |
| | She arrived in the a.m. |

Most dictionaries provide an alphabetical list of other abbreviations. For abbreviations in documentation of research sources, see pages 394–415.

Hyphen

Hyphens divide words at the right-hand margin and join two or more words used as a single adjective if they precede the noun but not if they follow it:

> com-puter
> the rough-hewn wood
> the all-too-human error
> The wood was rough hewn.
> The error was all too human.

Some other commonly hyphenated words:

- Most words that begin with the prefix self-. (Check your dictionary.)

> self-reliance
> self-discipline

- Combinations that might be ambiguous.

> re-creation [*a new creation*]
> recreation [*leisure activity*]

- Words that begin with **ex,** only if **ex** means "past."

> ex-faculty member
> excommunicate

- All fractions, along with ratios that are used as adjectives and that precede the noun (but not those that follow it), and compound numbers from twenty-one through ninety-nine.

> a **two-thirds** majority
> In a **four-to-one** vote, the student senate defeated the proposal.
> The proposal was voted down **four to one.**
> **Thirty-eight** windows were broken.

Capitalization

Capitalize the first words of all sentences, as well as titles of people, books, and chapters; languages; days of the week; the months; holidays; names of organizations or groups; races and nationalities; historical events; important documents; and names of structures or vehicles. In titles of books, films, and the like, capitalize the first word and all those following except articles or prepositions.

Items that are capitalized		
Joe Schmoe	Russian
A Tale of Two Cities	Labor Day
Protestant	Dupont Chemical Company
Wednesday	Senator Barbara Boxer
the *Queen Mary*	France
the Statue of Liberty	The War of 1812

Do not capitalize the seasons (**spring, winter**) or general groups (the **younger generation, the leisure class**).

Capitalize adjectives that are derived from proper nouns.

| Chaucerian English

Capitalize titles preceding a proper noun but not those following.

State Senator Marsha Smith
Marsha Smith, state senator

Capitalize words such as **street, road, corporation,** and **college** only when they accompany a proper noun.

Bob Jones University
High Street
The Rand Corporation

Capitalize **north, south, east,** and **west** when they denote specific locations, not when they are simply directions.

the South
the Northwest
Turn east at the next set of lights.

Use of Numbers

Numbers expressed in one or two words can be written out or written as numerals. Use numerals to express larger numbers, decimals, fractions, precise technical figures, or any other exact measurements.

543	2,800,357
$3\frac{1}{4}$	15 pounds of pressure
50 kilowatts	4,000 rpm

Use numerals for dates, census figures, addresses, page numbers, exact units of measurement, percentages, times with a.m. or p.m. designations, and monetary and mileage figures.

page 14	1:15 p.m.
18.4 pounds	9 feet
12 gallons	$15

Do not begin a sentence with a numeral. If your figure needs more than two words, revise your word order.

> Six hundred students applied for the 102 available jobs.
>
> The 102 available jobs brought 780 applicants.

Do not use numerals to express approximate figures, time not designated as a.m. or p.m., or streets named by numbers less than 100.

> about seven hundred fifty
>
> four fifteen
>
> 108 East Forty-second Street

sp Spelling

Take the time to use your dictionary for all writing assignments. When you read, note the spelling of words that give you trouble. Compile a list of troublesome words.

Application **A-13**

In these sentences, make any needed mechanical corrections in abbreviations, hyphens, numbers, or capitalization.

1. Dr. Jones, our english prof., drives a red maserati.
2. Eighty five students in the survey rated self-discipline as essential for success in college.
3. Since nineteen eighty seven, my goal has been to live in the northwest.
4. Senator tarbell has collected forty five hand made rugs from the middle east.
5. During my third year at Margate university, I wrote twenty three page papers on the Russian revolution.
6. 100 bottles of beer are on the wall.

Format Guidelines for Submitting Your Manuscript

Format Guidelines for Submitting Your Manuscript   **537**

Format Checklist   **538**

Format is the look of a page, the visual arrangement of words and spacing. A well-formatted manuscript invites readers in, guides them through the material, and helps them understand it.

FORMAT GUIDELINES FOR SUBMITTING YOUR MANUSCRIPT

1. *Use the right paper and ink.* Type or print in black ink, on 8½ × 11 inch, low-gloss, white paper. Use rag-bond paper (2 pounds or heavier) with a high fiber content (25 percent minimum).

2. *Use high-quality type or print.* On typewritten copy, keep erasures to a minimum, and redo all smudged pages. On a computer, print your hard copy on a letter-quality printer or a laser printer.

3. *Use standard type sizes and typefaces.* Standard type sizes for manuscripts run from 10 to 12 points—depending on the particular typeface. (Certain typefaces, such as pica, usually call for a 10-point type size whereas others, such as elite, call for a 12-point type size.) Use other sizes only for headings, titles, or special emphasis.

   Word-processing programs offer a variety of typefaces (or fonts). Except for special emphasis, use conservative typefaces; the more ornate ones are harder to read and inappropriate for most manuscripts.

4. *Number pages consistently.* Number your first and subsequent pages with arabic numerals (1, 2, 3), one-half inch from the top of the page and aligned with the right margin or centered in the top or bottom margin. For numbering pages in a research report, see pages 423, 445.

5. *Provide ample margins.* Small margins make a page look crowded and difficult, and allow no room for peer or instructor comments. Provide margins of at least 1½ inches top and bottom, and 1¼ inches right and left. If the manuscript is to be bound in some kind of cover, widen your left margin to 2 inches.

6. *Keep line spacing and indentation consistent.* Double-space within and between paragraphs. Indent the first line of each paragraph five spaces from the left margin. (Indent five spaces on a word processor by striking the Tab key.)

7. *Design your first page.* If your instructor requires a title page, see pages 421, 443. For the first page of a manuscript without a separate title page, follow the format your instructor recommends.

8. *Cite and document each source.* Consult Chapter 21. For designing "Works Cited" pages in a documented essay, see pages 464–68.

9. *Proofread your final manuscript.* On a word-processing program, spellcheckers and grammar checkers can reveal certain errors but are no substitute for your own careful evaluation.

How to Insert Corrections on Final Copy

If you need to make a few handwritten corrections on your final copy, use a caret (^) to denote the insertion:

                    MAKE
| If you need to^a few handwritten. . . .

Any page requiring more than three or four such corrections should be retyped or reprinted.

10. *Bind your manuscript for readers' convenience.* Do not use a cover unless your instructor requests one. Use a staple or large paper clip in the upper left-hand corner.

11. *Make a backup copy.* Print out or photocopy a backup paper, which you should keep—just in case the original you submit gets lost or misplaced.

FORMAT   CHECKLIST ☑

Before submitting any manuscript, evaluate its format by using the following checklist.

- ☐ Do paper and ink meet quality standards?
- ☐ Is the type or print neat, crisp, and easy to read?
- ☐ Are type sizes and typefaces appropriate and easy to read?
- ☐ Are pages numbered consistently?
- ☐ Are all margins adequate?
- ☐ Are line spacing and indentation consistent?

- ☐ Are the first and subsequent pages appropriately designed?
- ☐ Is each source correctly cited and documented?
- ☐ Has the manuscript been proofread carefully?
- ☐ Is the manuscript bound for readers' convenience?
- ☐ Has a backup copy been made?

Useful Web Sites and Electronic Library Resources

Useful Web Sites   **539**

Electronic Library Resources   **542**

USEFUL WEB SITES

The following sites are available to anyone with Internet access.

Search Engines

AltaVista <**http://www.altavista.com**> Offers a comprehensive Web catalog.

Deja News <**http://www.deja.com**> Searches for newsgroup discussions by key word.

Excite <**http://www.excite.com**> Includes Usenet postings.

Google <**http://www.google.com**> One of the most widely used search engines.

Infoseek <**http://www.infoseek.go.com**> Fast and easy to use.

Liszt Directory of Mailing Lists <**http://www.liszt.com**> Searches for listservs by key word.

Liszt Directory of Newsgroups <**http://www.liszt.com/news**> Searches for newsgroups by key word.

Savvy Search <**http://www.savvy search.com**> Can search over one hundred engines at once.

WebCrawler <**http://www.webcrawler.com**> Easy to use and comprehensive.

Subject Directories (or Catalogs)

The Argus Clearinghouse <**http://www.clearinghouse.net**> A useful site for beginning a research project.

The Internet Public Library <**http://www.ipl.org**> The gateway for countless Web sites, including many in this listing.

Library of Congress World Wide Web Home Page <**http://www.lcweb.loc.gov**> Provides access to the entire Library of Congress catalog.

Library of Congress World Wide Web Gateway <**http://www.lcweb.locgov/ z3950/gateway.html#other**> Provides easy access to countless different libraries.

WWW Virtual Library <**http://www.vlib.org**> An index listing hundreds of categories.

Yahoo! <**http://www.yahoo.com**> A popular and valuable tool for searching a subject on the Web.

Almanacs

The Almanac of Politics and Government <**http://www.polisci.com**> Focuses on U.S. and world political structures and history.

Global Statistics <**http://www.stats.demon.nl**> Provides worldwide statistical data.

Information Please Almanac <**http://www.infoplease.com**> A popular general almanac.

Associations and Organizations

Associations on the Net (AON) <**http://www.ipl.org/ref/AON**> Gateway to sites for countless associations and societies.

Idealist <**http://www.idealist.org**> Lists thousands of sites for nonprofit organizations.

International Organizations <**http://www.library.nwu.edu/govpub/idtf/ igo.html**> Lists sites for organizations worldwide.

Business Directories

Big Book <**http://www.bigbook.com**> A listing of U.S. businesses.

Europages <**http://www.europages.com**> A listing of European businesses.

Dictionaries

Dictionary.com <**http://www.dictionary.com**> Considered the top online dictionary in English.

Encyberpedia Dictionary <**http://www.encyberpedia.com/glossary.htm**> Lists all types of dictionaries available on the Internet.

Roget's Thesaurus <**http://www.thesaurus.com**>

WWWebster Dictionary <**http://www.m-w.com/netdict.htm**>

Encyclopedias

Encyberpedia <**http://www.encyberpedia.com/ency.htm**> Lists the various specialized encyclopedias on the Web.

Microsoft Encarta Concise Encyclopedia <**http://www.encarta.msn.com/find/default.asp?section=find**> Available free.

Encyclopedia Britannica <**http://www.britannica.com**> Available free.

Grolier's Encyclopedia <**http://www.grolier.com**> Usually available via your school library's Web page.

Journal Articles

Carl UnCover <**http://www.carl.org**> Indexes millions of articles from thousands of journals. Faxed copies of articles can be ordered for a fee.

Publist.Com <**http://www.publist.com**> A comprehensive index of articles from publications worldwide.

News Organizations

ABCNews.Com <**http://www.abcnews.go.com**>

MSNBC <**http://www.msnbc.com/news/default.asp**>

New York Times <**http://www.nytimes.com**>

National Public Radio <**http://www.npr.org**>

PBS Online NewsHour <**http://www.pbs.org/newshour**>

Time Magazine <**http://pathfinder.com/time**>

Washington Post <**http://www.washingtonpost.com**>

The Wire—News from the Associated Press <**http://www.wire.sp.org**> For breaking news from around the world.

U.S. Government Information

Federal Gateway <**http://www.fedgate.org**> The gateway for information on federal, state, and local government.

The National Security Archive <**http://www.seas.gwu.edu/nsarchive**> Provides access to formerly classified documents now available through the Freedom of Information Act (see page 358).

Government Documents <**http://www.sosu.edu/lib/govdocs**> A guide to federal government information and publications.

Writing and Research Guides

Researchpaper.com <**http://www.researchpaper.com**> Offers ideas for topics, a chat room, and tips and guidelines for research and writing.

Purdue Online Writing Lab <**http://www.owl.english.purdue.edu/introduction.html**> Offers all kinds of writing help.

ELECTRONIC LIBRARY RESOURCES

The following databases are easily searchable through your school library. Access is usually restricted to the school community via password. A sampling of likely databases in your library:

Applied Science and Technology Index

Art Index

Books in Print with Reviews

Contemporary Literary Criticism (InfoTRAC)

Expanded Academic ASAP (InfoTRAC). An excellent index to begin a search.

General Science Index

Humanities Index

MLA International Bibliography

Readers' Guide to Periodical Literature

Social Sciences Index

Ask your reference librarian about specific resources available at your school.

Allison, Jay. "About Men: Back at the Ranch" by Jay Allison from *The New York Times Magazine*, May 27, 1990. Copyright © 1990 by The New York Times Co. Reprinted by permission.

Angell, Roger. "On the Ball" from *Five Seasons* by Roger Angell. Copyright © 1972, 1973, 1974, 1975, 1976, 1977 by Roger Angell. Reprinted by permission of International Creative Management, Inc.

Baumeister, Roy F. "Should Schools Try to Boost Self Esteem?" by Roy F. Baumeister, as appeared in the Summer, 1996 issue of *American Educator*, the quarterly journal of the American Federation of Teachers. Reprinted by permission of American Federation of Teachers and the author.

Botstein, Leon. "Let Teenagers Try Adulthood" from the *New York Times,* May 1999. Copyright © 1999 by the New York Times Co. Reprinted by permission.

Britt, Suzanne. "Neat People vs. Sloppy People." From *Show and Tell* by Suzanne Britt. Copyright © 1982 by Suzanne Britt. Reprinted by permission of the author.

Brookhiser, Richard. "All Junk, All the Time." *National Review* 25 Nov. 1996: 73–74. © 1996 by National Review, Inc., 215 Lexington Avenue, New York, NY 10016. Reprinted by permission.

Brooks, John. *Telephone: The First Hundred Years* by John Brooks. New York: Harper & Row, Publishers, Inc., 1975, 1976.

Cousins, Norman. "How to Make People Smaller Than They Are." *Saturday Review*, December 1978.

Dillard, Annie. "Seeing" from *Pilgrim at Tinker Creek* by Annie Dillard. Copyright © 1974 by Annie Dillard. Reprinted by permission of HarperCollins Publishers, Inc.

Eighner, Lars. "On Dumpster Diving" from *Travels with Lizbeth: Three Years on the Road and on the Streets* by Lars Eighner. Copyright © 1993 by Lars Eighner. Reprinted by permission of St. Martin's Press LLC.

Goleman, Daniel. "Why the Brain Blocks Daytime Dreams" by Daniel Goleman. Copyright © 1976 by Sussex Publishers, Inc. Reprinted with permission from *Psychology Today* Magazine.

Goodman, Ellen. "The Company Man" from *Close to Home*. Copyright © 1979 by The Washington Post Company. Reprinted with the permission of Simon & Schuster.

Hampl, Patricia. "Grandmother's Sunday Dinner" from *A Romantic Education,* Copyright 1981 by Patricia Hampl. Reprinted with the permission of W. W. Norton & Company, Inc.

Hemingway, Ernest. From "Bull Fighting: A Tragedy" by Ernest Hemingway in *By-Line: Ernest Hemingway,* edited by William White. Copyright © 1967 by Mary Hemingway. Copyright © renewed 1995 by By-Line Ernest Hemingway, Inc.

Henry III, William A. "In Defense of Elitism" from *In Defense of Elitism.* Copyright 1994 by William A. Henry III. Reprinted with the permission of Doubleday, a division of Random House, Inc.

Hertzberg, Hendrick and David C. K. McClelland. "Paranoia" by Hendrick Hertzberg and David C. K. McClelland. Copyright © 1974 by *Harper's Magazine*. All rights reserved. Reproduced from the June issue by special permission.

Holmes, Thomas H. and R. H. Rahe. Table, "The Social Readjustment Rating Scale" by Thomas H. Holmes and R. H. Rahe from *Journal of Psychosomatic Research* 11(2), 1967: 213–18. Reprinted with permission from Elsevier Science.

INDEX

Abbreviations, 532–533

Abstract, guidelines for preparing an, 373, 374. 375

Abstract, for a research report (sample), 422, 423

Abstracts, of research sources, 357. *See also* Summaries and abstracts

Abstract versus concrete words, 144, 145

Academic tone, in writing, when to use or avoid, 37, 38, 147

Acceptable fragments, of sentences, 507–508

Action verbs
  for conciseness, 121, 126
  for instructions, 122, 222

Active voice, 121–122
  for conversational tone, 147, 149
  faulty shifts in, 518
  for instructions, 122, 222

Ad hominem attack, in argument. *See* Attacking your opponent

Agreement
  pronoun-antecedent (referent), 118, 514
  subject-verb, 513–514

Almanacs, in research, 355

Ambiguity, avoidance of, 118, 143, 149, 533

Ampersand, 407

Analogy
  faulty, in argument, 319
  versus comparison, 255

Analyzing a writing situation
  case study in, 29–30
  questions for, 22

Anecdote
  as essay introduction, 52
  as evidence, in research, 380

Antecedent, of a pronoun. *See* Pronoun references

APA documentation style, 394, 406–416

Apostrophe, 527–529

Appeals
  to emotion, irrational, 320–321
  to emotion, legitimate, 320–326
  to reason, 310–317
  to shared goals and values, 286–287

Appendix, to a research report, 460, 461, 462, 463

Appositive, 525

Arguing from ignorance, 320

Argument (persuasion)
  aims of, 162
  appeals to reason in, 310–317
  appeals to shared goals and values in, 286–287
  audience resistance to, 282–283
  case studies in, 294–296, 299–301
  connecting with an audience in, 282
  convincing reasons in, 284–285
  debatable point in, 283–284
  deduction in, 310, 311, 312, 314–317
  definition of, 282
  emotional appeals in, 320–326
  empathy in, 322–323
  ethical considerations in, 289, 290
  expert opinion in, 286
  humor in, 326
  illogical reasoning, avoidance of, 317–321, 382–385
  induction in, 310, 311, 312–314
  line of thought in, 287
  objective evidence in, 285–286
  reader questions about, 282
  refutation in, 287
  satire in, 325–326
  specific features of, 283
  standard shape for, 287–288
  support for, 284–287
  thesis (main point) in, 283–284
  tone in, 288–289, 323–324

Argument essay (samples), 292–293, 294–296, 297–298, 299–301, 302–303, 304–305, 325–326, 500–504

Argument (persuasion) guidelines, 288, 289

Argument outline (shape), 287–288

Arguments for various goals, 290–292

Assertions, in argument. *See* Claims; Thesis statement

Assumptions, underlying, in research, 382, 386

Attacking your opponent, in argument, 321

Attacking a strawperson, in argument, 321

Audience (readers)
   for college essays, 3
   defining your, 11, 12, 28–29, 51
   expectations, 3, 28–29, 86, 87, 100, 101
   intolerance for needless details, 28–29
   organizing for your, 33, 34–36
   tone and, 37, 38, 145–150

Audience, consideration of, in argument, 282, 283, 290–292

Audience resistance to argument, 282–283

Automated (computerized) tools for revising, 59, 76, 157

Automated searches for information. *See* Electronic information sources, in research

Bandwagon appeal, in argument, 320

Basis
   for classification, 211, 213
   for comparison, 257

Begging the question, in argument, 319

Bias
   in company literature, 362
   in preparing databases, 351
   in expert testimony, 286, 338, 359
   in information sources, 337, 376, 378
   in Internet newsgroups, 346
   in interpreting research findings and statistics, 381–382, 386
   in interview questions, 360
   in language use, 150, 151, 152, 153, 154
   in personal observation, 362
   in survey questions, 365

Bibliographic databases, in research, 350

Bibliographies, for given subjects, 354

Bibliography entry, for research sources, 369

Block pattern, in comparison and contrast, 257

Body section
   of an argument, 287–288

of an essay, 54–55

of any message, 9

of a paragraph, 97–98

Bookmarks, for Web sites, 348

Books, indexes to, in research, 356

Boolean operators, for electronic literature searches, 351–352

Brackets, use of, 370–371, 457, 531

Brainstorming, 32, 33, 34, 35

Browsers, for World Wide Web exploration, 348

Capitalization, rules for, 534

Card catalog, library, electronic entries, 355–356

Caret, to insert a correction, 537

Case, of a pronoun, 516–517

Causal reasoning, faulty, 318

Causation versus correlation, in research findings, 384–385, 387

Cause-and-effect (causal) analysis
   case study in, 247–250
   effect-to-cause reasoning in, 238, 239
   for explaining something, 236, 237
   faulty causal reasoning in, 239, 318
   guidelines for, 238, 239
   to make a point, 237–238
   probable, possible, and definite causes in, 236, 237, 238
   reader questions about, 234
   used beyond the classroom, 236

Cause-and-effect essay (samples), 241–242, 244–245, 248–250, 487–490

Certainty, assessing levels of, in research, 380–382, 386

Chronological order, 104, 107–108. *See also* Narration

Circular definition, avoidance of, 270

Citation indexes, in research, 357

Citing information sources. *See* Documentation

Claims, in argument, 268, 283, 284, 287, 288

Clarity, achievement of
   through definition, 265
   through examples, 285–286
   through sentence style, 118–122
   through specific and concrete language, 144, 145

Classification
   case study in, 218–219
   versus division, 209–210
   guidelines for, 213
   reader question about, 209

of a term, in definition, 269, 270
used to explain, 211, 212
used to make a point, 212
Classification essay (samples), 215–217, 218–219, 480–482
Cliché. *See* Triteness
Closing strategies, for essays, 55–56
Clutter words, 128
Coherence, 9, 103–112, 120–121
Collaborative writing. *See also* Peer reviewing and editing
benefits of, 5
decisions in, 5
evaluation sheet for, 41
guidelines for, 40–41
plan sheet for, 42
problems in, 5
via computer, 5, 352
Collective nouns, 513
Colloquialisms, 38, 154
Colon, 519, 522
Combining related ideas, for fluency, 131–132, 510
Comma
correct use of, 520, 523–526
faulty use of, 526
Comma splice, 510–512
Common knowledge, citing, in research, 393
Commonly confused words, 140–142
Compact disks (CD-ROMs)
in research, 350
listing of resources on, 542
Comparison and contrast
as analogy, 255
case study in, 262–264
combined, 253–254
for explaining something, 254
guidelines for, 257
for making a point, 254–255
reader questions about, 252
uses beyond the classroom, 254
Comparison-and-contrast essay (samples), 259–261, 262–264, 490–495
Comparison, using, in writing, 252
Completeness, of a message, criteria for, 89–90
Complex sentence, 523
Composing an essay. *See* Writing Process
Compound noun, 528
Compound sentence, 523
Computer, brainstorming with, 32
Computer guidelines for writers, 58–59

Computer, writing with a
benefits of, 5, 6
for brainstorming, 32
for collaborative projects, 6, 352
decisions in, 5, 6
guidelines for, 58–59
limitations of, 6
Computerized research, 5–6. *See also* Online sources, in research
Conciseness, 124–129
Conclusion
of an argument, 288
of an essay, 55–56
of a message, 9 (*see also* Essay conclusion)
of a syllogism, 314, 315
Concrete versus abstract language, 144–145
Conference proceedings, indexes to, 357
Confidential research sources, documenting, 393
Conjunctive adverbs, 511, 521. *See also* Transitions
Content, of an essay
questions for evaluating the, 17
revising the, 63, 68–75, 81, 83–91
Contraction, 148–149, 528, 529
Contrast, use of, in writing, 252–253
Conversational tone, 37, 147–149
Coordinating conjunctions, 508, 520, 523
Coordination, 132, 508–509
Copyright protection
of email, 353
of Internet sources, 349
Correlation, versus causation, in research findings, 318, 384–385, 387
Credibility of a message, criteria for, 84–85, 393
Crediting your information sources, 90–91, 392, 393, 394
Criteria for evaluating an essay. *See* Revision checklist
Critically analyzing information, guidelines for, 386, 387
Critical reading, 165–166
Critical thinking, in research, 332–339, 340
Cross-cultural considerations, in style, 129, 153, 154
Cultural context for writing, 153–154

Dangling modifiers, 119, 515, 516
Dashes, 532
Databases, online, for research, 350–351
Data mining (dredging), in research, 385, 387
Debatable point in argument, 283–284

Decision making in the writing process, case study in, 10–14
Deductive reasoning, 310, 311, 312, 314–317
Definition
    case study in, 277–279
    connotative, 266, 267
    denotative, 266, 267
    as essay introduction, 54
    expanded, 269, 270, 271
    guidelines for, 270, 271
    level of detail in, 268–270, 271, 272
    by negation, 271, 272
    reader questions about, 266
    as a sentence, 269. 270
    used beyond the classroom, 267–268
    as a synonym (parenthetical), 268, 269
Definition essay (samples), 275–276, 278–279, 495–500
Dependent (subordinate) clause, 507, 511
Description
    defined, 179
    as essay introduction, 53
    guidelines for, 183
    as objective view, 179–180, 181, 183
    as part of exposition, 179
    as part of narration, 179
    as persuasive strategy, 179, 181–182
    reader questions about, 179
    as subjective view, 180–181, 183
    used beyond the writing classroom, 182
Descriptive essay (samples), 180–181, 472
Details, in writing
    appropriate, 183, 188, 222, 472
    excessive, 33, 34, 88, 90, 201
    inadequate, 89, 90
Development strategies, 161, 162
Diction. *See* Word choice
Dictionaries, in research, 355
Diminutive word endings, in sexist usage, 153
Direct (second-person) address
    appropriate use of, 146, 149
    as essay conclusion ("call to action"), 56
    as essay introduction, 53
    incorrect use of, 149
Direct quotation, guidelines for, 370–372
Directories of organizations and institutions, in research, 355
Discovering useful ideas, 31–33
Division
    versus classification, 209–210
    guidelines for, 212

reader questions about, 209
    used to explain, 210
    used to make a point, 210–211
Division and classification essay (samples), 215–217, 217–219, 478–482
Documentation (citation), of research sources. *See also* Library; Research
    bibliography, 394
    of confidential sources, 393
    of electronic sources (*see* APA documentation style; MLA documentation style)
    endnotes, 394
    footnotes, 394
    purpose of, 392
    sources not requiring, 393
    sources requiring, 392
Documentation systems, commonly used
    APA style, for social sciences, 394, 406–416
    MLA style, for the humanities, 394, 395–406
Dominant impression, in description, 183
Drafting on the computer, guidelines for, 58–59
Drafting the essay, case study in, 56–58
Drafting stage, of the writing process, 10, 48–49

Editing, defined, 67
Editing the work of peers, guidelines for, 66, 67
Effect-to-cause analysis. *See* Cause-and-effect analysis
Either/or fallacy, in argument, 319
Electronic card catalog, 355–356
Electronic information sources, citing of, in a research paper
    APA style, 414–415, 434, 436
    MLA style, 401–406, 464–469
Electronic information sources, in research
    benefits of, 344, 345
    limitations of, 344, 345
    types of (*see* Online sources, in research)
Electronic library sources, list of, 542
Electronic magazines (E-zines), 346, 347
Electronic mail (Email)
    benefits of, 347
    citing sources from, 404, 415
    copyright protection of, 353
    guidelines for using, 353
    limitations of, 347
    research via, 347
Ellipsis, 153, 370, 530
Emotional appeals, in argument
    guidelines for making, 322

irrational, 320–321
legitimate, 321–326
Empathy, in argument, 322–323
Emphasis
through arrangement of facts or points, 85
through coordination, 131, 132, 508
through dashes, 532
of key words in a sentence, 120, 121
through paragraph placement, 55
through parallel construction, 109
by placing items first, 106
by placing items last, 106
through rhetorical questions, 324
through short sentences, 132–133
through subordination, 131, 132, 509, 510
Emphatic order, 104, 106
Encyclopedias, in research, 355
Endnotes. *See* Documentation
Enthymemes, 315–316
Essay
defined, 3
as a model for all writing, 3
as an organized message, 9
in relation to support paragraphs, 24, 25, 97
Essay body. *See also* Body section, of a message
defined, 54–55
cxample of, 57
function of, 54–55
supporting paragraphs in, 55, 57
variations in, 162, 163
Essay conclusion. *See also* Conclusion, of a message
closing strategies for, 55–56
defined, 55
example of, 55
function of, 55
Essay introduction. *See also* Introduction, to a message
defined, 50
example of, 50
function of, 50
hints for writing of, 54
opening strategies for, 51–54
thesis placement in, 51
tone in, 54
Essay length, 89
Essay shape, 9
et al., 397
Essay structure. *See* Essay shape
Ethical considerations
in shaping an argument, 289–290

in interpreting evidence, 339
in summarizing information, 375, 376
Ethical implications
of a definition, 271
of word choice, 121, 156–157
Ethical obligations
in reporting information, 151
in research, 334, 338
Ethical purpose of documentation, 392
Etymology of a term, in definition, 271
Euphemisms, 138–139, 154
Evaluating research findings, criteria for, 337, 338, 379–380
Evaluating research sources, 334, 336, 337, 376–379
Evidence
in research, evaluating, 379–380, 386
in support of an assertion, 285–286
Exaggeration. *See* Overstatement
Examples. *See also* Illustration
as an essay introduction, 53–54
to support an argument, 285–286
Exclamation point, 521, 529
Expanded definition, 269, 270, 271
Expert opinion
in argument, 286
evaluating of, 338
in research, 337, 338, 359
Expert testimony, limits of, 337, 338, 359
Exposition, 162
Expressive goal, in writing, 160, 161
Extended example, uses of, 197, 200

Fact. *See also* Opinion
in argument, 285, 287
credibility and, 84, 85
in developing a thesis, 28
opinion and, 84, 85
relative value of a, 84, 85
in research, 393
Factual databases, in research, 350
Fallacies, of logic. *See also* Argument
arguing from ignorance, 320
attacking your opponent, 321
attacking a strawperson, 321
bandwagon appeal, 320
either/or fallacy, 319
faulty analogy, 319
faulty causal reasoning, 318
faulty generalization, 312, 313, 315, 316, 317–318

Fallacies, of logic (*continued*)
  faulty statistical reasoning, 382–385
  faulty syllogism, 314, 315, 316
  irrational appeals to emotion, 320–321
  question begging, 319
  red herring, 320
  slippery-slope fallacy, 319
False dilemma. *See* Either/or fallacy
FAQs (frequently asked questions), on Internet news-
    group sites, 346
Faulty statistical reasoning, 382–385
Feminine versus masculine pronouns, use of, 152,
    153
First page, essay, format for, 537
First-person, appropriate use of, 149
Flaming, on the Internet, 353
Fluency, of sentences, 131–133
Focus, of a topic, 22, 27, 100, 101, 343
Font, 537
Footnotes. *See* Documentation
Formal tone, when to use or avoid, 36, 37, 38, 146,
    147, 148
Format
  checklist, for paper submission, 538
  guidelines, for paper submission, 537
Freedom of Information Act, 358, 359, 362
Freewriting, 10, 31
Full-text databases, in research, 350

Generalization
  in deductive reasoning, 314, 315, 316
  hasty, 317
  in inductive reasoning, 312, 313, 314
  overstated, 316, 317
  for the sake of diplomacy, 145
  unsupported (faulty), 312, 313, 315, 316,
    317–318
General-to-specific order, 104, 105
General words, versus specific, 143, 144, 145
Goals of writing, major, 160–161
Government publications, access tools for, 357–358
Group work, planning for, 40–41
Guides to literature, in research, 356

Handbooks, from specialized fields, in research, 355
Handwritten corrections on printed copy, 537
Hard evidence, versus soft, in research, 380
Headings, in a research report, 424, 425, 446, 447

Homepage, on the World Wide Web, 348
Humor, use of, in argument, 326
Hyphen, 533

Idioms, 154
Illogical reasoning, avoidance of, 317–321, 382–385
Illustration
  case study in, 201–206
  to explain, 198–199
  as extended example, 197, 200
  guidelines for, 201
  to make a point, 199–200
  reader questions about, 197
  as a series of examples, 197, 200
  used beyond the writing classroom, 198
Illustration essay (samples), 202–203, 204–206,
    475–478
Imperative mood, for instructions, 222, 518–519
Indefinite pronouns, 513, 514
Indention (indentation)
  of paragraphs, 98, 537
  of works-cited and reference entries, 395, 407
Independent (main) clause, 131, 132, 510, 521
Indexes to periodicals and proceedings, 356–357
Indirect question, 521
Indirect source, quoting of an, 398, 410
Inductive reasoning, 310, 311, 312–314
Infinitive, 506
Infinitive phrase, 120, 524
Inflated diction, 147–148
Informal tone, when to use or avoid, 36, 37, 38, 146,
    147
Information retrieval services, electronic. *See* Online
    sources, in research
Informative interviews, in research, 339, 360–361
Informative value, of any message, criteria for,
    86–89
Informed versus uninformed opinion, 84–85
Inoffensive usage, 38, 122, 129, 145, 152, 154
Inquiries, in research
  via email, 347, 359
  via letter, 359
  via phone call, 359
Inquiry checklist, for research, 389
Inserting corrrections in final copy, 537
Instruction essay (samples), 224–225, 227–228,
    482–484
Instructions. *See* Process analysis
Interjection, 524

Internet, the
    copyright protection of sources on, 349
    guidelines for evaluating sources on, 378–379, 386
    guidelines for researching on, 348, 349
    and plagiarism, 91
    resources on, 345–349, 355, 358. *See also* World
       Wide Web
Internet service providers, 345
Interpreting evidence and research findings, 380–382
Interviews, in research. *See* Informative interviews
In-text citations. *See* Documentation
Introduction. *See also* Essay introduction
    to a message, 9
    to an argument, 287
    to a quoted passage, 371
    to a survey, 364–365
Invention. *See also* Worthwhile content
    using your reading for, 166, 170, 172
    strategies for, 31–33
Ironic use of language, 146, 325, 530
Irrational appeals, in argument, 320–321
Italics, 530–531
"It" sentence openers, avoidance of, 125

Journal
    for recording personal impressions, 31
    for responding to your reading, 169, 175
Journalists' questions, for invention, 31–32

Key word. *See also* Boolean operators; Signal term
    for electronic information searches, 348, 351–352
    or phrase, in a sentence, 120, 121

Legal and ethical implications
    of definition, 271
    of word choice, 156–157
Levels of certainty, in research, 380–382, 386
Levels of reading, 165–166
Library
    abstracts, of written works, 357
    card catalog, 355–356
    government publications, 357–358
    guides to literature, 356
    indexes, 356–357
    microforms, 358
    online sources, 350–351. See also Internet; World
      Wide Web
    reference works, 354–355

Library chatrooms on the Internet, 347
Line spacing
    in a college paper, 537
    in a list of references, 407
    in a works-cited list, 395
Linking verbs, 517
List of references, in a research report, 406, 407, 416,
    434–437
Listservs, on the Internet, 346–347
Literature search, for a research report. *See* Library
Loaded questions, in interviews and surveys, 360,
    365
Loaded words, in argument, 324
Looping structure of the writing process, 14, 15

Mainframe databases, in research, 350–351
Main point. *See* Viewpoint
Major premise, in a syllogism, 314, 315
Manual searches, in research, 345
Manuscript format, guidelines for, 537
Margin of error, in statistics, 384, 387
Margins, 537
Masculine versus feminine pronouns, use of, 152, 153
Mean, versus median and mode, in statistics,
    383–384
Mechanical elements of writing, versus rhetorical
    elements, 62
Mechanics, of writing, 532–535
Messiness in the writing process, the need for, 3, 4
Microforms, in research, 358
Minor premise, in a syllogism, 314, 315
MLA documentation style, for research sources,
    394–406
Moderated *newsgroups*, on the Internet, 345
Modifiers
    compound, hyphenation of, 533
    dangling, 119, 515, 516
    defined, 118, 514
    misplaced, 119, 515
    nonrestrictive, 524, 525
    restrictive, 525
Mood, of verb, 518, 519

Name-calling, in argument, 331
Narration. *See also* Chronological order
    case study in, 193–95
    as development strategy, 162, 179
    guidelines for, 188

Narration (*continued*)
   to make a point, 184–189
   to merely report, 182–183, 184
   as a persuasive strategy, 185
   point of view in, 188
   reader questions about, 179
   used beyond the classroom, 184
Narrative essay (samples), 186–188, 190–192,
    193–195, 473–475
Needless details, avoidance of, 80–81. *See also* Select-
   ing, of writing material
Needless phrases, 125–126
Needlessly technical details, avoidance of, 88–89
Negative constructions, avoidance of, 120, 127–128
Neutral expressions, to avoid sexist usage, 152
Newsgroups, on the Internet, 345, 346
Newspapers, indexes to, 356
Nominalizations, 126–127
Nominative case, 516, 517
Nonrestrictive modifier, 524, 525
Notation, in a formal outline, 418
Notes, for recording research findings, 369, 370–373
Numbers
   correct use of, 534–535
   hyphenation of, 533
   plurals of, 529
   versus words, 382

Objective case, 516, 517
Objective evidence, 285–286
Objectivity, 150, 179–180
Offensive usage
   avoidance of, 38, 122, 129, 145, 152, 154
   examples of, 122, 154
   Online discussion groups. See *Listservs*;
    Newsgroups
Online sources, in research
   card catalog, 355–356
   compact disks, 350
   electronic versions of hard copy sources, 351
   email inquiries, 347
   Internet sources, 345–349
   mainframe databases, 350–351
   World Wide Web, 347–349
Opening strategies, for essays, 51–54
Opinion. *See also* Fact
   in argument, 284, 285
   common sense and, 85
   credibility and, 84, 85

fact and, 84, 85
   informed versus uninformed, 84–85, 311
   and research, 332
Opposing views, acknowledgment of, in argument,
    287, 289, 323
Order of ideas
   in an essay (*see* Shape, of writing)
   in a paragraph, 104–108
Order of importance. See Emphatic order
Organization (shape)
   of an essay, 17, 33, 34–36
   revising the, 81
   of a support paragraph, 97, 98
   of any useful writing, 9
Organizational publications, as research sources,
    359–362
Orienting statement, 53, 105, 183, 185. *See also* Topic
   statement
Outlining. *See also* Essay shape
   an argument, 287–288
   case study in, 33–36
   an essay, 33, 34, 36
   a research report, 417, 418, 419, 444, 445
Overlapping categories, in a classification, 213
Overstatement, 138, 289, 316, 317
Overstuffed (crammed) sentences, 119, 132, 510

Page numbering
   consistency of, 537
   in a research report, 423, 447
Paragraph coherence, 103–112
Paragraph function, 98
Paragraph length, 98–99
Paragraph structure. *See* Support paragraphs,
   shape of
Paragraph types, 97
Paragraph unity, 102–103
Parallelism, 108–109, 120
Paraphrasing
   defined, 372
   example of, 373, 456, 457
   guidelines for, 373
Parentheses, 531
Parenthetical elements, in a sentence, 524–525
Parenthetical reference
   APA style, 406–407
   MLA style, 394–395
Participial phrase, 524
Passive voice, 121, 122, 149, 518

Peer reviewing and editing guidelines, 66, 67
Peer revision, 66, 67
Period, 519, 529
Periodicals, indexes to, 357
Person (first, second, or third), 149, 222, 518. *See also*
    Direct address
Persona, 288–289. *See also* Tone
Personal bias, in research, management of, 381–382
Personal observation, in research, 362
Personal pronouns
    effective use of, 133, 147, 149
    ineffective use of, 33, 149
Persuasion. *See* Argument
Persuasive (argumentative) goals, in writing, 161,
    290–292
Plagiarism, 90, 91, 371, 372
Plain English, 147–148. *See also* Conversational tone
Planning an essay
    decisions in, 10, 12, 21–42
    questions for, 10, 12, 22, 30, 31, 32
Planning guide, for an essay, 38, 39
Planning stage of the writing process, 21–42
Plural, contractions to indicate, 527, 528, 529
Point-by-point pattern, for comparison and contrast,
    257
Point of view (person)
    faulty shifts in, 518
    in instructions, 222
    in narration, 188
Possessive case, 516, 517, 527–528
Possessive noun, 527
Possessive pronoun, 517, 527
Precise language, 139–143
Prefaces, needless, 128–129
Premises, in deductive argument, 310, 311, 312, 314,
    315
Prepositional phrase, 524
Prepositions, overuse of, 126
Primary sources, in research, 344
Privacy issues, with Email, 353
Process analysis. *See also* Chronological order
    case study in, 227–228
    to explain events, 221
    guidelines for giving instructions, 222
    as instructions, 221–222, 223
    to make a point, 223
    reader questions about, 221, 223
    used beyond the classroom, 220–221
Process essay (samples), 224, 225, 227–228, 229–230,
    231–232, 482–486

Profanity, 38
Pronoun, 118
Pronoun case, 516–517
Pronoun references, 118, 514
Pronouns to improve coherence, 110
Proofreading, 62, 76, 537
Proposal essay (samples), 302–303, 498–500
Proposals, 291
Public records, as a research source, 359, 362
Puffery, 90
Punctuation, 519–532
Purpose, for writing, deciding on a, 22–23
Purpose statement, for an informative interview, 360.
    See also Statement of purpose

Qualifiers
    appropriate, 129, 316
    needless, 54, 129
Question begging, in argument, 319
Question mark, 520–521
Questionnaires, in research, 359, 364–365
Questions. *See also* Rhetorical questions
    as essay conclusion, 55
    as essay introduction, 52
Questions for evaluating writing, 17, 64
Quotation
    brackets in a, 370, 371, 531
    ellipsis in a, 370
    as essay conclusion, 56
    as essay introduction, 52
    example of a, 372
    of an indirect source, 398, 410
    punctuation of, 525, 529
    reasons for direct, 370
Quotation marks, 529–530
Quoting long passages, 371
Quoting the work of others, guidelines for, 370–372

Rationalization, as faulty reasoning, 318, 381
Reader(s). *See* Audience
Reading
    critically evaluating the, 170
    different levels of, 165, 166
    highlighting and annotating key passages in, 169,
        175–176
    as an invention strategy, 166
    and then writing, guidelines for, 175–176
    questions for critical, 165

Reading (*continued*)
  questions for responding to, 166
  responding to, a case study in, 167–172, 172–175
  strategies for writers, 166
  summarizing the, 170
Reading and writing, guidelines for, 175–176
Recording research findings, guidelines for, 369
Recursiveness
  in the research process, 339, 340
  in the writing process, 14, 15
Red herrring, in argument, 320
Redundancy, 124
Referential goal, in writing, 160, 161
Reference, of pronouns, 118, 514
References, list of, in APA style, 416, 407, 416, 434–437
Reference works, library, 354–355
Refereed publications, in research, 377
Reliability of information sources, 376–379
Repetition
  needless, 109, 125
  useful,109, 125
Research. *See also* Documentation; Library
  achieving adequate depth in, 336–337
  asking the right questions in, 334
  defined, 332–333
  discovering a topic for, 333, 343, 344
  documenting sources for, 392–416
  electronic information sources in, 344, 345, 348, 350, 351, 352 (*see also* Online sources, in research)
  evaluating findings in, 337, 338, 379–380
  exploring a balance of views in, 334, 335, 336
  hard copy versus electronic sources in, 344–345
  Internet sources in, 345–349
  interpreting findings in, 338, 339, 380–382, 386–387
  library use in (*see* Library)
  note-taking in, 369, 370–373
  primary versus secondary sources in, 344
  Web pages. *See* World Wide Web
Research process
  checklist for the, 389
  defined, 332–339
  flowchart for the, 340
  tree chart for the, 334, 335, 439
Research project (sample), 438–469
Research report
  checklist for the, 420
  defined, 332–333
  drafting the, 418–419
  outline for, 418, 419, 444, 445
  in APA style, 421–437
  in MLA style, 444–469
  revising the, 419
Research sources, electronic versus hard copy, 344–345
Research sources, evaluation of
  for balance, 334, 335, 336
  for currency, 376–377
  for depth, 336–337
  for dependability, 377
  guidelines for, 378–379, 386
  for objectivity, 336, 337, 338
  for reputation, 377
  for reliability, 338
  for sponsorship, 377, 378
Research topic, guidelines for choosing a, 343–344
Responding to your reading, 166, 175–176
Restrictive modifier, 524
Reviewing, defined, 67
Reviewing the work of peers, guidelines for, 66, 67
Revising
  automated aids for, 59, 76, 157
  case study in, 64–66
  critical evaluation in, 64
  decisions in, 62–76
  defined, 62
  example of, 68–75
  from hard copy, 58–59, 76
  for paragraph structure, 81, 97–112
  with peers, 67
  for sentence clarity, 81, 118–122
  for sentence conciseness, 81, 124–129
  for sentence fluency, 81, 131–133
  top-down decisions in, 80–81
  for word choice, 82, 138–153
  for worthwhile content, 81, 83–92
  in the writing process, 10, 12, 14, 15, 62
Revision checklist
  for an essay, 63
  for a research report, 420
Rhetorical elements, of an essay, 62
Rhetorical questions, 324
Running heads, 425, 447
Run-on sentence, 512. *See also* Overstuffed sentences

Sarcasm, as an element of satire, 325
Satire in persuasion, appropriate use of, 325–326

Search engines, for the World Wide Web, 348, 349
Secondary sources in research, 344
Second-person address. *See* Direct address
Selecting, of writing material, 33, 34, 89, 90. *See also* Needless details, avoidance of
Semicolon, 519, 521, 522
Semiformal tone, 146, 147
Sensory details, in descriptive writing, 183
Sentence combining, 132–133, 510. *See also* Coordination; Subordination
Sentence definitions, 269, 270
Sentence errors, common, 505, –519
Sentence fragment, 505–508
Sentence length, 132, 133
Sentence outline, 35, 36, 444, 445
Sentence shifts, faulty, 518–519
Sentence style
    clarity in, 118–122
    conciseness in, 124–129
    fluency in, 131–133
Sentence variety, 14, 132–133
Sexist usage. *See also* Bias in language
    defined, 151
    guidelines for eliminating, 152, 153
Shape
    of an argument, 287–288
    of any useful writing, 9
Shifts that destroy coherence, 110, 518–519
Short sentences
    for emphasis, 132–133
    for instructions, 222
sic, 153, 531
Signal term, in a topic statement, 102
Slang, 37, 38, 147, 154
Slippery-slope fallacy, in argument, 319
Soft evidence, versus hard, in research, 380
Spamming, on the Internet, 353
Spatial order, 104, 107. *See also* Description
Specific versus general language, 143, 144, 145
Specific-to-general order, 104, 105
Spell checkers, limits of, 58–59, 76, 157
Spelling, 535
Statement of purpose, 23, 30
Statistical fallacies, avoidance of, 382–385, 386, 387
Statistics, in support of an assertion or argument, 285
Stereotyping, 318
Structural variations
    in essays, 162–163
    in support paragraphs, 101–102

Style
    definition of, 117
    questions for evaluating, 17. (*see also* Sentence style; Tone; Word choice)
Subject directories, for the World Wide Web, 348–349
Subordinating conjunctions, 507
Subordination, 131, 132, 507, 509, 510
Substandard usage, 37
Summaries and abstracts, preparing, 373, 374, 375
Summarizing information, guidelines for, 374, 375
Summarizing original quotations, in research, 456, 457
Summarizing your reading, 170, 176
Summary, as an essay conclusion, 55, 288
Support for an argument, subjective versus objective, 284–287
Support for an opinion, 84, 85
Support paragraphs
    defined, 97
    function of, 98
    length of, 97–98
    shape of, 88
    topic statement in, 97, 99–101
    variations in, 101–102
Surveys and questionnaires, in research, 359, 364–365
Syllogism, 314, 315. *See also* Deductive reasoning
Synonyms, 109, 139, 268

Technical reports, indexes to, 357
Tenses
    control of, in narration, 188
    faulty shifts in, 460
"There" sentence openers, avoidance of, 125
Thesis as framework for reader and writer, 23, 24
Thesis, derived from statement of purpose, 23
Thesis placement, in an essay, 28
Thesis statement
    absence of, 11, 24
    criteria for evaluating, 25–26
    defined, 23, 24
    function of, 23, 24
    guidelines for developing a, 27–28
    placement of, 28, 51
    in a research report, 417, 441, 449
    and topic statement, 24, 25, 97, 99
    variations in, 26
    when to compose your, 27
Title page, for a research report, 421, 423, 444, 445

Titles
abbreviations in, 532
capitalization in, 534
for essays, 49–50
italics, to indicate, 530–531
quotation marks enclosing, 530
Tone
in academic writing, 37–38
as an expression of the writer's attitude, 150
appropriateness of, 36–38, 145–150
in argument, 288, 289, 323, 324
decisions about, 36–38, 147
definition of, 145
guidelines for, 147
level of formality and, 36–38, 146, 147, 148
role of, 45
Topic, of an essay, discovering a, 22, 27. *See also*
Viewpoint
Topic, for research, discovering a, 343–344, 438–439
Topic statement (sentence)
defined, 24
focus of, 100–101
function of, 99, 100
relation to thesis, 24, 25, 97, 99
Transitional paragraphs, 97, 111
Transitions
commonly used, 111–112
defined, 110
to improve coherence, 110–112
in narration, 188
between paragraphs, 111
as sentences, 111
as whole paragraphs, 97, 1110
Triteness, 138
Troubleshooting advice, giving, in instructions, 222
Truncation of a word, in electronic searches, 352
Truth, a working definition of, 380–381
Type size, choice of, 537
Typeface, choice of, 537

Unity
in essays, 9, 55
in paragraphs, 102–103
Unmoderated newsgroups, on the Internet, 345
Usage
differing cultural expectations about, 129, 153, 154
inoffensive, guidelines for, 38, 122, 129, 145, 152, 154
nonsexist usage, guidelines for, 152, 153
Usenet. See Newsgroups, on the Internet

Viewpoint. *See also* Thesis statement; Topic statement
expressing a definite position, 8, 9, 11, 26
significance of, 26
in a thesis statement, 11, 26
in a topic statement, 99
Visuals, 453
Voice, 36–38, 121. *See also* Active voice; Passive voice;
Persona; Tone

Weak verbs, 126
Web. *See* World Wide Web
Web pages and sites, in research, 346, 347–349. *See
also* World Wide Web
Web sites, list of useful
almanacs, 540
associations and organizations, 540
business directories, 541
dictionaries, 541
encyclopedias, 541
journal articles, 541
news organizations, 541
search engines, 539
subject directories, 540
U.S. Government information, 542
writing and research guides, 542
Word arrangement, for coherence and emphasis,
120–121
Word choice, 139–143, 147–148
Wordiness, 124. *See also* Conciseness; Puffery
Word order, the role of, 120–121
Word processing, 58, 157, 537
Working outline, for a research report, 418, 419
Working thesis, for a research report, 417
Works-cited entries, MLA, 395–406
Works-cited (section), in a research report, 394, 395,
406, 464–469
World Wide Web. *See also* Internet
access to research sources, 346, 347–349, 355, 358
documenting sites on the, 402, 403, 404, 405, 406,
415
evaluating sources on the, 377, 378–379
sites, in research, 347–349
Worthwhile content
defined, 81, 83
discovery of (*see* Invention)
elements of, 83–92
selection of, 33, 34, 86, 90
Writers' questions
for evaluating an essay, 17, 64, 81, 165
for responding to reading, 166

Writing collaboratively by computer, 5, 352
Writing with a computer
  benefits of, 5, 6
  decisions in, 5, 6
  guidelines for, 58–59
  limitations of, 6
Writing about reading, 164–176
Writing goal, types of, 160–161

Writing process, the
  decisions in, 2, 5, 6, 9, 10, 11, 12
  defined, 2, 14
  illustration of, 10–14
  looping structure of, 14, 15
  parts of the, 14, 15
  versus writing product, 3
Writing, qualities of all good, 14

Editing, Revision, and Proofreading Symbols

Symbol	Problem	Page*
ab	incorrect abbreviation	532
agr p	error in pronoun agreement	514
agr sv	error in subject-verb agreement	513
apl	missing or misused possessive apostrophe	527
av	active voice needed	121
bias	biased language needs rephrasing	150
ca	pronoun in the wrong case	516
cap	capital letter needed	534
cl	word that merely adds clutter	128
comb	choppy sentences need to be combined	131
cont	faulty contraction	528
coord	coordination needed or faulty	508
cs	comma splice, links two sentences only by a comma	510
dgl	dangling modifier	119
euph	euphemism that misleads	138
frag	a fragment used as a sentence	505

Symbol	Problem	Page*
ital	italics needed for emphasis	530
mod	a modifying word or phrase misplaced	118
neg	negative construction needs rephrasing	127
nom	nominalization (nouns made from verbs)	126
num	error in the use of numbers	534
np	a needless phrase, creates wordiness	125
over	overstatement or exaggeration	138
par	parallel phrasing needed	120
pct	error in punctuation	519
[]/	brackets	531
:/	colon	522
,/	comma	523
--/	dash	532
.../	ellipses	530
!/	exclamation point	521
-/	hyphen	533
()/	parentheses	531
./	period	520
?/	question mark	520
"/"	quotation mark	529
;/	semicolon	521

*Numbers refer to the first page of major discussion in the text.